Handbook of Human and Social Conditions in Assessment

The *Handbook of Human and Social Conditions in Assessment* is the first book to explore assessment issues and opportunities occurring due to the real world of human, cultural, historical, and societal influences upon assessment practices, policies, and statistical modeling. With chapters written by experts in the field, this book engages with numerous forms of assessment: from classroom-level formative assessment practices to national accountability and international comparative testing practices, all of which are significantly influenced by social and cultural conditions. A unique and timely contribution to the field of educational psychology, the *Handbook of Human and Social Conditions in Assessment* is written for researchers, educators, and policymakers interested in how social and human complexity affect assessment at all levels of learning.

Organized into four sections, this volume examines assessment in relation to teachers, students, classroom conditions, and cultural factors. Each section is comprised of a series of chapters, followed by a discussant chapter that synthesizes key ideas and offers directions for future research. Taken together, the chapters in this volume demonstrate that teachers, test creators, and policymakers must account for the human and social conditions that shape assessment if they are to implement successful assessment practices which accomplish their intended outcomes.

Gavin T. L. Brown is Professor and Director of the Quantitative Data Analysis and Research Unit in the Faculty of Education and Social Work at the University of Auckland, New Zealand.

Lois R. Harris is a Senior Post-doctoral Research Fellow within the School of Education and the Arts at Central Queensland University, Australia.

Educational Psychology Handbook Series
Series Editor: Patricia A. Alexander

International Handbook of Research on
Conceptual Change, Second Edition
Edited by Stella Vosniadou

The International Guide to Student
Achievement
Edited by John Hattie and Eric M. Anderman

The International Handbook of
Collaborative Learning
*Edited by Cindy E. Hmelo-Silver,
Clark A. Chinn, Carol Chan, and
Angela M. O'Donnell*

Handbook of Self-Regulation of
Learning and Performance
*Edited by Barry J. Zimmerman and
Dale H. Schunk*

Handbook of Research on Learning
and Instruction
*Edited by Patricia A. Alexander and
Richard E. Mayer*

Handbook of Motivation at School
*Edited by Kathryn R. Wentzel and
Allan Wigfield*

International Handbook of Research on
Conceptual Change
Edited by Stella Vosniadou

Handbook of Moral and Character
Education
*Edited by Larry P. Nucci and Darcia
Narvaez*

Handbook of Positive
Psychology in Schools,
Second Edition
*Edited by Michael Furlong, Rich Gilman,
and E. Scott Huebner*

Handbook of Emotions in Education
*Edited by Reinhard Pekrun and Lisa
Linnenbrink-Garcia*

Handbook of Moral and Character
Education
*Edited by Larry Nucci, Tobias Krettenauer,
and Darcia Narvaez*

International Handbook of Research
on Teachers' Beliefs
*Edited by Helenrose Fives and Michelle
Gregoire Gill*

Handbook of Social Influences
in School Contexts: Social-
Emotional, Motivation, and
Cognitive Outcomes
*Edited by Kathryn R. Wentzel and
Geetha B. Ramani*

Handbook of Motivation at
School, Second Edition
*Edited by Kathryn R. Wentzel and
David B. Miele*

Handbook of Human and Social
Conditions in Assessment
*Edited by Gavin T. L. Brown and
Lois R. Harris*

Handbook of Human and Social Conditions in Assessment

Edited by
Gavin T. L. Brown and Lois R. Harris

Routledge
Taylor & Francis Group

NEW YORK AND LONDON

First published 2016
by Routledge
711 Third Avenue, New York, NY 10017

and by Routledge
2 Park Square, Milton Park, Abingdon, Oxon, OX14 4RN

Routledge is an imprint of the Taylor & Francis Group, an informa business

Library of Congress Cataloging-in-Publication Data
A catalog record for this book has been requested

ISBN: 978-1-138-81153-9 (hbk)
ISBN: 978-1-138-81155-3 (pbk)
ISBN: 978-1-315-74913-6 (ebk)

Typeset in Minion
by Apex CoVantage, LLC

Printed and bound in the United States of America by
Edwards Brothers Malloy on sustainably sourced paper

CONTENTS

FOREWORD
John Hattie

In my book *Visible Learning*, I begin by commenting on the harm that has been done within the field of education because of the common assumption that "everything seems to work" (Hattie, 2009a, p. 1). I argue that this sentiment has been extremely destructive as it has allowed schools and teachers to essentially ignore evidence about best practices and what actually supports optimal learning for diverse groups of students. The alternative to a data driven approach is to rely on tradition, instincts, and intuitions. While not all of these intuitions and traditions are wrong, evidence must provide the foundation for why we continue, modify, or cease particular practices; otherwise, we risk repeating unsuccessful strategies over and over again simply because that is 'always how we've done things' or because practitioners 'assume' the current outcomes are the best which can be achieved.

The major message is that educators should continually ask about their impact, and assessing student learning is the major way to determine this. Schools and teachers must ask themselves many questions when considering impact. Is there a shared understanding of what impact means in the school (and between schools)? What is a sufficient magnitude of impact or what does at least a year's growth look like for a year's input? Does every student make sufficient gain? Impact is a judgement, informed by evidence, best discussed not only among teachers and school leaders, but with students as well. Impact evidence includes test scores, but also students' work calibrated over time and students' voices about their evidence of progress and their learning. Collating these judgements requires triangulation. The many interventions (and yes, some have higher probability of impact than others) are not as critical as the impact of these interventions. There is a 'practice' of teaching; effective methods are known, and success is all around us in education. However, our eyes must be open to this success and it must be identified in a valid and dependable way.

This message places a heavy reliance on assessments. The nature and quality of assessment strongly impacts on the judgements of teachers, the estimation of effect-sizes, what is noticed in classroom observations, how student work is read and commented upon, and even upon how questions are answered in class. This *Handbook of Human and Social Conditions in Assessment* explores many aspects of these assessment methods, particularly focusing on the interplay between the people involved (e.g., teachers, students, other stakeholders), their context (e.g., cultural, policy, social), and assessment. It investigates the teachers' and students' understanding of assessment implementations, the classroom conditions, and the cultural and social effects of assessment, highlighting the many ways that human and social factors can potentially impact on the validity and reliability of assessment results.

The many concerns about assessment echo strongly when examining current practices and a closer look begins to uncover what a messy space can exist behind the supposed order and structure that 'objective' test scores and grades appear to provide. Many current practices (e.g., use of standardised testing for high-stakes decisions, awarding letter grades) are steeped in tradition, to the point where stakeholder groups (like parents) may have trouble defining educational success or failure without the terminology associated with them (Freeman, Mathison, & Wilcox, 2006). Parent and community beliefs that testing is objective and that it is appropriate to use these scores for comparative purposes (Brookhart, 2013) are utilised to defend existing high-stakes testing practices, despite concerns from teachers and students about the equity, validity, and reliability of such practices (Nichols & Berliner, 2007). It seems most parents have not seen a test score they do not like, even if their own child's score is not liked!

However, testing is not the only contentious area within educational assessment, where tradition, diverse stakeholder conceptions, and evaluative data about assessment validity, reliability, and effects at times collide. There is also considerable disagreement surrounding what is best in relation to more low-stakes classroom assessment practices, including formative interpretations. When Michael Scriven (1967) first introduced the notions of formative and summative evaluation, he was clear these referred to the timing (during = formative, end = summative) and not to specific tests or assessment modes. This is why the phrase 'formative and summative *tests*' is misleading—as most tests can be interpreted formatively or summatively. The current penchant for privileging 'formative assessment' is thus misleading. Too many will falsely privilege formative as good, summative as bad (which is nonsense because to understand the effects of our teaching, we need to monitor the former to maximize the latter). Many consider formative as more important, but often teachers do not consider the reliability of these measures when making these interpretations. Policy makers often start calling their favored tests 'formative' and it is easy to predict that most state and national tests will soon be relabeled as formative! The point that is being missed is that both formative and summative interpretations are critical, as summed up by the Bob Stake's adage (cited in Scriven, 1991)—"when the cook tastes the soup, it is formative; when the guests taste the soup, it is summative." Surely, the quality of formative interpretations is the basis for subsequent summative judgements.

There is every reason to ensure formative interpretations are highly reliable, as these judgements form the expectations and the moment-by-moment decisions about 'where to next' in the learning cycle. My team and I developed, as one example, the New Zealand e-asTTle reporting engine, which allows teachers to create a test related to what they are currently teaching. This content (along with other constraints such as reliability, test length, surface and deep items) is used by the system to create a test (from a very large database of millions of test permutations). The test can be administered via paper, on screen, or adaptively (Hattie, Brown, & Keegan, 2003). The feedback to teachers (and potentially their students) is immediate. This engine has been available, on a voluntary basis, for all New Zealand elementary and high schools and is still widely used 15 years after it was first introduced. All tests are calibrated on the same difficulty/curriculum progression and thus changes over time can be evaluated—and this provision to teachers of measures over time is particularly valuable. It is the role of schools to make sense of progressions; it is the purpose of curriculum to assist in mapping progression; and it is a major function of testing to provide over-time calibrated measures. The same test can be interpreted as formative or summative depending on when it is administered. The provision of such a calibrated test bank is particularly critical given that so many teacher tests are created to measure what has just been taught, at the end or summative stage; are rarely calibrated over time; and, moreover, these often measure achievement levels *and not* progress and achievement.

There are numerous books available to try to get teachers 'started' with formative and summative interpretations assessment (e.g., Brookhart & Nitko, 2008; Clarke, 2001; Clarke, Timperley, & Hattie, 2003). While there is a general sentiment that any kind of formative interpretation will generally be 'good' and improve learning, current research paints a worrying picture of what can happen when particular conditions are not met, particularly a lack of psychological safety in the classroom (Cowie, 2009; Harris & Brown, 2013). Student-led practices (e.g., self- and peer assessment, sharing of personal learning goals), in particular, require strong trust between teachers, students, and their classmates; how to establish this necessary environment is seldom explained in depth alongside the self- and peer assessment templates which teachers are encouraged to use. Hence, there is a clear need to consider within any assessment which practices are actually most effective and under what conditions, identifying threats and paying particular attention to how necessary conditions can be established.

The most critical aspect is the quality of the interpretations that the teachers and students make from any assessment. Of course, tests need high levels of information, precision, and validity, but the key concern relates to the quality of interpretations and actions that are made from the test scores. The NZ e-asTTle reporting engine (mentioned above) used backward design to maximise the correctness and consequences of interpretations (Wiggins & McTighe, 2005). The first part of the engine that was developed was the reports from the tests (for school leaders, teachers, students, and parents). Hundreds of focus groups were conducted asking two questions:

- What do you understand from these reports?
- What would you do next in light of this understanding?

If the users answered these incorrectly, the reports were modified. After creating interpretable and consequential reports, the items and tests then were developed (Hattie, 2009b). These reports were linked to resources that could be used to support students with the 'next steps' identified.

If tests reports are designed like this, with the end user in mind, there is less need for concepts like assessment literacy, which requires the users to learn the language of the measurement experts; this approach instead demands the latter learn and use the language of the user (Hattie & Brown, 2010). A major aim of e-asTTle was to move testing from an 'event' which informs students of their achievement to enabling a set of interpretations that can help the teachers and students understand their impact and know how best to modify their teaching and learning to maximise reaching the criteria of success of the lessons.

Clearly, the assessment of learning (and through this, the impact of teaching) is far from straightforward and is influenced strongly by the many ways users understand, interact with, interpret, and act on results. This handbook is a timely look at some of these messy spaces within assessment. As assessments are designed, taken, and evaluated by human beings (whose behavior is not always consistent or predictable), I agree with co-editors Gavin Brown and Lois Harris that it is high time that we took more notice of the effects these human factors may have on what we can and cannot infer from assessment tasks. Likewise, assessment does not occur in a vacuum: classroom, policy, and cultural influences significantly impact on how it plays out. The four sections of this book examine the human and social factors which seldom have gained much attention within mainstream assessment debates: the viewpoints of teachers and how these affect assessment selection, implementation, and use; the perspectives of students and how these might systematically impact on their self-efficacy, participation, and effort during particular assessment practices; the classroom context and how this social environment affects how students enact particular assessment practices; and last, the influence local, national, and global culture has on assessment policy and practice. In many ways, this is one of the first books highlighting the sociology of assessment.

Chapters within this book have been contributed by the leading experts in the field and synthesise cutting-edge research around what we currently know about these human and social factors within assessment, with recommendations for assessment design, policy, and practice. The book includes much about teachers' perceptions and uses of assessment, the role of preservice teacher education and professional development, and the language of assessment. Sections on students include the role of emotions, the environment, novel forms of assessment, the importance of self-regulation, students' multiple perceptions of assessment, the nature of feedback, and the increasing concerns with dishonesty and effort in testing. The classroom conditions relate to peer and self-assessment, privacy rights and equity, collaborative learning, the individual and social influences, and the optimal conditions for effective classroom assessment. The final section looks globally and explores how international assessments are influencing policies and practices, while also examining assessment from Confucian and Islamic perspectives, multicultural issues, and changes driven by technology.

This handbook attempts to shine a spotlight on some of the messy aspects of assessment which may be more convenient to ignore, and provides timely reminders for diverse stakeholders, including educational policy makers, school leaders, teachers, test designers, and academics. It synthesises what is currently known, identifying gaps which still need to be addressed, and provides recommendations for psychometric modelling, teacher education, and policy. There is a wide audience which will benefit from this book, from teachers and school leaders looking to better understand student assessment experiences and the classroom environment necessary for optimal assessment implementation, to test designers wanting to further refine measurement models to more specifically account for particular types of student variability, to policy makers hoping to make more informed decisions, to researchers looking for important and fruitful lines of research to pursue, and to teacher educators and professional-development providers hoping to improve their program's assessment education components in line with best-practice data. I hope that careful reading of this book will begin to break down assumptions about how assessment could and should be practiced, helping move us away from a reliance on tradition and the notion that 'anything goes' to a position where evidence leads to conditions where assessment better supports learning and provides fairer and more informative, valid, and reliable results for students in all educational sectors.

REFERENCES

Brookhart, S. M. (2013). The public understanding of assessment in educational reform in the United States. *Oxford Review of Education, 39*(1), 52–71. doi:10.1080/03054985.2013.764751

Brookhart, S. M., & Nitko, A. J. (2008). *Assessment and grading in classrooms.* Upper Saddle River, NJ: Pearson Merrill Prentice Hall.

Clarke, S. (2001). *Unlocking formative assessment: Practical strategies for enhancing pupil's learning in the primary classroom.* London: Hodder Education.

Clarke, S., Timperley, H. S., & Hattie, J. A. (2003). *Unlocking formative assessment: Practical strategies for enhancing students' learning in the primary and intermediate classroom* (New Zealand ed.). Auckland, NZ: Hodder Moa Beckett.

Cowie, B. (2009). My teacher and my friends help me learn: Student perspectives and experiences of classroom assessment. In D. M. McInerney, G.T.L. Brown, & G.A.D. Liem (Eds.), *Student perspectives on assessment: What students can tell us about Assessment for Learning* (pp. 85–105). Charlotte, NC: Information Age Publishing.

Freeman, M., Mathison, S., & Wilcox, K. C. (2006). Performing parent dialogues on high-stakes testing: Consent and resistance to the hegemony of accountability. *Cultural Studies ↔ Critical Methodologies, 6*(4), 460–473. doi:10.1177/1532708606288647

Harris, L. R., & Brown, G.T.L. (2013). Opportunities and obstacles to consider when using peer- and self-assessment to improve student learning: Case studies into teachers' implementation. *Teaching and Teacher Education, 36*, 101–111. doi:http://dx.doi.org/10.1016/j.tate.2013.07.008

Hattie, J. (2009a). *Visible learning: A synthesis of meta-analyses in education*. London: Routledge.

Hattie, J.A.C. (2009b). Visibly learning from reports: The validity of score reports. *Online Educational Research Journal*, 1–15. Retrieved from http://www.oerj.org/View?action=viewPDF&paper=6

Hattie, J. A., & Brown, G.T.L. (2010). Assessment and evaluation. In C. Rubie-Davies (Ed.), *Educational psychology: Concepts, research and challenges* (pp. 102–117). Abingdon, UK: Routledge.

Hattie, J.A.C., Brown, G.T.L., & Keegan, P. J. (2003). A national teacher-managed, curriculum-based assessment system: Assessment Tools for Teaching & Learning (asTTle). *International Journal of Learning, 10*, 771–778.

Nichols, S. L., & Berliner, D. C. (2007). *Collateral damage: How high-stakes testing corrupts America's schools*. Cambridge, MA: Harvard Education Press.

Scriven, M. (1967). The methodology of evaluation. In R. W. Tyler, R. M. Gagne, & M. Scriven (Eds.), *Perspectives of curriculum evaluation* (Vol. 1, pp. 39–83). Chicago, IL: Rand McNally.

Scriven, M. (1991). Beyond formative and summative evaluation. In M. W. McLaughlin & D. C. Phillips (Eds.), *Evaluation & education: At quarter century* (Vol. 90, Part II, pp. 19–64). Chicago, IL: NSSE.

Wiggins, G. P., & McTighe, J. (2005). *Understanding by design*. Virginia, VA: ASCD.

ACKNOWLEDGMENTS

A book always starts with an idea. For us, this seed was planted at the 2010 International Test Commission conference in Hong Kong, when Bruno Zumbo strongly indicated that there was a need for a more formal engagement with the social psychological aspects of assessment. We would like to formally thank Bruno for his enthusiasm for our approach to this topic, the feedback he gave on our ideas, and his permission to use the 'in vivo' versus 'in vitro' metaphor in our final chapter.

This seed germinated through our collaboration on the Measuring Teachers' Assessment Practices (MTAP) project in New Zealand, which was supported by a two-year postdoctoral fellowship for Lois from the Faculty of Education Research Development Fund. The fieldwork and analyses of the mixed methods data led us to a much deeper understanding of what actually happens in real-life, enacted classroom assessment. This work has led us to the somewhat provocative conclusion that the beliefs and actions of students and teachers are often undermining the good intentions and ideals of assessment for learning.

In relation to the production of the book itself, we have been fortunate to work with a great team of authors. The authors have responded wonderfully to the challenging feedback we gave them. The views of the authors are their own and have been developed in dialogue with us as editors—they might not have liked everything we had to say, but they engaged with it effortfully to improve the quality of their chapter and ultimately they have made valuable contributions to the field. Together we have worked to ensure that the quality of writing is clear, concise, and hopefully pleasurable to read, and we would like to thank them all for their efforts.

The volume also would not be published today without the tremendous enthusiasm and support from the team at Routledge. Rebecca Novack, Trevor Gori, and Matthew Friberg have been particularly instrumental. Rebecca guided us through the proposal and author recruitment stages, while Trevor and Matthew assisted with the many administrative tasks involved in compiling and preparing the volume itself. We would also like to thank Patricia Alexander, the general editor of the handbook series, for her unfailing enthusiasm and encouragement in helping us develop our ideas and recruit high-quality authors.

Finally, the true sacrifice has been made by our respective families who have been patient with us as we have put in long hours to get this volume to completion. Gavin's wife, Judith, has exhibited great patience and self-reliance in leaving him alone while he read, wrote, reviewed, and concentrated on this book during their sabbatical year on the road. Without her support, he could not have done this. It was also always nice to know his adult children showed interest in his work.

We'd also like to thank Lois' husband, Chris, and her small children, Alexander, Rebecca, and soon to arrive baby #3, for being tolerant of the late nights and early mornings. There have been numerous times where Alex and Becca have had to wait patiently for a story or a snack so Lois could "just finish one more chapter," and their love and support have been greatly appreciated.

Lois' children and Gavin's grandchildren have provided inspiration for why this work is important. We hope that this handbook will generate research, policy, practice, and pedagogy leading to assessment being used more optimally and realistically for learning. Will it happen before they begin school? That is up to the readers of this handbook who prepare teachers, write policies, analyze data, and conduct research into the human and social experience of educational assessment. We hope that this book will make a real difference and would like to sincerely thank all who have played a part in it.

1

VOLUME INTRODUCTION

The Human and Social Experience of Assessment: Valuing the Person and Context

Lois R. Harris and Gavin T. L. Brown

The human condition is not perfect. We are not perfect specimens, any of us. We're not robots.

Michael Ovitz (*Zeman, 2001*, paragraph 70)

INTRODUCTION

In our quest to improve educational assessment (e.g., increasing its validity, authenticity, accuracy, and learning benefits), it is easy to secretly wish that human beings (like robots) behaved in a consistent, predictable, and rational fashion. Rather than being content with total scores or ranking, educational stakeholders are currently seeking more diagnostic results from testing and assessment, but understanding how such methods might cope with the dynamism and complexity of classroom interactions is still a major challenge. Ideally, assessments should be able to measure human knowledge and behaviour with the same level of accuracy that we can achieve when calculating the speed of a ball descending a ramp. Imagine test designers' glee if students always interpreted and responded to items in consistent ways or if panels of teachers marking essay responses generated identical feedback and scores. Classroom teachers would love to know in advance exactly how their students would interpret and respond to their formative feedback and be able to plan knowing precisely what kind of assessment was best for each student.

However, we live in a complex social and psychological world where people are not governed by universal laws of motion, but instead by their intricate (and ever changing) systems of values and beliefs, cultural and social norms, political contexts, personal motivations, relationships with others, and perceptions of the world around them, just to name a few. Within educational contexts, these factors influence all areas of assessment, including: decisions within educational systems, schools, and classrooms about how learning will be assessed; individuals' (e.g., teachers and students) understandings of and kind of participation in assessment practices; and how responses to these assessment practices are evaluated, interpreted, and used. Educational assessment also has multiple and sometimes overlapping purposes (e.g., improvement, student accountability, school accountability [Brown, 2008]) and functions (Newton, 2007).

While these multiple purposes create difficulties for assessment validity and reliability (Bonner, 2013; Brookhart, 2003; Parkes, 2013), assessment models still generally expect the world of task and response or question and answer to be stable. When administering an assessment, educators anticipate student answers will be predictable in response to the difficulty of the question, its curriculum content, its cognitive demand, the probability of a student guessing the answer, and the sensitivity of the question to small changes in ability. In relying on observation and judgement, teachers expect that the scoring rubric or rules will be sufficient to consistently explain and describe student learning or diagnose needs. These models of behaviour make testing and assessment easier since they allow us to pretend the complexity of human existence does not exist within the world of educational assessment.

However, our observation, based on years of teaching and research, is that assessment is not so simple given the social environments within and surrounding classrooms at compulsory and tertiary education levels, let alone in vocational and workplace learning contexts. Classmates influence each other, often for good and sometimes, sadly, for ill. Although educators might wish for student honesty, truthfulness, and consideration, responses to teachers in the public forum of the classroom can be distorted by reluctance to exhibit non- or misunderstanding in front of others (Harris & Brown, 2013) in both face-to-face and online settings. Teachers may be frustrated or angered when, despite best efforts, students fail to grasp a new concept or skill; pupils' fear of the teacher's disappointment or anger may create further distortions in their responses to assessment practices in classroom settings. Student concerns about parent reactions to or the high-stakes consequences of their assessment results (e.g., promotion, retention, tertiary entrance, financial costs or rewards) can motivate further dishonest behaviour (e.g., plagiarism or various forms of cheating). Furthermore, teachers as evaluators may not always assess consistently or accurately due to factors including fatigue, time constraints, mood, biases (e.g., having a positive or negative relationship with or opinion of the student, the halo effect, etc.), inexperience, and differing interpretations of performance standards or criteria (Kahneman, 2011; Wyatt-Smith & Klenowski, 2012; Wyatt-Smith, Klenowski, & Gunn, 2010). Even when scoring is mechanical (e.g., computer marking of tests) or objective, a person originally designed the questions and set the parameters of what would be considered a correct answer (Brown, 2015), a set of decisions that might not be universally accepted as appropriate. Hence, human conditions impact assessment from design to implementation to scoring and these take place within a complex social environment.

Within this handbook, the term *human conditions* refers to how individuals understand, respond to, and interpret assessment. These individuals include assessment takers (normally students), assessment givers (usually teachers or administrators), and assessment users (i.e., teachers, administrators, students, or parents). To understand human conditions, multiple aspects must be explored. First, it is important to consider the beliefs, attitudes, perceptions, and/or conceptions of assessment that diverse stakeholders hold. Additionally, one must take into account their experiences, responses to, behaviours around, and emotions towards assessment. Hence, when we speak of human conditions, we are talking specifically about emotions, experiences, and beliefs which occur WITHIN an individual and influence how that person understands, engages with, and interprets assessment experiences and results.

In contrast, the term *social conditions* is used to refer to how assessment is experienced in group settings (e.g., classrooms) and how cultural, historical, and societal influences mediate those experiences. Students are educated and assessed in social settings which include adult teachers (who enact assessment practices within particular policy, social, and cultural environments) and peers (who impact on students' motivation, self-esteem, self-image, collaborative learning opportunities, etc.). These settings are contextualised by the educational and assessment policies of the jurisdiction, which may or may not align with the values, beliefs, and motivations of students, their parents, and their teachers. Hence, by social conditions, we refer to the interplay between the experiences of the individual and collectives to which those individuals belong at the level of classroom, policy, society, and culture.

Both human and social conditions must be understood as many contemporary educational policy reforms (especially Assessment for Learning [AfL]) highlight the need to consider both the intra- and interpersonal dynamics of assessment. AfL explicitly requires classroom assessment practices (e.g., peer and self-assessment) that involve students taking on the teacher's traditional role as assessor (Assessment Reform Group, 2002; Berry, 2008; Black et al., 2004; Stiggins, 2002; Swaffield, 2011); the interpersonal dynamics of teacher and learner now have to be extended to account for experiences as students assess each other or assess themselves in front of their classmates.

Understanding what assessment means in light of these human and social conditions is important for the design of assessments, the preparation and development of teachers, the quality of scoring and marking systems, the creation of appropriate policies, and the design of statistical models used to generate scores. This chapter will further explore the need for research into these important areas and provide an introduction to the subsequent chapters within this volume.

The Need for Research Into Human and Social Factors

Test responses are a function not only of the items, tasks, or stimulus conditions, but of the *persons* responding and the *context* of measurement. This latter context includes factors in the environmental background as well as the assessment setting (Messick, 1989, p. 14). Any educational assessment, from classroom based teacher observations to high-stakes standardised tests needs to be valid and reliable if it is to be used in educational decision-making. The modern approach to validity positions it as a series of arguments (Kane, 2006, 2013); specifically, validity is "an integrated evaluative judgement of the degree to which empirical evidence and theoretical rationales support the *adequacy* and *appropriateness* of *inferences* and *actions* based on test scores or other modes of assessment" (Messick, 1989, p. 13). Reliability is generally considered to be the "consistency, stability, dependability, and accuracy of assessment results" (McMillan, 2001, p. 65). However, as Bonner (2013) accurately points out, there is a need to rethink exactly how validity is constructed within the realm of classroom assessment in light of the differences between assessments administered for summative evaluation versus those for formative improvements in instruction or learning. While the consequences of some educational assessments may be greater than others (e.g., student held back due to low test scores vs. placed in the wrong within-class reading group vs. spent slightly more time on a concept than necessary because the teacher thought he had not understood), all invalid or unreliable assessments carry some type of inappropriate consequence for learners, teachers, and/or schools.

But what causes assessments to be invalid or unreliable? While invalid assessment sometimes occurs because inappropriate instruments are used to evaluate learning (e.g., instrument does not assess what students had actually been taught) or because of cultural or linguistic biases (e.g., students are tested in their second language prior to attaining adequate competence in the language of testing), problems can also arise when students respond to the assessment in particular ways or when inappropriate inferences are drawn from it, rather than from inherent flaws within the instrument or assessment method itself. For example, issues can occur because of inappropriate student responses to assessment tasks (e.g., cheating or lack of effort) or physical and psychological issues which negatively affect the student's performance on the day (e.g., illness, anxiety about the test, or unrelated personal worries which distract the student). When stakeholders are unaware of the human and social conditions influencing assessment, they are far more likely to fail to consider these threats to validity and reliability, undermining the appropriateness of their inferences from the data.

Also, without understanding human and social conditions, inferences based on assessment results are less likely to be valid. One particularly concerning misconception is around the accuracy of a score. Over 30 years ago, Messick (1984, p. 215, emphasis added) noted:

> Because student characteristics as well as social and educational experiences influence current performance, the interpretation and implications of educational achievement measures must be relative to intrapersonal and situational contexts. These points imply a strategy of comprehensive assessment in context that focuses on the processes and structures involved in subject-matter competence *as moderated in performance by personal and environmental influences*.

However, this message appears to have been largely overlooked within the mainstream assessment culture, especially in environments where high-stakes testing is the primary form of student and school accountability and evaluation. Current three-parameter item response psychometric models account for item difficulty, item discrimination, and the probability of guessing (Hambleton, Swaminathan, & Rogers, 1991). There are multiple statistical models for handling polytomous, as opposed to dichotomous, scoring systems, and for identifying the impact of human raters, tasks themselves, and interactions of tasks and raters upon the accuracy of those polytomous scores. Tools and procedures exist to minimise error introduced by emotional or biased markers. However, current models do not have the ability to detect alignment (e.g., were students taught what was tested?), interference caused by variation in students' emotional or physical states, students' inappropriate responses to assessment, and a host of other human variability in relation to academic evaluation. We still have little understanding of the intrapersonal and interpersonal factors in various situations such as classrooms, and this absence weakens the statistical models we use to estimate attainment or proficiency.

THE CHALLENGES TO ASSESSMENT VALIDITY

There seem to be three major types or conditions of assessment that need to be distinguished. Classroom assessments include formal (e.g., tests, assignments) and informal (e.g., observations, conversations, interactions) methods to inform teacher and student improvement action (i.e., formative) and evaluate and report on performance (i.e., summative). Some national (e.g., the United States' National Assessment of Educational Progress [NAEP] or New Zealand's National Monitoring Study of Student Achievement [NMSSA]) and international (e.g., PISA, TIMMS) external monitoring assessments aim to lightly sample and monitor the overall health of the schooling system. These assessments generally have low-stakes consequences for school-level participants on whose performance inferences depend, but may have significant impact at the system level. Then, there are external accountability assessments (e.g., the United States' No Child Left Behind [NCLB]), where student testing is used to directly evaluate the efficacy of schools and teachers and which carry high-stakes consequences for school administrators and teachers. Interestingly, education research, especially from the USA, has uncovered that many of the consequences of school accountability testing have been negative (Nichols & Berliner, 2007). Parallel to these high-stakes school accountability tests are high-stakes graduation (e.g., Hong Kong Diploma of Secondary Education), certification (e.g., Texas Examinations of Educator Standards), or entry (e.g., China's University Entrance Examination-*gao kao*) tests used to evaluate the competence or proficiency of individual students.

Throughout this volume and within the field, it is evident that there is much more research about the human and cultural responses and constraints within formal testing than there is about informal, interactive classroom assessments. Interestingly, there is much less research into the effects of the formal testing used in low-stakes monitoring than there is of high-stakes formal testing. Hence, throughout this volume, the authors have been careful to delineate which class of assessment the research they review applies to and they have been challenged to consider the generalisability and meaningfulness of their results beyond the context which this research has investigated.

Challenges for Testing Systems

While information about validity and reliability of high-stakes testing systems may be contained within detailed technical reports about particular educational assessment tools, in many cases, such details are seldom released to the public (Chamberlain, 2013; Gebril, this volume) or are not provided in a language that lay people are likely to understand. In cases where technical information about test reliability has been made public (e.g., England) and efforts have been made to engage with the public around these important issues, there have been huge challenges, with the media often sensationalising, misinterpreting, or misreporting test data (Newton, 2013). Newton (2013) has noted that while such media reports often contain some useful information, there is a risk that readers take away only the sensationalised headlines and data about measurement error (e.g., 30% of students may have received the wrong score); these simplistic take-home messages could potentially erode public confidence in the system. Such was the case with the innovative California Learning Assessment System, which was determined to have a tolerable standard error of 0.55 on a 1 to 6 scale (Cronbach, Bradburn, & Horvitz, 1995), and yet, the system was deemed by politicians to have failed and was subsequently abandoned. Such data certainly can undermine commonly held public assumptions about testing: that it is objective and that it is appropriate to use such data comparatively and competitively (Brookhart, 2013). While Brookhart's (2013) work focuses on an American context, the global trend to use testing for school accountability purposes (e.g., the Australian National Assessment Program—Literacy and Numeracy [NAPLAN]; Klenowski & Wyatt-Smith, 2012; Thompson, 2013) indicates these concerns apply to many other countries.

Diverse important decisions, including academic promotion, acceptance into tertiary or other selective programs, school funding, and in some jurisdictions, teacher promotion or dismissal, often rely heavily upon test scores. Without test scores, it is highly possible such decisions might be subject to collusion, nepotism, or corruption and, thus, lead to even worse outcomes; these concerns provide an argument for maintaining formal assessment systems, especially in conditions of rationed resources. Hence, it is relatively easy for policy makers and non-experts to treat assessment scores and grades as clear, reliable, and unequivocal measurements of the performance of children and schools, justifying their continued faith in the 'objectivity' and independence that the scores provide (Brookhart, 2013).

Indeed, almost universally, it would appear that scores (especially grades or percentages) function as a kind of currency that purchases opportunities (including personal, social, and economic) and which seem 'easy' to understand, even if inferences commonly derived may not be appropriate or warranted. The rationality of scores within most ecologies enables the development of a 'fast' thinking heuristic (i.e., System I thinking, Kahneman, 2011) in which high scores equate to quality. However, in educational environments, having such heuristics can deter stakeholders from engaging in the much harder and more time-consuming 'slow' thinking (i.e., System II thinking) where they carefully consider the validity and reliability of evidence and arguments and the legitimacy of inferences being drawn. Clearly, research into the human and social conditions in assessment sheds light on the 'objectivity' of educational assessments and potentially directs our attention to factors within student and school characteristics, cultures, and abilities that need to be taken into account when students are assessed. This knowledge encourages all stakeholders to reconsider their treatment of scores and grades as heuristics, especially in relation to high-stakes purposes.

Classroom Settings

While the importance of human and social conditions in large-scale (and often high-stakes) assessment may be fairly obvious, there are also major implications for classroom assessment practices. Within classroom assessment, suggestions exist as to how the validity and reliability of classroom assessments could be improved (e.g., Bonner, 2013; Parkes, 2013). The ambitions of formative assessment, and even more so in strong versions of Assessment for Learning (Swaffield, 2011), are that assessment helps students learn in terms of curriculum objectives, self-regulation of learning, and the development of their own personalised goals and ambitions. Classrooms are nonetheless complex social spaces in which 'strangers' are assembled into 'units' under the direction of a learning professional who has likewise eclectic and idiosyncratic perspectives on and practices of assessment (Cizek, Fitzgerald, Shawn, & Rachor, 1995; Kahn, 2000). However, there are few uniform and universal guidelines or standards for interactive-informal classroom assessments. Instead, individual teachers are left to decide if the instruments or processes they use are valid and reliable for their purposes. The complexity and uncontrollability of classrooms, then, set up conditions and circumstance in which, as Robert Burns (1785) put it, "the best-laid schemes o' mice an' men gang aft agley." Without understanding the complex social dynamics at work within their classrooms, teachers run the risk of introducing assessment practices which may decrease student motivation and effort (see Wise & Smith, this volume), increase their likelihood of cheating (see Murdock, Stephens, & Grotewiel, this volume), or increase the probability of disingenuous responding (see Andrade & Brown; Panadero; Cowie & Harrison, this volume).

However, acknowledging and exploring the messiness of the human and social space where assessment takes place is in no way an excuse to back away from the evaluation of learning. It is about unpacking the ignored error factors so that diverse stakeholders can more validly judge the meaning of a particular educational assessment practice.

It concerns warning teachers about threats to the validity of even highly prized formative assessment practices so that these threats can be minimised or, when possible, avoided. It is about valuing the voice of students around their own assessment experiences and what would improve them, not about making excuses or condemning particular groups to perpetual poor performance.

THE NEED FOR THIS HANDBOOK

A detailed examination of the human and social conditions that mediate assessment results is long overdue. Research in educational psychology has mostly focused on the psychology of learning and teaching rather than assessment and evaluation processes, while research in educational measurement predominantly focuses on statistical modelling or policy, rather than the human experience of assessment. It is only through better professional and public understanding of these complexities that misinterpretation and misuse of test scores (e.g., as in the United States [Nichols & Berliner, 2007] or internationally [see Teltemann & Klieme, this volume]) could be minimised. It is expected that improved teacher education and classroom practice in selecting and implementing assessment will arise with a more comprehensive understanding of human and social factors in assessment.

From a psychometric perspective, the approach has generally been to 'tighten the instrument' (Camilli, 1996) to reduce systematic sources of error in test scores; nevertheless, random unexplained sources of error continue to plague all tests and assessments. As Camilli (1996, p. 2) explains, "From a statistical point of view, numbers are fuzzy rather than precise creatures, and a statistician's concern is to keep the amount of fuzziness to a minimum." However, educators and members of the general public are not taught to view these numbers as 'fuzzy.' Also, for too long, the responses, attitudes, and beliefs of teachers and students have been treated as either random or irrelevant and consigned to 'error,' and this volume attempts to highlight conditions which undermine the validity of seemingly reliable assessments. The contributions of this volume shed considerable light on the random error component in assessment and argue that when these variables are taken into account, better assessment statistics and processes will arise. The goal of this volume is not to push the concerns of psychometrics and statistical modelling into the corner or treat them as irrelevant, but rather to improve such processes by offering a more complete understanding of construct-irrelevant factors which can be taken into account.

Assessment experts must also attend further to human and social conditions within assessment given the repositioning of the student's role within assessment which has occurred over the past couple of decades via the rise of the Assessment for Learning movement (Black & Wiliam, 1998) and growing focus on student self-regulation within learning and assessment (e.g., Boekaerts & Corno, 2005; Zimmerman, 2008). These foci have led to a move from students being relatively passive participants within assessment processes (who essentially had assessment done to them), to active participant in the process, at times co-constructing criteria and negotiating tasks and, at the very least, acting to accept or reject assessment and feedback. If educators view students as active participants in the assessment process, understanding their perspectives (as explored in Section 2) and how classroom and cultural factors might affect pupils (examined in Sections 3 and 4) become extremely important. For researchers and school leaders, understanding how teachers navigate these same complex human and social factors (explored in Section 1) is also of utmost importance.

Through the contributions within this handbook, we want to challenge educational stakeholders to contemplate the implications of assessment taking place within a multidimensional, social space (i.e., the classroom) and consider how these variables may help or hinder the quality of decisions based on assessment practices. We argue that human and social conditions must be understood by assessment creators and users because teachers and learners enact assessment practices in accordance with their own values and attitudes, regardless of the intentions of policy or test creators. We suggest that without understanding the human and social conditions that shape how assessments are implemented and understood, the assessment industry is unlikely to be effective and intended policy objectives are likely to remain unfulfilled.

Exploring the Human and Social Conditions in Assessment

Within this volume, chapters are grouped together into four sections. Section 1, Teachers and Assessment, explores teacher understandings and experiences of assessment implementation (Chapters 2–6). Section 2, Students and Assessment, examines the diverse ways students understand and participate in assessment practices (Chapters 7–13). Section 3, Classroom Conditions, explores different ways that the classroom environment impacts on and shapes both student and teacher behaviours within assessment (Chapters 14–20). Finally, Section 4, Cultural and Social Contexts (Chapters 21–29), examines how factors outside the classroom, like culture, educational policy, globalisation, and public perceptions impact upon assessment practices. Each section contains a series of chapters, followed by a discussant chapter (written by experts in the field) which synthesises major ideas from the section, offers their insight on the issues raised in light of their own research, and stimulates further thinking around the topics raised.

Section 1. Teachers and Assessment

Chapter 2, by Sarah M. Bonner, synthesises literature on teachers' assessment perceptions generally and within the areas of AfL, summative assessment, and externally mandated testing. She argues that teachers perceive tensions within the broad domain of assessment, with generally positive perceptions about AfL and more negative perceptions about externally mandated testing, and that these cognitive conflicts may be exacerbated by external demands such as national mandates. She suggests that the impact of assessment on teachers in different positions in the system (e.g., teachers, middle managers, school leaders, etc.) should be examined, so that recommendations can made as to how policy makers and school-system administrators can develop policies and practices that take teacher beliefs into account.

Chapter 3, by Sharon L. Nichols and Lois R. Harris, focuses on the role assessment plays within school accountability policies and practices. It highlights recent school accountability policies within the United States, as these have created arguably one of the most rigid, pressure inducing systems across the globe, providing valuable lessons regarding the efficacy of using tests as the primary and, at times, sole indicator of educational quality. Nichols and Harris conclude that although tests can provide meaningful information, when they are used to make high-stakes decisions about teachers and their students, their usefulness and validity dissipate rapidly. They identify several alternatives from other international jurisdictions and provide recommendations for more meaningful approaches to educational accountability.

Chapter 4, by Mary F. Hill and Gayle E. Eyers, reviews studies investigating pre-service teachers' assessment learning, alongside their own work on the subject. The chapter discusses evidence around what is needed to create assessment capable beginning teachers. It raises issues regarding the complexities of teacher preparation for assessment, the effects of student and teacher preconceptions, and cultural implications. The authors suggest that moves to broadly integrate technology into assessment practices will further challenge teacher preparation for assessment. They also highlight the need for additional research regarding how to prepare teachers for using assessment formatively in developing countries.

Chapter 5, by Mei Lai and Kim Schildkamp, focuses on in-service teacher professional learning, in particular the use of assessment in data-based decision-making professional development (PD) programmes. The chapter profiles two case studies that demonstrate that it is possible for teacher in-service PD to simultaneously address teachers' attitudes and beliefs which prevent them from using data, and improve teacher knowledge about and skills in relation to analysing and using data. In both PD programmes discussed, the role of the PD is to develop teacher inquiry and adaptive expertise, treating teachers as joint partners and problem-solvers in relation to a common and shared problem. Both also develop professional learning communities which enable teachers to inquire into their practices, and the authors recommend this approach to maximise professional development benefits.

Chapter 6, by Judy M. Parr and Helen S. Timperley, discusses and synthesises the findings of the four chapters within this section, explaining how they collectively help us better understand teacher perspectives and experiences of formative and summative assessment. It notes the importance of examining the 'language' of assessment, raising questions about how assessment is discussed in different ways and whether terminology is clear. They also suggest further examination of how teachers see themselves as agents within the assessment process and of the consequences of assessment for all stakeholders, stressing that teachers' assessment attitudes and behaviours occur within specific contexts. The chapter provides numerous recommendations for policy and practice, and proposes the development of a matrix which categorises assessment purposes, associated ways of obtaining information, and the potential consequences of these actions in a way that considers contexts, discourse, and diverse stakeholder perspectives and uses. They believe that such a tool would help teaching professionals more easily see inconsistencies or potentially negative consequences within assessment practices.

Section 2. Students and Assessment

Chapter 7, by Elisabeth Vogl and Reinhard Pekrun, calls attention to the impact of achievement emotions on assessment processes and outcomes. The authors conclude that in line with research on test anxiety, any intense emotion that distracts attention away from the task at hand and compromises cognitive resources represents a potential threat to learning and to the validity of academic assessments. In contrast, positive task-focused emotions experienced in assessment situations, such as enjoyment of challenge and problem solving, may foster attention, motivation, and use of adequate strategies, thus making it possible to assess students' true capabilities. The authors summarise how learning environments and assessments can be designed in emotionally sound ways that support both students' learning and the valid evaluation of achievement.

Chapter 8, by Katrien Struyven and Joana Devesa, summarises the research that has been conducted on students' perceptions of novel forms of assessments. Novel assessments introduce innovations in terms of processes, formats, and/or requirements;

many represent a shift from a measurement model of a summative performance to a model where assessment is an integral part of the learning process. Results show that although educators are enthusiastic about novel forms of assessment, students are often initially less delighted about the innovative method(s). Resistance, as a consequence of the novelty effect, often triggers feelings of uncertainty, discomfort, and unease, resulting in students expressing their 'loyalty' towards more familiar assessment methods, such as paper-and-pencil tests and multiple-choice exams. However, reviewed research shows that students' perceptions are dynamic concepts that can be altered based upon experience with novel assessments. Drawing on students' perspectives, this chapter identifies aspects of novel tasks which students may not be comfortable with initially, provides recommendations about how to best introduce such tasks, and gives suggestions for research, policy, and practice in relation to novel tasks.

Chapter 9 provides Daniel L. Dinsmore and Hope E. Wilson's views concerning the impact of assessment on student self-regulation. They conclude that there is evidence that participation in assessment can be beneficial in terms of self-regulation, but that it is not the case that participation in particular assessment processes (e.g., self-assessment, peer assessment, teacher feedback, computer feedback) automatically fosters self-regulation. They argue that self-regulation throughout and after assessment is contingent on a variety of factors, including the learner's developmental characteristics, the nature of the task and domain, and the regulatory outcome desired (i.e., cognitive, motivational, and/or behavioural). While concluding that both self-assessment and teacher feedback appear important if assessment is to become part of a process of self-regulated learning, they identify numerous factors that practitioners and researchers must consider (i.e., the importance of investigating multiple aspects of causality, the need for consideration around if/when aspects of the self-regulation cycle can be studied in isolation, the importance of studying individuals' SRL development over time).

Chapter 10, written by Ana A. Lipnevich, David A. G. Berg, and Jeffrey K. Smith, focuses on how the nature of feedback, in the form of grades, comments, scores, or praise/criticism may relate to student emotional, cognitive, and behavioural responses to feedback. The authors examine some of the more prominent research in the field, summarise recent work done on the topic, and then present a tentative model for understanding how learners respond to formative feedback. Their model highlights the complexity of interactions throughout the feedback process, identifying multiple trigger points at which individual and social processes may prevent feedback from having its intended positive effects on learning.

In Chapter 11, Tamara B. Murdock, Jason M. Stephens, and Morgan M. Groteweil address the topic of academic dishonesty (i.e., cheating) and classroom assessment. Cheating has numerous deleterious effects on the assessment process: it disrupts the feedback-instruction cycle, biases summative evaluation, and reinforces classroom contexts where students see grades instead of learning as the goal of schooling. After reviewing the research on the frequency and methods of cheating, the authors examine the motivational, attitudinal, and instructional/contextual factors that appear to influence rates of classroom dishonesty. The chapter concludes with suggestions for educators about reducing academic dishonesty.

Chapter 12, written by Steven L. Wise and Lisa F. Smith, focuses on the validity challenges posed by students who do not give good effort on assessments. They show that any assessment—no matter how well designed—can be vulnerable to this problem, particularly when that assessment is administered under low-stakes conditions.

Wise and Smith discuss theoretical issues and research findings regarding test-taking motivation and provide a variety of strategies that assessment practitioners might use to mitigate this validity threat.

Chapter 13, by James H. McMillan, summarises what is known about student perceptions toward assessment and suggests a framework for understanding how these perceptions relate to learning and motivation. Based on extant empirical literature, a model for conceptualising student perceptions is presented that shows the relationships of these perceptions to all phases of the assessment cycle. The model provides an organisation for assessment practices that promote student attributions for success to moderate levels of effort, responsibility for performance, lessened anxiety, and positive emotions. He suggests that further study of students' perceptions toward assessment will elucidate the impacts of the assessment process on important educational outcomes.

Section 3. Classroom Conditions

Chapter 14, by Ernesto Panadero, analyses the evidence on the social and human aspects (e.g., motivation and emotion) of peer assessment. It reviews 26 articles that have been published since the first review of the topic was completed in 2009. Panadero draws two main conclusions based on this literature. First, he argues that formative uses of PA decrease the interpersonal problems that PA can elicit in students. Second, he suggests PA should not be implemented as a "side activity," but needs to be central to the curriculum to optimally fulfill its formative objectives.

Chapter 15, written by Robin D. Tierney and Martha J. Koch, explores the issue of privacy in classroom assessment. They argue that human beings living in social structures need privacy to thrive and develop and that students must be given privacy while learning. Drawing on literature, the authors identify that while technological advancements continue to enhance our ability to capture information, they also prompt concerns about privacy given that little has been done to safeguard students' privacy in most jurisdictions. They advocate that privacy rights should be included in teacher education programs and professional development initiatives for school leaders, and be openly discussed with students and parents. A proactive and collaborative approach between the technology sector and educational leaders is needed to find solutions for secure transmission and storage, develop policy for sharing and managing assessment information, and raise awareness and understanding about the importance of students' privacy rights for learning.

Chapter 16, by Tonya R. Moon, focuses on balancing the issue of diversity with equity within classroom settings through Tomlinson's (2001) framework of differentiation. In the chapter, she discusses the need for differentiated instruction and describes how assessment sits within this process, identifying that research around differentiated assessment, particularly within classroom contexts, is nascent but well-timed and urgently needed. She argues that future work is required to better understand how and under what circumstances the use of differentiated assessment removes barriers so that students have the best opportunity to demonstrate their learning.

Chapter 17, by Jan-Willem Strijbos, looks specifically at the assessment of collaborative learning (CL). Within the chapter, he reviews research which highlights the many assessment challenges which CL raises including issues relating to what should be assessed, how it should be assessed, and how such grades might be derived. He examines diverse literature around teacher CL assessment practices, student CL assessment experiences (including peer assessment of group members), and the impact technology is having on CL assessment. As one of the first reviews to deal with assessment in collaborative learning within a generally nascent field, he provides some tentative recommendations for practice and suggests the need for further discussion within the field around the role and desired outcomes of assessment within CL so guidelines can be established to help make teacher practices more consistent and valid.

Chapter 18, by Heidi L. Andrade and Gavin T. L. Brown, examines the individual and social influences on student self-assessment, including (a) intra-individual competence and confidence in self-assessment, (b) interpersonal relations with teachers/instructors who require students to conduct and perhaps share their self-assessments, (c) interpersonal relations with peers, in front of whom students are sometimes required to carry out self-assessments, and (d) the students' cultural context. The authors suggest that the power of self-assessment is dependent upon the conditions under which it is implemented. They argue that self-assessment should be implemented in a context likely to promote accuracy, suggesting they should not count toward grades, and perhaps be conducted in private. The authors recommend that self-assessment be structured as a form of self-regulated learning rather than as a formal assessment. They indicate that social response bias and response style can be managed to some degree by encouraging students to be honest and accurate. If feedback on consistency is given, it must be done in a supportive, constructive manner.

Chapter 19, by Bronwen Cowie and Christine Harrison, focuses in on the nature of classroom assessment with an emphasis on formative assessment/Assessment for Learning. They argue that, given the social and emotional impacts of classroom-based assessment, it is useful to consider teacher practice as lying along a continuum of formality whereby teachers generate information on student learning that can be used for formative or summative purposes (assessment for/of learning). They set out some of the ways teachers can generate and use information on student learning to inform their teaching and to assist students to monitor and advance their learning. They also raise some of the challenges teacher face in meeting the often conflicting accountability and learning demands arising from current policy and expectations for 21st century learning.

Chapter 20, by Susan M. Brookhart, discusses the findings from all the chapters in the classroom conditions section through a co-regulation of learning theoretical lens. Co-regulation acknowledges the joint influence of student self-regulation and regulation from other sources on assessment participation and student learning. She argues that considering co-regulation of learning illuminates our understanding of the general conditions of classroom assessment and is particularly helpful in describing differences between self- and peer assessment. This model also can help explain why certain classroom assessment practices are more effective than others. The chapter concludes with a compendium of recommendations, from the section chapters and other literature, for building assessments that work in classrooms.

Section 4. Cultural and Social Contexts

Chapter 21, by Janna Teltemann and Eckhard Klieme, reviews previous research on the effects of international assessments on education policies and practices. They show that many countries have reformed their education systems during the last 15 years, but raise doubts as to whether this is due to the soft governance mechanisms of international testing projects or if it is a logical response to the growing importance of education in modern economies. They argue that real effects of nations' differing assessment practices have hardly been identified, as most previous work has examined formal policies rather than enacted practices. They present their own approach to analysing changing school practices, drawing on data from the OECD PISA study, and call for more elaborate secondary analyses of international assessment data in order to more accurately evaluate the effectiveness of particular educational and assessment policies.

In Chapter 22, Bob Lingard and Steven Lewis argue that growing international adoption of top-down, test-based modes of educational accountability reflect the globalisation of more local 'Anglo-American' approaches to school accountability. They posit that this Anglo-American model is part of a broader neoliberal policy assemblage linked to the restructuring of the State and new modes of educational governance, including high-stakes testing, national curricula, an emphasis on literacy and numeracy standards, and marketisation and privatisation of various kinds. Drawing on theorising around the emergent relational, or topological, spatialities associated with globalisation, they show that context and culture do significantly influence how these accountabilities are locally enacted (e.g., in Australia versus Finland), with this varying uptake suggesting a decidedly 'vernacular' process of mediation. The chapter provides an evaluation of the Anglo-American model and calls for the development of an alternative 'authentic' model of educational accountability, one that reflects the broader societal purposes for schooling and which empowers local communities in conversation with their education authorities.

Chapter 23, by Kerry J. Kennedy, shares his understanding of teaching, learning, and assessment in Confucian heritage contexts based on reviewed literature and his extensive professional work in Hong Kong. He first reviews literature interrogating the influence of Confucian values, with a particular focus on Chinese educational contexts. He points out that the idea that there is one underlying cultural perspective is contested, with voices questioning the assumption that a single cultural perspective can be attributed to individuals simply because they occupy a common geographic space. Nevertheless, there is evidence, albeit inconclusive, that such values have influenced educational practice so that improvement, control, and accountability seem to provide the most salient rationale for assessment in what are called Confucian heritage cultures (CHCs). Assessment in these contexts, therefore, is not purely evaluative and takes on broader social purposes rather than simply being part of a 'testing' culture. This chapter concludes by advising that cultural assumptions should be subjected to research and stereotypes questioned.

Chapter 24 provides an insider view of assessment in the Islamic world by Egyptian scholar Atta Gebril. In the chapter, he focuses primarily on Arabic nations to show how in the last century, there has been rapid educational development, discussing how societies are seeking to define themselves under conditions of globalisation. Beginning with an introduction about Islam and history of education in Islamic countries, it then reviews research related to the characteristics of educational assessment within Islamic/Arabic societies, current assessment policies and practices, and the assessment challenges currently being experienced. He encourages readers to understand the incredible linguistic, geographic, ethnic, and cultural diversity characterising the Muslim world, but acknowledges that preserving/re-creating national identity and rationalising the distribution of limited educational opportunities have generally led such countries to adopt policies where assessment serves gate-keeping and accountability functions. While he suggests that alternative assessment approaches (e.g., Assessment for Learning) may help countries move away from such a strong accountability focus, he acknowledges that significant professional development and a shift in public ideas about the purpose of assessment would be needed for such implementations to be successful.

Chapter 25, by Fons J. R. van de Vijver, argues that if we want to achieve evidence-based assessment, we should reconceptualise the problem and adapt our procedures in multicultural assessment. He demonstrates that an adequate assessment of students in multicultural populations often requires a culture-informed, multidisciplinary approach. A taxonomy of bias and equivalence is presented to discuss problems of assessment. Special attention is paid to acculturation as a neglected factor in educational assessment in multicultural classrooms. He describes several cases of best practice, showing how these studies incorporated mixed methods procedures to ensure valid conclusions about performance and assessment tools.

Chapter 26 gives Chad W. Buckendahl's perspectives as a psychometrician on the general public's perceptions about assessment in education. At the heart of this chapter is a contention that the public's limited assessment literacy, based primarily on their own personal experiences and intuitive test theories, contributes to their perceptions regarding assessment policy and practice. This assertion is illustrated in one case (the United States) via longitudinal survey research about public perceptions about assessment. He suggests that educators play a key role in facilitating public assessment literacy development, arguing that it is their role to help students and their parents both understand assessment practices and use data coming from them. However, he acknowledges that as teachers often lack sufficient understanding themselves, particularly in relation to educational measurement, a first step might be to develop these professionals so they can then reach out to clear up misconceptions held by those in their local community. He also calls on the psychometric community to engage in further education and outreach and to develop strong relationships with media so appropriate messages, rather than misinformation, are disseminated.

In Chapter 27, Irvin R. Katz and Joanna S. Gorin review the evolving impact of technology on assessment, reflecting on how innovations may differently affect examinees and other assessment stakeholders. Framed by a historical overview, the authors discuss research that both (a) compares examinee performance on paper versus computer assessment and (b) investigates the role of examinees' familiarity or experience with technology as a means of understanding examinees' reactions to new technology-based assessments. Katz and Gorin note that although the literature on such comparisons offers some consistent results when comparing electronic with traditional testing formats, more research is needed in the case of innovative, interactive, technology-based assessments. The authors conclude that future research should move beyond coarse-grain comparison of assessment media, instead focusing on explanatory theories of differential performance that take into account richer (and more rigorous) measurement of technology familiarity as well as the design characteristics of computer-based assessment tasks.

In Chapter 28, Kadriye Ercikan and Guillermo Solano-Flores draw on their research on sociocultural context and assessment as a lens to synthesise main messages from the chapters within this section. The authors offer a conceptual framework for discussing two aspects of the dynamic relationship between assessment and sociocultural context: (1) the influence of culture and society on assessment, and (2) the influence of assessment on society. The authors highlight multiple examples of the strong bidirectional relationship between assessment and sociocultural context discussed in the chapters, drawing three conclusions. First, while bidirectional, the relationship between assessment and sociocultural context is not necessarily synergistic. Second, both within a country and in international test comparisons, standardisation does not necessarily ensure equity. Third, ignoring the relationship between assessment and sociocultural context leads to wrong expectations about the ways in which assessment can contribute to fair education reform.

The volume concludes in Chapter 29, where Gavin T. L. Brown and Lois R. Harris reflect on the current state of research knowledge around human and social conditions of assessment. We argue that the presence of error in all methods of data collection and interpretation is a problem that must be further acknowledged and discussed in relation to all forms of assessment, regardless of if they are used for high- or low-stakes purposes. Drawing on the in vivo/in vitro metaphor, we synthesise the threats to assessment validity and reliability discussed in the chapters. We argue that these threats are prevalent and often ignored in real classroom environments. The chapter considers implications from the volume for technology, psychometrics, and various purposes of assessment, attempting to envision something of what the future of assessment will be.

APPROACHES TO READING THIS VOLUME

While the book has been structured around individuals and groups, there are other thematic connections among the various chapters that the reader might wish to explore. We have attempted to insert cross-references to various chapters where appropriate, but there are numerous themes which have emerged across chapters. For example, interest in the impact of increasing the use of technology in assessment can be seen in chapters by Struyven and Devesa, Tierney and Koch, Strijbos, and Katz and Gorin. A number of chapters review policy developments in the last 50 years in OECD nations, with a special focus on the United States context; see Nichols and Harris; Lingard and Lewis; Teltemann and Klieme; and Buckendahl. While much of this work is focused on highly developed Western countries, there is interesting contrasting work from analyses of high-stakes public examination societies in chapters describing Confucian heritage cultures by Kennedy and the Islamic world by Gebril. Those interested in provisions for minority or special needs students would benefit from reading Moon and van de Vijver together. Multiple chapters also address issues around student-led assessment practices and their potential for self-regulation (e.g., Andrade & Brown, Panadero, Stribjos, Dinsmore & Wilson, Cowie & Harrison). While all authors have been asked to address implications for teacher preparation and professional development, chapters by Bonner, Hill and Eyers, and Lai and Schildkamp particularly address this theme.

Clearly, there is substantial crossover between Section 2 and Section 3, in which the student experience of being assessed, especially in a classroom context, is reviewed; research into self-regulation, emotional responses to assessment and feedback, cheating, and effort on tests plays itself out also in how students peer and self-assess, and so reading these sections interactively will be rewarding. Likewise, engaging with the four discussion chapters (Parr & Timperley, McMillan, Brookhart, and Ercikan & Solano-Flores) in conjunction with the final chapter by Brown and Harris provides a nice exploration and synthesis of major ideas within the volume. These are just a few of the numerous synergies we have found within the volume. We hope these tips help you appreciate the complexity and interconnectedness of the themes, issues, challenges, and priorities facing educational assessment.

Before you begin reading this volume, we would like to draw your attention to the cover graphic. The intersecting circles remind us of a handful of gravel being thrown into a still pond, disturbing its waters. The intersecting and overlapping circles and ripples represent the distorting and complicating effects that human and social factors have on the validity of educational assessments. We suggest that looking into the causes of those disturbances is a profitable exercise for improving the quality of educational assessment and decision-making arising from the sampling of student abilities, knowledge, and understanding. While individuals, cultures, and societies differ, it seems from reading the chapters in this volume that there are recurrent common themes around how assessment and evaluative practices impact on teachers, students, and cultures. An improved understanding of these common ripples will help us assess better. We believe that regardless of your role (e.g., teacher education, policy making, assessment research, or psychometrics), there is something for everyone who cares about the potential assessment has for improving life outcomes for learners, and we hope that you enjoy your journey through this messy terrain.

REFERENCES

Assessment Reform Group. (2002). *Assessment for learning: 10 principles. Research-based principles to guide classroom practice.* Cambridge, UK: Assessment Reform Group.

Berry, R. (2008). *Assessment for learning.* Hong Kong: Hong Kong University Press.

Black, P., Harrison, C., Lee, C., Marshall, B., & Wiliam, D. (2004). Working inside the black box: Assessment for learning in the classroom. *Phi Delta Kappan, 86*(1), 8–21.

Black, P., & Wiliam, D. (1998). Assessment and classroom learning. *Assessment in Education: Principles, Policy & Practice, 5*(1), 7–74.

Boekaerts, M., & Corno, L. (2005). Self-regulation in the classroom: A perspective on assessment and intervention. *Applied Psychology: An International Review, 54*(2), 199–231.

Bonner, S. M. (2013). Validity in classroom assessment: Purposes, properties, and principles. In J. H. McMillan (Ed.), *SAGE Handbook of research on classroom assessment* (pp. 87–106). Thousand Oaks, CA: SAGE.

Brookhart, S. M. (2003). Developing measurement theory for classroom assessment purposes and uses. *Educational Measurement: Issues and Practice, 22*(4), 5–12. doi:10.1111/j.1745–3992.2003.tb00139.x

Brookhart, S. M. (2013). The public understanding of assessment in educational reform in the United States. *Oxford Review of Education, 39*(1), 52–71. doi:10.1080/03054985.2013.764751

Brown, G.T.L. (2008). *Conceptions of assessment: Understanding what assessment means to teachers and students.* New York: Nova Science Publishers.

Brown, G.T.L. (2015, February). *The qualitative secret within quantitative research: It's not just about numbers.* Paper presented at the International Scientific Conference: Modern Approach to Social and Educational Research. Retrieved from http://bit.ly/1zSW16J

Burns, R. (1785). To a mouse, on turning her up in her nest with the plough. *Burns Country.* Retrieved December 4, 2015 from http://www.robertburns.org/works/75.shtml

Camilli, G. (1996). Standard errors in educational assessment: A policy analysis perspective. *Education Policy Analysis Archives, 4*(4), 1–17.

Chamberlain, S. (2013). Communication strategies for enhancing qualification users' understanding of educational assessment: Recommendations from other public interest fields. *Oxford Review of Education, 39*(1), 114–127. doi:10.1080/03054985.2013.764757

Cizek, G. J., Fitzgerald, S., Shawn, M., & Rachor, R. E. (1995). Teachers' assessment practices: Preparation, isolation and the kitchen sink. *Educational Assessment, 3*, 159–179.

Cronbach, L. J., Bradburn, N. M., & Horvitz, D. G. (1995). *A valedictory: Reflections on 60 years in educational testing.* Washington, DC: National Academy Press.

Hambleton, R. K., Swaminathan, H., & Rogers, H. J. (1991). *Fundamentals of item response theory.* Newbury Park, CA: Sage.

Harris, L. R., & Brown, G. T. L. (2013). Opportunities and obstacles to consider when using peer- and self-assessment to improve student learning: Case studies into teachers' implementation. *Teaching and Teacher Education, 36*, 101–111. doi: HYPERLINK "http://dx.doi.org/10.1016/j.tate.2013.07.008" \t "doilink" 10.1016/j.tate.2013.07.008

Kahn, E. A. (2000). A case study of assessment in a grade 10 English course. *The Journal of Educational Research, 93*, 276–286.

Kahneman, D. (2011). *Thinking, fast and slow.* London: Penguin Books.

Kane, M. T. (2006). Validation. In R. L. Brennan (Ed.), *Educational measurement* (4th ed., pp. 17–64). Westport, CT: Praeger.

Kane, M. T. (2013). Validity and fairness in the testing of individuals. In M. Chatterji (Ed.), *Validity and test use: An international dialogue on educational assessment, accountability and equity* (pp. 17–53). Bingley, UK: Emerald Group.

Klenowski, V., & Wyatt-Smith, C. (2012). The impact of high stakes testing: The Australian story. *Assessment in Education: Principles, Policy & Practice, 19*(1), 65–79. doi:10.1080/0969594x.2011.592972

McMillan, J. H. (2001). *Classroom assessment: Principles and practice for effective instruction* (2nd ed.). Boston, MA: Allyn & Bacon.

Messick, S. (1984). The psychology of educational measurement. *Journal of Educational Measurement, 21*(3), 215–237. doi:10.1111/j.1745–3984.1984.tb01030.x

Messick, S. (1989). Validity. In R. L. Linn (Ed.), *Educational measurement* (3rd ed., pp. 13–103). Old Tappan, NJ: MacMillan.

Newton, P. E. (2007). Clarifying the purposes of educational assessment. *Assessment in Education: Principles, Policy & Practice, 14*(2), 149–170.

Newton, P. E. (2013). Ofqual's reliability programme: A case study exploring the potential to improve public understanding and confidence. *Oxford Review of Education, 39*(1), 93–113. doi:10.1080/03054985.2012.760285

Nichols, S. L., & Berliner, D. C. (2007). *Collateral damage: How high-stakes testing corrupts America's schools.* Cambridge, MA: Harvard Education Press.

Parkes, J. (2013). Reliability in classroom assessment. In J. H. McMillan (Ed.), *SAGE handbook of research on classroom assessment* (pp. 107–123). Thousand Oaks, CA: SAGE.

Stiggins, R. J. (2002). Assessment crisis: The absence of assessment for learning. *Phi Delta Kappan, 83*(10), 758–765.

Swaffield, S. (2011). Getting to the heart of authentic assessment for learning. *Assessment in Education: Principles, Policy & Practice, 18*(4), 433–449. doi:10.1080/0969594X.2011.582838

Thompson, G. (2013). NAPLAN, MySchool and Accountability: Teacher perceptions of the effects of testing. *The International Education Journal: Comparative Perspectives, 12*(2), 62–84.

Tomlinson, C. A. (2001). *How to differentiate instruction in mixed-ability classrooms* (2nd ed.). Alexandria, VA: ASCD.

Wyatt-Smith, C., & Klenowski, V. (2012). Explicit, latent and meta-criteria: Types of criteria at play in professional judgement practice. *Assessment in Education: Principles, Policy & Practice, 20*(1), 35–52. doi:10.1080/0969594x.2012.725030

Wyatt-Smith, C., Klenowski, V., & Gunn, S. (2010). The centrality of teachers' judgement practice in assessment: A study of standards in moderation. *Assessment in Education: Principles, Policy & Practice, 17*(1), 59–75. doi:10.1080/09695940903565610

Zeman, N. (2001, April). Michael Ovitz, take two. *Vanity Fair.* Retrieved October 18, 2015 from http://www.vanityfair.com/news/2001/04/ovitz-200104

Zimmerman, B. J. (2008). Investigating self-regulation and motivation: Historical background, methodological developments, and future prospects. *American Educational Research Journal, 45*(1), 166–183.

Section 1

Teachers and Assessment

2

TEACHERS' PERCEPTIONS ABOUT ASSESSMENT

Competing Narratives

Sarah M. Bonner

I engaged in the task of writing this chapter expecting to find in the literature on teacher perceptions about assessment at best a tale of disorder, at worst a uniform negativity. Any student who has mastered introductory statistics can tell you that with these expectations, I felt a sense of dread. If teacher perceptions are essentially disorderly and unpredictable, they have no explanatory power; this is also true if they are invariant, whether at the negative or positive end of the spectrum.

Happily, my review of the literature has not confirmed my naïve expectations. There are many competing narratives about teacher assessment perceptions, but in reviewing the last 20 or so years of scholarship, I have come to recognize that the issue of competing narratives is itself a consistency. The story of teacher perceptions about assessment is no longer a story of confusion; it is a story of tension and conflict. That is progress of a sort, and certainly worth continued attention. Perceptions and behaviors deeply affect one another, and fixating on practice without due attention to perceptions may bear a cost. Perceptions matter, although their influence may be difficult to discern.

The chapter provides a selective review of empirical literature on teacher perceptions about student assessment in Grades K–12 internationally. Only studies whose major focus was on perceptions about assessment have been considered within the domain of this review. I have omitted scholarship on higher education and special needs assessment, which have unique traditions. An adequate discussion of issues in either field would merit a chapter of its own. Further, literature on teacher attitudes toward assessment when the subject assessed is the teacher her/himself (i.e., approaches to the evaluation of teachers by external reviewers) was beyond the scope of this chapter. Within those constraints, I have attempted to review and synthesize major trends in the empirical literature from the last 20 years.

An initial challenge in searching the literature was to decide on key words relevant to the term 'perceptions'. I included the following terms in my search: perception, conception, attitude, value, belief, and self-efficacy. Although each word has a unique meaning and connotations, I use 'perception' in this review as an umbrella term on the grounds that concepts, attitudes, values, and beliefs about assessment are all shaped by mental interpretations about perceived information and stimuli. I included perceptions about the self as a performer of assessment as well as perceptions about assessment processes and instruments. When summarizing relevant aspects of a particular study, I generally confined myself to those parts of the study that reported on teacher perceptions, concepts, attitudes, values, or beliefs, although many of the studies I reviewed described skills, practices, or self-report of practices as well.

I begin with an overview of scholarship that studies the structure of broadly defined concepts about assessment among teachers. I then review selected literature reporting teacher perceptions about classroom formative assessment or assessment for learning (AfL); grading, marking, and scoring summative assessments; and large-scale externally mandated assessment. Table 2.1 provides a summary of the reviewed empirical studies, which are dominated by cross-sectional survey methods. The discussion section teases out common themes from the diverse strands of scholarship, suggests directions for research, and explores implications for professional development and policy.

THE IMPORTANCE OF TEACHER BELIEFS

The theoretical framework adopted here draws on expectancy-value theory (e.g., Wigfield & Eccles, 2000), the theory of planned behavior (e.g., Ajzen, 1991), and the self-efficacy approach to understanding the relationship between belief and performance (e.g., Bandura, 1986). According to these related theories, beliefs flow from and express attitudes and values. Beliefs provide the basis for dispositions to act, which are profound predictors of behaviors (Ajzen, 1991; Bandura, 1986). From the perspective of motivation theory, individuals' attitudes and beliefs about how well they will do on an activity, and the value they ascribe to the activity, partly explain their persistence during performance of the activity (Wigfield & Eccles, 2000). Thus, teachers' beliefs, values, and self-efficacy or perception of competence in assessment (Bandura, 1986) and their perceived behavioral control over assessment (Ajzen, 1991) are expected to shape their assessment actions.

Because assessment is a professional responsibility as well as an individual activity, teachers are also affected in their perceptions and behaviors by the situational constraints of their sociocultural and policy contexts. New information from outside that is internally incompatible with prior beliefs generates stress or cognitive dissonance (Festinger, 1957). Although the "imposed physical and socio-structural environment is thrust upon people whether they like it or not" (Bandura, 1997, p. 156), individuals have leeway in how they construe and react to new information and conflicts. The amount of stress individuals experience relates to personal self-efficacy for tasks and characteristics of the environment (Bandura, 1997). In regard to teachers and assessment, teachers who believe in fulfilling their professional responsibilities and also believe that the purpose of assessment is to promote student learning may experience dissonance if they associate new duties with different assessment purposes (Festinger, 1957). They may, however, be able to learn from and synthesize competing beliefs if they perceive themselves to have high self-efficacy for assessment and to be in a supportive environment.

This chapter will demonstrate that teachers often hold conflicting beliefs about assessment. The relationship between their beliefs and their practices in assessment are likely affected by stress due to these internal conflicts, as well as contextual factors, external pressures, and professional development. This review and the discussion that follows take as a premise that it is desirable to resolve conflicts within teachers' beliefs systems and between those systems and the demands of the teaching profession in ways that support quality practices in assessment.

Table 2.1 Reviewed Empirical Studies on Teacher Perceptions About Assessment by Author (alphabetic order)

Source	Context	Preservice or In-service	Level/Content	Method/Design
Arkoudis & O'Loughlin, 2004	Australia	In-service	Primary & secondary ESL	Qualitative
Beydoğan, 2012	Turkey	Preservice	Preschool, primary generalist, secondary multiple content	Survey
Bonner & Chen, 2009	United States	Preservice	Primary generalist & secondary multiple content	Pre- post-survey
Bonner & Chen, 2012	United States	In-service	Primary generalist & secondary multiple content	Survey & interview
Brown, 2006	New Zealand & Australia	In-service	Primary generalist	Survey
Brown, 2009	New Zealand	In-service	Ages 10–12 generalist	Survey
Brown & Harris, 2009	New Zealand	In-service	Grades 5, 10 mathematics	Survey & interview
Brown & Michaelides, 2011	Cyprus & New Zealand	In-service	Primary generalist & secondary multiple content	Survey
Brown & Remesal, 2012	Spain & New Zealand	Preservice	Primary generalist & secondary multiple content	Survey
Brown, Harris, & Harnett, 2012	New Zealand	In-service	Primary generalist & secondary multiple content	Survey
Brown, Hui, Yu, & Kennedy, 2011	Hong Kong & China	In-service	Primary generalist & secondary multiple content	Survey
Brown, Lake, & Matters, 2011	Australia	In-service	Primary generalist & secondary multiple content	Survey
Büyükkarcı, 2014	Turkey	In-service	Primary English	Survey
Cicmanec, Johanson, & Howley, 2001	United States	In-service	Secondary mathematics	Survey
Cizek, Fitzgerald, & Rachor, 1995	United States	In-service	Primary generalist & secondary multiple content	Survey
Colby-Kelly & Turner, 2007	Canada	In-service	Secondary second language education	Survey, interview, document analysis
Davison, 2004	Australia and Hong Kong	In-service	Secondary English	Survey, think-alouds, interview
Dixon, Hawe, & Parr, 2011	New Zealand	In-service	Not stated	Interview, observation, document analysis

(Continued)

Table 2.1 (Continued)

Source	Context	Preservice or In-service	Level/Content	Method/Design
Gebril & Brown, 2014	Egypt	Preservice and in-service	Primary generalist & secondary multiple content	Survey
Green, Johnson, Kim, & Pope, 2007	United States	Preservice and in-service	Primary generalist & secondary multiple content	Survey
Griffith & Scharmann, 2008	United States	In-service	Primary science	Survey
Harris & Brown, 2009	New Zealand	In-service	Primary generalist & secondary multiple content	Interview
Hay & Macdonald, 2008	Australia	In-service	Secondary physical education	Interview & observation
Ingram, Louis, & Schroeder, 2004	United States	In-service	Secondary multiple content	Longitudinal with interview & focus group
James & Pedder, 2006	United Kingdom	In-service	Infant & primary generalist, secondary multiple content	Survey
Kerr, Marsh, Ikemoto, Darilek, & Barney, 2006	United States	In-service	Primary generalist & secondary multiple content	Longitudinal with interview & focus group
Klinger & Rogers, 2011	Canada	In-service	Grades 3, 6, 9 generalist	Survey
Llosa, 2008	United States	In-service	Primary English	Think-alouds
McMillan, 2001	United States	In-service	Grades 6–12 multiple content	Survey
McMillan, 2003	United States	In-service	Grades 5–12 multiple content	Interview
McMillan, Myran, & Workman, 2002	United States	In-service	Grades 3–5 multiple content	Survey
Milner, Sondergeld, Demir, Johnson, & Czerniak, 2012	United States	In-service	Primary science	Pre- post-survey & interview
Panadero, Brown, & Courtney, 2014	Spain	In-service	Primary generalist, secondary, post-secondary multiple content	Survey

Study	Country		Sample/Content	Method
Pope, Green, Johnson, & Mitchell, 2009	United States	In-service	Primary generalist and secondary multiple content	Critical incident response
Remesal, 2007	Spain	In-service	Primary generalist & secondary mathematics	Interview & document analysis
Remesal, 2011	Spain	In-service	Same sample as Remesal, 2007	Interview
Rieg, 2007	United States	In-service	Grades 7–9 multiple content	Survey
Sach, 2012	United Kingdom	In-service	Ages 4–9 generalist	Survey
Scholastic Gates Foundation, 2012	United States	In-service	Primary generalist and secondary multiple content	Survey
Segers & Tillema, 2011	The Netherlands	In-service	Secondary multiple content	Survey
Swan, Guskey, & Jung, 2014	United States	In-service	Grades 3–6 generalist	Survey
Tierney, Simon, & Charland, 2011	Canada	In-service	Grade 10 mathematics	Survey & interview
Torrance & Pryor, 1998	United Kingdom	In-service	Ages 5–7 generalist	Action research, interview, & observation
Volante, Beckett, Reid, & Drake, 2010	Canada	In-service	Primary generalist and secondary multiple content	Interview
Webb & Jones, 2009	United Kingdom	In-service	Primary generalist	Interview, observation, document analysis
Winterbottom, Brindley, Taber, Fisher, Finney, & Riga, 2008	United Kingdom	Preservice	Primary generalist & secondary multiple content	Survey
Wyatt-Smith, Klenowski, & Gunn, 2010	Australia	In-service	Primary generalist & secondary multiple content	Document analysis and analysis of 'teacher talk'
Young & Jackman, 2014	Grenada	In-service	Grades 7–9	Survey
Zhang & Burry-Stock, 2003	United States	In-service	Primary generalist & secondary multiple content	Survey

Note: Studies are cross-sectional and participants are in-service teachers unless otherwise noted.

THE STRUCTURE(S) OF TEACHER ASSESSMENT PERCEPTIONS

Is there a consistent underlying structure to how teachers perceive assessment? Validated measurements that confirm a replicable and interpretable latent structure would indicate that for at least some period of time and to some degree, individual teachers hold stable concepts about assessment. Individual differences in those conceptions might be useful to predict other relevant attitudes or behaviors. Understanding the dimensionality of teacher conceptions about assessment has the potential to help answer all kinds of questions about the effects of training and policy directives on outcomes.

Brown and colleagues (e.g., Brown, 2006; Brown & Harris, 2009; Brown et al., 2011; Brown & Michaelides, 2011; Gebril & Brown, 2014) have studied the dimensionality of teachers' conceptions about assessment extensively in multiple educational contexts over the last decade. Developed over several model-generation studies with New Zealand teachers and refined using factor analytic techniques, the Teachers' Conceptions of Assessment-III (TCoA-III) instrument assesses teachers' level of agreement with the following broad purposes of assessment: school accountability, student accountability, educational improvement, and the 'anti-purpose' conception that assessment is irrelevant. In New Zealand, Brown and Harris (2009) indicated that the four dimensions of teachers' conceptions were relatively independent of each other, and that teachers struggled to reconcile assessment for improvement and assessment for accountability purposes.

Several studies have attempted to confirm the TCoA-IIIA measurement model in different cultural and policy (e.g., low- versus high-stakes testing) contexts. Results thus far have not generally confirmed the factor structure found in New Zealand, where the official assessment policy is based on AfL principles. Brown et al. (2011) demonstrated that among teachers in Hong Kong and southern China, where the educational climate tends more toward high-stakes accountability, the measurement model differed; accountability was strongly related with improvement conceptions. Another factor structure was supported in Spain (Brown & Remesal, 2012), where the sample was composed of preservice teachers, and a study using TCoA items in the Netherlands identified yet another pattern (Segers & Tillema, 2011). Differences have been found even across contexts that are putatively similar in educational assessment policies. Using a revised measurement model, Brown and Michaelides (2011) demonstrated statistical invariance between teachers' conceptions in Cyprus and New Zealand, which have similar assessment policies; however, there were still fairly large differences between the Cypriot and New Zealand samples. Egypt has promoted educational policies to introduce formative assessment in classrooms, but Egyptian teachers' conceptions of the purposes of assessment still revealed different structural relations compared to those in New Zealand (Gebril & Brown, 2014). Like teachers in Hong Kong and China (Brown et al., 2011), Egyptian teachers associated school accountability with improvement purposes. These results suggest that the structure of teacher conceptions of assessment is not invariant across subgroups of the teaching population worldwide, although they may be internally consistent within or among some jurisdictions.

There is some evidence that teachers' perceptions about assessment covary with the level at which they teach, although it remains unclear whether this is due to structures and policies associated with different levels of schooling (e.g., primary and secondary), or whether it is due to the way prior beliefs about teaching, learning, and assessment influence teachers' job choices. Remesal (2007) contrasted the conceptions of assessment among primary and secondary teachers in Spain and discerned that secondary school teachers frequently held an 'accounting' conception of assessment related to authorizing and accrediting student performance, whereas primary school teachers more frequently were oriented to think of assessment for instructional purposes. She attributed teacher perceptual differences to policy differences at the secondary and primary school levels (Remesal, 2011). Brown et al. (2011) also detected significant variability among teachers working at different developmental levels in Queensland, Australia, where conceptions of primary teachers tended towards the improvement factor while conceptions of secondary teachers tended towards student accountability. At the time of the study in Queensland, a rigorous, externally monitored school-based assessment system existed only at the upper secondary level and only in some subject areas. Hence, while the observed differences might have related to the policy differences between the primary and secondary levels, they may also have related to other factors.

In sum, it appears that the structure of teacher beliefs about assessment in general is complex and varies by policy context and student development level. Individual factors not measured in these studies may also be at play in how teachers conceive of assessment. Teachers' perceptions about their decision-making authority within their educational system, their views about student motivation, and their own experiences as students are only a few of the many largely unexplored factors which may influence the way teachers internally organize concepts about assessment.

PERCEPTIONS ABOUT ASSESSMENT FOR LEARNING

Moving from assessment broadly defined to more constrained definitions, many researchers have endeavored to articulate teachers' sense of the value of AfL locally and internationally. Surveys in the last 15 years about teacher perceptions of AfL have consistently shown that teachers value AfL practices. Canadian teachers in second language classrooms at the pre-university level generally endorsed items about the value and importance of AfL practices such as feedback, student involvement, multiple methods, and student participation in generating success criteria (Colby-Kelly & Turner, 2007). In Grenada, both trained and untrained teachers espoused positive beliefs about using assessment to improve learning, correct misconceptions, and guide instruction (Young & Jackman, 2014). Winterbottom and colleagues (2008) found that teacher trainees in the United Kingdom (U.K.) valued assessment for promoting student autonomy and making learning explicit more than they valued a performance orientation. Using interviews as well as surveys, Büyükkarcı (2014) demonstrated that teachers at the primary school level in Turkey had generally positive perceptions about the value of AfL and a belief in making assessment an integral part of the learning process; Sach (2012) reported similar results through surveys of primary school teachers in the U.K. James and Pedder (2006) surveyed teachers in the U.K. about the classroom assessment practices they valued and their reports of their own practices. In general, teachers valued assessment practices that were consistent with the AfL framework, and did not value assessment practices that compared students to peers, summative assessment practices, or curriculum-oriented assessment planning.

Thus, multiple studies have shown that teachers internationally espouse beliefs in the value of AfL. It should be noted that most of these studies, which primarily rely on surveys, fail to capture the extent to which social desirability plays into teacher responses, or the likelihood that teachers will commit to the practice they espouse. In other words, these studies do not link cognitive expression of belief to actual behavior (Ajzen, 1991).

Specific AfL Practices: Peer and Self-assessment

Looking at the specific AfL practices of peer and self-assessment, several studies have shown that teachers perceive peer- and self-assessment techniques to be valuable (Bey-doğan, 2012; Büyükkarcı, 2014; Volante et al., 2010). However, teachers are relatively restrained in their support for peer and self-assessment. In Grenada, Young and Jack-man (2014) indicated that student self-monitoring and self-assessment were among items that were endorsed at low rates compared to other AfL practices, particularly among untrained teachers. In the U.K., James and Pedder (2006) indicated that peer assessment was a notable aspect of formative assessment that teachers in their sample did not strongly endorse. Also in the U.K., Sach (2012) discerned that teachers lacked confidence in the benefits of or their ability to implement several specific AfL strategies, particularly student self-assessment.

Variations in teacher perspectives on peer and self-assessment have been hypothesized to be partly a function of the developmental level at which they work. While both primary and secondary school teachers in New Zealand endorsed conceptions about the value of giving feedback to help students self-assess and using students and peers as a source of feedback (Brown et al., 2012), primary teachers agreed more strongly with items loading on both factors. On the other hand, Sach (2012) found that early primary school teachers were less likely to see the benefit of student learning from errors and peer assessment than middle-primary grade teachers. In a study of teachers in Spain, endorsement of the accuracy of student self-assessment rose markedly at the university level, but positive experience with self-assessment declined with grade level (Panadero et al., 2014). With these mixed results and only a handful of studies, research does not show a general trend relating support for peer and self-assessment to grade level.

Qualitative research has provided additional insight into teachers' mixed perceptions about peer and self-assessment (Dixon et al., 2011). Dixon and colleagues classified interview responses to questions about AfL along a continuum of perspectives, ranging from the 'assessment technician' to the 'assessment empowerer' (Dixon et al., 2011). Assessment technicians did not talk about the value of peer or self-assessment, and used language that placed students in a passive role rather than as agents in an assessment interaction. Those in the middle of the continuum tended to balance feasibility concerns against a perceived need for students to take an active role in assessment. Assessment empowerers espoused value for peer and self-assessment and used language that focused on student learning and development.

Overall, it appears that teachers generally support peer and self-assessment, but at a lower level of endorsement than many other AfL practices. Little is yet known about whether this is due to individual beliefs about student learning, characteristics of students, or other unmeasured factors.

Specific AfL Practices: Feedback

Research on teacher perceptions about feedback shows general support for use of non-evaluative or formative feedback, particularly at the primary level. In Turkey, Büyükkarcı (2014) found that primary school teachers held generally positive beliefs or perceptions about the value of giving non-evaluative feedback. In Canada, both primary and secondary groups perceived non-evaluative feedback as important (Volante et al., 2010). In New Zealand, teacher endorsement of specific feedback purposes and processes were reported to vary by student developmental level (Brown et al., 2012). Compared to secondary school teachers, primary school teachers agreed more strongly that feedback's main purpose was to improve learning, that it should be interactive, and that it must be timely. Perhaps not coincidentally, primary teachers in New Zealand also perceived a greater degree of school-level expectations related to their feedback practices.

Despite general endorsement at primary and secondary school levels, some researchers have found that feedback is an area of tension for teachers. Volante and colleagues (2010) described teachers as frustrated by conflicts between their assessment values and their self-perceived ability to implement feedback. Teachers felt challenged to reconcile giving formative feedback with reporting marks, and to implement peer assessment in ways that were educationally productive (Volante et al., 2010). Büyükkarcı (2014) discerned that teachers' beliefs about what 'should' be done in formative assessment matched poorly with their self-reported practices. For instance, Büyükkarcı reported a teacher who claimed that due to classroom crowding and curricular demands, students only received feedback on summative examinations, although the teacher recognized that this was not good practice (Büyükkarcı, 2014).

To summarize major trends in research on teacher perceptions about AfL, teachers generally endorse AfL practices such as using assessment to improve student learning and guide instructional responses. However, their beliefs about the general value of AfL sometimes conflict with their perceptions about certain practices, particularly peer and self-assessment and feedback, and their self-perceived ability to implement these practices in their own classrooms. Research has attempted to connect variability in teacher perceptions about AfL to student developmental level and local educational policy; however, there is insufficient work in these areas to discern a general trend. Individual differences in teacher self-efficacy and beliefs about student learning, as well as external factors, may also account for support of AfL.

PERCEPTIONS ABOUT GRADING, MARKING, AND SCORING SUMMATIVE ASSESSMENTS

There is a robust literature, especially in the United States (U.S.), indicating that the course grade or mark awarded summatively by school teachers is a "hodgepodge grade of attitude, effort, and achievement, created in an attempt to provide positive feedback to the student" (Brookhart, 1991, p. 36). Because much of the research basis for the 'hodgepodge' grade has been previously reviewed (Brookhart, 1994), only studies in the last 20 years will be discussed in this section. Cizek et al. (1995), taking up the charge from prior research, set the agenda for the next two decades when they demonstrated that from district to district, and teacher to teacher, grades combined a potpourri of elements, including formal and informal achievement information, and informal non-achievement information. Their conclusion was that teachers' individual and idiosyncratic values and beliefs about teaching strongly influenced their grading decisions, relative to contextual factors like district or school policies. The hodgepodge effect has been shown even within classrooms. In Canada, teachers espoused internally contradictory perceptions about grading; many surveyed teachers simultaneously believed that grades should reflect student performance on learning objectives, and that grades should reflect improvement (Tierney et al., 2011).

From this apparent disorder, researchers have attempted to infer coherent systems of beliefs from teacher self-report of grading practice or endorsement of practice. For instance, seeking to pull interpretable patterns from teachers' various conceptions about grading decisions through exploratory factor analysis, McMillan et al. (2002)

and McMillan (2001) reported that a non-achievement factor was an important grading dimension for many elementary teachers and secondary teachers. McMillan and colleagues labeled this dimension, characterized by using grades to report student qualities such as improvement, effort, and participation, as 'academic enabling'.

There is evidence that this and other dimensions of grading beliefs may be partly formed even before teachers are fully certified. Green et al. (2007) found no differences between preservice and in-service groups in perceptions about the ethics of a variety of grading practices including grading based on effort or growth. Bonner and Chen (2009), using vignettes to elicit implicit beliefs about grading decisions among preservice teachers, stated that preservice teachers already strongly espoused academic enabling approaches to grading. Further, high percentages, though not the majority, of preservice and in-service teachers in diverse samples have been shown to endorse using grades to manage student behavior by assessing late penalties, awarding zeros to address non-academic behaviors, and deducting points for misbehavior (Bonner & Chen, 2009; Green et al., 2007).

Little evidence has accumulated thus far that teachers' beliefs about awarding grades stem systematically from other individually held beliefs outside the grading or scoring domain. Cicmanec et al. (2001) found that teachers' orientation to pupil control was not a strong predictor of grading practice compared to contextual factors in the classroom such as class size and the proportion of students at-risk for failure. Bonner and Chen (2009) found only a small, though statistically significant, relationship between academic enabling beliefs and a constructivist orientation. However, research continues to suggest that knowledge and training relate to perceptions about grading and summative assessment. For instance, Tierney and colleagues (2011) reported that among teachers who experienced conflicts about grading, a plurality reported only some degree of awareness of recommended principles for grading.

Qualitative research has sought to explain in more depth why teachers endorse such diverse grading policies. McMillan (2003) proposed that teacher beliefs about the purposes of education in general (i.e., their educational philosophy) and their beliefs about the purposes of assessment (e.g., to motivate, to promote understanding) relate to the assessment practices they are likely to endorse. McMillan identified a desire among teachers to 'pull for' their students, resulting in a bias towards grading practices that are generally lenient or are heavily adapted to individual student needs (see also Bonner & Chen, 2009; Cizek et al., 1995). Davison (2004) asked senior secondary English language teachers in Australia and Hong Kong to verbalize their thinking as they graded responses to writing assessments. Davison classified teachers in groups along a continuum of assessment orientations, ranging from the 'assessor-technician' who was highly rule-bound, through the 'principled yet pragmatic professional', to the teacher at the extreme other end of the continuum who took a stance they termed 'assessor as God', expressing an intuitive and nearly omniscient understanding of students as individuals and little need for recourse to rules, standards, or objective assessment information during the grading process. The approach of this type of teacher-assessor makes an interesting contrast to the approach of the assessment empowerer (Dixon et al., 2011), especially in the case of a teacher classified as an AfL empowerer by Dixon and colleagues based on self-reported beliefs, but whose practice under observation was revealed to be characterized by high teacher control and only superficial engagement of students (Dixon et al., 2011).

To ameliorate internal and between-teacher conflicts, various methods to encourage teachers to stick to achievement or standards in grading have been implemented. Grades can be referenced to standards, or separate space on grade reports can be allotted to achievement and work habits, effort, or growth. There is thus far little evidence that reference to standards actually affects teachers' perceptions about the basis for awarding grades. Swan et al. (2014) reported that both teachers who did and did not use standards-based report cards indicated that they perceived standards-based grade reports to provide more and higher quality information compared to traditional grade reports. However, the teachers' perceptions about their own grading decisions were not measured. In Canada, in spite of implementation of a standardized system for reporting grades, Canadian teachers were found still to espouse grading based on improvement (Tierney et al., 2011). In Australia, physical education teachers continued to base their grades on internal expectations and intuitions about students, despite reference to standards in their discipline during the grading process (Hay & Macdonald, 2008). Further, no studies were found to indicate that separate reporting of achievement and effort has been linked to differences in teacher perceptions about how to award grades. Indeed, in the U.S., where most primary school grading includes separate marks for effort, primary school teachers still endorsed enabling approaches to grading (McMillan et al., 2002).

Studies that have looked particularly at the perceptions of teachers as they generate marks or scores on summative assessments provide insight into how teachers manage the complexities at play in their perceptions about grading. Llosa's (2008) qualitative study on teacher scoring processes and perceptions in the U.S. revealed that teachers struggled to resolve internal conflicts between beliefs about scoring for growth versus scoring on an absolute scale, and between perceptions of external pressure to meet particular score distributions versus desires to understand and focus on standards in scoring. In Australia, teachers were reported to arrive at grading decisions through a complex negotiation of cognitive and social factors which included, but was far from determined by, individual beliefs (Wyatt-Smith et al., 2010). Also in Australia, teachers participating in the scoring of large-scale language assessments were reported to experience anxiety and conflict between their roles as ESL teachers to use assessment to support learning and their roles as judges of student work (Arkoudis & O'Loughlin, 2004). In reviewing the literature on classroom summative assessment, Moss (2013) commented that even when teachers are aware of recommendations for grading practice, "they often see the realities of their classroom environments and other external factors imposed on them as prohibitive" (p. 252).

To summarize general trends in the literature on teacher perceptions about grading, many teachers believe that grading based on effort and non-achievement factors is a way of enabling students to succeed, and some consider it appropriate to use grades to manage student behavior. A complex and sometimes conflicted set of factors including teaching philosophy, teacher knowledge, and other sources of individual differences appear to shape these beliefs, which may be formed before professional experience begins. Research has not yet demonstrated that standards-referenced grading affects the factors teachers consider in making summative assessment decisions. Teachers have been reported to perceive tension between beliefs about AfL and expectations for summative assessment.

PERCEPTIONS ABOUT EXTERNALLY MANDATED ASSESSMENTS

Many, if not most, classroom teachers participate in the process of testing for accountability purposes in the schools, in terms of aligning their teaching to standards and performance expectations and responding to test results at the school or class level. In contexts where stakes are high, more teacher resources are often allocated to activities like test preparation, scoring, and results analysis. Teacher perceptions about externally mandated tests are likely to vary as a function of their involvement in such testing, as well as their individual perceptions about testing policies and practices (see Nichols & Harris, this volume).

Across several survey studies, teachers have been found to be neutral to negative about the value of externally mandated assessments. In Klinger and Rogers's (2011) survey of teachers in two provinces of Canada, the use of the provincial assessments was not seen as appropriate or related to the improvement of student achievement. Teachers were generally neutral about quality of data from the provincial assessments, and expressed concern that the assessments caused teachers to teach to the test. In a study of teachers in the U.S. by Scholastic, Inc. and the Gates Foundation (2012), teachers believed that standardized tests had value for broad reporting and accountability purposes, but did not consider tests to provide accurate or valid measurement of the skills and abilities of individual students. The large majority of teachers perceived that classroom formative assessments were more important measures of student achievement than were final exams or district and state examinations. In another U.S. study, one-third of elementary teachers believed that state or nationally mandated testing in reading and mathematics negatively impacted the teaching of science at the elementary level (Milner, Sondergeld, Demir, Johnson, & Czerniak, 2012). This is consistent with the findings of a larger survey study in the U.S. (Griffith & Scharmann, 2008), which found that more than half of sampled teachers perceived they had reduced instructional time in science since the onset of nationally mandated state accountability tests.

On the other hand, primary school teachers in New Zealand were found to associate school accountability assessment with deep learning (Brown, 2009). They associated standardized, formal formats with surface processing and with assessments intended to put students into categories, assign grades, or meet qualifications. In New Zealand, official policies support AfL, and standardized assessment for external reporting is not mandated until upper grades. The New Zealand case may indicate that negative perceptions about externally mandated assessments such as those cited above may relate to the nature of the assessments and how they are used, rather than to the notion of accountability itself. An assessment-based accountability system that does not result in categorizing individual students or rely on superficial selected-response format tests may be more palatable to some teachers. Nonetheless, in a phenomenographic study, Harris and Brown (2009) reported that even New Zealand teachers in their relatively low-stakes environment had concerns about teaching to the test and data manipulation on assessments used for external reporting.

Data Rich, Information Poor

Negativity in teacher perceptions about data quality and self-efficacy for interpretation of externally mandated tests results appears to be particularly salient in the U.S. In the wake of the No Child Left Behind legislation, standardized tests are used across the nation for accountability, and stakes for externally mandated tests are increasingly high. In interviews with teachers and school leaders working under a school-based Continuous Improvement framework in the U.S. (Ingram et al., 2004), many teachers preferred to judge their own effectiveness in reference to non-achievement student outcomes rather than test results, and even teachers who were concerned with test results were also concerned with non-achievement outcomes. Teacher-developed assessments and course grades were viewed by teachers, as well as school leaders, as better sources of information about teacher effectiveness than standardized test results, and teachers and school leaders sometimes preferred even informal information such as personal experience over information derived from external testing. Teacher interviews revealed mistrust of data quality, concern about data abuse, and a view of large-scale data use as a tradeoff for time with teaching (see also Brown & Harris, 2009). Also in the U.S., teachers in grades and content areas subject to state-mandated tests expressed frustration with the low information yield from test-based data (Bonner & Chen, 2012). One teacher described his professional situation as 'data-rich, information-poor.' Teachers' responses expressed a sense that school-based policies about the state testing program reflected narrow, constrained, and constraining ideas about learning and teaching. Such concerns and perceptions may lead to limited use of state test data in schools.

Some districts and school organizations in the U.S. have borrowed from industry to adopt a framework of organizational learning that relies heavily on data-based decision-making. Data-based decision-making among teachers and other school staff was studied intensively in three U.S. school districts (Kerr et al., 2006). Consistent with other studies, teachers questioned the quality of externally produced interim assessments and state test data, and perceived that classroom assessments provided more meaningful information. Further, many teachers, particularly those who were not given strong professional development on data use, perceived that they were not prepared to use assessment data in the ways their schools and districts would like. Related to the impact of professional development on teacher perceptions about their own assessment competencies, Zhang and Burry-Stock (2003) found that among U.S. teachers, those who had little training in assessment perceived themselves as less competent than their better trained peers in many aspects of assessment, including standardized testing.

Further, teachers appear to perceive tension between their beliefs about AfL and their beliefs about externally mandated tests and standardized test use. In interviews with primary school teachers in the U.K., Torrance and Pryor (1998) used phrases such as emotional turmoil and intense anxiety to describe the experiences of teachers who were trying to respond to increased assessment for accountability purposes while maintaining their internal beliefs about understanding young learners. According to the authors, questions about increases in assessment requirements for accountability provoked language that reflected great stress. Pope et al. (2009) indicated that teachers perceived frequent ethical dilemmas in assessment between institutional requirements for standardized testing and their own needs as teachers or their perceptions about student needs.

In summary, teachers have been shown to hold less than positive perceptions about externally mandated assessments, especially in the U.S. Perceptions of low test validity, low teacher self-efficacy for interpreting large-scale assessments, and lack of quality professional development have been reported as factors that inhibit large-scale test data use, and may be particularly salient in contexts where local or national policies encourage extensive use of standardized test data. Conflicts between beliefs about AfL and expectations or beliefs associated with large-scale testing may exacerbate negative perceptions about externally mandated assessments.

DISCUSSION

This review of the literature on teacher perceptions about assessment has revealed several consistent features in a diverse landscape. First, attempts to measure and understand broadly defined teacher conceptions about assessment show some consistencies in dimensions related to improvement and different accountability purposes, but also variability in conceptual structures between teacher groups, some of which may be due to the social context in which assessments are situated. Second, teachers across a variety of contexts perceive a positive value of AfL in theory, although they are sometimes less confident about their ability to enact some formative assessment practices. Third, teacher beliefs about the factors that they should include in their summative assessments and the processes they should use in awarding marks continue to diverge from professional recommendations, although one might have hoped that in the era of academic standards, more consistency in academic grading would be found. Fourth, perceptions about the value of assessment for accountability purposes range from neutral to negative, and in general, teachers prefer information from locally developed assessments to information from large-scale assessments.

Directions for Research on Teacher Perceptions

There are several areas where expanded research on teacher perceptions about assessment may improve understanding and practice. First, there is room for more focused review of the existing literature than this chapter has provided, especially in relation to change over time within local contexts. The educational landscape in many nations has undergone major shifts over the last two decades, which warrants studies that contrast current findings with prior accounts. Further, international policy implications of this review are beyond the scope of this chapter, but it is clear that work on many fronts needs to be done to understand fully the issues within those national educational assessment systems where practices and perceptions so evidently conflict.

Second, comparative studies that dig into questions of whether or how perceptions covary with student developmental levels, academic disciplines, or other teacher beliefs are needed to address gaps in the current literature. The trend seems to be that primary school teachers endorse AfL more than secondary school teachers, while secondary school teachers are more comfortable with assessment for student accountability. One can speculate that this is due to the traditional orientation of secondary school teachers to more formal assessments such as tests and quizzes (Frary, Cross, & Weber, 1993), or to generally lower stakes associated with testing at lower grades (e.g., New Zealand). However, no study was identified that was clearly able to demonstrate either connection, although research in these areas has begun to accumulate. International research that spans multiple levels of schooling needs to continue, and to be integrated with research that investigates other teacher belief systems. Also, little work has yet been done to compare teachers across multiple disciplines to understand if teachers hold discipline-specific perceptions about assessment.

Third, those interested in the area of AfL need to address issues in formative assessment where teachers struggle. Teachers' concerns about feedback seem to be primarily pragmatic, but nonetheless important. How can teachers effectively give timely and frequent feedback, and how can students effectively absorb it, given all the other pushes and pulls of the classroom environment? Regarding peer and self-assessment, there are issues possibly of a different nature. Although in this review I have treated them together, peer assessment and self-assessment are very different activities, and have different ways in which they impact learners (for more on self-assessment see Andrade & Brown, this volume; on peer assessment see Panadero, this volume). Each requires explicit coaching, practice, and development of student self-efficacy and/or communication and trust (Andrade & Valtcheva, 2009; Topping, 2013). Secondary school teachers in particular appear to doubt the value of some of these activities. More research needs to be performed to understand the nature of these doubts and to demonstrate positive impacts on learning through peer and/or self-assessment, especially at the secondary level. Without more evidence of impact on student learning, it is unlikely that secondary school teachers will be motivated to adopt peer or self-assessment widely.

Professional Development and Policy Implications

The dominant theme throughout this review has been one of tension and conflict. Teachers find it challenging to balance the expectations that surround externally mandated assessments with perceptions and beliefs that support AfL, when those two systems appear to be at odds. Introducing a special issue of *Language Testing*, Rea-Dickins asserted that "teachers find themselves at the confluence of different assessment cultures and faced with significant dilemmas in their assessment practices" (Rea-Dickins, 2004, p. 253). Teachers perceive that external pressures impact them both in how and what they assess (McMillan, 2003). They express negative emotions related to the conflicts between their own values and beliefs and external pressures, ranging from resignation to frustration to anger. Delandshere and Jones (1999) coined the phrase 'assessment paralysis' to describe the phenomenon of "tension between a call for change in curriculum and pedagogy on the one hand, and mandated tests that still reflect simplistic views of learning and curriculum on the other" (p. 238).

It may be a helpful heuristic to think of assessment practices as different colored fluids in a tube, constrained within a finite system of limited resources of time and training (Figure 2.1). Beliefs push and pull on the flow within and among types of practices. From this review, it is clear that there is a mismatch between how some teachers perceive space for different 'colors' of assessment should be allocated within the tube, and the actual allocation of space in local contexts, where time and human capacity also constrain implementation. Many teachers find themselves allocating more space to less valued activities related to accountability, and less space to more valued activities related to AfL. Discrepancies between espoused beliefs and practice (e.g., James & Pedder, 2006) are likely to be most common in contexts where AfL and accountability systems lack integration.

In an ideal system, AfL and accountability are integrated rather than divergent. In an integrated system, when additional practices are incentivized or mandated at the AfL side of Figure 2.1, there is a coordinated reduction in mandates at the accountability end, or the new assessment practices are designed to serve dual purposes of assessment for accountability and AfL. Such an integrated system appears to be in place in

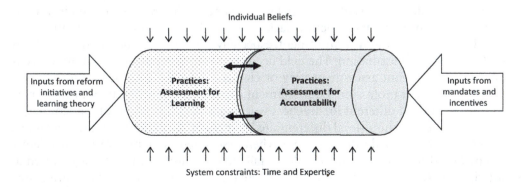

Figure 2.1 A System of Assessment Practice

New Zealand, for instance, particularly at the primary school level (Brown, 2009). Where integration is absent, 'pushes' at different ends of the system occur without reference or even in competition with one another. For instance, in some contexts such as the U.S., teachers and school administrators as well find it challenging to exercise whatever positive beliefs they hold about AfL, because higher-level mandates require emphasis on accountability testing to ensure a school's organizational survival. Under such circumstances, practices on the far end of the accountability side are increased, and in the space for AfL, either space is reduced or pressure builds. This can result in a reduction of instructional time for AfL, as discussed in Büyükkarcı (2014), or it can result in attitudes like that of the assessor-technician (Davison, 2004) or in the 'safe' simulation of AfL practices (Dixon et al., 2011).

When AfL and accountability practices are perceived to be very strongly at odds, the system may reach a limit. In that case, the result may be the suppression of internal values, inability to adopt desired strategies, and increasing frustration about a perceived disconnect between internal values and system values. There are myriad ways in which teachers can undermine a system whose values they do not support, from out-and-out corruption (e.g., cheating, Amrein-Beardsley, Berliner, & Rideau, 2010) to insidious behaviors that impact classroom climate. For some teachers, such frustration can end in burnout or exiting the profession. Delandshere and Jones (1999) stated "the dilemmas and struggles experienced by teachers should be regarded as an integral part of learning and change. But it is also possible that if left unassisted, these teachers will become overburdened by conflicts and the inconsistency of the goals they are expected to pursue" (p. 238).

What can be done to prevent such a negative outcome, when teacher beliefs don't align with dispositions to act in accordance with expectations? There is qualitative evidence that teacher perceptions about assessment can change with professional development. Webb and Jones (2009) studied the challenges and trepidations that six primary school teachers perceived over a two year period of professional development on formative assessment in the U.K. Their work suggests that development of teachers into successful formative assessment practitioners is a long-term process, and a teacher's developmental trajectory depends, at least in part, on his or her prior beliefs and motivation (see also Black, Harrison, Lee, Marshall, & William, 2003). Kerr and colleagues (2006) described a long-term process of professional development in the U.S. to improve data-driven decision-making among teachers and other school staff, and similarly found that the process was challenging and its effects were partly moderated by teacher beliefs (see also Ingram et al., 2004). Even researchers with extensive success in teacher professional development in assessment have asserted that a major hurdle to be overcome is developing coherence between teachers' AfL practices and their responsibilities for summative assessment (Black et al., 2003). Professional development can work, but it takes time and commitment, especially when prior beliefs and perceptions conflict with new information. The field needs improved understanding of how teachers' perceptions about assessment vary or change under different leadership models and given different professional development experiences. Further, if assessment perceptions are indeed different for teachers working at different levels of student development, studies of school-level differentiated professional development are warranted.

This review has made the case that when assessment systems are independently designed for different purposes and don't 'talk' to one another, the actions required to participate in them are more likely to compete for resources and create cognitive conflicts for teachers. However, AfL and accountability systems do not need to be viewed as separate systems. Under the framework of systemic validity (Frederiksen & Collins,

1989), particular educational assessments in a given context may be seen as components of a single, complex, and dynamic system. An assessment system has systemic validity when it supports all its purposes without conflict. Assessment choices of multiple stakeholders, including teachers, provide feedback to the system that determines its future. Teacher beliefs about assessment may lead them to make choices that support or detract from the overall goals of the entire system. Teachers' beliefs may influence them to adopt practices that support educationally valid purposes of their system, or that undermine the larger aims of their system, or whose principles and purposes lack educational validity but which other parts of their system requires. Implementation of educational mandates will be fuller and less fraught with tension when policy makers show flexibility by generating and sustaining assessment policies that support valid educational goals at all levels of the system and attend to the beliefs, values, and attitudes of diverse stakeholders, including teachers.

REFERENCES

Ajzen, I. (1991). The theory of planned behavior. *Organizational Behavior and Human Decision Processes, 50*(2), 179–211.

Amrein-Beardsley, A., Berliner, D. C., & Rideau, S. (2010). Cheating in the first, second, and third degree: Educators' responses to high-stakes testing. *Education Policy Analysis Archives, 18*(14), 1–33.

Andrade, H., & Valtcheva, A. (2009). Promoting learning and achievement through self-assessment. *Theory into Practice, 48*(1), 12–19.

Arkoudis, S., & O'Loughlin, K. (2004). Tensions between validity and outcomes: Teacher assessment of written work of recently arrived immigrant ESL students. *Language Testing, 21*(3), 284–304.

Bandura, A. (1986). *Social foundations of thought and action: A social cognitive theory.* Englewood Cliffs, NJ: Prentice Hall.

Bandura, A. (1997). *Self-efficacy: The exercise of self-control.* New York: Freeman.

Beydoğan, H. O. (2012). Evaluation of pre-service teacher's attitudes towards peer assessment. *International Journal of Academic Research, 4*(6), 60–69.

Black, P., Harrison, C., Lee, C., Marshall, B., & William, D. (2003). *Assessment for learning.* Berkshire, UK: Open University Press.

Bonner, S. M., & Chen, P. P. (2009). Teacher candidates' perceptions about grading and constructivist teaching. *Educational Assessment, 14*(2), 57–77.

Bonner, S. M., & Chen, P. P. (2012, April). *Teacher use of state test data for classroom instructional purposes.* Paper presented at the annual meeting of the American Educational Research Association, Vancouver.

Brookhart, S. M. (1991). Letter: Grading practices and validity. *Educational Measurement: Issues and Practice, 10*(1), 35–36.

Brookhart, S. M. (1994). Teachers' grading: Practice and theory. *Applied Measurement in Education, 7*(4), 279–301.

Brown, G.T.L. (2006). Teachers' conceptions of assessment: Validation of an abridged version. *Psychological Reports, 99*, 166–170.

Brown, G.T.L. (2009). Teachers' self-reported assessment practices and conceptions: Using structural equation modelling to examine measurement and structural models. In T. Teo & M. S. Khine (Eds.), *Structural equation modeling in educational research: Concepts and applications* (pp. 243–266). Rotterdam, NL: Sense Publishers.

Brown, G.T.L., & Harris, L. R. (2009). Unintended consequences of using tests to improve learning: How improvement-oriented resources heighten conceptions of assessment as school accountability. *Journal for Multidisciplinary Education, 6*(12), 68–91.

Brown, G.T.L., Harris, L. R., & Harnett, J. (2012). Teacher beliefs about feedback within an assessment for learning environment: Endorsement of improved learning over student well-being. *Teaching and Teacher Education, 28*, 968–978.

Brown, G.T.L., Hui, S. K. F., Yu, F.W.M., & Kennedy, K. J. (2011). Teachers' conceptions of assessment in Chinese contexts: A tripartite model of accountability, improvement, and irrelevance. *International Journal of Educational Research, 50*, 307–320.

Brown, G.T.L., Lake, R., & Matters, G. (2011). Queensland teachers' conceptions of assessment: The impact of policy priorities on teacher attitudes. *Teaching and Teacher Education, 27*(1), 210–220.

Brown, G.T.L., & Michaelides, M. P. (2011). Ecological rationality in teachers' conceptions of assessment across samples from Cyprus and New Zealand. *European Journal of Psychology of Education, 26*, 319–337.

Brown, G.T.L., & Remesal, A. (2012). Prospective teachers' conceptions of assessment: A cross-cultural comparison. *The Spanish Journal of Psychology, 15*, 1–19.

Büyükkarcı, K. (2014). Assessment beliefs and practices of language teachers in primary education. *International Journal of Instruction, 7*(1), 107–120.

Cicmanec, K. M., Johanson, G., & Howley, A. (2001, April). *High school mathematics teachers: Grading practice and pupil control ideology.* Paper presented at the annual meeting of the American Educational Research Association, Seattle, WA.

Cizek, G., Fitzgerald, S., & Rachor, R. (1995). Teachers' assessment practices: Preparation, isolation, and the kitchen sink. *Educational Assessment, 3*(2), 159–179.

Colby-Kelly, C., & Turner, C. E. (2007). AfL research in the L2 classroom and evidence of usefulness: Taking formative assessment to the next level. *The Canadian Modern Language Review, 64*(1), 9–38.

Davison, C. (2004). The contradictory culture of teacher-based assessment: ESL teacher assessment practices in Australian and Hong Kong secondary schools. *Language Testing, 21*, 305–334.

Delandshere, G., & Jones, J. H. (1999). Elementary teachers' beliefs about assessment in mathematics: A case of assessment paralysis. *Journal of Curriculum & Supervision, 14*(3), 216–240.

Dixon, H. R., Hawe, E., & Parr, J. (2011). Enacting assessment for learning: The beliefs practice nexus. *Assessment in Education: Principles, Policy & Practice, 18*(4), 365–379.

Festinger, L. (1957). *A theory of cognitive dissonance.* Stanford: Stanford University Press.

Frary, R. B., Cross, L. H., & Weber, L. J. (1993). Testing and grading practices and opinions of secondary teachers of academic subjects: Implications for instruction in measurement. *Educational Measurement: Issues and Practice, 12*(3), 23–30.

Frederiksen, J. R., & Collins, A. (1989). A systems approach to educational testing. *Educational Researcher, 18*(9), 27–32.

Gebril, A., & Brown, G.T.L. (2014). The effect of high-stakes examination systems on teacher beliefs: Egyptian teachers' conceptions of assessment. *Assessment in Education: Principles, Policy & Practice, 21*(1), 16–33.

Green, S. K., Johnson, R. L., Kim, D., & Pope, N. S. (2007). Ethics in classroom assessment practices: Issues and attitudes. *Teaching and Teacher Education, 23*, 999–1011.

Griffith, G., & Scharmann, L. (2008). Initial impacts of no child left behind on elementary science education. *Journal of Elementary Science Education, 20*(3), 35–48.

Harris, L. R., & Brown, G. T. (2009). The complexity of teachers' conceptions of assessment: Tensions between the needs of schools and students. *Assessment in Education: Principles, Policy & Practice, 16*(3), 365–381.

Hay, P. J., & Macdonald, D. (2008). (Mis) appropriations of criteria and standards-referenced assessment in a performance-based subject. *Assessment in Education: Principles, Policy & Practice, 15*(2), 153–168.

Ingram, D., Louis, K. S., & Schroeder, R. G. (2004). Accountability policies and teacher decision making: Barriers to the use of data to improve practice. *Teachers College Record, 106*(6), 1258–1287.

James, M., & Pedder, D. (2006). Beyond method: Assessment and learning practices and values. *Curriculum Journal, 17*(2), 109–138.

Kerr, K. A., Marsh, J. A., Ikemoto, G. S., Darilek, H., & Barney, H. (2006). Strategies to promote data use for instructional improvement: Actions, outcomes, and lessons from three urban districts. *American Journal of Education, 112*(4), 496–520.

Klinger, D. A., & Rogers, W. T. (2011). Teachers' perceptions of large-scale assessment programs within low-stakes accountability frameworks. *International Journal of Testing, 11*, 122–143.

Llosa, L. (2008). Building and supporting a validity argument for a standards-based classroom assessment of English proficiency based on teacher judgments. *Educational Measurement: Issues & Practice, 27*(3), 32–42.

McMillan, J. H. (2001). Secondary teachers' classroom assessment and grading practices. *Educational Measurement: Issues and Practice, 20*(1), 20–32.

McMillan, J. H. (2003). Understanding and improving teachers' classroom assessment decision making: Implications for theory and practice. *Educational Measurement: Issues and Practice, 22*(4), 34–43.

McMillan, J. H., Myran, S., & Workman, D. (2002). Elementary teachers' classroom assessment and grading practices. *The Journal of Educational Research, 95*(4), 203–213.

Milner, A. R., Sondergeld, T. A., Demir, A., Johnson, C. C., & Czerniak, C. M. (2012). Elementary teachers' beliefs about teaching science and classroom practice: An examination of Pre/Post NCLB testing in science. *Journal of Science Teacher Education, 23*, 111–132.

Moss, C. M. (2013). Research on classroom summative assessment. In J. H. McMillan (Ed.), *SAGE handbook of research on classroom assessment* (pp. 235–255). Thousand Oaks, CA: SAGE Publications, Inc.

Panadero, E., Brown, G., & Courtney, M. (2014). Teachers' reasons for using self-assessment: A survey self-report of Spanish teachers. *Assessment in Education: Principles, Policy & Practice, 21*(4), 365–383.

Pope, N., Green, S. K., Johnson, R. L., & Mitchell, M. (2009). Examining teacher ethical dilemmas in classroom assessment. *Teaching and Teacher Education, 25*(5), 778–782.

Rea-Dickins, P. (2004). Understanding teachers as agents of assessment. *Language Testing, 21*(3), 249–258.

Remesal, A. (2007). Educational reform and primary and secondary teachers' conceptions of assessment: The Spanish instance, building upon Black and William (2005). *The Curriculum Journal, 18*(1), 27–38.

Remesal, A. (2011). Primary and secondary teachers' conceptions of assessment: A qualitative study. *Teaching and Teacher Education, 27,* 472–482.

Rieg, S. A. (2007). Classroom assessment strategies: What do students at-risk and teachers perceive as effective and useful? *Journal of Instructional Psychology, 34*(4), 214–225.

Sach, E. (2012). Teachers and testing: An investigation into teachers' perceptions of formative assessment. *Educational Studies, 38*(3), 261–276.

Scholastic and the Bill and Melinda Gates Foundation. (2012). *Primary sources: 2012. America's teachers on the teaching profession.* Retrieved December 7, 2014 from http://www.scholastic.com/primarysources/pdfs/Gates2012_full.pdf

Segers, M., & Tillema, H. (2011). How do Dutch secondary teachers and students conceive the purpose of assessment? *Studies in Educational Evaluation, 37,* 49–54.

Swan, G. M., Guskey, T. R., & Jung, L. A. (2014). Parents' and teachers' perceptions of standards-based and traditional report cards. *Educational Assessment, Evaluation and Accountability, 26,* 289–299.

Tierney, R. D., Simon, M., & Charland, J. (2011). Being fair: Teachers' interpretations of principles for standards-based grading. *The Educational Forum, 75*(3), 210–227.

Topping, K. (2013). Peers as a source of formative and summative assessment. In J. H. McMillan (Ed.), *SAGE handbook of research on classroom assessment* (pp. 395–412). Thousand Oaks, CA: SAGE Publications, Inc.

Torrance, H., & Pryor, J. (1998). *Investigating formative assessment: Teaching, learning and assessment in the classroom.* Buckingham, UK: Open University Press.

Volante, L., Beckett, D., Reid, J., & Drake, S. (2010, May). *Teachers' views on conducting formative assessment within contemporary classrooms.* Paper presented at the annual meeting of the American Educational Research Association, Denver, CO.

Webb, M., & Jones, J. (2009). Exploring tensions in developing assessment for learning. *Assessment in Education: Principles, Policy & Practice, 16*(2), 165–184.

Wigfield, A., & Eccles, J. S. (2000). Expectancy-value theory of achievement motivation. *Contemporary Educational Psychology, 25,* 68–81.

Winterbottom, M., Brindley, S., Taber, K. S., Fisher, L. G., Finney, J., & Riga, F. (2008). Conceptions of assessment: Trainee teachers' practice and values. *Curriculum Journal, 19*(3), 193–213.

Wyatt-Smith, C., Klenowski, V., & Gunn, S. (2010). The centrality of teachers' judgement practice in assessment: A study of standards in moderation. *Assessment in Education: Principles, Policy & Practice, 17*(1), 59–75.

Young, J.E.J., & Jackman, M. G. (2014). Formative assessment in the Grenadian lower secondary school: Teachers' perceptions, attitudes and practices. *Assessment in Education: Principles, Policy & Practice, 21*(4), 398–411.

Zhang, Z., & Burry-Stock, J. (2003). Classroom assessment practices and teachers' self-perceived assessment skills. *Applied Measurement in Education, 16*(4), 323–342.

3

ACCOUNTABILITY ASSESSMENT'S EFFECTS ON TEACHERS AND SCHOOLS

Sharon L. Nichols and Lois R. Harris

School accountability systems provide information to the public about how schools are performing, demonstrating that the public and/or private funds entrusted to them are leading to improved student outcomes (Cizek, 2001). Parents and taxpayers reasonably want to know if schools are doing their job. After all, businesses are held accountable, so why shouldn't schools (and those who work in them)? Despite the 'soundness' of this logic, creating a balanced and fair accountability system in education is difficult for many reasons. In business, the bottom line is easy to agree upon (profit) and measure. By contrast, in education, the desired outcomes are many (e.g., citizenship, knowledge, interest in and value for learning) and are far more difficult to measure.

While there are many potential ways to judge school success (e.g., success of graduates in the workforce, school completion rates, parent/student satisfaction surveys, or measures of student creativity), within the Anglo-American model of school accountability (see Lingard & Lewis, this volume), test scores have been promoted as a cost effective and efficient way to accomplish multiple evaluative goals. In this model, tests provide evidence of students' academic progress, but are simultaneously used to evaluate and make decisions about the effectiveness of teachers and schools. Within such an accountability system, tests are considered 'high-stakes' since there are significant consequences that can follow students' positive or negative performance, both for individual students and their teachers and schools. Following the ideology of business, where successes are judged by profit margins, here schools, teachers, and their students are judged by test scores.

Using tests to evaluate students and determine who merits particular promotions or opportunities is not new. China's *keju* system, spanning over 1,300 years (AD 605–1905), used tests to "identify and recruit the most capable and virtuous individuals into government instead of relying on members of the hereditary noble class" (Zhao, 2014, p. 32). These tests were extremely high-stakes since doing well could offer a way out of poverty and into positions of nobility and power; however, these stakes primarily affected examinees and their families. Student accountability and school accountability are two distinctly different purposes for assessment (Brown, 2008). While student accountability assessment systems (like the keju) are designed to hold the student responsible for his or her learning, in test-based school accountability systems, a somewhat more recent phenomenon (Giordano, 2005; Herman & Haertel, 2005), results are used to determine the teacher and/or school's effectiveness and justify educational reforms.

The form and function of nations' educational accountability systems vary in two main ways. First is the locus of control. An accountability system can be directed and managed by the national government, primarily by local control, or by a mix of the two. Second, different indicators are often used; while some systems (e.g., most American states) rely primarily on one indicator (e.g., results from a battery of tests), in other systems (e.g., Finland, New Zealand) multiple measures of performance are considered (e.g., teacher observations and diverse evidence of student achievement). Accountability systems of all types may exert a level of pressure on educators to perform; however, that pressure varies enormously depending on the number and type of indicators present within the system, and the consequences attached. Undoubtedly, educators working in contexts where control is centralized and only a single indicator (e.g., test scores) is used experience the greatest pressure as the measure is narrower in focus and demands are more rigid and monolithic (i.e., the indicator is not adapted to local conditions).

The United States is an example of a country that has adopted an accountability system in which students' standardized test performance is often used as the *single* indicator of educational quality. Nationwide, students who attend public schools are subject to annual standardized tests, the results of which are often used to make decisions about the quality of their school, effectiveness of their teacher, and their academic progress. Administrators, teachers, and students are held accountable to these test scores by a system of high-stakes consequences that are triggered by students' performance. When students do well, educators are rewarded (e.g., positive publicity about the school and teacher promotion or bonuses), but if students do poorly, everyone is subject to punishing outcomes (e.g., sanctions or replacement of teaching staff). Importantly, the number and types of consequences attached to test scores varies even throughout the U.S.

The use of tests as the sole measure of educational quality is irresponsible and highly problematic. Such tests have been designed to examine what individual students know and can do, but school accountability systems use them to infer the quality of the teacher and school, usually without considering or controlling for other external factors that also influence student performance (e.g., effects of the child's previous teachers/schools; parental influences; student variables like effort during test-taking, motivation to learn at school, health and well-being). Unfortunately, humans are very quick to adopt simplistic causal explanations (e.g., scores are low, so bad teaching is to blame), even when such conclusions are not warranted (Kahneman, 2011). Those outside of the psychometric community seldom understand the limitations of assessments (e.g., measurement error), and the role of statistical processes (e.g., regression to the mean) on score increases and decreases (Gardner, 2013).

Eminent social scientist Donald Campbell warned us a long time ago about what can happen when a single indicator is used for high-stakes decision-making. He argued, "the more any quantitative social indicator is used for social decision-making, the more subject it will be to corruption pressures and more apt it will be to distort and corrupt the social processes it was intended to monitor" (Campbell, 1976, p. 49). Thus, reliance on test scores, which can be viewed as a single indicator, to measure something as complicated as the process of education is likely to corrupt and distort that process, rendering the results invalid for any purpose.

It is difficult (and beyond the scope of this chapter) to examine all types of account-ability systems and their effects internationally—not only do educational policies vary widely, but they change over time. Instead, we take a case study approach, reviewing what is known about the effects of educational accountability in the United States on teachers and teaching, focusing on high-stakes testing as mandated under the No Child Left Behind act of 2001 (NCLB, 2001) and the subsequent 2009 Race to the Top (RttT) grant program (U.S. Department of Education, 2009). Under these policies, the U.S. has implemented one of the most rigid, centrally imposed educational accountability systems in the world. This case explores what we have learned about the effects of these policies on teachers and serves as a cautionary tale for other countries who entertain similar ideologies of educational oversight. The discussion examines the generalizabil-ity of these findings to other contexts and provides some examples of alternative sys-tems that may serve accountability purposes without the strong negative consequences found within the U.S. system.

A BRIEF HISTORY OF HIGH-STAKES TESTING IN THE U.S.

Virtually any test students take could be considered a high-stakes situation for the pupil, since good or bad performance has consequences (e.g., higher/lower grade point averages, tertiary entry, or job assignments). Of course, the pressures associated with these stakes vary widely depending on the type of test a student takes (e.g., college-entry vs. classroom-based) and the kind of educational goals he/she has in mind at the time (i.e., how important is this test to me?). In contrast to these everyday tests, in this chapter we use the term high-stakes testing specifically to refer to an *externally imposed* system of standardized testing where scores are used to hold administrators and teachers accountable for what students have (or have not) learned on an annual basis (Giordano, 2005; McDonnell, 2005).

The theory of action (or rationale) for high-stakes testing suggests that by tying significant consequences (i.e., incentives and punishments) to students' test score per-formance, teachers and their students will be motivated to work harder and more effec-tively, resulting in learning gains over time and a reduction in ongoing achievement gaps between student groups (Carnoy, Elmore, & Sisken, 2003; Raymond & Hanushek, 2003). In the United States under NCLB and RttT, high-stakes testing accountability is the mechanism adopted to transform and improve how schools function, teachers teach, and students learn (Jennings, 2015).

Testing and School Reform

The practice in the United States of using standardized tests to make decisions about teachers and students partly stems from decades of 'manufactured' discontent about the quality of America's public school system (Berliner & Biddle, 1995; Glass, 2008). This ongoing criticism leveled at public schools was occasionally made more salient by certain sociopolitical events. For example, Russia's 1957 satellite launch was used as evidence that the U.S. education system was rapidly falling behind, particularly in science and math (Bracey, 2008). Later, *A Nation at Risk* (National Commission for Excellence in Education, 1983) argued that the American school system was eroding rapidly, so if solutions were not found and implemented immediately, America's very economic vitality would be devastated. More recently, critics have pointed to America's average test performance on international tests (e.g., PISA) as 'proof' that it is failing to prepare students to compete globally (Armario, 2010; Berliner, Glass, and Associates,

2014; Duncan, 2010). Over time, the narrative that America's public school system is 'failing' or is in 'crisis' has helped to spur widespread support for the use of high-stakes testing (Glass, 2008; Ravitch, 2011, 2013).

Accountability Policies Featuring High-stakes Testing

For at least a century, various regions of the U.S. have experimented with high-stakes testing as a strategy for reform (Lavigne, 2014; Lavigne & Good, 2014). It was not until the early 1990s that high-stakes testing as a lever for reform was used more systematically. In the early 1990s, Texas began using standardized tests as a way to evaluate teachers and schools and to distribute significant consequences to schools (via public ranking systems), teachers (via tenure/promotion decisions), and students (diplomas were contingent on performance) (Craig, 2009). Texas school leaders and politicians touted the 'success' of this approach to school reform by holding up data that seemed to show student achievement and graduation rates were improving as a result of high-stakes testing policies. Although it was later shown that these successes were 'myths' (Haney, 2000), by 2001, politicians overwhelmingly (and unquestioningly) supported the promise of high-stakes testing accountability for transforming school outcomes through the bipartisan passage of the No Child Left Behind act (NCLB, 2001) (Nichols & Berliner, 2007a).

NCLB is a complex piece of federal legislation that made states' access to federal education tax dollars contingent on their compliance with its requirements. While containing many mandates, the central feature focused on here is the high-stakes testing component. Specifically, states had to implement five key steps to be in compliance with federal law. First, all states had to define and distribute a set of core academic standards across all grade levels and subjects. States then had to develop a battery of criterion-referenced standardized tests in core subject areas (i.e., math, reading, and science) that would gauge students' progress against these grade level standards. Next, states identified cut-score targets that would define academic proficiency levels (i.e., what score constitutes proficient vs. failing, etc.). Next, states had to develop a set of aggregate proficiency targets each school was expected to meet annually (dubbed Adequate Yearly Progress or AYP). AYP spelled out annual achievement targets that would ultimately lead to 100% of students passing the battery of tests by the year 2014. And lastly, all states had to implement a system of escalating consequences for schools if they failed to meet AYP targets. Although states varied widely in their target goals and test proficiency cut-scores, all faced a system of consequences based primarily on how students performed on the state battery of tests.

Race to the Top (RttT) was the follow-up policy to NCLB. RttT is a $4 billion competitive grants program that incentivized states to reorganize their policies to align with federal government educational reform goals. The primary feature of RttT was the use of tests to evaluate teachers. Although this was embedded throughout NCLB, with RttT the use of tests, growth scores, and other indicators to evaluate teachers became an even more central focus (Lavigne & Good, 2014). Whereas NCLB was a comprehensive approach to school reform that used high-stakes testing systems as its main platform to evaluate schools, teachers, and students, RttT encouraged states to explicitly use standardized tests to gauge teacher 'effectiveness.' It required that teachers be evaluated primarily (although not necessarily solely) on student growth (i.e., improvement in student achievement on tests over time).

Since its release, 18 states and the District of Columbia have received RttT grants. The outcome has been that states vary even more in terms of the role standardized tests play in making high-stakes decisions about educational leaders and teachers. Although some states continue to rely primarily on students' standardized test performance for distributing consequences, in other states (such as those who received RttT grants), evaluation systems may rely on multiple indicators (test scores, and/or growth scores, and/or value added scores, and/or observation measures) and focus more centrally on using these scores to make decisions about teachers (i.e., recruitment, retention, and firing). Although states vary somewhat in terms of the number of indicators used for evaluating teachers, the core feature of high-stakes accountability testing persists and, in many states, educators continue to face higher (or increasing) pressures tied to student testing.

INTENDED AND UNINTENDED CONSEQUENCES OF HIGH-STAKES ACCOUNTABILITY TESTING

Since the mandated institution of high-stakes accountability tests in the U.S. in 2001, we have come to learn a great deal about the intended and unintended effects of high-stakes testing practices on teachers and their students within the United States (Boohrer-Jennings, 2005; Jones, Jones, & Hargrove, 2003; Nichols & Berliner, 2007a; Valenzuela, 2005). While it was the intention of the law to increase student learning and reduce ongoing and pervasive achievement gaps (as measured by tests), there is still no strong evidence either of these goals have been achieved. Additionally, data from the U.S. suggest that the NCLB and RttT high-stakes testing systems have affected preservice and in-service teachers in numerous ways.

Achievement

Isolating the impact of high-stakes testing on student achievement trends over time is challenging because these effects are often confounded with other variables (Koretz, 2008). Still, most data available seem to suggest that high-stakes testing does not improve student learning and, in some cases, may undermine it. For example, Nichols, Glass, and Berliner (2006, 2012) examined the relationship between their empirically derived measure of accountability pressure across 25 states and its relationship to student achievement as measured by the low-stakes National Assessment of Education Progress (NAEP). Their examination of NAEP trends in fourth and eighth grade math and reading revealed that high-stakes testing seemed to be positively connected to fourth grade math achievement, but was largely unconnected to eighth grade math and fourth and eighth grade reading achievement. Importantly, in some cases, high-stakes testing was inversely related to reading. Nichols et al. (2006) argued that these results suggest that high-stakes testing may incentivize greater teaching to the test (more easily done around the fourth grade curriculum), explaining why they found a positive relationship in fourth grade math only. Others have found similar results (Braun, 2004; Dee & Jacob, 2009; Rosenshine, 2003). Data suggest that high-stakes testing has not had the desired effects of increasing student achievement (Grodsky, Warren, & Kalogrides, 2009; Jennings & Bearak, 2014; Nichols, 2007; Reardon, Atteberry, Arshan, & Kurlaender, 2009; Winters, Trivitt, & Greene, 2010), reducing the achievement gap (Braun, Chapman, & Vezzu, 2010; Braun, Wang, Jenkins, & Weinbaum, 2006; Timar & Maxwell-Jolly, 2012), or increasing graduation rates (Holme, Richards, Jimerson, & Cohen, 2010; Marchant & Paulson, 2005).

There is also evidence of unintended (and largely negative) consequences from these policies. As Campbell's law suggests, when teachers are pressured to get students to pass a particular test, undesirable effects, such as deleterious instructional practices, often result (Nichols & Berliner, 2007a; Perlstein, 2007; Ryan, 2004).

Preparing to Become a Teacher

There are connections between how students experience school and how they see education later as a teacher (Anderson, 2001; Flores & Day, 2006, Hollingsworth, 1989). For example, preservice teachers' pedagogical and instructional understandings and worldviews about learning are shaped by their previous experiences (Anderson, 2001; Hollingsworth, 1989), making it reasonable to infer that the experience of taking high-stakes tests as students might inform their practice as teachers. As Hollingsworth (1989, p. 168) suggests, our previous experiences act as "filters for processing program content and making sense of classroom contexts."

There have been few studies to examine this connection as it relates specifically to high-stakes testing contexts. One exception comes from Brown (2010), who conducted a qualitative study with eight female preservice teacher candidates from Texas—a state with a long history of high-stakes testing. Brown (2010) reported that most of the candidates believed that the tests they had taken as students were not too difficult. While initially their perceptions of teaching seemed simplistic (e.g., teachers only teach to the test), Brown (2010) found that upon probing, their understandings were actually more complex. According to one candidate, the role of the teacher is to get "the student ready for society—socially, academically, and emotionally" (p. 483). This suggests that a history of classroom experiences dictated by tests and testing do not necessarily restrict preservice teachers' views of the broader purposes of schooling.

Initial ideas about being a teacher and the role of assessments in teaching, however, are also shaped through teacher education experiences (Barnes, Fives, & Dacey, 2015). Studies suggest that preservice teachers experience conflict between their classroom observations and their learning in teacher preparation classes (Brown, 2010; Gerwin, 2004). For example, Brown (2010) found that during field experiences, teacher candidates' beliefs about what constitutes 'good' teaching grew more conflicted as they observed their cooperating teachers spending a great deal of time preparing students for the state test. Particularly salient was the issue of how to develop important skills like critical thinking, while simultaneously teaching what would be on the state test, goals often in direct conflict (Au, 2007). Given limited class time, beginning teachers may worry that excessive test preparation activities will squeeze out the more authentic, spontaneous, and critical inquiry based activities modeled as effective pedagogy in their teacher preparation program.

There are also issues relating to preservice teachers' understandings of test bias, discipline boundaries, and academic achievement. Doppen's (2007) Ohio study found that while preservice social studies teachers were able to articulate opinions about fair and unfair uses of testing, they were seldom able to identify actual bias within test items or propose viable alternatives to multiple-choice testing. These gaps made most candidates unprepared to effectively enter debates around assessment and accountability or identify what was or was not appropriate content to test within their discipline. Brown and Goldstein's (2013) study of preservice teachers revealed their confusion and uncertainty about what academic achievement actually meant. This stemmed from conflicts between their initial concept of achievement as the demonstration of academic progress versus the NCLB position that achievement only occurred when a specific proficiency target (measured solely via tests) was reached. Barrett (2009) also found that preservice and new teachers experienced internal and external conflicts whereby internal altruistic motivations to teach were increasingly frustrated by perceptions of external control perpetrated by high-stakes testing systems. It remains unclear how preservice and new teachers may deal with these somewhat conflicting ideas about their role (i.e., complex notions around holistic education versus the pressures to teach to the test), and this area certainly warrants further research and greater attention in teacher education programs.

Being a Teacher Under High-stakes Testing

High-stakes accountability testing has significantly impacted in-service teachers within the United States; their work has intensified and expanded (Valli & Buese, 2007) and their relationships with students and instructional autonomy has been affected (Watanabe, 2007). Valli and Buese (2007) conducted a mixed methods longitudinal (2001–2005) study of approximately 150 fourth and fifth grade reading and mathematics teachers, examining how instructional practices changed as NCLB implementation began. They found teachers' autonomy and control were undermined by NCLB's curriculum demands as teachers were often expected to move through curriculum at prescribed times. Simultaneously, teachers had to interpret and use test data to provide differentiated instruction and tutoring in a strategic way to make sure underperforming students passed the test, thus increasing their workload. Tensions emerged as prescribed curriculum pacing was often at odds with the philosophy of differentiated instruction where the pace of and approach to learning is adjusted to suit the individual learner (Moon, this volume). While encouraging teachers to increase differentiation is a potentially positive effect of this testing regime, the mandate that all students be at the same place at the same time, coupled with the pressure of making sure all content on the test is 'covered,' make effective differentiation extremely difficult, especially within schools that serve disproportionately high numbers of poor and minority students (Holme et al., 2010; Orfield, Losen, Wald, & Swanson, 2004; Vasquez Heilig & Darling-Hammond, 2008).

Valli and Buese (2007) identify that changes in teachers' roles have significant consequences for their pedagogies, relationships with students, and well-being. The barrage of tests and work associated with their administration, scoring, and interpretation interfered with teachers' abilities to establish quality relationships with students. Many teachers believed the constant testing was demoralizing to students, especially those struggling: "Do we have to keep slapping it in their face?" (Valli & Buese, p. 548). In short, the emphasis on tests disrupted teachers' abilities to invest quality time with students, making tests not "worth the price of diminished relational roles with their students" (Valli & Buese, p. 548).

There are few large-scale studies to examine the connection between high-stakes testing practices and teacher work satisfaction. Although Grissom, Nicholson-Crotty, and Harringon's (2014) large-scale study examining NCLB's impacts on teacher satisfaction seemed to show little to no effect (with the exception of a small effect on perceptions of teacher cooperation), their aggregate findings likely masked the wide variation in teachers' experiences across high and low socioeconomic status (SES) contexts in the U.S. Research focusing on teachers who work in high poverty contexts has found that they experience heightened pressures as a result of high-stakes testing (Abrams, Pedulla, & Madaus, 2003; Johnston-Parsons, & Wilson, & The Teachers at Park Street Elementary, 2007; Nichols & Berliner, 2007a; Nichols et al., 2006; Pedulla, Abrams, Madaus, Russell, Ramos, & Miao, 2003; Perlstein, 2007), leading to greater teacher dissatisfaction and lowered morale (McNeil & Valenzuela, 2001; Vasquez Heilig & Darling-Hammond, 2008). Initially, accountability labels (i.e., forms of sanctions where schools are identified as underperforming) tended to trigger teacher motivation to improve via increased effort and time, new approaches, attendance at professional development workshops, and greater collaboration to address challenges (Finnegan & Gross, 2007; Johnston-Parsons et al., 2007). However, the research suggests that over time these challenges were too great for the teachers alone to overcome (Berliner, 2013, Biddle, 2014), and they eventually became demoralized. Numerous qualitative studies (Barksdale-Ladd & Thomas, 2000; Taylor, Shepard, Kinner, & Rosenthal, 2003) illustrate the concerns teachers have relating to pressure caused by the tests (which may cause some to leave the profession) and the feeling that their autonomy and professionalism is being undermined.

Another unfortunate byproduct of high-stakes testing systems has been the creation of conditions under which some teachers turn to overt and covert forms of cheating and manipulation to help bolster their students' scores on these tests (Amrein-Beardsley, Berliner, & Rideau, 2010; Nichols & Berliner, 2007b). Data suggest those in low-performing contexts are far more likely to engage in inappropriate manipulations of test conditions or data (Jacob & Levitt, 2003). Teacher cheating may take many different forms, from telling students some questions ahead of time, allowing students more time or support than guidelines stipulate, or, in extreme cases, changing student answers on their tests. Teacher motives can vary as well. Some undoubtedly are acting to retain their jobs, while others may be concerned about the impact of continued failure on student well-being or their own promotion (Amrein-Beardsley et al. 2010). Regardless of the motivation, such manipulations undermine the validity of scores being used to make decisions about students, teachers, and schools.

The pressures of high-stakes testing throughout the U.S. have influenced teachers' instructional approaches. While Au's (2007) review of U.S. studies from 1992–2006 suggests that in 25% of studies high-stakes testing led to positive curriculum changes (e.g., broadening of curriculum, increase of collaboration and student-centered pedagogies, and integration of knowledge), the majority showed evidence of narrowing curriculum, test-centered pedagogies, and increasing fragmentation of knowledge. Au (2007) concluded that the nature of the test itself strongly influenced its effects upon curriculum. Most studies suggest the curriculum has been narrowed significantly, with tested subjects and content receiving greater time and attention (Jennings & Bearak, 2014; Vasquez Heilig, Cole, & Aguilar, 2010). Data also suggest testing-pressures may alter how certain subjects are taught. For example, in English, the pressures of testing may restrict creativity and compromise learning, subsequently undermining overall test validity (Au & Gourd, 2013). Watanabe's (2007) study of middle school English teachers in North Carolina indicated tests and test preparation took time away from broader learning objectives within the subject, undermined student motivation for reading literature, decreased collaborative activities, and made writing instruction "less like a real writer writes" (p. 335). Journell's (2010) study of social studies teachers found many were hesitant to use class time to discuss relevant current political events (e.g., the 2008 presidential election) as such discussions would take time away from preparation for a high-stakes end-of-year U.S. Constitution test. Those in school contexts where students had a history of not passing these tests were even less willing to engage with students about relevant contemporary events within their subject.

Curriculum restrictions and adjustments may be even more egregious for special education teachers who are forced to narrow the curriculum to meet the needs of the test as opposed to the specific needs of the student (Johnston-Parsons et al., 2007). An additional problem for special education teachers has to do with diagnosing and assessing students with disabilities, as decisions about student labeling may impact what test accommodations (or exemptions) the student can receive. For example, low performing students (who are disproportionately low income, minority, and/or students for whom English is a second language) are more likely to be categorized into special education programs in high-stakes accountability environments (Artiles, 2011; Harry & Klingner, 2014). This is done to take low scorers out of the general testing pool to improve the school's average test performance, and increase the chances that the school can avoid sanctions or negative publicity (Figlio & Getzler, 2006; Jacob, 2005).

There is evidence that high-stakes testing under NCLB and RttT has created further issues in relation to the distribution of teachers and their turnover. Although it is difficult to directly connect these policies with teacher turnover given many other confounding variables, there is a large body of literature that correlates teacher turnover to the undesirable working conditions often prevalent within low SES schools (Adamson & Darling-Hammond, 2012; Loeb, Darling-Hammond, & Luczak, 2005). These already challenging working conditions have only worsened under NCLB. For example, Clotfelter, Ladd, and Vigdor (2007) found that in North Carolina, where accountability policies based on high-stakes testing had been administered since 1996–1997, teacher turnover and retention rates worsened in low performing schools. The pressures of getting students to pass tests in contexts where the challenges of teaching are already high make teachers more likely to leave (Valli & Buese, 2007).

Reback, Rockoff, and Schwartz (2011) conducted a national study of teachers' perceptions of their working conditions in schools where short-term incentive pressures to pass the state test were greatest. In these contexts, they found that teachers, especially untenured ones, reported great concerns around job security and how test scores would impact their careers. They concluded that:

> our results also raise questions concerning whether NCLB pressure motivates both tenured and untenured teachers alike, whether talented teachers are discouraged from working in schools with little chance of meeting NCLB requirements, and whether schools neglect low-stakes subjects if their performance lags far below NCLB standards.
>
> (Reback et al., 2011, p. 23)

High-stakes testing has also informed teacher placement decisions. Both Cohen-Vogel (2011) and Fuller and Ladd (2012) found that principals would strategically reassign better teachers to tested grades (where test results impacted the school) and lower quality teachers to untested grades. Principals also reported relying heavily on standardized test scores as valid indicators of which teachers to hire, to which grade levels they would be assigned, and who needed particular professional development (Cohen-Vogel, 2011). Under RttT, the use of test scores for these kinds of decisions has grown in popularity and importance since states are more strategically designing accountability systems with teacher effectiveness in mind.

Policies may also impact where teachers choose to work. Achinstein, Ogawa, and Speiglman (2004) found that a combination of teacher characteristics and backgrounds, and local and state level policy climates influenced the types of teaching conditions teachers preferred. Their mixed methods case study found that accountability pressures combined with local school management practices may lead to two groups of teachers: ones who prefer more autonomy, flexibility, and opportunity to be creative in the classroom and ones who prefer structured, scripted curriculum and direct day-to-day instructions about teaching goals. In short, the pressures of testing combined with managerial philosophies of schools may entice specific types of teachers to particular working environments.

LESSONS FROM U.S. HIGH-STAKES TESTING ACCOUNTABILITY SYSTEMS

Data suggest that high-stakes testing under NCLB and RttT has made teaching conditions more intense and less desirable, often eroding teachers' autonomy and motivation to teach. Although there are accounts of test-based pressures initially inspiring greater teacher motivation (Johnston-Parsons et al., 2007), ongoing judgments of failure are demoralizing and undermining (Finnegan & Gross, 2007). Collectively, these factors are undoubtedly leading to higher teacher turnover, especially in lower performing schools. Additionally, there appears to be credible evidence that school and teacher actions are undermining the validity of such tests by teaching to the test, manipulating some conditions (e.g., which teachers are at which grade levels), and, in extreme cases, through dishonest behavior. These factors raise the question whether such data can be credibly used for any purpose at all.

It appears that learning to teach under accountability systems like NCLB and RttT poses a complex challenge for preservice teachers because there are often conflicts between the 'best practice' pedagogy being taught at university and the enacted practices they observe and are encouraged to take up within schools. It seems important that teacher preparation programs find a way to capitalize on these tensions to help teachers in training become mindful advocates of their future profession. All too often, new teachers internalize the expectations and norms of their school, which is problematic in schools where the primary emphasis is on passing a test. Ideally, new teachers in this context should be better prepared to counter these realities by drawing on appropriate pedagogical skills learned in their training programs, but at a minimum, teacher education programs must give preservice teachers time and space to honestly discuss these tensions and co-construct some basic strategies to help them adhere, as much as possible, to best practice pedagogy.

The flaws in the accountability system under NCLB and RttT appear twofold. First, there is an overreliance on test scores as the main indicator of student progress. As Campbell's (1976) law accurately predicts, the reality is that whenever there is overreliance on a sole indicator of performance or success, the processes it is designed to measure are likely to be corrupted, in this case via cheating, teaching to the test, and other forms of school gaming (e.g., reassignment of teachers to particular year levels). Regardless of how the corruption occurs, it ultimately means that such test scores no longer accurately measure the learning they are meant to describe, making them invalid not only for decision-making purposes, but also for any kind of diagnostic purposes that could help teachers better support learners. Here, the problem is not with the test per se; it is with the fact it is the sole (or strongest) indicator of performance. Even if testing were swapped with some other form of assessment (which would then become a sole indicator), many similar consequences would arise.

Second, the use of strong sanctions as punishment when unrealistic targets are not met further demoralizes schools that are already struggling and appears to contribute to teacher attrition. These issues pose serious problems for educational equity. With the U.S. education system (and many globally), populations are not homogenous, meaning individual schools may have differing reasons for failing to meet set performance targets. This does not mean that targets should not be set and that poor performance from low SES and minority students should be accepted as inevitable; rather, instead of sanctions, perhaps flexible systems of support should be implemented which are long-term and driven by those who understand the unique challenges facing the particular school and students it serves.

Darling-Hammond and Rustique-Forrester (2005) noted that statewide assessments systems in the U.S. can have positive outcomes when tests are of high quality, teachers are supported and highly involved in the development and scoring of the tests, and when stakes are medium or low. When assessments are used to evaluate students and their teachers for diagnostic and/or formative evaluative purposes (and when those tests are well developed and teachers are highly supported and involved), they can offer great benefits to a society looking to improve educational processes and outcomes. But attaching high-stakes consequences to those indicators instantly increases the likelihood of corruption and distortion and renders the indicator invalid. Ultimately, it is how the test is used rather than the instrument itself that is the problem.

CONCLUSION

High-stakes testing for accountability purposes is likely to continue to thrive in societies where competition (rather than collaboration) and a business model of reform relying on bottom line outcomes are seen as the best drivers of improvement. Within educational contexts, while competition may increase motivation for some, it can be a potentially destructive mechanism, because creating winners also creates losers. Unsurprisingly, as the U.S. case illustrates, the 'losers' under NCLB and RttT are the teachers and students who work in and attend schools serving the most vulnerable. While such tests may shine a spotlight on low performing students and this may lead to increased help for some (Cizek, 2001), for schools where such students make up the majority of the population, the task of meeting benchmarks can become overwhelming, and when sanctions rather than support are offered, real academic improvement becomes unlikely (Biddle, 2014).

Although in high-stakes accountability systems, like that created by NCLB and RttT, it is easy to view 'the test' as the source of all problems, the real issue is that heavy sanctions are tied to the outcomes of interest. Adopting this kind of approach has not proved effective for creating long-term desired changes within educational settings or other workplaces, as such systems tend to undermine intrinsic motivation (Deci, Koestner, & Ryan, 1999; Kohn, 1999; Lepper, Corpus, & Iyengar, 2005). When constructed well and used responsibly, it may be appropriate to use educational assessment to identify schools and students who are not meeting requirements. However, rather than using test scores to shame, blame, or punish, they should be used to identify areas for support and improvement. In lieu of punitive accountability systems, greater social, psychological, and financial investments into our schools and our teachers are needed, alongside better programs to support the physical health and well-being of the students coming to the school. For example, in Finland (where students regularly score highly on international assessments), schools provide comprehensive support; students receive meals, health care, and psychological counseling, and teachers are highly respected (Finnish National Board of Education, 2008).

Alternatives

While it is easy to identify problems with the Anglo-American accountability model, what alternatives exist? One seemingly simple solution might be to dilute the stakes attached to accountability measures. For example, within Australia, national literacy and numeracy testing data are collected, but without the extreme sanctions present in the U.S. system (e.g., closing schools, firing teachers); scores also have limited relationships to funding (Lingard & Lewis, this volume). However, such data are publicly reported on the MySchool website in a format that invites school comparisons by the public. Unsurprisingly, parents and the media actively use these data to compare, rank order, and label local schools. The pressure of publicly looking good has raised the stakes of this assessment and meant some undesirable practices linked to accountability (e.g., teaching to the test, trying to exempt kids from testing who may not perform well) are now being documented in Australia (Polesel, Rice, & Dulfer, 2013; Thompson, 2013). Hence, it seems that any time stakes are attached to single measures, the risks of corruption and distortion follow.

Other accountability approaches might allow for more holistic evaluations of teachers and schools. One such approach relies on school inspections or visits by an external team of evaluators. While not without its critics (Codd, 2005; Thrupp, 1998), such visits can potentially allow schools to demonstrate their progress in a richer way than test scores alone can capture. For example, in New Zealand, the Education Review Office visits schools every three years (although this cycle may be shortened or lengthened based on the school's perceived needs) (Crooks, 2011). During these visits, schools are allowed to select from a diverse range of tools (including standardized low-stakes tests and teacher judgments) to demonstrate effectiveness. Additionally, these visits examine the inputs as well as student outcomes, looking for evidence of particular practices like formative assessment; hence, evaluators can potentially make credible recommendations rather than just identifying achievement gaps. While such reports are publicly published in New Zealand on the ERO website, they are narrative and do not grade or score schools in ways which invite comparisons. However, the potential benefits of an inspection system will not occur if school evaluators overly rely on a rigid and narrow set of criteria and if criticism is not delivered in a constructive way.

Another accountability approach is to focus on the overall health of the system rather than monitor each individual school. Finland's accountability system has adopted this model; as Sahlberg (2011, p. 35) notes: "instead of test-based accountability, the Finnish system relies on the expertise and professional accountability of teachers who are knowledgeable and committed to their students and communities." Every year, a sample of schools participates in testing; however, the subject of these tests varies (e.g., mother tongue, mathematics, or other curriculum areas) and these results are not used for ranking schools; schools receive their own results back for development purposes (Ministry of Education and Culture, 2013). This light sampling process is similar to other low-stakes monitoring systems like National Education Monitoring Project (NEMP) in New Zealand and the National Assessment of Educational Progress (NAEP) system in the United States. However, in Finland this is the only external accountability measure used. While the highly competitive nature of admission into teaching (which is relatively unique to Finland) obviously contributes to public trust in teachers, this system provides food for thought for other nations as it exemplifies an alternative model of educational oversight and, importantly, one which appears to have avoided many of the educational problems associated with school accountability measures (e.g., narrowing curriculum). However, to implement a system like Finland's, there may need to be different public attitudes towards assessment than those found in the U.S., where citizens view testing as objective and believe in the comparative uses of such data (Brookhart, 2013; Buckendahl, this volume) and teachers and schools are regularly denigrated within the media (Nichols & Berliner, 2007a).

While there are clearly diverse school accountability models which can be drawn on, simply applying another jurisdiction's model is unlikely to be successful, especially where there are major differences in student compositions, or beliefs and values around educational accountability. Black and Wiliam (2005, p. 260) remind us that "the overall impact of particular assessment practices and initiatives is determined at least as much by culture and politics as it is by educational evidence and values." Clearly, there is a need for future research on the impact of culture and beliefs on the teacher uptake and public acceptance of new school accountability models that provide viable alternatives to systems which have previously relied on narrow measures.

Additionally, it is important to remember that while teachers are important change agents within schools, there are varying estimates about their actual contribution to student achievement. For example, Nye, Konstantopoulos, and Hedges (2004) attributed 7%–21% of student outcome variance to teachers, although Hattie (2003) estimated approximately 30%. Experts agree that the majority of variance is attributable to individual student and outside-the-school variables (Berliner, 2013), with socioeconomic status significantly impacting educational outcomes (Biddle, 2014). Hence, all school accountability systems must acknowledge and account for non-teacher sources of variance if trying to directly measure and reward teacher effectiveness.

Darling-Hammond (2012, p. 21) reminds us that "educational reforms based on conceptions of equity and capacity-building focusing on high-quality teaching and learning systems and access to good instruction for all students have proved to be more successful than educational reforms based on competition, incentives and sanctions." Hence, the challenge is to consider how, within the bounds of culture and social values, systems can be created within each jurisdiction which allow for transparency and the demonstration of progress, while still promoting equity. Additionally, it is important that such systems are designed to collaborate with teachers and school leaders rather than control them. It is only in systems where teachers, school leaders, and policy makers work together to provide appropriate evidence of student progress (see Lai & Schildkamp, this volume) derived from multiple measures that the corruption and distortion that Campbell's law predicts can be avoided.

REFERENCES

Abrams, L., Pedulla, J. J., & Madaus, G. (2003). Views from the classroom: Teachers' opinions of statewide testing programs. *Theory Into Practice, 42*(1), 18–28.

Achinstein, B., Ogawa, R. T., & Speiglman, A. (2004). Are we creating separate and unequal tracks of teachers? The effects of state policy, local conditions, and teacher characteristics on new teacher socialization. *American Educational Research Journal, 41*(3), 557–603.

Adamson, F., & Darling-Hammond, L. (2012). Funding disparities and the inequitable distribution of teachers: Evaluating sources and solutions. *Education Policy Analysis Archives, 20*(37). Retrieved from http://epaa.asu.edu/ojs/article/view/1053/1024

Amrein-Beardsley, A., Berliner, D. C., & Rideau, S. (2010). Cheating in the first, second, and third degree: Educators' responses to high-stakes testing. *Education Policy Analysis Archives, 18*(14), 1–33.

Anderson, L. M. (2001). Nine prospective teachers and their experiences in teacher education: The role of entering conceptions of teaching and learning. In B. Torff & R. J. Sternberg (Eds.), *Understanding and teaching the intuitive mind: Student and teacher learning* (pp. 187–215). Mahwah, NJ: Lawrence Erlbaum.

Armario, C. (2010, December 7). 'Wake-up call': U.S. students trail global leaders. *Associated Press Wire*. Retrieved from tinyurl.com/prelqy6

Artiles, A. J. (2011). Toward an interdisciplinary understanding of educational equity and difference: The case of the racialization of ability. *Educational Researcher, 40*(9), 431–445.

Au, W. (2007). High-stakes testing and curricular control: A qualitative metasynthesis. *Educational Researcher, 36*(5), 258–267.

Au, W., & Gourd, K. (2013). Asinine assessment: Why high-stakes testing is bad for everyone, including English teachers. *English Journal, 103*(1), 14–19.

Barksdale-Ladd, M. A., & Thomas, K. F. (2000). What's at stake in high-stakes testing: Teachers and parents speak out. *Journal of Teacher Education, 51*(5), 384–397.

Barnes, N., Fives, H., & Dacey, C. M. (2015). Teachers' beliefs about assessment. In H. Fives & M. G. Gill (Eds.), *The handbook of research on teachers' beliefs* (pp. 284–300). New York : Routledge.

Barrett, B. D. (2009). No Child Left Behind and the assault on teachers' professional practices and identities. *Teaching and Teacher Education, 25*(8), 1–8.

Berliner, D. C. (2013). Effects of inequality and poverty vs. teachers and schooling on America's youth. *Teachers College Record, 116*(1). Retrieved August 28, 2014 from http://www.tcrecord.org

Berliner, D. C., & Biddle, B. J. (1995). *The manufactured crisis: Myths, fraud, and the attack on America's public schools.* Reading, MA: Addison-Wesley.

Berliner, D. C., & Glass, G. V., & Associates. (2014). *50 myths and lies that threaten America's public schools: The real crisis in education.* New York: Teachers College Press.

Biddle, B. J. (2014). *The unacknowledged disaster: Youth poverty and educational failure in America.* New York: Sense Publishers.

Black, P., & Wiliam, D. (2005). Lessons from around the world: how policies, politics and cultures constrain and afford assessment practices. *Curriculum Journal, 16*(2), 249–261.

Boohrer-Jennings, J. (2005). Below the bubble: 'Educational triage' and the Texas accountability system. *American Educational Research Journal, 42*(2), 231–268.

Bracey, G. W. (2008). Disastrous legacy. *Dissent, 55*(4), 80–83.

Braun, H. (2004). Reconsidering the impact of high-stakes testing. *Educational Policy Analysis Archives, 12*(1), 1–40. Retrieved from http://epaa.asu.edu/epaa/v12n1/

Braun, H., Chapman, L., & Vezzu, S. (2010). The Black-White achievement gap revisited. *Education Policy Analysis Archives, 18*(21). Retrieved from http://epaa.asu.edu/ojs/article/view/772

Braun, H. I., Wang, A., Jenkins, F., & Weinbaum, E. (2006). The Black-White achievement gap: Do state policies matter? *Education Policy Analysis Archives, 14*(8). Retrieved from http://epaa.asu.edu/epaa/v14n8/

Brookhart, S. M. (2013). The public understanding of assessment in educational reform in the United States. *Oxford Review of Education, 39*(1), 52–71. doi:10.1080/03054985.2013.764751

Brown, C. P. (2010). Children of reform: The impact of high-stakes education reform on preservice teachers. *Journal of Teacher Education, 61*(5), 477–491.

Brown, G.T.L. (2008). *Conceptions of assessment: Understanding what assessment means to teachers and students.* New York: Nova Science Publishers.

Brown, K. D., & Goldstein, L. S. (2013). Preservice elementary teachers' understandings of competing notions of academic achievement coexisting in post-NCLB public schools. *Teachers College Record, 115*(1), 1–37.

Campbell, D. T. (1976). Assessing the impact of planned social change. Occasional Paper Series, #8.

Carnoy, M., Elmore, R., & Sisken, L. S. (Eds.). (2003). *The new accountability: High-schools and high-stakes testing.* New York: Routledge Farmer.

Cizek, G. J. (2001). More unintended consequences of high-stakes testing. *Educational Measurement: Issues and Practice, 20*(4), 19–27.

Clotfelter, C. T., Ladd, H. F., & Vigdor, J. L. (2007). Teacher credentials and student achievement: Longitudinal analysis with student fixed effects. *Economics of Education Review, 36*(6), 673–682.

Codd, J. (2005). Teachers as 'managed professionals' in the global education industry: The New Zealand experience. *Educational Review, 57*(2), 193–206. doi:10.1080/0013191042000308369

Cohen-Vogel, L. (2011). Staffing to the test: Are today's school personnel practices evidence based? *Educational Evaluation and Policy Analysis, 33*(4), 483–505.

Craig, C. J. (2009). The contested classroom space: A decade of lived educational policy in Texas schools. *American Educational Research Journal, 46*, 1034–1059.

Crooks, T. (2011). Assessment for learning in the accountability era: New Zealand. *Studies in Educational Evaluation, 37*(1), 71–77. doi:http://dx.doi.org/10.1016/j.stueduc.2011.03.002

Darling-Hammond, L. (2012). Two futures of educational reform: What strategies will improve teaching and learning? *Schweizerische Zeitschrift für Bildungswissenschaften, 34*(1), 21–38.

Darling-Hammond, L., & Rustique-Forrester, E. (2005). The consequences of student testing for teaching and teacher quality. In J. L. Herman, & E. H. Haertel (Eds.), *Uses and misuses of data for educational accountability and improvement* (pp. 289–319). The 104th Yearbook of the National Society for the Study of Education (part 2). Malden, MA: Blackwell.

Deci, E. L., Koestner, R., & Ryan, R. M. (1999). A meta-analytic review of experiments examining the effects of extrinsic rewards on intrinsic motivation. *Psychological Bulletin, 125*, 627–668.

Dee, T., & Jacob, B. (2009, November). The impact of No Child Left Behind on student achievement. *Journal of Policy Analysis and Management, 30*(3), 418–446.

Doppen, F. H. (2007). Pre-service social studies teachers' perceptions of high-standards, high-stakes. *International Journal of Sociology in Education, 21*(2), 18–45.

Duncan, A. (2010). Back to school: Enhancing U.S. education and competitiveness. *Foreign Affairs, 89*(6), 65–74.

Figlio, D. N., & Getzler, L. S. (2006). Accountability, ability and disability: Gaming the system? In T. J. Gronberg & D. W. Jansen (Eds.), *Improving school accountability: Check-ups or choice. Advances in applied microeconomics* (Vol. 14), pp. 35–49. New York: Elsevier.

Finnegan, K. S., & Gross, B. (2007). Do accountability policy sanctions influence teacher motivation? Lessons from Chicago's Low-performing schools. *American Educational Research Journal, 44*(3), 594–629.

Finnish National Board of Education. (2008). *Education in Finland.* Helsinki: Finnish National Board of Education.

Flores, M. A., & Day, C. (2006). Contexts which shape and reshape new teachers' identities: a multiperspective study. *Teaching and Teacher Education, 22,* 219–232.

Fuller, S. C., & Ladd, H. F. (2012, April). *School based accountability and the distribution of teacher quality among grades in elementary schools.* CALDER Working Paper, No. 75.

Gardner, J. (2013). The public understanding of error in educational assessment. *Oxford Review of Education, 39*(1), 72–92. doi:10.1080/03054985.2012.760290

Gerwin, D. (2004, March/April). Preservice teachers report the impact of high-stakes testing. *Social Studies, 95*(2), 71–74.

Giordano, G. (2005). *How testing came to dominate American schools: The history of educational assessment.* New York: Peter Lang.

Glass, G. V. (2008). *Fertilizers, pills, and magnetic strips: The fate of public education in America.* Charlotte, NC: Information Age Publishing.

Grissom, J. A., Nicholson-Crotty, S., & Harringon, J. R. (2014, December). Estimating the effects of No Child Left Behind on teachers' work environments and job attitudes. *Educational Evaluation and Policy Analysis, 36*(4), 417–436.

Grodsky, E. S., Warren, J. R., & Kalogrides, D. (2009). State high school exit examinations and NAEP long-term trends in reading and mathematics, 1971–2004. *Educational Policy, 23,* 589–614. doi:10.1177/0395909808320678

Haney, W. (2000). The myth of the Texas miracle in education. *Education Policy Analysis Archives, 8*(41). Retrieved from http://epaa.asu.edu/epaa/v8n41/index.html.

Harry, B., & Klingner, J. (2014). *Why are so many minority students in special education? Understanding race and disability in schools.* New York & London: Teachers College Columbia University.

Hattie, J. (2003, October). *Teachers make a difference: What is the research evidence?* Paper presented at the Australian Council for Educational Research, Auckland, NZ.

Herman, J. L., & Haertel, E. H. (Eds.). (2005). *Uses and misuses of data for educational accountability and improvement. The 104th yearbook of the National Society for the Study of Education, part II.* Malden, MA: Blackwell.

Hollingsworth, S. (1989). Prior beliefs and cognitive change in learning to teach. *American Educational Research Journal, 26,* 160–189.

Holme, J. J., Richards, M. P., Jimerson, J. B., & Cohen, R. W. (2010). Assessing the effects of high school exit examinations. *Review of Educational Research, 80*(4), 476–526. doi:10.3102/0034654310383147

Jacob, B. (2005). Accountability, incentives and behavior: The impact of high-stakes testing in the Chicago Public Schools. *Journal of Public Economics, 89*(5–6), 761–796.

Jacob, B. A., & Levitt, S. D. (2003). *Rotten apples: An investigation of the prevalence and predictors of teacher cheating.* National Bureau of Economic Research (NBER Working Paper No. 9413).

Jennings, J. J. (2015). *Presidents, congress, and the public schools: The politics of education reform.* Cambridge, MA: Harvard Education Press.

Jennings, J. L., & Bearak, J. M. (2014). "Teaching to the test" in the NCLB era: How test predictability affects our understanding of student performance. *Educational Researcher, 43*(8), 381–389.

Johnston-Parsons, M., & Wilson, M., & The Teachers at Park Street Elementary. (2007). *Success stories from a failing school: Teachers living under the shadow of NCLB.* Charlotte, NC: Information Age Publishing.

Jones, M. G., Jones, B., & Hargrove, T. (2003). *The unintended consequences of high-stakes testing.* Lanham, MD: Rowman & Littlefield.

Journell, W. (2010, Spring). The influence of high-stakes testing on high school teachers' willingness to incorporate current political events into the curriculum. *The High School Journal, 93*(3), 111–125.

Kahneman, D. (2011). *Thinking, fast and slow.* Sydney: Penguin Books.

Kohn, A. (1999). *Punishment by rewards.* New York: Houghton Mifflin.

Koretz, D. (2008). *Measuring up: What educational testing is really telling us.* Cambridge, MA: Harvard University Press.

Lavigne, A. L. (2014). Exploring the intended and unintended consequences of high-stakes testing evaluation on school, teachers, and students. *Teachers College Record, 116*, 1–29.

Lavigne, A. L., & Good, T. L. (2014). *Teacher and student evaluation: Moving beyond the failure of school reform.* New York: Routledge.

Lepper, M. R., Corpus, J. H., & Iyengar, S. S. (2005). Intrinsic and extrinsic motivational orientations in the classroom: Age differences and academic correlates. *Journal of Educational Psychology, 97*(2), 184–196.

Lingard, B., & Lewis, S. (2016). Globalization of the Anglo-American approach to top-down, test-based educational accountability. In G.T.L. Brown & L. R. Harris (Eds.), *Handbook of human and social factors in assessment* (pp. 387–403). New York: Routledge.

Loeb, S., Darling-Hammond, L., & Luczak, J. (2005). How teaching conditions predict teacher turnover in California schools. *Peabody Journal of Education, 80*(3), 44–70.

Marchant, G. J., & Paulson, S. E. (2005). The relationship of high school graduation exams to graduation rates and SAT scores. *Education Policy Analysis Archives, 13*(6). Retrieved from http://epaa.asu.edu/epaa/v13n6/

McDonnell, L. (2005). Assessment and accountability from the policymaker's perspective. In J. L. Herman & E. H. Haertel (Eds.), *Uses and misuses of data for educational accountability and improvement: The 104th yearbook of the National Society for the Study of Education, part II* (pp. 35–54). Malden, MA: Blackwell.

McNeil, L., & Valenzuela, A. (2001). The harmful impact of the TAAS system of testing in Texas. In G. Orfield & M. L. Kornhaber (Eds.), *Raising standards or raising barriers? Inequality and high-stakes testing in public education* (pp. 127–150). New York: Century Foundation Press.

Ministry of Education and Culture. (2013). Evaluation of education. Retrieved September 13, 2015 from http://www.minedu.fi/OPM/Koulutus/koulutuspolitiikka/koulutuksen_arviointi/?lang=en

Moon, T. R. (2016). Differentiated instruction and assessment: An approach to classroom assessment in conditions of student diversity. In G.T.L. Brown & L. R. Harris (Eds.), *Handbook of human and social factors in assessment* (pp. 284–301). New York: Routledge.

National Commission for Excellence in Education. (1983). *A Nation at risk: The imperatives for educational reform.* Washington, DC: US Department of Education, National Commission for Excellence in Education.

Nichols, S. L. (2007). High-stakes testing: Does it increase achievement? *Journal of Applied School Psychology, 23*(2), 47–64.

Nichols, S. L., & Berliner, D. C. (2007a). *Collateral damage: How high-stakes testing corrupts America's schools.* Cambridge, MA: Harvard Education Press.

Nichols, S. L., & Berliner, D. C. (2007b). The pressure to cheat in a high-stakes testing environment. In E. M. Anderman & T. Murdock (Eds.), *Psychological perspectives on academic cheating* (pp. 289–312). New York: Elsevier.

Nichols, S. L., Glass, G. V., & Berliner, D. C. (2006). High-stakes testing and student achievement: Does accountability pressure increase student learning? *Education Policy Analysis Archives, 14*(1). Retrieved July 20, 2009 from http://epaa.asu.edu/epaa/v14n1/

Nichols, S. L., Glass, G. V., & Berliner, D. C. (2012) High-stakes testing and student achievement: Updated analyses with NAEP data. *Education Policy Analysis Archives, 20*(20). Retrieved September 16, 2012 from http://epaa.asu.edu/ojs/article/view/1048

No Child Left Behind (NCLB) Act of 2001, 20 U.S.C.A. § 6301 *et seq.* (West 2003).

Nye, B., Konstantopoulos, S., & Hedges, L. V. (2004). How large are teacher effects? *Educational Evaluation and Policy Analysis, 26*(3), 237–257.

Orfield, G., Losen, D., Wald, J., & Swanson, C. (2004). *Losing our future: How minority youth are being left behind by the graduation rate crisis.* Cambridge, MA: The Civil Rights Project at Harvard University.

Pedulla, J. J., Abrams, L. M., Madaus, G. F., Russell, M. K., Ramos, M. A., & Miao, J. (2003, March). *Perceived effects of state-mandated testing programs on teaching and learning: Findings from a national survey of teachers.* Boston, MA: Boston College, National Board on Educational Testing and Public Policy. Retrieved January 7, 2004 from http://www.bc.edu/research/nbetpp/statements/nbr2.pdf

Perlstein, L. (2007). *Tested: One American school struggles to make the grade.* New York: Henry Holt & Co.

Polesel, J., Rice, S., & Dulfer, N. (2013). The impact of high-stakes testing on curriculum and pedagogy: a teacher perspective from Australia. *Journal of Education Policy*, 1–18. doi:10.1080/02680939.2013.865082

Ravitch, D. (2011). *The death and life of the great American school system: How testing and choice are undermining education.* New York: Basic Books.

Ravitch, D. (2013). *Reign of error: The hoax of the privatization movement and the danger to America's public schools.* New York: Alfred A. Knopf.

Raymond, M. E., & Hanushek, E. A. (2003, Summer). High-stakes research. *Education Next*, pp. 48–55.

Reardon, S. F., Atteberry, A., Arshan, N., & Kurlaender, M. (2009, April 21). *Effects of the California High School Exit Exam on Student Persistence, Achievement and Graduation* (Working Paper 2009–12). Stanford, CA: Stanford University, Institute for Research on Education Policy & Practice.

Reback, R. Rockoff, J., & Schwartz, H. L. (2011). *Under pressure: Job security, resource allocation, and productivity in schools under NCLB.* Working paper 16745, National Bureau of Economic Research. Retrieved December 16, 2014 from http://www.nber.org/papers/w16745

Rosenshine, B. (2003). High-Stakes testing: Another analysis. *Education Policy Analysis Archives, 11*(24). Retrieved from http://epaa.asu.edu/epaa/v11n24/

Ryan, J. (2004). The perverse incentives of the No Child Left Behind Act. *New York University Law Review, 79*, 932–989.

Sahlberg, P. (2011). Lessons from Finland. *The Professional Educator, Summer,* 34–38.

Taylor, G., Shepard, L., Kinner, F., & Rosenthal, J. (2003). *A survey of teachers' perspectives on high-stakes testing in Colorado: What gets taught, what gets lost* (CSE Technical Report 588). Los Angeles: University of California.

Thompson, G. (2013). NAPLAN, MySchool and Accountability: Teacher perceptions of the effects of testing. *The International Education Journal: Comparative Perspectives, 12*(2), 62–84.

Thrupp, M. (1998). Exploring the politics of blame: School inspection and its contestation in New Zealand and England. *Comparative Education, 34*(2), 195–209. doi:10.1080/03050069828270

Timar, T. B. and Maxwell-Jolly, J. (Eds.). (2012). *Narrowing the achievement gap: Perspectives and strategies for challenging times.* Cambridge, MA: Harvard Education Press.

U.S. Department of Education (2009, November). *Race to the top: Executive summary.* Washington, DC: US Department of Education. Retrieved from http://ed.gov/programs/racetothetop/executive-summary.pdf

Valenzuela, A. (Ed.). (2005). *Leaving children behind: How 'Texas-style' accountability fails Latino youth.* Albany, NY: State University of New York Press.

Valli, L., & Buese, D. (2007). The changing roles of teachers in an era of high-stakes testing accountability. *American Educational Research Journal, 44*(3), 519–558.

Vasquez Heilig, J., Cole, H., & Aguilar, A. (2010). From Dewey to No Child Left Behind: The evolution and devolution of public arts education. *Arts Education Policy Review, 111*, 136–145.

Vasquez Heilig, J., & Darling-Hammond, L. (2008). Accountability Texas-style: The progress and learning of urban minority students in a high-stakes testing context. *Educational Evaluation and Policy Analysis, 30*(2), 75–110.

Watanabe, M. (2007). Displaced teacher and state priorities in a high-stakes accountability context. *Education Policy, 21*(2), 311–368.

Winters, M. A., Trivitt, J. R., & Greene, J. P. (2010). The impact of high-stakes testing on student proficiency in low-stakes subjects: Evidence from Florida's elementary science exam. *Economics of Education Review, 29*, 138–146. doi:10.1016/j.econedurev.2009.07.004

Zhao, Y. (2014). *Who's afraid of the big bad dragon? Why China has the best (and worst) education system in the world.* New York: Jossey-Bass.

4

MOVING FROM STUDENT TO TEACHER

Changing Perspectives About Assessment
Through Teacher Education

Mary F. Hill and Gayle E. Eyers

INTRODUCTION

Preparing preservice teachers (PSTs) to use appropriate classroom assessment is important work. Assessment is used to make judgements about progress and achievement, often with reference to curriculum and qualification standards, norms, total scores, and ranks. It is the mechanism through which we know learners are making progress, how to proceed with teaching, and whether qualifications should be awarded. Furthermore, it is used to hold teachers to account, to rank schools and, in some jurisdictions, to contribute to making decisions about what teachers are paid. Therefore, teachers need to become both confident and competent in using assessment in trustworthy ways. However, perhaps even more important is how assessment is used in the daily life of the classroom to support learning during teaching. There is a growing body of evidence to show that assessment supports learning when it motivates students to keep on trying (Crooks, 1988; Stiggins, 2007); involves students in setting their own goals and assessing against these (Black & Wiliam, 1998; Earl, 2013; Sadler, 1989); leads to the provision of regular, helpful, and appropriate feedback (Grudnoff et al., 2015; Tunstall & Gipps, 1996); is used effectively and with integrity (Black, 2013); and, when it meets the various purposes required in teaching and schooling (Newton, 2007).

Despite the evidence about the importance of classroom assessment, studies of the assessment practices of classroom teachers consistently report inadequacy in their skills and knowledge (Brookhart, 1994; Campbell, 2013; Dixon, 2011; Hill, 2000; McMillan, Myran, & Workman, 2002; Stiggins, 1992). Campbell (2013) argues that preservice preparation has been less than adequate, and that formal instruction in assessment may also be overridden by either teaching practice experiences and/or certain personal characteristics of the PSTs themselves. Studies of PSTs have consistently demonstrated that when they begin teacher education, many have negative emotions regarding assessment (Crossman, 2007; Smith, Hill, Cowie, & Gilmore, 2014), value the formative worth of assessment but feel unable to implement it (Winterbottom, Brindley, Taber, Fisher, Finney, & Riga, 2008), and have different conceptions of assessment from those of practicing teachers (Brown, 2011; Brown & Remesal, 2012; Chen & Brown, 2013). Brown and Remesal (2012) argue that differences between teachers' and PSTs' assessment conceptions also have implications for teacher education. For example, they found that while practising teachers had a conception of valid assessments contributing to improved student learning, PSTs did not make this link and instead associated the validity factor with school accountability.

In a review of studies since the 1950s, Campbell (2013) documented that teachers' assessment knowledge and skills have been weak, and that there has been less than optimal teacher preparation for assessment (Goslin, 1967; Hills, 1977; Noll, 1955). Brookhart (2001), summarising the research from 1990–2001, concluded that pre-service teachers need more instruction in assessment including selecting and creating classroom assessments related to instructional goals, using assessment results to inform teaching and learning, using valid and reliable grading practices, and communicating assessment results to students and other stakeholders. In many places, and particularly in the USA where more extensive research exists, teacher preparation efforts focus mostly on the measurement and evaluation aspects of assessment, requiring PSTs to understand and demonstrate assessment of learning techniques such as test and item construction (Campbell, 2013; Cizek, 1995; Stiggins, 1991) and marking or grading (Barnes, 1985) associated with assessment *of* learning or summative assessment. Since the turn of the century, however, the emphasis in classroom assessment internationally has broadened to include assessment *for* learning, where formative assessment strategies are highlighted (Gipps, Brown, McCallum, & McAlister, 1995; Kane, 2006; McMillan et al., 2002; Quilter, 1998; Stiggins, 1995, 1998), and assessment *as* learning, where students in classrooms are encouraged to participate in their own assessment (Brown & Harris, 2013; Earl, 2013). Thus, research attention has begun to shift to finding ways to prepare PSTs to use assessment for multiple purposes, engage with the complex nature of classroom assessment, and be able to critique such practices in light of assessment purposes, principles, and philosophies (DeLuca & Klinger, 2010).

This chapter reviews empirical evidence regarding effective techniques for preparing teachers to competently and confidently use a full range of assessment practices in the support of learning. Typically, such assessment literacy has been defined as "the ability to design, select, interpret, and use assessment results appropriately for educational decisions" (Quilter, 1998, p. 4). However, definitions range from reasonably succinct measurement focused interpretations, such as "assessment-literate educators need to understand a relatively small number of commonsense measurement fundamentals" (Popham, 2006, p. 84) to all-inclusive descriptions that may or may not include self- and peer assessment (Cooper, 1997, pp. 516–8 and New Zealand Ministry of Education, 2007, p. 39). In this chapter we use assessment literacy in the wider sense to include the skills teachers need to implement assessment in classrooms effectively, as well as the capability to involve their own students in the assessment process as active participants (Black & Wiliam, 1998).

Richardson and Placier (2001) reviewed the teacher change literature and situated studies of teacher education within the category of *individual or small group* change focused on bringing about cognitive, affective, and behavioral changes. They argued that teacher change literature supports three conclusions:

(i) teacher change and learning is a cognitive process, not simply a surface level behavioural one;
(ii) individuals create their own new understandings based on the influences with which they come into contact;

(iii) the complexity of teaching and the diversity of contexts within which teaching (and thus assessment) occurs combine to make it impossible to adequately prepare teachers by training them in particular practices.

Changing preservice teachers' cognitions and beliefs is difficult but important because teachers' beliefs and conceptions have been shown to underpin how they teach (Fives & Buehl, 2012; Richardson & Placier, 2001). Teacher preparation can lead to cognitive change and shift orientations towards teaching practices that use assessment to enhance learning and for the range of assessment purposes required, but such changes are not always guaranteed nor necessarily deep-seated. Bolstered by evidence that desired changes did take place during student teaching experiences, Richardson and Placier (2001) hypothesised that the difficulty in changing cognition and shifting beliefs might be addressed through integrating coursework with more practical experiences during teacher education or through structural changes to teacher education that might embed it within a teaching career rather than occurring before the career begins. Our research questions, therefore, connected with Richardson and Placier's (2001) frame of PSTs' beliefs, conceptions, and confidence, and how and why they change through teacher education. The following questions have guided our review:

1. What are PSTs' assessment conceptions?
2. How do they change as a result of teacher preparation in assessment?
3. What is the relationship between preservice assessment teaching and PST assessment learning?
4. How does involvement in the practical use of assessment in classrooms influence PST learning in assessment?
5. What further factors affect PSTs' assessment learning?

METHOD

In our review of the literature, we examined studies of teacher preparation in assessment carried out in the compulsory schooling sector since 2000 to understand the scope and nature of studies as well as the empirical findings. For information about pre-2000 studies, Campbell (2013) is recommended. We used key terms including teacher candidates, preservice teachers, student teachers, initial teacher education (ITE), and assessment learning, assessment literacy, assessment theory, assessment practice, assessment education, beliefs about assessment, teacher education, teacher education programmes, and preservice teacher training. We searched using Google, Google Scholar, Education Resources Information Centre (ERIC), EBSCO, ProQuest Education Journals, and SAGE Full Text Journal Collection, and library and book catalogues. After checking the abstracts and titles, studies were excluded when they were:

- Not available from authors, the library, or the Internet
- In languages other than English
- Not connected with teacher preparation in the schooling sector
- Focused on assessment as measurement
- Conceptual, pedagogical texts or commentary pieces rather than empirical work.

Since the seminal reviews of Crooks (1988) regarding the effects of classroom evaluation on students, and Black and Wiliam (1998), which established the value of formative assessment for learning, there has been a gradual but incremental shift towards including assessment *for/as* learning as well as assessment *of* learning in teacher professional development programmes. While this began more prominently in the U.K. (Gipps et al., 1995; Harlen, Gipps, Broadfoot, & Nuttall, 1992) and New Zealand (Hill, 1995, 1999) well before 2000, it is a continuing global shift in assessment discourse and practice (Berry, 2011). This is evidenced through recent studies in the U.S. (Andrade & Cizek, 2010; Ruiz-Primo et al., 2012), Australia (Wyatt-Smith & Klenowski, 2014), China (Jiang, 2015), African nations (Braun & Kanjee, 2006), and elsewhere.

After reading and rereading, the studies were summarised and the main findings coded. From these summaries, possible themes related to the research questions were generated and tested against the evidence in the studies. Thematic categories were then assigned. These were (1) assessment conceptions (conceptions); (2) relationships between assessment teaching and preservice teacher learning (teaching); (3) involvement in practical use of assessment in classrooms (practice); (4) influences on preservice teacher learning such as alignment of theory and/or policy with practice, metacognitive influences, and differences in status (other influences). Both authors agreed on the thematic decisions for each study. Due to the qualitative nature of some of these studies, we have not attempted to use effect size measures with this data.

ASSESSMENT LEARNING IN PRESERVICE TEACHER EDUCATION

The main design, demographic, and thematic content, along with a brief description of each of the 22 identified studies is summarised in Table 4.1.

Assessment Conceptions

Many of the studies reviewed (14) included information about PSTs' conceptions of or beliefs about assessment, or had investigated their knowledge or confidence in using assessment. Some had tracked these conceptions these over time to follow how these aspects changed as a result of teacher preparation in assessment, but most had examined these aspects at just one point within the preparation programme. Thirteen of the studies used surveys to investigate PSTs' conceptions, beliefs, or confidence (or sometimes a mixture of these).

Using a survey, Brown (2011) investigated PSTs' conceptions of assessment and compared these with academic performance in an assessment course. The study showed that these PSTs had quite different patterns and effects in their conceptions of assessment than practicing teachers and high school students. In a follow-up study, Brown and Remesal (2012) compared preservice teachers' conceptions of assessment cross-culturally and with those of practising teachers. This study confirmed that in both countries, PSTs tended to have assessment conceptions different from in-service teachers. The differences in conceptions between countries were also significant, reinforcing the idea that assessment is culturally embedded and, that like teachers, PSTs' assessment conceptions reflect societal beliefs and practices (Brown & Remesal, 2012). These studies also indicated that along the life span of teacher experience, conceptions of assessment may change. Similar findings in the United States (Buck, Trauth-Nare, & Kaftan, 2010; DeLuca, Chavez, & Cao, 2012; Graham, 2005; Mertler, 2003), Oman (Alkharusi, Kazem, & Al-Musawai, 2011), and related studies in New Zealand (Eyers, 2014; Hill, Ell, Grudnoff, & Limbrick, 2014a; Smith et al., 2014) appear to confirm this progressive view of assessment conceptions.

Table 4.1 Summary Design, Demographic, Description, and Thematic Characteristics of Reviewed Studies on Assessment Preparation for Preservice Teachers

	Source	Design	Country	N	School level preparation	Description of study	Theme
1	Alkharusi et al. (2011)	Survey	Oman	279 PSTs 233 Tchrs	Middle School	Examined differences between preservice and in-service teachers' assessment knowledge, skills, and attitudes and the impact of classroom experience	2. teaching 3. practice
2	Brown (2011)	Survey	New Zealand	324 PSTs	Not available	Analysed relationship between preservice teachers' conceptions of assessment and academic performance in assessment course	1. conceptions
3	Brown and Remesal (2012)	Survey	New Zealand Spain	324 PSTs NZ 672 PSTs Spain	Not available Multiple levels and specializations	Compared preservice teachers' conceptions of assessment cross-culturally and to those of practising teachers	1. conceptions
4	Buck et al. (2010)	Action Research	United States	30 PSTs 1 TEs 3 Doc sts	Primary	Investigated reconceptualised preparation of preservice teachers to guide the teaching and learning process with formative assessment	1. conceptions 2. teaching 3. practise
5	Chen (2005)	Survey	United States	61 PSTs	Middle School Secondary	Investigated preservice teachers' assessment literacy and compared those with some teaching experience to those with no teaching experience	2. teaching 4. other influences
6	DeLuca, Chavez, Bellara, and Cao (2013)	Survey	United States	151 PSTs	Multiple levels and specialisations	Examined instructional strategies and course activities that supported preservice teachers' learning during mandatory assessment course	4. other influences

(Continued)

Table 4.1 (Continued)

	Source	Design	Country	N	School level preparation	Description of study	Theme
7	DeLuca et al. (2012)	Survey	United States	48 PSTs	Multiple levels and specialisations	Investigated how conceptions of assessment changed during assessment course and any links between changing conceptions and confidence in assessment practises	1. conceptions
8	DeLuca and Klinger (2010)	Survey	Canada	288 PSTs	Primary and Secondary	Examined assessment curriculum in one preservice teacher education program and identified perceived confidence levels in assessment theory and practise	1. conceptions 2. teaching 3. practise
9	DeLuca, Klinger, Searle, and Shulha (2010)	Multi-method	Canada	circa 700 PSTs per year × 3	Primary and Secondary	Traced the development of one preservice teacher education program's assessment curriculum development process	1. conceptions 2. teaching 3. practise 4. other influences
10	Eyers (2014)	Case Study	New Zealand	8 PSTs 1 TE 5 SL 5 Tchrs	Primary	Investigated preservice teachers' perceptions of how they learned about assessment in university and school practicum settings, as well as the educators' perceived roles in assessment learning	1. conceptions 2. teaching 3. practise 4. other influences
11	Graham (2005)	Content analysis	United States	38 PSTs	Secondary	Investigated changes in preservice teachers' assessment theories and practises over a year-long program and the impact of assessment literate mentor teachers	1. conceptions 2. teaching 3. practise
12	Hill et al. (2014a)	Multi-method	New Zealand	24 TEs 214 PSTs	Primary	Examined assessment curriculum within contexts of university courses and school practicum in relation to development of assessment literacy and confidence	1. conceptions 2. teaching 4. other influences

#	Author (Year)	Method	Country	Sample	Level	Description	Focus
13	Jiang, H. (2015)	Ethnography	China	7 PSTs	Middle School	Shadowed PSTs during a residential internship over four months and examined their assessment learning and use	3. practise 4. other influences
14	Maclellan (2004)	Content analysis	Scotland	30 PSTs	Primary	Examined evidence of preservice teachers' knowledge of assessment principles and methods	1. conceptions
15	Mertler (2003)	Survey	United States	67 PSTs 197 Tchrs	Secondary	Measured and compared assessment literacy of preservice teachers and in-service teachers	1. conceptions 2. teaching 3. practise
16	Nolen, Horn, Ward, and Childers (2011)	Case-based ethnography	United States	8 PSTs	Secondary	Investigated how and why preservice teachers took up or rejected assessment tools and practises promoted in the social worlds of university and schools in which they learned to teach and became novice teachers	3. practise 4. other influences
17	Siegel and Wissehr (2011)	Content analysis	United States	11 PSTs	Secondary	Investigated assessment preservice teachers' assessment literacy and disconnect between assessment for learning beliefs and understandings and their choice of traditional assessment practises in inquiry-based science units	2. teaching
18	Smith et al. (2014)	Multi-method	New Zealand	1054 PSTs 25 TEs	ECE and Primary	Examined preservice teachers' assessment learning during three-year undergraduate programs at four universities	1. conceptions 2. teaching 4. other influences
19	Taber, Riga, Brindley, Winterbottom, Finney, & Fisher, 2011	Interviews	England	17 PSTs		Examined trainees understanding of, and developing thinking about, assessment issues during their ITE course	3. practise

(Continued)

Table 4.1 (Continued)

	Source	Design	Country	N	School level preparation	Description of study	Theme
20	Volante and Fazio (2007)	Survey	Canada	69 PSTs	Primary	Examined the development of assessment literacy and the reliance on the mentorship and assessment literacy of associate teachers	1. conceptions 2. teaching
21	Wang et al. (2010)	Multi-method	Taiwan	215 PSTs	Primary	Investigated preservice teachers' conception of assessment and whether they are congruent with conceptions of learning science	1. conceptions
22	Winterbottom et al. (2008)	Survey	England	220 PSTs	Secondary	Compared similarities and differences between preservice teachers' assessment values and practices and to those of qualified teachers	1. conceptions

Studies commonly reported that PSTs indicate knowing very little about assessment when they enter teacher education (Graham, 2005; Smith et al., 2014; Volante & Fazio, 2007; Wang, Kao, & Lin, 2010). Some report limited assessment knowledge (Maclellan, 2004; Wang et al., 2010) and low levels of assessment confidence (Volante & Fazio, 2007) continuing into later stages of teacher education programmes. PSTs mostly hold summative beliefs about assessment on entry to teacher education (Brown, 2011; DeLuca et al., 2012, Hill et al., 2014a; Smith et al., 2014; Volante & Fazio, 2007), suggesting that these views result from their previous experiences as students in secondary schools and through gaining advanced qualifications (Graham, 2005). Hence, although PSTs enter teacher education programmes with preexisting assessment conceptions, beliefs, and knowledge, new PSTs often report feelings of fear and anxiety about assessment and view it as conceptually difficult.

However, since 2000, studies have reported shifts in PSTs' views towards treating formative assessment as important as a result of teacher education programs (Buck et al., 2010; DeLuca & Klinger, 2010; DeLuca et al., 2012; Eyers, 2014; Hill et al., 2014a; Smith et al., 2014). Studies that compared PSTs' assessment conceptions with those of practicing teachers (Alkharusi et al., 2011; Mertler, 2003; Winterbottom et al., 2008), and some that compared entry conceptions and knowledge with those held later in the teacher preparation programme (DeLuca et al., 2012; Eyers, 2014; Graham, 2005; Smith et al., 2014) have demonstrated that assessment conceptions change over time following explicit teaching and learning in assessment and through teaching experiences.

This changeability of beliefs may constitute a challenge to Pajares's (1992) suggestion that pedagogical beliefs and, therefore, assessment conceptions, are relatively stable. Alternatively, it may be that the changes in assessment beliefs being reported are in peripheral areas that are sensitive to contextual conditions, rather than in core beliefs (Green, 1971). Nonetheless, evidence from several studies suggests that by the end of their teacher education programmes, there are still values–practice gaps between what beginning teachers value and what they can put into practice (Smith et al., 2014; Winterbottom et al., 2008). These findings reinforce the direction of current efforts to increase assessment education within teacher preparation programmes.

Relationships Between Assessment Teaching and Preservice Teacher Learning

At least 11 studies since 2000 have investigated relationships between assessment teaching and PST assessment learning. Where measured, when compared with the in-service teachers who had had no preservice educational assessment course, those having taken a preservice educational assessment course, on average, knew more about educational assessment (Alkharusi et al., 2011; Chen, 2005; DeLuca & Klinger, 2010; Hill et al., 2014a; Smith et al., 2014). Conversely, DeLuca and Klinger (2010) found that undertaking curriculum and/or professional studies courses without an assessment course did not appear to support development of assessment confidence.

Even where studies found that preservice assessment education did change PSTs' assessment understandings and/or beliefs, these changes were often partial and did not affect all students within the programme. For example, Buck et al.'s (2010) action research with 30 PSTs found a substantial pre- to post-course difference in the preservice teachers' understanding of formative assessment in a science methods course where assessment was a focus. However, although there was an increase in formative understanding, some PSTs still thought of formative assessment as a series of continuous summative events and even PSTs with an adequate understanding of formative assessment were unable to thoroughly explain the importance of students' involvement in monitoring their own learning.

A large-scale, mixed methods study in New Zealand (Smith et al., 2014) also confirmed the partial nature of shift towards an enabling view of assessment following preservice assessment education. This study investigated the assessment learning of over 1,000 elementary and early childhood PSTs across four universities during their three-year undergraduate teacher education programmes. Three of these programmes included a specific educational assessment course but also taught assessment within specific curriculum methods and professional courses, while, at the fourth, assessment education was embedded within the curriculum methods and professional courses. Surveys with both Likert-type items and open-ended questions revealed significant positive differences in assessment knowledge and beliefs by the end of the second and third years of preparation. However, similar to Buck et al. (2010), the changes were neither uniform nor ubiquitous. Nonetheless, the third-year PSTs were able to view assessment from both teacher and student orientations regarding formative and summative assessments, drawing attention to some significant changes in their teacher identities and assessment understanding.

An analysis of the data for PSTs from one of the universities in the Smith et al. (2014) study demonstrated that all of the participants confirmed that the assessment course in the first semester of their second year of study had profoundly influenced their assessment learning (Hill et al., 2014a). The PSTs in that study stated that the timing of the assessment course, in the first semester of the second year of the programme, meant that knowledge gained could be applied in their second- and third-year practicum experiences following the course. This timing meant that there were more opportunities to practice what they had been learning before graduation.

Exploring the views of New Zealand PSTs in more depth, Eyers (2014) conducted four interviews each with eight PSTs across the final year of teacher education. A compulsory assessment course was undertaken during their second year directly before their second school practicum. All eight PSTs believed the course was one of the most powerful influences on their assessment learning, especially when they could make connections between the theory learned and the assessment practice being enacted in practicum classrooms. Other studies confirm such benefits of a specific course on assessment (DeLuca & Klinger, 2010; DeLuca et al., 2012; Hill, Gunn, Smith, Cowie, & Gilmore, 2014b; Siegel & Wissehr, 2011). The PSTs in Eyers's (2014) study described how the assessment teacher educator modelled pedagogical practices and activities (e.g., peer and class discussions, questioning, effective oral and written feedback, practice-based scenarios, and critical reflections) to elicit and modify the PSTs' assessment beliefs and preconceptions in order to trigger changes in their repertoire of assessment strategies and skills. Using formative assessment practices within the teacher education process helped build new assessment knowledge within the conceptual framework of the principles, purposes, and practices of assessment taught in the assessment course. Thus, both Eyers (2014) and Buck et al. (2010) found that making formative practices explicit to PSTs by using them in university classrooms served to mitigate the PSTs tendency to use more traditional forms of assessment such as tests. Such practices might also counter the inclination of PSTs, noticed by Siegel and Wissehr (2011), to revert to more traditional forms of assessment even after learning about and responding positively to the use of formative and equitable assessment techniques. Siegel and Wissehr (2011) discuss possible reasons, such as PSTs lacking knowledge of practical assessment strategies or perhaps not trusting their newly acquired strategies. They come to no conclusions, however, and propose this as an area for further investigation.

Thus, the studies reviewed here indicate that, for some PSTs, educational assessment classes focused on and modelling assessment for learning can and do support conceptual change towards assessment practices that support student learning. However, these changes appear to be different for individual PSTs and less than ubiquitous. Although such courses cannot fully prepare beginning teachers for their assessment roles, they can assist PSTs to understand the purposes, principles, policies, and practices they will be responsible for in their own classrooms. Furthermore, such courses play a part in preparing teachers to use assessment in the service of learning, as well as for accountability purposes, and in communicating assessment information to learners and their families. The evidence from these studies indicates that assessment education coursework, whether encountered as a separate course or crafted within methods courses, works in combination with teaching experience in classrooms, and it is to this practical use of assessment that we now turn.

Involvement in Practical Use of Assessment in Classrooms

Nine of the studies reviewed included evidence that supports the need for combining assessment learning with experiencing the use of assessment in real classrooms. Surveyed Omani PSTs who undertook a teaching practicum had, on average, higher levels of educational assessment knowledge, higher levels of perceived skillfulness in educational assessment, and more positive attitudes towards assessment (Alkharusi et al., 2011). Mertler (2003) likewise used a survey to compare the assessment literacy of PSTs with in-service teachers and found that practical experience in classrooms was necessary for teacher preparation in classroom assessment.

In Canada, DeLuca and Klinger (2010), using a survey, also identified practicum as an important site for the development of assessment knowledge and confidence. They pointed out that, in the absence of specific teaching of educational assessment, practicum becomes the primary site for learning about and using assessment. Furthermore, because many in-service teachers also lack assessment literacy, PSTs "will be exposed to idiosyncratic practices leading to inconsistent knowledge, practices and philosophies as a result" (DeLuca & Klinger, 2010, p. 434). Thus, while practical experience is certainly very important in assessment education, without specific assessment education, PSTs may focus mostly "on the practices of assessment without critical reflection on these practices" (DeLuca & Klinger, 2010, p. 436).

Several studies delved deeper into the ways in which PSTs learned about assessment through practical experiences in classrooms (Buck et al., 2010; Eyers, 2014; Graham, 2005; Hill et al., 2014b; Nolen et al., 2011; Smith et al., 2014; Taber et al., 2011). Graham (2005) had her 35 participants write answers to a series of questions and used content analysis to analyse the responses. Although PSTs reported many influences on their learning, teacher mentors were, for many, the single most powerful influence. They reported that through mentorship they developed a more comprehensive and dynamic understanding of assessment including the use of formative assessment.

Using sustained sequential interviewing, Eyers (2014) also found that having opportunities to practise assessment in classrooms was a powerful influence on assessment learning. The PSTs in her study began their second-year practicum as soon as their assessment course was completed. They reported that their new assessment knowledge began to make sense when they found it aligned with what was occurring in the classroom, supporting Darling-Hammond, Hammerness, Grossman, Rust, and Shulman's (2005) argument for entwining coursework and classroom experience. Sadly, such is not always the case. In some policy environments, what PSTs are taught and what they see happening in the name of assessment in the classroom may be very different (see Nichols & Harris, this volume, for more on this point).

Most in-service mentor teachers in Eyers's (2014) study modelled a range of assessment, practices including oral and written feedback, questioning, peer and self-assessment. They provided multiple opportunities to practice assessment so PSTs could put their learning into action and make clear links between theory and practice. They were supportive, engaged in ongoing conversations about assessment, and provided descriptive feedback about the PSTs' use of assessment in planning, teaching, and monitoring learning. However, Eyers (2014) noted, as did DeLuca and Klinger (2010), that not all mentor teachers provided the same opportunities to practise assessment or see it being effectively modelled. Additionally, as Nichols and Harris (this volume) note, well-founded assessment training of PSTs can be undermined within high-stakes accountability contexts when the pressure to get students to pass the tests overrides other learning objectives.

Variability in in-service mentor teachers' assessment understanding, their idiosyncratic use of assessment, and differing school practices and policies influence PSTs, thus heightening the need for coursework in assessment to provide a framework for critical reflection on practice. Several studies clearly demonstrated the negotiated nature of assessment learning and use of assessment (Jiang, 2015; Nolen et al., 2011; Taber et al., 2011). Power issues are a critical influence on the assessment practices that PSTs and newly qualified teachers (NQTs) could possibly use. In this regard, Nolen et al. (2011) investigated, using interviews and observations over four years, how and why eight PSTs in the USA took up or rejected assessment tools and practices promoted in the social worlds of university and schools in which they had learned to teach and become novice teachers. Using activity theory as a theoretical frame, this longitudinal study of a small number of participants enabled these researchers to look into the complexities of learning to use assessment practices in classrooms. They explained that through negotiating assessment practices such as rubrics, tests, grades, assignments, standardized test formats, and scores with mentors, colleagues, parents, students, and the school administrators who employed them, PSTs and NQTs shaped their practice to conform to the school culture and prevailing assessment practices.

Learning assessment through experience in real classrooms was also rated as highly influential in a study of a one year graduate programme in England where PSTs were participating in a supported apprenticeship model working alongside experienced teachers in a school, interspersed with periods of reflection, academic study, and research within a university context (Taber et al., 2011). In this secondary school setting, the PSTs mostly related to the use of summative practices, and felt that *"what they see and are guided to do in the classroom does not match up to the ideals that are widely discussed in the academic and professional literature they read, and the official guidance issued to them"* (Taber et al., 2011, p. 181, italics in the original).

Jiang (2015) followed eight PSTs during a four month practicum in a rural middle school in China to understand how they learnt about assessment. Their teacher preparation courses had focused almost exclusively on curriculum subject matter courses and their assessment preparation "was minimal and limited to abstract concepts about assessment, such as validity and reliability" (Jiang, 2015, p. 48). In China, the examination system continues to be the dominant system for educational mobility and, thus, the examinations themselves formed an essential ingredient of the everyday programme in school. Jiang's case study demonstrates how individual PST, mentor teacher, school, and cultural factors interacted in complex and often unexpected ways to influence how PSTs learned to teach within this examination-dominated environment. Even in one school, focused on the same tests and examinations, learning to use assessment developed in very different directions.

Thus, involvement in the practical use of assessment in classrooms is not unproblematic. While rated by PSTs as important and highly influential, when PSTs interact with different mentor teachers and students, the influence of these practical settings appears to be uneven. PSTs report less than optimum experiences in some settings (Jiang, 2015; Taber et al., 2011), which suggests that in practice teachers may or may not be implementing formative assessment, nor be involving students in their own assessment as promoted by strong versions of assessment *for* learning (Swaffield, 2011). Furthermore, their status as novices means that they must negotiate the use of innovative or less common assessment practices with those in authority over them. PSTs value opportunities to use assessment in classrooms but are continually interacting with, brokering, and sometimes deferring to, influences which shape their assessment conceptions and practices.

Other Influences on Preservice Teacher Learning

While it is clear that involvement in teaching and learning in both university and school settings is crucial to PSTs assessment learning, some of the studies reviewed indicate that this is a more complex process than it might at first appear (Maclellan, 2004). One aspect of this complexity relates to the PSTs themselves. In this regard Chen's (2005) survey indicated that those PSTs who had had prior teaching experiences before entering teacher education scored better across the seven standards for teacher competence in the educational assessment of students than those who had not. The DeLuca et al. (2010) survey indicated that explicit teaching of metacognitive skills such as goal setting, self-directed learning, and self-regulation strategies were helpful in assisting PSTs to develop a professional orientation to learning about assessment. This is connected to evidence from another study by DeLuca et al. (2013), which indicated that critical reflection and planning for learning by the PSTs was one of four pedagogical constructs that supported assessment learning. Similarly, Eyers (2014) found PSTs' metacognitive and self-regulation of learning skills influenced their ability to understand and use assessment practices. Developing knowledge and confidence in assessment was associated with more positive attitudes towards assessment and its uses.

In addition to the complexity of personal dimensions, Eyers (2014), Jiang (2015), and Smith et al. (2014) found assessment learning occurs differentially and in multiple contexts even in the same programmes. PSTs are influenced in their learning about assessment because of personal experiences, such as being parents, serving on school boards, undertaking assessments and examinations at university, and hearing experiences of family members and friends (Eyers, 2014). Jiang's (2015) study described how cultural, moral, and intellectual evaluative criteria served to differentiate every aspect of their teaching.

Furthermore, PST learning is not necessarily predictable, although it can be linked to broader policy and societal issues current at the time. For example, Smith et al. (2014) saw differential changes in two cohorts of graduating PSTs in relation to their knowledge and attitudes to standardised assessment. The earlier cohort had graduated before national standards were implemented and were less positive towards rating learners against such standards than the cohort who had been PSTs during the introduction of national standards.

Studies such as Eyers (2014), Jiang (2015), and Nolen et al. (2011) have observed how PSTs construct assessment meaning as they navigate their way through their teacher education courses, engaged in practicum settings, and then began teaching. These studies demonstrate that PSTs' status influences the way they make meaning about assessment. As indicated earlier, PSTs have to collaborate with, work under, and follow what others (e.g., mentor teachers, senior staff members, parents, peers, board members, and university faculty) have decided. Thus, PSTs' low status in the system means that they often cannot implement the assessment practices or principles that they have been taught about in university courses. Nolen et al. (2011) showed how teaching practices associated with assessment were not simply something that PSTs had more or less facility with, or accepted or rejected, but rather these "required constant situational negotiation" (p. 90). An important finding was the effect the PSTs' (and novice teachers') status had on their ability to negotiate the use of assessment. Thus, assessment preparation should include teaching PSTs how to negotiate with seniors towards desirable assessment practices known to support learning in culturally appropriate ways.

DISCUSSION

The findings in this chapter are consistent with the work of Richardson and Placier (2001) who stressed that teacher professional learning is a cognitive as well as a behavioural change process and involves individuals in creating their own understanding related to the influences into which they come into contact. Furthermore, as they argued, the complexity of teaching (and we would add assessment) and the diversity of contexts in which PSTs experience teaching (and assessment practices) present challenges to changing PST assessment attitudes, conceptions, and practices. At entry to teacher preparation, PST views and conceptions are generally different from those of more experienced teachers. Several of the studies reviewed supported Campbell's (2013) conclusion that PSTs enter teacher education knowing little about assessment, with low levels of confidence in implementing assessment and that their conceptions, beliefs and emotions can be difficult to change. Reasons for this include variability in whether assessment coursework is included in preservice programmes and the nature and appropriateness of such coursework for classroom practice. Additionally, in the USA, Campbell and Collins (2007) raised concerns that differing views regarding assessment among textbook authors may contribute to inconsistent assessment messages, suggesting a broader range of assessment topics and identification of essential content may be required to help better prepare teachers to make data-based decisions for improved student achievement. Variable outcomes in assessment preparation also relate to the extent to which assessment preparation is embedded within authentic teaching practice in school classrooms, and social factors such as national and local assessment policies. Personal factors also interact with the above influences to shape PSTs assessment knowledge and behaviours. These include PSTs' cultural, intellectual, and moral beliefs, and their experiences in different roles, such as also being parents or community leaders.

However, despite variability in assessment education outcomes, and in contrast with Richardson and Placier's (2001) review of the teacher change literature, many studies in this chapter demonstrate that with deliberate effort and planning, PSTs can begin teaching with positive attitudes, knowledge, and ability to use assessment appropriately in their social context. The findings of these studies, conducted since 2000, suggest that assessment conceptions and beliefs can and do change through participation in carefully designed assessment courses. This was particularly the case in Western countries such as Canada, New Zealand, the U.K., and the USA when educational assessment classes focused on, and modeled, assessment for learning in ways that supported conceptual change. Such courses assisted PSTs to understand the purposes, principles, policies, and practices they will be responsible for in their own classrooms. Studies in Canada (DeLuca et al., 2010), the USA (DeLuca et al., 2013), and New Zealand (Eyers, 2014; Smith et al., 2014) suggest that direct assessment education that provides a theoretical frame on which PSTs can build their assessment conceptions is important, particularly where that assessment education is congruent with assessment policies and practices within the societal system as a whole. And as noted earlier, the challenges are greater in societies where accountability assessment regimes may at times be at odds with what research has established as best practice.

Likewise, PSTs report practical experiences during their preparation programmes where they used assessment in classroom settings were critical to developing skills in using assessment confidently and competently. For example, findings from very different cultures such as China (Jiang, 2015) and New Zealand (Eyers, 2014) demonstrated that extended engagement in the use of assessment for teaching in school settings had powerful effects on PST assessment learning. Thus, consistent with Richardson and Placier (2001), PSTs create their own new understanding based upon what they already know and believe about assessment and the ideas with which they come into contact. However, as we have shown in this chapter, this is not a linear process. The complexity of teaching, the variability of contexts, schools, and systems, and the strong influence of individual PSTs' own beliefs, cognition, and decision-making point to the need for assessment preparation that acknowledges this complexity and is aligned with local conditions.

This chapter, therefore, both confirms and builds on the findings of Richardson and Placier (2001) indicating difficulty in "affecting cognitive change [in preservice programmes], particularly change in deep-seated beliefs" (p. 916). Our analysis indicates some difficulty in changing such beliefs, but also demonstrates that when aligned culturally and contextually, assessment courses can assist PSTs to think differently about assessment, and learn new practices. PSTs can become more positive about assessment and learn to use assessment for a range of purposes over the course of teacher preparation. Assessment learning is also impacted by human and social factors, such as idiosyncratic assessment practices that are often beyond the control of teacher educators (e.g., Kahn, 2000). Thus, there are implications for both teacher education in assessment, and for further research.

Implications for Teacher Preparation

The findings in this chapter confirm that teacher preparation in assessment is important and relevant. The studies reviewed, most of which were from Western developed nations, indicated that PSTs do learn from and value assessment coursework and practical classroom experiences in using assessment. However, assessment teaching is not always included in teacher education programmes. For example, even in New Zealand which has a strong assessment *for* learning system, only some universities and within them, some programmes, include specific assessment courses. Some jurisdictions and texts, limit assessment course subject matter to measurement and evaluation and some teacher education programmes do not include assessment content or courses (Jiang, 2015). Given the recent shifts in many countries to using assessment to measure students' progress towards meeting standards and support learning, as well as developing self-regulation, the evidence in this review supports a proactive approach to teacher preparation in assessment. What such preparation might look like will vary depending on the local context and assessment system requirements. However, drawing on Richardson and Placier (2001) and the findings in this chapter, such preparation needs to elicit and examine the assessment preconceptions of their PSTs, help them to build theoretical frames for assessment consistent with local contexts and conditions, and enable PSTs to collaborate in using assessment with mentors who themselves understand and use assessment appropriately.

Due to the human and social factors that impact PSTs, as well as time constraints, teacher educators need to be realistic in their expectations for PST assessment learning. For most PSTs, assessment knowledge and practice will continue to grow and change during their career, especially in the first few years of teaching. However, teacher educators are able to foster PSTs' orientation towards ongoing professional learning about assessment and encourage them to be flexible and adaptive in their classroom practice (DeLuca et al., 2010; Eyers, 2014). Preparing new teachers for the realities they will face as newly qualified teachers (Nolen et al., 2011) and not simply presenting assessment learning as training, seems advisable. Such steps could include initiatives that ensure that PSTs encounter school cultures and mentor teachers who model desirable assessment practices. Given the practice turn in teacher education (Reid, 2011; Zeichner, 2012) which, it is asserted, is needed to bridge the theory–practice gap, the results of the studies reviewed suggest it essential that PSTs be placed in classrooms where assessment practices are at least consistent with the assessment theory they are learning, and at best, where they see and learn to use a repertoire of assessment practices that prioritize learning.

Implications for Future Research

As well as surveying conceptions, beliefs, and knowledge, several studies reviewed in this chapter set out to explore how PSTs learn about assessment over time. Few studied large cohorts or tracked learning through the student to teacher journey. There appears to be little data available about the lasting contribution of PSTs' assessment learning to teachers' classroom practice, improved student learning, and the promotion of student engagement in their own assessment. Those that did follow PST assessment learning over time were small studies. These small-scale but intensive studies revealed that rather than considering teacher education in assessment as a linear process, PSTs were learning about and engaging in reflective thinking about assessment in more complex ways than most investigations into PST assessment learning have assumed to date.

Because teacher preparation occurs chronologically and events such as university courses and practical experiences occur one after the other, we tend to study assessment learning as a linear process as though it happens sequentially. This view, however, does not take into account factors such as the prior beliefs and conceptions of PSTs, the status of the mentor teacher, nor assessment texts and systems that continuously surround and impact upon PST learning simultaneously. Rather than viewing teacher education in assessment as a linear process, we suggest conceptualising it as a complex system. We need to understand more about how these simultaneous influences impact PST assessment learning. While small-scale studies can give us clues, larger investigations that trace the emergence of assessment learning would be helpful for informing the design of assessment preparation experiences.

Most of the studies reviewed were carried out in developed countries and all but three were from Western nations. We are aware, however, that preservice assessment education is occurring in other places. For example, the first author is a scientific advisor for a professional development project in South Africa aimed to increase the formative use of tests through preservice and in-service assessment education. We are also aware of initiatives in other places such as the Maldives, Tanzania, Kenya, and Uganda to prepare teachers to use assessment for formative as well as summative practices. Thus, there is scope for research regarding teacher preparation from new contexts and the particular challenges each presents.

Finally, several of the studies reviewed in this chapter raised important issues about cultural contexts for assessment learning. The findings demonstrated that societal influences shape assessment conceptions and practices (Brown & Harris, 2009). Therefore, it is entirely appropriate that teacher learning in assessment be further investigated, particularly in contexts where radical change is being attempted. For example, investigating initiatives to prepare teachers who can use assessment in ways that improve equity of outcomes is both needed and urgent. Other gaps were also apparent in the literature. For instance, despite the importance of grades and the effects that they have on people's lives, many teachers receive no teacher preparation regarding how grades should be decided or awarded. Other scholars have drawn attention to the need for instruction in this area (De Luca et al., 2013) and we do the same. Another issue is PSTs' ability to competently implement (and use the results from) assessment in psychometrically valid and reliable ways. We found no recent studies that addressed this issue. There is certainly much scope to learn more regarding assessment preparation.

REFERENCES

Alkharusi, H., Kazem, A. M., & Al-Musawai, A. (2011). Knowledge, skills, and attitudes of preservice and inservice teachers in educational assessment. *Asia-Pacific Journal of Teacher Education, 39*(2), 113–123. doi:10.1080/1359866X.2011.560649

Andrade, H. L., & Cizek, G. J. (2010). Preface. In H. L. Andrade & G. J. Cizek (Eds.), *Handbook on formative assessment* (pp. vii–xii). New York: Routledge.

Barnes, S. (1985). A study of classroom pupil evaluation: The missing link in teacher education. *Journal of Teacher Education, 36*(4), 46–49.

Berry, R. (2011). Assessment reforms around the world. In R. Berry & B. Adamson (Eds.), *Assessment reform in education: Policy and practice* (pp. 89–102). Dordrecht, NL: Springer.

Black, P. (2013). Formative and summative aspects of assessment: Theoretical and research foundations in the context of pedagogy. In J. H. McMillan (Ed.), *Sage handbook of research on classroom assessment* (pp. 167–78). Thousand Oaks, CA: Sage.

Black, P., & Wiliam, D. (1998). Assessment and classroom learning. *Assessment in Education: Principles, Policy & Practice, 5*(1), 7–74.

Braun, H., & Kanjee, A. (2006). Using assessment to improve education in developing countries. In H. Braun, A. Kanjee, E. Bettinger, & M. Kremer (Eds.), *Improving education through assessment, innovation and evaluation* (pp. 1–46). Cambridge, MA: American Academy of Arts and Sciences.

Brookhart, S. M. (1994). Teachers' grading: Practice and theory. *Applied Measurement in Education, 7*(4), 279–301.

Brookhart, S. M. (2001). *The "standards" and classroom assessment research.* Paper presented at the annual meeting of the American Association of Colleges for teacher Education, Dallas, TX. (ERIC Document Reproduction Service No. ED451189)

Brown, G.T.L. (2011). New Zealand prospective teacher conceptions of assessment and academic performance: Neither student nor practising teacher. In R. Kahn, J. C. McDermott, & A. Akimjak (Eds.), *Democratic access to education* (pp. 119–132). Los Angeles, CA: Antioch University Los Angeles, Department of Education.

Brown, G.T.L., & Harris, L. R. (2009). Unintended consequences of using tests to improve learning: How improvement-oriented resources engender heightened conceptions of assessment as school accountability. *Journal of MultiDisciplinary Evaluation, 6*(12), 68–91. Retrieved from https://tinyurl.com/o82pkv4

Brown, G.T.L., & Harris, L. (2013). Student self-assessment. In J. H. McMillan (Ed.), *Sage handbook of research on classroom assessment* (pp. 367–393). Thousand Oaks, CA: Sage.

Brown, G.T.L., & Remesal, A. (2012). Prospective teachers' conceptions of assessment: A cross-cultural comparison. *The Spanish Journal of Psychology, 15*(1), 75–89. doi:10.5209/rev_SJOP.2012.v15.n1.37286

Buck, G. A., Trauth-Nare, A., & Kaftan, J. (2010). Making formative assessment discernable to pre-service teachers of science. *Journal of Research in Science Education, 47*(4), 402–421. doi:10.1002/tea.20344

Campbell, C. (2013). Research on teacher competency in classroom assessment. In J. H. McMillan (Ed.), *Sage handbook of research on classroom assessment* (pp. 71–84). Thousand Oaks, CA: Sage Publications.

Campbell, C., & Collins, V. L. (2007). Identifying essential topics in general and special education introductory assessment textbooks. *Educational Measurement: Issues and Practice, 26*(1), 9–18.

Chen, J., & Brown, G.T.L. (2013). High stakes examination preparation that controls teaching: Chinese prospective teachers' conceptions of excellent teaching and assessment. *Journal of Education for Teaching, 39*(5), 541–556.

Chen, P. P. (2005). Teacher candidates' literacy in assessment. *Academic Exchange Quarterly, 62*(5), 62–66.

Cizek, G. J. (1995). The big picture in assessment and who ought to have it. *Phi Delta Kappan, 77*(3), 246–249.

Cooper, J. D. (1997). *Literacy: Helping children construct meaning.* Boston: Houghton Mifflin Company.

Crooks, T. J. (1988). The impact of classroom evaluation practices on students. *Review of Educational Research, 58*, 438–481. doi:10.3102/00346543058004438

Crossman, J. (2007). The role of relationships and emotions in student perceptions of learning and assessment. *Higher Education Research & Development, 26*(3), 313–327.

Darling-Hammond, L., Hammerness, K., Grossman, P., Rust, F., & Shulman, L. (2005). The design of teacher education programs. In L. Darling-Hammond & J. Bransford (Eds.), *Preparing teachers for a changing world: What teachers should learn and be able to do* (pp. 390–441). San Francisco, CA: Jossey-Bass.

DeLuca, C., Chavez, T., Bellara, A., & Cao, C. (2013). Pedagogies for preservice assessment education: Supporting teacher candidates' assessment literacy development. *The Teacher Educator, 48*(2), 128–142. doi:10.1080/08878730.2012.760024

DeLuca, C., Chavez, T., & Cao, C. (2012). Establishing a foundation for valid teacher judgement on student learning: The role of pre-service assessment education. *Assessment in Education: Principles, Policy & Practice.* Retrieved from http://dx.doi.org/10.1080/0969594X.2012.668870

DeLuca, C., & Klinger, D. A. (2010). Assessment literacy development: Identifying gaps in teacher candidates' learning. *Assessment in Education: Principles, Policy & Practice, 17*(4), 419–438.

DeLuca, C., Klinger, D. A., Searle, M., & Shulha, L. (2010). Developing a curriculum for assessment education. *Assessment Matters, 2*, 20–42.

Dixon, H. (2011). The problem of enactment: The influence of teachers' self-efficacy beliefs on their uptake and implementation of feedback-related ideas and practices. *Assessment Matters, 3*, 71–92.

Earl, L. M. (2013). *Assessment as learning: Using classroom assessment to maximize student learning* (2nd ed.). Thousand Oaks, CA: Corwin.

Eyers, G. (2014). *Preservice teachers' assessment learning: Change, development and growth.* Unpublished doctoral thesis, The University of Auckland, NZ.

Fives, H., & Buehl, M. M. (2012). Spring cleaning for the "messy" construct of teachers' beliefs: What are they? Which have been examined? What can they tell us? In K. R. Harris, S. Graham, & T. Urdan (Eds.), *APA educational psychology handbook: Individual differences and cultural and contextual factors* (Vol. 2, pp. 471–499). Washington, DC: APA.

Gipps, C., Brown, M., McCallum, B., & McAlister, S. (1995). *Intuition or evidence? Teachers and national assessment of seven-year-olds.* Buckingham, UK: Open University Press.

Goslin, D. A. (1967). *Teachers and testing.* New York: Russell Sage Foundation.

Graham, P. (2005). Classroom-based assessment: Changing knowledge and practice through preservice teacher education. *Teaching and Teacher Education, 21*, 607–621.

Green, T. F. (1971). *The activities of teaching.* New York: McGraw-Hill.

Grudnoff, L., Hill, M. F., Haigh, M., Cochran-Smith, M., Ell, F., & Ludlow, L. (2015). *Teaching for equity: Insights from international evidence.* Paper presented at the American Education Research Association Annual Meeting, Chicago, 19 April.

Harlen, W., Gipps, C., Broadfoot, P., & Nuttall, D. (1992). Assessment and the improvement of education. *The Curriculum Journal, 3*(3), 215–230.

Hill, M., Ell, F., Grudnoff, L., & Limbrick, L. (2014a). Practise what you preach: Initial Teacher Education students learning about assessment. *Assessment Matters, 7*, 90–110.

Hill, M., Gunn, A., Smith, L., Cowie, B., & Gilmore (2014b). Preparing teacher education students to use assessment. *Assessment Matters, 7*, 4–23.

Hill, M. F. (1995). Self assessment in primary schools: A response to student teacher questions. *Waikato Journal of Education, 1*, 61–70.

Hill, M. F. (1999). Assessment in self-managing schools: Primary teachers balancing learning and accountability demands in the 1990s. *New Zealand Journal of Education Studies, 34*(1), 176–185.

Hill, M. F. (2000). *Remapping the assessment landscape: Primary teachers reconstructing assessment in self-managing schools*. Unpublished doctoral thesis. Hamilton, NZ: Waikato University.

Hills, J. R. (1977). Coordinators of accountability view teachers' measurement competence. *Florida Journal of Education Research, 19*, 34–44.

Jiang, H. (2015). *Learning to teach with assessment: A student teaching experience in China*. Singapore: Springer.

Kahn, E. A. (2000). A case study of assessment in a grade 10 English course. *The Journal of Educational Research, 93*, 276–286.

Kane, M. T. (2006). Validation. In R. L. Brennan (Ed.), *Educational Measurement* (4th ed., pp. 17–64). Westport, CT: Praeger.

Maclellan, E. (2004). Initial knowledge states about assessment: Novice teachers' conceptualisations. *Teaching and Teacher Education, 20*, 523–535. doi:10.1016/j.tate.2004.04.008

McMillan, J. H., Myran, S., & Workman, D. (2002). Elementary teachers' classroom assessment and grading practices. *The Journal of Educational Research, 95*(4), 203–213.

Mertler, C. A. (2003). *Preservice versus inservice teachers' assessment literacy: Does classroom experience make a difference?* Paper presented at the Mid-Western Educational Research Association, Columbus, OH.

Newton, P. E. (2007). Clarifying the purposes of educational assessment. *Assessment in Education: Principles, Policy & Practice: Principles, Policy & Practice, 14*(2), 149–170.

New Zealand Ministry of Education. (2007). *The New Zealand Curriculum*. Wellington: Learning Media.

Nolen, S. B., Horn, I. S., Ward, C. J., & Childers, S. A. (2011). Novice teacher learning and motivation across contexts: Assessment tools as boundary objects. *Cognition and Instruction, 29*(1), 88–122. doi:10.1080/073 70008.2010.533221

Noll, V. H. (1955). Requirements in educational measurement for prospective teachers. *School and Society, 82*, 88–90.

Pajares, F. (1992). Teachers' beliefs and educational research: Cleaning up a messy construct. *Review of Educational Research, 62*(3), 307–332.

Popham, J. (2006). A dose of assessment literacy. *Improving Professional Practice, 63*(6), 84–85.

Quilter, S. M. (1998). *Inservice teachers' assessment literacy and attitudes toward assessment*. Unpublished doctoral dissertation, University of South Carolina, Columbia, SC.

Reid, J. A. (2011). A practice turn for teacher education? *Asia Pacific Journal for Teacher Education, 39*(4), 293–310.

Richardson, V., & Placier, P. (2001). Teacher change. In V. Richardson (Ed.), *Handbook of research on teaching* (4th ed., pp. 905–947). Washington, DC: American Educational Research Association.

Ruiz-Primo, M., Li, M., Willis, K., Giamellaro, M., Lan, M., Mason, H., & Sands, D. (2012). Developing and evaluating instructionally sensitive assessment in Science. *Journal of Research in Science Teaching, 49*(6), 691–712.

Sadler, R. (1989). Formative assessment and the design of instructional systems. *Instructional Science, 18*, 119–144.

Siegel, M. A., & Wissehr, C. (2011). Preparing for the plunge: Preservice teachers' assessment literacy. *Journal of Science Teacher Education, 22*, 371–391. doi:10.1007/s10972–011–9231–6

Smith, L. F., Hill, M. F., Cowie, B., & Gilmore, A. (2014). Preparing teachers to use the enabling power of assessment. In C. Wyatt-Smith, V. Klenowski, & P. Colbert (Eds.), *Designing assessment for quality learning* (Vol. 1, pp. 303–323). Dordrecht: Springer.

Stiggins, R. J. (1991). Relevant classroom assessment training for teachers. *Educational Measurement: Issues and Practice, 10*(1), 7–12.

Stiggins, R. J. (1992). *In teachers' hands: Investigating the practices of classroom assessment*. Albany, NY: State University of New York Press.

Stiggins, R. J. (1995). Assessment literacy for the 21st century. *Phi Delta Kappan, 77*(3), 238–245.

Stiggins, R. J. (1998). Confronting the barriers to effective assessment. *School Administrator, 55*(11), 6–9.

Stiggins, R. J. (2007). Conquering the formative assessment frontier. In J. H. McMillan (Ed.), *Formative classroom assessment: Theory into practice* (pp. 8–28). New York, NY: Teachers College Press.

Swaffield, S. (2011). Getting to the heart of authentic Assessment for Learning. *Assessment in Education: Principles, Policy & Practice, 18*(4), 433–449. doi:10.1080/0969594X.2011.582838

Taber, K. S., Riga, F., Brindley, S., Winterbottom, M., Finney, J., & Fisher, L. G. (2011). Formative conceptions of assessment: trainee teachers' thinking about assessment issues in English secondary schools. *Teacher development, 15*(2), 171–186.

Tunstall, P., & Gipps, C. (1996). Teacher feedback to young children in formative assessment: A typology. *British Educational Research Journal, 22*(4), 389–404.

Volante, L., & Fazio, L. (2007). Exploring teacher candidates' assessment literacy: Implications for teacher education reform and professional development. *Canadian Journal of Education, 30*(3), 749–770.

Wang, J.-R., Kao, H.-L., & Lin, S.-W. (2010). Preservice teachers' initial conceptions of assessment of science learning: The coherence with their views of learning science. *Teaching and Teacher Education, 26*, 522–529. doi:10.1016/j.tate.2009.06.014

Winterbottom, M., Brindley, S., Taber, K. S., Fisher, L. G., Finney, J., & Riga, F. (2008). Conceptions of assessment: Trainee teachers' practices and values. *The Curriculum Journal, 19*(3), 193–213.

Wyatt-Smith, C. & Klenowski, V. (2014). Elements of better assessment for the improvement of learning. In Claire Wyatt-Smith, Valentina Klenowski, & Peta Colbert (Eds.), Designing assessment for quality learning (pp. 195–210). Dordrecht, Netherlands: Springer.

Zeichner, K. (2012). The turn once again toward practice-based teacher education. *Journal of Teacher Education, 63*(5), 376–382.

5

IN-SERVICE TEACHER PROFESSIONAL LEARNING

Use of Assessment in Data-based Decision-making

Mei Kuin Lai and Kim Schildkamp

There is increasing international emphasis on using data as part of teacher decision-making to improve teaching practices and raise student achievement. This emphasis is often positioned as two competing agendas. On the one hand, there is a move to hold teachers and schools more externally accountable for student educational outcomes. In this case, assessment data are used to show the district, state, and/or school inspection office how well the school is performing (Coburn & Talbert, 2006; Diamond & Spillane, 2004; Schildkamp, Lai, & Earl, 2013; Wohlstetter, Datnow, & Park, 2008). This approach is generally associated with top-down (government or district driven), external accountability, and high-stakes testing (see Nichols & Harris, this volume).

On the other hand, there is a move to use assessment data as part of evidence-based teacher inquiry, an approach generally associated with bottom-up, internal school self-evaluation and low-stakes testing (Earl & Katz, 2006; Schildkamp et al., 2013). This approach includes the use of assessment data for decision-making, but positions assessment data as one of multiple sources of data, including other academic and non-academic information on learning (e.g., student engagement). These different agendas influence how assessment data are perceived and used as part of data-based decision-making, and school leaders and teachers often have to balance both agendas simultaneously.

Emerging evidence suggests that under certain conditions, using assessment data as part of teacher decision-making can contribute to improvements in teachers' knowledge and student achievement (Campbell & Levin, 2009; Carlson, Borman, & Robinson, 2011; Lai, Wilson, McNaughton, & Hsiao, 2014; Poortman, Ebbeler, & Schildkamp, 2015; Slavin, Cheung, Holmes, Madden, & Chamberlain, 2011; Timperley & Parr, 2009). Consequently, large-scale teacher in-service professional development (PD) in data-based decision-making has been implemented in diverse contexts (Campbell & Levin, 2009; Carlson et al., 2011; Lai, McNaughton, Amituanai-toloa, Turner, & Hsiao, 2009; Schildkamp & Poortman, 2015; Slavin et al., 2011; Timperley & Parr, 2009). An integral part of this PD is training in how to analyse and use assessment data for teacher decision-making.

In this chapter, we position teachers' use of assessment data as part of a data-based decision-making framework with an emphasis on using data for teacher inquiry. We identify some of the challenges to teachers' use of assessment data, paying particular attention to teachers' knowledge, and beliefs or attitudes towards the use of data. The bulk of the chapter focuses on two case studies of in-service teacher professional development (PD) where teachers have successfully learnt to use data to improve practices and student achievement. Finally, implications for teacher preparation and PD, policy priorities, and assessment frameworks are addressed.

USE OF ASSESSMENT WITHIN A DATA-BASED DECISION-MAKING FRAMEWORK

Data-based decision-making research aims to understand how teachers and school leaders use data (which may include assessment data) to make decisions. In this chapter, we focus on teachers' use of assessment data for formative purposes (i.e., improving teaching or learning; Black & Wiliam, 1998) within the wider data-based decision-making framework.

Our definition of 'data' in the context of data-based decision-making in schools is "information that is collected and organized to represent some aspect of schools" (Lai & Schildkamp, 2013, p. 10). This definition focuses on the multiple kinds of data, including assessment data, that teachers and school leaders need for decision-making (Lai & Schildkamp, 2013). It is deliberately broad to include any relevant information about students, parents, schools, and teachers derived from both qualitative (e.g., structured teacher reflections on classroom teaching) and quantitative (e.g., standardised testing) methods of analysis. Our definition of assessment data is not limited to formal assessment (e.g., standardized or national tests), but includes all data that are systematically collected and that a teacher can generate to assess his/her students, including informal assessment, such as teacher-made quizzes. The key element is that the data, formal or informal, must be systematically collected.

Our definition seeks to avoid the two common extremes when using assessment as part of a data-based decision-making framework: (1) when 'data' becomes narrowly defined as assessment data, particularly data from standardized assessments or national tests that are quantifiable (Nichols & Harris, this volume; Hamilton, Stecher, & Yuan, 2009), and (2) when assessment data (particularly data from standardised tests) are seen as less useful than individual teacher's experience or intuition or information gathered 'on-the-run' from students during a lesson (Schildkamp & Kuiper, 2010). Rather, we argue that both assessment and other forms of data can be used for teacher decision-making. Assessment data are an important source of evidence of what students are learning and what teachers might need to teach. However, assessment data alone are an insufficient basis for most teachers and school leaders to use when making good decisions. Assessment data in and of themselves do not indicate the "root causes behind the numbers" (Slavin et al., 2011, p. 3). Nor do they automatically indicate the most appropriate instructional changes a teacher or school leader needs to make to address student weaknesses; for this, they also need other data, such as information on current teaching and leadership practices and curricular goals (Lai & McNaughton, 2013b).

There is general consensus around the framework for analysing assessment data as part of data-based decision-making, albeit the name of the framework and its components varies across publications (Boudett & Steele, 2007; Earl & Katz, 2006; Lai & Schildkamp, 2013; Mandinach, Honey, Light, & Brunner, 2008; Marsh, 2012; Schildkamp & Poortman, 2015):

- The framework typically begins with a clear *purpose* for examining data, with the purpose typically framed as using data to improve teaching practice and improve student learning and achievement.
- Assessment and other *data are collected* to achieve that purpose.
- These data are then *analysed* to identify student strengths and learning needs.
- Teachers then *interpret* the various data sources and the possible actions to address the needs identified in the data. This is a sense-making process as the implications for future teaching actions based on the analysis of the data are often not self-evident (Mandinach et al., 2008; Marsh, 2012). Rather, teachers need to connect data with their own understanding, knowledge, and expertise to determine what the data mean and what needs to happen next.
- Based on the analysis and interpretation of the data, teachers use the data to *improve teaching and learning.*
- Teachers *evaluate* how they have used data, in terms of the success of their actions in achieving the purpose. The data that are acted on usually reshapes the purpose in some way, leading to another cycle of data collection, analysis, and interpretation. Thus, data use is a cyclic and iterative process.

The process is summed up in Figure 5.1.

In many countries, learning how to use data is not part of the teacher education curricula (Herman & Gribbons, 2001; Mandinach & Gummer, 2013). Yet, there is a general consensus that professional development (PD) in the use of data is needed, and is essential for improving the quality of schools (Desimone, 2009; Schildkamp & Kuiper, 2010; Wayman & Stringfield, 2006). This situation has led to the rise of in-service teacher PD on data use. The in-service PD typically provides support to schools to effectively use data for decision-making, based on the cycle presented above (Dunn, Jaafar, Earl, & Katz, 2013; Lai et al., 2014; Lai, McNaughton, Amituanai-Toloa, & Hsiao, 2009; Schildkamp & Poortman, 2015; Staman, Visscher, & Luyten, 2013).

It is worth noting the framework described above is focused on using data in desirable ways (Lai & Schildkamp, 2013; Weiss, 1998); that is, using data in 'conceptual' (i.e., change teacher's thinking) and/or 'instrumental' (i.e., change teachers practice) ways. However, it is possible within our framework to 'misuse' data (e.g., teachers teach to the test) or 'abuse' data (e.g., improve test scores by focusing only on students who are likely to improve) (Booher-Jennings, 2005), both of which are more likely to occur within high-stakes, external accountability systems. This does not mean that data should not be used for external accountability purposes. Using data for decision-making is important for both internal and external accountability, as schools are responsible for the quality of education they provide to students, and accountable to their school communities, the general public, and the government. Schools can use data to account for their functioning, although assessment data should only be one of several pieces of evidence concerning school quality (Coburn & Talbert, 2006; Diamond & Spillane, 2004).

Tensions and conflicts are likely to arise when it comes to using data for both accountability and improvement purposes (Hargreaves & Braun, 2013; Ingram et al., 2004).

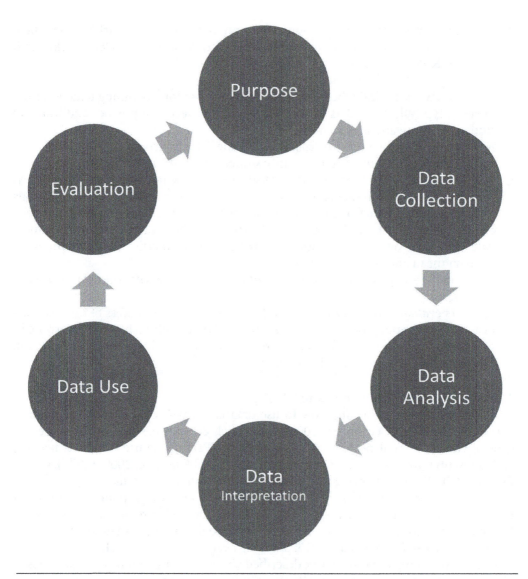

Figure 5.1 Typical Data Analysis Process

For example, Brown and Harris (2009) found that the policy introduction of using assessment for school-wide data-based improvement initiatives led some teachers to stop perceiving that the same assessment information could be used for classroom improvement purposes. However, it does not necessarily follow that high-stakes accountability uses will automatically result in negative teachers' attitudes towards using data. A recent national survey of professional (i.e., teacher, school leaders, pastoral care staff, etc.) attitudes towards the use of data in England found highly positive reports in the use of externally collected data, albeit teachers tended to use such data less (Downey & Kelly, 2013). However, respondents also reported a tension between the internal (i.e., for self-evaluation and improvement) and external (i.e., for accountability and public use) purposes of using data, with most wanting the former. Thus, it may not be the high-stakes accountability focus per se that is the issue behind the reluctance to use data, but when the high-stakes accountability focus is not shared by schools or teachers, or when the consequences for using data outweigh the benefits. The challenge is finding a balance between these two purposes, because as Earl and Katz (2006, p. 12) state: "Accountability without improvement is empty rhetoric, and improvement without accountability is whimsical action without direction."

CHALLENGES TO TEACHERS' USE OF STUDENT ASSESSMENT DATA

There is well-documented evidence of teacher reluctance to use data (including assessment data) for decision-making (Datnow, Park, & Wohlstetter, 2007; Earl & Katz, 2008; Marsh, 2012; Vanhoof, Van Petegem, & De Maeyer, 2009). Herman and Gribbons (2001, p. 18) call this a "siege mentality," where teachers become defensive about the use of data, and fear that data are only being used for blaming and shaming teachers specifically. In this chapter, we briefly present the common issues in the literature which are indicative rather than exhaustive of the challenges faced by teachers when using assessment data for decision-making.

Knowledge and Skills to Effectively Use Assessment Data

One of the biggest challenges teachers face when using assessment data for decision-making is the lack of knowledge and skills to use such data (Earl & Timperley, 2008; Schildkamp & Kuiper, 2010). To use assessment data for decision-making, teachers need knowledge and skills to enact the data analysis cycle (i.e., knowledge and skills to analyse, interpret, and use different forms of data for decision-making), including an understanding of how assessment data is positioned within the data analysis cycle. This is often referred to as data literacy (Earl & Katz, 2006; Mandinach, 2012; Marsh et al., 2006; Wohlstetter et al., 2008).

Teachers need other skills and knowledge, most notably pedagogical content knowledge (PCK) (Lai, McNaughton, & Zhu, 2015; Mandinach, 2012; Schildkamp & Poortman, 2015), and knowledge about their curriculum areas. Shulman (1986) defined PCK as subject matter content knowledge and knowledge of how to teach subject matter. Identifying an appropriate instructional strategy from assessment data requires knowledge of the content students struggle with, of a range of strategies which could be used to address students' weaknesses, and which strategy (out of a range of strategies) might be most appropriate given the students in the class. Teachers also often need awareness about their school organization, for example, the rules, norms, and structures in their organization, especially if they are working to simultaneously achieve a school-wide purpose, such as reducing grade repetition (Schildkamp & Poortman, 2015). Such understanding cannot be gained through preservice or possibly even in-service PD, but represents the tacit knowledge an organization holds and how that knowledge is communicated to its members.

Teachers' Attitudes and Beliefs

While a lack of knowledge and skills is an influencing factor, merely providing more PD will not necessarily result in teachers using data, if their beliefs in the importance of using assessment data are not addressed. A common problem faced is persuading some teachers that teaching and curriculum decisions based on assessment data may have as much or more value than decisions based on intuition and gut instinct (Ingram et al., 2004; Robinson & Lai, 2006; Timperley & Phillips, 2003). These teachers believe that their personal experience and theories are more powerful than assessment data in determining what students need to learn and how best to teach it. If these beliefs are not challenged or engaged with, then teachers will be less willing to use assessment data (Datnow et al., 2007; Marsh, 2012; Robinson & Lai, 2006; Schildkamp, Karbautzki, & Vanhoof, 2014). Indeed, a focus on changing teachers' theories of the value of assessment has been associated with interventions which have successfully changed teachers' thinking (Timperley & Phillips, 2003) and improved student learning (Lai & McNaughton, 2013a; Timperley & Parr, 2009).

Even if teachers believe in the importance of data, they may still choose not to use data in decision-making if they believe that they have no ownership over the data or the problem the data are being used to solve (Lai & McNaughton, 2013b; Schildkamp & Poortman, 2015). Teachers may choose not to use data if they feel that critical decisions about the assessment data (e.g., what data and for what purposes) are beyond their control, and if they feel that they are not primarily responsible to solve the problem the school is encountering (Lai & McNaughton, 2013b; Timperley & Phillips, 2003). This is a particularly pressing issue under conditions of high external accountability, where data might be used to blame and shame teachers (Booher-Jennings, 2005).

The degree to which teachers believe that a purpose can be reached and/or a problem can be solved using assessment data also influences the use of data. If teachers do not believe that they have the power to affect student learning, they are not likely to use assessment data to make changes in their teaching. This is a particularly salient issue in situations where the problem is widespread and historical, such as the low academic achievement of minority students in low socioeconomic communities (Lai, McNaughton, Amituanai-Toloa et al., 2009), and where even national initiatives to improve achievement have yielded smaller than desired effects (Borman, 2005). In such instances, teachers may feel that nothing they do can make a difference. Teachers that feel less efficacious are less willing to experiment to meet the needs of students, are less resilient in the face of difficulties and failure, and have lower persistence (McNaughton, 2002). If many teachers within the school feel less efficacious, then this may lead to a collective lack of efficacy (i.e., a group's shared belief in its capability to organize and execute actions required to achieve goals) (Bandura, 1995; Tschannen-Moran & Woolfolk Hoy, 2001). Strong collective efficacy in schools is associated with better student achievement outcomes (Bandura, 1995; Lai, McNaughton, Timperley, & Hsiao, 2009).

Finally, the degree to which teachers believe that they have the autonomy to make decisions based on data is also essential. This is called perceived autonomy in the theory of planned behaviour (Ajzen, 2005). Teachers may want to use data, own the problem, and feel efficacious; however, they may believe they lack the autonomy to make instructional changes. Although in some countries certain curriculum decisions cannot be made by individual teachers, there are many instructional decisions that can be made by teachers, even within these countries. As such, the perception of autonomy may be even more important than actual autonomy (Nieveen & Kuiper, 2012; Nieveen, Van den Akker, & Resink, 2010; Schildkamp et al., 2014).

Summarizing, in-service teacher PD around the use of assessment data is not just about developing the knowledge and skills to make sense of and use data. It also requires addressing teachers' attitudes and beliefs about using assessment data within their wider decision-making framework. Although we have presented some of the challenges to teacher attitudes and beliefs in the literature, these may work in differing combinations in different contexts, may change over time and across curriculum areas, and may be magnified by individual school circumstances.

IN-SERVICE TEACHER PD TO USE ASSESSMENT
DATA FOR DECISION-MAKING

Despite the challenges, there is some evidence that under certain conditions, there can be powerful effects when teachers and/or school leaders analyse and use data (including assessments) as part of in-service PD to reflect on and improve their own teaching. There is evidence of improvement in math and literacy achievement and increased high school certificate attainment using a range of methodologies including randomized control trials (Campbell & Levin, 2009; Carlson et al., 2011; Lai et al., 2014; McNaughton, Lai & Hsiao, 2012; Poortman et al., 2015; Slavin et al., 2011). However, some of these improvements were made in the context of other professional development (Lai et al., 2014; McNaughton et al., 2012); hence, the impact on student outcomes cannot be fully attributed to using data alone.

Although there are many teacher in-service PD programmes in data use for decision-making, most programs do not include a systematic research programme to evaluate and theorise the in-service teacher PD programme over an extended period of time. In what follows, we present two case studies, one from New Zealand (NZ) and the other from the Netherlands, which are representative rather than exhaustive of the teacher in-service PD data-use programmes, and where the effects on teacher knowledge and achievement have been studied over an extended period of time. These two cases represent recent PD which has improved teaching and achievement. A recent review on data-use PD found only two out of 74 PD programmes on data-use actually examined the effects of the data use programmes (Schildkamp et al., 2014b). The two cases both demonstrate, using similar PD principles, how to simultaneously address teachers' attitudes and beliefs and knowledge, and demonstrate that it is possible to shift teaching and learning by treating teachers as professionals with expertise to contribute to the data use process, rather than as technicians to implement an externally developed programme with fidelity. The cases are instances where we had insider knowledge which enabled us to provide a more in-depth perspective than is possible from a review of journal articles.

In these two PD models, the general PD process was to support teachers and school leaders' analysis and use of assessment and other data relevant to their context, with a PD focus on aspects of the model that teachers and school leaders might struggle with. The main in-service PD models used in this study were (in alphabetical order): Data Teams (DT) (Netherlands, Sweden, and England), a model that has been used since 2009, with emerging but positive evidence on improving teachers' attitudes and beliefs, as well as improving student achievement (Poortman, Ebbeler, Schildkamp, & Handelzalts, 2014, 2015; Schildkamp & Poortman, 2015); and the Learning Schools Model (LSM) (New Zealand, Australia), a model which has been used since 2003, with extensive evidence of improving student achievement over time and across different contexts (Lai et al., 2014; Lai, McNaughton, Amituanai-Toloa et al., 2009; McNaughton et al., 2012).

A comparison of key features of the in-service teacher PD is reported in Table 5.1.

Descriptions of the Teacher In-service PD Programs

Data teams. The DT programme provides PD on how to use data, with the immediate goal of developing teachers' data literacy and the ultimate goal of school improvement (i.e., solving the educational problem schools are experiencing using data) (Poortman et al., 2014; Schildkamp, Handelzalts, & Poortman, 2012; Schildkamp & Poortman, 2015).

Table 5.1 In-service Teacher Professional Development Features for the Data Teams and Learning Schools Model

Characteristic	Data Team Procedure	Learning Schools Model
PD format	• Two year programme • PD is delivered to individual schools • Focus is on a topic that the school chooses (e.g., grade repetition, mathematics achievement, English achievement) • Data teams of six to eight people in each school, including teachers and school leaders engage in the PD • Cascade model (i.e., data teams spread learning to other parts of the school) • Facilitators work with individual schools' data teams • Approximately 12–14 school meetings per year guided by an external facilitator • PD in the school's own context with the school's own data	• Three year programme • PD is delivered to clusters of schools and to individual schools in the cluster • Focus is on literacy • Inter-school (e.g., cross-schools principals group; cross-schools principals and literacy leaders groups) and intra-school (e.g., teachers, senior management team) professional learning communities (PLCs) are formed, and engage with the PD. • Cascade model (PLCs spread learning to other parts of the school) • Researchers and, in some cases, facilitators work with inter-school PLCs and in some intra-school PLCs. • Number of meetings varies by year and facilitated by either the researchers or school or literacy leaders. Phase 1, for example, involves three cross-school leaders PLCs, and two individual meetings per school with the entire staff. • PD in the school's own context with the school's own data and multiple schools' data from the cluster
PD content	• Teams define their own problem for which they want to use data • Eight step iterative and cyclic procedure; members go back and forth between the eight steps • Includes additional data analysis workshops focused on both qualitative and quantitative data analysis • Support provided by an external facilitator from the university, who participates in all meetings	• An achievement problem is collectively defined by all schools in the cluster working together with the researchers • PD content varies by phase, however collectively analyzing and using data occurs in all phases • Includes additional workshops on literacy teaching and sustainability
Resources	• Structured data use manual • Worksheets per step • Set procedures to analyse data with the support of two data analysis manuals	• PowerPoints of all sessions and workshops • Set procedure to analyse data • Research readings

The DT procedure has been implemented in over 50 schools in the Netherlands. The DT programme directly impacts on the staff and students that are part of the DT focus, and the number of staff and students directly involved in the programme varies with school and DT focus. However, the programme can also indirectly affect all staff and students, which is approximately 900 students per school, if the learning is shared by the DT to the wider school. Pilot programmes are currently being implemented in Sweden and England.

The DT programme consists of teams of four–six teachers and one–two (assistant) school leaders, who collaboratively use data to solve a selected educational problem within the school, using a structured eight-step approach:

1. Defining a common purpose (an educational problem and goals the team wants to focus their efforts on).
2. Developing hypotheses as to causes of the problem.
3. Collaboratively collecting data to investigate possible causes.
4. Checking the quality of the data for reliability and validity.
5. Collaboratively analysing data.
6. Collectively interpreting the data and drawing conclusions.
7. Implementing improvement measures.
8. Evaluating process and improvement measures.

Reports of outcomes are from a qualitative study of four schools, using observation data and interview data, and a larger study employing a quasi-experimental design with an intervention group of 10 schools, and a comparison group of 42 schools. The latter study included survey data (pre- and post-test), a data literacy assessment (pre- and post-test), interviews, observations, and student achievement results as part of the study. Triangulation across a range of data collection methods (e.g., observations, interviews, and a satisfaction questionnaire) showed that participation in the intervention led to a more positive data use attitude and high satisfaction about the support in the use of data (Poortman et al., 2014; Schildkamp & Poortman, 2015; Schildkamp et al., 2012). Also, DT teachers scored significantly higher on the data literacy post-test than on the pre-test ($d = 0.32$) and on a data use questionnaire of knowledge and skills ($d = 0.60$) (Poortman et al., 2014).

However, application of data use in the classroom showed mixed outcomes, with some teachers not able to use data in their classrooms without support. Other teachers were able to use data to make improvements in the classroom (Poortman et al., 2014; Schildkamp et al., 2012). The impact on achievement was similarly mixed. Some schools have been able to solve the achievement problem they were working on and raise achievement. For example, from the nine schools in the second project, so far, three schools have been able to solve their problem (large effect sizes ranging from $d = 0.54$ to 0.66). One team quit the project, one team was not able to solve the problem, and the other five teams are still working on it (Poortman et al., 2015). The same goes for several other DT projects, where the teams are still in the process of developing measures to solve their problems, and the research team is still collecting data on achievement of these teams.

Learning Schools Model

The LSM is a whole-school research and development intervention. The purpose of the intervention is to develop innovative teaching practices and improve student achievement. The in-service teacher PD is a component of the wider intervention and

PD design. The main in-service teacher PD consists of PD in using assessment data for decision-making, in teaching literacy, and in sustaining interventions. The LSM has been implemented in over 60 schools in New Zealand (NZ). As the LSM is a whole-school intervention, it directly impacts on all staff and students in the schools, impacting so far well over 10,000 children. A variation of the LSM was recently implemented in Australia.

The model comprises three phases, each phase lasting approximately a school year and involving teachers' collectively in analysing and using data. The model uses design-based research principles where each phase informs the subsequent phase. The three phases are: (1) Baseline profiling and collaborative analysis of data; (2) Professional development workshops based on Phase 1 findings with collaborative analysis of data; and (3) Sustainability of interventions and collaborative analysis of data. In Phase 1, teachers and researchers work in teams to collectively analyse the nature of the achievement problem (teachers and students' learning strengths and needs), analyse how to solve the problem, develop instructional strategies to solve the identified problem, and design PD workshops for teachers. In Phase 2, collective analysis in teams continues, and about 10 PD workshops are provided to teachers to develop teachers' knowledge and skills in literacy teaching. The workshops are based on the analysis of data in Phase 1. The impact of these workshops are assessed and refined for Phase 3. In Phase 3, collective analyses in teams continue, and in most applications of the model, teachers implement an action research project around an achievement issue in their classrooms. Additional workshops focus on developing the sustainability of the intervention.

The LSM has been replicated for over 15 years in five clusters of schools across diverse contexts (e.g., rural and urban; different socioeconomic communities; indigenous, ethnic minorities, and dominant ethnic group; high and low achievers) (Lai, McNaughton, Amituanai-Toloa et al., 2009; Lai et al., 2014; McNaughton et al., 2012). Gains were determined using quasi-experimental designs with comparison groups and, if appropriate, a determination of odds ratios. Hierarchical linear modeling (HLM) was used to check the variance in achievement.

Replication studies have consistently found statistically and educationally significant improvements in achievement across four clusters of schools ($n = 53$ schools) in reading, writing, and high school qualifications. The fifth cluster's study is ongoing, but initial results show the same positive trend. For example, in the four clusters, effect sizes were generally greater than or equivalent to similar interventions internationally (McNaughton et al., 2012). For example, effects sizes were $d = 0.50$ and 0.62 in a high school cluster (Lai et al., 2014); whereas, similar high school reading comprehension interventions reported effect sizes of 0.06 (Scammacca et al., 2007), and schooling improvement initiatives have more generally reported effect sizes of 0.20 for interventions of similar length (Borman, 2005). In two clusters, the effect size shifts meant that students were achieving at the average band of achievement by the end of the intervention from a pre-intervention start of about two years below national expected levels. Where it has been possible to track achievement of the clusters post-intervention, achievement improvements were sustained such that the rate of gain in literacy was the same as during the interventions (Lai et al., 2009).

Triangulation across a range of data collection methods during and after the intervention indicated that teachers used assessment data and other data to identify student learning needs, and improve their teaching practices (Lai & McNaughton 2008; Lai et al., 2014). For example, classroom observations indicated that teachers only checked for textual evidence when comprehending a text about once every 120 minutes, and the assessment data showed students seldom used textual evidence when comprehending.

After discussing these issues with teachers in PLCs, checking for evidence increased to every seven–eight minutes in a sample of classrooms.

Features of Teacher In-service PD

Our analysis of these effective PD models indicated seven common features.

Shared and Urgent Focus on Addressing Student Learning

Teacher motivation to invest time and energy into learning to use data for decision-making is a significant barrier to in-service PD on data-based decision-making. These PD models motivated teachers by focusing on an urgent problem of practice from the teachers' own context, rather than starting with a generic focus on how to use assessment data. This strategy capitalises on teachers' genuine interest in supporting their students to learn by positioning the PD on data use as a way of problem-solving difficult issues that teachers are grappling with. This approach is consistent with literature reviews focused on effective PD more broadly (Hawley & Valli, 1999; Timperley, Wilson, Barrar, & Fung, 2007).

The two models used slightly different ways of creating a shared and urgent focus. In the NZ case, the first phase of the intervention involved examining student assessment data from the schools to develop a common understanding of the extent and nature of the problem. In the Dutch model, the PD started with school participants identifying the pressing concerns of the school rather than with data. Data were then positioned in the PD as means to explore and solve this problem.

Ownership

Allied to the first feature is the importance of teacher ownership of the student learning problem and its solution. If teachers see others (e.g., government, students, parents) as mainly responsible for solving the issues, then they will not see the relevance of engaging in PD requiring them to use data to change instruction in their classrooms. This is especially salient in contexts of low socioeconomic status and ethnic minority communities with long-standing issues of low achievement. An allied strategy was taking teacher hypotheses about the data or problem seriously and testing them. In both PD programmes, discovering that some of teachers' own hypotheses about low achievement were not supported by the data increased ownership of the problem and willingness to examine their own practices as a possible cause. Resistance to owning the problem can also be overcome when teachers' own assessment data shows growth, illustrating that it is possible to shift achievement within the teachers' own context.

By doing this, teacher professional knowledge and complementary and reciprocal expertise to solve existing problems is acknowledged. This increases the chance that teachers will feel ownership over the data used for decision-making and the problem they are investigating, even if the assessment data are a nationally mandated assessment. This approach is vastly different to PD approaches that treat teachers as technicians whose sole role in the PD is to implement with fidelity a programme of instruction designed by others.

Relevance of the Data

Teachers' beliefs about the relevance of the data being used for decision-making matters to their engagement. Reliance on national data only, rather than local data, is relatively ineffective. In the Dutch and NZ cases, what data to collect, including which assessments to use, was negotiated between researchers or professional developers and the teachers and school leaders. Negotiations around what data to collect was an integral part of the PD to ensure that teachers understood and accepted the data being used. The case studies illustrate that the kind of data being used (e.g., tests vs. observations) may be less important than having teachers involved in determining the purpose and relevance of particular kinds of data. In both PD programmes, national as well as local data were used, as long as these were seen as relevant to improving student learning.

Structures and Protocols to Develop Data Use

Structures and protocols that provide a scaffold for teachers to develop their knowledge and skills in data use are needed. This can be in the form of a set procedure to analyse data (NZ case), or an eight step data use process (Dutch case); the latter includes a data analysis course, a manual, and worksheets. Such structures and protocols are particularly important because data use is something new to many teachers, and these structures and protocols provide scaffolds to teacher learning. For example, teachers reported that the Dutch eight step procedure presented the use of data in a systematic way, and ensured that all activities in a data cycle would be carried out. Without structure, it is easy for teachers to jump from their perceptions of the problem to the solution without collecting data to test their perceptions.

Developing Teachers as Adaptive Experts to Use Data

In all the PD models, teachers are treated as adaptive experts (Darling-Hammond & Bransford, 2005), who are deeply knowledgeable about what they do, how they do it, and why they do it, and are perceived to be flexible and adaptable in their practices. This approach positions in-service PD within the teacher-as-inquiry agenda. In the Dutch model, teachers were supported through the PD to analyse and discuss data, even though there was no direct PD in how to address the problems identified. The data may show a PD team what is causing the problem they are investigating, but the teachers, as experts, combine the data with their own knowledge and experience to develop and implement measures, and evaluate and further adapt those measures with data. The LSM employed a similar strategy, but in addition, provided PD to address identified problems from the data in instances where the teachers' capacity to address the problem might be limited. Specifically, in the three-phase NZ model, there is no initial PD to address the problems, but workshops develop pedagogical content knowledge to address identified student and teacher needs in the subsequent phases.

Professional Learning Communities to Support Data Use

PD seems to be more effective when it takes place in professional learning communities (PLCs). While there is debate around the definition of a PLC, here we use PLC to refer to a group of individuals who share and critically interrogate their practice using data in an ongoing and reflective way to improve teaching and learning. In both cases, PLC members discussed how to use assessment data plus other relevant data to improve teaching and student learning. These PLCs involved teachers (or a few teacher leaders), school leaders, and facilitators and researchers. All PLCs had a common focus on using data to improve student learning and also, learning from each other, taking collective responsibility to progress joint tasks, developing shared cognition and collective efficacy, apprenticing teachers into the norms of the group, and developing knowledge and skills in data use. The facilitators and researchers exemplied how to use data to improve teaching and learning, and become participants in developing solutions with schools. The expertise to use the data-use cycle is distributed across the facilitators, researchers, and teachers. PLCs also apprenticed teachers into the group norms of using data, as teachers new to the school or the process were part of the PLCs with more experienced teachers and learnt by observing discussions around how to analyse and use the data.

Interdependence With a Range of Learning Partners

In both cases, the PD on data use relied on interdependent partners (e.g., researchers, other schools) who supported teachers in learning how to use data. Interdependence means that teachers form complementary and mutually informed relationships with a range of partners with appropriate expertise to support them in data use (Lai & McNaughton, 2013a). The focus on interdependence reduces the emphasis on two extremes: too much reliance on external experts or too little dependence on external experts when the teachers lack the knowledge to identify and/or address the problems in their classroom (Lai & McNaughton, 2013a). Such partnerships maximize distributed cognition by having more divergent knowledge to understand a problem, test hypotheses, and solve the problem.

The features of in-service PD described here work in combination with each other, and the emphasis on particular features varies across the case studies and different times within a case. The specific combinations and emphases in each case study are based on data either collected before or during the PD. In this sense, the PD developers also used data as inquiry to reflect on and change their practices, often combining this reflective approach with more systematic design-based approaches to PD development. In both cases, there was an assumption of autonomy to make changes that were suggested by the data.

It is also worth emphasizing that PD provided to schools was over an extended period of time. Using assessment data for decision-making requires educators to consider current beliefs in relation to new knowledge (often from data), reflect on data, and construct new ways of thinking about the issues, all of which requires sufficient time for educators to come to grips with the new learning. Finally, both case studies are in the context of educational systems which are not typically associated with top-down high-stakes accountability and national testing, although each system has tests that are used nationally, and has national and/or regional accountability systems.

CONCLUSIONS AND IMPLICATIONS

The use of assessment data as part of a data-based decision-making cycle has the potential to lead to improved teaching and learning. However, to use assessment data effectively, teachers and school leaders need to acquire new knowledge and skills and be supported and challenged to reexamine their attitudes and beliefs about the usefulness of data in improving teaching and learning. The two case studies demonstrate that it is possible for teacher in-service PD to simultaneously address the aforementioned teachers' attitudes and beliefs, which prevent them from using data, and improve teacher knowledge and student learning. However, this is dependent on the form and content of the PD, and in how teachers are viewed in the PD model. Importantly, the PD models here view the role of the PD as developing teacher inquiry and adaptive expertise (Darling-Hammond & Bransford, 2005), treating teachers as joint partners and problem-solvers of a common and shared problem, and developing PLCs which enable teachers to inquire into their practices. In addition, the development of positive teacher attitudes and beliefs towards data was a central part of the PD, and developed through the process of acquiring knowledge on analysing and using data to solve urgent and collective problems experienced by the school.

Thus, the PD approach of the two case studies is highly respectful of existing teacher expertise and knowledge, but does assume an 'adequate' level of teacher knowledge to engage with the PD. It is unclear whether this type of PD can be used to increase teacher knowledge in instances where teacher knowledge is very low at the start of the PD. Testing the latter is important, because it is easy to have 'deficit thinking' that assumes teachers with low knowledge need a 'teacher-proof' curriculum and a PD approach where the teachers' sole role is to implement another's ideas with fidelity. The problem with such 'teacher-proof' PD approaches is that it violates many of the factors we have found to be effective in our PD. For example, teachers are likely to lose a feeling of ownership over the data and the outcomes if their only role is to implement with fidelity; they are less likely to buy into the PD approach as their theories have been ignored; and consequently, they are more likely to resist the proposed PD approaches. It may be that, in instances where teacher knowledge is very low, having additional content knowledge workshops to supplement the PD on the analysis of data will be sufficient to produce similarly positive effects on student learning.

While PD in the use of assessment data could profit from including the seven features of successful in-service PD models described in this chapter, any PD needs to be contextualized to the needs of teachers and school leaders undertaking the PD. These needs may differ within the same context, across different contexts within countries and across different countries, and even over time. Different cultural contexts mean that some forms of data become more difficult to collect, as the schools do not have shared norms around collecting and using such data. For example, in our experience, it is less common to collect detailed observations of teaching practice in some schools in Australia. That is not to say data on teaching practices cannot and should not be collected, but there needs to be greater negotiation around the value of collecting such data in that context.

Moreover, the accountability context may influence data use and data-use PD in different countries. For example, Schildkamp et al. (2014) found that the accountability system not only influenced which data were available to schools in Poland, Germany, England, Lithuania, and the Netherlands, but also for which purposes these data were being used. Too much pressure to use data, combined with too little support, leads to less effective data use. Effective data use required some pressure from the accountability system, but also support in terms of access to data, data analysis tools, and the availability of PD (Schildkamp & Lai, 2013). Thus, the case studies suggest that providing greater support to teachers and having less external punitive pressure might be more profitable in encouraging teachers to use data effectively to improve instruction.

However, independent of the country and accountability context, teachers and school leaders need to have sufficient autonomy to actually make changes in the curriculum and their instruction based on data. This requires policy support in the form of autonomy to make decisions based on data, and also the provision of tools and PD in the use of data. Where teacher autonomy is low (e.g., little freedom around curriculum decisions), it may still be possible to implement the data cycle on the parts of teaching over which the teacher has autonomy (e.g., instructional practices), though this may not bring about as robust results as reported in these two case studies.

A challenge to implementing the PD approaches as outlined here is that these PD approaches do not rely on workshops or similar traditional forms of PD. Therefore, there is sometimes the perception that PD in analysing data, in the way described here, is not PD. As such, some teachers prefer to reduce the focus on analysing data and focus more on learning new instructional moves to try in the classroom through more traditional PD workshops by 'experts.' The notion that the process of analysing data *is* PD in itself requires a change in mindset for some teachers, but these teachers often start to understand the importance of the PD once they see the impact on their students' learning. A related challenge for schools is finding the time to engage in these types of PD. Some schools actually prefer more conventional forms of PD (e.g., workshops) because these require less time, even though they are often less effective in addressing teacher and student learning; Van Veen et al. (2010) and Houtveen and Van de Grift (2012) both demonstrated the importance of having PD over a prolonged period of time.

Finally, some of the collective problems described in this chapter (e.g., grade retention, reducing long-standing disparities in achievement) are very complex. This requires perseverance by the participants to continue with the PD, even if it seems in the short term that the school is not closer to finding a solution. This is particularly the case at the start of the PD, where time is spent generating and testing hypotheses about the causes of the problems. This process is a powerful learning experience in analysing data to check assumptions, and contributes greatly to finding the solution. However, having to reject multiple hypotheses can be de-motivating, and it requires persistence to continue. It may be that teachers need greater support during this process to more quickly eliminate the less likely hypotheses and focus their attention on the more probable ones.

The case studies highlight two areas for future research. First, there is the need for more robust testing of the components of the in-service models with teacher learning and student data to better understand the relationships between the different features of the PD model and the impact on teaching and learning. A recent study by Lai et al. (2015) analysed observations of meetings where data are discussed, and used hierarchical linear modelling to test the relationship between discussing patterns in the data, the pedagogical content knowledge required to determine next instructional steps from the data, and achievement gain. Results indicated that neither discussing data nor pedagogical content knowledge alone had a relationship with achievement gains; however, a combination of the two was related to achievement. Analytic techniques, such as structural equation modelling of PD components, might be a useful way of testing the components of the in-service teacher PD with outcomes.

Second, there is the need for systematic, long-term, and replicable evidence on the impact of that PD on student achievement and teachers' knowledge, attitudes, and beliefs. While several PD programs are currently being developed and implemented to support schools in the use of data around the world, the evidence is less systematically collected.

Finally, while this chapter focuses on PD in the use of assessment data, we would like to stress that PD in the use of data should not start with how to use assessment data. It should start with a problem teachers want to solve or a goal that they want to reach with their students. This is the first step in addressing the changes in attitude and an increase in knowledge and skills to use data to increase student learning and achievement in schools.

REFERENCES

Ajzen, I. (2005). *Attitudes, personality and behavior* (2nd ed.). New York: Open University Press.

Bandura, A. (1995). Exercise of personal and collective efficacy in changing societies. *Self-Efficacy in Changing Societies*, 15, 334. doi:10.1017/CBO9780511527692

Black, P., & Wiliam, D. (1998). Assessment and classroom learning. *Assessment in Education: Principles, Policy & Practice, 5*, 7–74. doi:10.1080/0969595980050102

Booher-Jennings, J. (2005). Below the bubble: "Educational triage" and the Texas accountability system. *American Educational Research Journal, 42*(2), 231–268. doi:10.3102/00028312042002231

Borman, G. D. (2005). National efforts to bring reform to scale in high-poverty schools: outcomes and implications. In L. Parker (Ed.), *Review of research in education 29.* (pp. 1–28). Washington, DC: American Education Research Association. doi:10.3102/0091732X029001001

Boudett, K. P., & Steele, J. L. (2007). *Data wise in action. Stories of schools using data to improve teaching and learning.* Cambridge: Harvard Education Press.

Brown, G.T.L., & Harris, L. R. (2009). Unintended consequences of using tests to improve learning: How improvement-oriented resources engender heightened conceptions of assessment as school accountability. *Journal of MultiDisciplinary Evaluation, 6*(12), 68–91.

Campbell, C., & Levin, B. (2009). Using data to support educational improvement. *Educational Assessment, Evaluation and Accountability, 21*(1), 47–65. doi:10.1007/s11092–008–9063-x

Carlson, D., Borman, G. D., & Robinson, M. (2011). A multistate district-level cluster randomized trial of the impact of data-driven reform on reading and mathematics achievement. *Educational Evaluation and Policy Analysis, 33*(3), 378–398. doi:10.3102/0162373711412765

Coburn, C. E., & Talbert, J. E. (2006). Conceptions of evidence use in school districts: Mapping the terrain. *American Journal of Education, 112*(4), 469–495. doi:10.1086/505056

Darling-Hammond, L., & Bransford, J. (2005). *Preparing teachers for a changing world: What teachers should be able to learn and be able to do.* San Francisco, CA: John Wiley & Sons.

Datnow, A., Park, V., & Wohlstetter, P. (2007). *Achieving with data: How high-performing school systems use data to improve instruction for elementary students.* Los Angeles: Center on Educational Governance, Rossier School of Education, University of Southern California.

Desimone. (2009). Improving impact studies of teacher's professional development: toward better conceptualizations and measures. *Educational Researcher, 38*(3), 181–199. doi:10.3102/0013189X08331140

Diamond, J., & Spillane, J. (2004). High-stakes accountability in urban elementary schools: challenging or reproducing inequality?. *The Teachers College Record, 106*(6), 1145–1176. doi:10.1111/j.1467–9620.2004.00375.x

Downey, C., & Kelly, A. (2013). Professional attitudes to the use of data in England. In K. Schildkamp, M. K. Lai, & L. Earl (Eds.), *Data-based Decision Making in Education* (pp. 69–89). Springer Netherlands. doi:10.1007/978–94–007–4816–3_5

Dunn, R., Jaafar, S. B., Earl, L., & Katz, S. (2013). Towards data-informed decisions: From ministry policy to school practice. In K. Schildkamp, M. K. Lai, & L. Earl (Eds.), *Data-based decision making in education* (pp. 155–175). Dordrecht: Springer. doi:10.1007/978–94–007–4816–3_9

Earl, L., & Katz, S. (2006). *Leading in a data rich world.* Thousand Oaks, CA: Corwin Press.

Earl, L., & Katz, S. (2008). Getting to the core of learning: Using assessment for self-monitoring and self-regulation. In S. Swaffield (Ed.). *Unlocking assessment: Understanding for reflection and application* (pp. 123–137). London: Routledge.

Earl, L., & Timperley, H. (2008). *Professional learning conversations: Challenges in using evidence for improvement.* Amsterdam: Springer. doi:10.1007/978–1–4020–6917–8

Hamilton, L. S., Stecher, B. M., & Yuan, K. (2009). *Standards-based reform in the United States: History, research, and future directions.* Santa Monica: RAND Corporation.

Hargreaves, A., & Braun, H. (2013). Data-driven improvement and accountability. *Boston College: National Education Policy Center.* Retrieved October 24, 2013.

Hawley, W. D., & Valli, L. (1999). The essentials of effective professional development: A new consensus. In G. E. Darling-Hammond & Sykes (Eds.), *Teaching as a learning profession* (pp. 127–150). San Francisco: Jossey-Bass.

Herman, J. L., & Gribbons, B. (2001). *Lessons learned in using data to support school inquiry and continuous improvement: Final report to the Stuart Foundation.* Center for the Study of Evaluation, National Center for Research on Evaluation, Standards, and Student Testing, Graduate School of Education & Information Studies, University of California, Los Angeles.

Houtveen, T., & Van de Grift, W. J. C. M. (2012). Improving reading achievements of struggling learners. *School Effectiveness and School Improvement, 23*, 71–93. doi:10.1080/09243453.2011.600534

Ingram, D., Louis, K. S., & Schroeder, R. (2004). Accountability policies and teacher decision making: Barriers to the use of data to improve practice. *Teachers College Record, 106*(6), 1258–1287. doi:10.1111/j.1467–9620.2004.00379.x

Lai, M. K., & McNaughton, S. (2008). Raising student achievement in poor, urban communities through evidence-based conversations. In L. Earl & H. Timperley (Eds.), *Evidence-based conversations to improve educational practices* (pp. 13–27). Netherlands: Kluwer/Springer Academic Publishers.

Lai, M. K., & McNaughton, S. (2013a). An approach for developing effective research-practice partnerships: Lessons from a decade of partnering with schools in poor urban communities. In J. Duncan & L. Connor (Eds.), *Research partnerships within early years education: Relational expertise and knowledges in action* (pp. 49–70). New York: Palgrave MacMillan. doi:10.1057/9781137346889.0010

Lai, M. K., & McNaughton, S. (2013b). Analysis and discussion of classroom and achievement data to raise student achievement. In S. Schildkamp, M. K. Lai, & L. Earl (Eds.), *Data-based decision making in education: Challenges and opportunities* (pp. 23–48). Netherlands: Springer.

Lai, M. K., McNaughton, S., Amituanai-Toloa, M., Turner, R., & Hsiao, S. (2009). Sustained acceleration of achievement in reading comprehension: The New Zealand experience. *Reading Research Quarterly, 44*(1), 30–56. doi:10.1598/RRQ.23.3.2

Lai, M. K., McNaughton, S., Timperley, H., & Hsiao, S. (2009). Sustaining continued acceleration in reading comprehension achievement following an intervention. *Educational Assessment, Evaluation and Accountability, 21*(1), 81–100. doi:10.1007/s11092–009–9071–5

Lai, M. K., McNaughton, S., & Zhu, T. (2015). *The nature of collective pedagogical content knowledge in professional learning communities and its relationship with achievement.* Manuscript submitted for publication.

Lai, M. K., & Schildkamp, K. (2013). Data-based decision making: An overview. In K. Schildkamp, M. K. Lai, & L. Earl (Eds.), *Data-based decision making in education* (pp. 9–21). Netherlands: Springer. doi:10.1007/978–94–007–4816–3_2

Lai, M. K., Wilson, A., McNaughton, S., & Hsiao, S. (2014). Improving achievement in secondary schools: Impact of a literacy project on reading comprehension and secondary school qualifications. *Reading Research Quarterly, 49*(3), 305–334. doi:10.1002/rrq.73

Mandinach, E., Honey, M., Light, D., & Brunner, C. (2008). A conceptual framework for data-driven decision-making. In E. B. Mandinach & M. Honey (Eds.), *Data-driven school improvement: Linking data and learning* (pp. 13–31). New York: Teachers College Press.

Mandinach, E. B. (2012). A perfect time for data use: Using data-driven decision making to inform practice. *Educational Psychologist, 47*(2), 71–85. doi:10.1080/00461520.2012.667064

Mandinach, E. B., & E. S. Gummer. (2013). A systemic view of implementing data literacy in educator preparation. *Educational Researcher, 42*(1), 30–37. doi:10.3102/0013189X12459803

Marsh, J. A. (2012). Interventions promoting educators' use of data: Research insights and gaps. *Teachers College Record, 114*(11), 1–48.

Marsh, J. A., Pane, J. F., & Hamilton, L. S. (2006). *Making sense of data-driven decision making in education. Evidence from recent RAND research.* Santa Monica, CA: RAND Corporation.

McNaughton, S. (2002). *Meeting of minds.* Wellington, NZ: Learning Media.

McNaughton, S., Lai, M. K., & Hsiao, S. (2012). Testing the effectiveness of an intervention model based on data use: A replication series across clusters of schools. *School Effectiveness and School Improvement, 23*(2), 203–228. doi:10.1080/09243453.2011.652126

Nieveen, N., & Kuiper, W. (2012). Balancing curriculum freedom and regulations in the Netherlands. *European Educational Research Journal, 11*(3), 357–368. doi:10.2304/eerj.2012.11.3.357

Nieveen, N., Van den Akker, J., & Resink, F. (2010). *School-based curriculum development in the Netherlands.* Paper presented at the European Conference on Educational Research (ECER), Helsinki, Finland.

Poortman, C. L., Ebbeler, J., & Schildkamp, K. (2015, April). *School improvement effects of a data use intervention for teachers.* Paper presented at the American Educational Research Association conference, Chicago, IL.

Poortman, C. L., Ebbeler, J., Schildkamp, K., & Handelzalts, A. (2014, April). *Effects of a data team procedure on data use.* Paper presented at the American Educational Research Association, Philadelphia, USA.

Robinson, V.M.J., & Lai, M. K. (2006). *Practitioner research for educators: A guide to improving classrooms and schools.* Thousand Oaks, CA: Corwin Press.

Scammacca, N., Roberts, G., Vaughn, S., Edmonds, M., Wexler, J., Reutebuch, C. K., & Torgesen, J. K. (2007). *Interventions for adolescent struggling readers: A meta-analysis with implications for practice.* Portsmouth, NH: RMC Research Corporation, Center on Instruction.

Schildkamp, K., Handelzalts, A., & Poortman, C. L. (2012). Sustainability of data teams for school improvement. *Paper presented at the American Educational Research Association conference, April, Canada.*

Schildkamp, K., Heitink, M., Van der Kleij, F., Hoogland, I., Dijkstra, A., Kippers, W., & Veldkamp, B. (2014). Voorwaarden voor effectieve formatieve toetsing: Een praktische review [Prerequisites for formative assessment: A practical review]. Final Report NRO-PPO: dossier 405–14–530–002. Den Haag: NRO.

Schildkamp, K., Karbautzki, L., & Vanhoof, J. (2014). Exploring data use practices around Europe: Identifying enablers and barriers. *Studies in Educational Evaluation, 42*, 15–24. doi:10.1016/j.stueduc.2013.10.007

Schildkamp, K., & Kuiper, W. (2010). Data Informed Curriculum Reform: Which data, what purposes, and promoting and hindering factors. *Teaching and Teacher Education, 26*, 482–496. doi:10.1016/j.tate.2009.06.007

Schildkamp, K., Lai, M. K., & Earl, L. (2013). *Data-based decision making in education.* Dordrecht: Springer. doi:10.1007/978–94–007–4816–3

Schildkamp, K., & Poortman, C. L. (2015). Factors influencing the functioning of data teams. *Teachers College Record, 117*(4), 1–30. http://www.tcrecord.org. ID Number: 17851.

Shulman, L. S. (1986). Those who understand: Knowledge growth in teaching. *Educational Researcher, 15*(2), 4–14. doi:10.3102/0013189X015002004

Slavin, R., Cheung, A., Holmes, G., Madden, N., & Chamberlain, A. (2011). Effects of a data-driven district reform model. Retrieved from http://bit.ly/1MmrVEz

Staman, L., Visscher, A. J., & Luyten, H. (2013). The effects of professional development on the attitudes, knowledge and skills for data-driven decision making. *Studies in Educational Evaluation, 43,* 79–90. doi:10.1016/j.stueduc.2013.11.002

Timperley, H., & Parr, J. (2009). Chain of influence from policy to practice in the New Zealand literacy strategy. *Research Papers in Education: Policy and Practice, 24*(2), 135–154. doi:10.1080/02671520902867077

Timperley, H., & Phillips, G. (2003). Changing and sustaining teachers' expectations through professional development in literacy. *Journal of Teaching and Teacher Education, 19,* 627–641. doi:10.1016/S0742–051X(03)00058–1

Timperley, H., Wilson, A., Barrar, H., & Fung, I. (2007). *Best evidence synthesis iterations (BES) on professional learning and development.* Wellington, NZ: Ministry of Education.

Tschannen-Moran, M., & Woolfolk Hoy, A. (2001). Teacher efficacy: Capturing an elusive construct. *Teaching & Teacher Education, 17,* 783–805.

Van Veen, K., Zwart, R., Meirink, J., & Verloop, N. (2010). *Professionele ontwikkeling van leraren. Een reviewstudie naar effectieve kenmerken van professionaliseringsinterventies van leraren [Teacher professional development. A review of studies on effective characteristics of teacher professionalization interventions].* Leiden: ICLON/Expertisecentrum Leren van Docenten.

Vanhoof, J., Van Petegem, P., & De Maeyer, S. (2009). Attitudes towards school self-evaluation. *Studies in Educational Evaluation, 35,* 21–28. doi:10.1016/j.stueduc.2009.01.004

Wayman, J. C., & Stringfield, S. (2006). Data use for school improvement: School practices and research perspectives. *American Journal of Education, 112,* 463–468. doi:10.1086/505055

Weiss, C. H. (1998). Have we learned anything new about the use of evaluation?. *American Journal of Evaluation, 19*(1), 21–33. doi:10.1016/S1098–2140(99)80178–7

Wohlstetter, P., Datnow, A., & Park, V. (2008). Creating a system for data-driven decision-making: Applying the principal-agent framework. *School Effectiveness and School Improvement, 19*(3), 239–259. doi:10.1080/09243450802246376

6

SECTION DISCUSSION: TEACHERS AND ASSESSMENT

Enhancing Assessment Capability

Judy M. Parr and Helen S. Timperley

This section of the handbook has topics concerning teachers and assessment, in particular how teachers understand and respond to assessment practices and policies, and how their beliefs are affected and their knowledge of assessment is built. The topic of teachers and assessment is one that has assumed increased significance as notions of assessment and its functions have changed.

The function of student assessment is twofold (Allal, 2010; Bloom et al., 1971). One is to regulate students' progression through the educational system, which includes predictive assessments for admission and placement and summative assessment to certify the quality of achievement. The second is to adapt teaching and learning activities in a formative way, retroactively, or interactively. The latter purposes of assessment that are focussed on learning were brought to the fore through the seminal works of Crooks (1988), Sadler (1989), and Black and Wiliam (1998), which have directed attention to the use of assessment information as a means of making teaching more targeted to student learning needs and, therefore, more effective. Recent literature views assessment for learning as involving learners working in partnership with their teachers and peers to seek, reflect upon, and respond to information from dialogue, demonstration, and observation in ways that promote student autonomy and enhance ongoing learning (Klenowski, 2009; Swaffield, 2011). Students are no longer "the objects of their teacher's behaviour, [rather] they are animators of their own effective teaching and learning processes" (James & Pedder, 2006, p. 28). This view of assessment has focussed attention on teacher actions like feedback and the implementation of peer and self-assessment, practices that facilitate learners to use assessment information.

The major purposes of assessment are commonly viewed as involving accountability of students and schools on the one hand, and concerns around improvement in teaching and learning on the other. Earl and Le Mahieu (1997), in recognizing this, were among the first to argue for an approach whereby assessment would both improve learning and provide accountability. Similarly, Harlen (2005) pointed to the potential synergy, in terms of promoting learning, between formative and summative forms of assessment. So, although the purposes for assessment often continue to be positioned as polarized, particularly by those reporting on systems with high-stakes accountability, this portrayal of the relationship is simplistic. Even in these high-stakes systems, accountability is intended to drive improvement, although the evidence that it does so is sparse. On balance, most purposes include a mix of accountability and improvement. As Earl and Katz (2006) state: "accountability without improvement is empty rhetoric, and improvement without accountability is whimsical action without direction" (p. 31).

This chapter focuses on the theme of enhancing assessment capability. We intend to address the spirit of the title by bringing together the chapters, synthesizing, and discussing the significant findings; identifying themes, and expanding on their content. The aim is to suggest how, collectively, we might enhance our understanding of teacher perspectives and experiences of assessment. We extrapolate from the chapters with an interwoven discussion of what we need to further know about improving teacher assessment capability, in particular the processes and use of assessment by teachers. In doing this we draw heavily on our own context and experience. However, it should be acknowledged that the New Zealand context is far from typical. Features like self-governing schools, a broad, nonprescriptive curriculum, and no mandated large-scale testing but, rather, reporting against national standards for Years 1–18, based on overall teacher judgment, are major contributors to this atypicality. We aim to move the current discussion forward by suggesting issues that need to be resolved and areas that may be fruitful to explore. The first of these issues broadly concerns the way in which assessment is talked about.

THE 'LANGUAGING' OF ASSESSMENT

There is a lack of clarity around many of the concepts and terms in relation to teachers and assessment and this is reflected in the fact that assessment is 'languaged' in different ways among the chapters in this section. Hill and Eyers (this volume) focus primarily on the classroom, on formative assessment for learning as they term it. Bonner (this volume) places assessment into three categories: classroom formative assessment or assessment for learning; classroom summative assessment, grading, or marking; and large scale externally mandated assessment of student learning, whether low- or high-stakes. Nichols and Harris (this volume) are concerned with the latter, assessment that is externally mandated and high-stakes. They note that while not new, high-stakes testing has grown more popular in recent decades as a tool of educational reform (through accountability measures) in countries like the U.S.

The use of the terms high- and low-stakes contains an implied association with value; high-stakes detracts from the central focus on learning and the less intrusive low-stakes having greater value. High-stakes assessment is associated with an imposed system of rewards and punishments to incentivise teacher and student efforts (although evidence of its success in doing such is questioned) with low-stakes assessment having, by definition, little likelihood of serious punitive repercussions. Framing this issue of consequences in terms of assumed value may be simplistic in the same way that the dichotomy between accountability and improvement is simplistic with potential value needing to be positioned in more nuanced ways. In their chapter Lai and Schild-kamp (this volume) use the terms top-down, which relates to external accountability, high-stakes assessment, and bottom-up, which refers to internal accountability and low-stakes assessment. Reference is made in their chapter to literature that uses terms like internal (i.e., for self-evaluation and improvement) and external (i.e., for accountability and public use) purposes of using data from assessment. Similar to much of the literature they draw on, these authors acknowledge the tension between external accountability/high-stakes testing (typically achievement data) and using data for teacher inquiry (a wider range of evidence).

Part of this difficulty may stem from perceptions or misperceptions concerning the connotations of words like assessment and test. Research by Brown and Harris (2009) in the New Zealand context found that, despite the opportunities for teachers to engage with resources intended to support assessment for learning and improvement in teaching and learning (a software program, Assessment Tools for Teaching and Learning [asTTle], that enables teachers to create personalized but standardized tests for diagnostic purposes, and an intensive professional development program, Assess to Learn [AtoL]), they largely perceived assessment to be about school accountability. Perhaps the ongoing noticing of student behaviours and less formal means of considering learning in the classroom did not fit their conception of assessment. They did not see the opportunity for assessment to contribute to both purposes, particularly that a diagnostic test under their control could be useful in their improvement efforts in the classroom.

This aligns with Lai and Schildkamp's (this volume) claim that it is difficult for teachers (although, we would suggest, not impossible—see Parr et al., 2007, and Timperley, Parr, & Meissel, 2010) to use data simultaneously for teacher inquiry/student learning and for accountability. Such multiple uses may partly depend on the nature of the assessment and how decisions in relation to it are arrived at. But, arguably, the extent to which the gap can be bridged between the discrete and polarized use of assessments, for example those for accountability and more public use and those focused on self-evaluation and improvement, depends on working to ensure teacher conceptions of assessment and the practice of assessment reflect the current state-of-the-art knowledge. The knowledge base is considerably greater than in the 1990s, when assessment for accountability and learning appeared in relation to school reform. But it has some distance to go in terms of knowledge encompassing shared understandings communicated through shared language.

To move the field forward, there is a need to address the apparent lack of shared understanding among researchers and between researchers and education professionals as to what is being talked about with respect to assessment in its many guises by finding a means to capture accurately the nature and the function of these guises. As researchers and shapers of the field, we need some new thinking around how we 'language' talk relating to assessment. What assessment encompasses ranges widely and requires a much more nuanced and precise terminology. Current categorisations may not work for either research or practice contexts. The terms formative and summative assessment tend to depict a dichotomy often defined by the time in the learning when the assessment happens as well as the purpose for the assessment. But an assessment administered to evaluate learning may also inform further learning. Assessments can conceivably include elements of both and be used for multiple purposes. The use of the terms diagnostic versus evaluation-cum-judgement is also not quite right, as a judgement about whether a student has met a standard, for example, may involve the diagnosis of strengths and gaps in relation to the standard.

There are assessment tools that support both formative and summative, both diagnosis and an evaluative judgment. For example, the New Zealand tool, Assessment Tools for Teaching and Learning (asTTle v4/e-asTTle) (Ministry of Education, 2004, 2006) provides a detailed diagnostic assessment of various dimensions of reading, writing, and math as well as information about performance relative to national norms. In each of the areas, the tool is criterion-referenced to the national curriculum (in New Zealand a relatively broad, nonprescriptive document, Ministry of Education, 2007). The sophisticated software generates a 40 minute 'test,' tailored to teacher requirements whenever the teacher wishes to gain evidence of student learning and the success of teaching (Hattie & Brown, 2008; Hattie, Brown, & Keegan, 2003). For example, if a teacher has spent some time in writing instruction focusing on the communicative purpose of writing to persuade, the teacher can set the test so a prompt appropriate to that writing function is generated. Detailed rubrics are applied to scoring. Or if, in reading, the teacher has been working to build student ability to make inferences, a test can be constructed, at whatever curriculum level required, which contains items that will examine learning in this area. Using norms obtained from a large representative national sample of students in Years 4–12, the software can indicate where a class or year group is relative to norms or to other classes or groups like the teacher's students (in terms of socioeconomic status of school catchment area, gender, etc.). Class profiles of strengths and gaps are displayed, and the same can be obtained for individuals. The tool is an example of bridging or blurring the lines between formative and more diagnostic and evaluative, even accountability, assessment purposes. It would be interesting to establish whether, with presumably greater experience with the assessment tools and in a climate that now foregrounds teacher judgement of student performance relative to standards, teachers have developed differing views about assessment to those found by Brown and Harris (2009).

It is difficult to find terms that adequately describe the spectrum or combinations of purposes and that acknowledge the fact that assessment, particularly from a teacher perspective, actually involves a range of actions. Assessment includes (a) the rationale and the decision to gather information about learning and by what means; (b) the decision regarding what to attend to and notice in or from a particular activity; (c) the interpretation of what is perceived; and then (d) the decisions and actions that follow from these processes. All of these activities are situated in the contexts of school and wider policies which contribute in a complex way to teachers' understanding. The term classroom assessment is often used to encompass these actions. According to Jim McMillan in his introduction to the *Handbook of Research on Classroom Assessment* (2013), classroom assessment (CA) is a broad and evolving conceptualization of a process that teachers and students use in collecting, evaluating, and using evidence of student learning for a variety of purposes, including diagnosing student strengths and weaknesses, monitoring student progress toward meeting desired levels of proficiency, assigning grades, and providing feedback to parents. That is, CA is a tool teachers use to gather relevant data and information to make well-supported inferences about what students know, understand, and can do (Shavelson & Towne, 2002), as well as a vehicle through which student learning and motivation are enhanced (p. 2).

Notably, none of the current ways of talking about assessment, particularly about the actions in formative or classroom assessment, encompasses adequately the ongoing, interactive (after Cowie & Bell, 1999 who talk about interactive and planned) assessment for teaching and learning. Interactive assessment occurs when the student interacts with the components of the activity or task, including the teacher and other students, but also actions or materials that are designed to promote self-reflection on the part of the student (Allal, 2010) and/or designed to provide the teacher with information about students' learning. This type of assessment could be seen to form part of the tool kit of a teacher who constantly evaluates the success of his/her teaching through examining outcomes. In New Zealand, the National Curriculum document (Ministry of Education, 2007) in its brief statement about pedagogy describes teaching as "inquiry" (p. 35) and teachers as reflective practitioners able to adjust their practice in the light of evidence.

The present notion of assessment seldom includes a systematic consideration of the processes and outcomes of interactive assessment. Some (e.g., Brown, 2013) raise questions about the feasibility of evidence from interactivity, evidence that essentially forms part of a teacher's log-in-the-head (Timperley & Parr, 2004), contributing to assessment decision-making. But there are situations where a more systematic understanding of less visible forms of ongoing, interactive assessment seems warranted. Policy in New Zealand places the decision about whether a student meets (or is just or well below or just or well above) National Standards in Reading, Writing and Mathematics (Ministry of Education, 2009) squarely on an overall teacher judgement. Such a situation (and the awarding of a grade at the end of a course may be not dissimilar) would support the importance of being able to trace the layering of evidence and the contribution and interaction of various sources in forming a final judgment.

In the same way teachers work to come to shared understandings, for example, of a quality performance in writing, to improve assessment capability, we may need to start by building a shared understanding of concepts in assessment through a shared language. This would seem to be important to achieve, at least, amongst teachers within a common assessment context (perhaps at state or national level).

Shared language is relevant also, methodologically, in research investigations of, for example, teacher perceptions. Much of this research is conducted through surveys, which begs the question: *To what extent do researcher's categorisations or the language reflected in their items or employed in reporting their inferences from responses, actually align with what teachers have in their mind when responding?* Given the potential for a lack of shared understandings around the language of assessment and of conceptual confusion regarding the relationship between accountability and improvement, it is not surprising that research (see Bonner, this volume, whose chapter has a theme of competing narratives regarding teacher perceptions of assessment) has yielded various patterns and factor structures in terms of teacher perceptions of the purposes of assessment. As Bonner (this volume) observes, the international research shows that factor structures are not invariant across contexts. Perceptions about the purpose of assessment vary, for example, by country or across levels of schooling, and these perceptions may also be internally inconsistent. In some groups of teachers, the two broad purposes of assessment for accountability and assessment for improvement are found not to overlap. In New Zealand, for example, where an assessment for learning culture dominates, Brown and Harris (2009) indicated that the four dimensions of teachers' conceptions (school accountability, student accountability, educational improvement, and the 'anti-purpose' conception that assessment is irrelevant) were relatively independent of each other. This was not the case in Hong Kong or southern China, systems with high-stakes assessment designed primarily for accountability, where the measurement model differed; accountability was strongly related to improvement conceptions (Brown, Hui, Yu, & Kennedy, 2011), although what constituted improvement is unclear. It is highly possible that improvement may be viewed in terms of rates of passing high-stakes tests.

Bonner (this volume) suggests that studies of formative assessment (which she says is likely to be aligned more readily with improvement in teachers' minds), show teachers holding more positive views of such assessment practices. This may be oversimplifying and not differentiating those who walk the talk from those who espouse positive views but do not necessarily believe or engage in the associated assessment practices. The substantive work of James (2006) in the United Kingdom demonstrates that the rhetoric was far from the reality of the deep changes in pedagogy and relationships involved in assessment for learning. Some teachers may not endorse all of the practices associated with assessment for learning, especially those relating to peer and self-assessment. The lack of visibility of these practices in classrooms (Hawe & Parr, 2014; Hunter, Mayenga, & Gambell, 2006) may be a function of such a lack of belief in these practices or simply reflect the time and expertise it takes to embed them. There is a paucity of research in this area of assessment regarding teacher understandings. The area is also ripe for an analysis of what factors operate to constrain and to enable teachers' use of assessment for learning practices. Factors such as time, competing requirements, level of support from school leaders, and level of teacher knowledge and the opportunity to build this knowledge may be implicated in explaining why and to what extent teachers engage with the range of formative assessment meanings.

CONSEQUENCES OF ASSESSMENT

Alongside perceptions of the purpose (and often processes and instruments) of assessment, there is a need to consider the consequences for teachers in particular, both intended and unintended and both positive and negative. Perhaps, as a corollary to considering consequences, research should make efforts to evaluate how teachers can best employ different types and formats of assessment to improve learning and in what contexts, and whether there are instances where certain types of assessment do not have value or their value is significantly outweighed by detrimental accompaniments.

The nature of the sociopolitical context and the high-stakes accountability assessment that has been the response to calls for reform in the United States provides an example of potentially serious, but also unintended consequences. Notably, there exist a raft of consequences of varying degrees of severity like teacher dismissal, school shut down, and parents moving students to schools perceived as better. In some contexts, Nichols and Harris (this volume) note that the assessments are intended to serve as detectors (providing information) and effectors (promoting change). In terms of the latter, effectors, they suggest that research shows that high-stakes testing does not improve student learning. The authors note some potentially desirable, but demanding, practices like those involving differentiation of instruction. Although high-stakes testing generally garners bad press, there is suggestion of positive outcomes (Cizek, 2001), like increased knowledge about assessment, higher quality tests, and extended discussion by professionals within content areas, and the provision of higher quality professional development.

Although Nichols and Harris discuss practices like narrowing the curriculum and teaching to the test as less desirable, there are contrary views. For example, teaching to the test need not lead, necessarily, to undesirable consequences. In a book, appropriately titled *The Ambiguity of Teaching to the Test*, Monfils and colleagues (2004) talk of mixed benefits in New Jersey. While some teachers adjusted by becoming more aware of and interested in reform elements, others simply intensified conventional practice. Their research illustrates how some teachers engage in embedded test preparation—that is, make changes to their style of teaching to reflect the state standards and the content of the test. These teachers reported more inquiry-oriented teaching with the test motivating them to use small group instruction and manipulatives in math and science, to add new content and to use open-ended items in order to encourage students to do more writing, and to provide more oral explanations. Detrimental outcomes tended to be associated with an increase in decontextualized test preparation.

The unintended and largely negative consequences of assessment have focussed on high-stakes assessment, but other forms of assessment have consequences that have yet to be researched systematically. As noted above, formative, ongoing assessment may involve considerable workload for teachers. Implementing peer and self-assessment techniques requires both training of students, but also ongoing monitoring and feedback as to the efficacy of students' evaluative efforts.

Teachers' Roles and Identities

A further consideration of consequences relates to teacher perceptions about themselves as agents in assessment. How assessment is framed and played out in their particular context affects how teachers feel about themselves as professionals, and this impacts their practice. Nichols and Harris (this volume) point out that the nature of assessment not only affects pedagogy and relationships with students but also teachers' own well-being in terms of areas like commitment, satisfaction, stress, and professional identity. The professionalism and the degree of autonomy associated with the role that form an integral part of teacher identity is implicitly questioned when assessment is imposed and teachers have little or no input and when they may see little or no benefit to their work in supporting students to learn. Nichols and Harris (this volume) conclude, "Research focusing on teachers who work in high poverty contexts has found that they experience heightened pressures as a result of high-stakes testing, leading to greater teacher dissatisfaction and lowered morale" (p. 46), also noting that teachers in all contexts could potentially feel undermined by such external accountability systems. It is likely that this relationship between high-stakes testing and stress is complex and affected by the extent to which teachers are included, treated as professionals, and supported to engage with the process and utilise whatever it can offer. Lai and Schildkamp (this volume) touch on this theme of treating teachers as professionals, pointing out the importance of empowering teachers to be effective users of data, rather than as technicians who have to be trained to implement a particular practice with fidelity.

THE IMPORTANCE OF CONTEXT

Features of particular contexts may explain patterns of teachers' response towards assessment. As Black and Wiliam (2005) noted, the overall impact of assessment is as much determined by culture and policies as educational evidence and values. This area is one that would benefit from more cross-cultural, comparative research, which might examine how similar assessment practices play out in different contexts. There are other contextual variables that may also be important to examine. Bonner (this volume) suggests, for example, that perceptions about externally mandated assessment may be mediated by experience or there may be other mediators like local management practices. She notes that leadership and professional learning climates that promote a positive assessment culture are not well researched.

One potentially fruitful area for research arises from the work by Achinstein, Ogawa, and Speiglman (2004), cited by Nichols and Harris (this volume), that suggests a wider ripple effect of the interaction between teacher characteristics and backgrounds, and local and state level policy climates. The interaction of these factors conceivably may influence the types of teaching conditions teachers prefer: accountability pressures combined with local school management practices may lead to two groups of teachers, namely, those who prefer more autonomy, flexibility, and opportunity to be creative in the classroom and those who prefer structured, scripted curriculum, and direct day-to-day instructions about teaching goals. In short, the pressures of testing combined with managerial philosophies of schools may interact in ways that entice teachers with specific orientations to particular working environments. Nichols and Harris (this volume) and, similarly, Bonner (this volume), seem to be suggesting that perhaps leadership teams' reaction to, and support of, policies and teachers may mitigate or mediate responses to high-stakes assessment. As noted earlier, this may also be true for other approaches to assessment.

The issue requiring further research is the extent to which differing patterns of teacher perceptions or responses are the result of the context influencing understandings. The context which defines their experience may also influence how teachers understand and respond to the language that researchers use in relation to assessment. This area warrants investigation. Another question to consider is the influence of teacher preexisting dispositions and beliefs in response to new policies or changed assessment demands. Clearly, different methodologies, including longitudinal research designs and innovative means of analysis, may be needed to address such questions and to explore further the complexity of this area of differential response to assessment.

Assessment and Initial Teacher Education

Policy contexts intersect with other contexts, such as initial teacher education, the focus of the chapter by Hill and Eyers (this volume). Teacher education faces the challenge of preparing beginning teachers for the process of engaging in effective classroom assessment. We would add that it also needs to prepare teachers to question how they might learn from other assessments. The learning of preservice teachers arises from a complex interaction of input from lecturers and from practicum experiences. The latter includes the ideas and practices of supervising teachers and the broader assessment climate of the educational jurisdictions and the schools within them where students are placed to gain such practical experience. The policy climate regarding assessment impacts this preparation. Nichols and Harris (this volume) suggest that in the U.S., as a result of the assessment regime, new teachers are graduating within the context of a high-stakes system and pedagogical and instructional understandings are shaped by this context. A similar issue has been noted in other high-stakes examination systems like China (Chen & Brown, 2013). In general, preservice teachers struggle between what they are being taught about good teaching and their field experiences involving intense test preparation of students. To date, almost all studies of such effects involve small samples. Although the assessment regime may have the effect of preparing preservice teachers to 'teach to the test,' there is some evidence that they are able to develop more complex understandings of the function of assessment. However, the suggestion is that the overall effect is likely to be that preservice graduates will lack the training to question and critique the curriculum and the way learning is examined and evaluated. Further, when they become novice teachers, experienced teachers in their schools may prevent their implementing more innovative practices; Hill and Eyers (this volume) comment, in this regard, on the power differential between preservice and novice teachers, and established teachers.

While acknowledging the influences on the acquisition of dispositions and knowledge about assessment, including the assessment policy climate and the variable experiences in the field, Hill and Eyers (this volume) hold positive views regarding what can be achieved through teacher preservice education. They report that university-based classes in educational assessment have been shown to influence learning about assessment in ways that support conceptual change towards productive assessment practices. Of interest are the beliefs that preservice teachers initially hold and how these develop and change as a result of teacher preparation. While important, involvement in the practical use of assessment in the classroom during practicum/field experiences is not unproblematic; the lack of suitable role models often means the influence of these settings is uneven. While classroom teachers are often seen to be lacking in knowledge, their influence interacts with the content of preservice courses and the preservice teacher's personal beliefs and perceptions.

Critical reflection and planning for learning by the preservice teachers was one of four pedagogical constructs seen by Hill and Eyers (this volume) to support assessment learning. In their consideration of the literature, Hill and Eyers (this volume) contend that perspective building conversations potentially support preservice teachers' metacognitive understandings of assessment. They note that developing this metacognitive level of thinking regarding assessment and also cultivating students' self-regulation of learning skills influenced preservice student teachers' ability to understand and use assessment practices. This understanding supported them to implement effective classroom assessment and also to reflect critically on their assessment practices. This would seem to be critical as initial teacher education programs have to prepare students for a highly diverse range of contexts even within an educational system. Perhaps, for many preservice teachers, we would suggest, it is not until they are in their own classroom with the responsibility to monitor and report learning and with the immediate motivation to use the evidence they gather and observe to inform teaching and learning that they engage fully with assessment. It is within their current teaching context that they rework and clarify understandings of assessment.

Assessment and Professional Learning

Lai and Schildkamp (this volume) consider teacher professional learning in the area of assessment, beyond initial teacher education, as a context for developing teachers' beliefs and knowledge. The authors discuss data use with professionals in schools and focus on the varied forms of data employed for decision-making. The chapter examines the cyclical iterations involved in effective data use to identify problems and assess progress towards solutions. The piece is wide-ranging, dipping into areas such as professional learning communities and concepts like pedagogical content knowledge and adaptive expertise. The authors endorse the idea that we need more than achievement data for explanatory purposes. As Slavin and colleagues point out, assessment data per se do not "indicate the root causes behind the numbers" (Slavin, Cheung, Holmes, Madden, & Chamberlain, 2011, p. 3); they do not explain the reasons for the patterns nor indicate the appropriate changes.

A framework adopted for data use is presented in the chapter, namely, having a clearly established purpose for the data, typically to improve teaching, learning, and achievement; interpreting the meaning of the data and considering the possible actions (a sense-making process); then using this understanding to improve teaching and learning. One reservation we have about the framework is its tendency to simplify something that is complex and multidimensional. However, the chapter does identify challenges, including the necessary knowledge and skills to use data. Moderating factors like teacher attitudes and beliefs are touched on, as is the notion of the extent to which teachers consider data an efficacious way to solve a problem or issue (partly whether they consider they have the power to affect student learning), and this area in particular needs further investigation.

We agree with Lai and Schildkamp (this volume) that we need to know more about the effect of PD (and its nature) on teachers' knowledge and beliefs/attitudes about assessment. How does PD help teachers negotiate the challenges in their particular assessment context, which might include clearly communicating assessment matters to those they concern? How does engagement with particular PD components influence views but also build knowledge and skill? What requires more investigation is how PD changes teacher perceptions not only of their influence but of what assessment can provide for them and how the PD relates to helping them to acquire what they need to know about teaching their subject, including, sometimes, acquiring specific content knowledge in order to meet student needs identified from assessment. The use of smart tools (after Norman, 1988) by teachers when engaged in assessment, like detailed, curriculum-referenced scoring rubrics in writing (Parr, Glasswell, & Aikman, 2007) or developmental progressions in literacy (Parr, 2011) has a part to play in building teacher knowledge. While any form of PD around the use of data is likely to be helpful, our work (Parr & Timperley, 2008) showed that while teachers became more skilled in working out what their student data showed, this ability did not relate to the progress their class made. It suggested that practitioners are perhaps in need more of the knowledge of potentially effective practice and of how to implement such and, then, use data to monitor and evaluate the impact of this changed practice. While this notion moves the lens beyond the usual focus of assessment research, the broader area of use of assessment as a key lever in teaching and learning and in improving teacher knowledge and practice is a major area in need of further research.

CONCLUSION

Collectively, the chapters suggest multiple sources of influence on teacher perceptions and that the nature of such perceptions impact use of assessment. They help us to consider the interplay between actors and artefacts as teachers make choices about, implement, and act on, assessment. The chapters collectively reinforce the idea that the context matters in assessment and that teachers, their perceptions, and their learning, together with that of their students, are a key element in that context. However, we would venture to suggest also that the context of the researchers influences their choice of what is salient to investigate. In some contexts like the United States, issues around high-stakes assessment dominate the research agenda landscape while, in other countries, like New Zealand, the interest centers on teacher assessment for learning and on the ways in which teachers come to judgements about students. Other research (Parr, 2011, 2012), in contexts where assessment for learning dominates, considers the mediating layer of resources and tools that support teachers to conduct and utilize the information from various means of assessment according to the purposes and needs that are salient for them.

While the chapters represent a wide range of assessment topics and issues from the relatively narrow accountability function of assessment to the preparation of preservice teachers, there are significant gaps. These gaps are mirrored in the wider literature. One of these concerns teachers' actual practices in the classroom with respect to assessment and what prompts or motivates these practices. We know little about how teachers make decisions about what means or tools to use to obtain information about learning. What prompts them to choose one means over another? Do they possess the level of knowledge needed to make optimal choices? What are the multiple ways they may obtain assessment information about particular facets of learning and how do they piece this together to form a coherent picture of the patterns of development of individual students?

For example, what are teachers cued to notice when students produce a piece of writing, not only from the final product itself but from the various behaviours that led to this? The latter might include observation of engagement in the process and of the talk that happens around writing—the verbalisations, the questions asked of self and others, or the responses to questions, or the work or comments of others. Perhaps more importantly, we need greater insight into how teachers work with this information to support learning. We need to know much more about assessment as a pedagogical practice. This is where the line between the assessment literature and the instruction or pedagogical literature merges. As part of this richer picture, we need to understand what underpins pedagogical decisions about assessment from the interactive to the more planned forms of assessment.

Conceptually, there appears to be a lack of an integrative (or at least a multidimensional) model of perceptions including what teachers perceive as the purpose or purposes of assessment and what influences those perceptions, through to what influences judgements like grading and the use of particular practices like peer and self-assessment. Similarly, there is no model available of the likely contributors to, and mediators of, teacher stress or job satisfaction which allows us to examine direct and indirect relationships on outcomes related to such. None of the chapters in this section directly addresses this issue of building such models, although the findings they discuss may contribute to the variables and parameters to be considered. Also, there appears to be lacking a discussion or a methodological literature review examining the ways in which teacher perceptions, processes, and practices around assessment have been explored. These issues warrant attention by the field.

Educational assessments have many purposes and exist in many forms. Our response to this complexity is a call for more talk about and investigation of assessment that does not polarize or neatly box complex notions. While we agree with the numerous researchers (e.g., Black, 2013; Brown, 2008; Harlen, 2005) railing against dichotomies (e.g., between formative and summative or between accountability versus learning), moving forward is not unproblematic. An extension of the current focus on purposes for assessment makes the notion of a continuum of purposes for assessment appealing.

Perhaps instead we need to think about assessment in several dimensions. Not often considered are the objects of assessment and which of these is paramount in a particular instance. These objects include subject matter knowledge, both declarative and procedural, the progressive mastery of meaningful tasks that foster knowledge use in context (situated cognition), the metacognitive and conative dimensions of learning, and strategies of self-regulation (Allal & Durcey, 2000). Then, major dimensions would be the purposes of assessment and the associated means of obtaining information. Note the use of the plural in both cases; more than one means can be used to assess, and assessment can be designed to meet more than one purpose or to assess more than one object of learning.

Although these are the main dimensions, there are additional significant dimensions such as the locus of control, the level of aggregation of assessment information, and the time frame. For example, the issue of how information from classroom assessment is aggregated to evaluate performance at class, teacher, grade, school, and system level is important because, as Bonner (this volume) notes, this is likely to influence teachers' perceptions of assessment and the information they are prepared to send 'up the system.' So, information about students collected in a variety of ways and over time (e.g., test, observation, class work, etc.) can be used in varying combinations to make a single judgement about whether a student meets a standard at a particular point in time. But the information gathered to do this may also serve other purposes related to teaching and learning like identifying where targeted, direct teaching is needed, for which groups of students, and at what point this may be most powerful.

What emerges is more akin to a vector or matrix than either categorisations or a continuum of purposes. A starting point for unpacking this idea of a matrix, and more particularly the dimension of integration of evidence, could be the extensive review of assessment and evaluation systems across 15 participating countries in the OECD (2013). This review led to a recommendation that schools and systems bring together currently disparate and fragmented attributes of their assessment and evaluation systems into more comprehensive frameworks. The framework proposed is designed to assist learners, teachers, schools, and systems to identify how different sets of assessment information travel throughout an education system, the multiple purposes to which they are put, and the consequences that result. The purpose of the proposed framework is to bring transparency to how and what evidence from classrooms assessment is used at different levels of the system (student, teacher, leader, school, and system) and to make more explicit the relationships between different tools, purposes, and other aspects of the framework (OECD, 2013). In this way, inconsistencies and potentially negative consequences can be detected more easily.

We have repeatedly made the point throughout this discussion chapter that context matters and further development of this kind of framework could help to provide support for teachers to understand the multiple purposes their classroom-based assessment might serve in the jurisdictions where they work. One of the most important tasks for the assessment community at this point in time may be to assess how the matrix of purposes, tools, understandings, and language impact on and at times distort and potentially undermine each other within an overarching assessment and evaluation framework. In the operationalization of any such framework, it is important to identify how teachers' perceptions and assessment activities both influence and are influenced by what happens in the assessment and evaluation space that is increasingly occupying a prominent place in all of our education systems.

REFERENCES

Achinstein, B., Ogawa, R. T., & Speiglman, A. (2004). Are we creating separate and unequal tracks of teachers? The effects of state policy, local conditions, and teacher characteristics on new teacher socialization. *American Educational Research Journal, 41*(3), 557–603.

Allal, L. (2010). Assessment and the regulation of learning. In P. Peterson, E. Baker, & B. McGaw (Eds.), *International encyclopedia of education* (Vol. 3, pp. 348–352). Oxford, UK: Elsevier.

Allal, L., & Durcey, G. P. (2000). Assessment of—or in—the zone of proximal development. *Learning and Instruction, 10,* 137–152.

Black, P. (2013). Formative and summative aspects of assessment: Theoretical and research foundations in the context of pedagogy. In J. H. McMillan (Ed.), *SAGE handbook of research on classroom assessment* (pp. 167–178). Thousand Oaks, CA: Sage.

Black, P., & Wiliam, D. (1998). Assessment and classroom learning. *Assessment in Education: Principles, Policy and Practice, 5,* 7–73.

Black, P., & Wiliam, D. (2005). Lessons from around the world: How policies, politics and cultures constrain and afford assessment practices. *Curriculum Journal, 16*(2), 249–261.

Bloom, B. S., Hastings, J. T., & Madaus, G. F. (Eds.). (1971). *Handbook on formative and summative evaluation of student learning.* New York: McGraw-Hill.

Brown, G.T.L. (2008). *Conceptions of assessment: Understanding what assessment means to teachers and students.* New York: Nova Science Publishers. ISBN: 9781604563221

Brown, G.T.L. (2013). Assessing assessment for learning: Reconsidering the policy and practice. In M. East & S. May (Eds.), *Making a difference in education and social policy* (pp. 121–137). Auckland, NZ: Pearson.

Brown, G.T.L., & Harris, L. R. (2009). Unintended consequences of using tests to improve learning: How improvement-oriented resources heighten conceptions of assessment as school accountability. *Journal of Multi-Disciplinary Education, 6*(12), 68–91.

Brown, G.T.L., Hui, S. K. F., Yu, F.W.M., & Kennedy, K. J. (2011). Teachers' conceptions of assessment in Chinese contexts: A tripartite model of accountability, improvement, and irrelevance. *International Journal of Educational Research, 50,* 307–320.

Chen, J., & Brown, G.T.L. (2013). High-stakes examination preparation that controls teaching: Chinese prospective teachers' conceptions of excellent teaching and assessment. *Journal of Education for Teaching, 39*(5), 541–556. doi:10.1080/02607476.2013.836338

Cizek, G. J. (2001). More unintended consequences of high-stakes testing. *Educational Measurement: Issues and Practice, 20*(4), 19–27.

Cowie, B., & Bell, B. (1999). A model of formative assessment in science education. *Assessment in Education: Principles, Policy and Practice, 6,* 101–116.

Crooks, T. J. (1988). The impact of classroom evaluation practices on students. *Review of Educational Research, 58*(4), 438–481.

Earl, L. M., & Katz, S. (2006). *Leading in a data rich world.* Thousand Oaks, CA: Corwin Press.

Earl, L. M., & LeMahieu, P. G. (1997). Rethinking assessment and accountability. In A. Hargreaves (Ed.), *Rethinking educational change with heart and mind* (pp. 149–168). Alexandria, VA: ASCD.

Harlen, W. (2005). Teachers' summative practices and assessment for learning: Tensions and synergies. *Curriculum Journal, 16,* 207–223.

Hattie, J.A.C., & Brown, G.T.L. (2008). Technology for school-based assessment and assessment for learning: Development principles from New Zealand. *Journal of Educational Technology Systems, 36*(2), 189–201. doi:10.2190/ET.36.2.g

Hattie, J.A.C., Brown, G.T.L., & Keegan, P. J. (2003). A national teacher-managed, curriculum-based assessment system: Assessment tools for teaching & learning asTTle. *International Journal of Learning, 10,* 771–778.

Hawe, E., & Parr, J. M. (2014). Assessment for Learning in the writing classroom: An incomplete realisation. *Curriculum Journal, 25,* 210–237.

Hunter, D., Mayenga, C., & Gambell, T. (2006). Classroom assessment tools and uses: Canadian English teachers' practices for writing. *Assessing Writing, 11,* 42–65.

James, M. (2006) Assessment, teaching and theories of learning. In J. Gardner (Ed.), *Assessment and learning* (pp. 47–60). London: Sage.

James, M., & Pedder, D. (2006). Beyond method: Assessment and learning practices and values. *Curriculum Journal, 17*(2), 109–138. doi:10.1080/09585170600792712

Klenowski, V. (2009). Assessment for learning revisited: An Asia-Pacific perspective. *Assessment in Education: Principles, Policy & Practice, 16*(3), 277–282. doi:10.1080/09695940903319646

McMillan, J. H. (2013). Why we need research on classroom assessment. In J. H. McMillan (Ed.), *Sage handbook of research on classroom assessment* (pp. 3–16). Thousand Oaks, CA: Sage.

Ministry of Education. (2007). *The New Zealand curriculum.* Wellington, NZ: Learning Media.

Ministry of Education. (2009). *The New Zealand curriculum reading and writing standards for Years 1–8.* Wellington, NZ: Learning Media.

Ministry of Education and the University of Auckland. (2004). *Assessment tools for teaching and learning: AsTTle* (version 4). Wellington, NZ: Ministry of Education.

Ministry of Education and the University of Auckland. (2006). *e-asTTle: Assessment tools for teaching and learning* (version 7). Wellington, NZ: Ministry of Education.

Monfils, L. F., Firestone, W. A., Hickes, J. E., Martinez, M. C., Schorr, R. Y., & Camilli, G. (2004). Teaching to the test. In W. A. Firestone, R. Y. Schorr, & L. F. Monfils (Eds.), *The ambiguity of teaching to the test: Standards, assessment, and educational reform* (pp. 37–61). Mahwah, NJ: LEA.

Norman, D. (1988). *The psychology of everyday things.* New York, NY: Basic Books.

OECD (2013). *Synergies for better learning: An international perspective on evaluation and assessment.* Paris, France: OECD Publishing. doi:10.1787/9789264190658-en

Parr, J. M. (2011). Repertoires to scaffold teacher learning and practice in assessment of writing'. *Assessing Writing, 16,* 32–48.

Parr, J. M. (2012). *Shaping teachers' understandings in writing through repertoires of practice.* Paper presented at the Annual Meeting of American Educational Research Association, Vancouver, Canada, April.

Parr, J. M., Glasswell, K., & Aikman, M. (2007). Supporting teacher learning and informed practice in writing through assessment tools for teaching and learning. *Asia-Pacific Journal of Teacher Education, 35,* 69–87.

Parr, J. M., & Timperley, H. (2008). Teachers, schools and using evidence: Considerations of preparedness. *Assessment in Education: Principles, Policy and Practice, 15,* 57–71.

Parr, J. M., Timperley, H. S., Reddish, P., Jesson, R., & Adams, R. (2007). *Literacy professional development project: Identifying effective teaching and professional development practices for enhanced student learning.* Report to the Ministry of Education, NZ. Retrieved from http://www.educationcounts.govt.nz/publications/literacy/16813

Sadler, R. (1989). Formative assessment and the design of instructional systems. *Instructional Science, 18*, 114–144.

Shavelson, R. J., & Towne, L. (Eds.). (2002). Scientific research in education. Washington, DC: National Academy Press.

Slavin, R., Cheung, A., Holmes, G., Madden, N., & Chamberlain, A. (2011). *Effects of a data-driven district reform model*. Baltimore, MD: Johns Hopkins University, Center for Data-Driven Reform in Education (CDDRE).

Swaffield, S. (2011). Getting to the heart of authentic assessment for learning. *Assessment in Education: Principles, Policy & Practice, 18*(4), 433–449. doi:10.1080/0969594X.2011.582838

Timperley, H., & Parr, J. M. (2004). *Using evidence in teaching practice: Implications for professional learning*. Auckland, NZ: Hodder-Moa-Beckett.

Timperley, H., Parr, J. M., & Meissel, K. (2010). *Making a difference to student achievement in literacy: Final research report on the Literacy Professional Development Project. Report to Learning Media and the Ministry of Education*. Auckland, NZ: UniServices, University of Auckland.

Section 2

Students and Assessment

7

EMOTIONS THAT MATTER TO ACHIEVEMENT

Student Feelings About Assessment

Elisabeth Vogl and Reinhard Pekrun

Think about the last time your performance was assessed. Were you anxious or hopeful? Did you enjoy the assessment or were you frustrated by it? Were you proud or ashamed of your result? Did you envy, admire, or condemn your fellow examinees' outcomes? How did your examiner make you feel? Answers to these questions suggest that assessment situations arouse a multitude of different achievement-related emotions, including anxiety, frustration, and shame, but also positive emotions such as enjoyment, hope, or pride. Additionally, assessments are usually social situations conveying social evaluations of individual achievement that can trigger not only self-related emotions, but also emotions related to other people or their attainment. Moreover, emotions are not mere epiphenomena of assessments. Rather, emotions can influence motivation, activation of cognitive resources, learning behavior, and consequently students' assessment outcomes.

Maladaptive emotions, such as trait-like test anxiety or hopelessness, are problematic as they can hinder students from tapping into their full potential and may lead to sizable, systematic measurement error for many students. However, even though high-stakes testing and an audit culture is the standard in many school systems around the world today, the impact of assessment on students' emotions and the effects of these emotions on assessment are often overlooked. Measures to prevent maladaptive emotions and foster adaptive ones to ensure reliable and valid measurement of achievement are rarely implemented in assessment settings at schools or universities.

This chapter argues that research on assessment-related emotions needs to go beyond test anxiety and calls for research that explores the role of emotions in various types of assessments. We suggest guidelines for fostering favorable student emotions and preventing emotions that may harm the validity of achievement assessment.

CONCEPT OF ACHIEVEMENT EMOTIONS

Contemporary emotion researchers agree that emotions are complex, multifaceted phenomena which comprise an emotion-specific subjective affective experience or feeling, cognitive processes, motivational tendencies, expressive behavior, and physiological components (Kleinginna & Kleinginna, 1981; Scherer, 2009). For instance, test anxiety involves, among others, uneasiness and nervous feelings (affective component), worries about failing the exam (cognitive component), impulses to avoid the test situation (motivational component), an anxious facial expression characterized by open eyes and raised eyebrows (expressive component), and physiological changes such as an increased heart rate or perspiration (physiological component).

In line with the multi-componential nature of the emotion construct, emotions can be assessed by means of diverse measures such as self-report questionnaires; implicit assessment (e.g., IAT-Anxiety, Egloff & Schmukle, 2002); peripheral physiological and neuro-physiological measures (e.g., electrodermal activity, EEG); observation of nonverbal behavior (facial, gestural, and postural expression); or the prosodic features of verbal speech (Reisenzein, Junge, Studtmann, & Huber, 2014). Standardized self-report scales are the most widely used instruments to date, and have proven reliable, valid, and cost-effective (Hodapp & Benson, 1997; Pekrun et al., 2004; Zeidner, 1998), although they may be subject to socially desirable response style. Traditionally, emotion questionnaires focused on students' test anxiety; however, instruments such as the Test Emotions Questionnaire (TEQ; Pekrun et al., 2004) and the Achievement Emotions Questionnaire (AEQ; Pekrun, Goetz, Frenzel, Barchfeld, & Perry, 2011) have broadened this spectrum to include a variety of assessment-related emotions.

Assessments can trigger a variety of different types of emotions. Specifically, assessments of achievement can induce achievement emotions, which are defined as emotions that relate to achievement activities and their success and failure outcomes (Pekrun, 2006). Achievement emotions related to tests and exams are referred to as test emotions (Pekrun et al., 2004; Zeidner, 1998, 2014). *State test emotions* can occur during different temporal phases of assessment: (1) the forethought phase in which students prepare for the assessment, (2) the performance phase during the assessment, and (3) the self-reflection phase after the assessment in which students reflect on the assessment (Schutz & Davis, 2000; Zimmermann, 2000). It is important to discriminate between these phases or stages because they may be associated with different emotional experiences and may therefore call for different coping strategies (Folkman & Lazarus, 1985; Pekrun et al., 2004). Individual dispositions to experience test emotions in habitual ways constitute *trait-like test emotions* (Pekrun et al., 2004). Test anxiety, for instance, is often defined as a situation-specific personality trait that refers to the individual's tendency to react with extensive worry, intrusive thoughts, mental disorganization, tension, and physiological arousal when exposed to evaluative situations (Spielberger & Vagg, 1995). Since assessments are also frequently embedded in social situations, they can also induce social emotions directed towards the examiner or the other examinees, including social achievement emotions related to the attainment of others, such as empathy, 'Schadenfreude,' envy, contempt, or admiration (Hareli & Parkinson, 2008; Hareli & Weiner, 2002; Pekrun & Stephens, 2012).

The type of assessment might influence the frequency and intensity of different emotions. For instance, self-assessment might induce, in particular, self-related achievement emotions; peer assessment might trigger social achievement emotions; informal and formal tests administered by teachers can arouse achievement emotions that are especially intense due to high-stakes purposes of selection and placement.

Unfortunately, research on social achievement emotions in academic settings is still largely missing, with only few exceptions (e.g., Mosquera, Parrott, & de Mendoza, 2010; Van de Ven, Zeelenberg, & Pieters, 2011). Research has focused primarily on emotions related to written tests and exams administered by teachers, possibly because this is one of the most common assessment types in school and university settings, and because the format lends itself relatively easily to investigation.

Achievement emotions differ in terms of their *valence*, their degree of *activation*, and their *object focus*. Similar to circumplex models of affective states (e.g., Barrett & Russell, 1999), discrete achievement emotions can be categorized as positive (pleasant) or negative (unpleasant) as well as physiologically activating or deactivating. Accordingly, achievement emotions include positive activating emotions (e.g., enjoyment of the challenge implied by an exam, hope for success, pride in positive outcomes), positive deactivating emotions (e.g., relief or pleasant relaxation after taking a test), negative activating emotions (e.g., anger about the examiner, anxiety before an exam, or shame following failure), and negative deactivating emotions (e.g., hopelessness when failure cannot be avoided).

In addition to valence and activation, achievement emotions can be grouped according to their object focus as displayed in Table 7.1 (Pekrun, 2006). Activity emotions, such as enjoyment and frustration, refer to the activity (e.g., test taking) rather than the outcome of the activity. Other emotions relate in prospective (anticipatory) or retrospective ways to achievement outcomes (Pekrun et al., 2004). Anticipatory joy, hope, anxiety, and hopelessness can be classified as prospective achievement emotions; by contrast, retrospective joy, relief, pride, and shame relate to success and failure that were already obtained. Typically, prospective achievement emotions peak before and at the start of an assessment and retrospective achievement emotions after the assessment; however, both prospective and retrospective achievement emotions can be experienced at any time before, during, and after an assessment (e.g., relief about successful preparation prior to an exam).

OCCURRENCE OF ACHIEVEMENT EMOTIONS
RELATED TO ASSESSMENTS

Qualitative studies that explored students' affective responses to assessments using drawings and interviews about assessments found that students from primary school to university report negative reactions to assessment more frequently than positive ones. For instance, Carless and Lam (2014) found that primary school students associate assessments mostly with negative feelings even though they can bring a sense of satisfaction. This result may reflect the high-stakes consequences of assessment in Chinese contexts, because, in contrast, New Zealand primary school children drew relatively positive emotional responses to assessment (Harris, Harnett, & Brown, 2009). However, negative feelings towards assessments may continue in higher levels of education in Eastern (Hong Kong) as well as Western (U.K.) countries (Brown & Wang, 2013; McKillop, 2006). While negative responses mostly focus on the forethought phase and the performance phase, positive responses are more often related to having finished the test and achieved positive outcomes. The most frequently reported discrete negative emotion related to assessments is anxiety (e.g., Spangler, Pekrun, Kramer, & Hofmann, 2002), which underscores the high-stakes nature of many assessments in educational contexts such as in Germany.

In line with these findings, research on assessment-related emotions has focused on students' test anxiety. This research has predominantly examined anxiety and other negative emotions in the forethought phase and the self-reflection phase (e.g., Folkman & Lazarus, 1985; Smith & Ellsworth, 1987). Less is known about anxiety and other emotions during the performance phase (Schutz & Davis, 2000). This is likely due to ethical considerations, since examining students' emotions during testing might negatively influence their test results by interrupting their concentration and problem-solving efforts (Zeidner, 1995). Some studies indicate that negative emotions such as anxiety, hopelessness, and sadness peak at the beginning of a test (e.g., Goetz, Preckel, Pekrun, & Hall, 2007; Pekrun et al., 2004; Spangler et al., 2002). However, other negative emotions, such as anger, shame, and disappointment, are reported more often during and after a test (Goetz et al., 2007; Pekrun et al., 2004). Positive emotions, such as joy, pride, and relief, seem to increase during the process of completing the exam (see also Pekrun et al., 2004; Reeve, Bonaccio, & Winford, 2014; Spangler et al., 2002). Peterson, Brown, and Jun (2015) found a similar pattern of the dynamics of emotions during a three week period including all three phases of assessment: positive emotions decreased until the test date but increased afterwards; conversely, negative emotions, which did not increase greatly towards the test, did decrease afterwards.

ORIGINS AND DEVELOPMENT OF ACHIEVEMENT EMOTIONS

Given that assessment-related achievement emotions can relate to student achievement and well-being, researchers and practitioners alike would be well advised to attend to their origins, making it possible to design, based on evidence, assessment settings that foster favorable student emotions. In the following sections, we address individual variables as well as environmental factors as antecedents of these emotions and summarize evidence on their development over the school years.

Appraisals as Proximal Individual Antecedents

Cognitive appraisals have been identified as the proximal determinants of achievement emotions related to assessments. First, test anxiety studies described appraisals concerning threat of failure as causes of anxiety. In Lazarus' transactional stress model (Lazarus & Folkman, 1987), a person evaluates a potential threat in a given achievement setting (e.g., an exam) first in terms of the likelihood of failure (primary appraisal) and thereafter in terms of coping resources and options (secondary appraisal). According to this theory, a student may experience anxiety when failure on the exam is likely (primary appraisal) and coping resources are not sufficiently available; that is, that the outcome of the exam is perceived as uncontrollable (secondary appraisal).

Weiner (1985, 2007) discussed causal achievement attributions (i.e., explanations about the causes of success and failure in assessments, such as ability, effort, task difficulty, luck) as primary determinants of achievement emotions beyond anxiety. Exceptions are attribution-independent emotions that are directly instigated by perceptions of success or failure (e.g., happiness about success and sadness/frustration about failure). Three dimensions of causal attributions were proposed to play key roles in determining attribution-dependent emotions: the perceived locus of causality (internal vs. external causes of achievement; such as, ability vs. environmental circumstances); the perceived controllability of causes (e.g., subjectively controllable effort vs. uncontrollable ability); and the perceived stability of causes (e.g., stable ability vs. unstable chance). For example, the theory posits that pride is aroused when success is

Table 7.1 A Three-dimensional Taxonomy of Achievement Emotions (adapted from Pekrun & Stephens, 2012)

Object Focus	Positive[a]		Negative[b]	
	Activating	Deactivating	Activating	Deactivating
Activity	Enjoyment	Relaxation	Anger	Boredom
Outcome	Hope	Contentment	Anxiety	Hopelessness
	Pride	Relief	Anger	Disappointment
	Gratitude		Shame	

Note: [a] Positive = pleasant emotion.
       [b] Negative = unpleasant emotion.

attributed to an internal cause (ability or effort), whereas shame is experienced when failure is attributed to an internal and uncontrollable cause (lack of ability).

In Pekrun's (2006; Pekrun & Perry, 2014) control-value theory of achievement emotions, core propositions of the transactional stress model and attributional theory were integrated and expanded to explain a broader variety of emotions experienced in achievement settings (Table 7.1), including both outcome emotions related to success and failure (e.g., hope, anxiety, pride, and shame) and activity emotions (e.g., enjoyment and boredom). The theory posits that the joint action of control and value appraisals instigate different achievement emotions. Retrospective outcome emotions such as pride and shame are thought to be induced when success and failure, respectively, are perceived to be caused by internal factors implying control (or lack of control) over these outcomes. Prospective outcome emotions, such as hope and anxiety, are thought to be experienced if a person perceives control as moderate to low and focuses attention on anticipated success (hope) or anticipated failure (anxiety), respectively. If perceived control is high, anticipatory joy may be experienced, but if there is a complete lack of perceived control, hopelessness may ensue. Regarding activity emotions, the theory proposes, for example, that a student would enjoy taking a test when she feels competent to meet the demands of the exam and perceives the material as interesting. Boredom may be experienced when the test is perceived as lacking any relevance and does not match the examinee's ability (Pekrun, Goetz, Daniels, Stupnisky, & Perry, 2010).

Gender and Achievement Goals as Distal Individual Antecedents

Appraisal theories imply that more distal individual antecedents affect students' emotions by first influencing their appraisals. In this context, students' gender and their achievement goals have received particular attention. Empirical evidence shows that females generally experience more negative achievement emotions such as anxiety, hopelessness, shame, and boredom, as well as less enjoyment and pride than male students (Else-Quest, Higgins, Allison, & Morton, 2012; Hyde, Fennema, Ryan, Frost, & Hopp, 1990). However, recent research indicates that these emotional differences may be mediated by gender differences in appraisals, in line with propositions of Pekrun's (2006) control-value theory (Frenzel, Pekrun, & Goetz, 2007; Goetz, Bieg, Lüdtke, Pekrun, & Hall, 2013).

An extension of the control-value theory links achievement goals to achievement emotions and suggests that emotions can function as mediators of the effects of achievement goals on learning by promoting varied appraisals and focusing attention on the task versus the self (Daniels et al., 2009; Elliot & Pekrun, 2007; Linnenbrink & Pintrich, 2002a; Pekrun, Elliot, & Maier, 2006, 2009). It is posited that performance-approach goals focus attention on the controllability of the task and success, thus facilitating positive outcome emotions, such as hope and pride; whereas, performance-avoidance goals induce negative outcome emotions (e.g., anxiety, shame, and hopelessness) by focusing attention on uncontrollability and failure. In contrast, mastery goals focus attention on the controllability and positive values of task activities, thus promoting positive activity emotions (e.g., enjoyment) and reducing negative activity emotions (e.g., boredom). The empirical evidence is in line with these propositions (Huang, 2011; Pekrun et al., 2006, 2009).

The Influence of Learning Environments and Assessments

The impact of learning environments and assessments on achievement emotions is largely unexplored, with the exception of research on the antecedents of test anxiety (for reviews, see Wigfield & Eccles, 1990; Zeidner, 1998, 2007, 2014). However, goal structures in the classroom and social expectations, the design of assessments, as well as feedback and the consequences of assessments have been discussed as important factors influencing the experience of assessment-related emotions.

Goal Structures and Social Expectations

Goal structures in the classroom can influence the achievement goals students adopt (Murayama & Elliot, 2009; Urdan & Schoenfelder, 2006). The emotions students experience are mediated by these goals (Kaplan & Maehr, 1999; Roeser, Midgley, & Urdan, 1996). For instance, competitive goal structures are more likely to induce negative assessment emotions (e.g., test anxiety and hopelessness) since competition implies that some students fail (Zeidner, 1998).

Excessively high achievement expectations from teachers and parents can also induce negative emotions (e.g., anxiety, shame, and hopelessness) because they reduce students' sense of control and expectancies for success (Pekrun, 1992a). Surprisingly, cooperative classroom climate and social support from teachers and parents does not necessarily reduce test anxiety and often fails to correlate with students' test anxiety scores (Hembree, 1988). One possible explanation is that social support may actually increase pressure to perform, thus counteracting any beneficial effects of support (Pekrun & Stephens, 2012).

Design of Assessments

Lack of structure and transparency, as well as excessive task demands (e.g., lack of information regarding demands, materials, and grading practices), are associated with students' elevated test anxiety (Zeidner, 1998, 2007). These links are likely mediated by students' expectancies of low control and failure (Pekrun, 1992a). Furthermore, the format of test items has been found to be relevant. Specifically, open-ended formats, such as essay questions, induce more anxiety than multiple-choice formats (Zeidner, 1987), possibly because open-ended formats require more attentional resources (i.e., working memory capacity). In addition, there is evidence that practices such as permitting students to choose between test items, relaxing time constraints, and giving second chances (e.g., opportunities to retake a test) may reduce test anxiety

(Zeidner, 1998), presumably because perceived control and achievement expectancies are enhanced under these conditions.

Feedback and Consequences of Assessments

In environments involving frequent assessments, achievement outcomes shape individual appraisals and thus students' emotions. In addition, performance feedback is likely of primary importance for the arousal of achievement emotions. Recent findings suggest that achievement goals are significant mediators of the influence of anticipated feedback on emotions (Pekrun, Cusack, Murayama, Elliot, & Thomas, 2014). Self-referential feedback was found to have a positive influence on mastery goal adoption and consequently the experience of positive achievement emotions (i.e., hope and pride), whereas normative feedback positively influenced performance-approach and performance-avoidance goal adoption and consequently the experience of negative achievement emotions (i.e., anxiety and shame).

Besides the type of feedback, the social setting might influence emotions. Unfortunately, research on the emotional impact of feedback given by different people (e.g., authority figures vs. peers) is sparse. It seems, however, that peer pressure and fear of disapproval, which may undermine the motivation for participating in assessments, is an important topic that needs to be addressed in social assessment situations such as peer assessment. In this context, anonymous peer feedback may be one way to dampen negative perceptions of peer assessment and reduce negative emotions experienced in the process (e.g., Vanderhoven, Raes, Montrieux, & Rotsaert, 2015; see Panadero, this volume, for a review on peer assessment).

Development and Reciprocal Causation

Qualitative studies that have explored emotional responses to assessments indicate that older students have more negative emotional reactions to assessment than younger students, which can at least be partly explained by their increased awareness of the personal implications of test results (Brown & Wang, 2013; Harris et al., 2009). With the exception of test anxiety studies, quantitative empirical evidence on the development of discrete achievement emotions is scarce. At the beginning of elementary school, average scores for test anxiety are low but increase dramatically during the elementary school years (Hembree, 1988). After elementary school, average anxiety scores stabilize and remain at high levels throughout middle school, high school, and college. However, despite stability at the group level, anxiety can change in individual students, for instance due to a change in reference groups (e.g., when changing schools; Marsh, 1987; Preckel, Zeidner, Goetz, & Schleyer, 2008).

Emotions, their antecedents, and their effects, are thought to be linked by reciprocal causation over time (Linnenbrink & Pintrich, 2002b; Pekrun, 2006). In this sense, positive feedback loops (e.g., success on an exam induces pride which fuels motivation to prepare and succeed on the next exam), as well as negative feedback loops (e.g., failure on an exam induces anxiety which prompts more effort in learning and subsequent success) can be important.

EFFECTS ON LEARNING, ACHIEVEMENT, AND WELL-BEING

Emotions can be experienced at any stage of assessment and can influence achievement outcomes not only by affecting cognitive processes during the assessment, but also by impacting the cognitive and motivational processes present when preparing for the assessment. While experimental research has mostly focused on the effects of positive versus negative mood and its influence on information processing, links between discrete student emotions and academic performance have been mostly analyzed in field research in education.

Mood and Information Processing

Emotions have been found to consume cognitive resources (i.e., working memory resources) by focusing attention on the object of an emotion (Ellis & Ashbrook, 1988). For negative emotions, such as test anxiety, which have task-extraneous objects and produce task-irrelevant thinking (e.g., worries about impending failure), the impact can be detrimental because fewer resources are available for task completion (Meinhardt & Pekrun, 2003). By contrast, positive task-related emotions, such as enjoyment of learning, can focus attention on the task, thus being beneficial for achievement. However, it is also possible that some positive task-related emotions, such as over-excitement, may distract attention away from the task (Pekrun & Linnenbrink-Garcia, 2012).

Studies on mood-congruent retrieval (Levine & Burgess, 1997; Parrott & Spackman, 1993) find that positive mood facilitates the retrieval of positive self-related information, and negative mood facilitates the retrieval of negative self-related information. By implication, positive mood can foster positive self-appraisals and thus promote motivation to learn and boost performance; in contrast, negative mood can facilitate the retrieval of negative self-appraisals and thus hamper motivation and performance (Olafson & Ferraro, 2001). In addition, positive and negative mood can moderate the memory effects of assessment on learning (i.e., testing effect; Roediger & Karpicke, 2006). Specifically, emotions can influence retrieval-induced forgetting. Negative mood can undo forgetting, likely because it inhibits spreading activation in memory networks (Bäuml & Kuhbandner, 2007). Conversely, positive emotions should promote relational processing of information and with that retrieval-induced facilitation (Kuhbandner & Pekrun, 2013).

Positive mood has been found to promote flexible and creative ways to solve problems, whereas negative mood fosters more focused, detail-oriented, and analytical ways of thinking (Clore & Huntsinger, 2007; Fredrickson, 2001). One possible explanation is that mood is used as information to guide further action: positive affective states signal that 'all is well,' indicating that it is safe to explore, whereas negative states suggest that something is amiss, making it necessary to analyze the problem more closely. A different explanation suggests that affective states influence the mode of information processing. Positive affect facilitates spreading activation in memory networks, thus promoting creative thinking and top-down information processing (accommodation), whereas negative affect facilitates bottom-up processing driven by sensory perception (assimilation; Fiedler, Nickel, Asbeck, & Pagel, 2003; Kuhbandner et al., 2009).

Thus, experimental research indicates that experiencing positive or negative affective states may affect assessment outcomes by: (a) influencing the availability of cognitive resources to master a given task, (b) promoting or undermining motivation triggered by the retrieval of positive or negative appraisals, and (c) impacting the problem-solving process. However, because these studies may lack ecological validity for real-life achievement, it is difficult to generalize these findings to actual assessment situations.

Discrete Emotions and Achievement

Field research in education has analyzed links between discrete achievement emotions and students' academic performance. In doing so, this research takes into account differential effects of activating and deactivating emotions (e.g., anxiety vs. boredom) beyond the valence of emotions and differential effects of discrete emotions of equal valence and activation (e.g., anxiety vs. anger; Carver & Harmon-Jones, 2009). The empirical evidence implies that the overall effects of emotions on learning and assessment outcomes are inevitably complex and may depend on the interplay between different mechanisms and task demands. In addition, correlational findings need to be interpreted with caution since the links between emotions and performance are likely reciprocal. Nevertheless, it seems possible to derive inferences from the existing evidence.

Positive Emotions

The available evidence suggests that *activating positive emotions*, such as enjoyment, hope, and pride, can have beneficial effects on students' interest, effort, and academic performance by focusing attention on the task, promoting interest and intrinsic motivation, and facilitating the use of flexible cognitive strategies (Ainley & Ainley, 2011; Pekrun et al., 2004). In line with theory, findings by Reeve et al. (2014) suggest that positive activating emotion experienced immediately prior to an exam may facilitate performance by decreasing distraction. Interestingly, high school students' belief that assessments should be fun was found to correlate negatively with academic achievement (Brown & Hirschfeld, 2008; Brown, Peterson, & Irving, 2009; Hirschfeld & Brown, 2009). However, beliefs about the purpose of assessments do not necessarily reflect the actual emotional experiences related to assessments.

General positive affect has also been found to correlate positively with students' engagement (Linnenbrink, 2007). However, other studies have found null relations (Linnenbrink, 2007; Pekrun et al., 2009). One possible explanation for the inconsistent findings for positive affect may be that *deactivating positive emotions* such as relief or contentment may reduce task attention, undermine current motivation, and lead to superficial information processing. In conclusion, the evidence on positive emotions is currently too scant to warrant firm conclusions, but highlights the importance of carefully defining and differentiating between discrete achievement emotions and related but different constructs such as moods, beliefs, or perceptions and their effects on academic outcomes.

Negative Emotions

Activating negative emotions, such as anxiety, shame, and anger appear to exert complex effects. These emotions promote task-irrelevant thinking and reduce interest and flexible thinking, but can simultaneously strengthen effort to avoid failure (Pekrun, 2006). Meta-analytic reviews demonstrated that *test anxiety* correlated moderately negatively with various measures of academic achievement and cognitive ability (Ackerman & Heggestad, 1997; Hembree, 1988). However, correlations with performance variables have not been uniformly negative across studies. Zero correlations have sometimes been found, especially for state test anxiety (e.g., Díaz, Glass, Arnkoff, & Tanofsky-Kraff, 2001; Gross, 1990; Kantor, Endler, Heslegrave, & Kocovski, 2001). Findings suggest that *shame* related to failure at assessments negatively correlates with students' effort and academic achievement (Pekrun et al., 2004) and negatively predicts exam performance (Pekrun et al., 2009). However, if students continue to be committed to future academic goals and believe these goals are attainable, then their motivation may increase after they experienced shame following negative exam feedback (Turner & Schallert, 2001). Similarly, students' *anger* has been shown to correlate negatively with academic interest, motivation, and self-regulated learning (Pekrun et al., 2004). However, the overall correlations with academic performance, which range from zero to moderately negative, may depend on whether the anger is directed at another individual or at oneself (Boekaerts, 1994; Pekrun et al., 2004). Nevertheless, the benefits of negative activating emotions are probably outweighed by their overall negative effects on performance and interest for the vast majority of students. This is in line with findings by Reeve et al. (2014) suggesting that negative activating emotions (shame, anxiety, and anger) may hinder performance on exams by increasing distraction.

Deactivating negative emotions, such as hopelessness and boredom, seem to relate uniformly negatively to measures of learning and performance (Craig, Graesser, Sullins, & Gholson, 2004; Pekrun et al., 2010; Pekrun, Hall, Goetz, & Perry, 2014; Tze, Daniels, & Klassen, 2015) possibly because they reduce attentional resources, undermine both intrinsic and extrinsic motivation, and promote superficial information processing (Pekrun, 1992b, 2006).

Effects on Students' Well-being

In addition to the influence of test emotions on students' achievement, emotions related to assessment may also impact students' well-being and health. In particular, test anxiety has detrimental effects on students' psychological well-being (Zeidner, 1998, 2014). Furthermore, negative test emotions, such as anxiety, anger, shame, and hopelessness, have been found to correlate positively with perceived health problems, including cardiovascular problems, stomach problems, and sleep disturbances; by contrast, positive test emotions, such as hope, may be negatively related to health impairments (Pekrun et al., 2004). While more research is needed to explore the differential effects of discrete test emotions other than anxiety on various health factors, test anxiety research clearly indicates an urgent need to ameliorate excessive negative achievement emotions in students' academic careers.

EFFECTS OF ACHIEVEMENT EMOTIONS ON THE VALIDITY OF ASSESSMENTS

The cumulative evidence on direct and indirect effects of emotions on the outcomes of performance assessments cited here indicates that students' maladaptive emotions may limit the validity of assessments; that is, assessments no longer accurately reflect the construct of interest, such as a student's competency or ability. To secure the validity of achievement assessments, it needs to be ensured that differences in test scores reflect individual differences in the ability trait rather than differences in construct-irrelevant factors such as emotions (Haladyna & Downing, 2004; Lubke, Dolan, Kelderman, & Mellenbergh, 2003). Accordingly, the validity of an assessment would be reduced if examinees with equal levels of the ability trait but different emotional experiences have different probabilities of correctly answering test items. For example, if emotions alter test responses by modifying aspects of respondents' cognitive processes during the assessment, the validity of the assessment might be at risk (Bornstein, 2011).

More specifically, emotions can reduce the validity of test scores in two different ways. First, emotions could change the measurement properties of the assessment at the item level in terms of changing item properties such as factor loadings, intercepts, etc. For example, the measurement properties of an achievement test could differ across students with low, medium, and high test anxiety, which would imply that test scores cannot be compared across these groups of students. Terms such as measurement bias and test bias have been used to denote such a change of measurement properties (for different interpretations of these terms, see Warne, Yoon, & Price, 2014). This type of measurement bias has been examined in a few studies for effects of test anxiety using structural equation modeling (SEM). The findings are inconclusive. Using different approaches to SEM, Reeve and Bonaccio (2008) and Sommer and Arendasy (2014) found that test anxiety did not change the measurement properties of cognitive tests, whereas Halpin, da-Silva, and De Boeck (2014) reported that test anxiety differentially influenced responses to different test items, suggesting that measurement properties were not equivalent across levels of test anxiety.

Second, emotions can change the latent ability variable that is measured by an assessment, even if the item-level measurement properties of the assessment are preserved. In line with this possibility, Reeve and Bonaccio (2008) and Sommer and Arendasy (2014) found that respondents' test anxiety correlated with latent ability factors underlying responses to items on intelligence tests. Such correlational findings do not, however, necessarily indicate that achievement assessments are biased against test anxious individuals. These correlations can be explained in at least three ways: (1) anxiety could reduce ability scores due to negative effects on resources and motivation during the assessment (e.g., worrisome cognitions and task-irrelevant thoughts), thus altering test responses and endangering the validity of the assessment; (2) anxiety could undermine the development of abilities prior to the assessment, due to negative effects on cognitive resources and motivation during learning; (3) anxiety may simply reflect existing lack of ability, without impacting learning and assessment (the deficit hypothesis).

Longitudinal or experimental evidence would be needed to disentangle these three possibilities and investigate if emotions reduce the validity of assessments by influencing the measured factor during the assessment itself. One option to examine test score validity would be to investigate if experimental manipulations of respondents' states emotions during testing impact their test scores (Bornstein, 2011). As discussed earlier, experimental studies on mood and information processing found negative effects of mood on attention and memory, which indicates that the validity of assessments might in fact be at risk due to state emotions during testing. The existing longitudinal evidence suggests that students' test anxiety and their academic achievement are linked by reciprocal causation over time (Meece, Wigfield, & Eccles, 1990; Pekrun, 1992b), suggesting that test anxiety is in fact both a cause and an effect of reduced performance. However, this research has not clarified if test anxiety reduced students' performance during learning, during the assessment of performance, or both.

More research is needed to explore if and how emotions impact the validity of assessments. Given the practical relevance of this issue, it would be especially important to further examine possible biases induced by anxiety and other state and trait-like test emotions such as intense anger or overexcitement that may limit the cognitive resources available for responding to assessments in real life settings (e.g., in low- vs. high-stakes testing situations; Putwain, 2008).

IMPLICATIONS FOR EDUCATIONAL POLICY AND PRACTICE

To avoid possible bias, which harms construct validity, assessments need to be arranged in particular ways to avoid emotions that might hinder students being able to show their full potential. In line with this, some scholars have called for special arrangements for test-anxious students (Hill & Wigfield, 1984; Zuriff, 1997). Furthermore, to reduce students' maladaptive achievement emotions and promote adaptive emotions, the learning environment needs to be designed in an appropriate way. Teachers need to be made aware of the influence of emotions on learning and assessment, and educational policy should promote emotionally sound learning environments, including adequately designed assessment settings. Even though research on achievement emotions other than test anxiety is clearly at a nascent stage, the empirical evidence discussed earlier has a number of implications for how to reach these aims.

Goal Structures and Social Expectations

A classroom climate that positively influences students' emotions and achievement can be promoted by avoiding social comparison standards to assess achievement and by communicating realistic expectations about achievement outcomes. Grading based on social comparison promotes competitive classroom goals and should be avoided whenever possible. Although social comparison standards (i.e., normative standards) may be needed for purposes of placement and selection, use of criterion-oriented standards focused on mastery of the learning material, as well as use of intra-individual standards based on learning progress, are recommended to best serve teaching and learning. These standards are better suited to promoting a mastery goal climate in the classroom. Furthermore, teachers' and parents' expectations should reflect students' abilities: exaggerated or unrealistic expectations can negatively influence students' control perceptions and assessment-related emotions.

Design of Assessments

Drawing on test anxiety research, measures that increase perceived control and decrease the importance of failure can help to create favorable test emotions and decrease the impact of maladaptive test emotions on performance (Zeidner, 1998). To prevent uncertainty and lack of control that may lead to anxiety, teachers should provide detailed information about the assessment procedure, the structure of the assessment, and the grading practice used. Surprise assessments that have not been announced to students should be avoided, especially if these tests have important consequences.

Examiners should strive for moderate test difficulty that is matched to students' ability levels. To limit the demands put upon students' attention, formats that reduce working memory load such as multiple-choice items can be used. It is important to note however, that closed item formats may not adequately assess competencies that involve creative problem solving or writing skills, and are not suitable for tracing the strategies students used to solve tasks.

Testing without time pressure allows students to review their answers and correct their mistakes. Relaxed time constraints decrease test anxiety and increase the reliability of the assessment if information processing speed is not a key component of the construct being assessed. Anxiety can also be reduced by assuring greater control over the test situation by allowing students to choose between items of similar difficulty, providing external aids, and giving students second chances to retake a test or exam. This can increase students' expectations of success.

Naturally, some of these strategies, such as highly structured materials or easy test items, may be advantageous for test-anxious students but may prove less motivating for other students. Further, multiple-choice testing is not always an option and free item choice may create problems when scoring the test. As such, educational measures to reduce students' anxiety should be counterbalanced in the context of multiple goals for assessment.

Feedback and Consequences of Achievement

Students' self-confidence and positive emotions can be strengthened by using the following guidelines for feedback on achievement based on Pekrun (2014).

1. As noted earlier, teachers should be encouraged to use mastery and individual standards to evaluate students' achievement. The use of normative standards should be avoided wherever possible.
2. Repeated feedback about success emphasizing (even small) improvement in performance in terms of task mastery or individual standards can strengthen students' self-confidence over time and increase their positive achievement emotions. By contrast, repeated feedback about failure can undermine self-confidence and increase negative achievement emotions. This is especially true if feedback about failure is coupled with the message that failure is due to lack of ability.
3. Errors should not be regarded as information about lack of ability but as opportunities to learn. Students need to be aware that they can master the material if they invest effort. Attributional retraining can be helpful to build adaptive success and failure attributions (Haynes, Daniels, Stupnisky, Perry, & Hladkyj, 2010). Connections between students' academic effort and future academic success after failure can increase perceived control, thus strengthening positive achievement emotions, and reducing negative ones (Pekrun et al., 2006). However, effort must also be invested in adequate learning strategies.
4. Beyond evaluative feedback about success and failure, it is important to provide informational feedback about how students can improve their competencies and attain mastery. Detailed informational feedback, coupled with positive expectancies that mastery is possible, can strengthen students' confidence in their abilities and adaptive achievement emotions (e.g., Harris, Brown, & Harnett, 2014).
5. The consequences of assessment practices need to be considered, especially when implementing high-stakes testing that has serious consequences, such as decisions about students' career opportunities. High-stakes testing can increase positive achievement emotions for high-achieving students, but for low-achieving students, it increases frustration and shame about failure as well as anxiety and hopelessness related to the future (Pekrun, 2014). Therefore, high-stakes testing should be avoided whenever possible and instead a culture that uses assessments as a means of gaining information about how to develop mastery should be adopted.

CONCLUSIONS

Although assessments can induce a multitude of different emotions, empirical research to date has focused mostly on test anxiety and its effects on students' performance and well-being. This extensive body of research shows that test anxiety has detrimental consequences for most students. The existing findings also suggest that test anxiety may lead to a sizable systematic error in assessment results. Findings on test emotions other than anxiety are sparse, and research on social emotions related to assessments is largely missing. However, it is possible that any intense emotion that distracts attention away from the task at hand and compromises memory processes represents a potential threat to the validity of academic assessments. In contrast, positive task-focused emotions experienced in assessment situations, such as enjoyment of challenge and problem solving, should foster attention, motivation, and use of adequate strategies, and thus make it possible to assess students' true capabilities. As outlined in this chapter, learning environments and assessments can be designed in emotionally sound ways that support both students' learning and a valid assessment of achievement. Shaping classroom goal structures, achievement expectations, grading practices, the design of tests, and the feedback and consequences provided after the assessment may be especially important to help students develop adaptive, and reduce maladaptive, emotions to ensure that students can tap into their full potential.

REFERENCES

Ackerman, P. L., & Heggestad, E. D. (1997). Intelligence, personality, and interests: Evidence for overlapping traits. *Psychological Bulletin, 121,* 219–245. doi:10.1037/0033–2909.121.2.219

Ainley, M., & Ainley, J. (2011). Student engagement with science in early adolescence: The contribution of enjoyment to students' continuing interest in learning about science. *Contemporary Educational Psychology, 36,* 4–12. doi:10.1016/j.cedpsych.2010.08.001

Barrett, L. F., & Russell, J. A. (1999). The structure of current affect: Controversies and emerging consensus. *Current Directions in Psychological Science, 8,* 10–14. doi:10.1111/1467–8721.00003

Bäuml, K.-H., & Kuhbandner, C. (2007). Remembering can cause forgetting—but not in negative moods. *Psychological Science, 18,* 111–115. doi:10.1111/j.1467–9280.2007.01857.x

Boekaerts, M. (1994). Anger in relation to school learning. *Learning and Instruction, 3,* 269–280. doi:10.1016/0959–4752(93)90019-V

Bornstein, R. F. (2011). Toward a process-focused model of test score validity: Improving psychological assessment in science and practice. *Psychological Assessment, 23,* 532–544. doi:10.1037/a0022402

Brown, G.T.L., & Hirschfeld, G.H.F. (2008). Students' conceptions of assessment: Links to outcomes. *Assessment in Education: Principles, Policy and Practice, 15*(1), 3–17. doi:10.1080/09695940701876003

Brown, G.T.L., Peterson, E. R., & Irving, S. E. (2009). Beliefs that make a difference: Adaptive and maladaptive self-regulation in students' conceptions of assessment. In D. M. McInerney, G.T.L. Brown, & G.A.D. Liem (Eds.), *Student perspectives on assessment: What students can tell us about assessment for learning* (pp. 159–186). Charlotte, NC: Information Age Publishing.

Brown, G.T.L., & Wang, Z. (2013). Illustrating assessment: How Hong Kong university students conceive of the purposes of assessment. *Studies in Higher Education, 38,* 1037–1057. doi:10.1080/03075079.2011.616955

Carless, D., & Lam, R. (2014). The examined life: perspectives of lower primary school students in Hong Kong. *Education 3–13: International Journal of Primary, Elementary and Early Years Education, 42,* 313–329. doi:10.1080/03004279.2012.689988

Carver, C. S., & Harmon-Jones, E. (2009). Anger is an approach-related affect: Evidence and implications. *Psychological Bulletin, 135,* 183–204. doi:10.1037/a0013965

Clore, G. L., & Huntsinger, J. R. (2007). How emotions inform judgment and regulate thought. *Trends in Cognitive Sciences, 11,* 393–399. doi:10.1016/j.tics.2007.08.005

Craig, S. D., Graesser, A. C., Sullins, J., & Gholson, B. (2004). Affect and learning: An exploratory look into the role of affect in learning with AutoTutor. *Journal of Educational Media, 29,* 241–250. doi:10.1080/1358165042000283101

Daniels, L. M., Stupnisky, R. H., Pekrun, R., Haynes, T. L., Perry, R. P., & Newall, N. E. (2009). A longitudinal analysis of achievement goals: From affective antecedents to emotional effects and achievement outcomes. *Journal of Educational Psychology, 101,* 948–963. doi:10.1037/a0016096

Díaz, R. J., Glass, C. R., Arnkoff, D. B., & Tanofsky-Kraff, M. (2001). Cognition, anxiety, and prediction of performance in 1st-year law students. *Journal of Educational Psychology, 93,* 420–429. doi:10.1037/0022–0663.93.2.420

Egloff, B., & Schmukle, S. C. (2002). Predictive validity of an implicit association test for assessing anxiety. *Journal of Personality and Social Psychology, 83,* 1441–1455. doi:10.1037//0022–3514.83.6.1441

Elliot, A. J., & Pekrun, R. (2007). Emotion in the hierarchical model of approach-avoidance of achievement motivation. In P. A. Schutz & R. Pekrun (Eds.), *Emotion in education* (pp. 57–73). San Diego, CA: Academic Press.

Ellis, H. C., & Ashbrook, P. W. (1988). Resource allocation model of the effect of depressed mood states on memory. In K. Fiedler & J. Forgas (Eds.), *Affect, cognition, and social behavior* (pp. 25–43). Toronto: Hogrefe International.

Else-Quest, N. M., Higgins, S., Allison, C., & Morton, L. C. (2012). Gender differences in self-conscious emotional experience: A meta-analysis. *Psychological Bulletin, 138,* 947–981. doi:10.1037/a0027930

Fiedler, K., Nickel, S., Asbeck, J., & Pagel, U. (2003). Mood and the generation effect. *Cognition and Emotion, 17,* 585–608. doi:10.1080/02699930302301

Folkman, S., & Lazarus, R. S. (1985). If it changes it must be a process: Study of emotion and coping during three stages of a college examination. *Journal of Personality and Social Psychology, 48,* 150–170. doi:10.1037/0022–3514.48.1.150

Fredrickson, B. L. (2001). The role of positive emotions in positive psychology: The broaden-and-build theory of positive emotions. *American Psychologist, 56,* 218–226. doi:10.1037/0003–066X.56.3.218

Frenzel, A. C., Pekrun, R., & Goetz, T. (2007). Girls and mathematics —A "hopeless" issue? A control-value approach to gender differences in emotions towards mathematics. *European Journal of Psychology of Education, 22,* 497–514. doi:10.1007/BF03173468

Goetz, T., Bieg, M., Lüdtke, O., Pekrun, R., & Hall, N. C. (2013). Do girls really experience more anxiety in mathematics? *Psychological Science, 24,* 2079–2087. doi:10.1177/0956797613486989

Goetz, T., Preckel, F., Pekrun, R., & Hall, N. C. (2007). Emotional experiences during test taking: Does cognitive ability make a difference? *Learning and Individual Differences, 17,* 3–16. doi:10.1016/j.lindif.2006.12.002

Gross, T. F. (1990). General test and state anxiety in real examinations: State is not test anxiety. *Educational Research Quarterly, 14*(3), 11–20.

Haladyna, T. M., & Downing, S. M. (2004). Construct-irrelevant variance in high-stakes testing. *Educational Measurement: Issues and Practice, 23,* 17–27. doi:10.1111/j.1745–3992.2004.tb00149.x

Halpin, P. F., da-Silva, C., & De Boeck, P. (2014). A confirmatory factor analysis approach to test anxiety. *Structural Equation Modeling: A Multidisciplinary Journal, 21,* 455–467. doi:10.1080/10705511.2014.915377

Hareli, S., & Parkinson, B. (2008). What's social about social emotions? *Journal for the Theory of Social Behavior, 38,* 131–156. doi:10.1111/j.1468–5914.2008.00363.x

Hareli, S., & Weiner, B. (2002). Social emotions and personality inferences: A scaffold for a new direction in the study of achievement motivation. *Educational Psychologist, 37,* 183–193. doi:10.1207/S15326985EP3703_4

Harris, L. R., Brown, G.T.L., & Harnett, J. A. (2014). Understanding classroom feedback practices: A study of New Zealand student experiences, perceptions, and emotional responses. *Educational Assessment, Evaluation and Accountability, 26,* 107–133. doi:10.1007/s11092–013–9187–5

Harris, L. R., Harnett, J., & Brown, G.T.L. (2009). "Drawing" out student conceptions of assessment: Using pupils' pictures to examine their conceptions of assessment. In D. M. McInerney, G.T.L. Brown, & G.A.D. Liem (Eds.), *Student perspectives on assessment: What students can tell us about assessment for learning* (pp. 53–83). Charlotte, NC: Information Age Publishing.

Haynes, T. L., Daniels, L. M., Stupnisky, R. H., Perry, R. P., & Hladkyj, S. (2010). The effect of attributional retraining on mastery and performance motivation among first-year college students. *Basic and Applied Social Psychology, 30*(3), 198–207. doi:10.1080/01973530802374972

Hembree, R. (1988). Correlates, causes, effects, and treatment of test anxiety. *Review of Educational Research, 58,* 47–77. doi:10.3102/00346543058001047

Hill, K. T., & Wigfield, A. (1984). Test anxiety: A major educational problem and what can be done about it. *The Elementary School Journal, 85,* 105–125. doi:10.1086/461395

Hirschfeld, G.H.F., & Brown, G.T.L. (2009). Students' conceptions of assessment: Factorial and structural invariance of the SCoA across sex, age, and ethnicity. *European Journal of Psychological Assessment, 25,* 30–38. doi:10.1027/1015–5759.25.1.30

Hodapp, V., & Benson, J. (1997). The multidimensionality of test anxiety: A test of different models. *Anxiety, Stress & Coping, 10,* 219–244. doi:10.1080/10615809708249302

Huang, C. (2011). Achievement goals and achievement emotions: A meta-analysis. *Educational Psychology Review, 23,* 359–388. doi:10.1007/s10648–011–9155–x

Hyde, J. S., Fennema, E., Ryan, M., Frost, L. A., & Hopp, C. (1990). Gender comparisons of mathematics attitudes and affect: A meta-analysis. *Psychology of Women Quarterly, 14,* 299–324. doi:10.1111/j.1471–6402.1990.tb00022.x

Kantor, L., Endler, N. S., Heslegrave, R. J., & Kocovski, N. L. (2001). Validating self-report measures of state and trait anxiety against a physiological measure. *Current Psychology, 20*, 207–215. doi:10.1007/s12144–001–1007–2

Kaplan, A., & Maehr, M. L. (1999). Achievement goals and student well-being. *Contemporary Educational Psychology, 24*, 330–358. doi:10.1006/ceps.1999.0993

Kleinginna, P. R., & Kleinginna, A. M. (1981). A categorized list of emotion definitions, with suggestions for a consensual definition. *Motivation and Emotion, 5*, 345–379. doi:10.1007/BF00992553

Kuhbandner, C., Hanslmayr, S., Maier, M. A., Pekrun, R., Spitzer, B., Pastötter, B., & Bäuml, K.-H. (2009). Effects of mood on the speed of conscious perception: Behavioural and electrophysiological evidence. *Social Cognitive and Affective Neuroscience, 4*, 286–293. doi:10.1093/scan/nsp010

Kuhbandner, C., & Pekrun, R. (2013). Affective state influences retrieval-induced forgetting for integrated knowledge. *PloS ONE, 8*, e56617. doi:10.1371/journal.pone.0056617

Lazarus, R. S., & Folkman, S. (1987). Transactional theory and research on emotions and coping. *European Journal of Personality, 1*, 141–169. doi:10.1002/per.2410010304

Levine, L. J., & Burgess, S. L. (1997). Beyond general arousal: Effects of specific emotions on memory. *Social Cognition, 15*, 157–181. doi:10.1521/soco.1997.15.3.157

Linnenbrink, E. A. (2007). The role of affect in student learning: A multi-dimensional approach to considering the interaction of affect, motivation, and engagement. In P. A. Schutz & R. Pekrun (Eds.), *Emotion in education* (pp. 107–124). San Diego, CA: Academic Press.

Linnenbrink, E. A., & Pintrich, P. R. (2002a). Achievement goal theory and affect: An asymmetrical bidirectional model. *Educational Psychologist, 37*, 69–78. doi:10.1207/S15326985EP3702_2

Linnenbrink, E. A., & Pintrich, P. R. (2002b). The role of motivational beliefs in conceptual change. In M. Limón & L. Mason (Eds.), *Reconsidering conceptual change. Issues in theory and practice* (pp. 115–135). Dordrecht, The Netherlands: Kluwer Academic Publishers.

Lubke, G. H., Dolan, C. V., Kelderman, H., & Mellenbergh, G. J. (2003). On the relationship between sources of within- and between-group differences and measurement invariance in common factor model. *Intelligence, 31*, 543–566. doi:10.1016/s0160–2896(03)00051–5.

Marsh, H. W. (1987). The big-fish-little-pond effect on academic self-concept. *Journal of Educational Psychology, 79*, 280–295. doi:10.1037/0022–0663.79.3.280

McKillop, C. (2006). Drawing on assessment: Using visual representations to understand students' experiences of assessment in art and design. *Art, Design & Communication in Higher Education, 5*, 131–144. doi:10.1386/adch.5.2.131/6

Meece, J. L., Wigfield, A., & Eccles, J. S. (1990). Predictors of math anxiety and its influence on young adolescents course enrollment intentions and performance in mathematics. *Journal of Educational Psychology, 82*, 60–70. doi:10.1037/0022–0663.82.1.60

Meinhardt, J., & Pekrun, R. (2003). Attentional resource allocation to emotional events: An ERP study. *Cognition and Emotion, 17*, 477–500. doi:10.1080/02699930244000039

Mosquera, P.M.R., Parrott, W. G., & de Mendoza, A. H. (2010). I fear your envy, I rejoice in your coveting: On the ambivalent experience of being envied by others. *Journal of Personality and Social Psychology, 99*, 842–854. doi:10.1037/a0020965

Murayama, K., & Elliot, A. J. (2009). The joint influence of personal achievement goals and classroom goal structures on achievement-relevant outcomes. *Journal of Educational Psychology, 101*, 432–447. doi:10.1037/a0014221

Olafson, K. M., & Ferraro, F. R. (2001). Effects of emotional state on lexical decision performance. *Brain and Cognition, 45*, 15–20. doi:10.1006/brcg.2000.1248

Parrott, W. G., & Spackman, M. P. (1993). Emotion and memory. In M. Lewis & J. M. Haviland-Jones (Eds.), *Handbook of emotions* (pp. 476–490). New York: Guilford Press.

Pekrun, R. (1992a). The expectancy-value theory of anxiety: Overview and implications. In D. G. Forgays, T. Sosnowski, & K. Wrzesniewski (Eds.), *Anxiety: Recent developments in self-appraisal, psychophysiological and health research* (pp. 23–41). Washington, DC: Hemisphere.

Pekrun, R. (1992b). The impact of emotions on learning and achievement: Towards a theory of cognitive/motivational mediators. *Applied Psychology, 41*, 359–376. doi:10.1111/j.1464–0597.1992.tb00712.x

Pekrun, R. (2006). The control-value theory of achievement emotions: Assumptions, corollaries, and implications for educational research and practice. *Educational Psychology Review, 18*, 315–341. doi:10.1007/s10648–006–9029–9

Pekrun, R. (2014). *Emotions and learning* (Educational Practices Series, Vol. 24). International Academy of Education (IAE) and International Bureau of Education (IBE) of the United Nations Educational, Scientific and Cultural Organization (UNESCO), Geneva, Switzerland.

Pekrun, R., Cusack, A., Murayama, K., Elliot, A. J., & Thomas, K. (2014). The power of anticipated feedback: Effects on students' achievement goals and achievement emotions. *Learning and Instruction, 29*, 115–124. doi:10.1016/j.learninstruc.2013.09.002

Pekrun, R., Elliot, A. J., & Maier, M. A. (2006). Achievement goals and discrete achievement emotions: A theoretical model and prospective test. *Journal of Educational Psychology, 98*, 583–597. doi:10.1037/0022–0663.98.3.583

Pekrun, R., Elliot, A. J., & Maier, M. A. (2009). Achievement goals and achievement emotions: Testing a model of their joint relations with academic performance. *Journal of Educational Psychology, 101*, 115–135. doi:10.1037/a0013383

Pekrun, R., Goetz, T., Daniels, L. M., Stupnisky, R. H., & Perry, R. P. (2010). Boredom in achievement settings: Exploring control–value antecedents and performance outcomes of a neglected emotion. *Journal of Educational Psychology, 102*, 531–549. doi:10.1037/a0019243

Pekrun, R., Goetz, T., Frenzel, A. C., Barchfeld, P., & Perry, R. P. (2011). Measuring emotions in students' learning and performance: The Achievement Emotions Questionnaire (AEQ). *Contemporary Educational Psychology, 36*, 36–48. doi:10.1016/j.cedpsych.2010.10.002

Pekrun, R., Goetz, T., Perry, R. P., Kramer, K., Hochstadt, M., & Molfenter, S. (2004). Beyond test anxiety: Development and validation of the test emotions questionnaire (TEQ). *Anxiety, Stress & Coping: An International Journal, 17*(3), 287–316. doi:10.1080/10615800412331303847

Pekrun, R., Hall, N. C., Goetz, T., & Perry, R. P. (2014). Boredom and academic achievement: Testing a model of reciprocal causation. *Journal of Educational Psychology, 106*, 696–710. doi:10.1037/t21196–000

Pekrun, R., & Linnenbrink-Garcia, L. (2012). Academic emotions and student engagement. In S. L. Christenson, A. L. Reschly, & C. Wylie (Eds.), *Handbook of research on student engagement* (pp. 259–282). New York: Springer.

Pekrun, R., & Perry, R. P. (2014). Control-value theory of achievement emotions. In R. Pekrun & L. Linnenbrink (Eds.), *International handbook of emotions in education* (pp. 120–141). New York: Routledge.

Pekrun, R., & Stephens, E. J. (2012). Academic emotions. In K. R. Harris, S. Graham, T. Urdan, S. Graham, J. M. Royer, & M. Zeidner (Eds.), *APA educational psychology handbook* (Vol. 2, pp. 3–31). Washington: American Psychological Association.

Peterson, E. R., Brown, G. T., & Jun, M. C. (2015). Achievement emotions in higher education: A diary study exploring emotions across an assessment event. *Contemporary Educational Psychology, 42*, 82–96. doi:10.1016/j.cedpsych.2015.05.002

Preckel, F., Zeidner, M., Goetz, T., & Schleyer, E. J. (2008). Female 'big fish' swimming against the tide: The 'big-fish-little-pond effect' and gender-ratio in special gifted classes. *Contemporary Educational Psychology, 33*, 78–96. doi:10.1016/j.cedpsych.2006.08.001

Putwain, D. (2008) Do high stakes examinations moderate the test anxiety-examination performance relationship? *Educational Psychology, 28*, 109–118. doi:10.1080/01443410701452264

Reeve, C. L., & Bonaccio, S. (2008). Does test anxiety induce measurement bias in cognitive ability tests? *Intelligence, 36*, 526–538. doi:10.1016/j.intell.2007.11.003

Reeve, C. L., Bonaccio, S., & Winford, E. C. (2014). Cognitive ability, exam-related emotions and exam performance: A field study in a college setting. *Contemporary Educational Psychology, 39*, 124–133. doi:10.1016/j.cedpsych.2014.03.001

Reisenzein, R., Junge, M., Studtmann, M., & Huber, O. (2014). Observational approaches to the measurement of emotions. In R. Pekrun & L. Linnenbrink (Eds.), *International handbook of emotions in education* (pp. 580–606). New York: Routledge.

Roediger, H. L., & Karpicke, J. D. (2006). The power of testing memory: Basic research and implications for educational practice. *Perspectives on Psychological Science, 1*, 181–210. doi:10.1111/j.1745–6916.2006.00012.x

Roeser, R. W., Midgley, C., & Urdan, T. C. (1996). Perceptions of the school psychological environment and early adolescents' psychological and behavioral functioning in school: The mediating role of goals and belonging. *Journal of Educational Psychology, 88*, 408–422. doi:10.1037/0022–0663.88.3.408

Scherer, K. R. (2009). The dynamic architecture of emotion: Evidence for the component process model. *Cognition and Emotion, 23*, 1307–1351. doi:10.1080/02699930902928969

Schutz, P. A., & Davis, H. A. (2000). Emotions and self-regulation during test taking. *Educational Psychologist, 35*, 243–256. doi:10.1207/S15326985EP3504_03

Smith, C. A., & Ellsworth, P. C. (1987). Patterns of appraisal and emotion related to taking an exam. *Journal of Personality and Social Psychology, 52*, 475–488. doi:10.1037/0022–3514.52.3.475

Sommer, M., & Arendasy, M. E. (2014). Comparing different explanations of the effect of test anxiety on respondents' test scores. *Intelligence, 42*, 115–127. doi:10.1016/j.intell.2013.11.003

Spangler, G., Pekrun, R., Kramer, K., & Hofmann, H. (2002). Students' emotions, physiological reactions, and coping in academic exams. *Anxiety, Stress & Coping, 15*, 413–432. doi:10.1080/1061580021000056555

Spielberger, C. D., & Vagg, P. R. (Eds.). (1995). *Test anxiety: Theory, assessment, and treatment.* Washington, DC: Taylor & Francis.

Turner, J. E., & Schallert, D. L. (2001). Expectancy-value relationships of shame reactions and shame resiliency. *Journal of Educational Psychology, 93*, 320–329. doi:10.1037//0022–0663.93.2.320

Tze, V. M. C., Daniels, L. M., & Klassen, R. M. (2015). Evaluating the relationship between boredom and academic outcomes: A meta-analysis. *Educational Psychology Review.* doi:10.1007/s10648–015–9301-y

Urdan, T., & Schoenfelder, E. (2006). Classroom effects on student motivation: Goal structures, social relationships, and competence beliefs. *Journal of School Psychology, 44,* 331–349. doi:10.1016/j.jsp.2006.04.003

Van de Ven, N., Zeelenberg, M., & Pieters, R. (2011). Why envy outperforms admiration. *Personality and Social Psychology Bulletin, 37,* 784–795. doi:10.1177/0146167211400421

Vanderhoven, E., Raes, A., Montrieux, H., & Rotsaert, T. (2015). What if pupils can assess their peers anonymously? A quasiexperimental study. *Computers and Education, 81,* 123–132. doi:10.1016/j.compedu.2014.10.001

Warne, R. T., Yoon, M., & Price, C. J. (2014). Exploring the various interpretations of "test bias". *Cultural Diversity and Ethnic Minority Psychology, 20,* 570–582. doi:10.1037/a0036503

Weiner, B. (1985). An attributional theory of achievement motivation and emotion. *Psychological Review, 92,* 548–573. doi:10.1037/0033–295X.92.4.548

Weiner, B. (2007). Examining emotional diversity on the classroom: An attribution theorist considers the moral emotions. In P. A. Schutz & R. Pekrun (Eds.), *Emotion in education* (pp. 73–88). San Diego, CA: Academic Press.

Wigfield, A., & Eccles, J. S. (1990). Test anxiety in the school setting. In M. Lewis & S. M. Miller (Eds.), *Handbook of developmental psychopathology* (pp. 237–250). Boston, MA: Springer US.

Zeidner, M. (1987). Essay versus multiple-choice type classroom exams: The student's perspective. *The Journal of Educational Research, 80,* 352–358. doi:10.2307/27540265

Zeidner, M. (1995). Adaptive coping with test situations: A review of the literature. *Educational Psychologist, 30,* 123–133. doi:10.1207/s15326985ep3003_3

Zeidner, M. (1998). *Test anxiety: The state of the art.* New York: Plenum Press.

Zeidner, M. (2007). Test anxiety in educational contexts: What I have learned so far. In P. A. Schutz & R. Pekrun (Eds.), *Emotion in education* (pp. 165–184). San Diego, CA: Academic Press.

Zeidner, M. (2014). Anxiety in education. In R. Pekrun & L. Linnenbrink (Eds.), *International handbook of emotions in education* (pp. 265–288). New York: Routledge.

Zimmermann, B. J. (2000). Attaining self-regulation. A social cognitive perspective. In M. Boekaerts, P. R. Pintrich, & M. Zeidner (Eds.), *Handbook of self-regulation* (pp. 13–39). San Diego, CA: Academic Press.

Zuriff, G. E. (1997). Accommodations for test anxiety under ADA? *Journal of the American Academy of Psychiatry and the Law Online, 25*(2), 197–206.

8

STUDENTS' PERCEPTIONS OF NOVEL
FORMS OF ASSESSMENT

Katrien Struyven and Joana Devesa

NEW ASSESSMENTS FOR A NEW ERA

Teaching and learning are expected to cope with considerable changes in the contemporary era (e.g., technical and scientific advances within knowledge-based economies and societies are rapid and quickly become obsolete [Powell & Snellman, 2004]). Thus, individuals need to become competent, flexible, resourceful workers able to adapt themselves to ever-changing circumstances (Boud, 2000; Boud & Falchikov, 2006), and students need to go beyond mere factual knowledge acquisition to mastery of a wide range of skills and competencies that can be applied in diverse and changing situations (Brine, 2006; Knight, 2002; Stefani, 1998).

Assessment that is aligned with these educational goals must necessarily be different from previous practice. Traditional summative forms of assessment (e.g., short answers, true/false, or multiple-choice standardised tests) taken at the end of a module, semester, or school year often focus on the acquisition of low-level cognitive skills and consequently do not meet a knowledge-based society's expectations (Knight, 2002; Parke & Lane, 2007; Yildrim, 2004). To that end, new assessment practices, variously called *assessment for learning* (Stiggins, 2002); *alternative assessment* (Gipps & Stobart, 2003); *learning-oriented assessment* (Carless, 2007); *student-centred assessment* (White, 2009); *assessment for self-regulated learning* (Clarke, 2012); or *sustainable assessment* (Boud, 2000), have been being introduced in classrooms all over the world (Struyven, Dochy, & Janssens, 2005).

Seeking an agreed-upon definition of new assessment practices is no easy task (Gipps & Stobart, 2003), since the concept is an umbrella term sheltering many alternatives to traditional standardised testing, including self-assessment, peer assessment, portfolio assessment, technology-enhanced assessment, performance-based assessment, cooperative assessment, criterion-referenced assessment, authentic assessment, problem-based inquiries, viva voce, vignettes, reflective diaries, and journals, just to name a few. To complicate matters further, it is sometimes difficult to categorise innovations, since new assessments are flexible (e.g., a portfolio can include performance-based assessment, and if done electronically, also be a technology-based assessment; if done in group, it is also a cooperative assessment, etc.). What all of these assessments have in common is that they introduce an innovation of some sort, in terms of processes, formats, and/or requirements, representing a shift from a purely psychometric and measurement model of a summative performance to a model in which classroom assessment is promoted as an integral part of the learning process (Gipps & Stobart, 2003), including a formative component.

While many experts tend to endorse these new methods (e.g., Boud & Falchikov, 2006; Nicol & Macfarlane-Dick, 2006; Stiggins, 2002), how students perceive them is less known. Which formats do they classify as being novel? What are the advantages and pitfalls students normally associate with them? Do they see novel assessment as a rather homogeneous category, or do their perceptions differ greatly depending on the format in question? Do they favor or disfavour them over more traditional formats? If one is to truly understand the potential of novel methods of assessment, students' views and perceptions are a source of invaluable information. In what follows, we will summarise the main findings of research on novel assessments, examining factors that might be responsible for students' positive and/or negative perceptions, and how instructors could act in order to overcome challenges identified.

RESISTANCE TO CHANGE: A COMMON FIRST REACTION

The Novelty Effect: Swimming in Unknown Waters

An assessment task deemed *novel*, evoking the ideas of newness, unconventionality, unusualness, innovation, modernity, and break with tradition, is undoubtedly different from its traditional counterparts in terms of format, processes, requirements, and/ or purpose. Instead of the customary memorization of lecture notes and text materials that may be required by conventional assessments (Kuisma, 2007), portfolio assessments urge students to decide which products constitute proof of their learning (Blaikie, Schönau & Steers, 2004); self- and peer assessments force students to make judgements about the quality of their own assignments and those of their peers (Vu & Dall'Alba, 2007); criterion-referenced assessments may require students to define the criteria against which their work will be assessed (Stefani, 1998); cooperative assessments push them to learn how to make consensus-based decisions (McLaughlin & Simpson, 2004); and technology-enhanced assessments compel them to discover the educational potential of e-tools which they normally use for entertainment, or to figure out how to work with unknown software (Hämäläinen et al., 2011). For the majority of students, practices such as these constitute first-time experiences that force them to engage in completely unfamiliar tasks and to handle requirements they have never encountered before, ultimately pushing them out of their comfort zone (Bevitt, 2014). The novelty of such tasks, combined with their added cognitive complexity and the demand to assume a much more active role in the process, can lead to student dissatisfaction.

Compared with traditional assessments, students see novel formats as being time-consuming and imposing heavy workloads for students (and instructors) (Drew, 2001; Lizzio, Wilson, & Simons, 2002). Learners who experienced peer assessments, for example, resented the time consumed by having to revise and evaluate several pieces of work (Ballantyne, Hughes, & Mylonas, 2002). Portfolio assessments attract similar critique, being characterised as a lengthy, repetitive process of creation, extensive collection of information, and substantial evidence of reflection, making it difficult to keep up with work in other classes (Aydin, 2010; Kuisma, 2007; Struyven, Blieck, & De

Roeck, 2014). Peer assessment and feedback, despite their learning potential, may be opposed because many students regard the teacher as having the sole expertise for reliable assessment, especially if the work is to be graded or counted towards course grades (Kaufman & Schunn, 2011; Liu & Carless, 2006; Ozogul & Sullivan, 2009). If teachers fail to take these complaints seriously and do not accommodate students' needs, then the learning potential of the tasks is compromised (Cook-Sather, 2002; Prensky, 2005). Coutts, Gilleard and Baglin (2011), who measured first year undergraduate students' mood and intrinsic motivation, found that in weeks when the number of assessments was higher, students' tension, depression, anger, fatigue, and confusion increased, while vigour, interest, and enjoyment were significantly decreased. Students subsequently adopted surface approaches to learning and, in some cases, withdrew from the class or program (Bevitt, 2014; Drew, 2001; Struyven et al., 2005).

When being assessed in a new way, students often find it hard to fully grasp what is expected of them and may consider the requirements confusing due to assessment's more subjective nature or cryptic language (Arnold et al., 2005; Carless, 2006; Kuisma, 2007). One student involved in Kuisma's study (2007) described the frustration he experienced while engaging in a portfolio assessment: ". . . the direction is a problem. Initially, we don't know how to start doing it. It seems like a free-expression, because you don't know how to do it from the beginning . . . the instruction should be concise and precise . . ." (pp. 564–565). This opinion seems to be shared by most of the Dutch students involved in Blaikie et al.'s (2004) study, in which only 32% claimed to understand what assessors were looking for when evaluating their portfolios. Similarly, students interviewed by Bevitt (2014) complained that having to deal with unfamiliar assessment, such as writing an executive summary or preparing a presentation in partnership with colleagues, wasted a lot of time, since before they could start the task itself, they had to figure out what an executive summary exactly was, or how to work in a group.

Having to cast aside habits internalised through years of formal schooling, and adopt new procedures, normally causes students to experience a mild level of bewilderment and disconcert (Constantinescu & Alexandrache, 2014). Under certain circumstances, however, it can go further, with feelings of frustration, pressure, anxiety, stress, and being overwhelmed, with decreased motivation being reported (Bevitt, 2014). Bevitt (2014) found the novelty effect tainted some students' overall academic experience, disrupting their learning, with some considering dropping the course.

In many cases, the assessment causing the acute uneasiness is technology enhanced. Due to the rapid dissemination of digital technology in the past few decades, and growing prevalence and affordability of personal devices with persistent network connections (Alexander, Underwood, & Truell, 2005; Backer, 2010), virtually any format of assessment—from multiple-choice and short-answer questions (Dermo, 2009; Han & Finkelstein, 2013) to reflective journals (Gleaves, Walker, & Grey, 2007), portfolios (Chang et al., 2013; Struyven et al., 2014), and peer assessments (Lu & Bol, 2007; Trautmann, 2009; Wen & Tsai, 2006) can now assume an electronic version. Instructors see embracing technology as necessary because students are supposedly *digital natives*; hence, instructional approaches must adapt and embrace computers, Internet, video cameras, cell phones, video games, and all the other devices of the digital age (Conole et al., 2008; Prensky, 2001, 2005, 2007). However, while most students appreciate certain aspects of e-assessments linked to information delivery and communication (Gleaves et al., 2007; Walvoord et al., 2008; Wen & Tsai, 2006), several authors (Backer, 2010; Coulby et al., 2011; Jones et al., 2010) found that a consistent minority of students have what Terzis et al. (2013) called 'low computer self-efficacy', in which technology in general, and technology-enhanced assessment in particular, is perceived as difficult. Such students report having difficulties in operating unfamiliar software and view the technical issues associated with it, such as malfunctioning, incompatibility with their home or school devices, and poor Internet connections as major setbacks (Backer, 2010; Stone, 2014). As a consequence, some students claim that technology-enhanced assessments (also known as *e-assessments* [Dermo, 2009], *automated assessments* [Dreher, Reiners, & Dreher, 2011], or *computer-based assessments* [Terzis et al., 2013]) significantly hinder their learning since they add supplementary stress to the already unsettling experience of being assessed. Other students still have little confidence in the validity of electronic variants, exhibiting more positive attitudes towards the 'old-fashioned way' than to its online counterpart (Dermo, 2009; Wen & Tsai, 2006). Coulby et al. (2011) argue that this generation is less homogeneous in its use and appreciation of new technologies than many assume, with significant variations amongst students (Jones et al., 2010). Even those comfortable with the technologies may not feel automatically confident in using them in educational settings, especially in connection with assessment practices (Coulby et al., 2011). Margaryan, Littlejohn, and Vojt (2011) likewise reported that large numbers of the students in their study indicated that they never employed virtual chat, MP3 players, handheld computers, podcasts, simulation games, MySpace, YouTube, or blogs for learning. One-quarter had never heard of Google Scholar, were not familiar with Wikipedia, and did not know what a podcast was. Generally speaking, the authors concluded, students did not universally appear to understand the potential of technology to support learning.

Unlike novel assessments, traditional formats and their requirements are consistent with the internalised image of what an assessment ought to be. Consistency breeds predictability, which in turn leads to feelings of reassurance and comfort (Maag, 2009). Hence, it is unsurprising that, far from demanding lecturers to change their practice, students frequently express less confidence and more dislike towards unfamiliar tasks, whatever they might be, and tend to prefer classical methods of assessment in which they believe they are proficient (Margaryan et al., 2011; Moni, van Kraayenoord, & Baker, 2002). A higher level of confidence in their ability to perform a task in the old way meant that students with greater experience in those methods were reluctant to let go of "the coherence, status and competence they had already gained," while those who had yet not mastered the procedures were more receptive to new work methods (Constantinescu & Alexandrache, 2014, p. 71). 'Loyalty' towards familiar assessment methods was also observed in Garside et al.'s (2009) study, with students justifying their preference on the basis that they were already familiar with essays and had previously had good outcomes, which gave them comfort when undertaking the traditional assessment format.

Traditional Methods: A Summative Safe Harbor?

Traditionally, assessment lay in the hands of the teacher, whose purpose was to grade students and certify their knowledge, or lack thereof. Today, things have changed (Boud & Falchikov, 2006; McGarr & Clifford, 2013), and teachers are expected to use assessment as part of the learning process, during which student's knowledge, skills, and competencies are meant to develop in order to equip them for lifelong learners (Kean, 2012; McGarr & Clifford, 2013; Sluijmans, Dochy, & Moerkerke, 1999). It is, however, worth asking whether learners perceive and engage with assessment practices in the same way, since whether they do or do not has huge implications as their learning and achievement (Brown & Hirschfeld, 2007, 2008; Struyven et al., 2005).

Zeidner (1992) concluded that most students believed that assessment was a practice having little to do with enhancing learning, motivating students, or shaping classroom behaviour. Instead, Peterson and Irving (2008) found students thought of assessments as "a piece of paper with a whole bunch of questions" (p. 7) intended mainly to award a mark, with students showing preference for ones which they are familiar with and believe they may score well on (Garside et al., 2009). Donald and Denison (2001) and Fletcher et al. (2012) corroborated that most students still tend to view assessment as having primarily a *feedout function* (Knight, 2002), serving merely as a mechanism for gatekeeping and achievement certification. Consequently, students testified to feeling apprehensive upon realizing they would be assessed by portfolio instead of a traditional exam, because they were used to the exam format and did well on it: "I have always been a pretty good test-taker, and that served me well to get good grades throughout my educational career" (Altahawi et al., 2012, p. 222).

Even if the superiority of alternative assessments for learning gains is demonstrated, students often deprecate them in favour of practices considered easier and familiar, especially among students who are used to high level of success within the traditional system (Brown & Hirschfeld, 2008; McGarr & Clifford, 2013). Grades are, after all, strongly attached to the individual's pride and sense of worth as a learner (Peterson & Irving, 2008), even if students are well aware that they often reflect assessment-taking ability rather than actual learning (Walker, 2008). Parke and Lane (2007) found that a majority of elementary and middle school students (73%) preferred multiple-choice items, even though most (80%) recognized that performance-based tasks made them think harder. Herman, Klein, and Wakai (1997) reached the same conclusions, finding that most of more than 800 math students in 13 California middle schools agreed open questions were more challenging (83%) and interesting to solve (51%), and made them think harder (55%), but continued to prefer multiple-choice questions (60%). Thanks to their familiarity with this format (e.g., "we do stuff like multiple-choice every day" [p.10]), they found it easier to understand what was expected of them (65%), considered questions less complicated (58%), and thought they performed better (68%) with multiple-choice questions.

Such focus on the summative component tends to undermine the learning potential of novel types of assessment (Boud, 2000; van der Vleuten et al., 2010). Brown and Hirschfeld (2007, 2008) found that pupils who conceived of assessment as irrelevant, that is, as "essentially just a hoop to be jumped through, with no relevance or importance to them beyond passing" (Rust, 2002, p. 150), tended to have lower levels of achievement. This happens because when more importance is granted to grades and results rather than to understanding, it is not unusual for students to adopt what Carless (2002) calls a *product approach*, and Entwistle et al. (2001) describe as a *strategic* or *achieving approach*. Within this approach, assigned tasks are viewed as unwelcome external impositions and are executed with little personal engagement. Students become strategic in their use of time and effort, channeling all of their energy towards a product that will enable them to obtain a passing grade (Carless, 2002) and nothing more—long-term knowledge is not their concern (Struyven et al., 2005). They selectively disregard content believed unlikely to be assessed, and if certain tasks are not intended to be graded, then students are prone to not complete them at all, or to devote an insignificant amount of effort towards them (Gibbs & Simpson, 2004–05; Rust, 2002) since they feel that work not graded is worthless and irrelevant as it provides no sense of accomplishment (Peterson & Irving, 2008). The learning component of assessment seems to be disregarded by students, if they do not worry about actually learning the material and if they do not reflect on which skills and knowledge were gained by completing the assignments or how they might improve in the future (Carless, 2002, 2006; Rust, 2002). According to Carless (2002), it is a fairly common practice for students not to bother to collect marked assignments containing written feedback if they are made available after their grades have been disclosed, especially when they have had poor results. Stone (2014) agrees, mentioning the case of four students who reported not seeing the point of checking what they could have done better once they knew they had passed an assignment. As one high school student put it, "[I] just really care about the grade, not the comments or anything because at the end of the day, the grade gets you passed anyway" (Peterson & Irving, 2008, p. 11).

Students' Personal Characteristics and Assessment Preferences

Sometimes, preference for traditional assessments persists in spite of the instructor's best efforts to cultivate alternative attitudes. In the last few decades, several researchers have taken an interest in examining the extent to which students' learning strategies and personality traits condition their assessment preferences. Birenbaum and Feldman (1998) explored the relationships between learning patterns and attitudes towards open-ended and multiple-choice assessments among students in higher education. They discovered that pupils who had good learning skills and high confidence in their academic abilities tended to prefer constructed-response types of assessments, while weaker students showed more inclination towards multiple-choice examinations. Chamorro-Primuzic et al. (2005) found that Big Five personality traits (i.e., neuroticism, extroversion, openness to experience, agreeableness, and conscientiousness) were modestly but consistently related to like or dislike for specific assessment procedures. For example, students who were extroverts showed preference for oral examinations and cooperative assessment, while those exhibiting openness tended to dislike multiple-choice exams. Furnham, Batey, and Martin (2010) added that students who adopted deep approaches to learning favoured dissertations and oral exams, while those with achieving or strategic approaches preferred continuous assessment, and those with surface or memorization approaches were more likely to prefer multiple-choice questions, especially when the format calls for recognition and recall.

TOWARDS OVERCOMING RESISTANCE

The Importance of Hands-on Experience

Bevitt (2014) and Bartram and Bailey (2010) note students experience very little assessment variety throughout their schooling, with assessments being dominated by examinations. If educational systems keep on relying almost exclusively on traditional examinations, students are unlikely to prefer novel assessments (McGarr & Clifford, 2013). However, if given opportunities to show their competence via different assessment methods, there is a fair chance that preference for new methods might emerge (van de Watering et al., 2008). For example, pupils who had used performance-based tasks throughout the school year were significantly more likely to state a preference for them over multiple-choice exercises (Parke & Lane, 2007). Similarly, previous experience with peer assessment made students more receptive towards the process (Wen & Tsai, 2006). Martínez-Lirola and Rubio (2009) noticed that compiling a portfolio for the first time generated complaints about its difficulty, but those with some prior experience tended not to make this complaint. After engaging in novel reflective writing, management reports, and presentation assessments in their undergraduate program, some students expressed preference for these techniques (Bevitt, 2014).

Further, students' perceptions of assessment are not stable or unchangeable characteristics. Positive hands-on experiences with novel modes can lead to increased familiarity and, subsequently, feelings of mastery, transforming an initial negative response into acceptance, and even enthusiasm (Struyven, Dochy, & Janssens, 2008). For example, a learner-centred portfolio-assessment system built around competency standards and continuous formative feedback generated initial reservations from students (Altahawi et al., 2012); however, as work progressed and the students became accustomed to the task, they reported advantages and enjoyment: "My attitude on feedback shifted from the criticism to the constructive. The system seemed to be working for me to improve on many aspects of becoming a doctor that would not necessarily have been addressed otherwise" (p. 223). Similarly, students reported considerable levels of anxiety in their first viva voce assessment, but later conceded the assessment was 'student-friendly' and gave it more positive comments than negative ones (Pearce & Lee, 2009).

Fostering Understanding of What Novel Assessments Aim For

Change in assessment is often unwelcomed because of misunderstanding or lack of information (Maag, 2009). When teachers' assessment processes and expectations are unclear, then mismatches between the students' conceptions of the requirements and their own can be expected (Nicol & Macfarlane-Dick, 2006; Peterson & Irving, 2008). The quality of training and explanation may be viewed positively by instructors but not by students. This was especially the case in Vu and Dall'Alba's study (2007) where undergraduate students had to undergo multiple assessments (e.g., peer assessment, a viva voce). Due to inadequate preparation, students reported not understanding the criteria, being unsure of how to match their peers' performances with standards, and fearing their marking was unfair and inaccurate. Similarly, teacher trainers believed an e-portfolio system was effective for assessing preservice student teachers' competences during a teaching internship, but student teachers saw the portfolio as "a mere container" (p. 51) of assignments which assessed their reflective skills and academic writing more than teaching competencies (i.e., "But actually, what is meant to be assessed? The capacity of teaching, not the capacity of writing reports!" [p. 46]), and saw it as a summative tool since little interaction with teacher trainers was experienced (Struyven et al., 2014).

To make sure students understand the purpose of an unfamiliar assessment and know how to work towards its fulfillment, a number of conditions need to be in place, including: (a) time to familiarise students with the goals, criteria, and standards; (b) involvement of students in elaboration and development of such criteria (Carless, 2007; Lizzio et al., 2002; Topping, 1998); (c) provision of examples of poor, average, and good assignments (Carless, 2007; Orsmond, Merry & Reiling, 2002; Stefani, 1998); (d) opportunities for frequent engagement with the task (Ballantyne et al., 2002; Kean, 2012; White, 2009); and (e) continual and timely feedback at each stage of the procedure (Altahawi et al., 2012; Hanrahan & Isaacs, 2001; Kean, 2012). Rust (2002) suggests novel assessments should be introduced gradually, with students first marking papers according to given criteria and eventually moving on to be involved in the design and choice of assessment tasks, and the negotiation of the assessment criteria. As Carless (2006) noted, "students need to learn about assessment in the same way they engage with subject content" (p. 230). This groundwork must take place even in cases when it is reasonable for the assessor to assume that students are already familiar with the task, (e.g., art students should have experienced evaluation through a portfolio, a fairly common practice in the field [Blaikie et al., 2004]).

Nonetheless, each individual will have his or her own conceptions of what is 'novel' (Bevitt, 2014). Pupils' assessment careers depend on the fields they have studied, the teachers they had, or the schools they attended, and, in the same classroom, a format that is familiar to one learner might be completely novel for another (Bevitt, 2014; Moni et al., 2002). This individual-difference factor may be even greater for international students from examination societies studying in contexts where examinations are not the sole method of assessment (Bevitt, 2014).

When novel assessments are well implemented (as per the advice above), a positive hands-on experience is likely to ensue, with gains in engagement and learning (Han & Finkelstein, 2013). For example, students who were required to define the marking criteria against which their group projects would be evaluated thought that the task was demanding, but allowed them to set their own targets and use creativity, enhancing their motivation, self-regulation, and ownership of the process (Stefani, 1998). In preparation for assessment of their peers' oral presentations, students discussed their topics in planning groups, reported on progress, gave mini-presentations, and generated peer feedback using the same criteria sheets used for the final assessment (White, 2009); consequently, the majority of the students developed positive attitudes toward peer assessment, with 75% claiming to feel at ease with it, 79% believing the overall scores given by peers were fair and reasonable, and 66% feeling qualified to mark their peers.

The same gradual development of students' perceived sense of mastery has been observed in technology-enhanced assessments. The web-based system Calibrated Peer Review (CPR[1]) for tertiary (and secondary) education, for example, requires students to peruse guiding questions and review a set of calibration essays. Students who do not meet the expectations set by the instructor must retake the calibration trial a second time, assuring proficiency prior to the actual assessment of peers. Following this initial training period, students then evaluate the papers of three colleagues, and their own, knowing that they have adequately mastered the use of the assessment criteria; finally, they receive feedback on their essay from three peers (Balfour, 2013; Hartberg et al., 2008; Walvoord et al., 2008). This allows students to progressively become less reliant on instructors, while at the same time developing trust in their own and peers' judgement. Use of the CPR system has helped students become better technical reviewers and enabled them to learn the class material better (Margerum et al., 2007). Peerceptiv[2] goes further by requiring students to submit a second revised paper based on the feedback received, which is again reviewed by peers. Again students' comments were positive, indicating improvement in their writing, and a deeper understanding of the evaluation process (Cho, Schunn, & Wilson, 2006).

Recognizing Learning Gains

Higher education students have positively evaluated assessments which have "more emphasis on learning, on academic skills, rather than jumping through hoops for marks"; are formative, "not just a big exam at the end"; and provide effective feedback that "explained where you went wrong in the assignment" and gave "positive help and advice for improvement in the future" (Drew, 2001, pp. 319–320). Novel assessments tend to be seen by students as achieving these learning goals much more so than traditional ones. Sambell et al. (1997) reported that students viewed traditional assessments as detrimental to the learning process, while innovative assessments incited them to channel their efforts into trying to understand the material. Middle school students considered open-ended questions as being focused on the importance of the quality or depth of their explanations, their use of diagrams and graphs, and their reasoning more than multiple-choice questions (Herman et al., 1997). Similarly, being assessed via portfolio instead of a traditional exam changed student approaches to learning from "slavishly studying material that was assigned by the professor in order to get a high letter grade or percentage," and "simply memorizing the specifics needed to pass a test" to "view[ing] learning as an opportunity rather than a mandate" and "digging deeper, trying to get the big picture" (Altahawi et al., 2012, p. 223).

Many authors report students claiming novel assessments help them acquire valuable skills and competencies, not only for their ongoing academic careers, but also for future employability (Donald & Denison, 2001; Drew, 2001; Joughin, 1998; Lam, 2013; Schutt & Linegar, 2010). They suggest:

- Problem-based assessments seem to develop understanding of content knowledge, foster the acquisition of problem-solving skills, and permit formation of connections between ideas (Hmelo-Silver, 2004; Sulaiman, 2010);
- Vignettes facilitate greater understanding of course content and reflection (Jeffries & Maeder, 2004–2005; Walen & Hirstein, 1995);
- Authentic assessments allow students to see coherence between school work and that awaiting them in 'the real world,' building confidence and developing knowledge (Sambell et al., 1997; Wu, Heng, & Wang, 2015);
- Collaborative assessments teach how to deal with multiple perspectives, collaborate, and better communicate (Swan, Shen, & Hiltz, 2006);
- Viva voce gives the opportunity to demonstrate mastery of content and verbal skills, allowing application of theory to practice, and providing invaluable experience for job interviews (Carless, 2002; Joughin, 1998; Pearce & Lee, 2009);
- Portfolios foster reflection, creativity, and improved writing, permitting students to go beyond the simple memorization of facts (e.g., Altahawi et al., 2012; Kuisma, 2007; Martínez-Lirola & Rubio, 2009);
- E-assessments (e.g., Calibrated Peer Review (CPR), Peerceptiv, Turnitin, MyPeer Review, or PRAZE [Cho et al., 2006; Pearce, Mulder, & Baik, 2009; Sitthiworachart & Joy, 2004]) increase engagement and participation, stimulate new ideas and creativity, and generate more feedback, learning, and understanding (Backer, 2010; Liu & Carless, 2006; Schutt & Linegar, 2010).
- Peer feedback, whether mediated by technology or not, increases more carefully elaborated, long-thought, exhaustive feedback comments; timeliness of feedback; and more diverse types of feedback, all resulting in improved work (Cho et al., 2006; Trautmann, 2009; Vu & Dall'Alba, 2007). It is worth noting that anonymized conditions (i.e., assessor and assessee do not know whose work is being reviewed by whom) tend to generate more critical, higher-quality, and impartial feedback (Jessup, Connolly, & Tansik, 1990; Lu & Bol, 2007; Wen & Tsai, 2006). Note that students generally welcome a low proportion of course grades being based on peer-assessment marks—somewhere between 15% and 25% (Cheng & Warren, 1997; Wen & Tsai, 2006; White, 2009).

This list does not imply that the identified learning outcomes are exclusive or unique to the method. Multiple novel formats seem to elicit multiple skills and competencies. Critical thinking, for example, was identified as an outcome by students who had engaged in (a) technology-enhanced assessment (Backer, 2010), (b) portfolios (Martínez-Lirola & Rubio, 2008), and (c) peer assessment (Walvoord et al., 2008).

Improved academic writing has been established with (a) portfolios (Aydin, 2010; Lam, 2013), (b) reflective journals (Gleaves et al., 2007) and (c) various e-settings, such as forums, blogs, and wikis (Miyazoe & Anderson, 2010). Nonetheless, it is likely that certain novel assessments are associated with certain kinds of outcomes; for example, a literacy assignment that allows students to transform the stories they write into actual films via Flip cameras, Comic Life software, or YouTube video is likely to foster more creativity than a self-assessment (Schutt & Linegar, 2010). Hence, a variety of learning gains are associated with novel assessments in general, rather than with specific formats.

The Importance of Feedback

The main power behind a novel assessment's effectiveness seems to be the central role it gives to feedback (Boud, 2000; Nicol & Macfarlane-Dick, 2006). Feedback is an essential tool in the enhancement of learning (Nicol & Macfarlane-Dick, 2006; Voerman et al., 2014). Students view feedback as inextricably linked to assessment, relying on it to know what and how to improve (Peterson & Irving, 2008). In fact, when asked to identify barriers to effective assessment, students pointed to lack of feedback and follow-up as the main problems (Brown, 2011; Carless, 2006; Crook et al., 2012). Feedback must be *forward looking* (Carless, 2006; Gibbs & Simpson, 2004–05; Rust, 2002), that is, provide students information on how to bridge the gap between where they are and where they need to be. Learners think that this is better achieved when they are provided with honest and constructive criticism that offers guidance rather than empty praise and inflated encouragement (Peterson & Irving, 2008). While wanting feedback on all aspects of their performance (Drew, 2001), they especially appreciate it when directed at generic issues that can be applied in a large range of future situations, rather than just to the assignment in question (Carless, 2002, 2006). If students are to act upon the feedback received, however, they need to understand it. Therefore, students urge assessors to be precise, concrete, and employ user-friendly language in order to transmit their meaning since, as students testify, attempts at interpreting it can sometimes be overwhelming (Altahawi et al., 2012). Furthermore, timely feedback is important to give students time to work on improvements (Gibbs & Simpson, 2004–05; Langrish & See, 2008); but this may be problematic for novel formats which may take considerably longer to process for feedback.

A current emphasis in many novel assessment formats is its formative function, assessment *for* learning, to generate detailed feedback to learners in daily classroom practices. Some formats in particular, such as peer assessment and technology-enhanced assessment, claim to take the conventional feedback process further, enriching it by introducing new stakeholders and by experimenting with alternative channels to communicate advice to students. Stevens and Jamieson (2002) used Mindtrail, a computerised assignment-marking assistant that allows teachers to construct a detailed marking scheme with scales, check boxes, and comment fields against which each assignment will be evaluated, and collate all of these items into a report for the students. After using Mindtrail to mark two major assignments, 120 postgraduate students believed the tool was useful and that it had improved the teachers' feedback, which in turn had helped them to gain a better understanding of the level they had achieved in their work. Crook et al. (2012) showed that 80% of the students who received constructive criticism from their instructors using ASSET (i.e., online interactive resource involving a webcam or a camcorder and screen-capture software) liked the use of video as a way of receiving feedback, considering it to be timely, accessible, and more detailed, informative, comprehensible, and engaging. A real advantage was the ability to rewatch the video-recorded feedback multiple times.

CONCLUSIONS AND DISCUSSION

This review has identified strong enthusiasm for the potential of novel assessments to contribute to preparing students as lifelong learners capable of continuously acquiring the knowledge and skills needed to adapt themselves to the ever-changing circumstances of their future professional life. However, it is clear that the claims about novel assessments are limited to potential: they *can*, not that they *will* (Torrance, 2012). Whether their potential is met depends on how students perceive the assessment—its purpose, importance, usefulness, fairness, complexity, difficulty, etc.—and on how they approach the task based on these perceptions (Brown & Hirschfeld, 2007, 2008; Struyven et al., 2014); the literature suggests students aren't nearly as enthusiastic as educators.

Consistent with change scenarios, there is reluctance in letting go of the familiar in favour of novel assessments and all they entail—new formats, processes, requirements, and purposes (Margaryan et al., 2011; Moni et al., 2002; Sagie, Elizur, & Greenbaum, 1985). This is especially so because novel assessments are perceived as being more time-consuming, difficult, complex, and demanding than their traditional counterparts (Bevitt, 2014; Carless, 2006; Kuisma, 2007). Despite the promise of technology to make novel assessments feasible and manageable, a significant number of students claim to have low computer self-efficacy and struggle with the requirements of the tools of the digital age, raising doubts about the widespread notion that all contemporary students are digital natives (Coulby et al., 2011, Dermo, 2009; Jones et al., 2010).

Students fear they won't be able to reach the same level of competence they had already gained within the former system and that this will potentially lower their results (Altahawi et al., 2012; Garside et al., 2009). The vision of assessment as serving merely as a mechanism for gatekeeping and achievement certification seems to still dominate students' perceptions (Fletcher et al., 2012; Peterson & Irving, 2008; Zeidner 1992). Several authors (Boud, 2000; van der Vleuten et al., 2010) warn about the dangers of such unproductive conceptions of assessment, relating them with surface approaches to learning, preference for less complex evaluation practices, and, ultimately, with low levels of achievement. In fact, the validity of the assessment is jeopardised if students' perceptions are not in line with the expectations and objectives of the course and its assessment practices.

However, students' perceptions and preferences of assessment are not static characteristics (Struyven et al., 2008). While in some cases students seem to be motivated by personal traits (Birenbaum & Feldman, 1998; Chamorro-Primuzic et al., 2005; Furnham et al., 2010), they mostly depend on the way assessment is designed and implemented.

If initial suspicions towards novel formats of assessment are to be overcome, educators must provide students with opportunities to get familiar with the tasks, allowing them to develop a sense of mastery. However, increasing students' hands-on experience with new formats of assessment is only a partial answer to this challenge.

In addition, the variation of novel formats is huge, each associated with new assessment procedures, methods, and standards. As such, the predictability of how students will respond to each newly experienced format is low, filling students with feelings of uncertainty, doubt, and possible incompetence. A meaningful way to deal with the diversity and wide variation of novel assessment formats is by being selective in and conscious about the adoption and implementation of the format.

One way to limit the wide range of possible new experiences is to perceive assessment as a program (van der Vleuten et al., 2010), aimed at (1) encouraging learning throughout the process and (2) safeguarding the quality of the learning outcomes at the end of the program. The triangulation of different formats of assessment, involving diverse stakeholders at multiple moments of measurement helps to assess (a) the complex nature of learning as knowledge construction and processes and (b) the outcomes of learning as competence development. If agreement is attained about the competences, indicators, and criteria (Strijbos et al., 2015), the assessment path and process, including novel forms, becomes transparent, comprehensible, and predictable for students and, if a formative function is integrated, the assessment 'points' become strong vehicles for learning throughout the lessons, courses, and years of the program.

With the idea of assessment as a program, the traditional psychometric parameters for quality of assessment, such as reliability and validity, which are well established for conventional one-off measurements with single correct answers, become deficient for many forms of novel assessments aimed at measuring and enhancing more complex processes of learning, such as knowledge construction and competence development. As such, the quality of assessment needs to be conceived differently as 'sets' or 'systems,' with quality parameters that are distinct from the format, the educator, the assessor, and the subject or course for which the assessment is being used.

It should be no surprise that more research is needed on novel forms of assessment. Future studies, on the one hand, need to be longitudinal, with repeated observations of the same formats, so that the novelty effect is replaced steadily by the true assessment effect. On the other hand, research with a 'system' approach of assessment as an intervention may shed interesting light on the formative function of assessment over lessons, courses, and years.

One promising avenue for research on assessment interventions, as well as the headwaters by which new assessment practices enter educational practice, is teacher education. Student teachers are taught about conventional and emerging principles of classroom assessment. We can call attention to novel assessments' potential to positively impact learning, clarifying how the tasks promote the acquisition of knowledge, skills, and competences relevant to students' academic and professional life. However, if our goal is to have future teachers 'walk the talk,' it is important that teacher education programs be exemplars of quality assessment practices, including novel formats that aim at capturing and guiding complex processes of learning. Teacher education needs to teach as it preaches.

NOTES

1 Available at http://cpr.molsci.ucla.edu/Home.aspx
2 Available at http://www.peerceptiv.com/

REFERENCES

Alexander, M., Underwood, R., & Truell, A. (2005). Advantages and disadvantages of web-based assessment: The effect of experience on student perceptions. *Journal of Business and Training Education, 14*, 1–8.

Altahawi, F., Sisk, B., Poloskey, S., Hicks, C., & Dannefer, E. (2012). Student perspectives on assessment: Experience in a competency-based portfolio system. *Medical Teacher, 34*, 221–225.

Arnold, L., Shue, C. K., Kritt, B., Ginsburg, S., & Stern, D. (2005). Medical students' views on peer assessment of professionalism. *Journal of General Internal Medicine, 20*(9), 819–824.

Aydin, S. (2010). EFL writers' perceptions of portfolio keeping. *Assessing Writing, 15*, 194–203.

Backer, E. (2010). Using smartphones and Facebook in a major assessment: the student experience. *E-Journal of Business Education & Scholarship of Teaching, 4*(1), 19–31.

Balfour, S. P. (2013). Assessing writing in MOOCs: Automated essay scoring and calibrated peer review. *Research and Practice in Assessment, 8*, 40–48.

Ballantyne, R., Hughes, K., & Mylonas, M. (2002). Developing procedures for implementing peer assessment in large classes using an action research process. *Assessment & Evaluation in Higher Education, 27*(5), 427–441.

Bartram, B., & Bailey, C. (2010). Assessment preferences: A comparison of UK/international students at an English university. *Research in Post-Compulsory Education, 15*(2), 177–187.

Bevitt, S. (2014). Assessment innovation and student experience: A new assessment challenge and call for a multi-perspective approach to assessment research. *Assessment & Evaluation in Higher Education*, 1–17.

Birenbaum, M., & Feldman, R. A. (1998). Relationships between learning patterns and attitudes towards two assessment formats. *Educational Research, 40*(1), 90–98.

Blaikie, F., Schönau, D., & Steers, J. (2004). Preparing for portfolio-assessment in art and design: A study of opinions and experiences of exiting secondary school students' in Canada, The Netherlands and England. *The International Journal of Art & Design Education, 23*(3), 302–315.

Boud, D. (2000). Sustainable assessment: Rethinking assessment for the learning society. *Studies in Continuing Education, 22*(2), 151–167.

Boud, D., & Falchikov, N. (2006). Aligning assessment with long-term learning. *Assessment & Evaluation in Higher Education, 31*(4), 399–413.

Brine, J. (2006). Lifelong learning and the knowledge economy: Those that know and those that do not: The discourse of the European Union. *British Educational Research Journal, 32*(5), 649–665.

Brown, G.T.L., & Hirschfeld, G.H.F. (2007). Students' conceptions of assessment and mathematics: Self-regulation raises achievement. *Australian Journal of Educational and Developmental Psychology, 7*, 63–74.

Brown, G.T.L., & Hirschfeld, G.H.F. (2008). Students' conceptions of assessment: Links to outcomes. *Assessment in Education: Principles, Policy and Practice, 15*(1), 3–17.

Brown, S. (2011). Bringing about positive change in the higher education student experience: A case study. *Quality Assurance in Education, 19*(3), 195–207.

Carless, D. (2002). The 'Mini-Viva' as a tool to enhance assessment for learning. *Assessment & Evaluation in Higher Education, 27*(4), 353–363.

Carless, D. (2006). Differing perceptions in the feedback process. *Studies in Higher Education, 31*(2), 219–233.

Carless, D. (2007). Learning-oriented assessment: Conceptual bases and practical implications. *Innovation in Education and Teaching International, 44*(1), 57–66.

Chamorro-Primuzic, T., Furnham, A., Dissou, G., & Heaven, P. (2005). Personality and preference for academic assessment: A study with Australian University students. *Learning and Individual Differences, 15*, 247–256.

Chang, C., Tseng, K., Liang, C., & Cheng, T. (2013). Using e-portfolios to facilitate university students' knowledge management performance: E-portfolio vs. Non-portfolio. *Computers & Education, 69*, 216–224.

Cheng, W., & Warren, M. (1997). Having second thoughts: Student perceptions before and after a peer assessment exercise. *Studies in Higher Education, 2* (22), 233–239.

Cho, K., Schunn, C. D., & Wilson, R. W. (2006). Validity and reliability of scaffolded peer assessment of writing from instructor and student perspectives. *Journal of Educational Psychology, 98*(4), 891–901.

Clarke, I. (2012). Formative assessment: Assessment is for self-regulated learning. *Educational Psychology Review, 24*(2), 205–249.

Conole, G., de Laat, M., Dillon, T., & Darby, J. (2008). 'Disruptive technologies', 'pedagogical innovation': What's new? Findings from an in-depth study of students' use and perception of technology. *Computers & Education, 50*, 511–524.

Constantinescu, M., & Alexandrache, C. (2014). Resistance to changes in the field of the education. *Procedia—Social and Behavioral Sciences, 137*, 70–73.

Cook-Sather, A. (2002). Authorizing students' perspectives: Toward trust, dialogue and change in education. *Educational Researcher, 31*(4), 3–14.

Coulby, C., Hennessey, S., Davies, N., & Fuller, R. (2011). The use of mobile technology for work-based assessment: The student experience. *British Journal of Educational Technology, 42*(2), 251–265.

Coutts, R., Gilleard, W., & Baglin, R. (2011). Evidence for the impact of assessment on mood and motivation in first-year students. *Studies in Higher Education, 36*(3), 291–300.

Crook, A., Mauchline, A., Maw, S., Lawson, C., Drinkwater, R., Lundqvist, K., Orsmond, P., Gomez, S., & Park, J. (2012). The use of video technology for providing feedback to students: Can it enhance the feedback experience for staff and students?. *Computers and Education, 58*, 386–396.

Dermo, J. (2009). E-assessment and the student learning experience: A survey of student perceptions of e-assessment. *British Journal of Educational Technology, 40*(2), 203–214.

Donald, J. G., & Denison, B. (2001). Quality assessment of university students: Student perception of quality criteria. *The Journal of Higher Education, 72*(4), 478–502.

Dreher, C., Reiners, T., & Dreher, H. (2011). Investigating factors affecting the uptake of automated assessment technology. *Journal of Information Technology Education, 10*, 161–181.

Drew, S. (2001). Perceptions of what helps learn and develop in education. *Teaching in Higher Education, 6*(3), 309–331.

Entwistle, N. J., McCune, V., & Walker, P. (2001) Conceptions, styles and approaches within higher education: Analytical abstractions and everyday experience. In R. J. Sternberg & L. F. Zhang (Eds.), *Perspectives on cognitive, learning and thinking styles* (pp. 103–136). New York, Lawrence Erlbaum Associates.

Fletcher, R. B., Meyer, L. H., Anderson, H., Johnston, P., & Rees, M. (2012). Faculty and students conceptions of assessment in higher education. *Higher Education, 64*, 119–133.

Furnham, A., Batey, M., & Martin, N. (2011). How would you like to be evaluated? The correlates of students' preferences for assessment methods. *Personality and Individual Differences, 50*, 259–263.

Garside, J., Nhemachena, J. Z., Williams, J., & Topping, A. (2009). Repositioning assessment: Giving students the 'choice' of assessment methods. *Nurse Education in Practice, 9*, 141–148.

Gibbs, G., & Simpson, C. (2004–05). Conditions under which assessment supports students. *Learning and Teaching in Higher Education, 1*, 3–31.

Gipps, C., & Stobart, G. (2003). Alternative assessment. In T. Kellaghan & D. L. Stufflebeam (Eds.), *International handbook of educational evaluation* (pp. 549–575). Dordrecht/Boston/London: Kluwer Academic Publishers.

Gleaves, A., Walker, C., & Grey, J. (2007). Using digital and paper diaries for learning and assessment purposes in higher education: A comparative study of feasibility and reliability. *Assessment & Evaluation in Higher Education, 32*(6), 631–643.

Hämäläinen, M., Hyyrynen, V., Ikonen, J., & Porras, J. (2011). Applying peer-review for programming assignments. *International Journal on Information Technologies & Security, 1*, 3–17.

Han, J. H., & Finkelstein, A. (2013). Understanding the effects of professors' pedagogical development with clicker assessment and feedback technologies and the impact on students' engagement and learning in higher education. *Computers & Education, 65*, 64–76.

Hanrahan, S. J., & Isaacs, G. (2001). Assessing self- and peer-assessment: The students' views. *High Education Research & Development, 20*(1), 53–70.

Hartberg, Y., Gunersel, A. B., Simpson, N. J., & Balester, V. (2008). Development of student writing in biochemistry using calibrated peer review. *Journal of the Scholarship of Teaching and Learning, 2*(1), 29–44.

Herman, J. L., Klein, D.C.D., & Wakai, S. T. (1997). *American students' perspectives on alternative assessment: Do they know it's different?—CSE technical report.* Los Angeles, CRESST/University of California.

Hmelo-Silver, C. E. (2004). Problem-based learning: What and how do students learn?. *Educational Psychology Review, 16*(3), 235–266.

Jeffries, C., & Maeder, D. W. (2004–05). Using vignettes to build and assess teacher understanding of instructional strategies. *The Professional Educator, 27*(1–2), 17–28.

Jessup, L. M., Connolly, T., & Tansik, D. A. (1990). Toward a theory of automated group work: The deindividuating effects of anonymity. *Small Group Research, 21*(3), 333–347.

Jones, C., Ramanau, R., Cross, S., & Healing, G. (2010). Net generation or digital natives: Is there a distinct new generation entering university? *Computers and Education, 54*(3), 722–732.

Joughin, G., 1998. Dimensions of oral assessment. *Assessment & Evaluation in Higher Education, 23*(4), 367–378.

Kaufman, J. H., & Schunn, C. D. (2011). Students' perceptions about peer-assessment for writing: Their origin and impact on revision work. *Instructional Science, 39*(3), 387–406.

Kean, J. (2012). Show and tell: Using peer-assessment and exemplars to help students understand quality in assessment. *Practitioner Researcher in Higher Education, 6*(2), 83–94.

Knight, P. T. (2002). Summative assessment in higher education: Practices in disarray. *Studies in Higher Education, 27*(3), 275–286.

Kuisma, R. (2007). Portfolio assessment of an undergraduate group project. *Assessment & Evaluation in Higher Education, 32*(5), 557–569.

Lam, R. (2013). Two portfolio systems: EFL students' perceptions of writing ability, text improvement, and feedback. *Assessing Writing, 18*, 132–153.

Langrish, T., & See, H. (2008). Diverse assessment methods in group work settings. *Education for Chemical Engineers, 3*, 40–46.

Liu, N., & Carless, D. (2006). Peer feedback: The learning element of peer-assessment. *Teaching in Higher Education, 11*(3), 279–290.

Lizzio, A., Wilson, K., & Simons, R. (2002). University students' perceptions of the learning environment and academic outcomes: Implications for theory and practice. *Studies in Higher Education, 27*(1), 27–52.

Lu, R., & Bol, L. (2007). A comparison of anonymous versus identifiable e-peer review on college student writing performance and the extent of critical feedback. *Journal of Interactive Online Learning, 6*(2), 100–115.

Maag, J. W. (2009). Resistance to change: Overcoming institutional and individual limitations for improving student behaviour through PLCs. *Journal of the American Academy of Special Education Professionals, 4*(2), 41–57.

Margaryan, A., Littlejohn, A., & Vojt, G. (2011). Are digital natives a myth or reality? University students' use of digital technologies. *Computers and Education, 56*, 429–440.

Margerum, L. D., Gulsrud, M., Manlapez, R., Rebong, R., and Love, A. (2007). Application of calibrated peer review (CPR) writing assignments to enhance experiments with an environmental chemistry focus. *Journal of Chemical Education, 84*(2), 292–295.

Martínez-Lirola, M., & Rubio, F. (2009). Students' beliefs about portfolio evaluation and its influence on their learning outcomes to develop EFL in a Spanish context. *International Journal of English Studies, 9*(1), 91–111.

McGarr, O., & Clifford, A. M. (2013). 'Just enough to make you take it seriously': exploring students' attitudes towards peer assessment. *Higher Education, 65*, 677–693.

McLaughlin, P., & Simpson, N. (2004). Peer-assessment in first year university: How the students feel. *Studies in Educational Evaluation, 30*, 288–297.

Miyazoe, T., & Anderson, T. (2010). Learning outcomes and students' perceptions of online writing: Simultaneous implementation of a forum, blog, and wiki in an EFL blended learning setting. *System, 38*, 185–199.

Moni, K. B., van Kraayenoord, C. E., & Baker, C. D. (2002) Students' perceptions of literacy assessment. *Assessment in Education: Principles, Policy & Practice, 9*(3), 319–342.

Nicol, D. J., & Macfarlane-Dick, D. (2006). Formative assessment and self-regulated learning: A model and seven principles of good feedback practice. *Studies in Higher Education, 31*(2), 199–218.

Orsmond, P., Merry, S., & Reiling, K. (2002). The use of exemplars and formative feedback when using student derived marking criteria in peer and self-assessment. *Assessment & Evaluation in Higher Education, 27*(4), 309–323.

Ozogul, G., & Sullivan, H. (2009). Student performance and attitudes under formative evaluation by teacher, self and peer evaluators. *Educational Technology Research and Development, 57*(3), 393–410.

Parke, C. S., & Lane, S. (2007). Students' perceptions of a Maryland state performance assessment. *The Elementary School Journal, 107*(3), 305–324.

Pearce, G., & Lee, G. (2009). Viva voce (oral examination) as an assessment method: Insights from marketing students. *Journal of Marketing Education, 31*, 120–130.

Pearce, J., Mulder, R., & Baik, C. (2009). *Involving students in peer review: Case studies and practical strategies for university teaching.* The University of Melbourne.

Peterson, E. R., & Irving, S. E. (2008). Secondary students' conceptions of assessment and feedback. *Learning and Instruction, 18*, 238–250.

Powell, W. W., & Snellman, K. (2004). The knowledge economy. *Annual Review of Sociology, 30*, 199–220.

Prensky, M. (2001). Digital natives, digital immigrants part I, *On the Horizon, 9*(5), 1–6.

Prensky, M. (2005). Engage me or enrage me: What today's learners demand. *Educause Review, 40*(5), 60–65.

Prensky, M. (2007). Changing paradigms: from "being taught" to "learning on your own with guidance". *Educational Technology.* Retrieved October 22, 2014 from http://marcprensky.com/articles-in-publications/

Rust, C. (2002). The impact of assessment on student learning: How can the research literature practically help to inform the development of departmental assessment strategies and learner-centred assessment practices?" *Active Learning in Higher Education, 3*(2), 145–158.

Sagie, A., Elizur, D., & Greenbaum, C. W. (1985). Job experience, persuasion strategy and resistance to change: An experimental study. *Journal of Occupational Behavior, 6*, 157–162.

Sambell, K., McDowell, L., & Brown, S. (1997). 'But is it fair?': An exploratory study of student perceptions of the consequential validity of assessment. *Studies in Educational Evaluation, 23*(4), 349–371.

Schutt, S., & Linegar, D. (2010). Agents of engagement: Trialling the use of collaborative technology workshops to engage at-risk youth and teachers in VET, in: AVETRA 13th Annual Conference, Thursday, 8–Friday, 9 April, Surfers Paradise, Queensland.

Sitthiworachart, J., & Joy, M. (2004). Effective peer assessment for learning computer programming. *ACM SIGCSE Bulletin, 36*(3), 122–126.

Sluijmans, D., Dochy, F., & Moerkerke, G. (1999). The use of self-, peer- and co-assessment in higher education: A review of literature. *Studies in Higher Education, 24*(3), 331–350.

Stefani, L.A.J. (1998). Assessment in partnership with learners. *Assessment & Evaluation in Higher Education, 23*(4), 339–349.

Stevens, K., & Jamieson, R. (2002). The introduction and assessment of three teaching tools (WebCT, Mindtrail, EVE) into a post graduate course. *Journal of Information Technology Education, 1*(4), 233–252.

Stiggins, R. J. (2002). Assessment crisis: The absence of assessment for learning. *Phi Delta Kappan, 83*(10), 758–765.

Stone, A. (2014). Online assessment: What influences students to engage with feedback?, *The Clinical Teacher, 11*, 284–289.

Strijbos, J., Engels, N., & Struyven, K. (2015). Criteria and standards of generic competences at bachelor degree level: A review study. *Educational Research Review, 14*, 18–32.

Struyven, K., Blieck, Y., & De Roeck, V. (2014). The electronic portfolio as a tool to develop and assess pre-service student teaching competences: Challenges for quality. *Studies in Educational Evaluation, 43*, 40–54.

Struyven, K., Dochy, F., & Janssens, S. (2005). Students' perceptions about evaluation and assessment in higher education: A review. *Assessment & Evaluation in Higher Education, 30*(4), 331–347.

Struyven, K., Dochy, F., & Janssens, S. (2008). The effects of hands-on experience on students' preferences for assessment methods. *Journal of Teacher Education, 59*(1), 69–88.

Sulaiman, F. (2010). Students' perceptions of implementing problem-based learning in a physics course. *Procedia Social and Behavioral Sciences, 7*(C), 355–362.

Swan, K., Shen, J., & Hiltz, S. R. (2006). Assessment and collaboration in online learning. *Journal of Asynchronous Learning Networks, 10*(1), 45–62.

Terzis, V., Moridis, C. N., Economides, A. A., & Mendez, G. R. (2013). Computer based assessment acceptance: A cross-cultural study in Greece and Mexico. *Educational Technology & Society, 16*(3), 411–442.

Topping, K. J. (1998). Peer assessment between students in colleges and universities. *Review in Educational Research, 68*(3), 249–276.

Torrance, H. (2012). Formative assessment at the crossroads: Conformative, deformative and transformative assessment. *Oxford Review of Education, 38*(3), 323–342.

Trautmann, N. M. (2009). Interactive learning through web-mediated peer review of student science reports. *Educational Technology Research and Development, 57*(5), 685–704.

van de Watering, G., Gijbels, D., Dochy, F., & van der Rijt, J. (2008). Students' assessment preferences, perceptions of assessment and their relationships to study results. *Higher Education, 56*(6), 645–658.

van der Vleuten, C. P. M., Schuwirth, L. W. T., Scheele, F., Driessen, E. W., Hodges, B., Currie, R., & Currie, E. (2010). The assessment of professional competence: Building blocks for theory development. *Best Practice & Research Clinical Obstetrics and Gynaecology, 30*, 1–17.

Voerman, L., Korthagen, F. J. A, Meijer, P. C., & Simons, R. J. (2014). Feedback revisited: Adding perspectives based on positive psychology. Implications for theory and classroom practice. *Teaching and Teacher Education, 43*, 91–98.

Vu, T. T., & Dall'Alba, G. (2007). Students' experience of peer-assessment in a professional course. *Assessment & Evaluation in Higher Education, 32*(5), 541–556.

Walen, S. B., & Hirstein, J. (1995). Classroom vignette: An alternative assessment tool. *Teaching Children Mathematics, 1*(6), 362–365.

Walker, P. (2008). 'What do students think they (should) learn at college?' Student perceptions of essential learning outcomes. *Journal of the Scholarship of Teaching and Learning, 2*(1), 45–60.

Walvoord, M. E., Hoefnagels, M. H., Gaffin, D. D., Chumchal, M. M., & Long, D. A. (2008). An analysis of calibrated peer review (CPR) in a science lecture classroom. *Journal of College Science Teaching, 37*(4), 66–73.

Wen, M. L., & Tsai, C. (2006). University students' perceptions of and attitudes towards (online) peer assessment. *Higher Education, 51*(1), 27–44.

White, E. (2009). Student perspectives of peer assessment for learning in a public speaking course. *Asian EFL Journal, 33*, 1–36.

Wu, X. V., Heng, M. A., & Wang, W. (2015). Nursing students' experiences with the use of authentic assessment rubric and case approach in the clinical laboratories. *Nurse Education Today, 35*, 549–555.

Yildrim, A. (2004). Student assessment in high-school social studies in Turkey: Teachers' and students' perceptions. *International Review of Education, 50*(2), 157–175.

Zeidner, M. (1992). Key facets of classroom grading: A comparison of teacher and student perspectives. *Contemporary Educational Psychology, 17*(3), 224–243.

9

STUDENT PARTICIPATION IN ASSESSMENT

Does It Influence Self-regulation?

Daniel L. Dinsmore and Hope E. Wilson

Typically, assessment is viewed as a process in which a person with more expertise (e.g., a teacher) evaluates a more novice individual (e.g., a student) using multiple sources of information to make this evaluation (e.g., tests, observations of student behavior [AERA, APA, & NCME, 1999]). In these relationships, there is an assumed hierarchy between teacher and student in the evaluation process, with the teacher having considerable power over the student and, thus, potentially regulating students' behavior. However, the argument exists that children taking an active role in assessment increases their self-regulation (Nicol & Macfarlane-Dick, 2006), which, in turn, has been shown to have positive benefits for student achievement (Pintrich & De Groot, 1990).

From the perspective of theories of self-regulation (SR) and self-regulated learning (SRL), the removal of the assessment and evaluative processes further away from the student's direct sphere may be problematic. The goal of most models of self-regulation is for the individual to be able to monitor, control, and regulate his or her own cognitions, affect, and behaviors to reach certain internal or external goals (Zimmerman & Schunk, 2011). Typically, these models posit either interaction between person (student) and environment (i.e., social cognitive frameworks [Zimmerman, 1989]) or more internal cognitive processes (i.e., information processing frameworks [Winne, 1995]) by which individuals achieve their own cognitive and behavioral goals. For both these views, participation by the individual in all phases of learning, including assessment, is crucial to positive educational outcomes.

Thus, for multiple models of self-regulation there is a tension between the direct engagement or participation of students in assessment and evaluation proposed by self-regulation theories and models and assessment practices that remove evaluation from the self (and teacher) to test creators and evaluators that students do not interact with nor over whom they have any control. The purpose of this chapter is to systematically review studies that focus on the role of student involvement in assessment to better understand the relationship between assessment and self-regulation. Specifically, we will examine what configurations of assessment, task, and learner characteristics are helpful to foster student self-regulation.

THEORETICAL FRAMEWORK

Theoretically, a variety of factors may influence how assessment, task, and learner characteristics influence student self-regulation. In this chapter, we will consider the following factors: conceptions of self-regulation, the aspects of the learner themselves, characteristics of the task and task outcomes, and the manner in which feedback is given.

Conceptions of Self-regulation and Assessment

The effects of self-assessment versus external assessment on self-regulation may depend on various factors of the learning environment, as well as which model of self-regulation is considered (e.g., an information-processing model or a social-cognitive model). While models of self-regulation differ in significant ways (Dinsmore, Alexander, & Loughlin, 2008; Puustinen & Pulkkinen, 2001; Zimmerman & Schunk, 2011), for the purposes of this discussion we will reference Zimmerman's model; however, one could certainly use a different theoretical model of self-regulation to examine these relations. Indeed, distinguishing the types of SR may be important in tracking the different outcomes posited in each of the different models (e.g., Winne's model, with its stronger emphasis on cognition, versus Zimmerman's model, which emphasizes both cognition and motivation).

Zimmerman's model of self-regulation (1989) involves three types of self-regulation: covert (i.e., monitoring and adjusting cognitive and affective states), behavioral (i.e., self-observing and strategically adjusting performance processes), and environmental (i.e., observing and adjusting environmental conditions and outcomes). Figures 9.1 through 9.3 present conceptual models of how SR may be influenced (or not) by the assessment process using Zimmerman's model. Figure 9.1 describes a situation where self-assessment occurs with no external feedback (i.e., only using the learner's self-assessment). In this particular case, engaging in self-assessment would give a learner more incentive to rely on covert and behavioral SR since there would be no environmental feedback to prompt environmental SR. Given the outcome of the performance and the learner's own assessment of that outcome, it is possible that the learner could both change the strategies he or she employed during the task, as well as change his or her own thinking about the task (e.g., his or her self-efficacy for that task [Bandura, 1986]). This is not to say that it is guaranteed that a learner would engage in covert and behavioral SR, only that the potential for these two types of SR would be most likely in this assessment situation.

In Figure 9.2, where the evaluation comes from a source outside of the learner's context without any direct interaction between learner and evaluator, there may be little room or potential for the types of self-regulation described previously in Figure 9.1. The only direct path for the learner would come from the evaluator's feedback (an environmental determinant) to the individual's mental processing (e.g., his or her self-efficacy); thus, it is possible the learner might then engage in covert SR, but that likelihood could be low given the noncontextual nature of the feedback. For example, a low score on a test has the potential to change a learner's self-efficacy, but has less potential to spur change in the learner's own covert or behavioral self-regulation because there would typically be less contextual information for the learner in such feedback. This may be due to the evaluator having little notion of the classroom or learning environment. Although not instructed to, a learner who is highly self-regulatory could engage in covert and behavioral SR, but with little in the task to suggest or aid the learner in doing this, it is assumed these other types of SR would be rather infrequent.

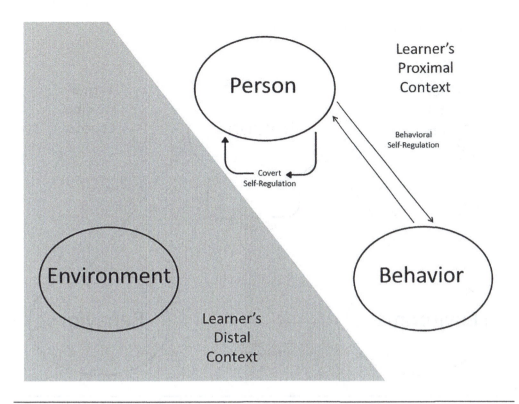

Figure 9.1 Conceptual Model of the Relation Between Self-regulation and Self-assessment. Adapted from Zimmerman (1989).

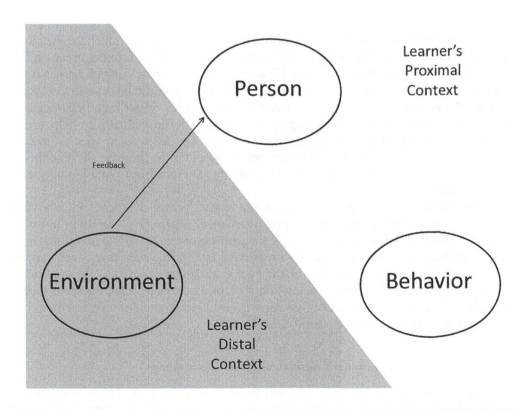

Figure 9.2 Conceptual Model of the Relation Between Self-regulation and Assessment from Noncontextual (off-site) Evaluator. Adapted from Zimmerman (1989).

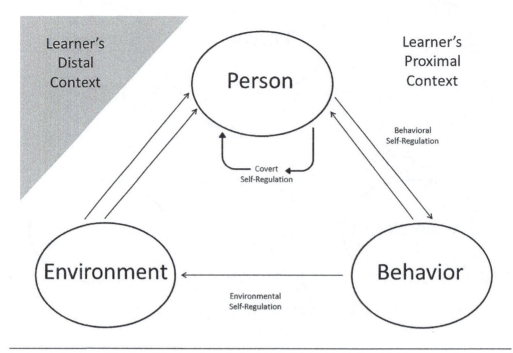

Figure 9.3 Conceptual Model of the Relation Between Self-regulation and Assessment That Includes Self-assessment and Feedback From a Contextually Relevant (i.e., on-site) Evaluator. Adapted from Zimmerman (1989).

Figure 9.3 presents a situation in which there is potential for all three forms of self-regulation—covert, behavioral, and environmental. This is a model in which the learner is expected to self-evaluate and is also provided feedback, which comes from a contextually relevant source (e.g., teacher or tutor). This could be described as scaffolded self-regulation in which the learner self-assesses his or her own behavior and mental processing, but can also engage in discourse with the evaluator to help adjust his or her own cognitive processing. In this regard, self-assessment with contextually situated evaluator feedback has the largest potential to increase the likelihood of self-regulatory activity on the part of the learner, thereby improving learning and performance.

Beyond whether the evaluator is part of the learner's immediate context, who that evaluator is may matter. For example, peer assessment is generally helpful in terms of student outcomes (Gonzalez de Sande & Godino-Llorente, 2014; Panadero, this volume) and metacognitive awareness (Kim & Ryu, 2013); however, this effect may be highly dependent on the credibility of the peer evaluator compared to the credibility of the instructor (Suen, 2014). Finally, the type of assessment (e.g., question types) may also play a broad role in how assessment influences regulation of learning and outcomes of learning (Sadler & Good, 2006).

Learner Characteristics and Assessment

When examining how assessment and self-regulation are related, it may be necessary to consider the developmental level of the student under consideration. While there is certainly a long line of research on the development of thinking and reasoning (Piaget, 1964), most models of SRL do not focus on development within the individual over time (i.e., intra-individual development), particularly compared to theories and models of metacognition (Dinsmore, 2014). Certainly in social-cognitive models of self-regulation, there is theorized to be linear change in self-regulation. It is critical that an examination of how assessment and SRL relate includes a look at how these relations may develop over time. For example, in Borkowski's (1996) more metacognitive model, development is also theorized to be linear, suggesting that as students' domain and topic knowledge grow, they become less reliant on self-regulation processes. Thus, one could extrapolate from two time points the growth of SR. On the other hand, linear additive models, such as the social-cognitive view, would hypothesize certain characteristics have the potential to more strongly relate to SR, as SR skills and processes develop over time and may influence each other in a reciprocal fashion. Thus, one may not be able to extrapolate the development of SR from any two time points.

Characteristics of the Task and Task Outcomes

The relation between assessment and self-regulation might also depend on the academic domain and the nature of the task that students engage in. Typically, models of self-regulation focus less on the nature of the domain and task at hand, with some exceptions. Increasing attention is being given to the effect of domain (Alexander, Dinsmore, Parkinson, & Winters, 2011), though Alexander and colleagues have concluded that that domain does matter, but there was insufficient evidence to draw firm conclusions. Nevertheless, within this chapter, domain will be included as a possible contributing factor in uncovering the relation between assessment and self-regulation.

Similarly, there are arguments about whether self-regulation is more state-like or trait-like. Boekaerts (1995) conceptualizes self-regulation as more trait-like (i.e., self-regulatory behaviors are stable across tasks), whereas Zimmerman's (1989) social-cognitive model is more state-like (i.e., unstable across tasks). Additionally, in related research areas of strategic processing, there are similar arguments. For deep- versus surface-level processing, there are those that argue for a more trait-like approach (Vermunt, 2005) and those that argue for a more state-like approach (Dinsmore & Alexander, 2012, 2015). Dinsmore and Alexander (2012, 2015) identified that task structure (i.e., ill-structured with multiple correct solutions and outcomes vs. well-structured with one correct solution path) impacted strategic processing. Thus, task structure will be included in this review.

Characteristics of the Assessment Feedback Given

The way in which feedback is given may also add to our understanding of how SRL and assessment relate. Given the prevalence of feedback in SRL models, it is important to examine how different types of feedback (i.e., solely self-assessment, assessment with an evaluator familiar with the learner and context, and assessment with an evaluator unfamiliar with the learner and context) might change the relation between assessment and SRL.

Boekaerts (1995) discussed the importance of goal striving, which feeds back internally to students' metacognitive knowledge or motivational beliefs. Likewise, Borkowski's (1996) model described how internal feedback shapes personal–motivational states that spur on further executive processes. Lastly, Pintrich's (2004) four-phase model described self-reflection as a critical element of the self-regulation process. While Winne and Hadwin (1998) certainly discussed internal reflection (i.e., metacognitive adaptation) where students examine their own study techniques relative to their metacognitive knowledge, they also examined students' evaluation of external feedback about the products of learning that help them adapt their standards for future tasks and future cycles in their model. Thus, the external feedback given is interpreted in light of the evaluation and standards a student possesses; the same external feedback may be interpreted differently by each student depending on how they evaluated that feedback and what their standards were for the task.

Social-cognitive models of self-regulated learning (Zimmerman & Schunk, 2011) also emphasize both internal and external feedback as being critical components in students' self-regulation. Bandura's (1986) model of reciprocal determinism suggests that three types of feedback can influence self-regulation. First, internal evaluations (i.e., covert self-regulation) can influence students' own mental processes (e.g., self-efficacy). Behavioral self-regulation occurs when students self-observe their actual behavior to strategically adjust performance processes (e.g., strategies). Finally, more toward the external side, students' environmental self-regulation includes adjusting both mental processes and behavior based on environmental conditions or outcomes, such as feedback from assessments for students in schools.

At the extreme end of the internal/external continuum are models of co-regulation. There are three facets of co-regulation that McCaslin and Hickey (2001) maintain as important factors: the unit of analysis should be relations between individuals, objects, and settings; the coordination of multiple social worlds, expectations, and goals are at the core of functioning; and, goal coordination is learned. Thus, according to this view, environmental and social factors (e.g., peer assessment) in an individual's sphere are important conditions that may help determine regulatory activity and ultimately learning.

Indeed, internal and external feedback related to self-regulation and metacognition have been studied quite extensively, particularly in research related to calibration (i.e., the relation between confidence and performance). Typically, the relation between students' confidence and performance is poor, with generally an overconfidence-underperformance effect found (Dunlosky & Rawson, 2012). However, much of the research on calibration focuses on internal processes (Parkinson, Dinsmore, & Alexander, 2010), with fewer studies examining the influence of external feedback. Thus, for this chapter, the type of feedback (as well as the timing of the feedback) will be a central focus to determine if internal, external, or a combination of the two types of feedback change the relation between assessment and SRL.

CURRENT ISSUES AND TRENDS

The historical and theoretical overview of self-regulation has helped to frame this examination of current issues and trends in the relation between assessment and self-regulated learning. These historical and theoretical aspects guided the questions for the literature review, as well as what information was categorized in the tables for this review.

The research questions are:

1. What types of assessments (i.e., selected response, constructed response, performance) and feedback have been examined in studies of self-regulation?
2. What has been the nature of the tasks and participants in studies that examine the relations between assessment and self-regulation?
3. What relations have been found between assessment and self-regulation in the current research literature?

METHODS

Search Criteria

Using a systematic literature review process, the pool of empirical studies was identified by searching PsycINFO using the keywords *self-regulation* and *assessment* from 2004–2014. Further delimiters included peer review, human subjects, and written in English. This initial pool contained 246 total articles. From this initial pool, studies that contained a student-involved assessment (i.e., self-assessment, peer assessment, or teacher feedback to students) and a measure of self-regulation or self-regulated learning were retained. Articles not included either had no assessment of learning or performance or no measure of self-regulation. The final study pool after this process resulted in 32 studies (Table 9.1).

Data Coding

Each study was coded for the response type of the assessment, evaluator, feedback timing, task domain, age of the participants, nature of the task, and how self-regulation was measured. While not coded, descriptions were also added to the table about the assessment feedback given, a brief description of the task, the analysis used to identify any relations between the assessment and self-regulation, and salient outcomes related to self-regulation.

Assessment Coding

Assessment coding included: response type; who the evaluator was; and, the timing of the assessment feedback. Assessment response types were coded as selected response, constructed response, performance, variable response, undetermined, and other. Selected response included assessments where individuals chose an answer from a list of available answer options. Constructed response included assessments where individuals were asked to supply their own responses to a question. Performance responses included assessments in which individuals were asked to engage in an extended task that resulted in a product or presentation of that activity. Variable response included studies that included both SR and one or more other types of response. Undetermined responses were those where there was not enough information to determine the type of assessment. The category of other was used for studies in which there was a description of the response type, but it did not fit into one of these categories, and for these we included a brief explanation in the table. There were also cases where multiple assessments with more than one response type were used.

With regard to the evaluator, the person who gave feedback was coded as self, teacher or tutor, peer, outside evaluator, or computer-derived feedback. Outside evaluators included cases where the evaluation was done by someone not in the same place as the individual being evaluated. With regard to feedback timing, feedback given in the same session as the assessment was coded as immediate; feedback given in a subsequent session was delayed; if a combination, it was coded variable; and if timing could not be determined, it was coded undetermined. In cases where there was no feedback, not applicable was recorded.

Nature of the Task and Participants

The domain in which the task was situated, as well as the structure of the task, were encoded. The task domain was coded as social science, medicine, languages, arts,

Table 9.1 Studies of Student-involved Assessment and Self-regulated Learning

Citation	Response Type	Evaluator	Description of Feedback	Feedback Timing	Domain	Age	Task Description	Task Structure	Analysis	SRL measure	Salient SRL outcomes
Andrade and Du (2007)	CR; Perf	S	N/A	N/A	Social Science	UG	Educational Psychology Criterion Referenced Self-Assessments	WS	Thematic	Focus Groups	Self-assessment helped students monitor learning but the transfer of self-assessment to performance was inconsistent.
Ashgar (2010)	O (dialogue)	S; P	Reciprocal Teaching	V	Medicine	UG	Physiotherapy Class	UD	Thematic (Phenomenological)	Interview	Feedback was motivational which, in turn, improved self-regulation.
Barber et al. (2012)	Sel	S	Conflicting Boxes in Sudoku Puzzle	V	Non-Academic	UG	Sudoku Puzzles	WS	Logistic Regression	Likert Scale Self-Report	Assessments of progress among highly self-aware individuals may facilitate adaptive self-regulation.
Bruning et al. (2013)	CR	O	Test Scores, Occurring After SR was Measured	D	Language	HS	Writing for a Standardized Test	IS	Correlation	Likert Scale Self-Report	Moderate correlation between SR measure (i.e., writing self-efficacy) and standardized test scores.
Casey et al. (2011)	UD	P	Marked Papers (No further details provided)	UD	Medicine	UG	Midwifery	UD	Thematic	Focus Groups	Participants perceived that peer assessment helped them calibrate their own self-assessments.
Cremaschi (2012)	Sel	S	N/A	N/A	Arts	UG	Practicing Piano	WS	ANOVA	Likert Scale Self-Report (MSLQ)	Practice checklist group had more metacognitive SR than control group, but no differences in self-efficacy or resource management.
Dannefer and Prayson (2013)	CR	S; T; P	Rubric	V	Medicine	PG	Professionalism (Case-Based Scenarios)	WS	Descriptive	Interview	Some evidence that the use of feedback helped to identify new areas for improvement.

Study											Findings
Eva and Regehr (2011)	Sel	S	Self-Assessment of Trivia Questions	I; D	Various	UG	Answering Trivia Questions	WS	ANOVA	Behavioral Observation	Self-assessment did improve performance.
Ferrão (2010)	Sel; CR	C	Percentage Correct	I	Mathematics	UG	Statistics Tests	WS	Means Testing	Preference for Different Forms of Assessment	Self-Regulation was not directly measured, although students had a preference towards self-assessment measures.
Grawitch, Granda, and Barber (2008)	Sel	S	N/A	N/A	Work-related	AD	Selected Work Tasks for Faculty, Staff, and Graduate Students	UD	Path Analysis	Likert Scale Self-Report	Self-assessed ambiguity and difficulty of tasks negatively predicted self-monitored performance.
Harris and Brown (2013)	V	S; T; P	Varied Depending on the Task	V	Various	MS; HS	Variable	V		Interview	Differences emerged in how students and teachers viewed assessment (e.g., accountability versus improvement) and how that translated to students perceptions of self-regulation via peer and self-assessment versus teacher assessment.
Hayes and Embretson (2013)	Sel	C	N/A	N/A	Social Science	UG	Psychology Test	WS		Likert Scale Self-Report	Standardized test procedure was positively related to SR (anxiety).
Ishimatsu, Miura, and Shinohara (2010)	Perf	C	N/A	N/A	Non-Academic	AD	A Central Target Letter Identification Task and a Peripheral Target Regularity Discrimination Task	WS		Interview	Older drivers reported more awareness of driving capabilities when given feedback.

(Continued)

Table 9.1 (Continued)

Citation	Response Type	Evaluator	Description of Feedback	Feedback Timing	Domain	Age	Task Description	Task Structure	Analysis	SRL measure	Salient SRL outcomes
Lizzio and Wilson (2013)	CR	S; T	Academic Recovery Workbook and Student-Tutor Dialogue	I	Social Science	UG	Course Exams	WS		None (Intervention)	SR was not directly measured, however students in the intervention group had higher performance.
Meng and Siren (2012)	Sel	S	Self-Rated Vision and Cognitive Functioning	N/A	Non-Academic	AD	None	UD		Interview	Self-assessments were associated with changes in driving behavior.
Miksza (2011)	Sel	S	N/A	N/A	Arts	MS	Practicing	WS		Likert Scale Self-Report	Ratings of practice efficiency correlated with SR items (time spent practicing).
Mullins and Devendorf (2007)	Perf	S; C	Journaling and Computer Feedback (depending on condition)	I	Non-Academic	UG	Naval Radar Simulation	WS		Likert Scale Self-Report and Diary	Assessment condition predicted goal-directed behavior, but only for the diary measure (not the Likert-type scales).
Panadero, Tapia, and Huertas (2012)	Perf	T	Performance Feedback Versus Process Feedback	I	Social Science	HS	Identifying Landscapes	WS		Likert Scale Self-Report and Online Measure	No differences in SR for type of self-assessment or feedback; some significant occasion effects (i.e., number of landscapes examined).
Panadero, Tapia, and Reche (2013)	Perf	T	Referred to Either Rubric or Scripts in Feedback	I	Social Science	UG	WebQuest	WS		Likert Scale Self-Report	Interaction between occasion and assessment type was significant for SR.

Rizzo and Belfiore (2013)	Sel	T	Student-Teacher Conference	D	Mathematics	MS	Standardized Mathematics Test	WS	None (Intervention)	Promotion of self-regulation through student-teacher conferencing (intervention) led to better performance.
Sargeant et al. (2010)	Sel	S	N/A	N/A	Various	UG; PG; AD	Variable	UD	Focus Groups	Participants reported using self-assessment to reflect, but did not necessarily consider it reflection.
Schelfhout, Dochy, and Janssens (2004)	UD	S; T; P	UD	UD	Business	UG	Class Work	UD	Interview	Self-assessment of cooperative learning did not foster cooperative skills. Teacher feedback was more useful because it served as a guide and provided instruction.
Steuer, Rosentritt-Brunn, and Dresel (2013)	Sel	S	N/A	N/A	Mathematics	MS	None	UD	Likert Scale Self-Report	Perceived error climate affects—partially mediated through students' individual reactions to errors—the quantity and self-regulation of students' effort. Perceived classroom environment, partially mediated by individual reaction to errors, affected SR.
Tal (2010)	CR	S; T	Reflective Writing; Mentor Feedback During a Teaching Episode	I	Language	UG	Preschool Teaching	IS	Journals	In one case, no external feedback was needed to prompt effective SRL, whereas in the other case, ineffective external feedback did not prompt self-reflection.

(*Continued*)

Table 9.1 (Continued)

Citation	Response Type	Evaluator	Description of Feedback	Feedback Timing	Domain	Age	Task Description	Task Structure	Analysis	SRL measure	Salient SRL outcomes
Tapia and Panadero (2010)	CR	S; T	Mastery or Performance Feedback	I	Social Science	HS	Learning about Landscape Characteristics	WS		Likert Scale Self-Report (GSSRQ) and Online (OLSRI)	Tenuous relation between self-assessment condition and SRL (self-efficacy and emotion regulation).
Turner and Husman (2008)	Sel	T	Exam Grade	D	Social Science	UG	Psychopharmacology Exam	WS		Interview	Self-assessment defined trajectories of cognitive, motivational, and emotional behaviors.
Violato and Lockyer (2006)	Sel	S; P	N/A	N/A	Medicine	AD	Assessment in Four Professional Domains	WS		Calibration	Self- and peer assessments resulted in differing calibration of performance to perceptions of performance.
Virtanen and Nevgi (2010)	Sel	S	Used MSLQ Scales	I	Various	UG	Unspecified	UD		Likert Scale Self-Report (MSLQ)	Female students scored moderately higher than male students on help-seeking strategies, utility value, and on performance anxiety.
Welsh (2012)	Sel	P	Through PebblePad	V	Social Science	UG	Educational Psychology Coursework	WS		Likert Scale Self-Report	Effects on SRL are undetermined from data presented.
Williford et al. (2013)	UD	V	Varied Depending on the Task	V	Non-Academic	PS	Naturalistic Preschool Observations	UD		Interview	Active and positive engagement with teachers resulted in higher SRL skills.

Xie and Andrews (2013)	Sel	S	N/A	N/A	Language	UG	Preparing for a Standardized English Proficiency Examination	WS	Likert Scale Self-Report (MSLQ)	No significant relationship between test use and SRL (test preparation).
Zou and Zhang (2013)	Sel; CR	T; C	Percentile Ranks and SRL for the Experimental; Traditional Score Report for the Control	D	Language	UG	Preparing for a Standardized English Proficiency Examination	WS	Likert Scale Self-Report (MAI)	New score reports resulted in improved SRL (metacognitive awareness).

Note: AD=Adults Not in Formal Schooling; C=Computer-Derived Feedback; CR=Constructed Response; D=Delayed; GSSRQ=General and Specific Self-Regulation Questionnaire; HS=High School; I=Immediate; IS=Ill-Structured; O=Outside Evaluator; OLSRI=On-Line Self-Regulation Index; MAI=Meta-cognitive Awareness Inventory; MS=Middle School; MSLQ=Motivated Strategies for Learning Questionnaire; P=Peer; Perf=Performance; PG=Postgraduate; PS=Pre-School; S=Self; Sel=Selected Response; SR=Self-Regulation; SRL=Self-Regulated Learning; T=Teacher or Tutor; UD=Undetermined; UG=Undergraduate; V=Variable; WS=Well-Structured mathematics, work-related tasks, non-academic tasks, or assessments that dealt with various domains. The structure of the task was coded as either well-structured if there was one solution path and one correct answer, or ill-structured if there were multiple solution paths with multiple correct answers. Tasks that were unclear (or if there was not a task) were coded as undetermined, and multiple tasks were coded as variable.

With regard to the nature of the participants, the age level of each sample was coded as preschool; Grades K–5 as elementary school; Grades 6–8 as middle school; Grades 9–12 as high school; undergraduates; postgraduates such as medical students; and adults not enrolled in formal schooling.

RESULTS AND DISCUSSION

The frequency and percentage of the coded characteristics are displayed in Table 9.2.

Table 9.2 Frequency and Percent of Studies Examining Assessment Factors

Category	Frequency	Percent
Response Type		
Selected	17	48.6
Constructed	8	22.9
Performance	5	14.3
Variable	1	2.8
Other	1	2.8
Undetermined	3	8.6
Feedback Timing		
Immediate	9	28.1
Delayed	5	15.6
Variable	6	18.8
Undetermined	1	3.1
No feedback	11	34.4
Evaluator		
Self	20	45.5
Teacher/tutor	11	25.0
Peer	7	15.9
Computer	5	11.4
Outside	1	2.2
Domain		
Social sciences	8	25.8
Medicine	4	12.9
Language arts	4	12.9
Performing arts	2	6.5
Mathematics	3	9.7
Work-related	1	3.2
Non-academic	5	16.1
Various	4	12.9

Table 9.2 (Continued)

Category	Frequency	Percent
Task Structure		
Well-structured	20	62.5
Ill-structured	2	6.3
Variable	1	3.1
Undetermined	9	28.1
Student Age		
Preschool	1	2.9
Elementary school	0	0.0
Middle school	4	11.4
High school	4	11.4
Undergraduates	19	54.3
Postgraduates	2	5.7
Adults	5	14.3

Types of Assessment and Feedback

With regard to response type, nearly half of the studies used some form of selected response. For academic subjects, this was primarily through the use of multiple-choice assessments (e.g., Hayes & Embretson, 2013). For non-academic assessment, this was primarily through the use of Likert-type scales (e.g., Barber, Grawitch, & Munz, 2012). Although the percentage of studies was much lower, there was quite a diverse range of constructed responses as well, ranging from portfolios (Dannefer & Prayson, 2013) to essays (Bruning, Dempsey, Kauffman, McKim, & Zumbrunn, 2013). Because the selected response format may have a relative advantage in terms of reliability (Linn & Gronlund, 2000; McMillan, 2014; Popham, 2011), there seems to be some doubt as to the practical application of constructed assessments, such as performance assessments. Nonetheless, selected response items may limit participants' ability to use feedback to self-assess their own learning because if assessment, and thereby knowledge, is in a highly structured form, there may be no need for a student to reflect on his or her own thinking or behavior; rather, the student can just adopt the structured knowledge as presented in the assessment.

When examining the types of feedback given, there was a range of fairly structured versus very general or broad feedback provided to students. More vague feedback included standardized and exam test scores (Bruning et al., 2013; Turner & Husman, 2008; Zou & Zhang, 2013) and percentages of questions correct or incorrect (Eva & Regehr, 2011; Ferrão, 2010). In contrast, Mullins and Devendorf (2007) used journaling as a way to provide specific feedback, but in a very open-ended way. Similarly, Rizzo and Belfiore (2013) examined feedback given during student-teacher conferences, which it may be assumed was more contextually situated than a standardized test score from an evaluator unfamiliar with the student, classroom, and school environment. Feedback including dialogue, such as in parent conferences or journals, should allow more engagement for students with regard to environmental self-regulation in Zimmerman's (1989) model.

Feedback varied as to when it was given. There was a fairly even distribution in terms of immediate versus delayed feedback (nine versus five studies respectively, with six being variable). This issue may be particularly important for self-regulation. On one hand, immediate feedback may be advantageous because, rather than demanding long-term memory processes, there may be immediate changes to monitoring and control processes related to cognition, self-efficacy, or behavior. On the other hand, delayed feedback, although it may be harder to remember the task performance, may allow the learner more time to reflect on his or her performance and make adjustments before feedback is given.

In terms of evaluator, self-feedback appeared to be most common, followed by teacher or tutor feedback, and peer feedback. There were quite a few studies that used multiple sources of feedback including: self and peer (Asghar, 2010); self and teacher (Lizzio & Wilson, 2013); self and computer (Mullins & Devendorf, 2007); teacher and computer (Zou & Zhang, 2013); and, self, teacher, and peer (Harris & Brown, 2013). These sources of feedback may be particularly important for processes of self-regulation. For covert self-regulation, self-evaluation may have a larger impact, particularly if examining self-regulation through an information-processing lens (Winne, 1995). We might also assume that peers would have more influence on changes in personal mental processes than teachers, as peers would have greater perceived similarity to the learner than a teacher (Bandura, 1986). For Vygotskyian approaches to self-regulation, there may be greater emphasis placed on the evaluator possessing enough knowledge to scaffold the learning through the use of helpful feedback. Thus, it may be particularly important to think about who is evaluating the assessment when predicting changes in self-regulation.

Nature of the Tasks and Participants

With regard to the domain of the study, not surprisingly, most of the studies were with social science tasks, with a majority of those being in either psychology or educational psychology classes. While other domains were modestly represented (e.g., mathematics), it was surprising that the other STEM disciplines (i.e., science, technology, and engineering) were not represented at all. Since domain may make a difference in self-regulatory processes (Alexander et al., 2011), this is an important consideration.

The tasks themselves and the structures of the task tended to be highly structured; with 63% of the tasks identified as well-structured, only 6% of the tasks were ill-structured, and the balance were undetermined (28%) or variable (3%). While it could be speculated that the dominance of selected-response assessments is responsible for the dominance of well-structured tasks, it was found that even the constructed-response assessments relied predominantly upon on well-structured tasks. This may be due to a prevalence of well-structured tasks in the classroom or possibly due to ease of administration and scoring on the part of the researchers. From a self-regulatory perspective, there may be a particular tension with the level of task structure. A task that is too highly structured may not allow the individual enough agency (Zimmerman, 1989); however, structure can help provide needed support for the learner (McCaslin & Hickey, 2001), and students may find it challenging to switch between tasks that are highly structured to those that are open-ended.

With regard to the developmental nature of the learner, we found that most studies examined college and university undergraduates (59%). As with the well-structured tasks, this could again be a function of ease on the part of researchers using their own students. Particularly striking was that there were no studies with elementary school students and only one study that examined preschool children's regulation of behavior (Williford et al., 2013). Since many models of self-regulation are developmental (e.g., McCaslin & Hickey, 2001; Zimmerman, 1989), from this corpus of studies it may be difficult to make inferences about younger students' ability to self-regulate when participating in assessment. Thus, most of the evidence applies to older adolescents and young adults.

Relations Between Assessment and Self-regulation

Methodological Considerations

Before discussing the relation between participation in assessment and its effects on self-regulation, it is important to take into account how self-regulation is measured and what analyses, if any, are conducted to demonstrate this relation. In terms of measures of self-regulation, there were 17 studies that relied on self-report to measure self-regulation. For example, Virtanen and Nevgi (2010) used the Motivated Strategies for Learning Questionnaire (MSLQ; Pintrich, Smith, García, & McKeachie, 1993). These self-report methods are potentially problematic for two reasons. First, there is the potential that monomethod bias could positively influence the relation between the two different constructs (Campbell & Fiske, 1959; Spector, 1994; Williams, Cote & Buckley, 1989), with shared variance a result of using the same method (self-report in this case), rather than a function of a real relation between the two constructs. Second, specific to self-regulation, many have suggested that self-report may be a problematic method of measurement (e.g., Dinsmore et al., 2008; Veenman, 2011) because individuals are being asked to reflect on their own reflections, which requires good metacognitive and self-regulatory skills in the first place.

Further, while the relations described between participation and assessment could be influenced by the method of analysis, there was quite a diversity of both quantitative and qualitative approaches. Within this pool of studies there were case studies (Harris & Brown, 2013), thematic analysis (Tal, 2010), phenomenological examinations (Asghar, 2010), analyses of means and variances (i.e., means testing, ANOVA, regression [Violato & Lockyer, 2006]), and structural equation models (Xie & Andrews, 2012).

Self-regulatory Benefits

Turning to the relations themselves, there were a wide variety of benefits from participation in assessment with regard to self-regulation. These were related to what part of self-regulation was measured (i.e., cognitive, motivational, emotional, and behavioral). However, there were studies that demonstrated no positive effects and mixed effects on self-regulation.

Cognitive Benefits

Cognitive self-regulatory benefits of participating in assessment included improved monitoring, awareness, judgments of learning, and reflections on learning. These positive effects included increased monitoring and awareness during (a) participation in coursework (Andrade & Du, 2007), (b) working on sudoku puzzles (Barber et al., 2012), (c) practicing musical instruments (Cremaschi, 2012), (d) driving (Ishimatsu et al., 2010), and (e) taking standardized tests (Rizzo & Belfiore, 2013; Zou & Zhang, 2013). However, participants' reflections about assessment might not always be conscious or intentional. In interviews, participants in Sargeant et al.'s (2010) study indicated that monitoring did increase, but they were not necessarily aware that this was occurring. Thus, it is possible that self-report measures might underreport the relation between participation in assessment and the positive relation with monitoring.

There were also benefits in terms of judgments of learning and reflections on learning. These were evident during medical case-based scenarios (Casey et al., 2011; Dannefer & Prayson, 2013) and professional situations in medicine (Violato & Lockyer, 2006). Finally, there were also differences in how participants viewed the assessment itself. Harris and Brown (2013) examined student and teacher views of assessment (accountability versus improvement) and how this might influence self-regulation using case studies. This examination highlights the need to think not only about the characteristics of the assessment itself, but also teachers' and students' beliefs about the purpose of assessment and how that might relate to students' views on learning and knowledge more generally. This might be particularly salient with regards to self-regulation, since students' epistemic beliefs have been associated with self-regulation (Bråten & Strømsø, 2005; Hofer & Sinatra, 2010; Muis, 2007).

Motivational and Emotional Benefits

There were also positive benefits from participation in assessment for motivational components of self-regulation. These included general aspects of motivation (Asghar, 2010), self-efficacy (Bruning et al., 2013), goals (Mullins & Devendorf, 2007), and effort regulation (Steuer et al., 2013). Interestingly, Virtanen and Nevgi (2010) found that there were gender effects on motivational self-regulation, with females having higher levels of help seeking, perceptions of task value, and anxiety than males.

Benefits were found for controlling of anxiety (Hayes & Embretson, 2013), regulating emotional discomfort (Meng & Siren, 2012), and controlling disturbing emotions (Tapia & Panadero, 2010). Further, Williford et al. (2013) found that constant use of feedback for preschool children's behavior helped them develop their emotional regulation over that year of study. On one hand, it is certainly possible that specific kinds of participation in assessment can help with emotional regulation during that assessment, but on the other hand, assessment might elicit negative emotions in the first place, reducing positive benefits.

Behavioral Benefits

Behavioral benefits (i.e., better performance) were found during assessments of driving behavior (Meng & Siren, 2012), time spent practicing a musical instrument (Miksza, 2011), and cooperative classroom behavior (Schelfhout et al., 2004; Williford et al., 2013). Schelfhout et al.'s (2004) examination of cooperative behavior was particularly interesting because they found that teacher assessment was actually better than self-assessment for this particular facet of behavioral self-regulation. Referring back to Figure 9.3, this may be good evidence that including teacher feedback (i.e., environmental determinants) may facilitate overall SR over having only self-assessment, where environmental feedback is not available.

No or Mixed Benefits

While most studies provided evidence of positive benefits from participation in assessment on self-regulation (albeit sometimes only a weak relation [Andrade & Du, 2007; Tapia & Panadero, 2010]), some studies showed mixed benefits while others showed no benefits at all. Studies demonstrating no effects included Eva and Regehr's (2011) study with trivia questions, Ferrão's (2010) study with statistics tests, Lizzio and Wilson's (2013) study of course exams, Panadero et al.'s (2012) study of landscape identification, and Xie and Andrews' (2012) study of students preparing for standardized English-language examinations. Although these were a minority of studies, it is possible that publication bias might also influence the evidence in this pool (Duval & Tweedie, 2000; Easterbrook, Gopalan, Berlin, & Matthews, 1991). Specifically, studies that show no relation between participation in assessment and self-regulation would be much less likely to be published, resulting in a corpus of studies skewed toward a significant, positive relation between the two constructs.

The mixed effects studies provided some of the most interesting findings. Cremaschi (2012) found that there were positive benefits in terms of metacognitive self-regulation with self-assessment of piano practice, but no benefits in terms of motivational self-regulation. Tal's (2010) qualitative study indicated that only some of the participants benefited from self-assessment. Finally, Panadero et al. (2013) did not find any direct effects of teacher feedback with landscape identification, but did find interaction effects with how often (i.e., by occasion) students engaged with their teacher in that feedback (i.e., the number of times they interacted in the feedback process changed how the feedback affected their learning). Thus, some familiarity or practice effects with that feedback may be necessary to realize self-regulatory benefits, and additionally, there may be other, as yet unidentified, characteristics of the learner that might offer affordances to benefiting from participation in assessment.

CONCLUSIONS

While there is certainly evidence that participation in assessment can be beneficial in terms of self-regulation, the case is certainly not convincing that participation in assessment—whether it be self-assessment, peer assessment, teacher feedback, or computer feedback—necessarily fosters self-regulation. Indeed, some authors have indicated their own skepticism:

> Increasingly it is being recognized that self-assessment as "a process of personal reflection based on an unguided review of practice and experience for the purposes of making judgments regarding one's own current level of knowledge, skills, and understanding as a prequel to self-directed learning activities that will improve overall performance and thereby maintain competence" (Eva and Regehr 2007, p. 81) is inherently flawed.
>
> (Eva & Regehr, 2011, p. 312)

While this skepticism is warranted in light of the mixed findings, we consider that the issue of the relation between assessment (particularly students' role in assessment) and self-regulation is a conditional one. In other words, one's ability to self-regulate during and following participation in assessment depends on a variety of factors, including the developmental characteristics of the learner, the nature of the task and domain under consideration, and the regulatory outcome desired (i.e., cognitive, motivational, or behavioral).

It is critical to consider the multidimensionality of the relations between assessment and self-regulation (Figures 9.1 through 9.3). For example, a very young child may benefit very little from participation in assessment since he or she may not have fully or adequately developed SRL competencies. So, the learner characteristics (i.e., his or her development of self-regulatory skills and abilities) will dampen the influence of participation in assessment on SRL. However, an older student who has developed some self-regulatory skills and abilities may benefit from participation in assessment, if certain conditions are met. For example, participation in assessment for a middle school student may influence self-regulation only if there are scaffolds (e.g., teacher input or well-structured tasks) in place to facilitate that regulation (or co-regulation). However, too great a reliance on well-structured tasks or assessments may not even require the student to self-regulate compared to an ill-structured task or constructed response assessment where self-regulation is necessary during task performance. In the former situation, there is no need for self-regulation to occur so there would be little need for SRL to develop; whereas, in the latter case, there is at least the potential for the relation of assessment to self-regulatory skills and abilities to become evident.

Most interesting to us were studies such as Cremaschi's (2012) where there were mixed benefits depending on what SRL outcome was examined (i.e., cognitive versus motivational). This underscores the importance of clarifying the model or view of SRL one takes. If one took purely a cognitive view of Cremaschi's results, one might conclude that indeed there was a strong relation between participation in assessment and SRL, whereas a social-cognitive view would conclude that the relation was significantly weaker. In other words, the theoretical lens and view of SRL is highly important in considering the relation between assessment and SRL.

Given the tenuous and conditional nature of the relation between participating in assessment and self-regulation, we suggest some directions for future research that more systematically investigates these multidimensional relations.

Implications for Research and Practice

One way to frame a systematic set of studies to examine this relation is through developmental systems theory and methodology. Developmental systems theory has recently been used as a lens to examine motivation (Kaplan, Katz, & Flum, 2012) and metacognition, self-regulation, and self-regulated learning (Dinsmore, 2014). Three aspects of developmental systems theory should be considered as new research is planned: the nature of development, the nature of categories, and notions of causality.

First, with regard to development, future research should focus on differences within an individual over time (i.e., intra-individual development) (Pintrich, Anderman, & Klobucar, 1994). These studies, with a few exceptions (Williford et al., 2013) examined solely differences between individuals (i.e., inter-individual differences) (Weinert & Helmke, 1995). Additionally, there is a need to examine participation in assessment for younger children, as there was only one study that used participants at the elementary school level or younger (Williford et al., 2013). This is especially salient since many models of self-regulation (Zimmerman & Kitsantas, 1997) posit developmental shifts over the life span (e.g., from process goals to outcome goals).

Second, we need to determine whether the facets of participation in assessment and self-regulation can be meaningfully broken apart and studied in isolation (i.e., a Cartesian-split mechanistic approach) or whether elements of self-regulation and participation in assessment must be viewed more holistically to determine their effects (i.e., a relational view). The interaction effects found by Panadero et al. (2013) may indicate that it may not be wise to isolate variables, but rather consider sets of conditions (e.g., views of assessment, epistemic beliefs about knowledge, type of assessment response), instead of attempting to isolate variance using variance partitioning approaches (e.g., ANOVA). In particular, latent approaches such as structural equation modeling may be particularly helpful in addressing this need.

Third, we should investigate multiple aspects of causality. The assumption for many of these studies (and the framing for this chapter) is that participation in assessment may facilitate or cause changes in self-regulation. However, this relation may not be unidirectional; indeed, it may be reciprocal, indicating the need for large-scale longitudinal studies across a broad developmental spectrum. In addition to efficient causal mechanisms (i.e., phenomena outside a thing which causes change to the thing) already demonstrated in these studies (e.g., self-assessment causes an increase in monitoring [Grawitch et al., 2008]), material (i.e., the aspect or change is determined by what the thing is made of), final (i.e., change caused by the aim or purpose of a thing; function), and formal (i.e., change caused by the arrangement of a thing; structure) causality should also be investigated (Overton, 2014). For example, Harris and Brown's (2013) finding that views of assessment may change as the function of assessment changes indicates that final causality might be very important in investigating the relation between participation in assessment and self-regulation.

Given the tentative nature of our conclusions, we want to be cautious in suggesting implications for practice. However, the complex nature of the relation between assessment and SRL should underscore the notion that there is not likely a one-size-fits-all model of assessment that would benefit learners' SRL. Rather, there will be an increasing necessity for teachers to better understand the multidimensional aspects of these relations when planning both formative and summative assessment.

In our view, particularly with younger learners, we see no evidence that these learners will spontaneously self-regulate if they are asked to self-assess without any additional feedback (Figure 9.1). Given the overconfidence-underperformance effect found in the calibration literature (Dunlosky & Rawson, 2012), it seems unlikely most students would be capable of evaluating their own work. This approach also ignores the third self-regulatory component in Zimmerman's (1989) model. On the other hand, an approach in which learners do not engage in any self-assessment (Figure 9.2) will likely miss opportunities to promote both covert and behavioral self-regulation.

Based on the findings from this review, we suggest approaches similar to that in Figure 9.3 that emphasizes both self-assessment and teacher feedback. These approaches have the highest likelihood of engaging students in all three forms of SR which, in turn, should increase performance in those tasks. However, it may be important to more closely examine the quality of the teacher feedback, self-assessment method, and tasks, since the type or amount of feedback may be dependent on a variety of factors such as the characteristics of the learner (e.g., his or her knowledge level) and the nature of the teacher-student relationship.

REFERENCES

Alexander, P. A., Dinsmore, D. L., Parkinson, M. M., & Winters, F. I. (2011). Self-regulated learning in academic domains. In B. Zimmerman & D. Schunk (Eds.), *Handbook of self-regulation of learning and performance* (pp. 393–407). New York: Routledge.

American Educational Research Association, American Psychology Association, & National Council on Measurement in Education. (1999). *Standards for educational and psychological testing.* Washington, DC: American Educational Research Association.

* Andrade, H., & Du, Y. (2007). Student responses to criteria-referenced self-assessment. *Assessment & Evaluation in Higher Education, 32,* 159–181. doi:10.1080/02602930600801928

* Asghar, A. M. (2010). Reciprocal peer coaching and its use as a formative assessment strategy for first-year students. *Assessment & Evaluation in Higher Education, 35,* 403–417. doi:10.1080/02602930902862834

Bandura, A. (1986). *Social foundations of thought and action: A social cognitive theory.* Englewood Cliffs, NJ: Prentice-Hall.

*Barber, L. K., Grawitch, M. J., & Munz, D. C. (2012). Disengaging from a task: Lower self-control or adaptive self-regulation? *Journal of Individual Differences, 33,* 76–82. doi:10.1027/1614–0001/a000064

Boekaerts, M. (1995). Self-regulated learning: Bridging the gap between metacognitive and metamotivation theories. *Educational Psychologist, 30*, 195–200.

Borkowski, J. G. (1996). Metacognition: Theory or chapter heading? *Learning and Individual Differences, 8*, 391–402.

Bråten, I., & Strømsø, H. I. (2005). The relationship between epistemological beliefs, implicit theories of intelligence, and self-regulated learning among Norwegian postsecondary students. *British Journal of Educational Psychology, 75*, 539–565.

* Bruning, R., Dempsey, M., Kauffman, D. F., McKim, C., & Zumbrunn, S. (2013). Examining dimensions of self-efficacy for writing. *Journal of Educational Psychology, 105*, 25–38. doi:10.1037/a0029692

Campbell, D. T., & Fiske, D. W. (1959). Convergent and discriminant validation by the multitrait-multimethod matrix. *Psychological Bulletin, 56*, 81–105.

* Casey, D., Burke, E., Houghton, C., Mee, L., Smith, R., Van Der Putten, D., & . . . Folan, M. (2011). Use of peer assessment as a student engagement strategy in nurse education. *Nursing & Health Sciences, 13*, 514–520. doi:10.1111/j.1442–2018.2011.00637.x

* Cremaschi, A. (2012). The effect of a practice checklist on practice strategies, practice self-regulation and achievement of collegiate music majors enrolled in a beginning class piano course. *Research Studies in Music Education, 34*, 223–233. doi:10.1177/1321103X12464743

* Dannefer, E., & Prayson, R. (2013). Supporting students in self-regulation: Use of formative feedback and portfolios in a problem-based learning setting. *Medical Teacher, 35*, 655–660.

Dinsmore, D. L. (2014, August). Perspectives on learning in the 21st century: Examining changing constructs, methods, and contexts. In L. Fryer (Chair), *20th Century Models of Student Learning at a 21st Century Crossroad*. Symposium presented at the biennial meeting of the European Association for Research on Learning and Instruction for SIG 4 Higher Education, Leuven, Belgium.

Dinsmore, D. L., & Alexander, P. A. (2012). A critical discussion of deep and surface processing: What it means, how it is measured, the role of context, and model specification. *Educational Psychology Review, 24*, 499–567. doi:10.1007/s10648–012–9198–7

Dinsmore, D. L., & Alexander, P. A. (2015). A multidimensional investigation of deep-level and surface-level processing. *Journal of Experimental Education.* doi:10.1080/00220973.2014.979126

Dinsmore, D. L., Alexander, P. A., & Loughlin, S. M. (2008). Focusing the conceptual lens on metacognition, self-regulation, and self-regulated learning. *Educational Psychology Review, 20*, 391–409. doi:10.1007/s10648–008–9083–6

Dunlosky, J., & Rawson, K. A. (2012). Overconfidence produces underachievement: Inaccurate self evaluations undermine students' learning and retention. *Learning and Instruction, 22*, 271–280. doi:10.1016/j.learninstruc.2011.08.003

Duval, S., & Tweedie, R. (2000). Trim and fill: A simple funnel-plot–based method of testing and adjusting for publication bias in meta-analysis. *Biometrics, 56*, 455–463.

Easterbrook, P. J., Gopalan, R., Berlin, J. A., & Matthews, D. R. (1991). Publication bias in clinical research. *The Lancet, 337*, 867–872.

Eva, K. W., & Regehr, G. (2007). Knowing when to look it up: A new conception of self-assessment ability. *Academic Medicine, 82*, 81–84.

* Eva, K. W., & Regehr, G. (2011). Exploring the divergence between self-assessment and self-monitoring. *Advances in Health Sciences Education, 16*, 311–329. doi:10.1007/s10459–010–9263–2

* Ferrão, M. (2010). E-assessment within the Bologna paradigm: Evidence from Portugal. *Assessment & Evaluation in Higher Education, 35*, 819–830. doi:10.1080/02602930903060990

Gonzalez de Sande, J. C., & Ignacio Godino-Llorente, J. (2014). Peer assessment and self-assessment: Effective learning tools in higher education. *International Journal of Engineering Education, 30*, 711–721.

* Grawitch, M. J., Granda, S. E., & Barber, L. K. (2008). Do prospective workday appraisals influence end-of-workday affect and self-monitored performance? *Journal of Occupational Health Psychology, 13*, 331–344. doi:10.1037/1076–8998.13.4.331

* Harris, L., & Brown, G.T.L. (2013). Opportunities and obstacles to consider when using peer- and self-assessment to improve student learning: Case studies into teachers' implementation. *Teaching and Teacher Education, 36*, 101–111.

* Hayes, H., & Embretson, S. E. (2013). The impact of personality and test conditions on mathematical test performance. *Applied Measurement in Education, 26*, 77–88. doi:10.1080/08957347.2013.765432

Hofer, B. K., & Sinatra, G. M. (2010). Epistemology, metacognition, and self-regulation: musings on an emerging field. *Metacognition and Learning, 5*, 113–120.

* Ishimatsu, K., Miura, T., & Shinohara, K. (2010). Age influences visual attention characteristics among accident-free and accident-involved drivers. *Japanese Psychological Research, 52*, 186–200. doi:10.1111/j.1468–5884.2010.00437.x

Kaplan, A., Katz, I., & Flum, H. (2012). Motivation theory in educational practice: Knowledge claims, challenges, and future directions. In K. R. Harris, S. Graham, T. Urdan, S. Graham, J. M. Royer, & M. Zeidner (Eds.), *APA educational psychology handbook, Vol. 2: Individual differences and cultural and contextual factors* (pp. 165–194). Washington, DC: American Psychological Association.

Kim, M., & Ryu, J. (2013). The development and implementation of a web-based formative peer assessment system for enhancing students' metacognitive awareness and performance in ill-structured tasks. *Educational Technology Research and Development, 61*, 549–561.

Linn, R. L., & Gronlund, N. E. (2000). *Measurement and assessment in teaching* (8th ed.). Upper Saddle River, NJ: Merrill.

* Lizzio, A. A., & Wilson, K. (2013). Early intervention to support the academic recovery of first-year students at risk of non-continuation. *Innovations in Education & Teaching International, 50*, 109–120. doi:10.1080/14703297.2012.760867

McCaslin, M., & Hickey, D. T. (2001). Self-regulated learning and academic achievement: A Vygotskian view. In B. J. Zimmerman & D. H. Schunk (Eds.), *Self-regulated learning and academic achievement: Theoretical perspectives* (pp. 227–252). Mahwah, NJ: Lawrence Erlbaum.

McMillan, J. H. (2014). *Classroom assessment: Principles and practice for effective standards-based instruction* (6th ed.). New York, NY: Pearson.

* Meng, A., & Siren, A. (2012). Cognitive problems, self-rated changes in driving skills, driving-related discomfort and self-regulation of driving in old drivers. *Accident Analysis & Prevention, 49*, 322–329. doi:10.1016/j.aap.2012.01.023

* Miksza, P. (2011). The development of a measure of self-regulated practice behavior for beginning and intermediate instrumental music students. *Journal of Research in Music Education, 59*, 321–338.

Muis, K. R. (2007). The role of epistemic beliefs in self-regulated learning. *Educational Psychologist, 42*, 173–190.

* Mullins, M. E., & Devendorf, S. A. (2007). Assessing goal-directed attention as an indicator of self-regulation: A comparison of two approaches. *North American Journal of Psychology, 9*, 229–250.

Nicol, D. J., & Macfarlane, D. (2006). Formative assessment and self-regulated learning: A model and seven principles of good feedback practice. *Studies in Higher Education, 31*, 199–218.

Overton, W. F. (2014). Relational developmental systems and developmental science: A focus on methodology. In P. C. M. Molenaar, R. M. Lerner, & K. M. Newell (Eds.), *Handbook of developmental systems theory & methodology* (pp. 19–65). New York: Guilford. Press.

* Panadero, E., Tapia, J. A., & Huertas, J. A. (2012). Rubrics and self-assessment scripts effects on self-regulation, learning and self-efficacy in secondary education. *Learning and Individual Differences, 22*, 806–813.

* Panadero, E., Tapia, J. A., & Reche, E. (2013). Rubrics vs. self-assessment scripts effect on self-regulation, performance and self-efficacy in pre-service teachers. *Studies in Educational Evaluation, 39*, 125–132.

Parkinson, M. M., Dinsmore, D. L., & Alexander, P. A. (2010, May). *Calibrating calibration: Towards conceptual clarity and agreement in calculation.* Paper presented at the annual meeting of the American Educational Research Association, Denver.

Piaget, J. (1964). Part I: Cognitive development in children: Piaget development and learning. *Journal of Research in Science Teaching, 2*, 176–186.

Pintrich, P. R. (2004). A conceptual framework for assessing motivation and self-regulated learning in college students. *Educational Psychology Review, 16*, 385–407.

Pintrich, P. R., Anderman, E. M., & Klobucar, C. (1994). Intraindividual differences in motivation and cognition in students with and without learning disabilities. *Journal of Learning Disabilities, 27*, 360–370.

Pintrich, P. R., & De Groot, E. V. (1990). Motivational and self-regulated learning components of classroom academic performance. *Journal of Educational Psychology, 82*, 33–40.

Pintrich, P. R., Smith, D. A., García, T., & McKeachie, W. J. (1993). Reliability and predictive validity of the Motivated Strategies for Learning Questionnaire (MSLQ). *Educational and Psychological Measurement, 53*, 801–813.

Popham, W. J. (2011). *Classroom assessment: What teachers need to know* (6th ed.). Boston, MA: Pearson.

Puustinen, M., & Pulkkinen, L. (2001). Models of self-regulated learning: A review. *Scandinavian Journal of Educational Research, 45*, 269–286.

* Rizzo, K., & Belfiore, P. J. (2013). Pairing student-teacher conferencing and self-regulation to increase mathematics performance in middle school students at risk for academic failure. *Journal of Evidence-Based Practices for Schools, 14*, 30–50.

Sadler, P. M., & Good, E. (2006). The impact of self- and peer-grading on student learning. *Educational Assessment, 11*, 1–31.

* Sargeant, J., Armson, H., Chesluk, B., Dornan, T., Eva, K., Holmboe, E., & . . . van der Vleuten, C. (2010). The processes and dimensions of informed self-assessment: A conceptual model. *Academic Medicine, 85*, 1212–1220.

* Schelfhout, W., Dochy, F., & Janssens, S. (2004). The use of self, peer and teacher assessment as feedback system in a learning environment aimed at fostering skills of cooperation in an entrepreneurial context. *Assessment & Evaluation in Higher Education, 29*, 177–201. doi:10.1080/0260293042000188465

Spector, P. E. (1994). Using self-report questionnaires in OB research: A comment on the use of a controversial method. *Journal of Organizational Behavior, 15*, 385–392.

* Steuer, G., Rosentritt-Brunn, G., & Dresel, M. (2013). Dealing with errors in mathematics classrooms: Structure and relevance of perceived error climate. *Contemporary Educational Psychology, 38*, 196–210.

Suen, H. K. (2014). Peer assessment for massive open online courses (MOOCs). *International Review of Research in Open and Distance Learning, 15*, 312–327.

* Tal, C. (2010). Case studies to deepen understanding and enhance classroom management skills in preschool teacher training. *Early Childhood Education Journal, 38*, 143–152. doi:10.1007/s10643–010–0395-z

* Tapia, J. A., & Panadero, E. (2010). Effects of self-assessment scripts on self-regulation and learning. *Infancia y Aprendizaje, 33*, 385–397.

* Turner, J. E., & Husman, J. (2008). Emotional and cognitive self-regulation following academic shame. *Journal of Advanced Academics, 20*, 138–173.

Veenman, M. V. (2011). Alternative assessment of strategy use with self-report instruments: A discussion. *Metacognition and Learning, 6*, 205–211.

Vermunt, J. D. (2005). Relations between student learning patterns and personal and contextual factors and academic performance. *Higher Education, 49*, 205–234.

* Violato, C., & Lockyer, J. (2006). Self and peer assessment of pediatricians, psychiatrists and medicine specialists: Implications for self-directed learning. *Advances in Health Sciences Education, 11*, 235–244.

* Virtanen, P., & Nevgi, A. (2010). Disciplinary and gender differences among higher education students in self-regulated learning strategies. *Educational Psychology, 30*, 323–347.

Weinert, F. E., & Helmke, A. (1995). Interclassroom differences in instructional quality and interindividual differences in cognitive development. *Educational Psychologist, 30*, 15–20.

* Welsh, M. (2012). Student perceptions of using the PebblePad e-portfolio system to support self- and peer-based formative assessment. *Technology, Pedagogy and Education, 21*, 57–83.

Williams, L. J., Cote, J. A., & Buckley, M. R. (1989). Lack of method variance in self-reported affect and perceptions at work: reality or artifact? *Journal of Applied Psychology, 74*, 462.

* Williford, A. P., Vick Whittaker, J. E., Vitiello, V. E., & Downer, J. T. (2013). Children's engagement within the preschool classroom and their development of self-regulation. *Early Education & Development, 24*, 162–187. doi:10.1080/10409289.2011.628270

Winne, P. H. (1995). Inherent details in self-regulated learning. *Educational Psychologist, 30*, 173–187. doi:10.1207/s15326985ep3004_2

Winne, P. H., & Hadwin, A. F. (1998). Studying as self-regulated learning. *Metacognition in Educational Theory and Practice, 93*, 27–30.

Xie, Q., & Andrews, S. (2012). Do test design and uses influence test preparation? Testing a model of Washback with structural equation modeling. *Language Testing, 30*, 49–70.

Zimmerman, B. J. (1989). A social cognitive view of self-regulated academic learning. *Journal of Educational Psychology, 81*, 329–339. http://dx.doi.org/10.1037/0022–0663.81.3.329

Zimmerman, B. J., & Kitsantas, A. (1997). Developmental phases in self-regulation: Shifting from process goals to outcome goals. *Journal of Educational Psychology, 89*, 29–36.

Zimmerman, B. J., & Schunk, D. H. (2011). Self-regulated learning and performance: An introduction and an overview. In B. J. Zimmerman & D. H. Schunk (Eds.), *Handbook of self-regulation of learning and performance* (pp. 1–12). New York: Routledge.

* Zou, X., & Zhang, X. (2013). Effect of different score reports of web-based formative test on students' self-regulated learning. *Computers & Education, 66*, 54–63.

* *Indicates articles included in the table.*

10

TOWARD A MODEL OF STUDENT RESPONSE TO FEEDBACK

Anastasiya A. Lipnevich, David A. G. Berg, and Jeffrey K. Smith

INTRODUCTION

"This C can't be right. I'm an A student."

If you are a teacher at almost any level, you will have heard this protest. But you have probably never heard, "This A can't be right. I'm a C student." There have certainly been situations where students have felt this, but they hardly ever express this sentiment. The simple complaint that one has received a grade that is lower than expected yields a wealth of information. As teachers, it tells us that:

1) The student has a strong sense of self-efficacy. The student is willing to hold on to that sense in the face of evidence to the contrary;
2) The student may have some difficulties in assessing his or her own abilities, or the quality of his or her work;
3) The student is upset. The negative affect associated with the grade may make it difficult for the student to effectively process any other aspect of this instructional setting; and
4) There is a disconnect that needs resolution.

In life, we receive feedback in many different settings (Kluger & DeNisi, 1996). We bake a pie that does not come out right; we pursue a relationship and get a positive response; or we submit a written piece of work and hear that our ideas have been well received. In some settings, we eagerly await the feedback; in others, we dread it. Some of us may generally like getting feedback, whereas others may not. Memories of our own student days allow us as teachers to empathise with our students' feelings about receiving feedback. Teacher feedback about student performance on a task is a powerful trigger of student emotions, which, in turn, have the potential to affect student engagement with the feedback, and ultimately, influence student achievement (Linnenbrink & Pintrich, 2002; Lipnevich & Smith, 2009b; also Vogl & Pekrun, this volume). This chapter focuses on how feedback, in the form of grades, comments, scores, or praise/ criticism may relate to how students respond to feedback (emotionally, cognitively, and behaviorally), and what they do with that feedback. We examine some of seminal research in the field, synthesize recent work done on the topic, and then present a tentative model for understanding how learners respond to formative feedback.

There have been numerous meta-analyses on the efficacy of formative feedback in student learning (Bangert-Drowns, Kulik, Kulik, & Morgan, 1991; Crooks, 1988; Hattie & Timperley, 2007; Kingston & Nash, 2011; Kluger & DeNisi, 1996; Shute, 2008). What we find in this meta-analytic work is that formative feedback is effective most of the time, and that certain characteristics of feedback are more effective than others. Our focus here is on a much narrower, but important, aspect of the feedback/learning process. We are interested in the inner workings of formative feedback, in particular the specific ways by which feedback influences what students do with the feedback and how it may affect their academic outcomes.

We begin this chapter by examining three seminal articles on formative feedback, two that present models that have been highly influential in the field (Hattie & Timperley, 2007; Kluger & DeNisi, 1996), and a third that presents a concrete set of recommendations for formative feedback based on a review of the research literature (Shute, 2008). We then examine a number of studies that look at the impact of formative feedback in experimental and quasi-experimental settings. The findings speak to the issue of the importance of how feedback is received by learners. In the final section, we propose a model of feedback that focuses on the relationship between the nature of the feedback and how students respond to it, and show how it relates to classroom practice and outcomes.

UNFOLDING FORMATIVE FEEDBACK

Ever since Scriven (1967) differentiated formative and summative evaluation, and Bloom (1970) applied the distinction to assessment, there have been various terms for the notion of feedback, formative assessment, and assessment for learning. Shute (2008) uses the phrase formative feedback, defining it as "information communicated to the learner that is intended to modify his or her thinking or behavior for the purpose of improving learning" (p. 154). We use this term and definition in this chapter.

The essential role of feedback in day-to-day instruction has been studied extensively over the past 30 years. Several meta-analyses and compendiums of reviewed literature have all come to a consistent conclusion: feedback works (Black & Wiliam 1998; Crooks 1988; Hattie & Timperley 2007; Shute, 2008). However, there are subtleties about *how and when* feedback works that are sometimes lost in the more general finding of feedback's overall effectiveness. In fact, some meta-analytic work suggests that feedback may negatively affect performance in up to one-third of cases (e.g., Bangert-Drowns et al. 1991; Kluger & DeNisi 1996). For example, in their meta-analysis of research in formative assessment, Kingston and Nash (2011) found that formative assessment practices, including feedback, were more effective in language arts than in mathematics or science. Studies have begun to unveil the exact mechanisms of how specific types of feedback may affect performance. In this section we discuss several models that describe how formative feedback may influence achievement and review recommendations for optimal uses of formative feedback.

Feedback Intervention Theory

In their review of the literature, Kluger and DeNisi (1996) found that in roughly one-third of the studies they examined, feedback had a negative impact on subsequent performance. In an effort to understand why feedback appeared to be effective in some settings and not in others, the authors developed what they call Feedback Intervention Theory (FIT) (Kluger & DeNisi, 1996, 1998). Their model focuses on feedback that provides information about the discrepancy between the individual's current level of performance and the desired standard of performance. Having understood the discrepancy between current and desired performance, the individual can: (a) choose to work harder, (b) lower the standard, (c) reject the feedback altogether, or (d) abandon their efforts to achieve the standard. Option selection depends upon how committed individuals are to the goal, whether the goal is clear, and how likely success will be if more effort is applied.

In FIT theory, when an individual receives feedback indicating that a goal has not been met, attention can be focused at one of three levels (broadly speaking): (a) the details of how to do the task, (b) the task as a whole, and (c) processes that the individual engages in doing the task (meta-task processes). Kluger and DeNisi (1996) argue that individuals typically process feedback at the task level, but that the feedback can influence the level at which the task is received and attended to. They note that if a task is well understood by the individual, receiving feedback containing details on how to perform the task can be detrimental to performance as such details draw attention away from the actual performance of the task (Kluger & DeNisi, 1998).

The FIT model provides meaningful insight into the processes that underlie how feedback influences performance; the impact of Kluger and DeNisi's work can be seen in much of the theoretical work that followed it (e.g., Hattie & Timperley's [2007] model). The FIT model is explicit and testable (Krenn, Wurth, & Hergovich, 2013), but the influence of a more industrial/organizational perspective on feedback (as compared to one directly related to issues of schooling) is obvious. There is a strong focus, for example, on feedback that lets individuals know if they are doing a particular task at a sufficient level. The assumption is that the individual knows how to do the task; hence, the purpose of the feedback concerns whether performance is up to expectation. But this is not often the case in educational settings. In classroom instruction, one is typically interested in the development of new skills, not the demonstration or repetition of ones that have already been mastered. Also, the FIT model does not place strong emphasis on the context in which the feedback is received, nor characteristics of the individual receiving the feedback, either in general, or in relation to the subject area and nature of the task under consideration. So, although one can consider FIT an excellent jumping-off point, there is room left for theoretical developments in the domain of instruction and learning.

Hattie and Timperley's Model

The next model considered is the work of Hattie and Timperley (2007). The influence of this seminal work is testified to by the fact that it had received well over 3,000 citations by the time of this writing. Hattie and Timperley take the same basic starting point as Kluger and DeNisi (1996), noting the main purpose of feedback is to close the gap between where an individual currently is and where he or she should be. Hattie and Timperley break this notion down into three issues: (a) the student's current status, (b) the desired status, and (c) the steps necessary to close the gap. Similarly to Kluger and DeNisi, they argue that students can increase their efforts, lower their expectations, or abandon their goals in response to less-than-ideal feedback. The researchers also add that the student can employ more effective strategies under the direct influence of the teacher, who may modify goals and help students to use better strategies to achieve the goal. With the concepts of goals, current status, and routes to close the gap in hand, Hattie and Timperley argue that each of these concepts can work at four different levels: (a) the task, (b) the processes that produce successful performance on the task, (c) self-regulation, and (d) the self. Thus, one might reasonably see the Hattie and Timperley typology of feedback as an elaboration of the Kluger and DeNisi model that is particularly well suited to the exigencies of the classroom setting.

Per Hattie and Timperley (2007), feedback at the level of the task can be as simple as informing the student as to whether an answer was correct or not (verification feedback), up to discussing why a right answer in a multiple-choice item was right and why the wrong answers were wrong. One also needs to take into consideration the nature and complexity level of the work on which feedback is being given. Knowledge level feedback at the correct/incorrect level is typically not generalizable beyond the specifics of the piece of information (e.g., knowing when WWI began will not help a student know when the War of the Roses ended). On the other hand, knowing if you managed to hit a golf ball straight can be very helpful in future attempts, so there are plentiful exceptions to the notion that verification feedback is limited in applicability.

Feedback about the processes that produced the performance on the task relates more to promoting a deeper understanding of the task than task level feedback. Such strategies might include error detection on the part of the student. It is interesting to note on this point that there is a bit of a 'flip' between the perspective of Kluger and DeNisi (1996) and Hattie and Timperley (2007). Kluger and DeNisi talk about a focus on the task as being at a higher level than a focus on the details of the task—a focus that might actually detract from performance. On the other hand, Hattie and Timperley argue that feedback with a focus on how successful performance on the task is produced, rather than how well the student did on the task represents a higher level of cognitive focus. This, perhaps, is due to the fact that in educational settings, the goal is to get the student to master the task, and in industrial settings, the goal is more commonly focused on seeing how well or how frequently the task can be performed.

Hattie and Timperley's third level of feedback (i.e., self-regulation) fundamentally does not exist in the Kluger and DeNisi model. Self-regulation involves a set of behaviors that students might engage in when learning or when performing a task. These include goal setting, planning, progress monitoring, help-seeking, evaluation of success, and attributions of success (Zimmerman, 2000; see also Dinsmore & Wilson, this volume). Feedback at a self-regulatory level might concern the students' plans for revising a piece of written work or reminding them to ask whether an answer to a math problem is reasonable in a given situation.

The fourth level of feedback concerns the self and is directly related to the Kluger and DeNisi (1996) model. Praise at this level would involve statements such as, "You're such a good mathematician!" or "You're a natural writer!" It draws students' attention away from the task and toward themselves as individuals. Hattie and Timperley (2007) point out that one should differentiate between self level praise that focuses on ability and praise that focuses on effort, and note that this distinction is often missed in the literature. Hattie and Timperley note that with the exception of feedback focused on the self, the nature and level of optimal feedback will depend upon what is being learned, where the student is in the acquisition of knowledge and skills, and the context of the learning situation.

Shute's Guidelines for Formative Feedback

Shute (2008) took a more applied approach to reviewing the literature on feedback. She synthesized research on formative feedback and generated a set of guidelines on how it should be created and delivered. Shute begins with a more elaborate definition of feedback than Kluger and DeNisi (1996) or Hattie and Timperley (2007). She identifies information concerning the gap between current and desired status as one type of feedback, and then includes two additional types of feedback: feedback that reduces the cognitive load of the student by providing needed information (e.g., a worked out example of how to approach a type of mathematics problem) and feedback that corrects misconceptions or misinterpretations.

Building on work from Bangert-Drowns et al. (1991), Shute (2008) argues that feedback provides learners with verification that their answer is correct (or not) and elaboration provides help to the learner on how to get to the correct answer. She examines the research literature concerning: (a) the impact of length and complexity of feedback, (b) the relationship between the nature and challenge of goals and learner motivation, (c) feedback as scaffolding, (d) the timing effects of feedback, (e) the influence of the ability level of the learner, (f) the learner's goal orientation (i.e., performance or learning), and (g) whether feedback was normative or self-referenced. Shute's guidelines for the optimal use of formative feedback are presented in four tables, one for things to do, one for things to avoid doing, one concerning the issue of timing, and one concerning individual differences in characteristics among learners.

With regard to things *to do*, Shute (2008) recommends (a) a focus on the task and not on the learner; (b) elaborated feedback presented in chunks that the student can handle; (c) being clear and straightforward; (d) being objective; and (e) focusing on learning goals. With regard to things not to do, she recommends: (a) not comparing students to others; (b) avoiding grades in most instances; (c) not using praise in most situations; (d) not using oral feedback; and (e) not focusing excessively on anaysing errors. With regard to issues of timing the provision of feedback, Shute recommends: (a) adjusting the timing to the situation, in particular, using immediate feedback for difficult tasks, but delayed for simple tasks; (b) using immediate feedback for procedural or motor skills; and (c) using delayed feedback to promote transfer. Her final set of recommendations concerns tailoring feedback to the needs of the individual learner: (a) stronger students can benefit from delayed and more indirect feedback whereas weaker students benefit more from immediate and specific feedback; and (b) low achieving students also appear to benefit from scaffolding and elaboration.

Finally, Shute (2008) calls for more research on individual differences among learners with regard to feedback and more work on motivational aspects of how feedback works. In particular, she calls for more work on the relationship between affect and outcomes.

Summary and Analysis

What can be seen in each of these three reviews is an attempt to move beyond questions of whether formative feedback works, and to ask when, where, and how it works. Formative feedback is no longer a blunt instrument that can be applied whenever learning needs a boost; we now have a much more nuanced and complex understanding of the role of formative feedback in instruction. But there are aspects of this work that need to be challenged and refined. To begin, there is the notion that feedback consists primarily of letting learners know where they are now and where they need to be.

Consider feedback in the development of writing skills. Unless one is working at a very micro level with a learning objective (e.g., proper use of the semicolon or developing good opening sentences), there is no real notion of what a goal is, nor a very definite notion of where the student is today. The whole process can be a movable feast, and the teacher needs to work within such a setting. If a student is writing about a topic he or she is very familiar with, and if the student is feeling venturesome, then an exciting and insightful piece might evolve. But if the student is not highly motivated, something less proficient will be seen. So what is the role of the teacher here? Is it to provide information on how good this piece is and how the piece could be improved? Is it to provide feedback that will facilitate the next piece of writing? Or to provide feedback as scaffolding the motivational zone of proximal development (Brophy, 2008)? If the underlying lesson concerned building paragraphs, but the student presents a stunningly good description of his grandfather, does the teacher ignore the lesson for the teachable moment of exploring the quality writing that the student has done?

Thus, given the complexity of learning goals and options, a sufficient formative feedback model must effectively address what goes on in schools. As Shute (2008) points out, learners vary and a model that does not take into account the manifold variations one encounters in students will be severely limited. One area of limitation that is not addressed extensively in the work reviewed here is how the learner receives the formative feedback. Student reactions (e.g., welcoming, resistance) can make all the difference in the world with regard to the efficacy of the feedback.

A CLOSE LOOK AT SOME RECENT WORK ON FORMATIVE FEEDBACK ON WRITING

There is a general consensus in the field that in order to be effective, feedback must encourage active processing of information on the part of the learner (Hattie & Timperley, 2007; Shute, 2008). In our research (Lipnevich, McCallen, Miles, & Smith, 2014; Lipnevich & Smith, 2009a, 2009b), we found that if students did not successfully engage with the feedback that they received, feedback would not enhance student learning. We examined differential effects of feedback on university students' performance, demonstrating that detailed comments, specific to an individual's work, were highly conducive to improvement on a writing task (Lipnevich & Smith, 2009a, 2009b). In the study, students participated in an essay writing and revision task. They were randomly assigned to one of three conditions: no feedback, detailed feedback from the instructor, or detailed feedback allegedly from a computer, but which was actually delivered by the experimenter, masked as computer-generated. Each of these three conditions was crossed with two factors: praise (receiving praise or not) and grade (receiving a preliminary grade or not). We found that detailed descriptive feedback was most effective when delivered without praise or grades. Interestingly, we also found that students who perceived the detailed feedback as coming from an instructor regarded it as more helpful than those who perceived the feedback as coming from a computer. Additionally, if praise was delivered along with grades, the negative impact of grades was ameliorated. It should be noted that in this study, students received their feedback in a scheduled class session as a part of the course they were taking, and were given the opportunity to increase their score by working on their draft based on the feedback received. Thus, the motivation to engage with the feedback was high.

In follow-up focus group discussions with students who participated in the experiment (Lipnevich & Smith, 2009b), students unanimously concurred that detailed comments were the more effective form of feedback. Grades were seen as potential obstacles to improvement, particularly by students who believed they received them from the instructor. Students who received high marks on the first draft of their work often said that they had little motivation to modify their draft, and some even indicated that they were afraid that changes might result in lower grades. Students who received low initial grades were often greatly demoralized by seeing their marks. Students considered praise pleasant but the least influential form of feedback, useful only for balancing the demotivating effect of grades. Taken together, these findings present strong evidence that providing university students with individualized, descriptive feedback specific to their work, and allowing them to make revisions based on that information, leads to significant improvement in writing performance.

These findings led us to consider the key player in the feedback scenario: the teacher providing the feedback. Unarguably, educators play a crucial role in providing effective feedback to improve student writing. Teachers value the practice of giving feedback (Brown, Harris, & Harnett, 2012; Hyland & Hyland, 2001) and actively use feedback in the process of teaching writing to students (Matsumura, Patthey-Chavez, Valdes, & Garnier, 2002), realizing that the quality of feedback messages influences the extent of students' writing improvement (Reid, Drake, & Beckett, 2011; Ruiz-Primo & Furtak, 2007; Wiliam, Lee, Harrison, & Black, 2004). Kingston and Nash (2011) noted that the quality of feedback and the way it is used matters greatly and that the implementation of feedback is often "left to the discretion of the teachers implementing formative assessment" (p. 34). Hence, carefully constructed feedback messages on students' written work can lead to enhanced performance, and educators' roles in this process are important. However, providing high quality feedback responses in communicating with students about their writing, such as delivering extensive, individualized comments, is time-consuming and may be impractical for teachers in many situations. The question arises as to whether more efficient forms of feedback can be found.

To that end, we designed a study that investigated the effects of what we refer to as generic, standardized written feedback on student performance (Lipnevich et al., 2014). Two forms of standardized feedback (a detailed rubric and essay exemplars) were utilized in an experimental design with undergraduate students at three U.S. college campuses. Students completed a draft of an essay as part of their course requirements and were then randomly assigned to receive a detailed rubric, essay exemplars, or both a rubric and essay exemplars for use in revising their work. The results revealed that all three conditions led to improvement that was significant and strong in terms of effect size. The rubric condition produced the biggest net growth in performance, with students who received rubric alone generating an effect size of $d = 1.0$, as compared to the other two conditions (effect sizes of $d \approx 0.50$ in each condition).

Andrade and her colleagues (Andrade, 2005, 2008; Andrade, Du, & Mycek, 2010) note that effective rubrics in writing clarify learning goals, guide educators' feedback on students' progress toward the goals, and allow students to judge their final writing product based on the degree to which they have met the learning goals. However, in her research, provision of rubrics as part of a feedback process varied in their effectiveness according to how they were used and the characteristics of the student participants. We speculate that the essential difference between her findings and ours is that we were working with students who were older and more advanced with regard to general academic abilities. Panadero and Jonsson (2013) reviewed the literature on using rubrics as formative feedback in a variety of settings, and generally found rubrics to be effective. However, in a quasi-experimental study, rubrics were found to not be effective in helping students to develop a multimedia presentation (Panadero, Alonso-Tapia, & Reche, 2013).

To our knowledge, no studies have previously examined rubrics solely as a form of feedback in lieu of detailed, individualized feedback on a writing draft (as opposed to *prior* to writing an initial draft). Possibly, when working with relatively sophisticated students, presenting a detailed rubric only after students complete a draft of their essay makes this tool more effective. Particularly interesting is that the rubric condition produced better results than the rubric plus exemplars condition. Based on discussions with the participants, we speculate that students see exemplars as more useful to them, when in fact, rubrics are. We believe that students prefer exemplars because following a model is easier than assessing one's work against rubrics; however, assessing one's work against rubrics may well lead to a deeper level of processing by the students.

These studies and those of our colleagues in the field led us to the belief that we need a model to better understand the mechanisms through which learners receive feedback, how they react to it, and what they do about it. The following section presents an initial attempt at the development of such a model.

TOWARD A MODEL OF THE IMPACT OF FEEDBACK ON STUDENTS

There have been a number of models of feedback presented in the research literature (Bangert-Drowns et al., 1991; Hattie & Timperley, 2007; Narciss & Huth, 2004) with varying degree of success in terms of utility and applicability. With a number of models extant, one might reasonably ask why another is being developed. The answer here is relatively straightforward. The models that exist provide a good general overview of the feedback/learning process, but do not focus on how the feedback is received by the individual. What are the characteristics of individuals that lead to different reactions to feedback? How can feedback be tailored to a given situation to maximize the reception that it receives? Is feedback primarily a function of the nature of the setting or a more enduring characteristic of the individual?

Our goal in the model is to examine what occurs in the feedback/learning process between the time when the student receives the feedback and the time when the student takes action on that feedback (or chooses not to do so). That is, we want to consider what causes students to eagerly engage the feedback they receive, reject it, or simply ignore it. If feedback is not acted upon, it is not likely to be effective in enhancing learning. Thus, we see this model as an attempt to explicate the process that underlies the efficacy (or lack thereof) of feedback. The model (Figure 10.1) begins with the context within which the student/feedback interaction takes place. Not all feedback is the same and not all students are the same. Feedback that is effective for one student may not be effective for the next; the efficacy will depend on a number of factors. We examine each component of the model in order.

Context

To begin, assessments have consequences for students, and these consequences affect how the student behaves on the assessment (Smith & Smith, 2002; Wolf & Smith, 1995), and how he or she receives the assessment feedback. A student waiting on college entrance examination scores is in an entirely different state of mind than a student showing a math problem to a teacher as she walks through the classroom aisles. High consequence or high-stakes feedback is much more likely to produce anxiety than low consequence feedback. Does the student view this feedback as formative or summative? Is it supportive or judgmental? The setting in which the feedback is received matters as well. Is this feedback coming from a teacher whom the student trusts and likes, or is it impersonal, or coming from a source that the student views as untrustworthy, or even antagonistic toward the student's best interests? Contexts differ and they matter.

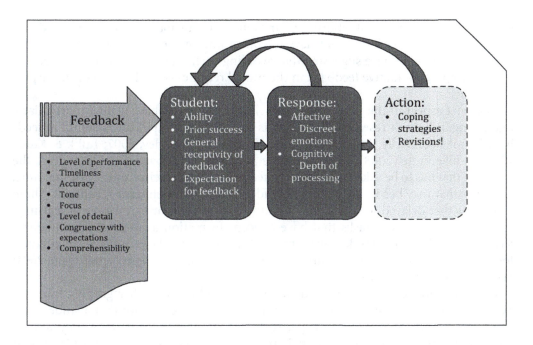

Figure 10.1 Feedback—Student Interaction Model

Yang and Carless (2013) attempt to integrate the plethora of factors that influence successful provision of feedback into a manageable taxonomy, with context of feedback taking a prominent position. They discuss three main areas of dialogic feedback that have to be considered when educators design instructional feedback: cognitive, social-affective, and structural. In regards to the cognitive dimension, students should be able to utilize feedback from peers and teachers to self-regulate their own performance. This process can be facilitated by trusting relationships among participants (social-affective dimension). Further, the strategy of using a multistage assignment or using technology to facilitate feedback use (structural dimension) also influences the overall acceptance and utilization of feedback messages. Other studies also show that context of feedback has the potential of changing the degree to which it will be utilized (Carless, Salter, Yang, & Lam, 2011).

Feedback

The model starts with feedback that is presented to students. Feedback can vary on a number of characteristics, and the individual efficacy of these for learning has been examined in a number of studies and summarized elsewhere (Hattie & Timperley, 2007; Kingston & Nash, 2011). The first thing we might consider is the degree of success in demonstrating that learning has occurred communicated by the feedback. In other words, according to the feedback being given, how close has the student gotten to the learning objective? Feedback on an assignment, essay, or test that is highly positive and communicates excellent performance is likely to be received more positively than feedback that suggests poor performance (Lipnevich & Smith, 2009b). For example, studies have shown that individuals tend to (a) process positive information about one's performance much faster than negative information and (b) take credit for their successes while attributing their failures to outside influences (Sedikides & Strube, 1997). Feedback does not have to communicate a level of performance at all, and our own studies have suggested that avoiding such evaluations is effective. Nonetheless, keeping evaluative feedback in the model requires consideration of this aspect of feedback.

The next aspect in the model is the timeliness of the feedback. This is particularly interesting in light of research that suggests that the most rapid turnaround on feedback is not necessarily the most effective (Hattie & Timperley, 2007; Kulik & Kulik, 1988). While Shute (2008) provides advice as to when feedback should be given, the question that has to be asked here is: Is the feedback being received at the optimal time, whatever that may be? In her review of evidence on the timeliness of feedback, Shute concludes that delayed feedback may be superior for promoting transfer of learning, especially in relation to tasks that have concept formation as their goal. Immediate feedback, on the other hand, may be more efficient, particularly in the short run and for procedural skills (i.e., programming and mathematics) (Corbett & Anderson, 2001; Ferguson, 2011; Schroth, 1992).

A third characteristic of the feedback is its accuracy. A teacher grading multiple essays over a weekend may well miss or misread an excellent point that a student has made, and make a comment on the paper that is not relevant, or perhaps is quite simply wrong. Brackett, Floman, Ashton-James, Cherkasskiy, and Salovey (2013) present evidence showing that teacher emotions affect accuracy of marking. The authors reveal that emotions may bias the grades teachers assign to their students, such that positive and negative emotions influence grade assignment in emotion-congruent ways. Another aspect to feedback accuracy has to do with its *honesty*. If a student gets a "Great Job!" on the top of a paper that he/she knows is less than a great job, then all the feedback contained therein could be called into question. As teachers, we all know that there are some written papers that have little in the way of strengths, and yet markers often do not want to be unduly negative (Nikolakakos, Reeves, & Shuch, 2012). Nonetheless, being honest with the student may really be the best route toward student growth (Boekaerts & Cascallar, 2006).

This leads to the issue of tone, which may be *the* most critical aspect of feedback, with regard to the emotional reaction that students experience. There is a world of difference between, "This doesn't make sense," and "I'm having some trouble following your argument here." One can expect different emotional reactions to "another simple math mistake," and "Tom, please check these answers for simple math errors." The difference is in the *tone* with which honest feedback is given. Furthermore, some students may have more difficulty than others in properly perceiving the intended tone of the written feedback (Brookhart, 2011).

A fifth issue is the focus of feedback. Feedback might focus upon what Hattie and Timperley (2007) refer to as the task level of the work, or it might focus on issues of self-regulation, or it may focus on trivial aspects of the student work. For example, feedback might be focused on the reasonableness of answers in math problems, or the story line in a piece of writing. Imagine the difference in formative feedback that pointed out all the grammatical errors in a piece of writing compared to one that encouraged the student to do a read-through of a piece of writing concentrating on catching and correcting grammatical errors, and perhaps provided an example of how to do so (Ferguson, 2011).

A sixth aspect of feedback is level of detail, which has to do with the sheer magnitude and specificity of the feedback that the student receives. This might range from a simple letter or number grade on a third grade math assignment to pages of scholarly commentary on a Ph.D. thesis draft. Has the student received enough feedback to effectively engage the material, or so much that the student is overwhelmed? Finding the right level of detail can be a challenge for the senders of feedback, often because teachers or peers may not have a good sense of how it is being received (Brookhart, 2011; Ferguson, 2011).

A seventh aspect of feedback is comprehensibility, which refers to accessibility and appropriateness of the feedback for the student receiving it. Is the sophistication of the feedback consonant with the ability of the student to process it? "Subject/verb agreement" as a comment on an essay is not helpful to a student who does not know what subject/verb agreement means and who may lack the resources or motivation to find out. This characteristic of feedback concerns the ability of the student to cognitively process the level at which the feedback is being delivered (Ferguson, 2011).

The final aspect of feedback is its congruency with expectations. Congruency with expectations is jointly a function of the nature of the feedback and the nature and disposition of the student. We include it with feedback because the student dispositions are reasonably stable and outside the immediate control of the feedback giver in any one feedback situation, whereas the feedback itself is variable. Congruence between the feedback itself and the students' expectations for feedback is important. At any level of performance, there may be a match or a mismatch between what the student receives and what he or she expected. Such mismatches may have very different consequences for how the feedback is received and acted upon (Eva, Armson, Holmboe, Lockyer, Loney, Mann, & Sargeant, 2012). For example, the literature on self-enhancement that comes from the field of economics shows that, in the context of performance assessment, feedback signaling performance below the expected level combined with one's perception of personal responsibility for that performance is the key trigger of self-enhancement (Audia & Brion, 2007). As a result, individuals will be more likely to attend selectively to positive indicators and ignore negative indicators (Baumeister & Cairns, 1992), or take full credit for successes and search for external excuses for failures (Bettman & Weitz, 1983; Jordan & Audia, 2012).

The feedback side of the model is complex because there are a number of issues to consider that can be reasonably expected to impact on how the feedback is received. What is critical is to acknowledge that not all feedback is the same with regard to how students will react to it.

Student

The second important factor in the feedback/response model is the student, each of whom is likely to react differently to the same feedback (Brown & Hirschfeld, 2007; Carless, 2006; Poulos & Mahony, 2008; Weaver, 2006). Some students are going to be generally more or less receptive to feedback, while others may react unpredictably and possibly inconsistently depending on the context and the nature of the feedback (Eva et al., 2012). In looking at how students respond to feedback, an interesting question arises almost immediately: Are some students generally more receptive to feedback across a variety of settings than other students? Or, is response to feedback highly dependent on the context and nature of the situation (Harris, Brown, & Harnett, 2014)?

Just like other psychological concepts, (e.g., self-efficacy, academic emotions) feedback may have to be examined as situated in two different planes; that is, (a) state, transient and situation-specific response to feedback and (b) trait, a more typical response to feedback. The latter characteristic is likely to be significantly impacted by subjective beliefs, just like academic emotions (Goetz, Lüdtke, Nett, Keller, & Lipnevich, 2013; Goetz et al., 2014; see also Vogl & Pekrun, this volume). This distinction between state and trait response to feedback is consistent with dual-process models of higher-order cognition. According to these models, individuals' state response to feedback would primarily reflect System 1 processes (fast, automatic, impulsive, perceptual), whereas a trait response to feedback would be indicative of System 2 processes (slow, controlled, reflective, analytic) (Kahneman, 2011; Strack & Deutsch, 2004). The question that we should ask ourselves is: How modifiable is this characteristic? Let us look at the characteristics of the student that might affect how he or she responds to feedback.

The first factor to consider is the current ability of the student with regard to the material under consideration. Is this a highly able student or one who struggles in this area? This is critical because the ability of the student is going to influence the design of the feedback for the student. More able students might be generally more receptive to feedback on their work, whereas weaker students may be more tentative or resistant toward feedback, although the literature is not robust on this matter (Dutro & Selland, 2012; Eva et al., 2012; Reay & Wiliam, 1999).

A second factor, closely related to the student ability, is the student's prior success. None of us like to do things that we do poorly and feedback that is going to point out our lack of success, especially if delivered in a social (e.g., classroom) setting (Stiggins, 2007). In contrast, if students feel and perceive that this is an area in which they do well and are successful, then the feedback they are about to receive is more likely to be welcomed. Thus, prior success sets the stage for how current feedback is received by the student.

A third characteristic of students concerning feedback is their general receptivity to feedback. Does a particular student enjoy getting feedback in general or dread it? Or does this depend on the setting for the student? General receptivity of feedback was found among a group of college undergraduates to be a more powerful predictor of emotional reaction to the feedback than feedback's congruency with expectations (Smith, Berg, Kendall-Smith, & Lipnevich, 2013). This result is consistent with Harris et al. (2014), which showed New Zealand schoolchildren had a generally positive disposition toward receiving feedback. Hence, it would seem to be a mistake to ignore students' general tendency to be positive or negative toward feedback.

In sum, the student side of the model has to do with how able the student is, what his or her history of feedback is within this subject area, whether the student generally likes or dislikes getting feedback, and what kind of feedback the student expects to receive for this work.

Response

By 'response' to feedback, we mean how the student receives the feedback both affectively and cognitively. It is what occurs within the self as the student peruses the feedback. The first response may well be an emotional one of joy, sadness, anger, or anxiety. It may be cognitive as well, including disbelief, agreement, realization that a point is well made by the teacher, or a belief that the teacher didn't understand what the student was saying. The affective side of this equation would be a series of discrete emotions. Studies have consistently shown that discrete emotions of the same valence have differential links with achievement and other outcomes (Goetz, Zirngibl, Pekrun, & Hall, 2003; Pekrun, Goetz, Titz, & Perry, 2002). Pekrun's (2006) control-value theory posits that feedback should be expected to affect students' emotions, which, in turn, will affect achievement-related behaviors. More specifically, students' academic achievement should positively relate to enjoyment and pride, and negatively to anger, anxiety, shame, and hopelessness (see Vogl & Pekrun, this volume).

The cognitive side of the equation also concerns a number of distinct items. First, the student has to comprehend the feedback. This means not just "does the student understand what is here," but also, and perhaps more importantly, "does the student take the feedback on board; does the student take the time and have the ability to process the feedback?" Processing includes depth of processing. Is the student able to not only see how the feedback applies to the situation at hand, but how that information can be generalized to new and different situations?

The cognitive and affective aspects of the response to feedback interact with one another. The more the student understands what the teacher is saying, the more likely the student is to have a positive response. And the more the student has a positive response to the feedback, perhaps because of its tone, the more likely the student is to spend the time and effort to comprehend what is being said (Brookhart, 2011).

Action

The final aspect of the model concerns the action that the student takes with regard to the feedback. Feedback that is not acted upon is essentially useless for student performance. So the question becomes one of what the student does with the feedback. This is dependent upon a number of factors (e.g., the degree to which the student has received useful and usable information about his/her performance; whether the student has comprehended that information; the tone of the feedback, its congruence with expectations, and the general receptivity of the student to feedback). These factors will hopefully put the student in a frame of mind where he/she is disposed to work sufficiently hard with the feedback received so as to improve performance.

Actions also include the general coping approach that students take. As we have already mentioned, feedback has the potential of eliciting strong, and sometimes negative, affect. The student's coping strategy determines whether or not a student takes action and what kind of action it will be. There are many different taxonomies of coping, but most models encompass Lazarus and Folkman's (1984) initial distinction between problem-focused and emotion-focused coping (Folkman & Moskowitz, 2004, provide a review of coping models). A further distinction is often made between emotion-focused and avoidant coping (Parker & Endler, 1996). These coping styles aim to reduce stress that could have been caused by feedback in different ways. In problem-focused coping, individuals deal adaptively with stress by resolving the root cause of the stressful situation and, consequently, improving their performance (e.g., going carefully through comments and methodically addressing each one). In contrast, in emotion-focused coping, students would tend to maladaptively focus on their emotional responses to the stressor. So, a student may feel sorry for him- or herself, or could blame the instructor who provided negative feedback. Likewise, in avoidant coping, students would maladaptively try to avoid the feedback stressor as much as possible (e.g., going shopping or playing video games instead).

Overall, coping styles have been linked with personality traits, life satisfaction, academic achievement, and a range of well-being measures; hence, it is not too fanciful to speculate that they should affect the coping response of students as a result of feedback received (Carver, & Connor-Smith, 2010; Diener, Lucas, & Scollon, 2006; MacCann, Fogarty, Zeidner, & Roberts, 2011).

A Walk-through of the Model

Feedback is received in context. It may be a process of feedback and a subject area where the student is comfortable or not about what is occurring. The feedback will have some level of consequence associated with it. It may be viewed as entirely supportive or it may have great import for the student and, thus, be anxiety-producing. It may be in a classroom environment that is friendly to feedback or be a competitive space and source of social comparison. Within the context, the feedback is delivered to the student. It may be detailed or sparse, aligned with the student's level or not. It may be painfully honest but delivered in a strongly supportive fashion, or be unpleasantly judgmental. It may match what the student is expecting or be wildly discrepant. The student receiving it will either be strong in this subject or not, have had good experiences with feedback, or perhaps be generally wary of getting feedback.

When the student receives the feedback, these feedback design factors come into play. They produce affective and cognitive responses that are often tightly interdependent. The student may experience dismay, joy, a feeling of pride, or embarrassment; worry about how parents or peers will react; have a sense of having disappointed the teacher or themselves in their performance, or of having made the teacher proud. In reading through the feedback, the student might be baffled by the comments or fully appreciative of them. He/she might only be able to generate a surface comprehension of what the teacher means or might be able to use the teacher comments as a springboard to an in-depth comprehension of where to go next. From this well-spring of affect and cognition, the student acts adaptively or maladaptively. He/she works on the assignment, processes the suggestions made by the teacher or perhaps discounts what has been said in order to save face and self-esteem. And finally, both the response to the feedback and the actions that the student takes reflect on who the student is, what the student knows and can do in this area, and how the student will respond in the next cycle of feedback. The feedback may trigger responses which generalize across settings and subject areas or remain specific to situations highly similar to this one.

It is our hope that this model helps to unfold the complexities of how students respond to feedback and highlight productive areas for future research. In the absence of empirical verification of the proposed model, we can only speculate as to how this might impact teachers in classrooms. But it is possible to look at the model, and reflect on what is established in the literature on formative feedback. We would suggest that, in addition to the excellent recommendations provided by Shute (2008), teachers are mindful of what they say to students via formative feedback. One might use the metaphor of a conversation in thinking about formative feedback. The teacher has begun the conversation by providing instruction and asking the student to generate a product (e.g., an essay, a lab report, a mathematics homework assignment) based on that instruction. The student picks up the conversation and responds to the request of the teacher. Now the ball is back in the court of the teacher. What will the teacher say next to the student? What will be the nature and content of that communication? For a student at the high school or tertiary level, this communication back from the teacher, tutor, or professor may be the only direct communication with the teacher for a substantial period of time. They are only words, but they come from us as teachers, and we know that the words of teachers can be powerful; we should choose them carefully.

REFERENCES

Andrade, H. G. (2005). Teaching with rubrics: The good, the bad, and the ugly. *College Teaching, 53*, 27–30.

Andrade, H. (2008). Self-assessment through rubrics. *Educational Leadership, 65*(4), 60–63.

Andrade, H. L., Du, Y., & Mycek, K. (2010). Rubric-referenced self-assessment and middle school students' writing. *Assessment in Education: Principles, Policy, & Practice, 17*(2), 199–214.

Audia, P. G., & Brion, S. (2007). Reluctant to change: Self-enhancing responses to diverging performance measures. *Organizational Behavior and Human Decision Processes, 102*(2), 255–269.

Bangert-Drowns, R. L., Kulik, C. L. C., Kulik, J. A., & Morgan, M. T. (1991). The instructional effect of feedback in test like events. *Review of Educational Research, 61*, 213–238.

Baumeister, R. F., & Cairns, K. J. (1992). Repression and self-presentation: when audiences interfere with self-deceptive strategies. *Journal of Personality and Social Psychology, 62*(5), 851.

Bettman, J. R., & Weitz, B. A. (1983). Attributions in the board room: Causal reasoning in corporate annual reports. *Administrative Science Quarterly*, 165–183.

Black, P., & Wiliam, D. (1998). Inside the black box: Raising standards through classroom assessment. *Phi Delta Kappan, 80*(2), 139–148.

Bloom, B. S. (1970). Toward a theory of testing which includes measurement, evaluation, and assessment. In M. C. Wittrock & D. E. Wiley (Eds.), *The evaluation of instruction* (pp. 25–50). New York, NY: Holt, Rinehart, & Winston.

Boekaerts, M., & Cascallar, E. (2006). How far have we moved towards the integration of theory and practice in self regulation? *Educational Psychology Review, 18*(3), 199–210. doi:10.1007/s10648–006–9013–4

Brackett, M. A., Floman, J. L., Ashton-James, C., Cherkasskiy, L., & Salovey, P. (2013). The influence of teacher emotion on grading practices: A preliminary look at the evaluation of student writing. *Teachers and Teaching: Theory and Practice, 19*(6), 634–646. doi:10.1080/13540602.2013.827453

Brookhart, S. M. (2011). Educational assessment knowledge and skills for teachers. *Educational Measurement: Issues and Practice, 30*(1), 3–12.

Brophy, J. (2008). Developing students' appreciation for what is taught in school. *Educational Psychologist, 43*(3), 132–141.

Brown, G.T.L., Harris, L. R., & Harnett, J. (2012). Teacher beliefs about feedback within an assessment for learning environment: Endorsement of improved learning over student well-being. *Teaching and Teacher Education, 28*(7), 968–978. doi:10.1016/j.tate.2012.05.003

Brown, G.T.L., & Hirschfeld, G.H.F. (2007). Students' conceptions of assessment and mathematics: Self-regulation raises achievement. *Australian Journal of Educational and Developmental Psychology, 7*, 63–74.

Carless, D. (2006). Differing perceptions in the feedback process. *Studies in Higher Education, 31*(2), 219–233.

Carless, D., Salter, D., Yang, M., & Lam, J. (2011). Developing sustainable feedback practices. *Studies in Higher Education, 36*(4), 395–407.

Carver, C. S., & Connor-Smith, J. (2010). Personality and coping. *Annual Review of Psychology, 61*, 679–704.

Corbett, A. T., & Anderson, J. R. (2001). Locus of feedback control in computer-based tutoring: Impact on learning rate, achievement and attitudes. In *Proceedings of ACM CHI 2001 conference on human factors in computing systems* (pp. 245–252). New York: ACM Press.

Crooks, T. J. (1988). The impact of classroom evaluation practices on students. *Review of Educational Research, 58*(4), 438–481.

Diener, E., Lucas, R. E., & Scollon, C. N. (2006). Beyond the hedonic treadmill: Revising the adaptation theory of well-being. *American Psychologist, 61*(4), 305–331.

Dutro, E., & Selland, M. (2012). "I Like to Read, but I Know I'm Not Good at It": Children's perspectives on high-stakes testing in a high-poverty school. *Curriculum Inquiry, 42*(3), 340–367.

Eva, K. W., Armson, H., Holmboe, E., Lockyer, J., Loney, E., Mann, K., & Sargeant, J. (2012). Factors influencing responsiveness to feedback: on the interplay between fear, confidence, and reasoning processes. *Advances in Health Sciences Education, 17*(1), 15–26.

Ferguson, P. (2011). Student perceptions of quality feedback in teacher education. *Assessment & Evaluation in Higher Education, 36*(1), 51–62.

Folkman, S., & Moskowitz, J. T. (2004). Coping: Pitfalls and promise. *Annual Review of Psychology, 55*, 745–774.

Goetz, T., Frenzel, A. C., Hall, N. C., Nett, U. E., Pekrun, R., & Lipnevich, A. A. (2014). Types of boredom: An experience sampling approach. *Motivation and Emotion, 38*(3), 401–419.

Goetz, T., Lüdtke, O., Nett, U. E., Keller, M. M., & Lipnevich, A. A. (2013). Characteristics of teaching and students' emotions in the classroom: Investigating differences across domains. *Contemporary Educational Psychology, 38*(4), 383–394.

Goetz, T., Zirngibl, A., Pekrun, R., & Hall, N. C. (2003). Emotions, learning and achievement from an educational–psychological perspective. In P. Mayring & C. von Rhoeneck (Eds.), *Learning emotions: The influence of affective factors on classroom learning* (pp. 9–28). Frankfurt am Main: Peter Lang.

Harris, L. R., Brown, G. T., & Harnett, J. A. (2014). Understanding classroom feedback practices: A study of New Zealand student experiences, perceptions, and emotional responses. *Educational Assessment, Evaluation and Accountability, 26* (2), 107–133.

Hattie, J., & Timperley, H. (2007). The power of feedback. *Review of Educational Research, 77*(1), 81–112.

Hyland, F., & Hyland, K. (2001). Sugaring the pill: Praise and criticism in written feedback. *Journal of Second Language Writing, 10*(3), 185–212.

Jordan, A. H., & Audia, P. G. (2012). Self-enhancement and learning from performance feedback. *Academy of Management Review, 37*(2), 211–231.

Kahneman, D. (2011). *Thinking, fast and slow*. London: Penguin Books.

Kingston, N., & Nash, B. (2011). Formative assessment: A meta-analysis and a call for research. *Educational Measurement: Issues and Practice, 30*(4), 28–37.

Kluger, A. N., & DeNisi, A. (1996). The effects of feedback interventions on performance: A historical review, a meta-analysis, and a preliminary feedback intervention theory. *Psychological Bulletin, 119*(2), 254.

Kluger, A. N., & DeNisi, A. (1998). Feedback interventions: Toward the understanding of a double-edged sword. *Current Directions in Psychological Science, 7*(3), 67–72.

Krenn, B., Wurth, S., & Hergovich, A. (2013). The impact of feedback on goal setting and task performance: Testing the feedback intervention theory. *Swiss Journal of Psychology, 72*(2), 79–89.

Kulik, J. A., & Kulik, C. L. C. (1988). Timing of feedback and verbal learning. *Review of Educational Research, 58*(1), 79–97.

Lazarus, R. S., & Folkman, S. (1984). *Stress, appraisal, and coping*. New York: Springer.

Linnenbrink, E. A., & Pintrich, P. R. (2002). Achievement goal theory and affect: An asymmetrical bidirectional model. *Educational Psychologist, 37*(2), 69–78.

Lipnevich, A. A., McCallen, L. N., Miles, K. P., & Smith, J. K. (2014). Mind the gap! Students' use of exemplars and detailed rubrics as formative assessment. *Instructional Science, 42*(4), 539–559.

Lipnevich, A. A., & Smith, J. K. (2009a). The effects of differential feedback on student examination performance. *Journal of Experimental Psychology: Applied, 15*(4), 319–333.

Lipnevich, A. A., & Smith, J. K. (2009b). "I really need feedback to learn": Students' perspectives on the effectiveness of the differential feedback messages. *Educational Assessment, Evaluation and Accountability, 21*(4), 347–367.

MacCann, C., Fogarty, G. J., Zeidner, M., & Roberts, R. D. (2011). Coping mediates the relationship between emotional intelligence (EI) and academic achievement. *Contemporary Educational Psychology, 36*(1), 60–70.

Matsumura, L. C., Patthey-Chavez, G. G., Valdes, R., & Garnier, H. (2002). Teacher feedback, writing assignment quality, and third-grade students' revision in lower- and higher- achieving urban schools. *The Elementary School Journal, 103*(1), 3–25.

Narciss, S., & Huth, K. (2004). How to design informative tutoring feedback for multimedia learning. In H. M. Niegemann, D. Leutner, & R. Brünken (Eds.), *Instructional design for multimedia learning* (pp. 181–195). Münster: Waxman.

Nikolakakos, E., Reeves, J. L., & Shuch, S. (2012). An examination of the causes of grade inflation in a teacher education program and implications for practice. *College and University, 87*(3), 2–13.

Panadero, E., Alonso-Tapia, J., & Reche, E. (2013). Rubrics vs. self-assessment scripts effect on self-regulation, performance and self-efficacy in pre-service teachers. *Studies in Educational Evaluation, 39*(3), 125–132.

Panadero, E., & Jonsson, A. (2013). The use of scoring rubrics for formative assessment purposes revisited: A review. *Educational Research Review, 9*, 129–144.

Parker, J. D. A., & Endler, N. S. (1996). Coping and defense: An historical overview. In M. Zeidner & N. S. Endler (Eds.), *Handbook of coping: Theory, research, application* (pp. 3–23). New York: Wiley.

Pekrun, R. (2006). The control-value theory of achievement emotions: Assumptions, corollaries, and implications for educational research and practice. *Educational Psychology Review, 18*(4), 315–341.

Pekrun, R., Goetz, T., Titz, W., & Perry, R. P. (2002). Academic emotions in students' self-regulated learning and achievement: A program of qualitative and quantitative research. *Educational Psychologist, 37*(2), 91–105.

Poulos, A., & Mahony, M. J. (2008). Effectiveness of feedback: The students' perspective. *Assessment & Evaluation in Higher Education, 33*(2), 143–154.

Reay, D., & Wiliam, D. (1999). 'I'll be a nothing': structure, agency and the construction of identity through assessment [1]. *British Educational Research Journal, 25*(3), 343–354.

Reid, J. L., Drake, S., & Beckett, D. (2011). Exploring teacher and administrator perceptions of assessment in the face of new assessment policies. *Canadian Perspectives: Education Coast to Coast to Coast, 1*(1). Retrieved from http://www.canadianperspectivesjournal.ca/uploads/1/5/8/2/15827834/1-1-1-sm.pdf

Ruiz-Primo, M. A., & Furtak, E. M. (2007). Exploring teachers' informal formative assessment practices and students' understanding in the context of scientific inquiry. *Journal of Research in Science Teaching, 44*, 57–84.

Schroth, M. L. (1992). The effects of delay of feedback on a delayed concept formation transfer task *Contemporary Educational Psychology, 17*(1), 78–82.

Scriven, M. (1967). The methodology of evaluation. In R. Tyler, R. Gagne & M. Scriven (1967) *Perspectives on curriculum evaluation* (AERA Monograph Series—Curriculum Evaluation). Chicago: Rand McNally and Co.

Sedikides, C., & Strube, M. J. (1997). Self-evaluation: To thine own self be good, to thine own self be sure, to thine own self be true, and to thine own self be better. *Advances in Experimental Social Psychology, 29*, 209–269.

Shute, V. J. (2008). Focus on formative feedback. *Review of Educational Research, 78*(1), 153–189.

Smith, J. K., Berg, D., Kendall-Smith, M., & Lipnevich, A. A. (2013). Response to feedback: How we perceive what we receive. Paper presented at annual meeting of the New Zealand Association for Research in Education, Dunedin, NZ.

Smith, L. F., & Smith, J. K. (2002). The relationship of test-specific motivation and anxiety to test performance. *Psychological Reports, 91*, 1011–1021.

Stiggins, R. (2007). Assessing through the student's eyes. *Educational Leadership, 64*(8), 22–26.

Strack, F., & Deutsch, R. (2004). Reflective and impulsive determinants of social behavior. *Personality and Social Psychology Review, 8*(3), 220–247.

Weaver, M. R. (2006). Do students value feedback? Student perceptions of tutors' written responses. *Assessment & Evaluation in Higher Education, 31*(3), 379–394.

Wiliam, D., Lee, C., Harrison, C., & Black, P. (2004). Teachers developing assessment for learning: Impact on student achievement. *Assessment in Education, 11*, 49–64.

Wolf, L. F., & Smith, J. K. (1995). The consequence of consequence: Motivation, anxiety, and test performance. *Applied Measurement in Education, 8*, 227–242.

Yang, M., & Carless, D. (2013). The feedback triangle and the enhancement of dialogic feedback processes. *Teaching in Higher Education, 18*(3), 285–297.

Zimmerman, B. J. (2000). Attaining self-regulation: A social cognitive perspective. In M. Boekaerts & P. R. Pintrich (Eds.), *Handbook of self-regulation* (pp. 13–39). San Diego, CA: Academic Press.

11

STUDENT DISHONESTY IN THE FACE OF ASSESSMENT

Who, Why, and What We Can Do About It

Tamera B. Murdock, Jason M. Stephens,
and Morgan M. Grotewiel

Academic assessment serves numerous functions: providing feedback for future instruction; communicating information about students' achievement; facilitating placement decisions; documenting accomplishments for a wider audience; and, especially in the USA, evaluating the yearly progress of teachers and school districts. Although cheating is a problem on external assessments such as national exams, the focus of this chapter is on internal assessments teachers design or select, because cheating in this context more immediately disrupts the critical feedback function of assessment.

We begin with a review of the behaviors that constitute academic dishonesty and the prevalence of these behaviors. Subsequently, we examine research that informs our understanding of academic dishonesty through various theoretical lenses, including personality theories, achievement motivation theories, and theories of moral development and neutralization. We next review the literature on contextual factors influencing academic dishonesty, and conclude with a brief summary of suggestions for classroom practice.

TYPES OF ACADEMIC DISHONESTY

Academic dishonesty can be conceptualized as any dishonest or unfair act intended to produce a more favorable outcome. More narrowly defined, 'cheating' behaviors result in students gaining assessment 'points' in a way that is against policy or regulation. In keeping with much of the literature, we use 'cheating' interchangeably with 'academic dishonesty.'

Cheating behaviors range from the seemingly innocuous (e.g., resubmitting a paper originally written for another class without the instructor's permission) to the extreme (e.g., stealing an exam key). Numerous scholars (Newstead, Franklyn-Stokes, & Armstead, 1996; Pavela, 1997; Stephens, Young, & Calabrese, 2007) have created typologies to help bring some conceptual order to this diverse domain. Pavela (1997) described four general types of academic dishonesty: (1) cheating—"using or attempting to use any unauthorized materials, information, or study aids in any academic exercise" (e.g., using "cheat sheets" during an exam); (2) fabrication—the "intentional and unauthorized falsification or invention of any information or citation in an academic exercise" (e.g., falsifying lab results or references); (3) facilitating academic dishonesty—"intentionally or knowingly helping or attempting to help another to [cheat, fabricate, or plagiarize]"; and (4) plagiarism—"intentionally or knowingly representing the words or ideas of another as one's own in any academic exercise" (pp. 104–105). Other similar typologies (e.g., Newstead et al., 1996) also capture cheating that alters the assessment context in one's favor (e.g., lying for an extension) without resorting to actually using information that is false or not one's own.

The rise (and now ubiquity) of the Internet and other digital technologies over the past two decades has led researchers to distinguish between conventional or traditional cheating and digital or online cheating (Stephens et al., 2007). This distinction is really one of means and not type; dishonesty in the above typologies can be carried out via conventional or digital means. However, these typologies do not explicitly capture 'paid contract cheating,' such as the recent example involving the use of online ghost-writing services by hundreds of university students in Australia (Visentin, 2015).

PREVALENCE OF ACADEMIC DISHONESTY

Although the term epidemic has been used to characterize the problem of academic cheating since the 1980s (Haines, Diekhoff, LaBeff, & Clark, 1986, p. 342), the exact prevalence is difficult to gauge because of a reliance on self-reporting and the lack of agreed-upon definitions. Within these limitations, several seminal large-scale studies can help us estimate the cheating prevalence across academic levels.

Our literature review yielded only one large-scale study (Brandes, 1986) assessing self-reported cheating among elementary students. The sample included 1,037 sixth grade students (i.e., 11- to 12-year-olds) from 45 elementary schools and 2,265 high school students (76% from Grade 11, age 17–18) from 105 high schools in California. Both age groups indicated that they engaged in the same three (of 11) behaviors with the highest frequency, though rates were higher among the high school students: plagiarism, 42% versus 52%; copying off another person during a test, 39% versus 75%; using crib notes during an exam, 28% versus 74%. Moreover, whereas 86% of the elementary students indicated that they had witnessed someone cheat during an examination, almost all (97%) high school students had witnessed it.

Although it is imprudent to generalize from a single study—conducted decades ago in one country—these results suggest that academic dishonesty occurs among relatively young learners, increases with age, and is witnessed by students at very high rates, which may suggest that more students cheat than are willing to admit to it.

Middle and High School Students

The Josephson Institute of Ethics has surveyed a nationally representative group of U.S. high school students biannually since 1998. In 2006, the survey was distributed to both middle and high school students. Of the 1,800-plus middle school students in Grades 6–8, 38% admitted to having cheated on an examination in the past year versus 60% of the over 34,000 high school students (Josephson Institute of Ethics, 2006). Admitted Internet plagiarism rates were 24% and 33%, respectively. Between 2006 and 2010, the rates of these behaviors remained within 4 points of the baseline rates, suggesting little change in cheating prevalence, given the +/- 3% margins of error (Josephson Institute of Ethics, 2006, 2008, 2010). Notably, however, exam cheating rates were only 51% in the 2012 survey, suggesting a potential decline in this behavior, while Internet plagiarism rates remained relatively constant (Josephson Institute of Ethics, 2012). These data also provide direct evidence that cheating is underestimated in self-reports: over 25% of the students said they lied on at least one question on this survey.

Although the vast majority of research on high school cheating has been in the United States, the problem is not unique to that nation. On a retrospective survey of New Zealand adults (Colmar Brunton, 2012), 52% of participants indicated that they had cheated during high school on an exam or homework assignment. In a recent survey of 92 junior and senior high school 'high-achieving' Hong Kong students, 90% of the students admitted to engaging in at least one of the nine assessed cheating behaviors, with the highest rates of cheating occurring on out of class work (i.e., homework, papers) followed by in-class examinations (Nora, 2009). In contrast, only 19% of Taiwanese high school students admitted to cheating on an exam or quiz (Tsai, 2012). Although these studies also provide evidence for the international scope of classroom dishonesty, given the different sampling techniques and survey questions employed, strong claims are not possible concerning cultural differences in cheating prevalence.

University Students

One of the largest and longest-running studies of academic dishonesty aggregates cross-sectional data from an eight year time period (2003–2010) on 149,161 university students in the United States and Canada (McCabe, Butterfield, & Treviño, 2012). An average of 65% of students admitted to at least one of the nine behaviors surveyed, with 42% collaborating when not permitted; 36% copying a few sentences in a paper without attribution; 30% receiving test answers or questions from someone who had already taken the test; and 14% copying from another student on a test or exam.

Cross-cultural comparisons of cheating are more prevalent at the university level than among younger students. Notable is a study with 1,097 university junior, senior, and graduate level students in Hong Kong that was based on McCabe et al.'s (2012) work. Ma, McCabe, and Liu (2013) found that 70%–80% of the students copied or collaborated on out of class work and just under 50% admitted to having copied from another student during an exam and/or brought unauthorized notes. A similar investigation among 2,068 Taiwanese college students found that approximately 85% of students had cheated on a test at least once, and close to 80% had cheated on assignments (Lin & Wen, 2007).

In addition to these large-scale surveys, numerous smaller scale studies shed light on differences in student beliefs and behaviors across various regions of the world. For example, Stephens, Romakin, and Yukhymenko (2010) reported higher rates of cheating and more favorable attitudes towards it among Ukrainian versus U.S. university students. A similar discrepancy was found in a comparison of 1,443 U.S. business students with 192 from Poland (Lupton, Chapman, & Weiss, 2000) with more cheating and tolerance of it among Polish students. Hence, there is consistent evidence of high cheating rates across university students from a range of cultures in industrialized nations.

PERSONALITY PREDICTORS OF ACADEMIC DISHONESTY

Personality theorists study internal, individual forces (e.g., traits, attitudes) that predict future behavior (Society for Personality and Social Psychology, 2015). Although psychological researchers debate the malleability of personality traits (e.g., Helson,

Jones, & Kwan, 2002; Helson & Kwan, 2000), a recent meta-analysis suggested that personality changes over time and is shaped by experience (Roberts, Walton, & Viechtbauer, 2006); thus, there is hope that even students inclined to cheating may respond favorably to anti-cheating initiatives and classroom practices that encourage learning. Below we briefly describe the research on cheating that is framed with one of three broad personality paradigms before turning a more focused attention to several specific personality variables (e.g., impulsivity) that serve as logical points for intervention.

Broad Personality Paradigms

A recent meta-analysis synthesized 17 studies that have examined cheating among high school and college students from the vantage of the *Big Five* personality factors (i.e., extraversion, agreeableness, conscientiousness, openness to experience, and neuroticism) (Giluk & Postlethwaite, 2015). Conscientiousness and agreeableness emerged as the strongest predictors of less self-reported cheating. Neuroticism (i.e., low emotional stability and a tendency to experience unpleasant emotions), openness to experience (i.e., tendency to seek out and integrate experiences), and extraversion (i.e., positive emotions, energy, assertiveness, sociability) were not reliably related to cheating.

A second typology, the *Dark Triad*, refers to a personality cluster of three unique but overlapping characteristics: narcissism, Machiavellianism, and psychopathy (Paulhus & Williams, 2002). Narcissism is defined by grandiosity, entitlement, dominance, and superiority. Machiavellianism involves a proclivity towards coldness, manipulation, and exploitation. Psychopathy is characterized by high impulsivity and thrill-seeking and low empathy and anxiety. Although distinct, these characteristics are likely to occur together, with moderate to strong correlations among them (e.g., Paulhus & Williams, 2002). Evidence from two Canadian studies suggests that (a) psychopathy predicts increased cheating above and beyond the Big Five personality factors and several types of perfectionism (Nathanson, Paulhus, & Williams, 2006) and (b) the effect of psychopathy is mediated by unrestrained achievement and moral inhibition (Williams, Nathanson, & Paulhus, 2010), suggesting that people with more psychological symptomatology cheat because they single-mindedly pursue achievement with little concern for the moral implications of their behavior. Menon and Sharland (2011) found that another 'dark' personality trait, Machiavellianism, uniquely predicted cheating beyond narcissism, academic entitlement, and academically dishonest attitudes. Together, these results suggest that academic cheating is associated with some personality traits generally deemed negative by society.

Finally, people with Type A personalities are easily aroused, competitive, and aggressive, whereas people with Type B personalities are more easygoing and creative (Davis, Pierce, Yandell, Arnow, & Loree, 1995). In several experimental studies, college students with Type A personalities cheated more than students with Type B personalities (Davis et al., 1995; Perry, Kane, Bernesser, & Spicker, 1990). However, self-report data have shown no effect (Huss, Curnyn, Roberts, & Davis, 1993) or negative effects (Weiss, Gilbert, Giordano, & Davis, 1993) of Type A personality on cheating, making it hard to reach a definitive conclusion about 'Type,' but also alerting us to the potential confounds of method (self-report versus experiments with behavioral outcomes) in this research.

Other Personality Traits

Sensation-seeking, Impulsivity, and Self-control

Sensation-seeking (i.e., the need to have exciting, novel, or intense experiences) and impulsivity (i.e., the tendency to act without thinking) tend to be highly correlated (McTernan, Love, & Rettinger, 2014), and self-control (i.e., the ability to resist impulses in the face of external demands) tends to inversely and strongly correlate with impulsivity (Duckworth & Kern, 2011). As theorized, impulsivity, sensation-seeking, and low self-control have all been found to predict cheating behavior in most studies (Anderman, Cupp, & Lane, 2009; Bolin, 2004; DeAndrea, Carpenter, Shulman, & Levine, 2009; McTernan et al., 2014; Tibbetts & Myers, 1999). For example, among a sample of adults, McTernan et al. (2014) found sensation-seeking and impulsivity predicted five types of cheating, including school cheating. Likewise, Anderman et al. (2009) reported that impulsivity predicted even higher levels of cheating among high school students who had already reported extensive cheating. Finally, Bolin (2004) found low self-control to be associated with more favorable attitudes toward cheating and increased cheating behavior among university students.

Locus of Control

Locus of control concerns individuals' feelings of control over their own lives and life events: as people's perceived locus of control becomes more internal/less external, they tend to have more actual self-control (Rotter, 1966). The vast majority of studies of academic cheating among high school and college students find that people with a stronger external locus of control are more likely to cheat (Forsyth, Pope, & McMillan, 1985; Karabenick & Srull, 1978; Leming, 1980).

Across the personality literature, the evidence suggests that students with higher levels of cognitive and emotional regulation and those who assume greater responsibility for their behavior (i.e., internal locus of control and conscientiousness) are less likely to engage in academically dishonest behaviors. Beyond these factors, most evidence for personality predictors of cheating is fairly weak (see Whitley, 1998, for a thorough review).

Achievement Motivation and Cheating

There is a general consensus among achievement motivation theorists that a person's perceived competence to complete a task (i.e., self-efficacy) and their reasons for engaging or not engaging in the task are two central determinants of their achievement behavior (e.g., Reeve, 2014). Similarly, one's academic confidence and academic purpose have both been reliably linked to students' tendency to cheat (Murdock & Anderman, 2006).

Academic Aptitude and Confidence

In a study of university students, those with lower previous academic accomplishment reported cheating more frequently than higher ability students (Newstead et al., 1996). However, this association was moderated by gender, such that cheating was more common for males with low ability than females with the same aptitude, with gender differences disappearing at higher ability levels. Similarly, Tang and Zuo (1997) found that male cheaters had lower GPAs than male non-cheaters, but there was no difference in GPA for females. Numerous other studies have documented small to moderate inverse correlations between academic competence and cheating at middle school (Anderman & Midgley, 2004), high school (Finn & Frone, 2004), and university (Finn & Frone, 2004; Michaels & Miethe, 1989; Roig & DeTommaso, 1995; Scheers & Dayton, 1987); these relationships were sometimes moderated by variables such as gender (Scheers & Dayton, 1987), perceived performance goal structure (Scheers & Dayton, 1987), school identification (Finn & Frone, 2004), and self-efficacy (Finn & Frone, 2004). Furthermore, in one experimental study, when university students were given the opportunity to cheat in six self-grading situations, rates of dishonesty were higher among lower achieving students (Ward & Beck, 1990). Several correlational (Roberts, Anderson, & Yanish, 1997) and experimental (Williamson & Assadi, 2005) studies have found no relationship between GPA and cheating.

One possible explanation for the few non-significant findings in studies of GPA and cheating may be a failure to include information on the academic norms of the students in the study. For example, in the Brandes's (1986) survey discussed earlier, stratified cluster sampling was used to capture schools with a range of average achievement levels on the state assessment. Schools were then grouped into one of five performance quintiles. Across all quintiles, there was the expected inverse relationship between GPA and reported cheating. However, comparisons between students attending high schools in Q1 (lowest quintile), Q3 (middle quintile), and Q5 (upper quintile) yielded several interesting findings. Although various methods of cheating on exams occurred at higher rates in Q5 schools compared to Q1 schools, the discrepancies were not consistent across achievement levels. For example, while 'A' students at high performing (Q5) schools were less likely to cheat on exams than 'A' students at Q1 schools, as GPA declined, this trend reversed itself. Among students with GPAs of B+ or below, there were higher cheating rates in the higher-performing (Q5) versus lower-performing (Q1) schools. The authors suggest that these differences reflect the role that the norms for 'good performance' in a given context have on who cheats.

Finally, whereas GPA is an indicator of actual accomplishments, self-efficacy is an individual's belief in his or her ability to execute the skills needed to bring about some desired outcome (Bandura, 1986). Higher levels of academic-self efficacy have been associated with the selection of more difficult tasks, task engagement, and persistence, and more accurately predict these behaviors than GPA (Pajares, 1996). Consistent with these findings, moderate inverse correlations between self-efficacy and cheating have been found among students in middle (Murdock, Hale, & Weber, 2001; Tas & Tekkaya, 2010) and high school (Bong, 2008) in the United States (Finn & Frone, 2004), and among Australian university students (Marsden, Carroll, & Neill, 2005). One source of low self-efficacy information is the physiological arousal that occurs with fear or anxiety (Bandura, 1986). As expected, self-reported cheating has been correlated with a fear of failure (Schab, 1991), test anxiety (Malinowski & Smith, 1985), and worry over performance (Anderman, Griesinger, & Westerfield, 1998). Together, these results suggest that one's competence, self-assessed competence, and normative expectations for competence all influence cheating behavior.

Academic Purpose

Links between academic purpose and dishonesty have been most often studied from the vantage of Achievement Goal Theory (AGT) (Ames, 1992). When students are motivated towards mastery, called mastery goals, learning goals, or task-orientation, they see ability as malleable, evaluate their success based on personal standards, approach their school tasks with a desire to learn, and are willing to expend effort to improve their competence. Students with a performance orientation are motivated to validate their ability by outperforming others and/or showing how easily they can accomplish something.

Empirical investigations of achievement goals and cheating span three decades. In their seminal study of middle school students, Anderman and colleagues (1998) found that mastery goals at all levels (i.e., personal, classroom, and school) were negatively correlated with cheating beliefs and behaviors, whereas classroom extrinsic and school performance goals were positively associated with cheating behavior. In subsequent years, numerous researchers have explicitly adopted AGT to study cheating attitudes and behaviors. In general, stronger endorsement of mastery goals has been associated with less favorable attitudes about cheating (Anderman et al., 1998; Murdock et al., 2001; Stephens & Gehlbach, 2007, Stephens et al., 2010) and less engagement in cheating behavior (Anderman et al., 1998; He, Gou, & Chang, 2015; Marsden et al., 2005; Murdock et al., 2001; Stephens et al., 2010; Tas & Tekkaya, 2010); although stronger performance or extrinsic goals have been positively related to both attitudinal (Anderman et al., 1998; Murdock et al., 2001; Stephens, & Gehlbach, 2007) and behavioral cheating outcomes (Anderman et al., 1998; Marsden et al., 2005; Murdock et al., 2001; Stephens & Gehlbach, 2007; Tas & Tekkaya, 2010).

In sum, when students are interested in a task, desire to truly understand it, feel that it might benefit their personal development, and see themselves as having strong agency or intrinsic motivation to accomplish it, they are less likely to cheat. Likewise, when students' interest is low, they are doing something simply to achieve a certain level of performance, they are uninterested in the task or see it as having no value, or they feel forced to achieve due to external factors (e.g., family pressure, GPA requirements), they are more likely to cheat.

Beliefs About Cheating: Morality and Rationalization

Students' beliefs about whether, when, and why cheating is or is not acceptable are a large focus of the extant literature on academic dishonesty. The attention to this topic is likely due to three related factors: (a) students' beliefs about the acceptability or wrongness of academic dishonesty are robust predictors of their cheating behavior (Bushway & Nash, 1977; Whitley, 1998); (b) many students who believe cheating is wrong, report doing it anyway (Anderman et al., 1998; Honz, Kiewra, & Yang, 2010; Jordan, 2001; Stephens & Nicholson, 2008); and (c) students' beliefs about the acceptability or wrongness of cheating are highly contextualized, such that they cheat more when they can externalize blame or otherwise 'neutralize' responsibility for their behavior (Diekhoff et al., 1996; Haines et al., 1986; LaBeff, Clark, Haines, & Diekhoff, 1990; McCabe, 1992; Michaels & Miethe, 1989; Pulvers & Diekhoff, 1999; Stephens et al., 2007). In short, a critical mediator of the oft-observed 'judgment-action gap' (Blasi, 1980) is the extent to which students rationalize cheating behavior.

'I Believe It's Wrong, but . . .'

Believing that cheating is serious (Anderman et al., 1998), unacceptable (Honz et al., 2010), wrong (Wangaard & Stephens, 2011), or unjustifiable (Jordan, 2001) is a significant protective factor against cheating behavior, but does not make students immune from cheating. For example, Wangaard and Stephens (2011) found that over 50% of the 3,600 high school students they surveyed simultaneously admitted to cheating while reporting that they believed cheating was wrong. Similarly, in a survey of 100 high school students, the majority of the students admitted to engaging in behaviors that they identified as cheating (Honz et al., 2010).

'I'm Not Responsible'

One of the prime ways to avoid unpleasant self-recriminations created by belief-behavior incongruity is through the deployment of 'mechanisms of moral disengagement' (Bandura, 1986) or 'neutralization techniques' (Sykes & Matza, 1957). These mechanisms reduce or even negate one's responsibility by attributing one's conduct to others or situational contingencies. Several studies have demonstrated a strong positive association between cheating and neutralization among secondary (Evans & Craig, 1990; Stephens & Gehlbach, 2007; Zito & Mcquillan, 2011) and tertiary students (Diekhoff et al., 1996; Haines et al., 1986; LaBeff et al., 1990; McCabe, 1992; Michaels & Miethe, 1989; Pulvers & Diekhoff, 1999; Stephens et al., 2007).

In a large-scale study of undergraduates, McCabe (1992) found denial or displacement of responsibility to be most prevalent mechanisms; that is, 61% of students who reported cheating rationalized their cheating by blaming others and/or some aspect of the situational context. Similarly, Evans and Craig (1990) found displacement of responsibility to the teacher to be most pronounced among college-bound and high achieving high school students. More recently, Murdock, Beauchamp, and Hinton (2008) found that the tendency to blame teachers was a direct predictor of actual cheating behavior.

Given that some of the cross-cultural studies already discussed have documented differences in cheating attitudes (e.g., Lupton et al., 2000; Stephens et al., 2010), further investigations of academic integrity across cultures would benefit from explicit assessments of how neutralization techniques are used.

INSTRUCTIONAL AND ASSESSMENT FACTORS

Assessment Format and Context

In a series of experimental studies in the 1970s and '80s, Houston (1986) demonstrated that incidences of copying off of peers on exams can be reduced by seating students next to less- versus better-known classmates (Houston, 1986) and seating students in every other row with a free row in between (Houston, 1976). Alternate forms of multiple-choice exams were only found to reduce cheating when students were surrounded by classmates taking different versions of the exam and when both the order of the questions and the answers were scrambled across versions; simply scrambling the questions (Houston, 1983) or providing alternative versions to each row of students did not reduce copying (Houston, 1976).

Although the above studies are quite dated, they demonstrate the importance of considering how easy or difficult it is for students to cheat. Moreover, 20 years later, many of the measures Houston found to be effective were also among those perceived as most effective for deterring test cheating in a sample of 1,672 U.S. university students; that is, 82% agreed that scrambling test items was an effective deterrent and 67% suggested the use of two or more exams (Hollinger & Lanza-Kaduce, 1996). Other endorsed strategies focused on making it more difficult to cheat by using assessments that were not objective (i.e., essays) and/or ones in which students are more likely to be caught due to lower student-teacher ratios (70%) and the use of more proctors (68%).

Similarly, college students in Genereux and McLeod's (1995) study ranked type of exam (essay versus multiple choice) as second of 21 possible strategies for decreasing cheating and spacing in the exam room as the fourth of 21 most effective strategy for reducing unplanned cheating.

Plagiarism Detection Software

Many high schools and universities have turned to plagiarism detection (e.g., Turnitin) to reduce violations of academic integrity on term papers, essays, and course work. When students submit assignments to these types of database systems, they can be compared to all information currently on the Internet (e.g., published papers, academic proceedings) and to assignments other students turned in to the system. Feedback is provided to the student or instructor about which sections are not original along with information about the sources of their copying. Studies conducted on the effectiveness of this software across several countries (in Botswana, Batane, 2010; in England, Betts, Bostock, Elder, & Trueman, 2012; in the U.S., Martin, 2005) found declines in rates of plagiarism when this software was used. Still other data show that providing explicit instruction on how to paraphrase leads to less plagiarism than simply using electronic detection alone (Chao, Wilhelm, & Neureuther, 2009). This instructional aspect may be particularly important, as Heather (2010) has demonstrated that students can easily game the software by creating a document that can 'pass the Turnitin test' despite substantial amounts of plagiarism.

Honor Codes

Honor codes provide a formal mechanism for communicating an institutional commitment to integrity. Traditional honor codes typically (a) detail which behaviors constitute dishonesty, (b) outline the penalties for dishonesty, and (c) require students to affirm that they understand and will actively uphold the policy (i.e., report students who cheat), and will be involved in judicial processes around integrity violations (McCabe, Treviño, & Butterfield, 2002). Modified honor codes typically do not require formal pledges to report peers who cheat. Lower dishonesty rates have been found at institutions with traditional honor codes versus institutions with no honor codes (McCabe & Treviño, 1993, 1997). More recently, McCabe et al. (2002) found that modified honor codes were better than no honor codes, but less effective than traditional honor codes in reducing cheating.

Shu, Gino, and Bazerman (2011) demonstrated that participants' moral disengagement and motivated forgetting increased after they had been dishonest; however, participants who read or signed an honor code were significantly less likely to cheat and did not exhibit a subsequent increase in moral disengagement. In a related study, university students who completed a brief tutorial on plagiarism at the beginning of the semester significantly reduced their plagiarism on a subsequent essay assignment later in the same semester (Dee & Jacob, 2010). Together, these studies highlight the power of increasing the moral saliency of cheating through a situational reminder or contract.

Despite these known practices for making cheating more difficult and less frequent, data suggest that many instructors do not take even cursory measures (e.g., proctoring exams) to reduce cheating (Graham, Monday, O'Brien, & Steffen, 1994). Indeed, although most students believe the instructor is responsible to ensure ethical assessment behavior (McCabe et al., 2002), and that cheating is inversely related to instructor's concern about cheating and vigilance about detection (Genereux & McLeod, 1995), they also indicate that many of their teachers at both the high school (McCabe, 1999) and college level are aware of dishonesty and ignore it (Ng, Davies, Bates, & Avellone, 2003). Studies of instructors themselves support students' beliefs that faculty members often ignore cheating (Keith-Spiegel, Tabachnick, Whitley, & Washburn, 1998) and/or do not take proactive stances to reduce unethical behavior (Graham et al., 1994). Data from the United States suggest that instructors are reluctant to take action against cheating because it is uncomfortable, time-consuming, difficult to prove, and is perceived to potentially result in retaliation (Keith-Spiegel et al., 1998). Given that norms and rules of schooling likely differ widely across context, cross-cultural studies of teachers' attitudes and behaviors when confronted with cheating are much needed.

CLASSROOM CONTEXTUAL FACTORS

Classroom Goal Structure

Classrooms that emphasize the value of effort and learning by highlighting personal improvement, encouraging risk-taking, permitting work to be redone, and deemphasizing social comparisons are said to have mastery goal structures. In contrast, classrooms with performance goal structures place a premium on ability and conditions that foster competition and comparisons among students. Several studies have examined one-time associations between perceived classroom goal structure and cheating attitudes and/or cheating behavior. For example, Anderman et al. (1998) found that middle school 'cheaters' saw their classes as significantly more performance-focused than non-cheaters. Similarly, Murdock et al. (2001), reported that cheating among students in middle school math and science classrooms was predicted by decreased perceptions of mastery goal structures and increased perceptions of performance goal structures, even after controlling for students' own achievement (i.e., GPA) and personal motivation (i.e., personal goals and efficacy).

To determine how changes in context affect behavior, Anderman and Midgley (2004) studied changes in students' math cheating, motivation, and perceived classroom context as they transitioned from middle school to high school. Students who reported going from classes with high mastery to low mastery goal structures and from low performance to high performance environments also reported increased cheating. Conversely, moving from a low to high mastery context was accompanied by a decrease in cheating.

Several studies provide more conclusive evidence that the relations between goal structures and cheating are not simply due to differences in individual classroom perceptions, but rather shared views of what is happening in that context. For example, a recent investigation among seventh graders in Turkey found lower rates of cheating to be associated with classrooms where there were higher aggregated (i.e., mean across students) student views of the teachers' use of mastery oriented classroom practices (Tas & Tekkaya, 2010). Moreover, this classroom level variable was a better predictor of dishonesty than the student's own personal level of mastery-oriented beliefs. Similarly, in a field experiment, Van Yperen, Hamstra, and van der Klauw (2011) found an increase in cheating behavior when performance approach goals were imposed on university students. Finally, other experimental evidence for the influence of goal structures comes from studies using hypothetical vignettes to manipulate the portrayed classroom goal structure. High school students viewed cheating as less justifiable and likely in classrooms portrayed with mastery versus performance goal structures

(Murdock, Miller, & Kohlhardt, 2004); similar results have been obtained among university students with the same vignette methodology (Day, Hudson, Dobies, & Waris, 2011; Murdock, Miller, & Goetzinger, 2007).

Other studies outside the goal theory tradition demonstrate how contexts that emphasize grades and ability over engagement and learning are more apt to lead to cheating; peer pressure, pressure for financial aid, boring classes, and high-stakes examinations have all been associated with cheating behavior among high school and university students (Schraw et al., 2007). Whitley's (1998) review of the literature reported moderate correlations between cheating and various conditions that increase the pressure for success, including competition, high academic workload, and reward for success. Finally, in a survey of over 600 students in Grades 7–12, self-reported cheating increased in classrooms where grading was normative and competition between students was emphasized (Evans & Craig, 1990).

Teacher Pedagogical and Interpersonal Caring

Many scholars have examined how students' cheating attitudes and behaviors are affected by the quality of their relationship with their teacher or 'teacher caring' (for a review, see Anderman, Freeman, & Mueller, 2007). Teacher caring includes both *interpersonal* caring, characterized by behaviors such as warmth and knowing students' names, and *pedagogical* caring, as demonstrated by being prepared to teach and using fair assessment practices. Two studies undertaken among university students found that students were more apt to cheat when they perceived the assessment practices in the classroom were unfair (Genereux & McLeod, 1995; Graham et al., 1994). Another correlational study suggests students cheat less when the teacher is approachable, responsive, and pedagogically competent (Rabi, Patton, Fjortoft, & Zgarrick, 2006). Similarly, Murdock et al. (2001) found that high school students' self-reported cheating was inversely related to perceptions of the degree to which teachers evidenced 'competence and commitment' (i.e., pedagogical caring) as well as the interpersonal respect they communicated in the classroom.

High school students who read vignettes portraying poor pedagogy and/or low caring judged cheating to be more acceptable, blamed teachers more and students less for cheating, and predicted increased likelihood of cheating than those reading good pedagogy and/or high caring vignettes (Murdock et al., 2004). Follow-up investigations with university undergraduate (Study 1) and graduate (Study 2) students that manipulated pedagogical competence (better versus worse) and classroom goal structure (mastery versus performance) found similar results: better pedagogy and mastery goal structures were both associated with less predicted cheating and the assignment of blame for cheating more to students than to teachers (Murdock et al., 2007). A replication and extension of this study by Day et al. (2011) found similar effects of portrayed pedagogy on cheating attitudes using a sample of undergraduate business students.

Social Norms

It is well established in social psychology that peers can have a powerful effect on each other's norms, beliefs, and behaviors (Asch, 1951; Sherif, 1936). Norms are theorized to exist at two levels; that is, the collective level that comprises the (often unwritten) "codes of conduct that either prescribe or proscribe behaviors that members of a group can enact" (Lapinski & Rimal, 2005, p. 129), and the psychological level that is concerned with how individuals construe (or misconstrue) those norms. It is these *perceived norms* that are often of most consequence in determining behavior, and the ones most often assessed in the research on cheating behavior.

Empirical studies investigating the relationships between perceived peer norms and academic dishonesty among university students date back at least half a century (Bowers, 1964; Jordan, 2001; McCabe & Treviño, 1993; McCabe & Treviño, 1997; McCabe, Treviño, & Butterfield, 2001; Stephens et al., 2007). McCabe and Treviño (1997) found peer norms to be the strongest predictors of cheating in their multi-campus investigation of individual and contextual influences related to cheating. Specifically, students' perceived peer disapproval for academic dishonesty negatively predicted self-reported cheating, while perceived engagement in cheating behavior was a significant positive predictor of self-reported cheating. Results from O'Rourke et al.'s (2010) survey of university students indicated that the relationship between knowledge of peer cheating and self-reported cheating was moderated by cheating valence. Students who viewed cheating as unacceptable were largely unaffected by direct knowledge of peer cheating, while those who regarded cheating to be more acceptable were significantly more likely to cheat in the presence of cheating peers. However, in an experimental study exploring conformity versus awareness as explanations for the power of peer norms on cheating behavior, Fosgaard, Hansen, and Piovesan (2013) found that, although cheating among males was not affected by increased awareness of cheating (i.e., the suggestion of cheating as an option), it was significantly greater when it was suggested that their peers had cheated (i.e., conformity). Female participants were unaffected by conformity, but cheated significantly more in the awareness condition.

SUMMARY AND DISCUSSION

Taken together, this review on dishonesty provides implications for educators, policy makers, and psychometricians.

Educators and Teacher Educators

Teacher preparation programs should help prepare teachers to create norms where academic honesty is valued. As noted above, academic integrity can be promoted through the introduction of honor codes, creation of seating arrangements and assignment/test formats that make cheating more difficult, and the use of available technology to check for plagiarism. Many students see integrity as a part of a teacher's job—failing to use the resources available to deter it communicates to students that it does not matter. Equally important, teachers need to have a plan to attend to students during assessment and to take action when they perceive that their students are not being honest. Among other things, we need to discourage excuses. No one likes to identify themselves as a 'bad person,' and people are, thus, much more likely to cheat when they can externally justify their behavior. Often, these excuses are externalizations of blame onto the teacher or someone else in their lives. Supporting teachers and future teachers to facilitate discussions among their students about excuses and the function they serve might also promote integrity.

Fostering intrinsic motivation/autonomy and mastery goals is equally important, and teaching future teachers how to create mastery goal structures should also improve rates of honesty. Teaching practices that promote motivation also discourage cheating. For example, frequent formative assessments that provide students with developmental and complex tasks that are engaging and allow for some choices might both foster motivation and deter dishonesty. Grading practices that allow students the opportunity to relearn things if they did not master them the first time and emphasize personal improvement over normative performance also encourage mastery.

We also need to remember the importance of what are sometimes called soft skills (e.g., communication, self-regulation, social skills) and consider the development of these skills both worthy of instructional time at the K–12 level and as an important learning outcome for those who are in teacher education programs. Recall that students with high levels of impulsivity tend to cheat more than others, as do students who feel worried or pressured that they cannot meet time demands. Explicitly teaching students how to manage both their emotions (see Vogl & Pekrun, this volume, for more on achievement emotions) and their time demands can be a helpful deterrent to cheating and also promote success more generally.

Finally, teacher education should help teachers develop the skills needed to create caring relationships with students. Having a teacher who is seen as caring not only increases student engagement, it decreases cheating and students' tendency to neutralize cheating. Soliciting feedback from students to improve one's pedagogy, making sure that assessment is fair (i.e., aligns with what has been taught, is a good presentation of the material, and at an appropriate level of difficulty), and making the effort to communicate warmth and respect for students all might reduce dishonesty.

Policy Makers

Current trends in assessment policies and practices in some jurisdictions (see Nichols & Harris, this volume) largely focus on promoting greater accountability for both teachers and students. This outcomes focus may well be contributing to the epidemic of cheating (e.g., Callahan, 2004). Cheating scandals on high-stakes tests are revealed with increasing frequency, involving both students themselves and teachers/administrators who are worried about how test scores are used to assess the performance of their classroom or school. Current responses to these instances of dishonesty are largely to focus on improving the 'detection industry' rather than looking the root causes and meaning of the incidents themselves.

For example, we might examine the alignment between what we want our students to know and how they are assessed in classrooms versus in higher-stakes settings. Current trends in teacher education encourage the use of multiple assessments that allow students varied opportunities to demonstrate their knowledge, yet it is largely multiple-choice examinations that determine entrance into special educational tracks, selection into higher education, or awards of credit (such as Advanced Placement exams in the United States, where college credit can be earned for a high school class). This disconnect might encourage cheating on classroom assessments, as they are seen as 'busy work to get done,' and on the higher-stakes examinations because of the associated possible benefits.

Burgeoning rates of classroom cheating and grade inflation combine to make it difficult for external audiences to trust the relationship between learning and grades as evidenced in the classroom. Moving conversations away from accountability (i.e., are these schools doing their job?) towards student learning might alleviate some of these pressures, increase learning, and decrease the motivation for dishonesty. As currently employed, high-stakes standardized assessment are used to gauge success at classroom or school levels (i.e., what percent of student are at or above grade level?), but are not used to improve the learning of individual students.

For example, we might advocate for policies that encourage using high-stakes test results to set goals and educational plans for individual students based on their current performance. If a student is two levels below grade level in mathematics, for example, satisfactory progress for this student might be to advance the equivalent of at least one grade in the upcoming academic year, or better still, to master a set of specific skills that he or she currently does not have. At a minimum, students and parents should receive feedback about what skills have been mastered in the current year that were under-developed in previous years. As currently implemented, students who are below grade level are likely to continuously hear the same negative feedback rather than information about what skills they have been able to develop.

Psychometrics

The psychological measurement of cheating behavior and its correlates dates back nearly a hundred years to Hartshorne and May's (1928) classic *Studies in Deceit*. Since that time, numerous theories and techniques have been employed to measure cheating and the psychological factors thought to be associated with it. If there is a single point of agreement among the disparate models and measures used to assess cheating, it is that it is widespread. In short, regardless of the measure used to assess cheating behavior (e.g., self-report survey, plagiarism detection software, experimental manipulation, etc.) many, and often most, students cheat. At this point, the challenge for psychometricians interested in cheating behavior is not the development of more valid and reliable detection of cheating. This is not say that more and better measures of cheating, programs that detect it, or prompts that elicit it, would not be welcomed. However, that true challenge confronting scholars interested in the problem of cheating is its reduction.

Toward that end, the past decade has been an especially fruitful period of empirical research on academic dishonesty and interventions designed to reduce it. Several studies reviewed in this chapter (Dee & Jacob, 2010; Fosgaard et al., 2013; Shu et al., 2011) illustrate how relatively small interventions can affect cheating behavior. More such studies are needed, and interventions that prove robust need to be scaled up and disseminated effectively. At present, much of what has been learned about cheating does not appear to be systematically informing practice. This needs to change, and scholars from many fields have a role to play in promoting academic integrity.

REFERENCES

Ames, C. (1992). Achievement goals and the classroom motivational climate. In D. H. Schunk, J. L. Meece, D. H. Schunk, & J. L. Meece (Eds.), *Student perceptions in the classroom* (pp. 327–348). Hillsdale, NJ, England: Lawrence Erlbaum Associates, Inc.

Anderman, E. M., Cupp, P. K., & Lane, D. (2009). Impulsivity and academic cheating. *Journal of Experimental Education, 78*, 135–150.

Anderman, E. M., Freeman, T. M., & Mueller, C. E. (2007). The "social" side of social context: Interpersonal and affiliative dimensions of students' experiences and academic dishonesty. In E. M. Anderman & T. B. Murdock (Eds.), *Psychology of academic cheating* (pp. 203–228). Burlington, MA: Elsevier Academic Press.

Anderman, E. M., Griesinger, T., & Westerfield, G. (1998). Motivation and cheating during early adolescence. *Journal of Educational Psychology, 90*, 84–93.

Anderman, E. M., & Midgley, C. (2004). Changes in self-reported academic cheating across the transition from middle school to high school. *Contemporary Educational Psychology, 29*, 499–517.

Asch, S. E. (1951). Effects of group pressure upon the modification and distortion of judgments. In H. Guetzkow (Ed.), *Groups, leadership and men; research in human relations* (pp. 177–190). Oxford, UK: Carnegie Press.

Bandura, A. (1986). *Social foundations of thought and action: A social cognitive theory.* Englewood Cliffs, NJ: Prentice-Hall.

Batane, T. (2010). Turning to Turnitin to fight plagiarism among university student. *Educational Technology & Society, 13*(2), 1–12.

Betts, L. R., Bostock, S. J., Edler, T. J., & Trueman, M. (2012). Encouraging good writing in first-year psychology students: An intervention using Turnitin. *Psychology Teaching Review, 18*(2), 74–81.

Blasi, A. (1980). Bridging moral cognition and moral action: A critical review of the literature. *Psychological Bulletin, 88*(1), 1–45.

Bolin, A. U. (2004). Self-control, perceived opportunity, and attitudes as predictors of academic dishonesty. *The Journal of Psychology: Interdisciplinary and Applied, 138*, 101–114. doi:10.3200/JRLP.138.2.101–114

Bong, M. (2008). Effects of parent-child relationships and classroom goal structures on motivation, help-seeking avoidance, and cheating. *Journal of Experimental Education, 76*, 191–217.

Bowers, W. J. (1964). *Student dishonesty and its control in college.* New York: Columbia Bureau of Applied Research.

Brandes, B. (1986). *Academic honesty: A special study of California students.* Sacramento, CA: California State Department of Education. Retrieved from ERIC database. (ED272533)

Bushway, A., & Nash, W. R. (1977). School cheating behavior. *Review of Educational Research, 47*, 623–632. doi:10.2307/1170002

Callahan, D. (2004). *The cheating culture: Why more Americans are doing wrong to get ahead.* Orlando, FL: Harcourt.

Chao, C.-A., Wilhelm, W. J., & Neureuther, B. D. (2009). A study of electronic detection and pedagogical approaches for reducing plagiarism. *Delta Pi Epsilon Journal, 51*(1), 31–24.

Colmar Brunton. (2012). Lying, cheating, stealing. Retrieved from http://www.colmarbrunton.co.nz/index.php/news/lying-cheating-stealing

Davis, S. F., Pierce, M. C., Yandell, L. R., Arnow, P. S., & Loree, A. (1995). Cheating in college and the Type A personality: A reevaluation. *College Student Journal, 29*, 493–497.

Day, N. E., Hudson, D., Dobies, P. R., & Waris, R. (2011). Student or situation? Personality and classroom context as predictors of attitudes about business school cheating. *Social Psychology of Education: An International Journal, 14*, 261–282.

DeAndrea, D. C., Carpenter, C., Shulman, H., & Levine, T. R. (2009). The relationship between cheating behavior and sensation-seeking. *Personality and Individual Differences, 47*, 944–947. doi:10.1016/j.paid.2009.07.02

Dee, T. S., & Jacob, B. A. (2010). Rational ignorance in education: A field experiment in student plagiarism. National Bureau of Economic Research (NBER Working Paper #15672). Retrieved from http://www.nber.org/papers/w15672.pdf

Diekhoff, G. M., LaBeff, E. E., Clark, R. E., Williams, L. E., Francis, B., & Haines, V. J. (1996). College cheating: Ten years later. *Research in Higher Education, 37*(4), 487–502.

Duckworth, A. L., & Kern, M. L. (2011). A meta-analysis of the convergent validity of self-control measures. *Journal of Research in Personality, 45*, 259–268. doi:10.1016/j.jrp.2011.02.004

Evans, E. D., & Craig, D. (1990). Adolescent cognitions for academic cheating as a function of grade level and achievement status. *Journal of Adolescent Research, 5*(3), 325–345.

Finn, K. V., & Frone, M. R. (2004). Academic performance and cheating: Moderating role of school identification and self-efficacy. *The Journal of Educational Research, 97*(3), 115–122. doi:10.3200/JOER.97.3.115–121

Forsyth, D. R., Pope, W. R., & McMillan, J. H. (1985). Students' reactions after cheating: An attributional analysis. *Contemporary Educational Psychology, 10*, 72–82. doi:10.1016/0361–476X(85)90007–4

Fosgaard, T. R., Hansen, L. G., & Piovesan, M. (2013). Separating Will from Grace: An experiment on conformity and awareness in cheating. *Journal of Economic Behavior & Organization, 93*(0), 279–284. doi:10.1016/j.jebo.2013.03.027

Genereux, R. L., & McLeod, B. A. (1995). Circumstances surrounding cheating: A questionnaire study of college students. *Research in Higher Education, 36*(6), 687–704.

Giluk, T. L., & Postlethwaite, B. E. (2015). Big five personality and academic dishonesty: A meta-analytic review. *Personality & Individual Differences, 72*, 59–67. doi:10.1016/j.paid.2014.08.027

Graham, M. A., Monday, J., O'Brien, K., & Steffen, S. (1994). Cheating at small colleges: An examination of student and faculty attitudes and behaviors. *Journal of College Student Development, 35*, 255–260.

Haines, V. J., Diekhoff, G. M., LaBeff, E. E., & Clark, R. E. (1986). College cheating: Immaturity, lack of commitment, and the neutralizing attitude. *Research in Higher Education, 25*, 342–354.

Hartshorne, H., & May, M. A. (1928). *Studies in deceit.* New York: Macmillan.

He, T. H., Gou, W. J., & Chang, S. M. (2015). Parental involvement and elementary school students' goals, maladaptive behaviors, and achievement in learning English as a foreign language. *Learning and Individual Differences, 39*, 205–210.

Heather, J. (2010). Turnitoff: Identifying and fixing a hole in current plagiarism detection software. *Assessment & Evaluation in Higher Education, 35*(6), 647–660.

Helson, R., Jones, C., & Kwan, V. S. Y. (2002). Personality change over 40 years of adulthood: Hierarchical linear modeling analyses of two longitudinal samples. *Journal of Personality and Social Psychology, 83*, 752–766.

Helson, R., & Kwan, V. S. Y. (2000). Personality development in adulthood: The broad picture and processes in one longitudinal sample. In S. Hampson (Ed.), *Advances in personality psychology* (Vol. 1, pp. 77–106). London: Routledge.

Hollinger, R. C., & Lanza-Kaduce, L. (1996). Academic dishonesty and the perceived effectiveness of counter-measures: An empirical survey of cheating at a major public university. *NASPA Journal, 33*(4), 292–306.

Honz, K., Kiewra, K. A., & Yang, Y. S. (2010). Cheating perceptions and prevalence across academic settings. *Mid-Western Educational Researcher, 23*(2), 10–17.

Houston, J. P. (1976). Amount and loci of classroom answer copying, spaced seating, and alternate test forms. *Journal of Educational Psychology, 68*, 729–735. doi:10.1037/0022–0663.68.6.729

Houston, J. P. (1983). Alternate test forms as a means of reducing multiple-choice answer copying in the class-room. *Journal of Educational Psychology, 75*, 572–575. doi:10.1037/0022–0663.75.4.572

Houston, J. P. (1986). Classroom answer copying: Roles of acquaintanceship and free versus assigned seating. *Journal of Educational Psychology, 78*, 230–232. doi:10.1037/0022–0663.78.3.230

Huss, M. T., Curnyn, J. P., Roberts, S. L., & Davis, S. F. (1993). Hard driven but not dishonest: Cheating and the Type A personality. *Bulletin of the Psychonomic Society, 31*, 429–430.

Jordan, A. E. (2001). College student cheating: The role of motivation, perceived norms, attitudes, and knowl-edge of institutional policy. *Ethics & Behavior, 11*, 233–247.

Josephson Institute of Ethics. (2006). *2006 report card on the ethics of American youth.* Los Angeles, CA: Author. Retrieved from https://charactercounts.org/programs/reportcard/2006/index.html

Josephson Institute of Ethics. (2008). *2008 report card on the ethics of American youth.* Los Angeles, CA: Author. Retrieved from https://charactercounts.org/programs/reportcard/2008/index.html

Josephson Institute of Ethics. (2010). *2010 report card on the ethics of American youth.* Los Angeles, CA: Author. Retrieved from https://charactercounts.org/programs/reportcard/2010/index.html

Josephson Institute of Ethics. (2012). *2012 Report card on the ethics of American youth.* Los Angeles, CA: Author. Retrieved from https://charactercounts.org/programs/reportcard/2012/index.html

Karabenick, S. A., & Srull, T. K. (1978). Effects of personality and situational variation in locus of control on cheat-ing: Determinants of the congruence effect. *Journal of Personality, 46*, 72–95. doi:10.1111/j.1467–6494.1978.tb00603.x

Keith-Spiegel, P., Tabachnick, B. G., Whitley, B. J., & Washburn, J. (1998). Why professors ignore cheating: Opinions of a national sample of psychology instructors. *Ethics & Behavior, 8*, 215–227. doi:10.1207/s15327019eb0803_3

LaBeff, E. E., Clark, R. E., Haines, V. J., & Diekhoff, G. M. (1990). Situational ethics and college student cheating. *Sociological Inquiry, 60*, 190–198. doi:10.1111/j.1475–682X.1990.tb00138.x

Lapinski, M. K., & Rimal, R. N. (2005). An explication of social norms. *Communication Theory, 15*(2), 127–147. 10.1111/j.1468–2885.2005.tb00329.x

Leming, J. S. (1980). Cheating behavior, subject variables, and components of the internal–external scale under high and low risk conditions. *The Journal of Educational Research, 74*(2), 83–87.

Lin, C.-H. S., & Wen, L.-Y. M. (2007). Academic dishonesty in higher education—a nationwide study in Taiwan. *Higher Education, 54*, 85–97. doi:10.1007/s10734–006–9047-z

Lupton, R. A., Chapman, K. J., & Weiss, J. (2000). American and Slovakian university business students' attitudes, perceptions and tendencies toward academic cheating. *Journal of Education for Business, 75*(4), 231–241.

Ma, Y., McCabe, D. L., & Liu, R. (2013). Students' academic cheating in Chinese universities: Prevalence, influenc-ing factors, and proposed action. *Journal of Academic Ethics, 11*, 169–184. doi:10.1007/s10805–013–9186–7

Malinowski, C. I., & Smith, C. P. (1985). Moral reasoning and moral conduct: An investigation prompted by Kohl-berg's theory. *Journal of Personality and Social Psychology, 49*, 1016–1027. doi:10.1037/0022–3514.49.4.1016

Marsden, H. T., Carroll, M., & Neill, J. T. (2005). Who cheats at university? A self-report study of dishonest academic behaviours in a sample of Australian university students. *Australian Journal of Psychology, 57*(1), 1–10.

Martin, D. F. (2005). Plagiarism and technology: A tool for coping with plagiarism. *Journal of Education for Business, 80*(3), 149–152.

McCabe, D. L. (1992). The influence of situation ethics on cheating among college students. *Sociological Inquiry, 62*, 365–374. doi:10.1111/j.1475–682X.1992.tb00287.x

McCabe, D. L. (1999). Academic dishonesty among high school students. *Adolescence, 34*, 681–687.

McCabe, D. L., Butterfield, K. D., & Treviño, L. K. (2012). *Cheating in college: Why students do it and what educa-tors can do about it.* Baltimore, MD: The Johns Hopkins University Press.

McCabe, D. L., & Treviño, L. K. (1993). Academic dishonesty: Honor codes and other contextual influences. *Journal of Higher Education, 64*(5), 522–538.

McCabe, D. L., & Treviño, L. K. (1997). Individual and contextual influences on academic dishonesty: A multi-campus investigation. *Research in Higher Education, 38*, 379–396.

McCabe, D. L., Treviño, L. K., & Butterfield, K. D. (2001). Dishonesty in academic environments: The influence of peer reporting requirements. *Journal of Higher Education, 72*(1), 29–45.

McCabe, D. L., Treviño, L. K., & Butterfield, K. D. (2002). Honor codes and other contextual influences on academic integrity: a replication and extension to modified honor code settings. *Research in Higher Education, 43*, 357–378.

McTernan, M., Love, P., & Rettinger, D. (2014). The influence of personality on the decision to cheat. *Ethics & Behavior, 24*, 53–72.

Menon, M. K., & Sharland, A. (2011). Narcissism, exploitative attitudes, and academic dishonesty: An exploratory investigation of reality versus myth. *Journal of Education for Business, 86*, 50–55.

Michaels, J. W., & Miethe, T. D. (1989). Applying theories of deviance to academic cheating. *Social Science Quarterly, 70*, 870–885.

Murdock, T. B., & Anderman, E. M. (2006). Motivational perspectives on student cheating: Toward an integrated model of academic dishonesty. *Educational Psychologist, 41*(3), 129–145.

Murdock, T. B., Beauchamp, A. S., & Hinton, A. M. (2008). Predictors of cheating and cheating attributions: Does classroom context influence cheating and blame for cheating?. *European Journal of Psychology of Education, 23*(4), 477–492.

Murdock, T. B., Hale, N. M., & Weber, M. J. (2001). Predictors of cheating among early adolescents: Academic and social motivations. *Contemporary Educational Psychology, 26*, 96–115. doi:10.1006/ceps.2000.1046

Murdock, T. B., Miller, A. D., & Goetzinger, A. (2007). Effects of classroom context on university students' judgments about cheating: Mediating and moderating processes. *Social Psychology of Education, 10*, 141–169. doi:10.1007/s11218-007-9015-1

Murdock, T. B., Miller, A., & Kohlhardt, J. (2004). Effects of classroom context variables on high school students' judgments of the acceptability and likelihood of cheating. *Journal of Educational Psychology, 96*, 765–777.

Nathanson, C., Paulhus, D. L., & Williams, K. M. (2006). Predictors of a behavioral measure of scholastic cheating: personality and competence but not demographics. *Contemporary Educational Psychology, 31*, 97–122.

Newstead, S. E., Franklyn-Stokes, A., & Armstead, P. (1996). Individual differences in student cheating. *Journal of Educational Psychology, 88*, 229–241.

Ng, H.W.W., Davies, G., Bates, I., & Avellone, M. (2003). Academic dishonesty among pharmacy students. *Pharmacy Education, 3*, 261–269. doi:10.1080/15602210310001643375

Nora, W.L.Y. (2009). *Motives of cheating among secondary school students: The role of self efficacy, peer attitudes, and behavior.* Hong Kong: University of Hong Kong. Retrieved from http://hdl.handle.net/10722/123912

O'Rourke, J., Barnes, J., Deaton, A., Fulks, K., Ryan, K., & Rettinger, D. A. (2010). Imitation is the sincerest form of cheating: The influence of direct knowledge and attitudes on academic dishonesty. *Ethics & Behavior, 20*, 47–64.

Pajares, F. (1996). Self-efficacy beliefs in academic settings. *Review of Educational Research, 66*(4), 543–78.

Paulhus, D. L., & Williams, K. M. (2002). The dark triad of personality: Narcissism, Machiavellianism, and psychopathy. *Journal of Research in Personality, 36*(6), 556–563. doi:10.1016/S0092-6566(02)00505-6

Pavela, G. (1997). Applying the power of association on campus: A model code of academic integrity. *Journal of College and University Law, 24*, 97–118.

Perry, A. R., Kane, K. M., Bernesser, K. J., & Spicker, P. T. (1990). Type A behavior, competitive achievement-striving, and cheating among college students. *Psychological Reports, 66*, 459–465. doi:10.2466/PR0.66.2.459–465

Pulvers, K., & Diekhoff, G. M. (1999). The relationship between academic dishonesty and college classroom environment. *Research in Higher Education, 40*(4), 487–498.

Rabi, S. M., Patton, L. R., Fjortoft, N., & Zgarrick, D. P. (2006). Characteristics, prevalence, attitudes, and perceptions of academic dishonesty among pharmacy students. *American Journal of Pharmaceutical Education, 70*, 73–81.

Reeve, J. M. (2014). *Understanding motivation and emotion.* Hoboken, NJ: John Wiley & Sons.

Roberts, B. W., Walton, K. E., & Viechtbauer, W. (2006). Patterns of mean-level change in personality traits across the life course: A meta-analysis of longitudinal studies. *Psychological Bulletin, 132*, 1–25.

Roberts, P., Anderson, J., & Yanish, P. (1997, October). *Academic misconduct: Where do we start?* Poster presented at the Annual Conference of the Northern Rocky Mountain Educational Research Association. Retrieved from ERIC.

Roig, M., & DeTommaso, L. (1995). Are college cheating and plagiarism related to academic procrastination? *Psychological Reports, 77*, 691–698. doi:10.2466/pr0.1995.77.2.691

Rotter, J. B. (1966). Generalized expectancies for internal versus external control of reinforcement. *Psychological Monographs: General and Applied, 80*, 1–28.

Schab, F. (1991). Schooling without learning: Thirty years of cheating in high school. *Adolescence, 26,* 839–847.

Scheers, N. J., & Dayton, C. M. (1987). Improved estimation of academic cheating behavior using the randomized response technique. *Research in Higher Education, 26,* 61–69. doi:10.1007/BF00991933

Schraw, G., Olafson, L., Kuch, F., Lehman, T., Lehman, S., & McCrudden, M. T. (2007). Interest and academic cheating. In E. M. Anderman & T. B. Murdock (Eds.), *Psychology of academic cheating* (pp. 59–106). Burlington, MA: Elsevier Academic Press.

Sherif, M. (1936). *The psychology of social norms.* Oxford, UK: Harper.

Shu, L. L., Gino, F., & Bazerman, M. H. (2011). Dishonest deed, clear conscience: When cheating leads to moral disengagement and motivated forgetting. *Personality and Social Psychology Bulletin, 37*(3), 330–349. doi:10.1177/0146167211398138

Society for Personality and Social Psychology. (2015). What is social/personality psychology? Retrieved from http://spsp.org/what-socialpersonality-psychology

Stephens, J. M., & Gehlbach, H. (2007). Under pressure and underengaged: Motivational profiles and academic cheating in high school. In E. M. Anderman & T. B. Murdock (Eds.), *Psychology of academic cheating* (pp. 107–134). Burlington, MA: Elsevier Academic Press.

Stephens, J. M., & Nicholson, H. (2008). Cases of incongruity: Exploring the divide between adolescents' beliefs and behavior related to academic dishonesty. *Educational Studies, 34*(4), 361–376.

Stephens, J. M., Romakin, V., & Yukhymenko, M. (2010). Academic motivation and misconduct in two cultures: A comparative analysis of US and Ukrainian undergraduates. *International Journal for Educational Integrity, 6,* 47–60.

Stephens, J. M., Young, M. F., & Calabrese, T. (2007). Does moral judgment go offline when students are online? A comparative analysis of undergraduates' beliefs and behaviors related to conventional and digital cheating. *Ethics & Behavior, 17,* 233–254. doi:10.1080/10508420701519197

Sykes, G. M., & Matza, D. (1957). Techniques of neutralization: A theory of delinquency. *American Sociological Review, 22,* 664–670.

Tang, S., & Zuo, J. (1997). Profile of college examination cheaters. *College Student Journal, 31,* 340–346.

Tas, Y., & Tekkaya, C. (2010). Personal and contextual factors associated with students' cheating in science. *Journal of Experimental Education, 78,* 440–463.

Tibbetts, S. G., & Myers, D. L. (1999). Low self-control, rational choice, and student test cheating. *American Journal of Criminal Justice, 23,* 179–200. doi:10.1007/BF02887271

Tsai, C.-L. (2012). Peer effects on academic cheating among high school students in Taiwan. *Asia Pacific Education Review, 13*(1), 147–155. 10.1007/s12564–011–9179–4

Van Yperen, N. W., Hamstra, M. R. W., & van der Klauw, H. (2011). To win, or not to lose, at any cost: The impact of achievement goals on cheating. *British Journal of Management, 22,* S5–S15. doi:10.1111/j.1467–8551.2010.00702.x

Visentin, L. (2015). Macquarie University revokes degrees for students caught buying essays in MyMaster cheating racket. *The Sydney Morning Herald.* Retrieved from http://www.smh.com.au/national/education/macquarie-university-revokes-degrees-for-students-caught-buying-essays-in-mymaster-cheating-racket-20150528-ghba3z.html

Wangaard, D. B., & Stephens, J. M. (2011). *Creating a culture of academic integrity: A tool kit for secondary schools.* Minneapolis, MN: Search Institute.

Ward, D. A., & Beck, W. L. (1990). Gender and dishonesty. *Journal of Social Psychology, 130,* 333–339.

Weiss, J., Gilbert, K., Giordano, P., & Davis, S. F. (1993). Academic dishonesty, Type A behavior, and classroom orientation. *Bulletin of the Psychonomic Society, 31,* 101–102.

Whitley, B. J. (1998). Factors associated with cheating among college students: A review. *Research in Higher Education, 39,* 235–274.

Williams, K. M., Nathanson, C., & Paulhus, D. L. (2010). Identifying and profiling scholastic cheaters: Their personality, cognitive ability, and motivation. *Journal of Experimental Psychology: Applied, 16,* 293–307.

Williamson, W. P., & Assadi, A. (2005). Religious orientation, incentive, self-esteem, and gender as predictors of academic dishonesty: An experimental approach. *Archive for the Psychology of Religions, 27,* 137–158. doi:10.1163/008467206774355411

Zito, N., & McQuillan, P. J. (2011). "It's not my fault": Using neutralization theory to understand cheating by middle school students. *Current Issues in Education, 13*(3), 1–25.

12

THE VALIDITY OF ASSESSMENT WHEN STUDENTS DON'T GIVE GOOD EFFORT

Steven L. Wise and Lisa F. Smith

We assess a student's achievement to find out something about what the student knows and can do. Obtaining valid information requires that we have a good assessment that has been competently developed. But that is not sufficient. Valid information also requires that the student is motivated to devote enough effort to the assessment that the resulting information accurately reflects his or her knowledge, skills, and abilities. In this chapter, we examine the issue of motivation in an assessment context. We will focus our discussion on student testing, because the bulk of the relevant research to date has addressed test-taking motivation. It should be emphasized, however, that most of the issues discussed apply to all forms of student assessment.

The importance of test-taking motivation has been long recognized. Over a century ago, Thorndike (1904) noted the importance of effort in task performance, stating that "all our measurements assume that the individual in question tries as hard as he can to make as high a score as possible . . . we rarely know the relation of any person's effort to his maximum possible effort" (p. 228). Later, Cronbach (1960) commented on the unique role of motivation and its importance in the measurement of people:

> In making a physical measurement—for instance, weighing a truckload of wheat—there is no problem of motivation. Even in weighing a person, when we put him on the scale we get a rather good measure no matter how he feels about the operation. But in a psychological test the subject himself must place himself on the scale, and unless he cares about the result he cannot be measured.
>
> (p. 52)

The idea that test score validity depends on the effort expended by the student is logical and straightforward, and its veracity is not in doubt. Yet, this idea has thus far had little impact on our psychometric models, which tacitly assume that if we administer a test item to a student, the student will give good effort. Because they make no allowance for unmotivated students, the psychometric models currently used make a universal assumption of motivated test taking (Wise, 2015). In reality, however, test takers frequently do not behave effortfully. In these instances, measurement is distorted and validity diminished.

Although low motivation can affect the scores from any assessment, it has historically been of greatest concern with scores from assessment programs that are low-stakes from the student's perspective. There are two reasons for this. The first, and most obvious reason is that low motivation is far more prevalent when there are no personal consequences for students associated with test performance. The second reason concerns differences between high- and low-stakes assessments in terms of who is responsible for motivation. In high-stakes assessment, motivation is viewed as the responsibility of the test taker, who presumably has something meaningful to gain by doing well on the test. In contrast, in low-stakes assessment, the responsibility for test-taking motivation rests largely with those giving the test, who need to motivate students to give good effort despite the absence of personal consequences. That is, while many assessments are high-stakes for the test givers, they are often low-stakes for the test takers. Test-taking motivation, however, is driven primarily by the perspective of the test taker.

Throughout this chapter, we discuss low test-taking motivation and its effects on test performance. As we will show, the impact of low motivation has been found to be sizable, particularly with low-stakes tests, in which there are few consequences for students on the basis of their performance. In addition, we will consider the terms 'motivation,' 'engagement,' and 'effort' in a test-taking context as synonymous, in the sense that a *motivated* test taker is *engaged* to give good *effort* during a test event.

THE IMPACT OF LOW MOTIVATION ON VALIDITY

The most obvious impact of unmotivated test taking is that the student's score is likely to substantially underestimate what that student knows and can do. Because teachers use assessment information to understand the instructional needs of their students, decisions made about the needs of unmotivated students will be based on misleading information. This may result in the student being placed in lower learning groups or classes, or given special instruction on academic material that he or she already knows. At the same time, there are opportunity costs, because less instructional time will be available that could be directed toward helping the student master new material that he or she is ready to learn. Thus, the presence of test scores from unmotivated students can waste time, cause confusion, and render the educational process less efficient. Moreover, such test scores potentially have an adverse impact on school or teacher evaluation decisions.

Test scores are often aggregated for a variety of purposes, and the presence of non-effortful test taking affects each of these uses. Such data are often used to develop test norms that are used by students, teachers, and parents to help them interpret student test performance. Because scores resulting from non-effortful test taking tend to be negatively biased, their presence will, in turn, exert a negative bias on test norms.

Aggregated data are also used in several ways when developing tests and assessing their psychometric properties. First, in studies with multiple-choice tests, low motivation affects reliability estimation by spuriously inflating values of coefficient alpha (Wise & DeMars, 2009). Second, because low motivation introduces construct-irrelevant variance, non-effortful test taking attenuates the correlations of test scores with external variables (Wise, 2009). Third, non-effortful test taking can bias item statistics and calibrations (Wise & DeMars, 2006). Finally, differential item functioning (DIF) can be observed that is attributable to subgroups exhibiting differential mean effort, rather than to an item's content (DeMars & Wise, 2010).

Aggregated test score data are often used for research purposes—both in basic research and in the evaluation of educational programs. Because non-effortful responses to test items are correct at a rate similar to those from random responding, their presence in data can weaken the statistical power of significance tests (Osborne & Blanchard, 2011) or falsely indicate significant interaction effects (Wise & DeMars, 2010). In addition, when aggregated test scores are used to compare entities (e.g., schools, states, countries), mean differences in test-taking motivation can distort cross-entity comparisons of test performance (Elköf, Pavešič, & Grønmo, 2014; Setzer, Wise, van den Heuvel, & Ling, 2013).

THEORETICAL CONSIDERATIONS

Pintrich and Schunk (2002) defined motivation as "the process by which goal-directed activity is instigated and sustained" (p. 5). In the context of assessment, the relevant goal-directed activity is a student giving good effort throughout the assessment event. The expectancy-value theory of achievement motivation (Eccles, 1983) is commonly used to explain student assessment behavior. Drawing on this theory, Pintrich (1988; 1989; Pintrich & De Groot, 1990) provided a model of motivation that relates individual student characteristics and dispositions to the nature of the task at hand. In Pintrich's model, a student's motivation to complete a task is a function of three components: (a) expectancy of success on the task; (b) task value, or the importance of success to the student; and, (c) affective and emotional reactions to the task. Applying Pintrich's model to test taking, a student's motivation is a function of how well the student expects he or she will do on the test, the value to the student of doing well, and emotional reactions the student has to the testing situation (e.g., test anxiety).

Although an expectancy-value model provides a useful conceptualization of assessment motivation, it provides a somewhat limited explanation of observed student test-taking behavior. For example, Wolf, Smith, and Birnbaum (1995) found that students tended to give less effort to items on a test that were mentally taxing, especially when they did not know the material for that item. They suggested broadening the importance component of the expectancy-value model to include the estimated amount of effort needed to arrive at an item's correct answer. In addition, a student's test-taking motivation can vary during a test event (Wise, 2006; Wise & Kong, 2005; Wolf et al., 1995). These factors suggest that a test event should not be considered a unitary entity, and that fully understanding the dynamics underlying test-taking motivation requires that other factors be considered beyond student characteristics and dispositions.

An alternative perspective is provided if we conceptualize a test event as a series of encounters between the student and a test item, with each encounter occurring within a particular context. How much effort the student gives to a particular item can be influenced by characteristics of the student or item and the context in which the item was administered.

Based on this alternative perspective, we developed a demands-capacity model of test-taking effort (Wise & Smith, 2011). In this model, the amount of effort exhibited by a student for a particular test item is a function of two primary model components. The first component is the item's *resource demands*, which represents the amount of effort that must be expended by the student to correctly answer the item. The second component is the student's *effort capacity*, which is the amount of effort that the student is willing to devote to answering the test item. Two important features of the demands-capacity model are that resource demands can vary across items, and a student's effort capacity can change during a test event. An item's resource demands are determined by factors such as item difficulty, mental taxation, or the amount of reading required to answer the item. In comparison, a student's effort capacity has a more complex set of determinants including test consequences, internal factors such as attitudes about assessment, the student's experiences with previous items, and other external factors related to the testing environment (e.g., comfort level, distractions, etc.).

Under the Wise and Smith (2011) model, the central idea is that when a student is administered an item, student response effort is determined by the relative levels of the student's effort capacity and the item's resource demands. If effort capacity is higher, the student will respond effortfully. If, however, the item's resource demands exceed the student's current level of effort capacity, then a non-effortful response (e.g., an omitted answer or a random response) will occur. Whenever there are important consequences for the student (e.g., performance affects grades, or acceptance into university), effort capacity will typically greatly outweigh resource demands, and effortful responding will occur throughout the test event. However, in low-stakes testing, test-taking effort will largely be driven by internal factors, which may or may not engender a sufficient and consistent level of effort capacity throughout the test event.

From a validity perspective, the absence of test-taking motivation represents a construct-irrelevant factor that can negatively distort test scores (Haladyna & Downing, 2004; Messick, 1984). Most consumers of test scores (e.g., parents, employers, admissions officers, evaluators, etc.), however, tend to interpret test scores as uncontaminated measures, assuming that a student's responses to test items reflect only his or her knowledge, skills, and abilities relevant to the target measurement domain (Wise, 2015). Because measurement models rarely account for test-taking motivation, it is important to identify unmotivated test taking when it occurs to avoid validity threats. Identification of such scores indicates to consumers of assessment results that test scores should be interpreted cautiously.

MEASUREMENT OF TEST-TAKING MOTIVATION

To address the measurement challenges posed by unmotivated test taking, we need effective methods for measuring it. Such methods require consideration of the nature of unmotivated test taking and its characteristic behaviors. There are several different approaches, each with advantages and limitations.

Measures Based on Observation

Unmotivated students may appear to show little interest in their tests. One approach to measuring students' motivation would be through observations by educators during the test event. For example, school psychologists who give individually administered cognitive and psychological tests to students often use this approach. They are trained to observe a student during testing and to stop testing if they believe that the student's score would be invalid due to low motivation.

However, observational measures suffer from several disadvantages within classroom contexts. First, whenever students are tested in groups, it may be difficult to simultaneously assess the motivation of each individual student. Second, observational data tend to be more expensive to collect than that from other types of measures. Third, such observational measures provide only a generalized assessment of test-taking motivation, and would be of little value in assessing changes in a student's motivation during a test event. For these reasons, observational measures of motivation have limited practical value.

Self-report Measures

The most commonly used method for assessing test-taking motivation is through administration of self-report measures that students complete after they have taken their tests. Such scales typically consist of a small number of Likert-type items. These scales can be administered very quickly and generally have high internal consistency reliability. In the U.S., the most commonly used measure is the 10-item Student Opinion Survey (SOS [Sundre & Moore, 2002]), which is a revised version of a scale originally developed by Wolf and Smith (1995). The SOS has two 5-item subscales measuring the test's importance to the student and the amount of effort expended by the student, respectively.

Despite their popularity, self-report measures have two primary limitations. First, it is difficult to know how truthful students' responses are. Some students might not admit to being unmotivated if they feel that doing so would have negative consequences (e.g., punishment or being required to retake the test). Conversely, students who think they did not do well and who generally attribute failure to lack of effort (Pintrich & Schunk, 2002) might report being unmotivated to justify poor performance. Self-report motivation scales also require students who were unmotivated during the test to faithfully complete the motivation scale, a problematic assumption at best. These caveats are not intended to discourage the use of self-report motivation scales, but to make users aware of their potential limitations.

The second drawback of motivation scales is that they typically provide only general information about a student's test-taking motivation. This makes it difficult to identify when students responded effortfully during only a portion of their test event. Thus, self-report scales are also limited in the information they can provide.

Objective Measures Based on Student Behavior

Another class of test-taking motivation measures is based on student behaviors that can be objectively identified. Such behaviors include the student's pattern of responses to the administered items, and the time the student takes to respond to items.

Person Fit Statistics

A motivated test taker would be expected to produce a response pattern that is consistent with the difficulty levels of the items administered. Person fit statistics compare a student's response pattern to a theoretical measurement model, with aberrant patterns indicating poor model fit. For example, a random pattern (Meijer, 2003), in which most responses are incorrect and response correctness is unrelated to item difficulty, may indicate unmotivated test taking.

A key advantage of person fit is that because it is based on observed responses of students to test items, it is not vulnerable to the response biases characteristic of self-report measures. Person fit, however, has two important limitations. First, person fit statistics are sensitive to a variety of sources of misfit, which render them difficult to interpret. For example, in addition to detecting random response patterns, person fit has been found to identify student cognitive misconceptions (Tatsuoka, 1996) and curricular differences among schools (Harnisch & Linn, 1981), as well as cheating, lucky guessing, creative responding, or careless responding (Meijer, 1996). Hence, although random responding would be expected to result in poor person fit, observing poor person fit does not necessarily imply random responding. The second limitation of person fit statistics is that they, like self-report measures, focus on the entire test event as the unit of analysis. Because of these limitations, person fit statistics have not been widely used in practice to assess test-taking motivation.

Response Time Effort

During the past decade, as computer-based tests (CBTs) have become more common, researchers have begun to explore motivation measures based on item response time. These research efforts extended the work of Schnipke and Scrams (2002), who studied the behavior of test takers at the end of timed, high-stakes CBTs. They found that as time was running out, some test takers began rapidly responding to remaining items in hopes of getting some correct by chance. Based on these observations, Schnipke and Scrams identified two types of test-taking behavior. In *solution behavior*, test takers effortfully seek to determine the correct answer. In *rapid-guessing behavior*, test takers quickly respond to items in an essentially random fashion.

Wise and Kong (2005) investigated the data from *untimed, low-stakes* tests and discovered rapid guessing occurring throughout test events. They hypothesized that rapid guessing in this context indicated test taker disengagement, leading to non-effortful responding. Based on this, Wise and Kong developed a measure of test-taking effort called *response time effort* (RTE), which equals the proportion of a test taker's item responses that were solution behaviors, as opposed to rapid-guessing behavior. They proposed five research hypotheses that support the validity of RTE as a measure of test taker motivation. Wise and Kong found support for each hypothesis in this and subsequent studies (Wise, 2015).

As with person fit statistics, RTE has the advantage of being based on observable test taker behavior and can be sensitive to unmotivated test taking any time during a test event. It does, however, have two limitations. First, because RTE is based on response time, its use is practically limited to CBTs. Second, RTE was intended to be used with selected-response items, and its usefulness with constructed-response items is unclear.

THE DYNAMICS OF TEST-TAKING MOTIVATION

Performing well on an achievement test requires that the student has sufficient knowledge to score well, and sufficient motivation to demonstrate what he or she knows. This idea that test performance is a joint function of knowledge and motivation has important implications for test score validity, because test score interpretation becomes equivocal. Although this is most clearly seen in the interpretation of low performance (i.e., did the student score poorly because of low knowledge, low motivation, or both?), test-taking motivation can potentially influence the interpretation of all but the highest scores. To complicate matters, test-taking motivation is rarely an all-or-none matter, with students showing varying degrees of effort to a test. Moreover, students rarely behave non-effortfully throughout their entire test event; studies of RTE have found that most students exhibiting rapid-guessing behavior do so for fewer than half of their test items (DeMars, 2007; Swerdzewski, Harmes, & Finney, 2011; Wise & Cotten, 2009; Wise & DeMars, 2010; Wise & Kong, 2005).

The vulnerability of low-stakes achievement tests to the distortive effects of test-taking motivation represents an inconvenient truth to those who wish to use such tests and interpret their scores. Promoting and maintaining test score validity, however, demands that we recognize the impact of motivation in low-stakes testing, and better understand when, how, and why test-taking motivation affects scores. To that end, this section discusses what has been learned about the dynamics of test-taking motivation and its effects on validity. Factors influencing test-taking motivation group into three general categories: the context in which testing occurs, characteristics of the item, and characteristics of the student.

Contextual Characteristics

Test consequences for students represent by far the strongest factor affecting test-taking motivation. Wise and DeMars (2005) synthesized 15 studies of test-taking motivation, and found that examinees tested under low-consequence conditions exhibited test performances averaging over one-half standard deviation lower than that of examinees from higher-consequence conditions. Subsequent studies have found similar effect sizes (Eklöf & Knekta, 2014; Smith & Smith, 2002; Sundre & Kitsantas, 2004).

Apart from test consequences, myriad contextual factors can affect motivation, especially in low-stakes settings. The time of day that testing occurs has been found to be associated with rapid-guessing behavior, with mean RTE decreasing throughout the school day (Wise, Ma, Kingsbury, & Hauser, 2010). The physical setting in which testing occurs is important. A setting that is noisy, too hot or cold, has other instructional activities occurring nearby, or has other distracting elements can affect students' focus and attention. Moreover, taking a test in unfavorable conditions may suggest to the student that the test is unimportant, further diminishing motivation. Although these considerations constitute normal operational procedure recommendations for the administration of standardized tests, they are not always followed in practice—with potentially adverse consequences for test-taking motivation.

The test proctor can affect a student's test-taking motivation. If the proctor is disliked by the student or inattentive to the group's test-taking engagement, motivation may decrease. Occasionally teachers are required to administer tests that they perceive to have little value; here, they may—consciously or unconsciously—exhibit behavior that invites unmotivated test taking from their students.

Test-taking motivation may also be affected by peers. A large group test session may foster a sense of anonymity, with students believing unmotivated test taking will go unnoticed by the proctor—particularly if other students appear unmotivated. Additionally, if students are allowed to leave the testing room upon test completion, remaining students may shift to rapid-guessing behavior to finish their tests to leave and join their friends.

While many signals and cues in the testing room can potentially diminish a student's test-taking motivation, some can also have positive effects. Testing students in a quiet, comfortable room with attentive proctors who encourage motivated test taking is most likely to yield test scores that are undistorted by low motivation.

A student's level of motivation to respond to an item may be influenced by the experience of having taken the items that precede it. The degree to which previous items were engaging and challenging would influence the value component according to expectancy-value theory. Likewise, how well the student perceives he or she did during the previous portion of the test would influence the expectancy component when responding to the current item.

The development of response time–based measures of test-taking motivation has revealed an additional contextual issue for low-stakes tests. Rapid guessing has been associated with the position of the item on a test: the later an item appears, the more likely it is to receive rapid-guessing behavior (Lee & Jia, 2014; Setzer et al., 2013; Wise, 2006; Wise, Pastor, & Kong, 2009). Such item position effects may be due to test speededness or to fatigue or boredom (Wise et al., 2009; Wolf et al., 1995).

Item Characteristics

Diverse item characteristics have been found to be related to test-taking motivation. Reading items have higher rates of rapid guessing than math items (Wise et al., 2010). Mentally taxing items are associated with lower effort levels (Wise et al., 2009; Wolf et al., 1995). Essay items elicit lower levels of motivation than multiple-choice items (Sundre, 1996; Sundre & Kitsantas, 2004). DeMars (2000) found constructed-response items were lowered by lack of test consequences more than multiple-choice items. In studies of rapid-guessing behavior on multiple-choice items, motivation was lower on longer items (Setzer et al., 2013; Wise, 2006; Wise et al., 2009). However, Wise et al. (2009) found that inclusion of an item graphic was associated both with higher motivation and mitigated the item position effect on motivation, possibly because these items were more engaging. Collectively, these results are generally consistent with the demands-capacity model, as items that require more from the student (e.g., constructed response or additional reading) have higher resource demands, which is somewhat offset by the possible capacity-enhancing effect of item graphics.

Item difficulty would be expected to influence test-taking motivation, because items that are too easy provide little challenge, while items that are too difficult would be discouraging. Consequently, students find moderately challenging tasks the most intrinsically motivating (Pintrich & Schunk, 2002), with research somewhat supporting these expectations. Wolf et al. (1995) found the level of item difficulty was predictive of the differences in item difficulties from consequential and non-consequential testing conditions. However, Wise et al. (2009) found item difficulty to be predictive of rapid-guessing behavior, while Wise (2006) did not.

Computerized adaptive testing (CAT), which is designed to adjust to the students' ability levels and administer items of moderate difficulty for each individual, provides a new context in which to explore item difficulty's impact on motivation. Because item difficulty is matched to student achievement level, it has been claimed that CAT is more motivating than fixed-length tests, consistent with motivation research that has found that individuals find moderately challenging tasks the most intrinsically motivating. Hence, CAT should yield higher scores because it reduces a construct-irrelevant factor that can negatively distort test scores. A study of the claim (Wise, 2014), however, found that although some students report being more motivated during CAT, these motivational differences do not appear to be accompanied by higher test performance.

Student Characteristics

There are clearly numerous transient physical and emotional states that students could experience (e.g., hunger, fatigue, illness, depression, anxiety, grief), which could understandably lead to lower motivation during a particular test event. There are, however, a number of stable student characteristics that are associated with a predisposition to low motivation.

Researchers have found differential mean motivation across different demographic groups of test takers. One of the most frequently observed correlates is gender. Numerous studies have found that males are much more likely to exhibit low test-taking motivation than females (DeMars, Bashkov, & Socha, 2013; DeMars & Wise, 2010; Eklöf, 2007; Setzer et al., 2013; Swerdzewski, Harmes, & Finney, 2009; Wise & Cotten, 2009; Wise & DeMars, 2010; Wise, Kingsbury, Thomason, & Kong, 2004; Wise et al., 2010). There is also evidence that low motivation in school-aged students becomes more prevalent with age. Wise et al. (2010) found, using the same type of low-stakes adaptive achievement test across a variety of U.S. grades, that the occurrence of rapid guessing increased steadily between Grades 3 through 9 (roughly ages 9–14). This increase may be due, at least in part, to either the increasing desire for independence that students tend to develop during those years, or to an increased reluctance to give effort to an activity that has no personal value or benefit. Similar findings were reported by Eklöf and Knekta (2014), who studied Grade 8 and Grade 12 students in Sweden.

Student levels of test-taking motivation have been found to be associated with a variety of student academic dispositions and personality constructs. Several studies investigated achievement goal orientation and found motivation to be positively related to mastery approach and performance approach orientations (Barry, Horst, Finney, Brown, & Kopp, 2010; Swerdzewski et al., 2009; Waskiewicz, 2012) and negatively related to work avoidance (Barry et al., 2010; DeMars et al., 2013; Swerdzewski et al., 2009; Waskiewicz, 2012). Swerdzewski et al. (2009) compared U.S. university students who either attended or failed to attend a required assessment session (i.e., attendance served as a surrogate for test-taking motivation) and found group differences on test performance and on several dispositional variables. Wise and Cotten (2009) investigated the relationship between rapid-guessing behavior and student responses to the Student Conceptions of Assessment inventory (SCoA [Brown, Irving, Peterson, & Hirschfeld, 2009]), and found that three of the four SCoA subscales predicted student test-taking motivation. Self-reported motivation has been found to be positively related to conscientiousness and agreeableness (Barry et al., 2010; DeMars et al., 2013), and non-attendance at a university assessment session was associated with higher levels of psychological reactance (Brown & Finney, 2011).

Research on test-taking motivation has uncovered a diverse set of causes and correlates, and has shown that the factors influencing motivation can come from the student taking a test, the test items, and the context in which testing is done. How these factors interact in determining how effortfully a student responds to a test item, however, is still being established.

ADDRESSING THE VALIDITY THREAT

While test-taking motivation is complex and has impact on the validity of score-based inferences, we now focus on the question of what can be done about the problem.

Increasing Test Consequences

Increasing the consequences for test performance can have a strong positive impact on student effort during low-stakes tests. For example, test performance could count toward a student's course grade (DeMars, 2000; Smith, & Smith, 2002; Sundre, 1999; Sundre & Kitsantas, 2004; Wolf & Smith, 1995) or students could be required to attain a sufficient score in order to graduate. However, any shift to higher-stakes testing brings with it a set of validity issues, such as (a) an increased need for secure testing to prevent cheating, (b) heightened concerns about the effects of test anxiety (also a construct-irrelevant factor) on validity, and (c) the need for more frequent development of new test forms. Hence, increasing the stakes of testing, although highly likely to improve student motivation, will generally require more resources than many test givers could afford.

An alternative way to increase test consequences would be to provide material incentives contingent on examinee test performance. Multiple studies have found positive effects of incentives on motivation and/or performance (Berlin et al., 1992; Braun, Kirsch, & Yamamoto, 2011; Duckworth, Quinn, Lynam, Loeber, & Stouthamer-Loeber, 2011; Marsh, 1984; Steedle, Zahner, & Kugelmass, 2014; Terry, Mills, & Sollosy, 2008). Other studies, however, have found incentives to have no effects (O'Neil, Abedi, Miyoshi, & Mastergeorge, 2005) or to have positive effects only for some examinees (Baumert & Demmrich, 2001; O'Neil, Sugrue, & Baker, 1996).

As a serious method for improving test-taking motivation, incentives suffer from two drawbacks. The first is practical; the cost of providing meaningful monetary incentives for test performance will exceed the budgets of most, if not all, testing programs. The second drawback is that the use of incentives can distort test score distributions in unpredictable ways, and may exacerbate achievement gaps (Braun et al., 2011).

Increase the Value of Test Performance to Students

In many low-stakes assessment programs, students receive little or no feedback regarding their scores or how the scores are to be used. A cost-effective approach to increasing students' perceived value of test performance would be to provide information to them regarding (a) how well they have done and how to interpret their scores and (b) who will receive the resulting test scores and/or how they are to be used. Several studies have investigated different types of instructions that could be given to students to increase the test's value to the student. These studies have reported mixed success. Merely providing feedback about test performance to students after low-stakes tests does not appear to improve either test-taking motivation or test performance (Baumert & Demmrich, 2001; Wise, 2004).

Finney, Sundre, Swain, and Williams (2014) randomly assigned college students taking a low-stakes assessment, both as incoming freshman and mid-year sophomores, to receive instructions that either (a) they would receive test scores reported only to them, (b) their scores would be reported to their faculty, or (c) their scores would be averaged with others and the aggregated results would be used for institutional effectiveness. They found that test consequences did not affect value-added estimates of achievement. Kornhauser, Minahan, Siedlecki, and Steedle (2014) experimentally studied the effects of instructions for the Collegiate Learning Assessment, which emphasized that students were representing their university, and that test performance had real consequences for their institution. These special instructions, which were intended to appeal to the academic citizenship of the students, improved neither test-taking motivation nor performance.

Other studies have had more positive results. Brown and Walberg (1993) found that elementary school students taking the Iowa Test of Basic Skills who were given special instructions to do as well as possible for themselves, their parents, and their teachers, performed significantly better than students in a control condition. Liu, Bridgeman, and Adler (2012) randomly assigned college students taking the ETS Proficiency Profile to receive instructions that they would either (a) receive no feedback on test performance (control) with scores to be used only for research purposes, (b) have their scores sent to their college or potential employers, or (c) have their scores averaged with others and the average sent to their college. Students in the two treatment conditions reported higher motivation and performed significantly better than students in the control condition. In a later study, Liu, Rios, and Borden (2015) randomly assigned students taking the Proficiency Profile to treatment conditions in which they were told that either (a) their score would have no consequences on their grade but they were encouraged to do their best or (b) their scores could be used in aggregate for institutional assessment and that this assessment may affect the academic ranking of their institution and affect the future value of their diploma. As with their previous study, they found that instructions indicating higher consequences resulted in greater motivation and test performance.

Although test instructions can have positive effects on test takers, one cannot assume that they will in a given context. Assessment practitioners are, therefore, encouraged to empirically determine the types of instructions that are likely to be effective with the assessment being administered to their particular population of students. Such instructions may appeal to academic citizenship, students' feelings of ownership over their test performance, or may communicate explicit consequences associated with their test performance being disseminated to others. Of course, it should be noted that these types of instructions can potentially have unexpected negative effects; for example, if the students of an unpopular teacher were told that student test performance would be used to evaluate that teacher, they may be motivated to perform poorly on the test.

Use Items That Are Resistant to Low Motivation

Unmotivated test taking appears to affect the responses to constructed-response items more than multiple-choice items (DeMars, 2000). Mentally taxing items appear to be more vulnerable to the effects of low motivation (Wolf et al., 1995), and the more reading required, the higher the likelihood of rapid-guessing behavior (Wise, 2006; Wise et al., 2009). Collectively, these findings suggest that the most desirable types of items, from a motivational standpoint, would be multiple-choice items that require little reading and are not mentally taxing. Of course, this is not realistic because it unduly constrains effective measurement of the target achievement domain. The measurement of higher-order skills typically requires items with cognitive complexities that render them highly vulnerable to low motivation.

The lesson for measurement practitioners is that when low-stakes assessments are used, there may be practical limits to what one can ask students to do during a test event. Short tests that have items with low resource demands are most likely to be responded to effortfully. More complex, mentally taxing items might be highly desirable to use in a low-stakes context, but if the demands of these items exceed the effort capacity of the students, non-effortful responding is likely to occur and the test event will be a wasted assessment opportunity. The unique challenge of low-stakes testing is to effectively measure what a student knows and can do, using items with resource demands that are within the constraints of limited student effort capacity.

Motivation Reporting and Filtering

Some amount of unmotivated test taking is inevitable even under the best of circumstances, and it is important that a plan is in place to deal with its occurrence. When individual students will be judged on the basis of their test performance, the most powerful step that measurement practitioners can take is to simply report information about test-taking motivation to anyone who will interpret these scores. This might be done by establishing some threshold criterion value on the motivation measure being used, and classifying as invalid any scores whose motivation values surpass the threshold value. For example, Wise (2015) describes an *individual score validation* procedure in which scores would be invalidated for any unspeeded test event during which more than 10% of the item responses were classified as rapid guesses. This criterion would indicate scores deemed too potentially distorted by rapid guessing to be trustworthy. A score classified as invalid for this reason should be noted as such on the student's score report, which would alert educators and parents to interpret that score cautiously. Although the idea of identifying motivation-invalidated scores on score reports seems logical and straightforward, to our knowledge no operational assessment program is currently doing this.

As discussed earlier, test scores are frequently aggregated and analyzed for diverse psychometric purposes, such as item calibration, norms development, and miscellaneous psychometric analyses (e.g., reliability estimation, differential item functioning, and studies to support the validation of score interpretations). Hence, another reason one might seek to classify scores as motivation invalid would be to delete these scores from psychometric data analyses. This process, termed *motivation filtering* (Sundre & Wise, 2003; Wise & DeMars, 2005), has been investigated as a method to improve the quality of test data (DeMars, 2007; Liu et al., 2015; Rios, Liu, & Bridgeman, 2014; Steedle, 2014; Swerdzewski et al., 2011; Waskiewicz, 2011; Wise, 2009; Wise & Cotten, 2009; Wise & DeMars, 2005, 2010; Wise & Kong, 2005; Wise, Wise, & Bhola, 2006). The typical finding from these studies is that, after filtering invalid scores, mean test performance increases, and correlations of test scores with external criteria tend to increase (even though filtering usually reduces the variance of the test score data which typically *reduces* correlations). Interestingly, although motivation filtering has the effect of lowering coefficient alpha, this is due to coefficient alpha values being spuriously high when data from unmotivated test takers are included (Wise, 2006; Wise & DeMars, 2009). Although some statisticians discourage its use (Sijtsma, 2009; Teo & Fan, 2013), coefficient alpha continues to be widely used; the spurious boost in alpha due to motivation may give a false sense of security regarding a test's reliability.

The use of motivation filtering requires the assumption that test-taking effort is unrelated to a student's true achievement level. Otherwise, if motivation and true achievement were positively related, then filtering out the less motivated students would also filter out the less able students, which would undesirably distort the distribution of scores one was trying to analyze. However, studies of this assumption have generally found correlations between motivation and other measures of student academic ability to be near zero or to show very weak positive relationships (see Steedle, 2014 for a summary).

Effort-moderated IRT Model

One of the advantages of measuring test-taking motivation using item response time is that it classifies each item as either solution or rapid-guessing behavior. This led Wise and DeMars (2006) to propose a modified item response theory (IRT) model that ignores rapid guesses. Wise and DeMars found that when rapid guessing was present in test data, their effort-moderated IRT model exhibited better model fit, more accurately estimated item parameters, and yielded student scores that exhibited higher correlations with external variables than a standard IRT model. Kong (2007) reported similar findings in an expanded investigation of multiple IRT models.

The effort-moderated model assumes that if a student's non-effortful behavior does not apply to too many items, then the effortful portion of the test event can still be used to calculate a viable score. For example, if a student gave rapid guesses to 20% of the items, the effort-moderated model would compute a score based on the student's responses to the other 80%. Effort-moderated scoring assumes that the item responses that were not rapid guesses were, in fact, effortful. Wise and Kingsbury (2015) found support for this assumption.

Effort-monitoring CBT

Both motivation filtering and effort-moderated scoring represent post hoc strategies that measurement professionals could use to reduce the impact of unmotivated test taking. When computer-based, multiple-choice tests are used, a more proactive approach is available that may serve as a deterrent to non-effortful responding. Wise, Bhola, and Yang (2006) introduced an *effort-monitoring CBT*; during a test event, the computer monitors for rapid-guessing behavior. If a student exhibits a threshold number of rapid guesses, the computer displays a warning message that encourages the student to give more effort. In an experimental study of the effects of such messages, Wise et al. (2006) found that receiving a warning message resulted in a sharp decrease in rapid-guessing behavior and higher correlations of test scores with external criteria. In a follow-up study, Kong, Wise, Harmes, and Yang (2006) replicated these results, and also found a significant improvement in test performance for rapid guessers who received warnings. Hence, it is possible to intervene during a test event to curtail a substantial amount of rapid-guessing behavior and thereby improve validity.

CONCLUSIONS

Measurement practitioners who want to reduce the impact of low motivation on test score validity have an array of options available to them. Test stakes can be raised, more motivating instructions can be given to students, items with fewer resource demands can be used, score reports can indicate motivation invalid scores, motivation filtering can be employed, and effort-moderated scoring or effort-monitoring CBTs can be used. Note that many of these options can be used in combination to enhance their effects. For example, DeMars (2007) found that the use of effort-moderated scoring in combination with motivation filtering was more effective than effort-moderated scoring alone.

The ultimate lesson is that valid measurement of a student's achievement, in any context, requires an understanding of test-taker psychology as well as of psychometrics. Without adequate student effort, it is difficult to assess achievement, and this chapter has explored many of the issues relevant to test-taking motivation.

When assessment occurs outside a formal testing context (e.g., during classroom assessment activities) students may be less likely to behave non-effortfully. There are several reasons for this. First, during classroom assessments, students may be less likely to feel a sense of anonymity; that is, if they do not try on the assessment, it would more likely to be noticed by the teacher. Second, non-test assessments, which are often more formative in nature, may be viewed by students as having greater a connection to their own learning. Third, non-test assessments are often completed in smaller groups that can be monitored by the teacher, who can take corrective action, provide feedback, or suspend the assessment if the students are not giving good effort. It should be noted, however, that motivation on classroom assessments has received little research attention; hence, less is known about the dynamics of student motivation with these types of assessments.

There has been a great deal of growth in research on test-taking motivation in recent years, as evidenced by three-quarters of the references for this chapter dated 2000 or later. Part of the reason for this growth is increased interest in the impact of motivation on the validity of scores from several low-stakes, high-profile national and international assessments (e.g., NAEP, PISA, or TIMSS). Another reason is that the advent of computer-based assessment has brought with it key developments in the use of response time–based measures of motivation. These measures have allowed us to look inside test events, item by item, in ways that were not possible before, and have provided researchers with a richer understanding of the dynamics of test-taking effort. Moreover, the response time–based measurement of motivation has led to several promising new tools for addressing the challenges to validity posed by unmotivated test taking, such as effort-moderated scoring or effort-monitoring tests.

Despite the knowledge that has been gained over the past two decades, and innovations that have emerged to measure and manage the effects of unmotivated test taking, these efforts have, thus far, had limited impact on practice. A major obstacle is that those interpreting test scores continue to unquestioningly accept the universal assumption of motivated test taking that was noted by Thorndike (1904) and is perpetuated in the psychometric models used today. The validity of assessment when students do not give good effort depends on educators' ability to incorporate what we know about test-taking motivation into the way we administer our assessments and interpret their scores. This will require increasing the sensitivity of educators, policy makers, and other key stakeholders to the problem, and enhancing their understanding of strategies for effectively dealing with unmotivated students during the assessment process.

REFERENCES

Barry, C. L., Horst, S. J., Finney, S. J., Brown, A. R., & Kopp, J. P. (2010). Do examinees have similar test-taking effort? A high-stakes question for low-stakes testing. *International Journal of Testing, 10*, 342–363.

Baumert, J., & Demmrich, A. (2001). Test motivation in the assessment of student skills: The effects of incentives on motivation and performance. *European Journal of Psychology of Education, 16*, 441–462.

Berlin, M., Mohadjer, L., Waksberg, J., Kolstad, A., Kirsch, I., Rock, D., & Yamamoto, K. (1992). An experiment in monetary incentives. *Proceedings of survey research methods section* (pp. 393–398). American Statistical Association: Alexandria, VA.

Braun, H., Kirsch, I., & Yamamoto, K. (2011). An experimental study of the effects of monetary incentives on performance on the 12th-grade NAEP reading assessment. *Teachers College Record, 113*, 2309–2344.

Brown, A. R., & Finney, S. J. (2011). Low-stakes testing and psychological reactance: Using the Hong Psychological Reactance Scale to better understand compliant and non-compliant examinees. *International Journal of Testing, 11*, 248–270.

Brown, G.T.L., Irving, S. E., Peterson, E. R., & Hirschfeld, G.H.F. (2009). Use of informal-interactive assessment practices: New Zealand secondary students' conceptions of assessment. *Learning and Instruction, 19*, 97–111.

Brown, S. M., & Walberg, H. J. (1993). Motivational effects on test scores of elementary students. *Journal of Educational Research, 86*, 233–236.

Cronbach, L. J. (1960). *Essentials of psychological testing (2nd Ed.)* New York: Harper & Row.

DeMars, C. E. (2000). Test stakes and item format interactions. *Applied Measurement in Education, 13*, 55–77.

DeMars, C. E. (2007). Changes in rapid-guessing behavior over a series of assessments. *Educational Assessment, 12*, 23–45.

DeMars, C. E., Bashkov, B. M., & Socha, A. B. (2013). The role of gender in test-taking motivation under low-stakes conditions. *Research & Practice in Assessment, 8*, 69–82.

DeMars, C. E., & Wise, S. L. (2010). Can differential rapid-guessing behavior lead to differential item functioning? *International Journal of Testing, 10*, 207–229.

Duckworth, A. L., Quinn, P. D., Lynam, D. R., Loeber, R., & Stouthamer-Loeber, M. (2011). Role of test motivation in intelligence testing. *Proceedings of the National Academy of Sciences, 108*, 7716–7720.

Eccles, J. (1983). Expectancies, values, and academic behaviors. In J. T. Spence (Ed.), *Achievement and achievement motives* (pp. 75–146). San Francisco: Freeman.

Eklöf, H. (2007). *Gender differences in test-taking motivation on low-stakes tests—A Swedish TIMSS 2003 example.* Paper presented at the annual meeting of the American Educational Research Association, Chicago.

Eklöf, H., & Knekta, E. (2014, April). *Different stakes, different motivation? Swedish studies of test-taking motivation in different assessment contexts.* Paper presented at the annual meeting of the American Educational Research Association, Philadelphia.

Elköf, H., Pavešič, B. J., & Grønmo, L. S. (2014). A cross-national comparison of reported effort and mathematics performance in TIMSS Advanced. *Applied Measurement in Education, 27,* 31–45.

Finney, S. J., Sundre, D. L., Swain, M., & Williams, L. M. (2014, April). *Are value-added estimates influenced by test consequences in large-scale, low-stakes testing contexts?* Paper presented at the annual meeting of the American Educational Research Association, Philadelphia.

Haladyna, T. M., & Downing, S. M. (2004). Construct-irrelevant variance in high-stakes testing. *Educational Measurement: Issues and Practice, 23*(1), 17–27.

Harnisch, D. L., & Linn, R. L. (1981). Analysis of item response patterns: Questionable test data and dissimilar curriculum practices. *Journal of Educational Measurement, 18,* 133–146.

Kong, X. J. (2007). *Using response time and the effort-moderated model to investigate the effects of rapid guessing on estimation of item and person parameters.* Unpublished doctoral dissertation, James Madison University.

Kong, X. J., Wise, S. L., Harmes, J. C., & Yang, S. (2006, April). *Motivational effects of praise in response-time based feedback: A follow-up study of the effort-monitoring CBT.* Paper presented at the annual meeting of the National Council on Measurement in Education, San Francisco.

Kornhauser, Z. G. C., Minahan, J., Siedlecki, K. L., & Steedle, J. T. (2014, April). *A strategy for increasing student motivation on low-stakes assessments.* Paper presented at the annual meeting of the American Educational Research Association, Philadelphia.

Lee, Y., & Jia, Y. (2014). Using response time to investigate students' test-taking behaviors in a NAEP computer-based study. *Large-scale Assessments in Education, 2*(8). doi:10.1186/s40536–014–0008–1

Liu, O. L., Bridgeman, B., & Adler, R. M. (2012). Measuring learning outcomes in higher education: Motivation matters. *Educational Researcher, 41,* 352–362.

Liu, O. L., Rios, J. A., & Borden, V. (2015). The effects of motivational instruction on college students' performance on low-stakes assessment. *Educational Assessment, 20,* 79–94.

Marsh, H. W. (1984). Experimental manipulations of university student motivation and their effects on examination performance. *British Journal of Educational Psychology, 54,* 206–213.

Meijer, R. R. (1996). Person-fit research: An introduction. *Applied Measurement in Education, 9,* 3–8.

Meijer, R. R. (2003). Diagnosing item score patterns on a test using item response theory-based person-fit statistics. *Psychological Methods, 8,* 72–87.

Messick, S. (1984). The psychology of educational measurement. *Journal of Educational Measurement, 21,* 215–237.

O'Neil, H. F., Abedi, J., Miyoshi, J., Mastergeorge, A. (2005). Monetary incentives for low-stakes tests. *Educational Assessment, 10,* 185–208.

O'Neil, H. F., Sugrue, B., & Baker, E. L. (1996). Effects of motivational interventions on the National Assessment of Educational Progress mathematics performance. *Educational Assessment, 3,* 135–157.

Osborne, J. W., & Blanchard, M. R. (2011). Random responding from participants is a threat to the validity of social science research results. *Frontiers in Psychology, 1,* 1–7.

Pintrich, P. R. (1988). A process-oriented view of student motivation and cognition. In J. S. Stark & R. Mets (Eds.), *Improving teaching and learning through research* (pp. 55–70). San Francisco: Jossey-Bass.

Pintrich, P. R. (1989). The dynamic interplay of student motivation and cognition in the college classroom. In C. Ames & M. Maehr (Eds.), *Advances in achievement and motivation* (Vol. 6, pp. 117–160). Greenwich, CT: JAI Press.

Pintrich, P. R., & De Groot, E. V. (1990). Motivational and self-regulated learning components of classroom academic performance. *Journal of Educational Psychology, 82,* 33–40.

Pintrich, P. R., & Schunk, D. H. (2002). *Motivation in education: Theory, research, and applications* (2nd ed.). Upper Saddle, NJ: Merrill Prentice-Hall.

Rios, J. A., Liu, O. L., & Bridgeman, B. (2014). Identifying low-effort examinees on student learning outcomes assessment: A comparison of two approaches. *New Directions for Institutional Research, 2014*(161), 69–82.

Schnipke, D. L., & Scrams, D. J. (2002). Exploring issues of examinee behavior: Insights gained from response-time analyses. In C. N. Mills, M. T. Potenza, J. J. Fremer, & W. C. Ward (Eds.), *Computer-based testing: Building the foundation for future assessments* (pp. 237–266). Mahwah, NJ: Lawrence Erlbaum Associates.

Setzer, J. C., Wise, S. L., van den Heuvel, J. R., & Ling, G. (2013). An investigation of test-taking effort on a large-scale assessment. *Applied Measurement in Education, 26,* 34–49.

Sijtsma, K. (2009). On the use, the misuse, and the very limited usefulness of Cronbach's alpha. *Psychometrika, 74*, 107–120. doi:10.1007/S11336–008–9101–0

Smith, L. F., & Smith, J. K. (2002). Relation of test-specific motivation and anxiety to test performance. *Psychological Reports, 91*, 1011–1021.

Steedle, J. T. (2014). Motivation filtering on a multi-institution assessment of general college outcomes. *Applied Measurement in Education, 27*, 58–76.

Steedle, J. T., Zahner, D., & Kugelmass, H. (2014, April). *Test administration procedures and their relationships with effort and performance on a college outcomes test.* Paper presented at the annual meeting of the American Educational Research Association, Philadelphia.

Sundre, D. L. (1996, April). *The role of examinee motivation in assessment: celebrity, scene stealer, or cameo?* Paper presented at the annual meeting of the National Council on Measurement in Education, New York.

Sundre, D. L. (1999, April). *Does examinee motivation moderate the relationship between test consequences and test performance?* Paper presented at the annual meeting of the American Educational Research Association, Montreal.

Sundre, D. L., & Kitsantas, A. (2004). An exploration of the psychology of the examinee: Can examinee self-regulation and test-taking motivation predict consequential and non-consequential test performance? *Contemporary Educational Psychology, 29*, 6–26.

Sundre, D. L., & Moore, D. L. (2002). The student opinion scale: A measure of examinee motivation. *Assessment Update, 14*(1), 8–9.

Sundre, D. L., & Wise, S. L. (2003, April). *'Motivation filtering': An exploration of the impact of low examinee motivation on the psychometric quality of tests.* Paper presented at the annual meeting of the National Council on Measurement in Education, Chicago.

Swerdzewski, P. J., Harmes, J. C., & Finney, S. J. (2009). Skipping the test: Using empirical evidence to inform policy related to students who avoid taking low-stakes assessments in college. *Journal of General Education, 58*, 167–195.

Swerdzewski, P. J., Harmes, J. C., & Finney, S. J. (2011). Two approaches for identifying low-motivated students in a low-stakes assessment context. *Applied Measurement in Education, 24*, 162–188.

Tatsuoka, K. K. (1996). Use of generalized person-fit indices, zetas for statistical pattern classification. *Applied Measurement in Education, 9*, 65–76.

Teo, T., & Fan, X. (2013). Coefficient alpha and beyond: Issues and alternatives for educational research. *Asia-Pacific Education Researcher, 22*, 209–213. doi:10.1007/s40299–013–0075-z

Terry, N., Mills, L., & Sollosy, M. (2008). Student grade motivation as a determinant of performance on the Business Major Field ETS Exam. *Journal of College Teaching & Learning, 5*, 27–32.

Thorndike, E. L. (1904). An introduction to the theory of mental and social measurements. Oxford: Science Press.

Waskiewicz, R. A. (2011). Pharmacy students' test-taking motivation-effort on a low-stakes standardized test. *American Journal of Pharmaceutical Education, 75*(3), Article 41.

Waskiewicz, R. A. (2012). Achievement goal orientation and situational motivation for a low-stakes test of content knowledge. *American Journal of Pharmaceutical Education, 76*(4), Article 65. doi:10.5688/ajpe76465

Wise, S. L. (2006). An investigation of the differential effort received by items on a low-stakes, computer-based test. *Applied Measurement in Education, 19*, 93–112.

Wise, S. L. (2009). Strategies for managing the problem of unmotivated examinees in low-stakes testing programs. *Journal of General Education, 58*, 152–166.

Wise, S. L. (2014). The utility of adaptive testing in addressing the problem of unmotivated examinees. *Journal of Computerized Adaptive Testing, 2*, 1–17.

Wise, S. L. (2015). Effort analysis: Individual score validation of achievement test data. *Applied Measurement in Education, 28*, 237–252.

Wise, S. L., Bhola, D., & Yang, S. (2006). Taking the time to improve the validity of low-stakes tests: The effort-monitoring CBT. *Educational Measurement: Issues and Practice, 25*(2), 21–30.

Wise, S. L., & Cotten, M. R. (2009). Test-taking effort and score validity: The influence of student conceptions of assessment. In D. M. McInerney, G.T.L. Brown, & G. A. D. Liem (Eds.), *Student perspectives on assessment: What students can tell us about assessment for learning* (pp. 187–205). Greenwich, CT: Information Age Press.

Wise, S. L., & DeMars, C. E. (2005). Low examinee effort in low-stakes assessment: Problems and potential solutions. *Educational Assessment, 10*, 1–17.

Wise, S. L., & DeMars, C. E. (2006). An application of item response time: The effort-moderated IRT model. *Journal of Educational Measurement, 43*, 19–38.

Wise, S. L., & DeMars, C. E. (2009). A clarification of the effects of rapid guessing on coefficient alpha: A note on Attali's Reliability of Speeded Number-Right Multiple-Choice Tests. *Applied Psychological Measurement, 33*, 488–490.

Wise, S. L., & DeMars, C. E. (2010). Examinee non-effort and the validity of program assessment results. *Educational Assessment, 15*, 27–41.

Wise, S. L., & Kingsbury, G. G. (2015, April). *Modeling student test-taking motivation in the context of an adaptive achievement test.* Paper presented at the annual meeting of the National Council on Measurement in Education, Chicago, IL.

Wise, S. L., Kingsbury, G. G., Thomason, J., & Kong, X. (2004, April). *An investigation of motivation filtering in a statewide achievement testing program.* Paper presented at the annual meeting of the National Council on Measurement in Education, San Diego.

Wise. S. L., & Kong, X. (2005). Response time effort: A new measure of examinee motivation in computer-based tests. *Applied Measurement in Education, 18*, 163–183.

Wise, S. L., Ma, L., Kingsbury, G. G., & Hauser, C. (2010, May). *An investigation of the relationship between time of testing and test-taking effort.* Paper presented at the annual meeting of the National Council on Measurement in Education, Denver, CO.

Wise, S. L., Pastor, D. A., & Kong, X. J. (2009). Understanding correlates of rapid-guessing behavior in low stakes testing: Implications for test development and measurement practice. *Applied Measurement in Education, 22*, 185–205.

Wise, S. L., & Smith, L. F. (2011). A model of examinee test-taking effort. In J. A. Bovaird, K. F. Geisinger, & C. W. Buckendal (Eds.), *High-stakes testing in education: Science and practice in K-12 settings* (pp. 139–153). Washington, DC: American Psychological Association.

Wise, V. L. (2004). *The effects of the promise of test feedback on examinee performance and motivation under low-stakes testing conditions* (Unpublished doctoral dissertation). University of Nebraska-Lincoln, Lincoln, NE.

Wise, V. L., Wise, S. L., & Bhola, D. S. (2006). The generalizability of motivation filtering in improving test score validity. *Educational Assessment, 11*, 65–83.

Wolf, L. F., & Smith, J. K. (1995). The consequence of consequence: Motivation, anxiety, and test performance. *Applied Measurement in Education, 8*, 227–242.

Wolf, L. F., Smith, J. K., & Birnbaum, M. E. (1995). Consequence of performance, test motivation, and mentally taxing items. *Applied Measurement in Education, 8*, 341–351.

13

SECTION DISCUSSION: STUDENT PERCEPTIONS OF ASSESSMENT

James H. McMillan

Over the past decade, new lines of research on student perceptions of assessment have been generated that have significant implications for understanding how assessment impacts student learning and motivation. Some time ago, Crooks (1988) pointed out that assessment's impact on students is mediated by how the students' perceptions about the assessment, including students' affective reactions, are responded to and internalized by the students. However, Brown, McInerney, and Liem (2009) and Brown and Hirschfeld (2007) pointed out that the literature on students' assessment-related perceptions since that time has not been extensive. The first volume that devoted significant attention to students' perceptions of assessment was Brown (2008), which discussed both student and teacher conceptions about assessment, based primarily on empirical work done in New Zealand and Australia. This was followed by McInerney, Brown, and Liem's (2009) edited book in which chapter authors described research pertaining to student perceptions of assessment, summarizing empirical evidence about what assessment means to students. This volume included several chapters that described the development of quantitative surveys to measure perceptions toward assessment. The editors pointed out that student voice is "remarkably absent" in the literature on assessment (Brown et al., 2009, p. 5).

The landscape of studies focused on student perceptions of assessment has changed. There is now a growing body of literature on student beliefs about assessment that will greatly enhance our understanding of how students prepare for, engage in, and react to assessment, and how resultant beliefs, emotions, and perspectives affect learning and motivation. This chapter reviews and synthesizes this emerging literature to show what has been researched, what it means, and implications for practice and future research, developing a model that shows the relationships of the components to the process of assessment.

WHY STUDY STUDENT PERCEPTIONS OF ASSESSMENT?

There is considerable precedent for establishing the important role of human perception as a critical intervening influence on emotions and behavior (Patrick, Skinner, & Connell, 1993; Weiner, 2012), and there is every reason to believe that perceptions are related in important ways to other achievement-related constructs such as self-regulation, self-efficacy, and motivation (Schunk, 1992; Schunk & Meece, 1992). Clearly, how people perceive, think about, and react to events, objects, and other people is important in understanding and promoting positive behavior and lessening undesirable behavior, such as academic dishonesty. Furthermore, we know that there are cultural and other normative influences on perceptions, and that, over time, perceptions are shaped by experience (Bandura, 1986; Lakoff & Johnson, 1999). So it is somewhat curious that relatively little attention has been paid toward student perceptions of assessment. Perceptions can refer to many things, from awareness and basic recognition to deeper meaning, understanding, and interpretation. Whether termed 'perceptions' or 'conceptions,' the nature of this characteristic is essentially what students think, believe, and feel, comprising of cognition (thinking) and emotion (feeling) (Ajzen, 2005; Fabrigar, MacDonald, & Wegener, 2005; Ostrom, 1969; Rosenburg & Hovland, 1960).

There is growing acceptance that terms such as *beliefs*, *conceptions*, and *perceptions* generally refer to cognitive understandings, descriptions, and evaluations of and affective responses about things in a person's world (Fives & Buehl, 2012; Rubie-Davies, Flint, & McDonald, 2011). Since they are highly personalized and develop over time, the cultural context in which one establishes perceptions is critical to what is understood. Furthermore, some perceptions may be stable across contexts, while others are subject to situational differences (Pekrun, 2006). Our broader understanding of students' conceptions of assessment, then, will likely depend on contextual differences across cultures, and may even change among different teachers in the same culture. Essentially a socio-constructivist perspective, this view has been recognized by many as a needed theory to understand student beliefs (Moll, 2014). Based on the work of Vygotsky (1978), perceptions, thinking, and learning from a socio-constructivist view are socially and culturally mediated (Shepard, 2000). Applied to assessment, this suggests students' reactions to assessments, their subsequent performance, and feedback they receive are determined in part by the social context from which students construct meaning.

Regardless of the particulars of how perceptions may be influenced by socio-constructivist determinants, it is clear that students' cognitions and feelings are part of the assessment process, and these perceptions and emotions will affect learning and motivation (Boekaerts & Cascallar, 2006; Brown, 2008; Brown & Hirschfeld, 2008). One challenge is to establish a framework that takes into account perspectives students bring to any assessment event, influenced by both sociocultural factors and the more specific effects of particular assessment experiences. Together, these factors will help explain what students mentally and emotionally process about the assessment event, and why there can be a high diversity of thoughts and reactions to the same assessment (Chu, Guo, & Leighton, 2014; Moni, Van Kraayenoord, & Baker, 2002).

Cognitive beliefs concerning importance or value, and affective reactions such as enjoyment, like, or dislike, may be either consistent or inconsistent with one another. That is, it is possible to both value something and dislike it, while it is also possible to believe something is important and enjoyable. When cognitive and affective components are consistent, overall attitudes are stronger (McMillan, 2014). Research on test anxiety (Pekrun & Bühner, 2014) already recognizes the importance of looking at both components, something the assessment research field would do well to emulate.

An important area of study that has indirectly investigated student perceptions, certainly the impact of assessment results, is the extensive amount of research on student attributions for performance success and failure. At its core, this research has clearly established that meaning to the student, based on a number of factors, is a mediated process that has implications for learning, motivation, and self-efficacy (Gipps & Tunstall, 1998; Weiner, 2005). That is, if high effort and high expectations culminate in poor performance, leading to feelings of shame and distress, surely these emotions fuel questions about competence. While much of the attribution literature is based on experimental studies, using staged scenarios, there is no question that this line of research has supported the essential role of student perceptions of evaluative tasks. Perceptions of such factors as effort, task difficulty, peer performance, and item quality are determinants of attributional meanings. For example, students who view an assessment as easy, yet perform poorly, may attribute failure to lack of ability, which could diminish motivation, leading to hopelessness. Self-efficacy may be enhanced when students exert moderate levels of effort for difficult tasks and experience success. Since perceptions may be conceptualized in a number ways, and are related to different theoretical frameworks, it is important to identify the more influential types of perceptions that impact on learning behavior and motivation.

LITERATURE ON STUDENT PERCEPTIONS TOWARDS ASSESSMENT

Table 13.1 summarizes the major dimensions of elementary and secondary students' perceptions of assessment that have been reported by both quantitative and qualitative investigations since 1996, though most have been published after 2000. The initial literature search was limited to empirical investigations within compulsory schooling published between 1995–2014, using as descriptors 'student perceptions,' 'student beliefs,' 'student attitudes,' and 'student conceptions,' with 'assessment' and 'test.' ERIC, PsycINFO, and Google Scholar databases were searched, with identified articles, books, and reports used to find additional studies. For each study, the age of students, country, nature of perceptions, and behavioral consequences were identified. The nature of perceptions category identified the type or characteristic of assessment which students were discussing (e.g., an accountability or classroom assessment), and the composition of these attitudes (i.e., beliefs [cognitive component] and emotions [affective component]). Studies examining secondary students are listed first, followed by studies of several or all grade levels, then those at only the elementary level. It is organized this way because, as Brown, Peterson, Irving, & Hirschfeld (2009) pointed out, there may be important differences in perceptions related to age.

The search found three substantial lines of research on student perceptions of assessment, one preliminary line of research, and a number of individual studies. Each of the three major lines of research has a large number of studies that have replicated and refined a particular conceptual framework about student perceptions, primarily at the secondary level. Much of the research in these three lines report results from the development of surveys to assess students' perceptions. For example, in one major line of studies, there has been extensive research reported on the validity of dimensions used to describe student perceptions toward assessment from the student self-report survey *Student Conceptions of Assessment*. As listed in Table 13.1, Gavin Brown and others have demonstrated the validity of six fundamental student perception scales (type as interactive-informal or more formal test, improvement of teaching and learning, irrelevance, external attribution, and enjoyment). The scales originated primarily from previous research on teachers' conceptions of assessment (Brown, 2011). This may have resulted in a less than comprehensive exploration of student perceptions, especially in light of other research that has demonstrated additional perceptual categories (e.g.,

Table 13.1 Summary of Empirical Investigations of Elementary and Secondary Students' Perceptions of Assessment

Line of Research or Study	Grade Level(s)	Country(ies)	Perception Component		
			Assessment Task-Related	Beliefs	Affect
Brown and colleagues: (Brown, 2011; Brown & Harris, 2012; Brown & Hirschfeld, 2007, 2008; Brown et al., 2009; Brown, Peterson & Irving, 2009; Hirschfeld & Brown, 2009; Hue, Leung, & Kennedy, 2014; Segers & Tillema, 2011; Weekers, Brown, & Veldkamp, 2009)	Primarily secondary	New Zealand, Netherlands, Hong Kong	• Interactive-informal/formal-test like • Teacher controlled or for school accountability	• Improves teaching and learning • Reject as irrelevant (e.g., bad, inaccurate, unfair)	• Enjoyment
Pekrun and colleagues (Pekrun, 2006; Pekrun, Cusack, Murayama, Elliot, & Thomas, 2014; Pekrun et al., 2004; Pekrun, Elliot, & Maier, 2006, 2009; Pekrun, Goetz, Frenzel, Barchfeld, & Perry, 2011; Pekrun, Goetz, Titz, & Perry, 2002)	Secondary	Germany, UK, US, Australia			• Hope • Anxiety • Hopelessness • Pride • Relief • Shame • Enjoyment/joy • Anger
Dorman and colleagues; Alkharusi: (Alkharusi, 2007, 2009, 2011; Alkharusi, Aldhafri, & Alnabhani, 2014; Cavanagh, Waldrip, Romanoski & Dorman, 2005; Dorman, Fisher, & Waldrip, 2006; Dorman & Knightly, 2006a; Dorman & Knightly, 2006b; Dorman, Waldrip & Fisher, 2008; Gao, 2012)	Secondary	US & International (primarily Germany, Oman)	• Alignment (Congruence with planned learning) • Authenticity • Student input/consultation • Transparency of purpose • Fairness (able to complete/right level/differentiation		

Study	Level	Country			
Gao, 2009	High school	Hong Kong	• Feedback	• Value for learning • Fairness	• Anxiety
Harris, Harnett, & Brown, 2009	Intermediate and high school	New Zealand	• Type of assessment outcome • Time		• Anxiety • Positive emotion • Confusion • Boredom
Irving, Peterson, & Brown, 2008; Lee, 2007; Tjeerdsma, 1997	Secondary	New Zealand, Hong Kong, Netherlands	• Trustworthiness of source • Source • Encouragement • Mode of feedback • Feedback error correction	• Relevance to standards • Motivation	• General emotional reaction
Pajares & Graham, 1998	Middle school	US	• Honesty • Feedback error correction • Encouragement	• Accuracy • Motivation	• General emotional reaction
Peterson & Irving, 2008	Secondary	New Zealand	• Encouragement • Feedback error correction • Honesty	• Relevance • Value/usefulness • Motivation	• General emotional reaction
Havnes, Smith, Dysthe, & Ludvigsen, 2012	High school	Norway	• Feedback quality • Mistakes • Criteria • Peer assessment • Follow up	• Feedback usefulness	
Brookhart, Walsh, & Zientarski, 2006	Middle school	US	• Difficulty • Effort	• Value/usefulness • Self-efficacy • Goal orientation	

(Continued)

Table 13.1 (Continued)

Line of Research or Study	Grade Level(s)	Country(ies)	Perception Component		
			Assessment Task-Related	Beliefs	Affect
Williams, 2014	Middle school	New Zealand	• Type of feedback • Targets • Correct/incorrect • Improvement	• Usefulness	
Harris, Brown, & Harnett, 2014	Primary, intermediate, high school	New Zealand	• Focus on improvement/correction • Source • Trustworthiness of source • Focus on general praise		• General emotional response
Brookhart & Bronowicz, 2003	Elementary, secondary	US	• Difficulty • Effort • Self-efficacy • Goal orientation	• Relevance/Importance • Self vs. others' opinions	
McMillan & Turner, 2014	Elementary, middle	US	• Teacher or accountability • Accuracy • Difficulty • Error correction • Goal orientation • Self-efficacy • Effort	• Value/usefulness • Ability • Attributions for performance	• Anxiety, nervousness • Happiness • Pride • Temporary distress

Reference	Grade level	Country	Constructs	
Lowe & associates: (Lowe, 2014; Lowe & Ang, 2012; Lowe, Grumbein, & Raad, 2011; Lowe & Lee, 2008; Lowe et al., 2008; Wren & Benson, 2004)	Elementary, secondary	US	• Worry • Autonomic hyper-arousal response • Social concerns • Cognitive interference • Task-irrelevant behavior	
Tunstall & Gipps, 1996	Elementary	UK	• General emotional reaction	• Source • Relevance to standards
Remesal, 2009	Elementary	Spain		• Goal orientation • Context • Grades
Lichtenfeld, Pekrun, Stupnisky, Reiss, & Murayama, 2012	Elementary	US; Germany	• Enjoyment • Anxiety • Affect	• Value for learning
Atkinson, 2003	Elementary	Scotland		• Difficulty • Effort • Grades • Self-assessment • Peer assessment

Pekrun and associates, and Dorman and associates [Table 13.1]), and because much of the research has been conducted in countries without extensive accountability testing, such as New Zealand. Nevertheless, it is significant to find that secondary students differentiate among test characteristics, affect, and beliefs about the value of assessment for improving teaching and learning.

A second line of research, also focused on the validity of different components of student perceptions through instrument development, has been conducted by Jeffrey Dorman and colleagues, as well as Hussain Alkharusi and associates. They have researched another student self-report survey, the *Perceptions of Assessment Tasks Inventory*, and demonstrated that students' conceptions could be organized into five assessment-task factors (i.e., alignment, authenticity, student involvement, transparency, and fairness). In contrast to the *Student Conceptions of Assessment* survey, which has used primarily New Zealand student populations for instrument development, the *Perceptions of Assessment Tasks Inventory* has been developed with mostly U.S. and German student populations. This difference in populations and contexts may explain why there are some differences in components of perceptions, though some overlap clearly exists (e.g., controlled by teacher or for accountability is similar to purpose, irrelevance to authenticity and fairness, and student input to interactive-informal).

A different extensive line of research, within the wider context of academic emotions, has been established by Reinhard Pekrun and others, who have completed a significant amount of research on the multidimensionality of assessment-related emotions (Pekrun & Bühner, 2014). Also relying on student self-report inventories, primarily the *Test Emotions Questionnaire* and *Achievement Emotions Questionnaire*, this line of research has demonstrated that emotions related to assessment are quite varied (e.g., hope, anxiety, relief, and joy), with sometimes subtle but important differences. Notably, this work differentiates between relatively stable emotions (trait) and those related to a specific point in time (state).

Other individual studies with secondary level students show some overlap with the more extensive lines of research, as summarized, but also show differences. In particular, assessment-related characteristics such as difficulty, accuracy, errors and mistakes, effort, goal orientation, feedback, general emotional reactions, and self-efficacy are suggested as important perceptions. There is also some overlap among the studies (e.g., value, importance, or relevance; whether tests are for accountability or not; and specific affective components such as anxiety and enjoyment).

An emerging line of research on test anxiety, at both the elementary and secondary levels, has been initiated by Lowe and colleagues. While not as extensive and well-developed as the aforementioned three, these investigations also focus on the development of student self-report instruments (*Test Anxiety Inventory for Children and Adolescents* and *Test Anxiety Measure for Adolescents*). These measures have been validated as identifying several components of student anxiety, including cognitive interference, physiological arousal, social concerns, engaging in task irrelevant behaviors, and worry.

While there is much less research with younger students, especially quantitative investigations of instrument development that reveal components of perceptions [notable exceptions are Brown & Harris (2012) and Hue et al. (2014)], the studies show that there are similar perceptions related to characteristics of assessment, affect, and beliefs about the value and importance of assessment. In particular, studies at the elementary level find that students tend to associate assessment with generally positive or negative emotions, such as happiness, pride, satisfaction, distress, and/or anxiety, and value the information from assessment that shows how much they understand.

Students are keenly aware of the difficulty of assessments. Younger students tend to make clear connections between effort studying and their performance, generally accepting the results from assessment as fair and accurate, with more emphasis on improvement and correction of errors (McMillan & Turner, 2014).

When evaluating this body of work overall, it appears that study of these perceptions is still in its infancy, and, consistent with Brown et al.'s (2009) findings, much more delineation of the nature of student perceptions and the relationship of these perceptions to learning and motivation is needed. While possible robust perceptual components have been identified through instrument development, additional research is needed to provide a more thorough and accurate description of these perceptions. The very credible research that has been conducted in the three major lines and one emerging line of research needs further replication with other student populations in countries with different assessment policies. Cultural differences may be critical to how students view and react to assessment.

Furthermore, components that have been verified through student self-reports are limited to the nature of the questions that have been used. It is possible that different components would emerge as important with the inclusion of additional items. One perspective that could be examined in more detail would be differences between perceptions about classroom versus accountability assessment. It seems possible that students' views about classroom assessment, with potentially greater connection between learning and tests, would generate different perceptions than large-scale accountability tests that are frequently far removed from the learning process. With these caveats in mind, there are some trends from this research that summarize the findings as related to the process of assessment and can be used to generate a useful framework.

A FRAMEWORK FOR UNDERSTANDING STUDENT PERCEPTIONS TOWARDS ASSESSMENT

The framework suggested in Figure 13.1 consists of three well-established phases of assessment—before, during, and after assessment (McMillan, 2014; Peterson, Brown, & Jun, 2015), with student perceptions drawn from the review related to each phase. The *before* phase of the framework consists of perceptions and emotions that, in turn, influence preparation effort, expectations for success, and emotions (e.g., anxiety) that occur prior to taking the assessment. Consistent with McMillan and Turner's (2014) qualitative investigation and earlier research on emotions (Pekrun & Bühner, 2014), perceptions toward assessment in the before phase can be dichotomized into either *trait* or *state* characteristics.

Trait-related perceptions are those that are based on relatively stable and consistent personality dispositions that students bring to most assessment tasks, regardless of the specific assessment event (e.g., goal orientation, positive expectations, self-efficacy, attributional style, and expectations for success). For example, students who have developed a mastery orientation over time tend to view assessment as a means for knowing if they understand the content or can accomplish the skill, and what deficits need to be ameliorated. Students who in general attribute success and failure to controllable factors, such as effort and study skills, may be less anxious than students who attribute success and failure to uncontrollable factors, such as test difficulty. Stable traits of individuals also could include beliefs about the accuracy and validity of assessment in general, and a belief in the value of assessment in general, beyond what is elicited by a specific assessment.

Phase

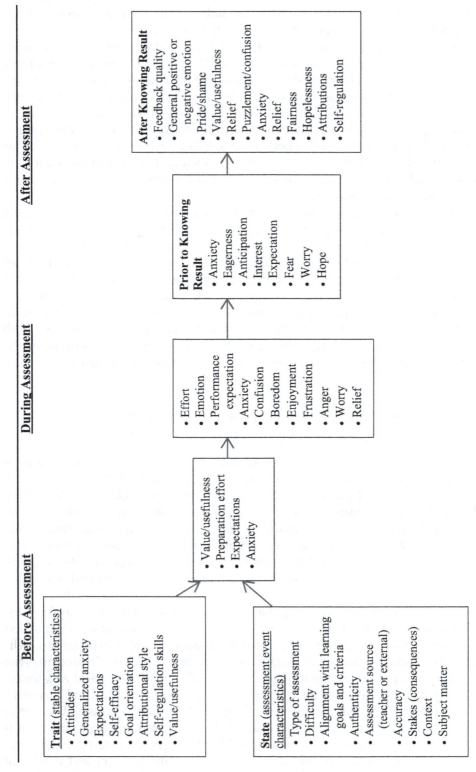

Figure 13.1 Framework Showing How Student Perceptions Toward Assessment Relate to the Assessment Process

The *state* dimension is influenced by the features of a specific assessment event or situation, depending on the nature of assessment on a single occasion. As a result, states vary from time to time. That is, some assessments are difficult, some easy, some long and others short, some consist of constructed-response items, others selected-response items. States also vary with respect to the subject matter being assessed, what Pekrun and Bühner (2014) term 'course/domain-specific' achievement emotions in their research. Struyven and Devesa (this volume) assert that alternative or 'novel' types of assessment (e.g., self- and peer assessment, performance-based, portfolio, and technology-based assessments), may engender different student initial perceptions. Especially within higher education, students may view non-traditional forms of assessment with suspicion, wary of potential problems with fairness and grading, even though they may understand the value of skills that are emphasized. Most importantly, perhaps, Struyven and Devesa remind us that regardless of the type of assessment, student perceptions depend mostly on how the chosen assessment is designed, implemented, and scored. That is, the type of assessment may not be as important as the quality of the items and/or task and its relevance, alignment with what was studied, administration, and scoring process. At lower grade levels, students may be less guarded about novel assessment since their tendency is to be less performance and more mastery/learning oriented (McMillan & Turner, 2015).

Brown and colleagues (e.g., Brown, 2011; Brown et al., 2009), in concluding that students differentiate between interactive informal assessments and those that are more formal, as well as between those that are teacher-controlled versus those used for school accountability, provide evidence for differences in state characteristics. Dorman and colleagues (e.g., Dorman & Knightley, 2006a, 2006b; Dorman et al., 2006), and research by Irving et al. (2008), confirm that students recognize whether assessments are aligned with planned learning, criteria, and standards; if they are transparent in purpose; and whether they are authentic. Several investigations suggest that students know the value and usefulness of specific assessments, and some research documents that students' anxiety is greater with some types of assessments (McMillan & Turner, 2014; Struyven & Devesa, this volume). Murdock, Stephens, and Grotewiel (this volume) show how beliefs about the value of assessments, as either performance or mastery oriented, predict academic dishonesty.

Trait and state factors influence behavior, affective predilections, and perceptions of value about the upcoming assessment. An important behavior is the level of effort that students exert in preparing for the assessment (Atkinson, 2003; Brookhart & Bronowicz; 2003, Brookhart et al., 2006; McMillan & Turner, 2014). Effort is critical in determining how students think about assessment results (McMillan & Turner, 2014), obviously impacting on what and how much is learned, and also clearly influencing motivational constructs (McMillan & Turner, 2014). Wise and Smith (this volume) point out that effort varies considerably and impacts the validity of assessment results. For example, McMillan and Turner (2015) found that when students exerted little effort, poor performance was taken less seriously than when moderate or great effort was exerted. The development of healthy self-efficacy and internal, controllable attributions depends on exerting an appropriate amount of effort in preparing for an assessment. Self-regulation is developed as students experience different levels of success in relation to their effort. Expectations about performance are partly based on the amount of effort that is exerted preparing for the assessment. Expectations are also influenced by state characteristics such as the type of assessment. Some students are more confident about doing well on multiple-choice rather than constructed-response type items, or on tests similar to those on which they have been successful in the past.

Perceived value and anxiety also result from both trait and state characteristics. Brown and colleagues have demonstrated that students differentiate between teacher-controlled and external tests, and it is likely that assessments with greater relevance to and alignment with classroom learning are seen as more valuable. Assessments seen as irrelevant would elicit less motivation and effort. McMillan and Turner (2014) have found that longer tests are viewed as more difficult, resulting in greater anxiety. It is also likely that anxiety toward assessment in general and related emotions, such as worry, influence expectations as well as effort and related behaviors. Murdock, Stephens, and Grotewiel (this volume) identify that relatively stable traits (e.g., personality, goal orientation, and academic confidence) are connected to beliefs about cheating and academic dishonesty.

Perceptions and emotions are also elicited *during* an assessment event. Effort may impact on how carefully students read questions, focus, apply appropriate learning strategies, and check answers. Emotions such as hope, relief, anxiety, and contentment are elicited (Vogl & Pekrun, this volume), often influenced by perceptions of difficulty, preparation effort, and expectations about performance. Harris et al. (2009) confirmed that confusion and boredom may occur during assessment. Wise and Smith (this volume) remind us that the expectancy/value model of motivation (a) determines (to a certain extent) student effort while test-taking, (b) identifies that factors beyond student dispositions also impact effort, (c) suggests that motivation varies by test item, depending on how much effort is required to answer the item (resource demands), and (d) impacts on students' willingness to exert effort to come up with an answer (effort capacity).

After the assessment is completed, a range of emotions and cognitions will be evident. It is useful to think about these as first occurring before receiving results and then after receiving results (e.g., grade, score, mistakes or learning errors). Immediately following performance, emotions include relief, hope, happiness, satisfaction, distress, and fear, and probably help confirm perceptions related to fairness and difficulty. Once results are received, in conjunction with feedback, studies indicate that students will experience a range of emotions, and, depending on effort and expectations, will form beliefs that influence subsequent behavior and motivational dispositions (Irving et al. 2008; Lowe, 2014; McMillan & Turner, 2014).

Many of the investigations in Table 13.1 confirm that a dominant initial emotional reaction is general, either positive or negative (Harris et al. 2009; Irving et al. 2008; Lee, 2007; Pajares & Graham, 1998; Peterson & Irving, 2008; Tjeerdsma, 1997). Peterson et al. (2015) found that students draw a meaningful relationship between results and achievement emotions only after feedback is received. McMillan and Turner (2014) found that when students receive results, they focus on whether wrong answers were the result of silly mistakes or not knowing the correct answer. When careless errors were made, immediate negative emotions, such as anger, disappointment, and other distress reactions were temporary, without lasting effects. They also found that more enduring emotions and cognitions are formed when students study, form a positive expectation for success, then find out that they did not know the content or could not perform the skill. Clearly, most students are happy when they obtain a high score or grade, even when little effort was exerted (success with little effort can sometimes support attributions of ability, which is not undesirable unless taken to an extreme). When students realize they are wrong, they will hopefully acknowledge and accept feedback (Harris et al., 2014), then determine what they need to work further on and exert subsequent effort in learning.

While students may become worried or have anxiety based solely on performance, depending on consequences, lasting effects are more likely to occur when they have exerted some level of effort. Emotions such as hopelessness, shame, and pride, and cognitions such as confidence and expectations, will have impact beyond what is experienced with the specific assessment event. The alignment of effort with results may also be important for the development of self-regulation, especially when students make learning errors and, subsequently, take steps to study more in order to do better in the future (Andrade, 2013). This suggests that self-regulation may be developed most effectively when students exert effort for moderately difficult assessments that sometimes result in having wrong answers because of a deficit in knowledge and/or skills. That is, development of self-regulating skills is dependent, in part, on having tasks which the student has not yet fully mastered. By knowing what was not sufficiently understood, in the context of what effort was expended preparing for the assessment, students are able to link outcomes to the manner in which they studied. In this way, they learn about how to control their actions, an essential component of self-regulation.

IMPLICATIONS OF THE STUDENT PERCEPTIONS OF ASSESSMENT FRAMEWORK FOR THE SECTION CHAPTERS

Daniel Dinsmore and Hope Wilson (this volume), and Katrien Struyven and Joana Devesa (this volume) delineate some important *before* elements related to the assessment process, such as the genre of assessment (e.g., selected-response, constructed-response, performance-based, technology-enhanced, or portfolio); the nature of the evaluator (instructor, peers, or student for self-assessment); the domain being assessed; and the developmental stage of the student. These factors are shown to influence self-regulation, anxiety, and emotional regulation. Of particular note is the point that the purpose of assessment, and student views about knowledge, learning, and testing in general, are linked to self-regulation. If one of the goals of education is to enhance self-regulation, these *before* factors need to be carefully considered and addressed. That is, students need to be taught how assessment is important for their learning, rather than how assessment is used summatively. These authors remind us that much research is needed to show how student involvement in assessment improves self-regulation. The important role of feedback, both from the student in self- and/or peer assessment and the teacher, is also emphasized.

Elisabeth Vogl and Reinhard Pekrun (this volume) provide a comprehensive summary of how emotions intersect with all phases of the assessment process. The authors point out how test anxiety exists as both a trait and state emotion (reflected in Figure 13.1), and explain why it is important to differentiate between the forethought phase (before; prospective), the performance phase (during), and the self-reflective phase (after; retrospective). Anxiety, accompanied sometimes with debilitating effects, is described as an emotion and perception that can exist in all phases of the assessment process, not simply in the before phase as described by Dinsmore and Wilson (this volume). While most studied as anticipatory anxiety, it is clear that this disposition can have major impacts on the reliability of scores and validity of inferences. The negative effects of anxiety can be directly addressed via interventions that help students to cope with their anxiety, or correct cognitive distortions (e.g., thinking it's all or nothing or projecting unsupported or illogical negative outcomes, or 'the end of the world'). These could be termed test-taking skills, ones that are very fair, because they enhance the accuracy of results and promote a more balanced, healthy perspective about assessment.

As previously pointed out, effort is a key disposition for understanding student perceptions toward assessment tasks and results. Effort is purposeful engagement, an important behavioral consequence of motivation. Before an assessment event, effort is evidenced by student preparation and studying. Wise and Smith (this volume) point out that effortful studying is in part determined by the nature of the test and consequences, and in part by trait characteristics. They summarize how contextual factors (e.g., high- or low-stakes consequences, time of day, test proctor, physical setting, climate), and the difficulty of the items effect levels of effort both before and during the assessment. For example, challenging items and those of moderate difficulty generally enhance motivation, as does an assessment that has high-stakes consequences. This suggests that perceptions of consequences of lower-stakes tests, such as quizzes or classroom tests, may be important for motivation. In the absence of high stakes, if students perceive assessment as contributing to their understanding, essentially a formative purpose that impacts the perceived value of the assessment, motivation could be enhanced. Item difficulty, if at the appropriate level, can also enhance motivation. If items are perceived to be too difficult or too easy, motivation is undermined, especially for low-stakes tests. According to Wise and Smith, low-stakes tests are more vulnerable to less effort than high-stakes tests.

Finally, a significant point made by Wise and Smith (this volume), is that lack of effort leads to poor assessment validity. This has implications for perceptions students have after completing an assessment and finding out how they performed. With moderate effort students will value outcomes more and be able to connect effort to success. This connection helps develop self-regulation and self-efficacy. Low effort is related to lack of value, especially intrinsic value, even with high scores or grades. As summarized by Lipnevich, Berg, and Smith (this volume), perceptions of feedback will also be related to effort, since feedback about performance when little effort was expended is likely to be dismissed. In their model of feedback, Lipnevich et al. show that descriptive, individualized feedback that focuses on the student's cognitive processes elicits value to the student and enhances learning and self-regulation. If feedback is more descriptive than evaluative, or is vague, emotional reactions are more likely to be muted, with more confusion and frustration. When specific and individualized, feedback leads to a more reasoned perspective, one that allows meaningful connection between effort and expectations. According to Lipnevich et al., both cognitive and affective response elements interact with one another. Feedback using the right tone and connecting strongly to the work is more likely to generate a positive emotional response, making it more likely that students will focus and internalize the information provided, and adopt a more problem-oriented coping strategy rather than an emotion-focused, avoidant coping response.

The chapter by Murdock, Stephens, and Grotewiel (this volume) on academic dishonesty relates to the framework by showing how trait and state characteristics, particularly at the *before* stage, are related to dishonesty beliefs and cheating. Traits such as goal orientation, self-efficacy, locus of control, and other personality types are related to tendencies to justify dishonesty. Beliefs about the seriousness of cheating, a trait characteristic, predict actual cheating. State characteristics, such as classroom goal orientation and social norms, that are part of teacher-created assessment contexts, also establish *before* factors that influence beliefs about dishonesty and cheating. The authors indicate that some students will cheat even when they know it is wrong, pointing out how instructional strategies *during* assessment, including seating arrangements and exam formats, can reduce cheating. Furthermore, they encourage adoption of mastery oriented approaches because performance oriented ones may encourage students to 'win' at all costs, including cheating.

IMPLICATIONS FOR PRACTICE AND POLICY

Implications for practice from the section chapters are presented in Table 13.2. They are organized by the before, during, and after phases of assessment, and indicate the benefits that derive from each suggestion. Many of the implications are practices to implement before assessment, which target state-related factors within the control of teachers and schools concerning the nature of the assessment and how students are prepared for and involved in the process. Careful teacher planning can address these variables.

Implications for Practice

Following the logic of Figure 13.1, a final set of implications for teaching, which essentially integrates Tables 13.1 and 13.2, is posited.

1. Consider Students' Varied Perceptions Toward Assessment

The research is clear that students hold a variety of perceptions, with both affective and cognitive components, and different perceptions may need differing teacher responses. Teachers need to know the range and nature of their students' perceptions of assessment, essentially being able to see and understand assessment through the eyes of the student (Hattie, 2009). This will enable a better match between instruction, assessment, and feedback, and guide teachers to give more individualized attention to students with particularly unhealthy perceptions. Teachers also need to consider how student perceptions differ at each stage of the assessment process—before, during, and after assessment. Attention should be directed toward cognitions and affect that are likely at each phase, especially those that are demonstratively adaptive (Figure 13.1). For example, perceptions of difficulty are best addressed before assessment, while noting what students feel and think while taking an assessment will help in understanding their subsequent reactions to their actual performance.

2. Take Time to Understand Students' Trait Characteristics

There are many good reasons for helping students to understand their trait tendencies toward assessment, especially when it comes to emotional anticipation, anxiety, and motivation. Knowing these dispositions will enable teachers to directly address misconceptions about ability, expectations, dysfunctional levels of anxiety, and other negative emotions. By determining student study habits and other methods of preparation, teachers can promote positive behaviors that will lead to students' confidence and realistic expectations, as well as provide opportunities for students to connect effort and strategies with outcomes, which is important for self-regulation.

3. Stress Assessment Relevance and Value

When students perceive that assessments are important and helpful, they are more engaged in learning and less likely to cheat. Feedback is taken more seriously and can be more easily related to preparation and performance. Teachers need to emphasize the learning benefits of assessments to lessen performance goal orientation, lack of effort in preparation, and lack of focus while taking assessments. When students make mistakes or learning errors, negative emotions, such as disappointment or even despair,

Table 13.2 Implications for Practice From Section Chapters

Implication	Section Chapter					
	Dinsmore & Wilson	Vogl & Pekrun	Wise & Smith	Lipnevich, Berg, & Smith	Struyven & Devesa	Murdock, Stephens, & Grotewiel
Before Assessment						
Increase student participation in assessment (e.g., self-assessment & interaction with teacher)	• Promotes self-regulation • Lessens anxiety				• Promotes student understanding of criteria	
Emphasize mastery/learning rather than performance	• Promotes self-regulation • Increases motivation					• Lessens academic dishonesty
Make sure students are prepared		• Lessens anxiety				
Give students strategies for coping with anxiety while completing assessments		• Lessens anxiety				• Lessens academic dishonesty
Keep assessments clearly structured and transparent		• Lessens anxiety • Enhances positive expectations				
Avoid excessively demanding assessment tasks		• Lessens anxiety, confusion, hopelessness, and negative expectations				• Lessens academic dishonesty
Use moderately challenging assessment tasks and items that require moderate effort			• Increases intrinsic motivation • Enhances value			

Strategy	Effects
Use novel forms of assessment	• Lessens anxiety
	• Promotes understanding of quality work
	• Engages students
	• Sharpens students' evaluation skills
	• Promotes thinking skills
	• Focuses on the process of learning
Use technology-enhanced assessments	• Allows immediate feedback, novelty, and ease of retesting
	• Lessens academic dishonesty

During Assessment

Strategy	Effects
Ensure appropriate context for taking assessments	• Increases motivation
Provide sufficient time to complete the assessment	• Lessens anxiety

After Assessment

Strategy	Effects
Provide self-referenced feedback	• Enhances mastery goal orientation, hope
	• Lessens shame and hopelessness
	• Enhances self-confidence
	• Enhances confidence in abilities
	• Elicits positive coping strategies
Focus on connection between achievement and effort after failure	
Provide detailed, informational feedback	• Promotes positive emotional response and problem-oriented coping strategies
	• Improves self-regulation
Use descriptive feedback that focuses on process	• Mutes negative emotions

need to be channeled into value for further learning. Brown (2011) gives suggestions for turning maladaptive emotions, beliefs, and assessment-related behaviors into adaptive ones that will enhance subsequent learning. While many students understand that misconceptions, making mistakes, or having errors in understanding can lead to improved achievement (McMillan & Turner, 2015), others need to adopt this perspective, with the help of teachers, other students, and parents.

4. Use a Variety of Moderately Challenging, Untimed, Relatively Short Assessments in Appropriate Contexts

There are many reasons for giving students moderately difficult assessments that are not too long. Moderate difficulty promotes effort in preparation, positive expectations, a healthy dose of anxiety, and effort attributions for both success and failure. Assessments that are too easy or difficult may result in lack of effort, hopelessness, or unhealthy anxiety. Students tend to be intrinsically motivated by challenge, especially if they perceive the task to be fair and attainable, and if they view being wrong as helpful to their learning. Timed assessments lead to anxiety, fear, and other negative emotions, and lead to external attributions for failure. The assessment environment needs to be designed to allow individual focus, without undue interruptions. This leads to positive expectations, less anxiety, and fewer distractions.

5. Emphasize Teacher-controlled, Classroom Assessments

Students clearly differentiate between classroom and accountability-driven assessment, and there seem to be different perceptions of both value and affect toward each type. Classroom assessments have the greatest potential to establish positive perceptions about relevance, purpose, fairness, and feedback that can have more powerful impacts on learning and motivation and the development of self-regulatory skills. Accountability tests, on the other hand, are more likely to elicit greater negative affect, such as debilitating anxiety, fear, hopelessness, and shame because these types of assessment are seen as less connected to students' lessons and studying, with primarily extrinsic rewards and little or no feedback. Classroom assessments need to be well designed to align closely to prior learning and study, which enhances the effect of feedback and development of self-regulation. Wise and Smith (this volume) explain that there is little stake for individual students with high-stakes assessments that are used for school and teacher accountability. As a result, there is much less reason for exerting effort to do well.

6. Involve Students in Assessment

Student perceptions of assessment may vary based on their involvement with all aspects of the assessment process, from understanding criteria to using feedback for further learning. This may or may not include self-assessment or peer assessment, though it appears that these approaches elicit primarily positive perceptions. What is most important is for students to think that they are partners in assessment, and that assessment is part of the learning process. Panadero (this volume) and Andrade and Brown (this volume) both note the importance of including appropriate monitoring and training of student-generated evaluations of work. As students engage in establishing goals, evaluating their own learning, and determining next steps, they essentially become evaluators of their own learning, a process that is related to enhanced motivation and achievement (Hattie, 2009).

7. Focus Attention on Effort and Test Preparation

Perceptions of assessment appear to be more positive when students have had adequate preparation and know appropriate strategies for learning, and answering questions. Without the right level of preparation effort, perceptions are likely to be negative or dismissive, even when doing well, and lead to low motivation. Exerting effort also increases the likelihood feedback may be used for the development of self-regulation.

8. Keep Feedback Self-referenced to Learning and Focused on Strategies to Learn and Improve Effort

Try to avoid performance-oriented or norm-referenced feedback and extrinsic rewards. It is best to provide feedback about why something was missed and what can be done to study further for enhanced understanding. Here it is helpful to identify learning strategies for students to enhance confidence, positive expectations, and responsibility. Since effort is malleable, it is useful for students to understand that either the amount of effort and/or how effort was expended can be controlled for more positive performance in the future.

Policy Implications

There are also implications for policy, though these are more speculative than grounded in research. Given the current emphasis on formative assessment and student growth in learning, as contrasted to static performance, it may make sense to use student perceptions of assessment, as well as achievement results, for accountability purposes. Knowing perceptions of effort, difficulty, and perceived value of assessment results could provide helpful information that contextualizes student performance (e.g., assessments that students do well on but are not perceived as challenging could lead to effective professional development that helps teachers create more challenging tests). If students perceive assessments more as helpful tools for enhancing learning, rather than documenting achievement, this may suggest that teachers have been effective in communicating to students how the results of assessment should be used for learning, and why assessment is important.

The implication of research on student perceptions is that it is important to understand the consequences of assessment policy on beliefs and emotions that are generated and encouraged, and how these impact both short-term and long-term learning and motivation. If assessment policy results in a disconnect between performance and learning, perhaps there is a proclivity for students to view assessment as less positive and helpful. Students need to hold the belief that assessment is essential to know what is understood, and to identify what further learning is needed. Teachers need to know about the nature of student perceptions to better understand and account for the impact of assessment. We now have sufficient understanding about the nature of student perceptions about assessment, and their potential impact on learning and motivation, that policy makers would be wise to consider these perceptions in designing assessment and accountability programs, as well as teachers' professional development programs.

CONCLUSION

Based on existing conceptual frameworks and theories about student motivation, effort, beliefs, and emotions, research is now emerging to show what student perceptions toward assessment look like, how they can be understood, and how teachers and policy makers can use this knowledge for more effective learning. This section contains some excellent thinking about important studies that help us understand how student beliefs and affect, and other noncognitive traits and perceptions, are related to assessment.

The framework presented has organized an analysis of the research using the phases of an assessment sequence, and this is suggested as a reasonable organization for guiding future research. It is clear that student emotions, beliefs, and perceptions exist, vary among students, and can have significant impact on learning and motivation, and we now have strong conceptualization of their nature and how they can be operationalized and measured. Teachers can monitor these attitudes throughout all phases of the assessment cycle and design assessments appropriately so that students are guided toward healthy perceptions, positive emotions, lessened anxiety, and greater responsibility for performance. There is promise in this line of research for greater understanding of how students' conceptions mediate, for good or for worse, both the validity and impact of the assessments they must prepare for and complete.

REFERENCES

Alkharusi, H. (2007). *Effects of teachers' assessment practices on ninth grade students' perceptions of classroom assessment environment and achievement goal orientations in Muscat science classrooms in the sultanate of Oman.* (Unpublished Ph.D.). Kent State University, College of Education, Health, and Human Services / Department of Educational Foundations and Special Services.

Alkharusi, H. (2009). Classroom assessment environment, self-efficacy, and mastery goal orientation: A causal model. *Proceedings of the 2nd International Conference of Teaching and Learning (ICTL 2009)*, INTI University College, Malaysia.

Alkharusi, H. (2011). Development and datametric properties of a scale measuring students' perceptions of the classroom assessment environment. *International Journal of Instruction, 4*(1), 105–120.

Alkharusi, H., Aldhafri, S., & Alnabhani, H. (2014). Classroom assessment: Teacher practices, student perceptions, and academic self-efficacy beliefs. *Social Behavior and Personality, 42*(5), 835–856.

Andrade, H. L. (2013). Classroom assessment in the context of learning theory and research. In J. H. McMillan (Ed.), *Sage handbook of research on classroom assessment* (pp. 17–34). Thousand Oaks, CA: Sage Publications, Inc.

Atkinson, P. (2003). *Assessment 5–14: What do pupils and parents think?* (No. Spotlight No. 87). Edinburgh, UK: The SCRE Centre, University of Glasgow.

Ajzen, I. (2005). *Attitudes, personality and behavior* (2nd ed.). New York: Open University Press.

Bandura, A. (1986). *Social foundations of thought and action: A social cognitive theory.* Englewood Cliffs, NJ: Prentice-Hall.

Boekaerts, M., & Cascallar, E. (2006). How far have we moved toward the integration of theory and practice in self-regulation? *Educational Psychology Review, 18*(3), 199–210. doi:10.1007/s10648–006–9013–4

Brookhart, S. M., & Bronowicz, D. L. (2003). 'I don't like writing. it makes my fingers hurt': Students talk about their classroom assessments. *Assessment in Education, 10*(2), 221–242. doi:10.1080/0969594032000121298

Brookhart, S. M., Walsh, J. M., & Zientarski, W. A. (2006). The dynamics of motivation and effort for classroom assessments in middle school science and social studies. *Applied Measurement in Education, 19*(2), 151–184.

Brown, G.T.L. (2008). *Conceptions of assessment: Understanding what assessment means to teachers and students.* New York: Nova Science Publishers, Inc.

Brown, G.T.L. (2011). Self-regulation of assessment beliefs and attitudes: A review of the students' conceptions of assessment inventory. *Educational Psychology, 31*(6), 731–748. doi:10.1080/0143410.2011.599836

Brown, G.T.L., & Harris, L. R. (2012). Student conceptions of assessment by level of schooling: Further evidence for ecological rationality in belief systems. *Australian Journal of Educational and Developmental Psychology, 12*, 46–59.

Brown, G.T.L., & Hirschfeld, G. (2007). Students' conceptions of assessment and mathematics achievement: Self-regulation raises achievement. *Australian Journal of Educational & Developmental Psychology, 7*, 63–74.

Brown, G.T.L., & Hirschfeld, G. (2008). Students' conceptions of assessment: Links to outcomes. *Assessment in Education: Principles, Policy & Practice, 15*(1), 3–17. doi:10.1080/09695940701876003

Brown, G.T.L., Irving, S. E., Peterson, E. R., & Hirschfeld, G.H.F. (2009). Use of interactive-informal assessment practices: New Zealand secondary students' conceptions of assessment. *Learning and Instruction, 19*(2), 97–111.

Brown, G.T.L., McInerney, D. M., & Liem, G.A.D. (2009). Student perspectives of assessment: Considering what assessment means to learners. In D. M. McInerney, G.T.L. Brown, & G. A. D. Liem (Eds.), *Student perspectives on assessment: What students can tell us about assessment for learning* (pp. 1–21). Charlotte, NC: Information Age Publishing.

Brown, G.T.L., Peterson, E. R., & Irving, S. E. (2009). Beliefs that make a difference: Adaptive and maladaptive self-regulation in students' conceptions of assessment. In D. M. McInerney, G.T.L. Brown, & G.A.D. Liem (Eds.), *Student perspectives on assessment: What students can tell us about assessment for learning* (pp. 159–186). Charlotte, NC: Information Age Publishing.

Cavanagh, R., Waldrip, B., Romanoski, J., & Dorman, J. (2005). Student perceptions of classroom assessment. *Annual Conference of the Australian Association for Research in Education*, Sydney.

Chu, M. W., Guo, Q., & Leighton, J. P. (2014). Students' interpersonal trust and attitudes towards standardized tests: Exploring affective variables related to student assessment. *Assessment in Education: Principles, Policy & Practice, 21*(2), 167–192. doi:10.19080/0969594X.2013.844094

Crooks, T. (1988). The impact of classroom evaluation practices on students. *Review of Educational Research, 58*(4), 438–481.

Dorman, J. P., Fisher, D. L., & Waldrip, B. G. (2006). Classroom environment, students' perceptions of assessment, academic efficacy and attitude to science: A LISREL analysis. In D. Fisher & M. S. Khine (Eds.), *Contemporary approaches to research on learning environments: Worldviews* (1st ed., pp. 1–28). Singapore: World Scientific.

Dorman, J. P., & Knightley, W. M. (2006a). Initial use of the Perceptions of Assessment Tasks Inventory (PATI) in English secondary schools. *Educational Studies, 32*(1), 47–58.

Dorman, J. P., & Knightley, W. M. (2006b). Development and validation of an instrument to assess secondary school students' perceptions of assessment tasks. *Educational Studies, 32*(1), 47–58. doi:101.1080/03055690500415951

Dorman, J. P., Waldrip, B. G., & Fisher, D. L. (2008). Using the Student Perceptions of Assessment Questionnaire (SPAQ) to develop an assessment typology for science classes. *Journal of Science Education, 1*(9), 13–17.

Fabrigar, L. R., MacDonald, T. K., & Wegener, D. T. (2005). The structure of attitudes. In D. Albarracin, B. T. Johnson, & M. P. Zanna (Eds.), *The handbook of attitudes* (pp. 79–124). New York: Lawrence Erlbaum Associates.

Fives, H., & Buehl, M. M. (2012). Spring cleaning for the "messy" construct of teachers' beliefs: What are they? Which have been examined? What can they tell us? In K. R. Harris, S. Graham, & T. Urdan (Eds.), *APA educational psychology handbook: Individual differences and cultural and contextual factors* (Vol. 2, pp. 471–499). Washington, DC: APA.

Gao, M. (2009). Students' voices in school-based assessment of Hong Kong: A case study. In D. M. McInerney, G.T.L. Brown, & G.A.D. Liem (Eds.), *Student perspectives on assessment: What students can tell us about assessment for learning* (1st ed., pp. 107–130). Charlotte, NC: Information Age.

Gao, M. (2012). Classroom assessments in mathematics: High school students' perceptions. *International Journal of Business and Social Science, 3*(2), 63–68.

Gipps, C., & Tunstall, P. (1998). Effort, ability, and the teacher: Young children's explanations of success and failure. *Oxford Review of Education, 24*(2), 149–166.

Harris, L. R., Brown, G.T.L., & Harnett, J. A. (2014). Understanding classroom feedback practices: A study of New Zealand student experiences, perceptions, and emotional responses. *Educational Assessment, Evaluation, and Accountability, 26*, 107. doi:10.1007/s11092–013–9187–5

Harris, L. R., Harnett, J. A., & Brown, G.T.L. (2009). "Drawing" out student conceptions: Using pupils' pictures to examine their conceptions of assessment. In D. M. McInerney, G.T.L. Brown, & G.A.D. Liem (Eds.), *Student perspectives on assessment: What students can tell us about assessment for learning* (1st ed., pp. 53–83). Charlotte, NC: Information Age Publishing, Inc.

Hattie, J. (2009). *Visible learning: A synthesis of meta-analyses in education.* London: Routledge.

Havnes, A., Smith, K., Dysthe, O., & Ludvigsen, K. (2012). Formative assessment and feedback: Making learning visible. *Studies in Educational Evaluation, 38*, 21–27.

Hirschfeld, G.H.F., & Brown, G.T.L. (2009). Students' conceptions of assessment: Factorial and structural invariance of the SCoA across sex, age, and ethnicity. *European Journal of Psychological Assessment, 25*(1), 30–38.

Hue, M., Leung, C., & Kennedy, K. J. (2014). Student perception of assessment practices: Towards 'no loser' classrooms for all students in the ethnic minority schools in Hong Kong. *Educational Assessment, Evaluation, and Accountability, 26*, 1–21. doi:10.1007/s11092–014–9205–2

Irving, S. E., Peterson, E. R., & Brown, G.T.L. (2008). Feedback and academic achievement: The relationship between students' conceptions of feedback and achievement. *Paper Presented at the 6th Biennial Conference of the International Test Commission*, Liverpool, UK.

Lakoff, G., & Johnson, N. (1999). *Philosophy in the flesh: The embodied mind and its challenge to Western thought*. New York: Basic Books.

Lee, I. (2007). Feedback in Hong Kong secondary writing classrooms: Assessment for learning or assessment of learning? *Assessing Writing, 12*(3), 180.

Lichtenfeld, S., Pekrun, R., Stupnisky, R. H., Reiss, K., & Murayama, K. (2012). Measuring students' emotions in the early years: The Achievement Emotions Questionnaire-Elementary School (AEQ-ES). *Learning & Individual Differences, 22*(2), 190–201.

Lowe, P. A. (2014). The Test Anxiety Measure for Adolescents (TAMA): Examination of the reliability and validity of the scores of a new multidimensional measure of test anxiety for middle and high school students. *Journal of Psychoeducational Assessment. 32*(5), 404–416. doi:10.1177/0734282913520595

Lowe, P. A., & Ang, R. P. (2012). Cross-cultural examination of test anxiety among US and Singapore students on the Test Anxiety Scale for Elementary Students (TAS-E). *Educational Psychology, 32*(1), 107–126. doi:10.1080/01443410.2011.625625

Lowe, P. A., Grumbein, M. J., & Raad, J. M. (2011). Examination of the psychometric properties of the Test Anxiety Scale for Elementary Students (TAS-E) scores. *Journal of Psychoeducational Assessment, 29*(6), 503–514. doi:10.1177/0734282910395894

Lowe, P. A., & Lee, S. W. (2008). Factor structure of the Test Anxiety Inventory for Children and Adolescents (TAICA) scores across gender among students in elementary and secondary school settings. *Journal of Psychoeducational Assessment, 26*(3), 231–246.

Lowe, P. A., Lee, S. W., Witteborg, K. M., Prichard, K. W., Luhr, M. E., Cullinan, C. M., . . . Janik, M. (2008). The Test Anxiety Inventory for Children and Adolescents (TAICA): Examination of the psychometric properties of a new multidimensional measure of test anxiety among elementary and secondary school students. *Journal of Psychoeducational Assessment, 26*(3), 215–230. doi:10.1177/0734282907303760

McInerney, D. M., Brown, G.T.L., & Liem, G.A.D. (Eds.). (2009). *Student perspectives on assessment: What students can tell us about assessment for learning*. Charlotte, NC: Information Age Publishing.

McMillan, J. H. (2014). *Classroom assessment: Principles and practice for effective standards-based instruction* (6th Ed.). Boston: Pearson Education, Inc.

McMillan, J. H., & Turner, A. B. (2014). Understanding student voices about assessment: Links to learning and motivation. *Paper Presented at the Annual Meeting of the American Educational Research Association*, Philadelphia.

McMillan, J. H., & Turner, A. B. (2015). Student perceptions of assessment as related to goal orientation. *Annual Meeting of the American Educational Research Association*, Chicago.

Moll, L. C. (2014). *L. S. Vygotsky and education*. New York: Routledge.

Moni, K. B., van Kraayenoord, C. E., & Baker, C. D. (2002). Students' perceptions of literacy assessment. *Assessment in Education: Principles, Policy & Practice, 9*(3), 319–342.

Ostrom, T. M. (1969). The relationship between the affective, behavioral, and cognitive components of attitude. *Journal of Experimental Social Psychology, 5*(1), 12–30.

Pajares, M. F., & Graham, L. (1998). Formalist thinking and language arts instruction: Teachers' and students' beliefs about truth and caring in the teaching conversation. *Teaching and Teacher Education, 14*(8), 855–870.

Patrick, B. C., Skinner, E. A., & Connell, J. P. (1993). *Journal of Personality and Social Psychology, 65*(4), 781–791. doi:10.1037/0022–3514.65.4.781

Pekrun, R. (2006). The control-value theory of achievement emotions: Assumptions, corollaries, and implications for educational research and practice. *Educational Psychology Review, 18*, 315–341.

Pekrun, R., & Bühner, M. (2014). Self-report measures of academic emotions. In R. Pekrun & L. Linnebrink-Garcia (Eds.), *International handbook of emotions in education* (1st ed., pp. 561–579). New York: Routledge.

Pekrun, R., Cusack, A., Murayama, K., Elliot, A. J., & Thomas, K. (2014). The power of anticipated feedback: Effects on students' achievement goals and achievement emotions. *Learning & Instruction, 29*, 115–124.

Pekrun, R., Elliot, A. J., & Maier, M. A. (2006). Achievement goals and discrete achievement emotions: A theoretical model and prospective test. *Journal of Educational Psychology, 98*, 583–597. doi:10.1037/0022–0663.98.3.583

Pekrun, R., Elliot, A. J., & Maier, M. A. (2009). Achievement goals and achievement emotions: Testing a model of their joint relations with academic performance. *Journal of Educational Psychology, 101*, 115–135. doi:10.1037/a0013383

Pekrun, R., Goetz, T., Frenzel, A. C., Barchfeld, P., & Perry, R. P. (2011). Measuring emotions in students' learning and performance: The Achievement Emotions Questionnaire (AEQ). *Contemporary Educational Psychology, 36*, 36–48. doi:10.1016/j.cedpsych.2010.10.002

Pekrun, R., Goetz, T., Perry, P. R., Kramer, K., Hochstadt, M., & Molfenter, S. (2004). Beyond test anxiety: Development and validation of the Test Emotions Questionnaire (TEQ). *Anxiety, Stress & Coping, 17*(3), 287–316.

Pekrun, R., Goetz, T., Titz, W., & Perry, R. P. (2002). Academic emotions in students' self-regulated learning and achievement: A program of qualitative and quantitative research. *Educational Psychologist, 37*, 91–105. doi:10.1207/S15326985EP3702_4

Peterson, E. R., Brown, G.T.L., & Jun, M. C. (2015). Achievement emotions in higher education: A diary study exploring emotions across an assessment event. *Contemporary Educational Psychology, 42*, 82–96. doi:10.1016/j.cedpsych.2015.05.002

Peterson, E. R., & Irving, S. E. (2008). Secondary school students' conceptions of assessment and feedback. *Learning and Instruction, 18*, 235–250. doi:10.1016/j.learninstruc.2007.05.001

Remesal, A. (2009). Accessing primary pupils' conceptions of daily classroom assessment practices. In D. M. McInerney, G.T.L. Brown, & G.A.D. Liem (Eds.), *Student perspectives on assessment: What students can tell us about assessment for learning* (pp. 25–52). Charlotte, NC: Information Age Publishing, Inc.

Rosenberg, M. J., & Hovland, C. I. (1960). Cognitive, affective and behavioral components of attitudes. In M. J. Rosenberg, & C. I. Hovland (Eds.), *Attitude organization and change: An analysis of consistency among attitude components* (pp. 1–14). New Haven: Yale University Press.

Rubie-Davies, C. M., Flint, A., & McDonald, L. G. (2011). Teacher beliefs, teacher characteristics, and school contextual factors: What are the relationships? *British Journal of Educational Psychology, 82*(2), 270–288. doi:10.1111/j.2044–8279.2011.02025.x

Schunk, D. H. (1992). Theory and research on student perceptions in the classroom. In D. H. Schunk & J. L. Meece (Eds.), *Student perceptions in the classroom* (pp. 3–24). Mahwah, NJ: Lawrence Erlbaum Associates, Inc., Publishers.

Schunk, D. H., & Meece, J. L. (Eds.). (1992). *Student perceptions in the classroom.* Mahwah, NJ: Lawrence Erlbaum Associates, Inc., Publishers.

Segers, M., & Tillema, H. (2011). How do Dutch secondary teachers and students conceive the purpose of assessment? *Studies in Educational Evaluation, 37*, 49–54.

Shepard, L. A. (2000). The role of assessment in a learning culture. *Educational Researcher, 29*(7), 4–14.

Tjeerdsma, B. L. (1997). Comparison of teacher and student perspectives of tasks and feedback. *Journal of Teaching in Physical Education, 16*(4), 388.

Tunstall, P., & Gipps, C. (1996). 'How does your teacher help you to make your work better?' children's understanding of formative assessment. *Curriculum Journal, 7*(2), 185–203.

Vygotsky, L. S. (1978). *Mind in society: The development of higher psychological processes.* Cambridge, MA: Harvard University.

Weekers, A. M., Brown, G.T.L., & Veldkamp, B. P. (2009). Analyzing the dimensionality of the students' conceptions of assessment (SCoA) inventory. In D. M. McInerney, G.T.L. Brown, & G. A. Liem (Eds.), *Student perspectives on assessment: What students can tell us about assessment for learning* (pp. 133–158). Charlotte, NC: Information Age Publishing, Inc.

Weiner, B. (2005). Motivation from an attributional perspective and the social psychology of perceived competence. In A. J. Elliot & C. S. Dweck (Eds.), *Handbook of competence and motivation* (pp. 73–84). New York: Guilford.

Weiner, B. (2012). *An attributional theory of motivation and emotion.* New York: Springer.

Williams, J. A. (2014). 'You know what you've done right and what you've done wrong and what you need to improve on': New Zealand students' perspectives on feedback. *Assessment in Education: Principles, Policy & Practice, 17*(3), 301–314. doi:10.1080/0969594X.2010.496249

Wren, D. G., & Benson, J. (2004). Measuring test anxiety in children: Scale development and internal construct validation. *Anxiety, Stress & Coping, 17*(3), 227–240.

Section 3

Classroom Conditions

14

IS IT SAFE? SOCIAL, INTERPERSONAL, AND HUMAN EFFECTS OF PEER ASSESSMENT

A Review and Future Directions

Ernesto Panadero

"With great power there must also come great responsibility."
(Uncle Ben to Peter Parker, in Lee & Ditko, 1962)

INTRODUCTION

Peer assessment (PA) occurs when people of equal status assess each other's work; most commonly in education, the peer is a classmate or a student from the same institution. Assessing a peer activates a significant number of cognitive, motivational, and emotional processes and has potential to enhance the assessor's and the assessee's learning (van Gennip, Segers, & Tillema, 2009). Mainly for this reason, formative assessment/assessment for learning (FA/AfL) advocates, including myself, consider peer assessment, along with self-assessment, to be central aspects of FA/AfL practices (Panadero & Alonso-Tapia, 2013; Reinholz, 2015). Additionally, peer assessment gives students power in the assessment process; that is, they can express their perspective and share responsibility (Dixon, Hawe, & Parr, 2011). This involves multiple social and human factors that need to be taken into account because peer assessment does not happen in a vacuum; rather it produces thoughts, actions, and emotions as a consequence of the interaction of assessees and assessors.

While there have been many studies on peer assessment, the social and human factors have been relatively overlooked and attention to these dimensions is relatively recent (Strijbos et al., 2009; van Gennip et al., 2009). Two reasons might explain this growing interest: (1) increased implementation of PA as a result of Black and Wiliam's (1998) seminal review on formative assessment and (2) van Gennip et al.'s (2009) review of interpersonal and social issues in PA. The van Gennip et al. paper reviewed much research on PA and learning outcomes and was a seminal synthesis of the four articles available at the time concerning interpersonal variables; after this, there was an increase in the number of studies on the topic. This chapter will first examine definitions of peer assessment, followed by a review of the main findings from reliability research into 'traditional' PA (i.e., giving an evaluative score, grade, or rating, with little or no explanation or justification for the evaluation). Then, research that explores social aspects of PA and 'new approaches' to PA (i.e., giving rationale, explanation, or description that informs, improvements) will be reviewed. In this research, if peer scoring accuracy is explored, it is always in interaction with other aspects (e.g., Panadero, Romero, & Strijbos, 2013), amplifying our understanding of the phenomena. Because this new PA research has a shorter tradition, I will conclude with specific recommendations for future research.

Definition of Peer Assessment and Learning Benefits

Definitions of peer assessment range from the process whereby groups of individuals rate their peers (Dochy, Segers, & Sluijsmans, 1999; Falchikov, 1995) to a consideration of "the amount, level, value, worth, quality or success of the products or outcomes of learning of peers of similar status" (Topping, 1998, p. 250). Others would consider it to be a form of collaborative learning (Kollar & Fischer, 2010; Strijbos, Ochoa, Sluijsmans, Segers, & Tillema, 2009). PA can range from asking the students to give a grade to a peer's work (i.e., peer grading/marking) (Falchikov, 1995) to expecting them to give and/or discuss specific feedback (Strijbos et al., 2009). Different PA practices seem to lead to differences in the depth of learning and the use of self-regulated learning strategies (van Gennip, 2012a). The idea that there are different types of PA is not new (Topping, 1998, 2012; van Gennip et al., 2009; Van Zundert, Sluijsmans, & Van Merriënboer, 2010). The effects of different PA forms have been studied; for example, the advantages of using a rubric to support PA over an open-ended format of PA (i.e., asking the students to PA unguided) (Panadero, Romero, & Strijbos, 2013) and the benefits of guided PA where students discuss the role of the assessor and how to grade peers' work (van Gennip, 2012a) have both been established.

A crucial argument for the use of PA is that it enhances both learning and performance in two distinct ways (Corgnet, 2012; Topping, 1998; van Gennip et al., 2009; van Zundert et al., 2010). First, the assessee whose work is assessed receives direct feedback on how to improve. Second, the assessor, by evaluating a peer's work, becomes more aware of his or her own strengths and weaknesses. In other words, peer assessment enhances self-assessment capability (Dochy et al., 1999; Reinholz, 2015) and students' self-regulated learning, with peers acting as co-regulators of their assessee peers (Panadero, Jonsson, & Strijbos, 2016). Hence, PA is an opportunity for students to learn more. Overall, most students have positive attitudes towards PA and report having learning gains (Bryant & Carless, 2010; Orsmond, Merry, & Reiling, 1996; van Zundert et al., 2010), even though those gains are not always substantiated in empirical studies (Li & Steckelberg, 2004).

Peer Assessment Research Focusing on Reliability

Traditionally, there has been considerable research into the reliability and/or validity and/or accuracy of peer scores (e.g., Panadero et al., 2013). Reliability generally focuses on the consistency of student peer marks with teacher or tutor marking. Validity has to do with the appropriateness of peer comments, corrections, or grades. Accuracy has to do with the truthfulness or veridicality of peer assessment. In other words, good PA might be that which (a) corresponds with teacher evaluations, (b) is appropriate to the work being evaluated, and (c) aligns with the reality of the work under consideration. More detailed discussions of these distinctions are available in Panadero et al. (2013) and to a lesser extent in Topping (2003, 2012). Peers can produce assessments in a manner consistent with their teachers (Topping, 2012) as demonstrated across different narrative reviews (Topping,

1998, 2003, 2012; van Zundert et al., 2010) and a meta-analysis (Falchikov & Goldfinch, 2000). The reliability of PA is greater when a number of pedagogical conditions are present, such as involving students in discussion about the criteria, avoiding a large numbers of peers in a peer assessment group, considering the level of expertise of the students, practicing how to peer assess over time, and receiving teachers' feedback about the PA conducted (Falchikov & Goldfinch, 2000; Strijbos et al., 2009; Topping, 2003).

However, the focus of PA research has been dominated by one practice; that is, "peer rating . . . often in combination with open comments" (Strijbos et al., 2009, p. 388). Additionally, the focus of PA research has been on summative purposes (e.g., aspects of grading); Topping (1998) reported that in 31 higher education studies the focus was "on scores and grades awarded by peers rather than through a focus on more open ended formative feedback" (p. 257). It may be that research into the reliability of PA continues, despite its robust establishment, because, although researchers and instructors would like to include PA as a legitimate part of student summative evaluations to improve assessment efficiency and validity, they still feel uncomfortable doing so given assessment is traditionally viewed as a teacher's responsibility (Magin, 2001). Potentially, if students are accurate peer assessors, then teachers could use PA to save time (Sadler & Good, 2006); however, since teachers have to devote time to teach students how to do PA and give them opportunities to practice (Strijbos et al., 2009; Topping, 1998), it remains unclear if instructor time would actually be saved via these processes. Additionally, hardly ever is there any consideration of how PA accuracy might directly affect the learning of the assessor or assessee (Topping, 1998) which is a crucial aspect that this type of PA research has yet to explore.

Moreover, students and teachers seem to not yet feel comfortable in allowing a peer or student score to count towards the final grade in a course (Panadero & Brown, 2016; Wen & Tsai, 2006). Therefore, we need to clarify the social and interpersonal variables that play a role in PA.

PEER ASSESSMENT RESEARCH FOCUSING ON INTERPERSONAL VARIABLES

Because PA can be conceptualized as a collaborative learning activity, it is clear that the social aspects of PA need to be considered, as varied PA practices will elicit different interpersonal variables (van Gennip, 2012a). Attention to social factors is needed because well-implemented PA should decrease negative social problems (e.g., negative situations like tension among peers because of peer scoring) (Topping, 2012).

Social Actors in PA: Students and Teachers

Students

The roles of assessor and assessee are not identical and have different psychological and interpersonal consequences (Panadero et al., 2013; van Zundert et al., 2010). As the assessor, the student must pass some sort of judgment on a peer and as an assessee the student must experience, and hopefully learn from, that judgment. Research that has differentiated between these contrasting roles is scarce (van Zundert et al., 2010).

Panadero et al. (2013) explored correlations between comfort as assessor and perceived fairness as assessee, finding small correlations, supporting the contention that students distinguish between the two roles. Further, the same study found students in PA groups gave moderately positive ratings of comfort when acting as assessor, and more negative comfort attitudes as assessee. This reluctance to being assessed by peers has been found elsewhere where students have indicated a preference for teacher judgments (Bryant & Carless, 2010; Gao, 2009; Harris & Brown, 2013; Peterson & Irving, 2008). A significant problem seems to be authority; that is, students do not perceive their peers as an authoritative source unlike more traditional sources (e.g., instructors or books) (Strijbos et al., 2009). In sum, the main actors of PA, the students, have some concerns, not with the process of PA itself or how much they can learn from it, but with their roles as assessors and assessees.

Teachers

Overall, teachers are positive about PA, reporting that it enhances learning and self-regulated learning strategies (Bryant & Carless, 2010; Harris & Brown, 2013; Lindblom-Ylänne, Pihlajamäki, & Kotkas, 2006; Panadero & Brown, 2015, 2016; Topping, 2012). Additionally, preservice teachers appear to hold similarly positive views that PA can enhance learning and the use of learning strategies (Karaca, 2009; Koc, 2011; Wen & Tsai, 2006). However, recent research has shown that teachers consider PA ineffective in reducing their workload. For example, Panadero and Brown (2016) found that 95% of 1,510 Spanish teachers reported that PA did not save them any time. Additionally, one-third to half the teachers indicated problems with PA having to do with reliability, student mistrust of peer scores, and the creation of social problems in classroom groups.

Teachers may also need to consider parents' perceptions of PA. The 2001 U.S. Supreme Court Case of Falvo v. Owasso School System (Sadler & Good, 2006) examined the appropriateness of peer assessment; in this situation, a sixth-grade boy with learning disabilities was teased after receiving low scores on a peer-graded quiz. This case resulted in a federal ruling that prohibited peer grading in six states of the USA. Sadler and Good (2006) noted that a case about the appropriateness of disclosing grades to classmates via peer grading turned into a case against peer grading itself. Since peer assessment involves children, the opinions and attitudes of their parents also matter for successful implementation of PA, an issue explored more by Buckendahl (this volume).

HUMAN AND SOCIAL VARIABLES IN PEER ASSESSMENT: EMPIRICAL EVIDENCE

Review Criteria

In searching the literature, the following criteria were used: (1) empirical evidence of the effect of PA on social or human factors or vice versa had to be available; (2) the study had to be to published and peer reviewed, including doctoral dissertations; and (3) articles had to be available in English. Articles related to clinical psychology applications were excluded. Searches in PsycINFO were conducted without and with year restriction (>2009) for the following combinations of key terms: PA + 'motivation'; + 'emotion'; + 'interpersonal'; + 'psychological safety'; + 'friendship'; + 'value diversity'; + 'value congruence' in abstracts. While anonymity is a crucial variable in PA (e.g., Vanderhoven et al., 2015), it has not been included in the search because few studies exploring its effect on interpersonal and human variables have been conducted. The searches identified a total of 191 abstracts which were read, and 16 relevant articles were identified. Another 10 relevant papers were identified from the reference lists of papers already included in the review. The basic content of the 26 selected articles is captured in Table 14.1 and is used to create a narrative review following Dochy's (2006) guidelines. A meta-analysis could not be conducted due to the lack of consistent definition of PA and the high number of descriptive studies.

Table 14.1 lists the articles by the author's name in chronological order of publication. The sample column reports information regarding the study sample as provided by the authors (i.e., number of students, gender distribution, mean age, academic subject, educational level, and country). The research method and data collection column captures the study design and instrumentation information as supplied by the authors. With regards to the classification of the research method used, the taxonomy by Montero and León (2007) was used. Four types of research methods have been used: (a) experimental with random assignment of individual participants to the experimental conditions (experimental design with random group, ERG), (b) experimental with random assignment of classroom groups to the experimental conditions (experimental design with random intact groups, ERIG), (c) implementation of PA in an educational setting to explore the effects with no control group (descriptive design with structured observation, DSO), and (d) a qualitative approach design using case study (multiple case study, MCS). The variables of interest column presents the focus of the study as relevant to this chapter. The type of PA column describes the relevant characteristics of the PA implementation, including the task for PA, whether PA was anonymous or not, the use of scoring tools, and whether feedback was face-to-face or not, and so on. It is important to point out that differences in the quality and quantity of information provided in the table are attributable primarily to the differences in the level of detail in the original manuscripts study (e.g., if the details of the PA implementation were missing, that cell would have less information).

Ten themes were identified in the selected studies:

(1) motivation, having to do with the reasons or goals students have for performing PA and the effects of PA on motivation;
(2) emotion, focused on the feelings connected to PA and its implementation;
(3) social factors, related to aspects of social connections, such as enhancing peer scores to be more liked by classmates;
(4) friendship, the potentially biasing effect of prior relations on PA (note: while this is also a social factor, a number of studies exploring it have made it the most salient factor, so it was decided to treat it as its own theme);
(5) trust in the self as assessor, focusing on belief that one can be a good assessor;
(6) trust in the other as assessor, related to having confidence in a peer who is capable of performing PA;
(7) fairness/(dis)comfort, referring to beliefs about the appropriateness of PA and the student's level of comfort within assessor and/or assessee roles;
(8) psychological safety, focusing on the extent to which students feel safe to give sincere feedback as an assessor and do not fear inappropriate negative feedback as an assessee;
(9) value diversity/congruence, referring to the level of goal similarity between assessor and assessee; and
(10) interdependence, examining the degree to which assessors and assessees are mutually dependent on each other.

However, because of similarity between these themes, the empirical evidence is aggregated in three major themes. Intra-individual motivations, emotions, perceptions of

Table 14.1 Summary of Studies on PA and Interpersonal Variables or Human Factors (chronological order of publication)

#	Study	Sample	Research Method & Data Collection	Variables of interest	Type of PA
1	Falchikov, 1995	N=13, 12 female; age M=20 years, 11 months. Students in developmental psychology course for degree in biological science. Scotland.	DSO. Self-reported data via an instrument (named self-evaluation sheet) with 7 questions (3 open ones and 4 continuum choices, e.g., fair vs. unfair).	Fairness and friendship	Short oral presentations were evaluated by classmates. Assessors were anonymous. Students were given list of 4 criteria plus a form to identify 'best feature' and 'weaknesses.' Scores were given in a 20-point scale and counted towards the final grade.
2	Hunter & Russ, 1996	Second and last year university music students. Ireland.	DSO Data are comments from the participants.	Fairness and friendship	Musical performances were PA, first by same year students, later by more senior students. PA was scaffolded with report outlines and criteria. Scoring agreement was checked.
3	Stanier, 1997	N=36; university students in geography courses. United Kingdom.	DSO. It seems to be self-reported data via an evaluation questionnaire with 6 questions, but also there are more data, although source is not reported.	Motivation and students' perceptions for PA	Group work was peer assessed. Assessors used a discussed set of criteria.
4	Topping, Smith, Swanson, & Elliot, 2000	N=12; 10 female; Age M=31. Educational psychology postgraduate students. Scotland.	DSO. Data are analysis of the students' PA feedback forms and questionnaire with 24 questions including choose an option (e.g., Y/N) and open questions.	Discomfort	A written academic report was PA. Reciprocal PA by pairing the students was implemented with face-to-face interactions and detailed feedback. Assessors filled out a report also filled by the staff and later exchanged with the assessee.

	Study	Sample	Method & Data	Construct	Description
5	Lin, Liu, & Yuan, 2002	N=57; 88% male, senior students vocational school and N=41 (85% male) university students. Taiwan.	DSO. Comparison between secondary and higher education students' attitudes towards PA. Self-reported, questionnaire with 11 questions, 5-point Likert items.	Trust in other as assessor	Different PA procedures for secondary and university students. Random assignment of assessors that used given criteria to assess. Only the university students could make changes after online peer feedback.
6	Sluijsmans, Brand-Gruwel, & van Merriënboer, 2002	N=93; 19 male; age M=20.7. Preservice teachers. The Netherlands.	ERIG. Self-reported data: questionnaire 72 items, 5-point Likert scale, and forms.	Trust in self as assessor	PA of videotaped lessons created by groups. Each student assessed 3 groups and gave qualitative PA.
7	Li & Steckelberg, 2004	N=48. Students in instructional technology course. USA.	ERG. Self-reported survey with 11 items, 5-point Likert.	Trust in other as assessor	Webquests were assessed. Online PA with randomly chosen assessors that used a given rubric. Assessees could, after PA, make changes to their work.
8	Wen & Tsai, 2006	N=280; Male 58%. Preservice teachers. Taiwan.	DSO. Self-reported survey on perceptions of PA vs. online PA (34 5-point Likert items).	Fairness	The study was exploring perceptions on PA from previous learning experience. There was no PA implementation within the study.
9	McMahon, 2009	N=5. University students enrolled towards a Bachelor's degree or a Certificate of Higher Education. Ireland.	MCS. Self-reported data via structured critical reflection.	Motivation and confidence as assessor	PA was organized in recursive iterations within the five participants meetings. PA was non-anonymous with detailed feedback in one-to-one and group instances.
10	Johnson & Winterbottom, 2010	N=28 girls from a rural comprehensive school aged 11–18. UK.	DSO. Self-report data (questionnaires: PALS & IMI), interviews, classroom observations, and video records of PA events. Students grouped via prior attainment.	Motivation (goal orientation)	Face-to-face PA opportunities were given.

(Continued)

Table 14.1 (Continued)

#	Study	Sample	Research Method & Data Collection	Variables of interest	Type of PA
11	McConlogue, 2010	N=82 engineering students. UK.	DSO. Self-report data via a questionnaire and focus group. PA implemented with two different samples (i.e., Level 5 and Level 7 of the curriculum).	Fairness	Level 5 assessed 4 to 5 anonymized peers' coursework assignments, each assignment evaluated by 4 to 5 assessors. Assessees received their work with all grades and feedback. In the Level 7 group, the PA was identical with the addition of prior discussion of assessment criteria.
12	van Gennip, Gijbels, Segers, & Tillema, 2010	N=118 employees from 4 organizations. The Netherlands.	DSO. Self-report data (questionnaires).	Trust, psychological safety, value diversity, interdependence, and transparency	Participants were assessed on their work performance via questionnaires by 3 or 4 persons (work colleague, manager, inferior, or customer) in a 360° feedback process.
13	van Gennip, Segers & Tillema, 2010	N=62 male secondary-vocational education students aged 16–19. The Netherlands.	ERG. Control and PA condition. 17 groups of 3 to 5 students in a project-based course. Only experimental groups received PA training. Self-reported data using validated questionnaires.	Trust, psychological safety, value diversity, interdependence, and predictors of perceived learning	Experimental condition received PA training. Each student evaluated the other groups' work using a form including agreed criteria as a classroom. Control group was evaluated by teacher.
14	Willey & Gardner, 2010	N=89 engineering students. Australia.	DSO. Self-report online survey had mixture of free response and 4-point rating items.	Fairness and comfort	SPARK^{PLUS} software for self-assessment and PA. Software provided anonymous written feedback and scores.

#	Study	Sample	Design/Method	Variables	Description
15	Carvalho, 2012	$N=120$; 73% age 21–25 years. Business higher education students, 7 different cohorts, in teams of 5–8 members. Portugal.	DSO. Self-report survey data with 4 Likert-point items.	Friendship-marking, fairness, and comfort	PA among teammates working on a collaborative learning activity.
16	Cheng & Tsai, 2012	$N=23$. First year university students. Age $M=18.74$, 8 males. Taiwan.	DSO. Self-reported data (interview). Note: students were also asked about their conceptions and learning approaches to explore how these interacted with the PA variables studied.	Trust in the self and the other, psychological safety, interdependence and value diversity	Online anonymous PA with grading (100-point scale) and comment making (feedback). Each student assessed 5 classmates. PA was done in five different tasks, so each student received 25 PA evaluations during the semester.
17	Corgnet, 2012	$N=66$. University students. Spain.	ERG. 3 conditions: Asymmetric Peer Evaluations (APE); Symmetric Peer Evaluations (SPE); Equal Split Conditions (EQS). Self-report (questionnaire).	Friendship, motivation	The peers evaluated members of same work group using a questionnaire.
18	Hou & Cheng, 2012	$N=65$. University students in multimedia production working in groups of 3. Taiwan.	DSO. Self-report (questionnaire).	Emotional state	Online forum commentaries on videos created and posted online by small groups of two or three students.
19	van Gennip, 2012b	$N=106$, males; Ages 15–18. Vocational school students in project-based course. The Netherlands.	ERIG. 3 conditions: control, PA, and PA+ (enhanced). Self-report (questionnaire).	Psychological safety and value congruency	PA conditions received PA training and PA+ condition received extra training on the role of assessors. Group work final product was assessed by the rest of classmates using a form with 11 criteria.

(Continued)

Table 14.1 (Continued)

#	Study	Sample	Research Method & Data Collection	Variables of interest	Type of PA
20	Harris & Brown, 2013	Three teachers and their students from primary, intermediate, and secondary education. New Zealand.	MCS. Classroom observation (narrative field notes), further analysis of the video recordings, students' work samples, focus group interviews, and individual teacher interviews.	Social factors in students' perceptions on PA (e.g., friendship bias)	Researchers observed natural instances of PA in the classroom including rubric-guided essay marking.
21	Kim & Ryu, 2013	$N=122$ Preservice teachers aged $M=21.57$ ($SD=1.4$). Korea.	ERG. 3 conditions: enhanced Web-based PA, traditional PA, and traditional self-assessment.	Metacognition, performance, and motivation (confidence and satisfaction)	Traditional PA condition = rubric-based scoring of non-anonymous peer work. Enhanced PA = online use of WFPAS software.
22	Panadero, Romero, & Strijbos, 2013	$N=209$; 87% female preservice teachers in Learning and Development II course, aged $M=22.17$ ($SD=3.92$). Spain.	ERIG. Two conditions created from 4 classroom groups assigned randomly to control PA and rubric PA. Self-report data (questionnaires and open questions).	Friendship construct validity bias, perceived comfort as PA assessor, and perceived fairness as assessee	Control PA = gave a grade and feedback to the work from a non-anonymous peer. Rubric PA = rubric with different criteria guiding grading and feedback.
23	Cheng, Hou, & Wu, 2014	$N=65$; 58 female. University students in advanced communication technology workshop aged 18–19. Taiwan.	DSO. Students worked in 21 groups of 2, 3, or 4 members. Self-report data on emotions based on the PA received (using the self-assessment manikin).	Emotions: emotional responses to PA comments	Peers commented anonymously online to group projects on YouTube. Assessees could decide to reply to those comments or not.

	Sample	Method	Focus	Description
24 Hwang, Hung, & Chen, 2014	N=167; age 12. Elementary students in 10-week natural science course. Taiwan.	ERIG. Control and experimental conditions, three classroom groups assigned to each. Self-report data via two scales, one questionnaire, and one open-ended questionnaire.	Motivation	PA condition = random assignment of work marked according to guidelines. Control group = no PA, instructor assessed work.
25 Vanderhoven, Raes, Montrieux, Rotsaert, & Schellens, 2015	N=69; 72% female; age range 15–16. Grade 9 and 10 secondary students in groups of 2 or 3. Belgium.	ERIG. Two conditions: traditional non-anonymous PA and experimental with anonymous computer-assisted PA. Mixed method data: self-reported questionnaire, observation of the logbook, semi-structured interviews with teacher and students, and open question at the end of the questionnaire.	Anonymity in relation to social effects (peer pressure and fear of disapproval), discomfort with PA, and emotions towards PA	Small-group presentations after PA training. Traditional non-anonymous PA = public raising score cards to evaluate presentation. Experimental, anonymous = computerized system to evaluate peer presentations.
26 Wilson et al., 2015	N=228. University students. Australia.	DSO. Self-report: survey, interview to selected students and 11 teachers.	Fairness and workload (temporality for students)	Anonymous PA using a massive online tool serving 2,793 students from different courses.

fairness, and discomfort are grouped into *intra-individual factors in PA*, while inter-individual social factors, friendship, and safety are grouped into *interpersonal aspects of PA*. The third group consists of cognitive issues to do with the confidence or trust in the competence of the peer as assessor, the self as an assessor, group commitment to values, and sense of task interdependence, referred to as *cognitive aspects of PA*.

Intra-individual Factors in PA

PA is usually conceptualized as an activity that enhances students' motivation as they take more control of their learning (e.g., Topping, 1998). However, as students might also feel powerful negative emotions (e.g., embarrassment) because of classmate feedback, these negative experiences have to be considered in examining students' motivations around PA. Of the six studies exploring motivation, four focused on a general concept of motivation; that is, if students were satisfied and willing to perform PA in the future (Hwang et al., 2014; Kim & Ryu; 2013, McMahon, 2009; Stanier, 1997), all of which reported students liking PA. Only two studies explored more specific aspects of motivation. Johnson and Winterbottom (2010) found that after implementing PA (and also self-assessment), students self-reported a decrease in learning goals, although the qualitative classroom observations suggested they performed more learning oriented actions. Corgnet (2012) studied how different acquaintance levels and money-sharing rules affected motivation for PA, finding that, to maintain intrinsic motivation, when working groups consist of friends it was better to have fixed sharing rules, while in teams with low acquaintanceship, making the amount of money to be received dependent on peer rating was a better sharing method.

A student's sense of fairness or (dis)comfort in PA is another emotional response in which contradictory results have been found. Some studies indicate that students perceive PA as unfair (Carvalho, 2012; McConlogue, 2010; Vanderhoven et al., 2015; Wen & Tsai, 2006; Willey & Gardner, 2010; Wilson, Diao, & Huang, 2015) and something they are not comfortable with (Carvalho, 2012; Vanderhoven et al., 2015). A sense of fairness in PA can lead to a positive acceptance of PA, greater comfort in PA, and less friendship bias marking (Carvalho, 2012; Panadero et al., 2013). Friction among teammates within a collaborative learning activity generated negative emotions (Carvalho, 2012). However, other studies indicate confidence in the fairness of PA (Falchikov, 1995; Hunter & Russ, 1996; Panadero et al., 2013), with students expressing comfort with it (Panadero et al., 2013). Part of the explanation for these contradictory results may lie in low or biased response rates (Wilson et al., 2015), lack of detail about the measurement of fairness (Falchikov, 1995; Hunter & Russ, 1996), or shortness of intervention (Panadero et al., 2013). In sum, PA can be a problematic assessment procedure in terms of perceived fairness by students.

Just as fairness has contradictory evidence, so does student emotion within PA. Hou and Cheng (2012) found PA had unclear effects on student emotional patterns. Cheng et al. (2014) found that the students who received more comments via peer feedback on YouTube responded more to the comments and expressed more positive emotions to their peers' neutral or positive comments. On the other hand, students who received fewer responses showed more negative emotions to critical and even encouraging messages by their peers. Vanderhoven et al. (2015) found that students in an anonymous PA condition reported more positive feelings towards PA. Hence, it is difficult to derive robust conclusions from so little research other than that PA affects students' emotions. Students' perceptions of PA fairness and (dis)comfort are problems in the classroom unless PA addresses and overcomes these valid concerns.

Interpersonal Aspects of PA

Social and interpersonal factors are important in PA, especially when PA is not anonymous (Cheng & Tsai, 2012). The importance of psychological safety for the effective functioning of PA is now well established (van Gennip et al., 2009; van Gennip, Gijbels et al., 2010); Cheng and Tsai (2012) found that students with higher psychological safety chose deeper learning approaches to their online PA. When PA participants feel safe, they have greater confidence that the peer assessor will make a valuable contribution. Two interventions that enhanced psychological safety were seen in van Gennip, Segers et al. (2010), where a control group was compared to a PA training group with enhanced safety measures, and in van Gennip, (2012b), that compared a control group against two different PA interventions with the PA conditions surpassing the control group on psychological safety. These studies show that training students to perform PA can increase their perceptions of psychological safety.

PA with one's friends is assumed to be psychologically safe, but also tends to lead to a friendship scoring bias. Two studies found students reported inflating PA scores in order to enhance relationship with peers (Carvalho, 2012; Harris & Brown, 2013), while Panadero et al. (2013) showed that students over-scored peers regardless of friendship level. Falchikov (1995) found that one of the least liked features of PA was marking friends, a reason why Hunter and Russ (1996) used students from more advanced courses to score second year music students. Hence, anonymity in PA may reduce peer pressure and fear of disapproval (Cheng & Tsai, 2012, Panadero et al., 2013; Vanderhoven et al., 2015).

Nonetheless, despite friendship bias, the relationships of peer marks to instructor grades are positively correlated and, thus, potentially valid (Falchikov & Goldfinch, 2000; Panadero et al., 2013). However, the direction and strength of friendship bias is not consistent; different rules of sharing the money awarded to the team for the group work (Corgnet, 2012) and different types of PA—just asking students to conduct unguided PA versus rubric PA— (Panadero et al., 2013) impact degree of bias. Social aspects are crucial to PA, impacting the validity and meaning of PA. Three of the studies showed that students feel social pressure while performing PA when scoring their peers (Carvalho, 2012; Harris & Brown, 2013) or in comparison to a non-anonymous PA (Vanderhoven et al., 2015). This scoring bias perception is actually transmitted to the peer score in the form of inflation, sometimes regardless of friendship level, and has been decreased using rubrics (Panadero et al., 2013). Therefore, there seems to be a tendency to over-score friends in non-anonymous PA.

Cognitive Aspects of PA

For PA to be an effective learning strategy, students must have confidence in themselves and their peers as evaluators (van Gennip et al., 2009). Generally, students report difficulties and problems in trusting that their peers can give competent assessments and feedback about their work (Harris & Brown, 2013; Lin et al., 2002; van Gennip, Segers et al., 2010), although this is not always consistently found (Li & Steckelberg, 2004). Students also express concern that it is not appropriate to do PA because it is not their job (Willey & Gardner, 2010; Wilson et al., 2015). The higher the trust in the other as assessor, the deeper the learning approaches towards PA (Cheng & Tsai, 2012). Therefore, trust in the other is something we want to promote.

Nonetheless, efforts to induce greater trust among peers in PA have not always had positive impact: van Gennip, Segers et al. (2010) and Sluijsmans et al. (2002) found better performance and more development of PA skills in their PA condition in comparison to the control groups, but these interventions had no effect on trust in either the self as assessor or the other as assessor. On the other hand, McMahon (2009) showed a major effect on trust in themselves as assessors through a very intensive intervention. Similarly, Topping et al. (2000) also found increased trust in PA when participants in their intensive intervention were given training in PA; the training focused on developing experience with PA, using anonymous reporting initially, and reporting only positive aspects of performance. Additionally, greater expertise in the PA assessor is associated with the assessee having greater trust in a peer's assessment (Cheng & Tsai, 2012; Willey & Gardner, 2010). Greater transparency about feedback also helps raise trust (van Gennip, Gijbels et al., 2010). In sum, trust in PA does not happen automatically and intensive practice and interaction seems to increase it.

Since PA, at least with a formative purpose, requires peers to collaborate with each other to conduct and accept evaluations, it is important that they have a shared understanding of what effective PA looks like, beyond mastery of techniques. To visualize this, when students have contrasting beliefs about the point of PA (e.g., one student believes that PA is just about scoring a peer's work without further interaction, while another believes differences in opinion lead to interesting discussion in which lies the potential of PA), this is known as value diversity, as opposed to value congruence. The studies explored here showed that the more value congruence in PA (or the less value diversity), the more trust there is and the more valuable the PA results (van Gennip, 2012b; van Gennip, Gijbels, et al., 2010; van Gennip, Segers et al., 2010); deeper learning approaches are also activated (Cheng & Tsai, 2012). Additionally, it has been found that, at the same time, PA interventions can increase value congruency (van Gennip, 2012b; van Gennip, Segers et al., 2010). Therefore, practice in PA must be a requirement for students to gain trust in the whole process; recent research supports this idea (Panadero & Brown, 2016). Furthermore, students who share the belief that greater learning occurs through the PA process (i.e., interdependence), rather than valuing independence or self-reliance, have a greater trust in each other (van Gennip, Gijbels, et al., 2010) and deeper learning approaches (Cheng & Tsai, 2012), both of which have been shown to be important to the quality of PA.

However, whether value congruency and interdependence can be generated in anonymous, randomly assigned products (e.g., online PA), contexts where the students barely interact, is unknown, but it could be the case that because the students do not interact, they have differentiated goals (e.g., here I act as an assessor, here I am an assessee) and without interaction, the alignment of goals can prove rare. In contrast, it seems that value congruency and interdependence play an important role when intensive types of PA are implemented (e.g., face-to-face feedback), because the interaction of assessor–assessee can produce such shared goals.

In sum, while it seems like value diversity/congruence have some connection to PA, they have not been explored much further than van Gennip's work. One of the reasons is that, while value diversity/congruence are applicable in collaborative learning situations where the goals are shared (or at least they should be), in classroom PA such shared goals are much less frequently the case. Peer assessment practices can happen in isolated contexts (e.g., online anonymous PA) where the goals of assessors and assessees are divergent: the assessor evaluates and produces a score and/or feedback, while the assessee interprets and reacts to that information. It is actually the case that van Gennip et al. (2009) borrowed value diversity/congruence from collaborative learning research and the connection to the assessment field they established is not yet robust. Therefore, that connection needs to be clarified in further attempts to use value diversity/congruence in PA by first clarifying how assessor and assessee's goals can be aligned.

DISCUSSION

This review has shown that there are different ways to conceptualize and implement PA and that there are human and social effects of differing PA implementations on students that need further exploration. Additionally, the effect of PA in individual differences is a completely unexplored area (e.g., how PA might be affected by different beliefs, personality), as a one size fits for all approach to PA is unlikely to have a uniform impact. Fortunately, since 2009, the PA field has focused more on these aspects and less on scoring accuracy, but this is an incomplete journey. Research indicates that more intensive PA implementations produce better human and social outcomes, especially as students gain a deeper understanding of the complexities of PA (McMahon, 2009; Topping et al., 2000). While more superficial approaches to PA (e.g., peer marking), are not wrong, they are not enough because (a) they do not guarantee enough peer feedback and other interactions that lead to more learning, (b) they do not explain why the grades have been awarded, and (c) nondisclosure can increase perceptions of unfairness and discomfort. These issues do not support the conclusion that summative approaches to PA should stop per se because there are grading-oriented approaches to PA (e.g., using rubrics to classify and comment on peer work) that can promote students' learning when well implemented (Harris & Brown, 2013). In sum, the conclusion is that superficial approaches that focus almost exclusively on getting students to generate a score can be detrimental for interpersonal relationships in the classroom and do not guarantee more learning because peer scores without further feedback do not help assessees understand why their work is at a particular level or how to go about improving it. Therefore, if PA is to be used for summative purposes, it is important that such evaluations include some justification of the result, along with suggestions for improvement so the assessee can reflect on the result and potentially apply the feedback to future learning situations.

However, teachers need to understand the limited scope if such approaches are adopted. We cannot expect students to learn as much from anonymous peer marking, where the assessee receives little feedback, as compared to PA, where the assessees and assessors interact and rich feedback is provided. The more interaction and peer feedback we want to provide, the longer PA will take, the more psychosocial variables will need to be monitored, and the more PA will have to become a central part of the curriculum. Therefore, if a teacher wants to implement a shallow approach to PA because the main goal is to have students score each other, he or she will have to be aware of the negative social consequences that peer marking and lack of peer feedback could bring.

Along this line, if a major goal of PA is to enhance learning, then greater focus on content accuracy (i.e., substantively appropriate information) becomes more important than scoring accuracy. Formative types of PA which focus on learning (Corgnet, 2012; Li & Steckelberg, 2004; Reinholz, 2015; Sluijsmans, Brand-Gruwel, & van Merriënboer, 2002; Van Zundert et al., 2010) usually require more social interaction as assessors provide more specific feedback or even interact face-to-face or via a computer with the assessees (Kollar & Fischer, 2010; Strijbos et al., 2009; van Gennip et al., 2009). Thus, interpersonal variables may be of greater relevance when PA research is focused on content and learning goals rather than simply on the consistency of student scoring with that of teachers or tutors.

This review has highlighted a large number of areas where insufficient research has been conducted. Within the field of intra-individual factors, more research is needed comparing different PA implementations as there seem to be differential effects. For example, research is needed into: (a) the role of goal orientation in PA activation,

(b) the effect of PA formats on motivation and emotions, (c) the impact of anonymity and exposure, in both face-to-face and online contexts, upon emotion and motivation, (d) the effects of cultural differences, and (e) how the effect of classroom motivational climate (Alonso-Tapia & Fernandez, 2008) might affect PA (especially psychological safety, trust, fairness, and [dis]comfort).

Although the nationality of the research samples have been included in Table 14.1, it cannot be concluded that the results reflect cultural or social group characteristics; rather the diversity indicates that international interest in PA is robust. Current research has not considered a wide breadth of possible emotional responses to PA, suggesting, for example, that research with the broader range of emotions in the Academic Emotions Questionnaire might be useful (Pekrun, Goetz, Titz, & Perry, 2002).

Likewise, research into the interpersonal dimensions needs to consider: (a) the impact of friendship on PA scoring and content accuracy, while not limiting the evidence to self-reported data; (b) the effect of possible interventions to reduce student tendencies to over-score; (c) the impact on friendship when PA requires a negative evaluation; (d) the effect of different PA types on more general social classroom climate, (e) the impact of different qualities of peer feedback (e.g., positive vs. negative; deep vs. superficial) upon assessees' emotions, motivations, and their ability to process such feedback, and (f) the emotions and motivations of assessors while giving different evaluations (e.g., positive vs. negative; low vs. high quality of peer work).

Research has shown that trust between peers in PA is not just a question of personality or attitude, but also depends on the competence of peers doing the evaluations. Hence, research is needed into the effect of assessor and assessee expertise and its influence on the quality of PA and the human and social impact.

This review also highlights some important implications for policy and practice. The first and more important is that we should not underestimate the interaction of PA and human and interpersonal variables. PA has an effect at the motivational and emotional level and can trigger powerful feelings such as unfairness and discomfort (like all other forms of educational assessment). Therefore, we need to implement PA in ways that minimize such negative effects. The studies reviewed here show that the 'deeper' the PA (i.e., more feedback and assessor-assessee interaction), the better results in the intra- and interpersonal variables studied here. But this comes with the 'cost' of taking more classroom time, as students need to be taught and scaffolded as to how to perform PA, and given the space and time for interaction. In other words, PA in such cases becomes a central part of the curriculum. This is the way PA reaches its full potential for enhancing students' self-regulation and learning. If teachers still prefer to use a summative approach (e.g., peer marking) to PA, they need to be aware of the possible tensions this could create, alongside possible decreases in student interest in PA: student evaluation is important and if the PA approach is shallow, this will impact students' liking of the process.

Can PA still be used for summative purposes? While formative uses are preferable, if we want to use PA for grading students, we need to be aware of the following: (a) it will take considerable time for the teacher to train and scaffold students to do this effectively, so it may not actually save time, (b) assessors need to provide a rationale for their score, (c) the use of assessment criteria (e.g., rubrics) will enhance the reliability and decrease friendship bias, and (d) the use of anonymity has to be considered carefully in terms of the learning benefits, if any, that it could produce (i.e., while anonymity may help assessors focus more on the content than the person who created the work, potentially decreasing bias, it is unknown if feedback written anonymously without much consideration of the recipient is as effective at connecting with the person and inspiring appropriate action to improve). In sum, PA implementations should be planned thoughtfully, not as a trial-and-error adventure.

These facts have at least three important implications. First, assessment for learning should be more critical of PA stances that merely award grades or scores without explanation; such approaches at least require students to be involved in assessment and, thus, have some value, but learning and self-regulated learning are not central to them. Therefore, assessment for learning proponents need to clearly position themselves against the indiscriminate use of PA, because shallow implementation might produce more harm than good. Second, preservice teachers and in-service teachers should be trained in PA implementation and, additionally, have experience themselves within PA as both assessors and assesses, as recent research has shown this is crucial for teachers' future use of PA in their classrooms (Panadero & Brown, 2016). Special emphasis should be given to the human and social PA factors analysed here, which are of major interest for the classroom climate. And, third, in terms of the psychometric analysis of PA, researchers need to move the focus from grade/scoring accuracy towards content accuracy, which is more beneficial for PA promotion of learning and self-regulated learning.

CONCLUSION

This chapter began with a well-known quote: "With great power there must also come great responsibility." Peer assessment is an educational practice with strong social and human effects. Assessors must be aware that their feedback and grade will affect the assessee. But researchers should also take note: for a long time the field has claimed that PA is a reliable source of information in terms of scoring accuracy. Now, we need to start exploring what happens in PA interactions and how it affects learning, not only the cognitive side of it (how much students learn), but also the motivational, emotional, and interpersonal aspects. Otherwise, we will continue along, trapped in our own research spider web, condemned to research the same topic (scoring accuracy) over and over again.

ACKNOWLEDGEMENTS

This research was funded by the Spanish Ministry (Ministerio de Economía y Competitividad) via Ramón y Cajal funding granted to the author (File id. RYC-2013–13469). Special thanks to Jan-Willem Strijbos for being always on the 'other side' and helping me reflect about the content from this chapter. Also thanks to the editors, Gavin Brown and Lois Harris, for their great job editing the chapter, and to Keith Topping and Jeltsen Peeters, who helped providing inaccessible manuscripts.

REFERENCES

Alonso-Tapia, J., & Fernandez, B. (2008). Development and initial validation of the classroom motivational climate questionnaire (CMCQ). *Psicothema, 20*(4), 883–889.

Black, P., & Wiliam, D. (1998). Assessment and classroom learning. *Assessment in Education: Principles, Policy & Practice, 5*(1), 7–73. doi: 10.1080/0969595980050102

Bryant, D. A., & Carless, D. R. (2010). Peer assessment in a test-dominated setting: Empowering, boring or facilitating examination preparation? *Educational Research for Policy and Practice, 9*(1), 3–15. doi:10.1007/s10671–009–9077–2

Carvalho, A. (2012). Students' perceptions of fairness in peer assessment: Evidence from a problem-based learning course. *Teaching in Higher Education, 18*(5), 491–505. doi:10.1080/13562517.2012.753051

Cheng, K. H., Hou, H. T., & Wu, S. Y. (2014). Exploring students' emotional responses and participation in an online peer assessment activity: A case study. *Interactive Learning Environments, 22*(3), 271–287. doi:10.10 80/10494820.2011.649766

Cheng, K. H., & Tsai, C. C. (2012). Students' interpersonal perspectives on, conceptions of and approaches to learning in online peer assessment. *Australasian Journal of Educational Technology, 28*(4), 599–618.

Corgnet, B. (2012). Peer evaluations and team performance: When friends do worse than strangers. *Economic Inquiry, 50*(1), 171–181. doi:10.1111/j.1465-7295.2010.00354.x

Dixon, H. R., Hawe, E., & Parr, J. (2011). Enacting Assessment for Learning: The beliefs practice nexus. *Assessment in Education: Principles, Policy & Practice, 18*(4), 365–379. doi:10.1080/0969594X.2010.526587

Dochy, F. (2006). A guide for writing scholarly articles or reviews for the Educational Research Review. *Educational Research Review.* Retrieved from http://www.journals.elsevier.com/educational-research-review/

Dochy, F., Segers, M., & Sluijsmans, D. (1999). The use of self-, peer- and co-assessment in higher education. A review. *Studies in Higher Education, 24*(3), 331–350. doi:10.1080/03075079912331379935

Falchikov, N. (1995). Peer feedback marking: Developing peer assessment. *Innovations in Education & Training International, 32*(2), 175–187. doi: 10.1080/1355800950320212

Falchikov, N., & Goldfinch, J. (2000). Student peer assessment in higher education: A meta-analysis comparing peer and teacher marks. *Review of Educational Research, 70*(3), 287–322.

Gao, M. (2009). Students' voices in school-based assessment of Hong Kong: A case study. In D. M. McInerney, G.T.L. Brown, & G.A.D. Liem (Eds.), *Student perspectives on assessment: What students can tell us about assessment for learning* (pp. 107–130). Charlotte, NC: Information Age Publishing.

Harris, L. R., & Brown, G.T.L. (2013). Opportunities and obstacles to consider when using peer- and self-assessment to improve student learning: Case studies into teachers' implementation. *Teaching and Teacher Education, 36*(0), 101–111. doi:10.1016/j.tate.2013.07.008

Hou, H. T., & Cheng, K. H. (2012). Analyzing the latent emotional transfer pattern (LETP) of a learning community in an online peer-assessment activity. *British Journal of Educational Technology, 43*(4), E113-E116. doi:10.1111/j.1467-8535.2012.01301.x

Hunter, D., & Russ, M. (1996). Peer assessment in performance studies. *British Journal of Music Education, 13*(01), 67–78. doi:10.1017/S0265051700002953

Hwang, G. J., Hung, C. M., & Chen, N. S. (2014). Improving learning achievements, motivations and problem-solving skills through a peer assessment-based game development approach. *Educational Technology Research and Development, 62*(2), 129–145. doi:10.1007/s11423-013-9320-7

Johnson, N., & Winterbottom, M. (2010). Supporting girls' motivation in science: A study of peer- and self-assessment in a girls-only class. *Educational Studies, 37*(4), 391–403. doi: 10.1080/03055698.2010.508605

Karaca, E. (2009). An evaluation of teacher trainees' opinions of the peer assessment in terms of some variables. *World Applied Sciences Journal, 6*(1), 123–128.

Kim, M., & Ryu, J. (2013). The development and implementation of a web-based formative peer assessment system for enhancing students' metacognitive awareness and performance in ill-structured tasks. *Educational Technology Research and Development, 61*(4), 549–561. doi:10.1007/s11423-012-9266-1

Koc, C. (2011). The views of prospective class teachers about peer assessment in teaching practice. *Educational Sciences: Theory & Practice, 11*(4), 1979–1989.

Kollar, I., & Fischer, F. (2010). Peer assessment as collaborative learning: A cognitive perspective. *Learning and Instruction, 20*(4), 344–348. doi:10.1016/j.learninstruc.2009.08.005

Lee, S., & Ditko, S. (1962, August 15). Spider Man. *Amazing Fantasy, 15,* 1–11.

Li, L., & Steckelberg, A. (2004). *Using peer feedback to enhance student meaningful learning.* Paper presented at the Conference of the Association for Educational Communications and Technology, Chicago, USA.

Lin, S. S. J., Liu, E. Z. F., & Yuan, S. M. (2002). Student attitudes toward networked peer assessment: Case studies of undergraduate students and senior high school students. *International Journal of Instructional Media, 29*(2), 241–254.

Lindblom-Ylänne, S., Pihlajamäki, H., & Kotkas, T. (2006). Self-, peer- and teacher-assessment of student essays. *Active Learning in Higher Education, 7*(1), 51–62. doi:10.1177/1469787406061148

Magin, D. (2001). Reciprocity as a source of bias in multiple peer assessment of group work. *Studies in Higher Education, 26*(1), 53–63. doi:10.1080/03075070020030715

McConlogue, T. (2010). But is it fair? Developing students' understanding of grading complex written work through peer assessment. *Assessment & Evaluation In Higher Education, 37*(1), 113–123. doi:10.1080/0260 2938.2010.515010

McMahon, T. (2009). Combining peer-assessment with negotiated learning activities on a day-release undergraduate-level certificate course (ECTS level 3). *Assessment & Evaluation In Higher Education, 35*(2), 223–239. doi:10.1080/02602930902795919

Montero Garcia-Celay, I., & León, O. (2007). A guide for naming research studies in Psychology. *International Journal of Clinical and Health Psychology, 7*(3), 847–862.

Orsmond, P., Merry, S., & Reiling, K. (1996). The importance of marking criteria in the use of peer assessment. *Assessment & Evaluation In Higher Education, 21*(3), 239–250. doi:10.1080/0260293960210304

Panadero, E., & Alonso-Tapia, J. (2013). Self-assessment: Theoretical and practical connotations. When it happens, how is it acquired and what to do to develop it in our students. *Electronic Journal of Research in Educational Psychology, 11*(2), 551–576. doi:10.14204/ejrep.30.12200

Panadero, E., & Brown, G.T.L. (2015). *Higher education teachers' assessment practices: Formative espoused but not yet fully implemented.* Paper presented at the Fifth Assessment in Higher Education Conference 2015, Birmingham, (UK).

Panadero, E., & Brown, G.T.L. (2016). Teachers' reasons for using peer assessment: Positive experience predicts use. *European Journal of Psychology of Education.* doi: 10.1007/s10212-015-0282-5

Panadero, E., Jonsson, A., & Strijbos, J. W. (2016). Enhancing ownership, relinquishing control: Scaffolding students regulated learning through involvement via Assessment for Learning. In D. Laveault & L. Allal (Eds.), *Assessment for Learning: Meeting the challenge of implementation.*

Panadero, E., Romero, M., & Strijbos, J. W. (2013). The impact of a rubric and friendship on construct validity of peer assessment, perceived fairness and comfort, and performance. *Studies in Educational Evaluation, 39*(4), 195–203. doi:10.1016/j.stueduc.2013.10.005

Pekrun, R., Goetz, T., Titz, W., & Perry, R. P. (2002). Academic emotions in students' self-regulated learning and achievement: A program of qualitative and quantitative research. *Educational Psychologist, 37*(2), 91–105. doi:10.1207/S15326985EP3702_4

Peterson, E. R., & Irving, S. E. (2008). Secondary school students' conceptions of assessment and feedback. *Learning and Instruction, 18*(3), 238–250.

Reinholz, D. (2015). The assessment cycle: A model for learning through peer assessment. *Assessment & Evaluation in Higher Education,* 1–15. doi:10.1080/02602938.2015.1008982

Sadler, P. M., & Good, E. (2006). The impact of self- and peer-grading on student learning. *Educational Assessment, 11*(1), 1–31.

Sluijsmans, D.M.A., Brand-Gruwel, S., & van Merriënboer, J. J. G. (2002). Peer assessment training in teacher education: Effects on performance and perceptions. *Assessment & Evaluation in Higher Education, 27*(5), 443–454. doi:10.1080/0260293022000009311

Stanier, L. (1997). Peer assessment and group work as vehicles for student empowerment: A module evaluation. *Journal of Geography in Higher Education, 21*(1), 95–98. doi:10.1080/03098269708725413

Strijbos, J. W., Ochoa, T. A., Sluijsmans, D.M.A., Segers, M.S.R., & Tillema, H. H. (2009). Fostering interactivity through formative peer assessment in (web-based) collaborative learning environments. In C. Mourlas, N. Tsianos, & P. Germanakos (Eds.), *Cognitive and emotional processes in web-based education: Integrating human factors and personalization* (pp. 375–395). Hersey, PA: IGI Global.

Topping, K. J. (1998). Peer assessment between students in colleges and universities. *Review of Educational Research, 68*(3), 249–276.

Topping, K. J. (2003). Self and peer assessment in school and university: Reliability, validity and utility. In M. Segers, F. Dochy, & E. Cascallar (Eds.), *Optimising new modes of assessment: In search of qualities and standards* (Vol. 1, pp. 55–87). Netherlands: Springer.

Topping, K. J. (2012). Peers as a source of formative and summative assessment. In J. H. McMillan (Ed.), *Handbook of research on classroom assessment* (pp. 395–412). Los Angeles: SAGE.

Topping, K. J., Smith, E. F., Swanson, I., & Elliot, A. (2000). Formative peer assessment of academic writing between postgraduate students. *Assessment & Evaluation in Higher Education, 25*(2), 149–169. doi:10.1080/713611428

van Gennip, N. (2012a). Arranging peer assessment: The role of interpersonal beliefs *Assessing together. Peer assessment from an interpersonal perspective* (Vol. PhD, pp. 45–57): Universiteit Leiden.

van Gennip, N. (2012b). *Assessing together. Peer assessment from an interpersonal perspective.* (PhD), Universiteit Leiden.

van Gennip, N., Gijbels, D., Segers, M., & Tillema, H. H. (2010). Reactions to 360° feedback: The role of trust and trust-related variables. *International Journal of Human Resources Development and Management, 10*(4), 362–379. doi:10.1504/IJHRDM.2010.036088

van Gennip, N. A. E., Segers, M.S.R., & Tillema, H. H. (2009). Peer assessment for learning from a social perspective: The influence of interpersonal variables and structural features. *Educational Research Review, 4*(1), 41–54. doi:10.1016/j.edurev.2008.11.002

van Gennip, N.A.E., Segers, M.S.R., & Tillema, H. H. (2010). Peer assessment as a collaborative learning activity: The role of interpersonal variables and conceptions. *Learning and Instruction, 20*(4), 280–290. doi:10.1016/j.learninstruc.2009.08.010

van Zundert, M., Sluijsmans, D., & Van Merriënboer, J. (2010). Effective peer assessment processes: Research findings and future directions. *Learning and Instruction, 20*(4), 270–279. doi:10.1016/j.learninstruc.2009.08.004

Vanderhoven, E., Raes, A., Montrieux, H., Rotsaert, T., & Schellens, T. (2015). What if pupils can assess their peers anonymously? A quasi-experimental study. *Computers & Education, 81*, 123–132. doi:http://dx.doi.org/10.1016/j.compedu.2014.10.001

Wen, M. L., & Tsai, C. C. (2006). University students' perceptions of and attitudes toward (online) peer assessment. *Higher Education, 51*(1), 27–44. doi:10.1007/s10734–004–6375–8

Willey, K., & Gardner, A. (2010). Investigating the capacity of self and peer assessment activities to engage students and promote learning. *European Journal of Engineering Education, 35*(4), 429–443. doi:10.1080/03043797.2010.490577

Wilson, M. J., Diao, M. M., & Huang, L. (2015). 'I'm not here to learn how to mark someone else's stuff': An investigation of an online peer-to-peer review workshop tool. *Assessment & Evaluation In Higher Education, 40*(1), 15–32. doi: 10.1080/02602938.2014.881980

15

PRIVACY IN CLASSROOM ASSESSMENT

Robin D. Tierney and Martha J. Koch

At a recent conference where researchers and teachers met to explore classroom assess-ment practice, a teacher described her use of a tablet-based application to capture the collaborative problem-solving of her elementary students. She explained that the 'app' records what students write and draw on the tablet and creates an audio recording of their conversation. She described the valuable insights she gains about students' think-ing and group work skills from these recordings. She saves them online so that she can review them from home where she often plans lessons. She also shares the recordings with students when conferencing with them, with parents during interviews, and with other teachers working with the same students. To demonstrate the app, she played a recording of three students engaged in problem-solving. We could see their thoughts emerge through the diagrams they drew and by listening to their conversation.

An enthusiastic discussion of the ways this app might enrich assessment practice ensued. Then one teacher lamented that she would not be able to use the app since her district prohibits online storage of student data. Others wondered about stu-dent privacy since the recordings were being shared with other students and their parents. A question about the ethics of recording young students was raised. Might they forget they were being recorded? Some felt this forgetting could result in a more accurate record of student thinking, while others were concerned it might compro-mise each student's privacy—that is, the privacy of their thoughts as they learn. Many expressed uncertainty about the security of data stored in "the cloud," which prompted further discussion of issues around the use of assessment apps.

This vignette is an account of a conversation that the second author witnessed. While it began with the benefits of an assessment tool, it quickly turned to a discussion of ethi-cal and professional concerns. This discussion resonated with us because we have noted in our experience as educators and researchers that worthwhile classroom assessment (CA) activities are sometimes at odds with students' need for and right to privacy. In this chapter we explore privacy in CA as a fundamental issue that predates the digital era, and we look at how technology creates more complex issues that urgently need to be addressed. Digital technologies, ranging from applications downloaded by individual teachers to comprehensive data management programs adopted by school systems, are increasingly used in many educational contexts. A recent technology survey in the United States (U.S.) indicated a 57% increase in expenditure on pre-kindergarten to Grade 12 educational assessment from 2010 to 2013, with revenues from this sector of the market estimated to be almost $2.5 billion (Richards & Stebbins, 2014). The survey also revealed that demand for technology related to large-scale assessments has slowed and much of the increase in expenditure is the "widespread demand for more and better formative assessments" (Richards & Stebbins, 2014, p. 2).

The changing demand in the technology market reflects a broader shift in CA theory and practice. CA has traditionally focused on assessment *of* learning (AoL), where student work is graded and achievement is summarized in order to place, select, or certify students. Increasingly, teachers and students also engage in assessment practices where ongoing monitoring and feedback are used to support learning. This form of assessment has been referred to as formative evaluation (Bloom, Madaus, & Hastings, 1971), formative assessment (Black & Wiliam, 1998), assessment *as* learning (Earl, 2003), and assessment *for* learning (AfL) (Assessment Reform Group, 1999). Though these terms differ in origin and meaning, they all emphasize that CA should be embedded within learning activities and that its primary purpose should be to support teaching and learning. We use the term AfL as it is currently endorsed in the education community (Gordon Commission, 2013). We also recognize that effective CA practice includes both AfL and AoL (Black, 2013; Earl, 2003; Harlen, 2006) and that digital technology holds enormous promise for both aspects of CA (Kong et al., 2014). While technology has been used to increase efficiency in administering and scoring large-scale tests for some time, it is now becoming a central feature of CA practice (see Katz & Gorin, this volume).

CA rarely figured into discussions about privacy, and vice versa, until quite recently. Legal cases related to student privacy tend to involve search and seizure or drug testing in schools (Crook & Truscott, 2007; Hachiya, Shoop, & Dunklee, 2014), and the attractions of digital technology for CA often garner more attention than the risks. However, with the pervasive use of technology for collecting, sharing, and storing information, and increasingly frequent breaches of data security in education (Herold & Davis, 2014), more attention is now being placed on student privacy. The Offices of Privacy Commissioners in Ontario, Canada, and in New Zealand, for example, have published resources specifically for schools on the privacy of student information (Cavoukian, 2011; Dalziel, 2009). In the U.S., 83 bills introduced in 32 states in 2014 related to the privacy of student information (Ujifusa, 2014), and the federal government established the Privacy Technical Assistance Center (PTAC) to inform stakeholders about student privacy (United States Department of Education, 2014).

Despite this recent surge of concern, student information systems with serious flaws are still being used (Hui, 2014), and current research highlights significant, unresolved issues in the privacy of student information (Reidenberg et al., 2013). A paradox that further complicates the issue is that while much concern is voiced about protecting privacy, personal information is often willingly shared in exchange for small benefits such as free apps or shopping coupons (Allen, 2011). The idea of having 'nothing to hide' is sometimes used to justify inattention to online privacy. Privacy experts are quick to counter this misconception because it essentially equates privacy with secrecy and overlooks its importance in both human development and autonomy in a democratic society (Moore, 2013; Solove, 2011).

Recent events suggest the tide may be turning against the great "electronic data giveaway" (Allen, 2011, p.156) that has marked the past few decades. A notable example is the community protest in the U.S. that led to the demise of InBloom, a multistate student data service (Kharif, 2014). However, a danger accompanying the rise in awareness around privacy issues is that some reactions may be counterproductive for classroom teaching and learning. For example, one state proposal would have barred teachers from accessing their own students' assessment results (Ujifusa, 2014).

The question at this point, and the focus of this chapter, is how to protect student privacy while using CA to its full potential. We explore the dilemmas inherent in this question from the premise that effective CA requires the frequent observation of students during learning activities and that CA can be greatly enhanced through the use of digital technology. At the same time, students require privacy in order to learn effectively (Davis, 2001; Moore, 2013), and the privacy of their personal information is a right (Crook & Truscott, 2007). To explore this question, we begin by clarifying our use of terms and providing a brief historical overview of privacy and its legislation. We then identify five beneficial aspects of CA that are in tension with privacy rights and consider the implications of these tensions for policy and practice.

KEY DEFINITIONS

Debate over the exact definition of privacy is ongoing (Bygrave, 2010), but experts agree that it is a nebulous (Bygrave, 2013, p. 77; Payton & Claypoole, 2014, p. 2) and multidimensional concept (Finn, Wright, & Friedewald, 2013; Moore, 2013). In discussing educational law and ethics, Crook and Truscott (2007) define the *right to privacy* as the right of an "individual to choose the time, circumstances, and extent of his personal presence, property, thoughts, feelings, or information being shared with or withheld from others" (p.105). Applying this definition to CA, the privacy of student records is an evident concern, but less obvious factors such as the privacy of students' thoughts and feelings while learning must also be considered. As such, we use *student information or data* to mean not only information contained in formal records (e.g., report cards), but also less formal information gathered in ongoing CA practice, such as a teacher's observations and anecdotal records about students.

Two other terms related to privacy appear in assessment literature. *Confidentiality* is the "duty to protect and hold in strict confidence all information concerning the person who is the subject of the professional relationship" (Dalziel, 2009, p. 7). Teachers' ethical codes or standards of practice, like those of other professions where sensitive information is shared, often refer to maintaining the confidentiality of student data (e.g Ontario College of Teachers, 2012). *Anonymity*, defined as "freedom from identification" (Westin, 1967), differs in that it is not necessarily required in CA, but can be used as a technique for fairer assessment. For instance, student anonymity may be used to avoid bias in the marking process. Thus in discussing CA, we use privacy, confidentiality, and anonymity as related but distinct terms.

PRIVACY—FROM BASIC DESIRE TO LEGISLATED RIGHT

Tracing the evolution of privacy from a basic desire to a legislated right sheds light on how it has become an increasing concern in educational contexts.

The Desire for Privacy

Most animals living in social structures, including humans, exhibit a desire for privacy (Moore, 1998; Westin, 1967). Even when cooperation within a community is beneficial, some degree of privacy is desirable. Privacy confers dignity and allows for the development of individual thought and identity (Payton & Claypoole, 2014). Privacy seems most coveted when it is threatened by curiosity, or the desire for knowledge (Bygrave, 2010; Westin, 1967). Curiosity can be constructive, such as when it motivates student learning, but it can also be detrimental when fueled by the desire for material gain or power over others (Allen, 2011; Solove, 2006). Technological advancements have facilitated our ability to profit from information about others, and consequently such advancements tend to be followed by increased concerns about privacy. The development of photographic and printing technology, for example, allowed late-19th-century newspapers to publish photographs, which increased sales. This spurred an article by Warren and Brandeis (1890/2005), which is now acknowledged as the first argument for privacy law in the U.S. (DeCew, 2013; Periñán, 2012). In recent years, the "unprecedented explosion of information technology" (Cavoukian, 2012, p. 19) has raised new concerns about privacy, particularly around intrusive security measures and the insecurity of data storage (Finn et al., 2013; Solove, 2006; Westin, 2003). Despite the complexity of life in an information society, the essential contradiction remains the same. While we seek privacy with tools such as password protection and encryption technology, we are enticed by social media, reality television, and video-sharing websites. Knowledge about people is not only power, it is business, and as U.S. technology market statistics reveal, student data is now big business (Lingard & Lewis, this volume; Richards & Stebbins, 2014).

Privacy as a Human Right

Privacy has long been a privilege of wealth and power, and it has been considered a human right only in relatively recent history. Major social, economic, and political changes followed by world wars in the first half of the 20th century underscored the need for a human rights agreement. This led to the United Nations Declaration of Human Rights (UNDHR) in 1948, which contained the first explicit recognition of privacy as a human right (United Nations, 1948, Article 12). The UNDHR established a foundation for international human rights law (United Nations, 2014), and subsequent treatises have maintained privacy as a human right. The European Union (EU) now leads the development of privacy law with comprehensive regulations around the collection and use of personal information (Bygrave, 2010).

Children were not immediately recognized in human rights legislation. Throughout much of history, children were considered property, belonging either to the state or a parent (Hinchey, 2001). They were not granted distinct rights as capable and autonomous beings until the 1989 United Nations Convention on the Rights of the Child (UNCRC). The UNCRC states that "no child shall be subjected to arbitrary or unlawful interference with his or her privacy, family, home or correspondence, nor to unlawful attacks on his or her honour and reputation" (United Nations, 1989, Article 16). The UNCRC has been ratified by 194 countries (excluding only Somalia, South Sudan, and the U.S.), and it is the most widely accepted international agreement in history (Committee on the Rights of the Child, 2014). Although the UNCRC has been criticized from the left as a platitude that masks urgent need for reform, and from the right for neglecting children's duties and usurping parental authority, many consider it a milestone in the evolution of children's status (Collins, 2013; Freeman, 2000).

Development of Privacy Law

While international treaties such as the UNCRC guide the development of regional law and policy (Crook & Truscott, 2007), the process is also influenced by cultural differences in the interpretation of privacy (Bygrave, 2013; Moore, 2013; Periñán, 2012). Differences in privacy law in the EU and the U.S. provide a notable example. Privacy is protected in the EU with one omnibus law, the Privacy Directive of 1995, and revisions underway will make it even more comprehensive (Schwartz & Solove, 2014). In contrast, the U.S. has a legal "patchwork" (Allen, 2011, p. 156) of privacy laws enacted over time for different sectors, including health care, finance, and education (DeCew, 2013; Payton & Claypoole, 2014; Westin, 2003). Whereas privacy in the EU is considered a fundamental right, in the U.S. it is one important consideration among others, particularly law enforcement, security, and business interests (Payton & Claypoole, 2014; Schwartz & Solove, 2014). Other industrialized nations tend to fall between the EU and the U.S., with more countries (e.g., Australia, Canada, Israel, and Switzerland) adopting privacy laws similar to the EU model (DeCew, 2013; Payton & Claypoole, 2014).

Most privacy laws do not refer specifically to children, perhaps because a parent or guardian typically represents children until they reach the age of majority. As minors, children are vulnerable to a "darker side of privacy" (DeCew, 2013, p. 15) because laws intended to protect privacy can also be used to hide abuse at home or school (Allen, 2013). An additional tension in establishing children's rights stems from differing views of parents' rights. Parental authority, which was incontestable in earlier centuries, has gradually been tempered as child protection services have become more common (Hinchey, 2001). At present in many jurisdictions, parents' rights tend to be balanced with their responsibility to care and provide, but children's privacy rights are still legally relegated to their parents.

The Organisation for Economic Co-operation and Development (OECD, 2012) reports that Internet use by growing numbers of children has created an urgent need for their protection. An array of laws, policies, and technological solutions have been developed to mitigate risks related to website content, marketing, privacy, and security for children (OECD, 2012). Although children's digital privacy is protected to some degree in many countries under the same laws as adults, much information is still collected from and about children online (Berson & Berson, 2006), including through educational databases (Herold & Davis, 2014). Given how rapidly technology is changing the privacy arena, the OECD has called for international cooperation and a more coordinated approach to better protect children's privacy.

Students' Privacy Rights in Education

In general, students' rights increased during the 1960s and 1970s, particularly rights to due process and to freedom of expression (Hinchey, 2001). More recent judicial decisions in North America have favored school safety over individual rights (Crook & Truscott, 2007; Shariff & Johnny, 2008). The increased frequency of school violence worldwide has augmented concerns about safety and prompted questions about the privacy of student records. Who should have access to these records, particularly if the mental health of a student is a concern? The answer is not always clear even for those involved in the collection, use, and disclosure of student data. In Ontario, Canada, for example, several acts at different levels of government apply to student data, creating a complex terrain for educators to navigate (Cavoukian, 2011). In the U.S., the *Family Education Rights and Privacy Act* (FERPA) protects the privacy of student records, but with some surprising exceptions. For instance, educational institutions can release 'directory information' without obtaining specific consent from parents as long as an option to 'opt out' is provided beforehand. Directory information can include a student's name, address, phone number, email address, birthplace, attendance, area of study, participation in clubs or teams, weight and height, awards and honors, schools attended, graduation date, and photograph (Hachiya et al., 2014). School records may also be viewed without parental consent for reasons relating to the student (e.g., inquiry by a social worker), to the school (e.g., a lunch program evaluation by government employee), or for research purposes (Russo & Osborne, 2014). Additionally, U.S. military personnel have access to student records for recruitment (United States Department of Education, 2002).

A related concern is the breadth of information that is protected in education. For example, the *Municipal Freedom of Information and Protection of Privacy Act* (MFIPPA) in Ontario, Canada, protects the confidentiality of students' files, which contains directory-type information and assessment reports, as well as other information such as yearbook photographs, field trip records, and honors lists (Cavoukian, 2011). This differs considerably from the U.S., where a Supreme Court decision (Owasso v. Falvo, 2002) established that information about students is not protected under FERPA unless it is contained in official records (Hachiya et al., 2014), which excludes much of the information gathered less formally in schools. While these sorts of regional differences should be remembered when thinking about privacy, there are also dimensions of CA practice that raise common concerns for privacy across educational contexts. We turn now to a discussion of these shared concerns.

BALANCING EFFECTIVE CLASSROOM ASSESSMENT PRACTICES WITH PRIVACY

We identify five overlapping dimensions of CA practice that create tension with regard to privacy: (1) ongoing assessment, (2) learning in public, (3) student involvement, (4) sharing information, and (5) storing data. For each of these dimensions, we first describe benefits for teaching and learning, and then explore associated privacy issues.

Ongoing Assessment

AoL uses tests and other procedures to describe achievement, usually following a unit or course of instruction, or at set times in the school calendar. While learning may occur as a result of AoL, particularly by academically successful students (Brookhart, 2001) or with enterprising teachers in the lead (Black & Harrison, 2001), the main purpose of AoL is to report on achievement. To effectively support learning for all students, CA must include both AoL and AfL (Harlen, 2006). AfL requires more than adding a "few techniques here and there—it organizes the whole teaching and learning venture around learning, and supports teachers in organizing the learning experiences of their students more productively" (Black, Harrison, Lee, Marshall, & Wiliam, 2003, p. 79). Teachers are encouraged to elicit, recognize, and respond to student learning in an ongoing, cyclical manner (Cowie & Bell, 1999). Students are encouraged to regulate their learning by setting goals and monitoring their progress, and to view mistakes and feedback as opportunities to learn (Earl, 2003; Moss & Brookhart, 2009).

Although the conceptualization of AfL as an ongoing process is widely accepted in assessment literature, it can be challenging for teachers to implement in practice. Morgan and Watson's (2002) case study, for example, revealed how easily a teacher might form an inaccurate understanding of a student's learning given the time constraints and simultaneous activities in a classroom. Technology can enable teachers to capture assessment information more frequently, more accurately, and in greater detail. It can be useful in providing prompt feedback to students and others, indicating not only if an item is answered correctly, but also potentially useful information such as length of time spent on each task. Furthermore, technology can increase the fairness of CA because accuracy does not depend on one observation. With sufficient time to review, analyze, and synthesize assessment information, teachers can use technology to benefit teaching and student learning.

At the same time, technology has the potential to exacerbate privacy issues, particularly if CA is implemented with the frequency of AfL but the intent of AoL. When this occurs, students become subject to continuous summative assessment (Dixon & Williams, 2003; Ecclestone, 2010). The use of continuous summative assessment is problematic for several reasons. First, it limits the leisure of mind that humans require for intellectual development (Moore, 2013). The Gordon Commission (2013) recognized this in noting that "having every learning (and teaching) action recorded and potentially used for consequential purposes is, arguably, an unnecessary invasion of the student's (and teacher's) right to engage freely in intellectual activity" (p. 136). Continuous summative assessment is not the same as AfL because it focuses on evaluation rather than learning. It is also problematic because students' deference to teachers' opinions, which occurs even in contexts that are favorable to AfL (Harris, Brown, & Harnett, 2014), may increase with less privacy of thought (Davis, 2001). Moreover, when learning activities are recorded, students may take fewer risks if they believe there could be repercussions after recordings are reviewed. An additional concern that has received less attention is the influence of construct-irrelevant information in recordings. Students may forget they are being recorded, as suggested in the opening vignette, resulting in inappropriate behavior being permanently captured. While this might permit an intervention that could be beneficial for classroom management or school safety, it could also be detrimental in its effect on teachers' perceptions and decisions.

Learning in Public

In their seminal review, Black and Wiliam (1998) noted that the public nature of classroom learning and assessment has generally been overlooked. They observed that "assessment processes are, at heart, social processes, taking place in social settings" (p. 56). Classroom learning and assessment have always been public in the sense that they unfold before others. Even in classrooms where individual desk work is the norm, information about student achievement is easily discernable. Wall charts with stars, stickers, or tallied points are often displayed to indicate progress; leveled reading groups are visibly demarcated; and student work is frequently posted for all to see. Beyond these physical indicators, oral questioning is used by teachers to understand students' thinking and guide pedagogy, and students hear and see teachers' feedback on each other's ideas and work. While some types of feedback have positive effects on student learning (i.e., descriptive, learning-oriented), some teachers also use the public nature of feedback for control and to motivate or punish students (Pryor & Torrance, 1998; Tunstall & Gipps, 1996).

Classroom practices that openly rank students, such as returning quizzes from highest to lowest score, are now less common, but students are still quite aware that they are on "public display and subject to teacher evaluation" (Cowie, 2005, p. 204). Some students worry about others seeing their assessment results, and will even inflate self-assessments as a self-protective measure (Harris & Brown, 2013). The importance of feelings and emotions in CA has increasingly been recognized (Harris et al., 2014; Vogl & Pekrun, this volume; Värlander, 2008), leading to greater emphasis on trust and respect in AfL practice (Birenbaum, Kimron, & Shilton, 2011; Shepard, 2006). Current professional materials encourage the cultivation of trust and respect in classrooms to permit more open discussion of mistakes, misconceptions, and triumphs in learning (Hattie, 2011; Moss & Brookhart, 2009).

Because CA is inherently social and aims to elicit student thinking, it is arguably an invasion of privacy even when its goals are constructive. For instance, learning activities often ask students to disclose personal information. As a case in point, primary school curricula in many jurisdictions include writing stories about family events, creating family trees, and bringing objects from home for 'show and tell.' While these types of activities have merit in terms of personalizing activities, empowering learners, and eliciting learning, they also compromise student privacy, which can increase pressure to conform and can constrain creative thinking (Davis, 2001; Solove, 2006). Hanafin, O'Donoghue, Flynn, and Shevlin (2009) maintain that such invasive activities make students vulnerable and habituate them to a culture of disclosure and surveillance. After studying 'circle-time' (i.e., a commonly used activity that encourages students to share thoughts) in primary schools in Ireland, Collins (2013) noted benefits such as enhancing students' social skills and promoting an equitable classroom environment. However, Collins (2013) also acknowledged the concerns raised by Hanafin and colleagues regarding the confidential information disclosed by young students, noting a significant "erosion" (p.432) in teachers' understanding of students' rights to abstain from participation. In effect, activities such as circle time can create an environment where it seems acceptable to coerce children to disclose personal information.

Compounding these concerns, Hanafin and colleagues (2009) point out that the audience in a classroom often includes a range of people. Along with teachers and students, there may be parent volunteers, teacher candidates, education assistants, and others. District leaders, social workers, maintenance staff, and school office personnel also have the opportunity to learn a great deal about students. Even if school records are securely stored and data are not intentionally shared, simple observation can reveal confidential information, such as which students receive curricular accommodations. CA standards (Joint Committee on Standards for Educational Evaluation, 2003) and privacy law for North American schools (e.g., FERPA, MFIPPA) specify that student information should only be shared with those with a legitimate interest (Cavoukian, 2011; Imber & van Geel, 2010). However, such laws generally do not protect information that is discerned through informal observation in schools. As a result, students' privacy depends on all members of a school community, as well as visitors, treating confidentiality as a matter of respect and moral responsibility regardless of their legal obligation.

Student Involvement

In current pedagogical theory, students are not passive recipients of teachers' evaluative judgments but are expected to take an active role in CA (Falchikov, 2007; Stiggins & Chappuis, 2005). In practice, teachers and students have always talked about assessment, but these conversations were typically focused on results and grades (Moss, 2003). Assessment conversations now also include talk about students' progress toward learning goals, and they help make criteria for success explicit (Ruiz-Primo, 2011; Willis & Adie, 2014). Assessment conversations that are based on peer and self-assessment (PASA) shift control from teachers and help students develop metacognitive skills (Shepard, 2006). Peer assessment (PA) has been found to be particularly effective not only in developing students' confidence and responsibility (Falchikov, 2007), but also for increasing student awareness that varied responses are acceptable and learning takes diverse paths (Värlander, 2008). In addition, when implemented as peer grading (i.e., scoring a quiz), PA can be useful for managing time and providing prompt results (Sadler & Good, 2006). For more on PA, see Panadero (this volume).

Despite these benefits, by allowing students to become more familiar with one another's strengths and weaknesses, PASA can compromise privacy. Whether students are using older tools (e.g., a document emailed between students) or newer applications to support collaboration, the use of technology for PASA increases this threat because students may make and post copies of work by other students (e.g., phone images, shared files, etc.). Some students may become "information brokers" (Berson & Berson, 2006, p. 136) who unwittingly reveal as much about others as themselves on social media (OECD, 2012). This information can become fodder for bullying in schools (Hanafin et al., 2009), which can promulgate rapidly online (Shariff & Johnny, 2008). Although lessons on responsible Internet use are now taught with greater frequency, privacy rights are not widely incorporated into curricula, and students may not fully understand the ramifications of posting comments or images online (OECD, 2012; Shariff & Johnny, 2008).

Bullying is especially problematic for students with disabilities (Paré, 2012). The U.S. Supreme Court case mentioned earlier (Owasso v. Falvo, 2002) involved a child with a disability who was mocked by peers after his scores were revealed through peer grading (Parry, 2002). Privacy law did not protect this student's psychological safety. In expressing discomfort with PA, students report that they have experienced or are concerned about negative effects within their peer group (Harris & Brown, 2013; Pryor & Lubisi, 2002). Several studies have revealed that students also prefer anonymity in giving peer feedback (Foley, 2013; Raes, Vanderhoven, & Schellens, 2013). Anonymity in PA can make the process less biased (Sadler & Good, 2006) and improve the substance of peer feedback (Howard, Barrett, & Frick, 2010). However, anonymity is not always possible. Student handwriting may be recognizable, for example, or an assessment may include recorded images. Furthermore, anonymity is not always desirable as the judicious use of some information contributes to fairer CA, such as knowledge of special circumstances requiring accommodation for a particular student (Moon, this volume). Thus, while student involvement in CA is clearly beneficial for learning, it also generates several thorny privacy concerns.

Sharing Information

In addition to assessment conversations between teachers and students, information about students is routinely shared outside the classroom. Various strategies are used to communicate with parents, from traditional report cards and conferences to newer digital approaches (Graham-Clay, 2005). While technology does not replace in-person conversations, it can support more frequent and effective communication with parents (Schweikert, 2014). There are now many online applications that teachers and parents can download to facilitate communication (see McCrea, 2013). Some are intended simply for short messages such as field trip reminders, while others allow parents and teachers to log-in and share detailed information about students. Using applications designed for early childhood education, teachers can add their observations to images of children engaged in activities for parents to see. Applications for older students often use a Web portal for students, parents, and teachers to communicate about attendance, homework, and grades. Communication with parents is a key factor in student success as it builds trust in the school community and enables parents to be actively involved in their children's learning (Borgonovi & Montt, 2012; Bryk & Schneider, 2003). The enhancement of communication with parents and students afforded by digital technology can support the effectiveness of CA.

Students' assessment results are also routinely shared among teachers and other professionals within schools. For example, diagnostic assessment results are shared by special education teachers for programming and placement purposes. These assessment conversations can support students' learning and help teachers improve their teaching and assessment practices (Johnston, 2003). Teachers and school leaders have been strongly encouraged in recent years to use the analysis of assessment results to improve teaching and learning (Hargreaves & Braun, 2013). Some jurisdictions use system-wide programs that make it possible for educators to enter, track, and share student achievement data. These programs often facilitate the development of individual learning plans for students, as well as improvement plans for schools. In this process, educators are expected to maintain the confidentiality of student data. The Ontario College of Teachers, for instance, refers to confidentiality in its ethical standards, and violation of such is considered professional misconduct (Government of Ontario, 1996).

Sharing information is essential for the effectiveness of CA practice, but there are privacy concerns relating to how and with whom it is shared. Students, parents, and teachers may use technology to communicate about assessment results without understanding the privacy risks. For example, a teacher might reply to a parent's email request for a student's assessment result without checking that it was a custodial parent who made the request, or without knowing whether the transmission was encrypted, or whether the online portal was secure. Ensuring that electronic communication is secure so that student data remains private tends to be overlooked in guidelines that aim to support effective home–school communication (for example, Harvard Family Research Project, 2013). With video recordings, there is the additional problem of more than one student being identifiable. Although campaigns for Internet awareness recommend caution in sharing identifiable information online (OECD, 2012), privacy legislation tends to predate this concern. A second major issue relates to who has access to student data. Generally, student data should only be shared with adults who have a 'legitimate' interest, but this may go beyond the academic purposes and relate to student health and safety, school or system administration, law enforcement, and external research (Cavoukian, 2011; Russo & Osborne, 2014). Furthermore, there is considerable variation in the interpretation of 'legitimate' across jurisdictions, and privacy laws are not always clear to stakeholders. For example, U.S. schools are supposed to notify parents of their right to opt out before student information is shared, but this is not always understood by parents and administrators, nor is it regularly enforced by the government (Zgonjanin, 2006).

Storing Data

The secure storage of student data is a necessity that has long posed administrative challenges. A significant change in the 21st century is the increased reliance on cloud-based storage that uses a "vast system of interrelated computer resources located remotely and accessible over a network" (Payton & Claypoole, 2014, p. 58). Reidenberg and colleagues (2013) studied the policies and procedures of a national sample of school districts in the U.S. and found that almost all (95%) used cloud-based services. These services provide benefits for districts including lower costs for hardware and personnel, and less risk of physical damage to files (Waters, 2010). Long-term benefits for teaching and learning may also be realized by preserving data for research purposes. Most significantly, cloud-based services allow data to be accessed more easily (Waters, 2010) and students can be efficiently tracked across systems and over time.

Technological advances in data storage have enabled a vast quantity of detailed evidence about students to be collected and saved in various formats, including text, images, and audio or video recordings. This can be beneficial in that providing students with multiple and varied opportunities to demonstrate learning increases the fairness of CA (Tierney, 2013). However, finding sufficient time to review and analyze the quantity of evidence that can now be gathered is problematic. Arguably, teachers can review assessment artifacts more frequently and conveniently with cloud-based storage. This allows instruction to be tailored more efficiently to students' needs. The use of cloud-based applications in classrooms is becoming common (Reidenberg et al., 2013) and is likely to increase given these benefits.

At the same time, the enormous potential of cloud computing to enhance CA is accompanied by several serious threats to privacy. Educational stakeholders, including those who make decisions about student data, are often not well informed about Internet security or privacy rights. Reidenberg and colleagues (2013) noted that cloud services in particular are "poorly understood, non-transparent, and weakly governed" (np). Many school districts in the U.S., for example, have signed contracts with cloud service providers that have poorly specified security provisions and do not restrict student data from being used or sold for marketing purposes (Reidenberg et al., 2013). Similarly, students and teachers routinely use applications to upload and download student work without understanding the security of the process. They may view security threats as outside of their control without realizing that their habits, such as sharing passwords or leaving computers on, also threaten the privacy of student data (Davis, 2009).

Another significant concern in the storage of student data is its permanency. While tracking student progress can have benefits for learning, it can also have negative consequences. School administrators often sign contracts for cloud services without clear terms about how long student data will be retained or how it will be destroyed (Reidenberg et al., 2013). Technology now makes it possible to link databases containing information retained from previous years, which allows comprehensive profiles to be assembled. Indeed, a student's entire learning history can now be recorded, including any mistakes or divergences which would otherwise be forgotten (Berson & Berson, 2006). Retained data can influence teachers' perceptions throughout a student's education, and have consequences for students later in their lives. As noted by the OECD (2012), the "persistent nature of personal information online" (p. 37) has cost more than a few job opportunities. The appeal of digital applications and cloud-based data storage for CA has resulted in rapid adoption, but inadequate attention has been paid to the immediate and long-term risks to student privacy.

IMPLICATIONS FOR IMPROVEMENT

Our review of privacy in CA suggests the need for improvement in the quality of CA practice, awareness of privacy rights, and the development of more effective privacy policies.

Quality of Classroom Assessment Practice

For CA to effectively inform teaching and support learning without unduly compromising students' privacy rights, teachers must attend to several points. First and foremost, creating an environment that enables CA to be used constructively requires that trust and respect be nurtured so that a sense of dignity prevails in the classroom. Without these conditions, students are unlikely to participate openly and honestly in learning and assessment activities. Some teachers actively cultivate a sense of community to encourage the constructive use of feedback and minimize any negative effects (Tierney, 2014). However, this skill takes time and considerable effort to develop (Wiliam, 2015).

The main purpose of CA must also be kept in mind so that the information gathered serves students appropriately. The ability to gather rich information about students and their learning with digital technology does not mean that every detail should be kept or used. Students need privacy of thought and the freedom to make mistakes as they learn. Furthermore, the vast quantity of data that can be gathered using digital technology exceeds what can actually be analyzed and used within the typical time constraints of CA. This can lead to situations where privacy risks are being taken without the realization of related benefits.

There is an essential tension between monitoring students' learning and respecting their privacy that needs to be openly discussed and better understood. Initial teacher education and professional development programs must support teachers in developing the professional judgment required to engage in effective and fair CA without unduly compromising privacy. For example, not all student self-assessments need to be disclosed to the teacher (Andrade & Brown, this volume). Emphasis must be placed on creating environments that are psychologically safe for learning and also on designing CA tasks or processes that respect students' privacy. This also suggests that teachers need to develop skills in drawing appropriate samples from masses of data in order to avoid making unjustified inferences. Consideration should be given to how much assessment data is gathered and stored in relation to what is needed or can feasibly be used. In addition, teachers will need support and guidance as they learn how to fairly and validly sample and summarize the available evidence.

Awareness of Privacy Rights

Children's rights have increasingly been recognized in recent decades, but changes in educational practice can be slow and competing concerns about school safety must also be considered. Students' privacy rights are now a matter of public concern largely because of the use of technology that facilitates collection, rapid analysis, and flexible storage of data. With the fate of one data services company fresh in mind, technology vendors appear to be improving their privacy policies (Kharif, 2014). However, there needs to be greater understanding that respecting privacy rights requires more than legal compliance, especially as law easily becomes obsolete with rapid developments in technology. Teachers and school leaders must more fully understand exactly what information is being gathered, retained, or sold when applications are downloaded for classroom use. Not only do they need to understand how privacy benefits learning, and how to mitigate threats to student privacy, they will also need to serve as leaders in raising parent and student awareness and respect for privacy rights. A first step in this process is to make use of existing resources that have been developed to promote a greater understanding of youth privacy (e.g., by Privacy Commissioners in Canada and New Zealand). All stakeholders in education need to have a better understanding of how student data systems work to be able to trust that the confidentiality of student data will be maintained when it should be. Most importantly, the educational community needs to recognize privacy as a fundamental human right. This will require professional development for educators, as well as broader public education campaigns.

Policy Development

Although educational policy must align with privacy laws, thinking about students' privacy should not be limited to the avoidance of litigation. To this end, the adoption of a broad definition of personal information, in line with the EU definition, would be useful. An area that could inform the development of policy for privacy in CA is research ethics. The process for ensuring the ethical conduct of research includes an explicit effort to balance the potential benefits of a proposed study with the potential for harm to participants. Moreover, researchers are required to specify how they will mitigate any anticipated harm (American Educational Research Association, 2000; Canadian Institutes of Health Research, Natural Sciences and Engineering Research Council of Canada, and Social Sciences and Humanities Research Council of Canada, 2014). While the confidentiality, safety, and dignity of research participants must be safeguarded, this does not mean that data cannot be collected, analyzed, and disseminated. Similarly, while attention must be paid to minimizing risks so that privacy rights are not compromised in CA, a balanced approach is needed to allow rich information to be gathered so that AfL can serve its purpose. Such an approach must begin with a concerted effort to make anticipated risks explicit and to indicate how those risks might be mitigated. The establishment of privacy review boards with stakeholders from a variety of areas of expertise, similar to institutional research ethics boards, could be an effective structure for overseeing major decisions about student privacy. To be cost-effective and logistically feasible, such an approach would likely need to be taken at the state or provincial level rather than by individual school districts.

Ultimately, policy development for privacy in CA will require leadership. Schools and districts should be encouraged to work with governmental bodies as they cannot be expected to have the legal expertise or technological sophistication necessary to fully develop privacy policies and ensure that contracts with service providers include adequate safeguards. Nor should they be entirely responsible for creating resources for professional development and family awareness. Government initiatives in these areas are also needed. While some excellent resources relating to privacy exist (e.g., the New Zealand Privacy Commission website), more are needed that focus on the privacy of student information and assessment data. To be accessible to all stakeholders, resources will need to be developed in multiple languages for different audiences.

CONCLUSION

Widespread breaches of data security on an unprecedented level have heightened concern about personal privacy in recent years. While technology may appear to be causing this concern, the desire for privacy actually predates written history and law. We agree with privacy experts in emphasizing that legislation and regulation, even if updated and maintained, is insufficient for the protection of student privacy (Cavoukian, 2012). A proactive and collaborative approach involving the technology sector, governmental agencies, and educational leaders is needed. We also suggest that privacy rights should be discussed with students as part of the curriculum in a manner similar to the focus on media literacy that has become a common feature of language arts curricula. The inclusion of students' privacy rights in initial teacher education programs and ongoing professional development for practicing teachers and school administrators is essential alongside broader public education. Action at all these levels must take place for students' privacy to be understood and respected throughout the classroom assessment process.

REFERENCES

Allen, A. L. (2011). *Unpopular privacy: What must we hide?* New York: Oxford University Press.

Allen, A. L. (2013). Privacy isn't everything: Accountability as a personal and social good. In A. D. Moore (Ed.), *Information ethics: Privacy, property, and power* (pp. 399–416). Seattle, WA: University of Washington Press.

American Educational Research Association. (2000). *Ethical standards of the American Educational Research Association* (3rd ed.). Washington, DC: AERA.

Andrade, H. L. (2010). Students as the definitive source of formative assessment: Academic self-assessment and the self-regulation of learning. In H. L. Andrade & G. J. Cizek (Eds.), *Handbook of formative assessment* (pp. 90–105). New York: Routledge.

Assessment Reform Group. (1999). *Assessment for learning: Beyond the black box.* Cambridge, UK: Cambridge University.

Berson, I. R., & Berson, M. J. (2006). Children and their digital dossiers: Lessons in privacy rights in the digital age. *International Journal of Social Education, 21*(1), 135–147.

Birenbaum, M., Kimron, H., & Shilton, H. (2011). Nested contexts that shape assessment for learning: School-based professional learning community and classroom culture. *Studies in Educational Evaluation, 37*, 35–48.

Black, P. (2013). Formative and summative aspects of assessment: Theoretical and research foundations in the context of pedagogy. In J. H. McMillan (Ed.), *Sage handbook of research on classroom assessment* (pp. 167–177). Thousand Oaks, CA: Sage.

Black, P., & Harrison, C. (2001). Self- and peer-assessment and taking responsibility: The science student's role in formative assessment. *School Science Review, 83*(302), 43–49.

Black, P., Harrison, C., Lee, C., Marshall, B., & Wiliam, D. (2003). *Assessment for learning: Putting it into practice.* Maidenhead, UK: Open University Press.

Black, P., & Wiliam, D. (1998). Assessment and classroom learning. *Assessment in Education: Principles, Policy & Practice, 5*(1), 7–74.

Bloom, B. S., Madaus, G. F., & Hastings, J. T. (1971). *Handbook on formative and summative evaluation of student learning.* New York: McGraw-Hill.

Borgonovi, F., & Montt, G. (2012). *Parental involvement in selected PISA countries and economies* (OECD Education Working Paper No. 73). (Trans.). Retrieved from http://www.oecd.org/officialdocuments/publicdisplaydocumentpdf/?cote=EDU/WKP%282012%2910&docLanguage=En

Brookhart, S. M. (2001). Successful students' formative and summative uses of assessment information. *Assessment in Education: Principles, Policy & Practice, 8*(2), 153–169.

Bryk, A. S., & Schneider, B. (2003). Trust in schools: A core resource for school reform. *Educational Leadership, 60*(6), 40–45.

Bygrave, L. A. (2010). Privacy and data protection in an international perspective. *Scandinavian Studies in Law, 56*, 165–200.

Bygrave, L. A. (2013, September). *Privacy as a cultural value.* Paper presented at the 35th International Conference on Data Protection and Privacy Commissioners, Warsaw, Poland.

Canadian Institutes of Health Research, Natural Sciences and Engineering Research Council of Canada, and Social Sciences and Humanities Research Council of Canada. (2014). *Tri-council policy statement: Ethical conduct for research involving humans.* Retrieved from http://www.pre.ethics.gc.ca/pdf/eng/tcps2–2014/TCPS_2_FINAL_Web.pdf

Cavoukian, A. (2011). *A guide to Ontario legislation covering the release of students' personal information.* Information and Privacy Commissioner, Toronto, ON, Canada.

Cavoukian, A. (2012). Privacy by Design [Leading Edge]. *IEEE Technology & Society Magazine, 31*(4), 18–19.

Collins, B. (2013). Empowerment of children through circle time: Myth or reality? *Irish Educational Studies, 32*(4), 421–436.

Committee on the Rights of the Child. (2014). *Ratification of the convention on the rights of the child.* Retrieved from http://www.ohchr.org/EN/HRBodies/CRC/Pages/CRCIndex.aspx

Cowie, B. (2005). Student commentary on classroom assessment in science: A sociocultural interpretation. *International Journal of Science Education, 27*(2), 199–214.

Cowie, B., & Bell, B. (1999). A model of formative assessment in science education. *Assessment in Education: Principles, Policy & Practice, 6*(1), 101–116.

Crook, K., & Truscott, D. (2007). *Ethics and law for teachers.* Toronto: Nelson Thomson Canada.

Dalziel, K. (2009). *Privacy in schools: A guide to the Privacy Act for principals, teachers and boards of trustees.* Wellington, NZ: Office of the Privacy Commissioner.

Davis, A. (2001). Do children have privacy rights in the classroom? *Studies in Philosophy and Education, 20*(3), 245–254.

Davis, M. R. (2009). Gradebooks take virtual approach: But online record-keeping poses data-security risks. *Education Week*, 30–31.

DeCew, J. (2013). Privacy. In E. N. Zalta, U. Nodelman, C. Allen, & R. L. Anderson (Eds.), *Stanford encyclopedia of philosophy*. Stanford, CA: Stanford University.

Dixon, H., & Williams, R. (2003). Teachers' understanding and use of formative assessment in literacy learning. *New Zealand Annual Review of Education*, 1–12.

Earl, L. M. (2003). *Assessment as learning: Using classroom assessment to maximize student learning*. Thousand Oaks, CA: Corwin Press.

Ecclestone, K. (2010). *Transforming formative assessment in lifelong learning*. Berkshire, UK: Open University Press, McGraw-Hill.

Falchikov, N. (2007). The place of peers in learning and assessment. In D. Boud & N. Falchikov (Eds.), *Rethinking assessment in higher education* (pp. 128–143). Abingdon, Oxon: Routledge.

Finn, R. L., Wright, D., & Friedewald, M. (2013). Seven types of privacy. In S. Gutwirth, R. Leenes, P. de Hert, & Y. Poullet (Eds.), *European data protection: Coming of age* (pp. 3–32). Dordrecht, Netherlands: Springer.

Foley, S. (2013). Student views of peer assessment at the International School of Lausanne. *Journal of Research in International Education, 12*(3), 201–213.

Freeman, M. (2000). The future of children's rights. *Children & Society, 14*(4), 277–293.

General Teaching Council for Scotland. (2012). *Code of professionalism and conduct*. Retrieved from http://www.gtcs.org.uk/standards/copac.aspx

Gordon Commission on the Future of Assessment in Education. (2013). *To assess, to teach, to learn: A vision for the future of assessment*. Princeton, NJ: ETS/Gordon Commission.

Government of Ontario. (1996). Ontario college of teachers act. Professional misconduct—Ontario regulation 437/97. Retrieved from http://www.e-laws.gov.on.ca/html/regs/english/elaws_regs_970437_e.htm

Graham-Clay, S. (2005). Communicating with parents: Strategies for teachers. *The School Community Journal, 16*(1), 117–129.

Hachiya, R. F., Shoop, R. J., & Dunklee, D. R. (2014). *The principal's quick reference guide to school law: Reducing liability, litigation, and other potential legal tangles* (3rd ed.). Thousand Oaks, CA: Corwin Press.

Hanafin, J., O'Donoghue, T., Flynn, M., & Shevlin, M. (2009). The primary school's invasion of the privacy of the child: Unmasking the potential of some current practices. *Educational Studies, 36*(2), 143–152.

Hargreaves, A., & Braun, H. (2013). *Data-driven improvement and accountability*. Retrieved from National Education Policy Centre website http://greatlakescenter.org/docs/Policy_Briefs/Hargreaves_DDIA_Policy.pdf

Harlen, W. (2006). On the relationship between assessment for formative and summative purposes. In J. Gardner (Ed.), *Assessment and learning* (pp. 103–117). Thousand Oaks, CA: Sage.

Harris, L. R., & Brown, G. T. (2013). Opportunities and obstacles to consider when using peer- and self-assessment to improve student learning: Case studies into teachers' implementation. *Teaching & Teacher Education, 36*, 101–111.

Harris, L. R., Brown, G. T., & Harnett, J. (2014). Understanding classroom feedback practices: A study of New Zealand student experiences, perceptions, and emotional responses. *Educational Assessment, Evaluation & Accountability, 26*(2), 107–133.

Harvard Family Research Project. (2013). *Tips for administrators, teachers, and families: How to share data effectively*. Retrieved from http://www.hfrp.org/publications-resources/browse-our-publications/tips-for-administrators-teachers-and-families-how-to-share-data-effectively

Hattie, J. (2011). *Visible learning for teachers*. Abingdon, Oxon: Routledge.

Herold, B., & Davis, M. R. (2014). Personal danger of data breaches prompts action. *Education Week, 33*(18), 1–11.

Hinchey, P. A. (2001). *Student rights: A reference handbook*. Santa Barbara, CA: ABC-CLIO.

Howard, C. D., Barrett, A. F., & Frick, T. W. (2010). Anonymity to promote peer feedback: Pre-service teachers' comments in asynchronous computer-mediated communication. *Journal of Educational Computing Research, 43*(1), 89–112.

Hui, T. K. (2014). Pearson data system hits a bumpy ride in North Carolina: Technical problems frustrating schools. *Education Week, 33*(23), 8.

Imber, M., & van Geel, T. (2010). *Education law*. New York: Routledge.

Johnston, P. (2003). Assessment conversations. *Reading Teacher, 57*(1), 90.

Joint Committee on Standards for Educational Evaluation. (2003). *The student evaluation standards: How to improve evaluations of students*. Thousand Oaks, CA: Corwin Press.

Kharif, O. (2014). Privacy fears over student data tracking lead to InBloom's shutdown. *Technology*. Retrieved from http://www.businessweek.com/articles/2014-05-01/inbloom-shuts-down-amid-privacy-fears-over-student-data-tracking

Kong, S. C., Chan, T.-W., Griffin, P., Hoppe, U., Huang, R., Kinshuk, . . . Yu, S. (2014). E-learning in school education in the coming 10 years for developing 21st century skills: Critical research issues and policy implications. *Journal of Educational Technology & Society, 17*(1), 70–78.

McCrea, B. (2013). 7 free Apps for keeping parents and teachers connected. *The Journal: Transforming Education Through Technology*. http://thejournal.com/articles/2013/06/11/7-free-apps-for-keeping-parents-and-teachers-connected.aspx

Moore, A. D. (2013). Privacy. In H. LaFollette, J. Deigh, & S. Stroud (Eds.), *The International Encyclopedia of Ethics* (Online ed.): Blackwell Publishing Ltd.

Moore, B. (1998). Privacy. *Society, 35*(2), 287–299.

Morgan, C., & Watson, A. (2002). The interpretive nature of teachers' assessment of students' mathematics. *Journal for Research in Mathematics Education, 33*(2), 78–110.

Moss, C. M., & Brookhart, S. M. (2009). *Advancing formative assessment in every classroom: A guide for instructional leaders*. Alexandria, VA: Association for Supervision & Curriculum Development.

Moss, P. (2003). Reconceptualizing validity for classroom assessment. *Educational Measurement: Issues and Practice, 22*(4), 13–25.

Ontario College of Teachers. (2012). *Foundations of professional practice*. Toronto, ON. Retrieved from http://www.oct.ca/~/media/PDF/Foundations%20of%20Professional%20Practice/Foundation_e.ashx

Organisation for Economic Co-operation and Development [OECD]. (2012). *The protection of children online: Recommendations of the OECD Council*. Organisation for Economic Co-operation and Development.

Paré, M. (2012). Inclusion of students with disabilities in the age of technology: The need for human rights guidance. *Education & Law Journal, 22*(1), 39–61.

Parry, G. (2002). Privacy rights in the classroom: Peer grading Supreme Court judgment. *Education & the Law, 14*(3), 173–180.

Payton, T. M., & Claypoole, T. (2014). *Privacy in the age of big data: Recognizing threats, defending your rights, and protecting your family*. Lanham, MD: Rowman & Littlefield.

Periñán, B. (2012). The origin of privacy as a legal value: A reflection on Roman and English law. *American Journal of Legal History, 52*, 183–201.

Pryor, J., & Lubisi, C. (2002). Reconceptualising educational assessment in South Africa: Testing times for teachers. *International Journal of Educational Development, 22*(6), 673–686.

Pryor, J., & Torrance, J. (1998). Formative assessment in the classroom: Where psychological theory meets social practice. *Social Psychology of Education, 2*, 151–176.

Raes, A., Vanderhoven, E., & Schellens, T. (2013). Increasing anonymity in peer assessment by using classroom response technology within face-to-face higher education. *Studies in Higher Education, 40*(1), 178–193.

Reidenberg, J., Russell, N. C., Kovnot, J., Norton, T. B., Cloutier, R., & Alvarado, D. (2013). *Privacy and cloud computing in public schools*. Fordham Law School, Center on Law and Information Policy. Retrieved from http://ir.lawnet.fordham.edu/clip/2

Richards, J., & Stebbins, L. (2014). Behind the data: Testing and assessment, a Pre K–12 US education technology market report. Washington, DC: Software & Information Industry Association.

Ruiz-Primo, M. A. (2011). Informal formative assessment: The role of instructional dialogues in assessing students' learning. *Studies in Educational Evaluation, 37*(1),15–24.

Russo, C. J., & Osborne, A. G. (2014). Student records and privacy. *School Business Affairs, 80*(4), 35–38.

Sadler, P. M., & Good, E. (2006). The impact of self- and peer-grading on student learning. *Educational Assessment, 11*(1), 1–31.

Schwartz, P. M., & Solove, D. J. (2014). Reconciling personal information in the United States and European Union. *California Law Review, 102*, 877–916.

Schweikert, G. (2014). Using technology to communicate with parents: Tool or taboo? *Exchange Magazine, May/June*, 62–64.

Shariff, S., & Johnny, L. (2008). Child rights in cyber-space: Protection, participation, and privacy. In T. O'Neill & D. Zinga (Eds.), *Children's rights: Multidisciplinary approaches to participation and protection* (pp. 220–244). Toronto, Canada: University of Toronto Press.

Shepard, L. (2006). Classroom assessment. In R. L. Brennan (Ed.), *Educational measurement* (4th ed., pp. 623–646). Westport, CT: National Council on Measurement in Education, American Council on Education and Praeger Publishers.

Solove, D. J. (2006). A taxonomy of privacy. *University of Pennsylvania Law Review, 154*(3), 477.

Solove, D. J. (2011). Why privacy matters even if you have 'nothing to hide'. *Chronicle of Higher Education, 57*(37), B11–B13.

Stiggins, R., & Chappuis, J. (2005). Using student-involved classroom assessment to close achievement gaps. *Theory Into Practice, 44*(1), 11–18.

Tierney, R. D. (2013). Fairness in classroom assessment. In J. H. McMillan (Ed.), *Sage handbook of research on classroom assessment* (pp. 125–144). Thousand Oaks, CA: Sage.

Tierney, R. D. (2014). Fairness as a multifaceted quality in classroom assessment. *Studies in Educational Evaluation, 43*, 55–69.

Tunstall, P., & Gipps, C. (1996). Teacher feedback to young children in formative assessment: A typology. *British Educational Research Journal, 22*(4), 389–404.

Ujifusa, A. (2014). State lawmakers ramp up attention on student-data privacy. *Education Week, 33*(28), 19–30.

United Nations. (1948). United Nations Universal Declaration of Human Rights. Retrieved from http://www.jus.uio.no/lm/un.universal.declaration.of.human.rights.1948/portrait.letter.pdf

United Nations. (1989). Convention on the Rights of the Child. Retrieved from http://www.ohchr.org/en/professionalinterest/pages/crc.aspx

United Nations. (2014). The Universal Declaration of Human Rights: Human Rights Law. Retrieved from http://www.un.org/en/documents/udhr/hr_law.shtml

United States Department of Education. (2002). Policy Guidance—Access to High School Students and Information on Students by Military Recruiters. Retrieved from http://www2.ed.gov/policy/gen/guid/fpco/hot topics/ht-10–09–02a.html

United States Department of Education. (2014). Protecting student privacy while using online educational services: Requirements and best practices. Retrieved from http://ptac.ed.gov/

Värlander, S. (2008). The role of students' emotions in formal feedback situations. *Teaching in Higher Education, 13*(2), 145–156.

Warren, S., & Brandeis, L. (1890/2005). The right to privacy. In A. D. Moore (Ed.), *Information ethics: Privacy, property, and power*. Seattle, WA: University of Washington Press.

Waters, J. K. (2010). Move it or lose it: Cloud-based data storage. *The Journal*. Retrieved from https://thejournal.com/Articles/2010/09/01/Move-It-or-Lose-It-Cloud-Based-Data-Storage.aspx

Westin, A. F. (1967). *Privacy and freedom*. New York: Atheneum.

Westin, A. F. (2003). Social and political dimensions of privacy. *Journal of Social Issues, 59*(2), 431–453.

Wiliam, D. (2015). Assessment: A powerful focus for the improvement of mathematics instruction. In C. Suurtamm (Ed.), *Assessment to enhance teaching and learning* (pp. 247–254). Reston, VA: National Council of Teachers of Mathematics.

Willis, J., & Adie, L. (2014). Teachers using annotations to engage students in assessment conversations: Recontextualising knowledge. *The Curriculum Journal, 25*(4), 495–515.

Zgonjanin, S. (2006). No child left (behind) unrecruited. *Connecticut Public Interest Law Journal, 5*(5), 167–196.

16

DIFFERENTIATED INSTRUCTION AND ASSESSMENT

An Approach to Classroom Assessment in Conditions of Student Diversity

Tonya R. Moon

Contemporary classrooms across the world from primary-age through post-secondary education are becoming more and more diverse (Ainscow, 2007; Aud, Fox, & Kewal-Ramani, 2010; Bartolo, 2008; Bradley, Noonan, Nugent, & Scales, 2008; Commonwealth of Australia, 2009; European Commission Directorate General for Education and Culture, 2003; Humphrey, . . ., & Wetso, 2006; Sperry, 1972). Perhaps the increasing diversity of the student population is best summarized by the Maltese National Minimum Curriculum (1999, cited in Adami, 2004):

> Each school is endowed with a vast repertoire of skills, experiences, and needs. The diversity, allied with the individual and social differences evident in the student population, enables and requires a pedagogy based on respect for and the celebration of differences.
>
> (p. 30)

Further amplification of this increasing diversity is seen by the growing numbers of refugees who are forced to relocate around the globe and move into classrooms without the acculturation (e.g., fluency in dominant language, parental support, cultural understanding) needed for school success (Dooley, 2009). This diversity results in learners entering classrooms from a wide range of backgrounds, including, but not limited to, differences in learners' understandings and command of a dominant language; learners' differences in racial, cultural, or gender identities; disability statuses; and variations in cognitive levels or lived experiences, all of which have implications for students' readiness to learn.

Readiness to learn is a developmental stage at which a child has the capacity to receive instruction at a given level of difficulty or to engage in a particular activity (*Dictionary*.com, 2015). While the increase in diversity in classrooms has been an ever-growing phenomenon, and one that is not anticipated to stop, there is mounting evidence to suggest that students' academic performances can increase when the methods of instruction match the cognitive levels, interests, and/or learning profiles of students (Abidin, Rezaee, Abdullah, & Singh, 2011; Ainley, Hidi, & Berndorff, 2012; Avci & Akinoğlu, 2014; Callahan, Moon, Oh, Azano, & Hailey, 2015; Dosch, & Zidon, 2014; Entwistle & Ramsden, 1983; Hidi, 1990; Jacobs, Lanza, Osgood, Eccles, & Wigfield, 2002; Jokinen, Heikkinen, & Morberg, 2012; Lepper, Corpus, & Iyengar, 2005; Messick, 1976; Renninger, 2000; Vygotsky, 1978). However, in many school contexts, it appears that the majority of today's educators do not systematically and proactively adjust their classroom instructional and assessment methods to respond to this trend in diversity (Gable, Hendrickson, Tonelson, & Van Acker, 2000; Guild, 2001; Powell, 2012). Differentiated instruction is a research-based model that is based on effective classroom practices that are adjusted to fit the diversity of readiness, interests, and learning profiles of students (Tomlinson et al., 2004). Framing the instructional model are several key elements: (1) high-quality curriculum; (2) continual assessment; (3) flexible grouping; (4) respectful tasks; (5) classroom community building; and (6) teaching up (Tomlinson et al., 2004). This term, differentiation, will be used throughout the chapter to refer to assessments and instructional activities that are adjusted proactively by the teacher to address the needs of students so that they can learn as efficiently as possible (Tomlinson et al., 2004).

The field of educational testing is guided by the *Standards for Educational and Psychological Testing* (American Educational Research Association [AERA], American Psychological Association [APA], & National Council on Measurement in Education [NCME], 2014). The major focus of the research in this area has been on the equity of assessment in the context of high-stakes standardized or large-scale testing with students who have some type of learning disability or are not native language learners and need specific modifications (Jordan, 2010; Kearns, 2011; Peters, & Oliver, 2009; Polesel, Rice, & Dulfer, 2014; Sireci, Scarpati, & Li, 2005). However as Jordan (2010, p. 142) notes, "Defining equity within the context of a diverse, multiracial, multiethnic, multilingual, and multicultural society . . . is problematic." While focusing most specifically on the American educational context, Jordan conducted an extensive review of the literature regarding the performance of diverse learners within the context of equity and noted that the consequences of high-stakes testing "have not helped advance the nation toward a more equitable schooling" (p. 142). Given this conclusion and recent advances in the areas of measurement, learning and motivation theory, and technology, there is a clear call for greater focus on classroom assessment instead of high-stakes assessment (McMillan, 2013; Pellegrino, 2014). Within this chapter, classroom assessment is defined as "the process of seeking and interpreting evidence for use by learners and their teacher to decide where the learners are in their learning, where they need to go and how best to get there" (Assessment Reform Group, 2002, pp. 1–2).

EQUITY IN CLASSROOM ASSESSMENT

It is well recognized that student abilities, interests, learning profiles, motivation, and other characteristics affect student learning and that these individual characteristics likely also impact assessment (Subban, 2006; Tomlinson & Moon, 2013a; Wang, Wang, Wang, & Huang, 2006). The basic premise of why assessment results are impacted by learners' differences is the idea that classroom assessment is a tool for improving student learning through its ability to guide and shape both curriculum and pedagogy (AfL, 2009). The student evidence produced by assessment is meant to guide the instructional decisions a teacher makes regarding the design and implementation of learning activities. This knowledge, along with the realities of the changing demographics of today's classrooms, necessitates that educators consider the need for assessments that can effectively, efficiently, and equitability accommodate the varying differences in students' readiness levels, interests, and ways of learning. Where differentiated instruction is understood as providing different avenues for students to acquire and make sense of content (Tomlinson, 2001), differentiated assessment provides various avenues for students to demonstrate their knowledge and understanding of the content (Tomlinson & Moon, 2013a).

The idea that assessment is more equitable when it is differentiated for varying student differences comes from several bodies of literature (Tierney, 2013). First, it emerges from theories that integrate learning, instruction, and assessment (Moon, 2005). Failing to recognize student differences and ignoring the ways in which instruction is carried out and assessment data are collected may ultimately impact student learning. At the simplest level, a fundamental concept in measurement is that a student's observed score (O) is equal to the student's true (T) score plus error (E) ($O = T + E$). Consider how this fundamental idea can play out in an assessment situation for a second language learner (L2). Errors in an L2 student's work in an assessment focused on mathematical problem solving may be due to the student's linguistic challenges, rather than the student's conceptual misunderstanding of the mathematics (Martiniello, 2008). The observed score might suggest low mathematical performance, when more accurately, the true score is masked by lack of language access to the problem. Failing to acknowledge this potential challenge and preventing the L2 student from demonstrating his or her knowledge, skills, and/or understandings through a different modality could have severe consequences, both short-term and long-term, for the student's learning of mathematics (e.g., being assigned to remedial mathematics classes; developing an incorrect self-perception of incapability in mathematics). The lack of language access is always problematic for school success (both in instruction and assessment) regardless of the specific content area (Aikens & Barbarin, 2008; Goldsmith, 2003; Schhneider, Martinex, & Owens, 2006). There are a myriad number of ways in which one might consider differentiated assessment. Consider the following scenario:

> A teacher gives an assessment that is intended to measure students' problem-solving ability. A student's ability to problem-solve in science is strong; however, her ability to use mental mathematics is problematic. If the teacher removes the aspect of mental math when assessing problem-solving and allows the student to use a calculator, this differentiated assessment better allows the student to demonstrate her problem-solving skills.

Other ways a teacher might differentiate assessments include: giving students options in demonstrating their understandings and skills (e.g., orally recording or typing on a computer instead of writing; providing directions in a native language for clarity; providing variations in organizational structures, such as stepwise directions, based on students' organizational skills; or allowance of more time). Whatever the mechanism for addressing student variance, what must remain constant across all versions of an assessment is the targeted learning objective (i.e., in the example given, problem solving).

Second, guidelines established in the field of special education in the U.S. (RTI Action Network, n.d.) or in other countries, sometimes under the heading of special assessment conditions (e.g., New Zealand Qualification Authority, n.d.) support the idea that the key to success in the classroom lies in having appropriate adaptations and accommodations made to all classroom activities, from instruction to assessment for students with disabilities and for many without disabilities (Luke & Schwarz, 2007). Third, it has been recognized that cultural diversity not only brings assets to the classroom through students' varied knowledge and skills, but additionally that this diversity must also be recognized in assessment (e.g., Fewster & MacMillan, 2002; Jiménez, 2005). It is important to appropriately recognize student diversity in classroom assessments, but any adaptations must be done in such a way as to construct assessment procedures that maintain measurement invariance (Venn, 2000). That is, the adaptation(s) must not alter the learning objectives that are being assessed regardless of groups or conditions.

Examples of successful (i.e., valid and reliable) adaptations have been seen in curriculum-based assessments (Fewster & MacMillan, 2002) and in the use of dynamic assessment (DA; Lantolf & Poehner, 2011). Overall, according to Tierney (2013), "the literature reveals that a shift is underway as convictions about equal treatment yield slowly to the realization that equitable practices result in fairer assessments, particularly in terms of supporting student learning" (p. 136). Yet, Tierney (2013) (see also Tierney & Koch, this volume) notes that consensus regarding the meaning of fair in the classroom assessment literature is limited and that there are common attributes which make assessments appropriate for individual learners (Poehner, 2011); that is, consideration of (a) bias (Popham, 2013), (b) opportunity to learn (Shepard, 2001, 2006), and (c) transparent communication (e.g., Guskey & Jung, 2012).

DIFFERENTIATED INSTRUCTION: RESPONDING TO THE NEEDS OF LEARNER VARIATION

Many scholars worldwide (Adebayo & Shumba, 2014; Cretu, 1998; George, 2005; Koutselini, 2008; Koutselini & Agathangelou, 2009; Prankerd & Lockley, 2011; Subban, 2006) have called for the need to account for students' individual differences, interests, and skills within curriculum and instruction in order to maximize each individual student's potential. Early discussions surrounding differentiation began with Stradling and Saunders (1993) defining differentiation as a pedagogical approach, rather than an organizational approach. Tomlinson (1999, 2001, 2003) further refined the term to indicate that differentiated instruction is a philosophy of teaching based upon the premise that students learn best when curriculum and instruction are designed proactively to address their differences in readiness, interests, and learning profiles, with the chief objective being to take advantage of every student's ability to learn. Thus, aligned and ongoing assessment guides teachers' decision-making related to curriculum and instructional choices. Because differentiated instruction is designed to be an effective means to address learners' variance, it avoids the one-size-fits-all curriculum (McBride, 2004). Rather, the philosophy links five classroom elements that work in tandem to prepare learners for the authentic work of a discipline: the classroom learning environment, the curriculum, instruction, classroom leadership and management, and assessment (Tomlinson & Moon, 2014). All are designed to create and support a community of learners through the differentiation of the content (i.e., what students learn), the process by which students access the content, and/or the product that students create as a result of learning the content.

There are four defining attributes of effective classrooms (National Research Council, 1999), of which all are also characteristics of a differentiated classroom. The foremost attribute of effective classrooms is that they are assessment-rich where data are used by teachers and students to help make forward progress in the learning journey. To move learning forward though, effective classrooms must also be student-centered, knowledge-centered, and community-centered. For each of these attributes, assessment becomes the glue that holds all of the attributes together. For example, in order to provide appropriate challenge and pacing for students through the escalation of one or more facets of a curriculum (student-centered and knowledge-centered) and to create a classroom environment (community-centered) where students feel safe to take risks and engage in the learning process, assessment information is critical to informing many adjustments including effectively varying the depth of the content, adjusting the abstraction of the ideas, and changing the complexity of the content.

Brief Overview of the Differentiated Instruction Model

Because the basis of the rationale for making assessment accommodations rests in the philosophy of differentiation, the five key elements upon which the philosophy rests are detailed.

Learning Environment

The learning environment refers to the physical and the affective tone of the classroom as students perceive it (Tomlinson & Moon, 2013b). The teacher's goal is to create a safe space where students can be challenged and grow to their fullest potential and where they can individually and collectively contribute to the work that will be done on a daily basis. In a differentiated classroom, this means that the physical environment and the social environment are responsive in that (a) students have access to materials from a range of levels and topics; (b) there are a variety of instructional groupings implemented in flexible ways that allow students to take part ownership of the construction of knowledge; (c) student choice is evident in the planning and implementing of instruction and in student products; and (d) the classroom climate is one of exploration, application, and high expectations. Because repeated research (Ahnert, & Milatz, Kappler, Schneiderwind, & Fischer, 2013; Allen, Gregory, Mikami, Hamre, & Pianta, 2013; Hamre & Pianta, 2001; Maldonado-Carreño & Votruba-Drzal, 2011; Roorda, Koomen, Spilt, & Oort, 2011) indicates that a teacher's emotional bond with students is a powerful contributor to their academic growth, it becomes a 'must have' condition for optimizing student learning.

Curriculum

Curriculum can be thought of as the 'what' of teaching. That is, the curriculum provides the plan for what teachers will teach and what students are expected to learn. According to Wiggins and McTighe (1998), quality curriculum should be based upon clearly defined learning goals that establish the knowledge, the understandings, and the skills that students should develop as a result of instruction. Furthermore, quality curriculum should engage students in the process of learning so that they develop deep and enduring understandings, rather than isolated or disconnected content.

Instruction

Instruction is how the written curriculum is translated into action with students. That is, instruction refers to the ways in which teachers deliver the curriculum and students engage in the learning experiences provided by the teacher. It is for this reason that instruction is at the heart of the philosophy of differentiation. Working in concert with quality curriculum, efficient and effective instruction is targeted so that students master the identified learning goals (e.g., KUDs = knowledge [K], understanding [U], and ability to do [D]), and is driven by pre-assessment (before instruction) and ongoing assessment (during instruction), and necessitates flexibility in classroom routines in a way that accommodates and supports varying learners' academic needs (Tomlinson & Moon, 2013b).

Classroom Leadership and Management

Classroom management is often considered synonymous with control (Tomlinson & Imbeau, 2013). However, a better way to conceptualize a teacher's role as the classroom instructional leader is the person who leads students through well designed processes and routines so that "students understand, contribute to, and participate in structures designed to facilitate learning" (Tomlinson & Moon, 2013b, p. 15). One aspect of effective classroom management is flexibility of instructional grouping arrangements. That is, grouping arrangements should be fluid (not static as in ability grouping [Kulik, 1992]) and can be an intentional mix of students with different abilities or skills, or students who need specific adaptations, or students who share the same interests or learning profiles (Radencich & McKay, 1995). Flexible classrooms allow students to engage with intellectually challenging ideas, to be risk-takers and problem-solvers in a safe environment, and to be collaborators.

Assessment

In a classroom that is based upon the philosophy of differentiation, persistent use of data (i.e., ongoing assessment) continually informs the instructional sequence and is instrumental to both students' and teachers' successes. Collecting and using data in a differentiated classroom occurs seamlessly across three phases: (1) the pre-assessment phase where data are used to plan for appropriate instruction based on students' readiness, interests, and/or learning profiles, (2) the ongoing phases where data are used to implement instruction and to adjust as needed based on students' needs, and (3) the evaluation phase where students are assessed on the degree that they mastered the specified KUDs and where teachers use the data to reflect upon the effectiveness or ineffectiveness of the implemented instructional events.

Brief Overview of the Assessment Framework Within a Differentiated Classroom

Consider this analogy: in a medical setting, primary care physicians are required to develop skills in patient history-taking (communication skills), conducting physical examinations (clinical skills), and counseling or patient management (knowledge). In many ways, there are parallels between the collection of data in medical settings and in a K–12 or post-secondary education setting. Teachers are analogous to the role of physicians and students to the patients, and it is the responsibility of the teacher to collect both accurate and sufficient data in order to make effective and efficient instructional plans that will allow students to successfully travel along the identified instructional journey. For the instructional journey to be one that allows students to successfully attain the identified KUDs, data must be collected, synthesized, and interpreted by the teacher with the curricular KUDs serving as guideposts.

In an effectively differentiated classroom, this involves using data in the three assessment phases (i.e., pre-, ongoing, and evaluation) to answer a series of questions that aid decision-making during the instructional cycle. Similar to the advice by others for effective student feedback (Hattie & Timperley, 2007; Kluger & DeNisi, 1996), sample assessment questions in differentiated assessment include:

- What are the most essential KUDs that students must master in this learning experience?
- What prerequisite KUDs are required for students to enter this learning experience?
- Where is each student in relation to the prerequisite KUDs or the targeted KUDs?
- Throughout the instructional sequence, where are students in their forward movement toward the specified KUDs?
- Are there indications that instruction needs to be adjusted for all or some students (the "what's next" question for each student)?

Using accurate and purposeful data to inform instructional decisions reflective of students' variation regarding their readiness, interests, and/or learning profiles allows the teacher to work on their behalf in developing their academic understandings and skills. Understanding that assessment should be age appropriate in both content and methods of data collection and that it should be linguistically appropriate is central to the collection of accurate and purposeful data. For example, if a teacher is attempting to collect data regarding a student's early reading skills and that student is a non-native language speaker, the teacher must recognize that assessment is easily confounded by language proficiency, especially for children who come from backgrounds with limited exposure to a native language. In this instance, the assessment would essentially be a measure of language proficiency rather a student's early reading skills.

CURRENT RESEARCH REGARDING ASSESSMENT IN DIVERSE CLASSROOMS

The literature is dominated by theoretical and empirical efforts directed toward large-scale assessment and accountability uses and largely ignores the importance of differentiation within assessment, except for students with formally diagnosed disabilities (who are usually exempted from, or given accommodations to, accountability testing). A recent handbook of *Research on Classroom Assessment* (McMillan, 2013), as well as work by Shepard (2001, 2006) have brought much-needed attention to developing a solid theoretical and empirical literature base focused specifically on classroom assessment. Within the U.S. context, research focused on accountability testing (Clarke et al., 2003; Hamilton et al., 2007; Jones, & Egley, 2004; Jones, Jones, & Hargrove, 2003; Koretz, Mitchell, Barron, & Keith, 1996; Moon, Callahan, & Tomlinson, 2003) has overwhelmingly demonstrated the unintended negative side effects of high-stakes testing (see also Nichols & Harris, this volume). Teachers indicate a narrowed curriculum, if a curriculum exists at all, with instruction focused predominantly on test preparation materials at the exclusion of other content areas. These types of negative side effects have also been reported in non-American contexts that employ some type of accountability testing (Collins, Reiss, & Stobart, 2010; Lingard, Martino, & Rezai-Rashti, 2013; Ydesen, 2013; see also Teltemann & Klieme and Lingard & Lewis, this volume). The net result is reduced access to non-tested content, skills, and dispositions.

In a review of the research, Mausethagen (2013) documented the negative side effects of accountability testing on teacher-student relationships and both the positive and negative effects on teachers' workplace environments across various international contexts. In the studies that were reviewed that focused on teacher-student relationships, the majority of the studies (23 of 28 studies) found that the increased emphasis on accountability had reduced the opportunities for teachers to develop strong relationships with students because of a shift in focus from "the child to the test and on the information required to learn for the test" (p. 20). The remaining six studies reported only a small negative influence of accountability testing on teacher-student relationships due to teachers' sense of ethical obligation to protect their students and the teachers having the perception that test scores were evidence of student success. Overall, Mausethagen reported less negative influence on teacher-student relationships in New Zealand, Portugal, and Finland as compared to the U.S., which may be further indication that systems with lower-stakes accountability systems have less negative consequences on classroom operations and teacher-student and teacher-teacher relationships. Furthermore, the atmosphere of high-stakes accountability has been noted to have negative influences on curriculum (Brighton et al., 2005; Brimijoin, 2005; Moon, Callahan, & Tomlinson, 2003). Researchers in these studies found the consistent pattern that the pressures of teaching to the high-stakes tests impeded teachers' willingness to establish a differentiated classroom.

There also exists a significant amount of research on the negative effects of high-stakes testing on students (Segool, Carlson, Goforth, Von Der Embse, & Barterian, 2013; Triplett & Barksdale, 2005; Watson, Johanson, Loder, & Dankiw, 2014) with Buck, Ritter, Jensen, and Rose (2010) noting studies showing negative impacts outnumber studies showing positive impacts nine to one. A significant limitation to these findings is that most studies used data from others who interpreted students' behaviors rather than relying directly on students' perspectives of the impact of high-stakes testing.

In the U.S., the mid-1990s and early 2000s saw a reconceptualization of the role of classroom assessment in student learning, based on advances in the cognitive learning sciences (National Research Council [NRC], 1999) and reform efforts supported by discipline-oriented professional organizations (e.g., International Reading Association and National Council of Teachers of English Joint Task Force on Assessment, [IRA/NCTE] 2010; National Council for Teachers of Mathematics [NCTM], 2000). Substantive new research on classroom assessment has been suggested (McMillan, 2013) because of (a) the well-documented negative effects of accountability testing on curriculum and instruction, (b) the increasing diversity in classrooms worldwide, (c) advances in understanding the roles that sociocultural influences and motivation play in learning (Gauvain Beebe, & Zhao, 2011), (d) the rediscovery of Vygotsky's Zone of Proximal Development (Allal & Ducrey, 2000) and Bruner's scaffolding theory (Wood, Bruner, & Ross, 1976), and (e) the recognition that new learning is shaped by prior knowledge (NRC, 1999) and cultural perspectives (Gauvain et al., 2011). According to Shepard (2000b) "the gathering and use of assessment information and insights must become a part of the ongoing learning process" (p. 1). The following section outlines the current research on the implementation of differentiated instruction and assessment along with the strengths and challenges associated with its implementation.

RESEARCH ON DIFFERENTIATED INSTRUCTION AND ASSESSMENT WITHIN A CLASSROOM SETTING

Research on Differentiated Instruction

There is developing evidence supporting the efficacy of differentiated instruction's role in supporting student learning across a variety of contexts, age levels, and content areas (Aliakbari & Haghighi, 2014; Brighton et al. 2005; Callahan et al., 2015; DeBaryshe,

Gorecki, & Mishima-Young, 2009; Dosch & Zidon, 2014; Karadag, & Yasar, 2010; Konstantinou-Katzi, Tsolaki, Meletiou-Mavrotheris, & Koutselini, 2013; Little, McCoach, & Reis, 2014; Santangelo & Tomlinson, 2009; Valiandes, 2015). Evidence also suggests that differentiated instruction is well received by the students themselves because of the instructional supports provided for access to materials (e.g., graphic organizers) and content, and the active learning and engagement environment (e.g., opportunities for choice) (Dosch & Zidon, 2014; Santangelo & Tomlinson, 2009). However, the research on students' perceptions of differentiated instruction has predominantly focused on students in higher education settings, and there is little known about elementary and secondary students' perceptions regarding differentiation.

Nonetheless, there is evidence that in implementing differentiated instruction, teachers encounter challenges (e.g., sustaining the practice over time) (Baumann, Hoffman, Duffy-Hester & Ro, 2000; Tobin & McInnes, 2008; Tobin & Tippett, 2014). Teachers cite challenges including lack of sufficient professional development on the topic (Edwards, Carr, & Siegel, 2006), leading to a lack of skills and self-efficacy in employing the philosophy (Dixon, Yssel, McConnell, & Hardin, 2014; Edwards et al., 2006).

Research on Differentiated Assessment

Despite the emphasis on differentiated instruction for addressing diverse learners' needs and the importance of alignment between learning objectives, instruction, and assessment (Martone & Sireci, 2009), less attention has been given to the efficacy of differentiated assessment and its role in student learning. In searching the empirically peer-reviewed literature using the key words *differentiated assessment* within the context of differentiation as defined by Tomlinson (1999; 2001) only three studies were located (Liao, 2015; Varsavsky & Rayner, 2013; Waters, Smeaton, & Burns, 2004). While the literature is scarce in the area of differentiated assessment within a differentiated classroom, the common finding across all three studies is that students in general are supportive of differentiated assessment.

Using a differentiated assessment approach aligned with Tomlinson's (2001) model of differentiation, Varsavsky and Rayner (2013) incorporated tiered activities driven by student choice representing differing complexity levels and abstractness in two Australian university science courses (i.e., biology and chemistry). Of the university students who self-selected to take the more complex tasks, the majority of students indicated that the more challenging task was intellectually stimulating and interesting. Other positive student comments about the more complex tasks included the benefit of working with others with similar interests and that the tasks were more fun than the standard assessment. Varsavsky and Rayner reported only one student questioning whether his/her choice was the right choice, due to concern that a higher grade might have been attained in the standard assessment. Of the students who chose not to engage in the more complex tasks, common reasons voiced included the potential impact on grades and the lack of confidence to tackle the academic challenge. Students, regardless of whether they took the more challenging tasks or not, reported appreciation for the opportunity of choice and indicated that they would like to see similar opportunities in later courses. In a differentiated classroom where choice is one avenue for addressing diversity (e.g., in interests, or learning profiles), students are consistently provided opportunities to engage in learning experiences matched to their needs. This principle of a differentiated classroom suggests that every learner must have access to tasks that are equally interesting and engaging and which provide equal access to essential understandings and skills. Differentiation, though, does not presume individualized tasks for each learner, but rather flexibility in task complexity, working arrangements, or modes of conveying learning so that students have a good fit much of the time (Tomlinson & Allan, 2000).

Liao (2015), working in English-speaking classes across universities in Taiwan, investigated students' perceptions regarding the validity and fairness of differentiated assessments and whether the students' perceptions differed because of variation in proficiency levels. Overall, regardless of proficiency level, there was, in general, positive learner perception of the differentiated assessments, with students indicating that the assessments were a fair practice, appropriately reflective of course objectives, and had a positive influence on learning. When looking within different proficiency levels, several students reported preferring the 'standard' assessment because it was perceived to be simple and fairer. Liao notes that these few students were from the group that the "traditional curricula and assessment typically target" (p. 53).

Waters et al. (2004), in conducting an action research study on differentiated authentic assessment in three high school science classrooms, found that although the majority of students favored the option of having choice and believed that the assessment format led to increased learning, there were students who preferred a traditional format of assessment (i.e., multiple-choice exams) with one student commenting "All I have to do is know the answer and not even understand it" (p. 98).

IMPLICATIONS FOR PRACTICE

Overall, the existing research on differentiated assessment is extremely limited and does not provide conclusive evidence of what works to balance the equity aspect with the student diversity aspect for the improvement of student learning. Despite the lack of research on differentiated assessment, based on findings from the existing research on classroom assessment in general, one could infer that insufficient professional preparation for developing and implementing differentiated assessment will be a major challenge for classroom teachers because of limited assessment literacy and the importance of assessment literacy in pedagogical content knowledge (Akutagawa, Miyuko, & Fernandez, 2014).

Professional Development in the Areas of Classroom Assessment and Student Diversity

The skills and understandings that are required for educators to collect assessment data and then to use those data to make valid instructional decisions are complex. Adding to the complex process is the general lack of teacher assessment literacy (Popham, 2006). Furthermore, research on teacher learning suggests that teachers who are the learners in a professional development setting should be treated the same way that teachers are expected to treat their students (Shepard, 2006) by addressing the diversity in their knowledge, skills, and understandings regarding classroom assessment.

Enhancing the classroom assessment literacy of educators, including administrators, principals, teachers, and classroom support personnel, requires ongoing differentiated professional development. For example, principals, teachers, and classroom support personnel need specific ongoing support in:

- aligning assessments with learning goals;
- the ways in which assessment data can be collected;
- how to analyze and interpret assessment data within a classroom context;

- how to use assessment data to plan appropriate instructional responses;
- how to provide effective and descriptive feedback to students,
- how to modify teaching based on quality assessment data to appropriately address student diverse learning needs; and
- dealing with specific issues (e.g., maintenance and troubleshooting) with data systems to store collected assessment data (more appropriate professional development for support personnel involved with instructional technology).

It is important to recognize that 'one-shot' traditional professional development opportunities are ineffective for creating teacher change in practice and have no effect on student achievement (Yoon, Duncan, Lee, Scarloss, & Shapley, 2007). Rather, studies (Blank, de la Alas, & Smith, 2008; Yoon et al., 2007) show that effective professional development occurs over time and is ongoing, requiring somewhere between 50 and 80 hours of instruction, practice, and coaching, all done within a content of expertise, before mastery is achieved. Much work has been done in the area of professional learning communities; records of practice as a mechanism for sustaining ongoing professional development have shown positive effects for teacher change and student achievement (Borko, 2004).

Developing a Research Framework in the Area of Classroom Assessment

Referring to his experience in creating, implementing, and studying the effects of classroom assessment, Shavelson (2008) wrote:

> After five years of work, our euphoria devolved into a reality that formative assessment, like so many other education reforms, has a long way to go before it can be wielded masterfully by a majority of teachers to positive ends.
>
> (p. 294)

Studying classroom assessment is a complex process. Student diversity, and the ways in which that diversity can be balanced equitably in an assessment context, further complicates an already complex process. It is well accepted that a variety of assessment techniques should be used to ensure sound measurement, but also should provide solid evidence about students' achievement of specified learning objectives. Yet, some research (Shavelson, Baxter, & Pine, 1992) suggests that interchanging the modality of assessment does have an impact on student performance. On the other hand, not allowing students to demonstrate their attainment of learning objectives in ways that best highlight their learning seems inappropriate. For example, requiring a student to communicate an understanding through a written piece of evidence rather than an oral piece, if writing is a weakness and is not one of the learning objectives, seems highly problematic. It is at this juncture that better understanding is needed in how to fairly balance students' diverse needs with equity within an assessment context.

While Shepard (2006) noted that a fundamental shift in the use of assessment as a tool for learning began in earnest during the late 20th century due to a variety of influences (e.g., increased accountability emphasis and its impact on instruction and student learning; measurement experts questioning the applicability of traditional notions of validity and reliability for classroom settings), she also noted that there is much needed research in the area. Approximately a decade later there is still much work to be done in establishing a body of knowledge about classroom assessment (McMillan, 2013). Given the current literature base on classroom assessment, it is important that a building-block approach be taken in order to accumulate needed knowledge in this area (McMillan, 2013). While there is some research (Smith, Hill, Cowie, & Gilmore, 2014; Hill & Eyers, this volume) that highlights the importance of changing preservice teachers' beliefs about assessment, little is known about how to actually impact assessment practice (Campbell & Evan, 2000; Grainger & Adie, 2014). It is important to understand that in many ways, while this area is ripe for research, it is akin to learning to fly a plane while building it.

Several areas of systematic study are needed in the field of classroom assessment. For example, many (Brookhart, 2003; Smith, 2003) have called for a reconceptualization of the psychometric concepts of validity and reliability for the classroom context. Classroom assessment, unlike large-scale assessment for accountability purposes, is a blending of measurement and instruction and, currently, these two concepts of reliability and validity stem from the tests-and-measurement model founded over 100 years ago and are primarily based on externally developed tests, like those used in high-stakes testing situations. The field of classroom assessment is in a state where these two concepts are in need of reconceptualization in order to accommodate the ever-evolving and dynamic nature between instruction and assessment.

At the same time, much has been learned about student learning and motivation (Pellegrino, Chudowsky, & Glaser, 2001) that has implications for developing a better understanding of the power classroom assessment has for developing student understanding. Specifically, the areas of learning and motivation highlight the importance of classroom assessment as, not only an end process, but also as a powerful player in the development process of student learning over time. For example, what role does self-regulation play in student learning and how can this be considered within a classroom assessment context (see Dinsmore & Wilson, this volume)? Shepard (2000a, b) noted that student learning is a socially mediated phenomenon in terms of expectations by self and by others, including interpersonal interactions and social norms, and that this social nature has implications for both teaching and assessment. What role do the expectations of self and others have on student performance in classroom assessments? How might adapting an assessment because of student diversity characteristics better capture what a student knows, understands, and is able to do, and how does that adaptation impact future expectations regarding performance? These are just a few of the questions that have the potential to transform instruction and assessment in today's diverse classrooms.

Much research on specific aspects of classroom assessment is needed (e.g., informal classroom assessment, providing feedback, types of adaptations that can be done without diluting or altering the focus of the assessment). While this type of research is needed, it is important to acknowledge the difficulty of conducting this type of research. For example, rigorous experimental studies where adaptations are made to classroom assessments to provide a more equitable assessment opportunity or experimental studies regarding the use of in-the-moment data (e.g., student response), how instructional modifications are made, and the subsequent impact on student understanding, may be impractical to carry out. In these instances, establishing an appropriate comparison that reflects what would have happened in the absence of such adaptation or the use of such data type is not an option. Shavelson and Towne (2002) group educational research questions into three types: (1) description (What is happening?); (2) cause (Is there a systematic effect?); and (3) process (Why or how is it happening?). The process of teaching and learning are complex ones and, as such, a variety of research methodologies must be recognized, employed, and accepted in order to move the field of classroom assessment forward.

CONCLUSION

In summary, research within the field of classroom assessment regarding differentiated assessment is nascent but well-timed and urgently needed. Contemporary classrooms around the globe are increasingly diverse and consequently students need vastly different learning conditions, instructional approaches, and ways to show what they have learned. Despite the complexity, the work of differentiating assessment across the learning cycle will facilitate more 'true' scores—and ultimately, better balance diversity with equity.

REFERENCES

Abidin, M.J.Z., Rezaee, A. A., Abdullah, H. N., & Singh, K.K.B. (2011). Learning styles and overall academic achievement in a specific educational system. *International Journal of Humanities and Social Science, 1*, 143–152.

Adami, A. F. (2004). Enhancing students' learning through differentiated approaches to teaching and learning: A Maltese perspective. *Journal of Research in Special Education Needs, 4*(2), 91–97. doi:10.1111/J.1471–3802.2004.00023x

Adebayo, A. S., & Shumba, C. B. (2014). An assessment of the implementation of differentiated instruction in primary schools, Kabwe district, Zambia. *European Scientific Journal, 10*(7). Retrieved from Eujournal.org/index.php/esj/article/view/2985/0.

AfL. (March, 2009). *Position paper on assessment for learning.* Third International Conference on Assessment for learning. Dunedin, NZ. Retrieved from www.fairtest.org/position-paper-assessment-learning.

Ahnert, L., Milatz, A., Kappler, G., Schneiderwind, J., & Fischer, R. (2013). The impact of teacher-child relationships on child cognitive performance as explored by a priming paradigm. *Developmental Psychology, 49*, 554–567. doi:10.1037/a0031283

Aikens, N. L., & Barbarin, O. (2008). Socioeconomic differences in reading trajectories: The contribution of family, neighborhood, and school contexts. Journal of Educational Psychology, 100, 235–251.

Ainley, M., Hidi, S., & Berndorff, D. (2012). Interest, learning, and the psychological processes that mediate their relationship. *Journal of Educational Psychology, 94*, 545–561. doi:10.1037/0022–0663.94.3.545.

Ainscow, M. (2007). Teacher development in responding to student diversity: The way ahead. In P. A. Bartolo, A. Mol Lous, & T. Hofsäss (Eds.), *Responding to student diversity: Teacher education and classroom processes* (pp. 1–22). Malta: University of Malta.

Akutagawa, T., Miyuko, M., & Fernandez, C. (2014). Knowledge of assessment: An important component in the PCK of chemistry teachers. *Problems of Education in the 21st Century, 62*, 124–147.

Aliakbari, M., & Haghighi, J. K. (2014). On the effectiveness of differentiated instruction in the enhancement of Iranian learners reading comprehension in separate gender education. *Procedia—Social and Behavioral Sciences, 98*, 182–189. doi:10.1016/j.sbspro.2014.03.405

Allal, L., & Ducrey, G. P. (2000). Assessment of— or in—the zone of proximal development. *Learning and Instruction, 10*, 137–152.

Allen, J. P., Gregory, A., Mikami, A. Y., Lun, J., Hamre, B., & Pianta, R. C. (2013). Observations of effective teacher-student interactions in secondary school classrooms. Predicting student achievement with the classroom assessment scoring system secondary. *School Psychology Review, 42*, 76–98.

American Educational Research Association, American Psychological Association, & National Council on Measurement in Education. (2014). *The standards for educational and psychological testing.* Washington, DC: Author.

Assessment Reform Group. (2002). *Assessment for learning: 10 principles. Research-based principles to guide classroom practice.* Cambridge, UK: Author.

Aud, S., Fox, M. A., & KewalRamani, A. (2010). *Status and trends in the education of racial and ethnic groups.* (NCES 2010–015). Washington, DC: Government Printing Office.

Avci, S., & Akinoğlu, O. (2014). An examination of the practices of teachers regarding the arrangement of education according to individual differences. *International Journal of Instruction, 7*(2). Retrieved from www.e-iji.net.

Bartolo, P. (2008). Preparing teachers for diversity. *Malta Review of Educational Research, 6*, 1–14.

Baumann, J. F., Hoffman, J. V., Duffy-Hester, A. M., & Ro, J. M. (2000). "The first r" yesterday and today. U.S. elementary reading instruction practices reported by teachers and administrators. *Reading Research Quarterly, 35*, 338–377.

Blank, R. k., de las Alas, N., & Smith, C. (2008). *Does teacher professional development have effects on teaching and learning? Evaluation findings from programs in 14 states.* Washington, DC: Council of Chief State School Officers.

Borko, H. (2004). Professional development and teacher learning: Mapping the terrain. *Educational Researcher, 33*(8), 3–15. doi:10.3102/0013189X033008003

Bradley, D., Noonan, P., Nugent, H., & Scales, B. (2008). *Review of Australian higher education: Final report.* Canberra: Department of Education, Employment and Workplace Relations.

Brighton, C. M., Hertberg, H. L., Moon, T. R., Tomlinson, C. A., & Callahan, C. M. (2005). *The feasibility of high-end learning in the diverse middle school classroom* (Monograph No. 05210). Storrs, CT: National Research Center on the Gifted and Talented, University of Connecticut.

Brimijoin, K. (2005). Differentiation and high-stakes testing: An oxymoron? *Theory into Practice, 44*, 254–261. doi:10.1207/s15430421tip4403_10

Brookhart, S. M. (2003). Developing measurement theory for classroom assessment purposes and uses. *Educational Measurement: Issues and Practice, 22*(4), 5–12. doi:10.1111/j.1745–3992.2003.tb00139.x

Buck, S., Ritter, G. W., Jensen, N. C., & Rose, C. P. (2010). Teachers says the most interesting things—An alternative view of testing. *Phi Delta Kappan, 91*(6), 50–54.

Callahan, C. M., Moon, T. R., Oh, S., Azano, A. P., & Hailey, E. P. (2015). What works in gifted education: Documenting effects of an integrated curricular/instructional model. *American Educational Research Journal, 52*, 1–31. doi:10.3102/0002831214549448.

Campbell, C., & Evan, J. A. (2000). Investigation of preservice teachers' classroom assessment practices during student teaching. *The Journal of Educational Research, 93*, 350–355.

Clarke, M., Shore, A., Rhoades, K., Abrams, L., Miao, J., & Li, J. (2003). *Perceived effects of state-mandated testing programs on teaching and learning: findings from interviews with educators in low-, medium-, and high-stakes states.* Retrieved from http://www.bc.edu/research/nbetpp/statements/nbr1.pdf

Collins, S., Reiss, M., & Stobart, G. (2010). What happens when high-stakes testing stops? Teachers' perceptions of the impact of compulsory national testing in science of 11-year-olds in England and its abolition in Wales. *Assessment in Education: Principles, Policy & Practice, 17*, 273–286. doi:10.1080/0969594X.2010.496205

Commonwealth of Australia, (2009) *Population flows: Immigration aspects 2007–08*, Migration and Visa Policy Division, Department of Immigration and Citizenship. Retrieved from www.immi.gov.au

Cretu, C. (1998). *Curriculum diferenfiat, Ji personalizat (Differentiated and personalized curriculum)*, vol. I, Iaşi. Romania: Polirom Publishing, "Talentum" Collection.

DeBaryshe, B. D., Gorecki, D. M., & Mishima-Young, L. N. (2009). Differentiated instruction to support high-risk preschool learners. *NHSA Dialog, 12*, 227–244.

Dixon, F., Yssel, N., McConnell, J. M., & Hardin, T. (2014). Differentiated instruction, professional development, and teacher efficacy. *Journal for the Education of the Gifted, 37*, 111–127. doi:10.1177/0162353214529042

Dooley, K. (2009). Re-thinking pedagogy for middle school students with little, no or severely interrupted schooling. *English Teaching: Practice & Critique, 8*(1), 5–19.

Dosch, M., & Zidon, M. (2014). "The course fit us": Differentiated instruction in the college classroom. *International Journal of Teaching and Learning in Higher Education, 26*, 343–357.

Edwards, C. J., Carr, S., & Siegel, W. (2006). Influences of experiences and training on effective teaching practices to meet the needs of diverse learners in school. *Education, 126*, 580–592.

Entwistle, N., & Ramsden, P. (1983). *Understanding student learning.* London: Croom Helm.

European Commission Directorate General for Education and Culture. (2003). *Improving education of teachers and trainers: Progress report.* Brussels: Author.

Fewster, S., & Macmillan, P. (2002). School-based evidence for the validity of curriculum-based measurement of reading and writing. *Remedial & Special Education, 23*, 149–158.

Gable, R. A., Hendrickson, J. M., Tonelson, S. W., & Van Acker, R. (2000). Changing disciplinary and instructional practices in middle school to address IDEA. *The Clearing House, 73*, 205–205.

Gauvain, M., Beebe, H., Zhao, S. (2011). Applying the cultural approach to cognitive development. *Journal of Cognition and Development, 12*, 121–133. doi:10.1080/15248372.2011.563481

George, P. S. (2005). A rationale for differentiating instruction in the regular classroom. *Theory into Practice, 44*(3), 185–193. doi:10.1207/s15430421tip4403_2

Goldsmith, S. M. (2003). Lost in translation: Issues in translating tests for non-English speaking, limited English proficient, and bilingual students. In J. E. Wall & G. R. Walz (Eds.), *Measuring up: Assessment issues for teachers, counselors, and administrators* (pp. 127–146). Austin, TX: PRO-ED.

Grainger, P. R., & Adie, L. (2014). How do preservice teacher education students move from novice to expert assessors? *Australian Journal of Teacher Education, 39*, 89–105.

Guild, P. B. (2001). Diversity, learning style and culture. Retrieved from education.jhu.edu/PD/newhorizons/strategies/topics/LearningStyles/diversity.html.

Guskey, T. R., & Jung, L. A. (2012). Four steps in grading reform. *Principal Leadership, 13*(4), 22–28.

Hamilton, L. S., Stecher, B. M., Marsh, J. R., McCombs, J. S., Robyn, A., Russell, J. L., Naftel, S., & Barney, M. E. (2007). *Standards-based accountability under No Child Left Behind: Experiences of teachers and administrators in three states.* Santa Monica, CA: Rand.

Hamre, B. K., & Pianta, R. C. (2001). Early teacher-child relationships and the trajectory of children's school outcomes through eighth grade. *Child Development, 72,* 625–638.

Hattie, J., & Timperley, H. (2007). The power of feedback. *Review of Educational Research, 77,* 81–112. doi:10.3102/003465430298487

Hidi, S. (1990). Interest and its contribution as a mental resource for learning. *Review of Educational Research, 60,* 549–571.

Humphrey, N., Bartolo, P. A., Calleja, C., Hofsaess, T., Janikova, V., Mol Lous, A., Vikiene, V., & Wetso, G. (2006). Understanding and responding to diversity in the primary classroom: An international study. *European Journal of Teacher Education, 29,* 3–5–318. doi:10.1080/02619760600795122

Jacobs, J. E., Lanza, S., Osgood, D. W., Eccles, J. S., & Wigfield, A. (2002). Changes in children's self-competence and values: Gender and domain differences across grades one through twelve. *Child Development, 73,* 509–527.

Jiménez, R. T. (2005). More equitable literacy assessments for Latino students. In S. J. Barrentine & S. M. Stokes (Eds.), *Reading assessment: Principles and practices for elementary teachers* (2nd ed., pp. 49–51). Newark, DE: International Reading Association.

Jokinen, H., Heikkinen, H. L. T., & Morberg, A. (2012). The induction phase as a critical transition for newly qualified teachers. In P. Tynjälä, M.-L. Stenström, & M. Saarnivaara (Eds.), *Transitions and transformations in learning and education* (pp.169–185). Dordrecht, The Netherlands: Springer.

Jones, B. D., & Egley, R. J. (2004). Voices from the frontlines: Teachers' perceptions of high-stakes testing. *Education Policy Analysis Archives, 12*(39). Retrieved from http://epaa.asu.edu/epaa/v12n39/

Jones, M. G., Jones, B. D., & Hargrove, T. Y. (2003). *The unintended consequences of high-stakes testing.* Lanham, MD: Rowman & Littlefield.

Jordan, W. J. (2010). Defining equity: Multiple perspectives to analyzing the performance of diverse learning. *Review of Research in Education, 43,* 142–178.

Karadag, R., & Yasar, S. (2010). Effects of differentiated instruction on students' attitudes towards Turkish courses: An action research. *Procedia-Social and Behavioral Sciences, 9,* 1394–1399. doi:10.1016/j.sbspro.2010.12.340

Kearns, L. L. (2011). High-stakes standardized testing and marginalized youth: An examination of the impact on those who fail. *Canadian Journal of Education, 34,* 112–130.

Kluger, A. N., & DeNisi, A. (1996). The effects of feedback interventions on performance: A historical review, a meta-analysis, and a preliminary feedback intervention theory. *Psychological Bulletin, 119,* 254–284.

Konstantinou-Katzi, P., Tsolaki, E., Meletiou-Mavrotheris, M., & Koutselini, M. (2013). Differentiation of teaching and learning mathematics: An action research study in tertiary education. *International Journal of Mathematical Education in Science and Technology, 44,* 332–349.

Koretz, D., Mitchell, K., Barron, S., & Keith, S. (1996). *The perceived effects of the Maryland School Performance Assessment Program.* (CSE Technical Report No. 409). Los Angeles: Center for the Study of Evaluation, University of California at Los Angeles.

Koutselini, M. (2008). Listening to students' voices for teaching in mixed ability classrooms: Presuppositions and considerations for differentiated instruction. *Learning and Teaching, 1,* 17–30.

Koutselini, M., & Agathanegelou, S. (2009). Human rights and teaching: Equity as praxis in mixed ability classrooms. In P. Cunningham (Ed.), *Proceedings of the Eleventh Conference of the Children's Identify and Citizenship in Europe (CCICE) Thematic Network: Human rights and citizenship education* (CD-ROM) (pp. 237–244). London: CiCe Publication.

Kulik, J. A. (1992). *An analysis of the research on ability grouping: Historical and contemporary perspectives* (Research Monogram 9204). Storrs, CT: University of Connecticut, The National Research Center on the Gifted and Talented.

Lantolf, J. P., & Poehner, M. E. (2011). Dynamic assessment in the classroom: Vygotskian praxis for L2 development. *Language Teaching Research, 15,* 11–33. doi:10.1177/1362168810383328

Lepper, M. R., Corpus, J. H., & Iyengar, S. S. (2005). Intrinsic and extrinsic motivational orientations in the classroom: Age differences and academic correlates. *Journal of Educational Psychology, 97,* 184–196. doi:10.1037/0022–0663.97.2.184.

Liao, H. C. (2015). EFL learner perceptions of differentiated assessment tasks. *English Teaching & Learning, 39,* 29–68. doi:10.6330/ETL.2015.39.1.02.

Lingard, B., Martino, W., & Rezai-Rashti, G. (2013). Testing regimes, accountabilities and education policy: Commensurate global and national developments. *Journal of Education Policy, 25,* 539–556. doi:10.1080/02689939.2013.820042.

Little, C. A., McCoach, D. B., & Reis, S. M. (2014). Effects of differentiated reading instruction on student achievement in middle school. *Journal of Advanced Academics, 25*, 384–402. doi:10.1177/1932202X14549250

Luke, S. D., & Schwarz, A. (2007). Assessment and accommodations. *Evidence for Education, 2*(1). Retrieved from www.parentcenterhub.org/repository/assessment-accommodations/.

Maldonado-Carreño, C., & Votruba-Drzal, E. (2011). Teacher-child relationships and the development of academic and behavioral skills during elementary school: A within- and between-child analysis. *Child Development, 82*, 601–616.

Martiniello, M. (2008). Language and the performance of English-language learners in math word problems. *Harvard Educational Review, 78*, 333–368.

Martone, A., & Sireci, S. G. (2009). Evaluating alignment between curriculum, assessment, and instruction. *Review of Educational Research, 79*, 1332–1361. doi:10.3102/0034654309341375

Mausethagen, S. (2013). A research review of the impact of accountability policies on teachers' workplace relations. *Educational Research Review, 9*, 16–33. doi:10.1016.j.edurev.2012.12.001

McBride, B. (2004). Data-driven instructional methods: "One-strategy-fits-all" doesn't work in real classrooms. *T.H.E. Journal, 31*(11), 38–40.

McMillan, J. H. (Ed.). (2013). *The SAGE handbook of research on classroom assessment.* Thousand Oaks, CA: SAGE.

Messick, S. (1976). Personality consistencies in cognition and creativity. In S. Messick & Associates (Eds.), *Individuality in learning* (pp. 4–22). San Francisco: Jossey-Bass.

Moon, T. R. (2005). The role of assessment in differentiation. *Theory into Practice, 44*, 226–233. doi:10.1207/s15430421tip4403_7

Moon, T. R., Callahan, C. M., & Tomlinson, C. A. (2003). Effects of state testing programs on schools with high concentrations of student poverty—Good News or Bad News? *Current Issues in Education* [On-line], *6*(8). Retrieved from http://cie.ed.asu.edu/volume6/number8

National Council of Teachers of Mathematics. (2000). *Principles and standards for school mathematics.* Reston, VA: Author.

National Research Council. (1999). *How people learn. Brain, mind, experience, and school* (Expanded Edition). Washington, DC: National Academies Press.

New Zealand Qualification Authority. (n.d.). *Special assessment conditions.* Retrieved from http://www.nzqa.govt.nz/providers-partners/assessment-and-moderation/managing-national-assessment-in-schools/special-assessment-conditions/

Pellegrino, J. W. (2014). Assessment as a positive influence on 21st century teaching and learning: A systems approach to progress. *Psicología Educative, 20*, 65–77.

Pellegrino, J. W., Chudowsky, N., & Glaser, R. (Eds.). (2001). *Knowing what students know: The science and design of educational assessment.* Washington, DC: National Academy Press.

Peters, S., & Oliver, L. (2009). Achieving quality and equity through inclusive education in an era of high-stakes testing. *Prospects, 39*, 265–279.

Poehner, M. E. (2011). Dynamic assessment: Fairness through the prism of mediation. *Assessment in Education: Principles, Policy, & Practice, 18*, 99–112. doi:10.1080/0969594X.2011.567090

Polesel, J., Rice, S., & Dulfer, N. (2014). The impact of high-stakes testing on curriculum and pedagogy: A teacher perspective from Australia. *Journal of Education Policy, 29*, 640–657. doi:10.1080/02680939.2013.865082

Popham, W. J. (2006). Needed: A dose of assessment literacy. *Educational Leadership, 63*, 84–85.

Popham, W. J. (2013). *Classroom assessment: What teachers need to know* (7th ed.). New York: Pearson.

Powell, D. (2012). A review of inclusive education in New Zealand. *Electronic Journal for Inclusive Education, 2*(10). Retrieved from http://corescholar.libraries.wright.edu/ejie/

Prankerd, S., & Lockley, J. (July, 2011). *Differentiated instruction in technology education.* Paper presented at the TENZ 2011: The Biennial Conference of Technology Education. Dunedin, NZ.

Radencich, M. C., & McKay, L. J. (1995). *Flexible grouping for literacy in the elementary grades.* Des Moines, IA: Allyn & Bacon.

Readiness. (2015). *Dictionary.com unabridged.* Retrieved from http://dictionary.reference.com/browse/readiness

Renninger, K. A. (2000). Individual interest and its implications for understanding intrinsic motivation. In C. Sansone & J. M. Harackiewicz (Eds.), *Intrinsic and extrinsic motivation: The search for optimum motivation and performance* (pp. 373–404). New York: Academic Press.

Roorda, D. L., Koomen, H.M.Y, Spilt, J. L., & Oort, F. J. (2011). The influence of affective teacher-student relationships on students' school engagement and achievement. *Review of Educational Research, 81*, 493–529. doi:10.3102/0034654311421793

RTI Action Network. (n.d.). *What is RTI?* Retrieved from http://www.rtinetwork.org/learn/what/whatisrti.

Santangelo, T., & Tomlinson, C. A. (2009). The application of differentiated instruction in postsecondary environments: Benefits, challenges, and future directions. *International Journal of Teacher and Learning in Higher Education, 20*, 307–323.

Schhneider, B., Martinex, S., & Owens, A. (2006). Barriers to educational opportunities for Hispanics in the U.S. In M. Tienda & F. Mitchell (Eds.), *Hispanics and the future of America* (pp. 179–227). Washington, DC: National Academies Press.

Segool, N. K., Carlson, J. S., Goforth, A. N., von der Embse, N., & Barterian, J. A. (2013). Heightened test anxiety among young children: Elementary school students' anxious responses to high-stakes testing. *Psychology in the Schools, 5*, 489–499.

Shavelson, R. (2008). Guest editor's introduction. *Applied Measurement in Education, 21*, 293–294. doi:10.1080/08957340802347613

Shavelson, R. J., Baxter, G. P., & Pine, J. (1992). Performance assessment: Political rhetoric and measurement reality. *Educational Researcher, 21*(4), 22–27.

Shavelson, R. J., & Towne, L. (Eds.). (2002). *Scientific research in education.* Washington, DC: National Academy Press.

Shepard, L. (2000a). The role of assessment in a learning culture. *Educational Researcher, 29*(7), 4–14. doi:10.3102/0013189X029007004

Shepard, L. (2000b). *The role of classroom assessment in teaching and learning.* (CSE Technical Report 517). Los Angeles: Center for the Study on Evaluation, National Center for Research on Evaluation, Standards, and Student Testing, University of California, Los Angeles.

Shepard, L. (2001). The role of classroom assessment in teaching and learning. In V. Richardson (Ed.), *Handbook of research on teaching* (4th ed., pp. 1066–1101). Washington, DC: AERA.

Shepard, L. (2006). Classroom assessment. In R. L. Brennan (Ed.), *Educational measurement* (4th ed.; pp. 623–646). Westport, CT: Praeger Publishers.

Sireci, S. G., Scarpati, S. E., & Li, S. (2005). Test accommodations for students with disabilities: An analysis of the interaction hypothesis. *Review of Educational Research, 75*, 457–490. doi:10.3102/003465430750004457

Smith, J. K. (2003). Reconsidering reliability in classroom assessment and grading. *Educational Measurement: Issues and Practice, 22*(4), 26–33. doi:10.1111/j.1745–3992.2003.tb00141.x

Smith, L. F., Hill, M. F., Cowie, B., & Gilmore, A. (2014). Preparing teachers to see the enabling power of assessment. In C. M. Wyatt-Smith, V. Klenowski, & P. Colbert (Eds.), *Designing assessment for quality learning* (pp. 303–323). Dordrecht, NL: Springer.

Sperry, L. (Ed.). (1972). *Learning and performance and individual differences.* Glenview, IL: Scott, Foresman, & Co.

Stradling, B., & Saunders, L. (1993). Differentiation in practice: Responding to the needs of all pupils. *Educational Research, 35*, 127–137.

Subban, P. (2006). *A research basis supporting differentiated instruction.* November, Adelaide: Australian Association for Research in Education Conference. Retrieved from http://www.aare.edu.au/06pap/sub06080.pdf

Tierney, R. D. (2013). Fairness in classroom assessment. In J. H. McMillan (Ed.), *SAGE handbook of research on classroom assessment* (pp. 125–144). Thousand Oaks, CA: SAGE.

Tobin, R., & McInnes, A. (2008). Accommodating differences: Variations in differentiated literacy instruction in Grade 2/3 classrooms. *Canadian Journal of Education, 28*, 784–801.

Tobin, R., & Tippett, C. D. (2014). Possibilities and potential barriers: Learning to plan for differentiated instruction in elementary science. *International Journal of Science and Mathematics Education, 12*, 423–443.

Tomlinson, C. A. (1999). *The differentiated classroom: Responding to the needs of all learners.* Alexandria, VA: ASCD.

Tomlinson, C. A. (2001). *How to differentiate instruction in mixed-ability classrooms.* (2nd ed.). Alexandria, VA: ASCD.

Tomlinson, C. A. (2003). *Fulfilling the promise of the differentiated classroom: Strategies and tools for responsive teaching.* Alexandria, VA: ASCD.

Tomlinson, C. A., & Allan, S. D. (2000). *Leadership for differentiating schools & classrooms.* Alexandria, VA: ASCD.

Tomlinson, C. A., Brighton, C. M., Hertberg, H., Callahan, C., Moon, T. R., Brimijoin, K., Conover, L., & Reynolds, T. (2004). Differentiating instruction in response to student readiness, interest, and learning profile in academically diverse classrooms: A review of the literature. *Journal for the Education of the Gifted, 27*(2/3), 119–145.

Tomlinson, C. A., & Imbeau, M. (2013). *Leading and managing a differentiated classroom.* Alexandria, ASCD.

Tomlinson, C. A., & Moon, T. R. (2013a). Differentiation and classroom assessment. In J. H. McMillan (Ed.), *SAGE handbook of research on classroom assessment* (pp. 415–430). Los Angeles: SAGE.

Tomlinson, C. A., & Moon, T. R. (2013b). *Assessment and student success in a differentiated classroom.* Alexandria, VA: ASCD.

Tomlinson, C. A., & Moon, T. R. (2014). *Assessment and student success in a differentiated classroom.* Alexandria, VA: ASCD.

Triplett, C. F., & Barksdale, M. A. (2005). Third through sixth graders' perceptions of high-stakes testing. *Journal of Literacy Research, 37,* 237–260. doi:10.1207/s15548430jlr3702_5

Valiandes, S. (2015). Evaluating the impact of differentiated instruction on literacy and reading in mixed ability classrooms. Quality and equity dimensions of education effectiveness. *Studies in Educational Evaluation, 45,* 17–26. doi:10.1016/j.stueduc.20015.02.005

Varsavsky, C., & Rayner, G. (2013). Strategies that challenge: Exploring the use of differentiated assessment to challenge high-achieving students in large enrollment undergraduate cohorts. *Assessment & Evaluation in Higher Education, 38,* 789–802. doi:10.1080/02602938.2012.714739

Venn, J. J. (2000). *Assessing students with special needs.* Upper Saddle River, NJ: Prentice-Hall.

Vygotsky, L. S. (1978). *Mind in society: The development of higher psychological processes.* Cambridge, MA: Harvard University Press.

Wang, K. H., Wang, T. H., Wang, W. L., & Huang, S. C. (2006). Learning styles and formative assessment strategy: Enhancing student achievement in web-based learning. *Journal of Computer Assisted Learning, 22,* 207–217. doi:10.1111/j.1365–2729.2006.00169.x

Waters, F. H., Smeaton, P. S., & Burns, T. G. (2004). Action research in the secondary science classroom: Student response to differentiated, alternative assessment. *American Secondary Education, 32,* 89–104.

Watson, C. E., Johanson, M, Loder, M., & Dankiw, J. (2014). Effects of high-stakes testing on third through fifth grade students: Student voices and concerns for educational leaders. *Journal of Organizational Learning and Leadership, 12*(1), 1–11.

Wiggins, G., & McTighe, J. (1998). *Understanding by design.* Alexandria, VA: ASCD.

Wood, D. J., Bruner, J. S., & Ross, G. (1976). The role of tutoring in problem solving. *Journal of Child Psychiatry and Psychology Review, 17,* 89–100.

Ydesen, C. (2013). Educational testing as an accountability measure: Drawing on twentieth-century Danish history of education experiences. *Paedogogica Historica, 49,* 716–733. doi:10.1080/00309230.2013.815235

Yoon, K. S., Duncan, T., Lee, S. W. Y., Scarloss, B., & Shapley, K. L. (2007). *Reviewing the evidence on how teacher professional development affects student achievement.* Washington, DC: U.S. Department of Education, Institute for Education Sciences. Retrieved from http://ies.ed.gov/ncee/edlabs

17

ASSESSMENT OF COLLABORATIVE LEARNING

Jan-Willem Strijbos

INTRODUCTION

Collaborative learning (CL) is a common practice at all levels of education. CL can be defined as a learning phenomenon where individuals in a social constellation (e.g., group, team, or community) within a physical and/or virtual environment, interact on the same or different aspects of a shared task to accomplish implicit or explicit shared and individual learning goals (e.g., domain-specific knowledge or skills, social skills, etc.). CL is structured by collaboration scaffolds (which can be faded if no longer needed) provided by an agent(s) within or outside of the social constellation (e.g., teacher, peer, self, technology) to guide interaction and increase the likelihood that social constellations and/or individuals can accomplish their goals. An agent(s) within or outside of the social constellation diagnoses and/or evaluates the constellation's and/or individual's accomplishment(s) against criteria and standards.

CL has been studied intensively since the 1970s (Gillies & Ashman, 2003 provide a detailed historical overview). The introduction of computers into CL shifted the behaviours being studied from individual cognitive learning gain (1970–1990) to how group process affect individual and group cognition (1990–present). As such, there are roughly two dominant foci in CL research: (1) understanding of (successful) CL practices, and (2) determining effective conditions for (successful) CL (Stahl, Koschmann, & Suthers, 2006; Strijbos, Kirschner, & Martens, 2004a).

Although it is common knowledge that assessment can strongly influence learning (Frederiksen, 1984), assessment has so far remained an under-researched issue within CL (De Hei, Strijbos, Sjoer, & Admiraal, 2016; Gillies & Boyle, 2010; Ross & Rolheiser, 2003: Strijbos, 2011; Van Aalst, 2013) and implicit in diverse theoretical and methodological positions on learning in CL (Lipponen, Hakkarainen, & Paavola, 2004; Stahl et al., 2006; Strijbos & Fischer, 2007). Key to the assessment of CL is the operationalization of relevant CL processes and outcomes and their subsequent measurement. The assessment of CL is directly shaped by what is measured; however, this is more than merely measurement because it also contains a statement on the quality and value of the CL process or product in relation to pre-specified assessment criteria and standards.

Assessment criteria, in turn, are shaped by the purpose of assessment. Broadly two purposes are distinguished: summative and formative (Harlen & James, 1996; Scriven, 1967). Summative assessment is essentially evaluative in nature and typically takes place after a learning phase, whereas formative assessment is essentially diagnostic in nature and typically takes place during a learning phase. Assessment purposes are not connected to specific assessment formats. Distinguishing both purposes can be useful, but it should be kept in mind that any assessment, when communicated to a student, involves the use of feedback information; whether this use is more summative (evaluative) or more formative (diagnostic) is an issue of interpretation rather than one of absolutes.

WHY AND WHAT TO ASSESS?

Understanding current CL assessment practices requires revisiting the theoretical origins of the CL approaches developed in the 1970s and 1980s, at the time referred to as 'cooperative learning.' CL methods developed at that time targeted primary education and were later adapted for secondary and higher education. However, any CL setting can induce 'social loafing' and/or 'free-riding.' Social loafing is the tendency to reduce individual effort when working in a group as compared to individual effort expended when working alone (Williams & Karau, 1991). Free-riding exists when an individual does not bear a proportional amount of the CL process and yet s/he shares the benefits of the group (Kerr & Bruun, 1983). Two CL mechanisms were introduced early on to counter these tendencies; individual accountability (Slavin, 1980) and positive (goal) interdependence (Johnson, 1981). Individual accountability refers to the extent to which group members are held individually accountable for jobs, tasks, or duties central to group performance. Positive interdependence refers to the degree to which the performance of a single member is dependent on the performance of all other members, and vice versa. Nowadays, it is agreed that individual accountability and positive interdependence are both crucial mechanisms for productive interaction in any CL approach (Cohen, 1994; Strijbos, Martens, & Jochems, 2004).

Common to all CL approaches developed in the 1970s and 1980s, and widely used ever since, is the premise that achievement is the principal outcome variable, typically measured in terms of 'scores' on (standardized) individual tests or quizzes, reflecting the assumption that all individual students must master the same learning material and/or skill. With respect to assessment of CL, Slavin's (1995, 1996) operationalization of individual accountability is of particular interest because it achieves individual accountability through assessment, and treats the individual and group level as intertwined (i.e., group rewards enhance student learning only if group rewards are based on the individual improvement of all group members). Hence, the issue of assessment of CL is not new, but historically reflected (a) an evaluative purpose and (b) acted as a mechanism to foster interaction. To date, researchers agree that all group members must perform a fair share of the task and that problems arise when one or several group members do not (Ross & Rolheiser, 2003; Stahl et al., 2006; Strijbos, Kirschner et al., 2004a). However, lack of effort or diverse degrees of effort by one or several group members is a frequent student complaint regarding unsatisfactory experiences with CL and their subsequent call for differentiated assessment (Barfield, 2003; Strijbos, Martens, Jochems, & Broers, 2007; Stuart, 1994). It is unclear how CL can best be assessed, let alone how such differentiation can best be accomplished.

Challenges for the Assessment of CL

Since the outcomes that are considered relevant directly govern what is assessed, the conceptualization of 'learning' in CL is crucial. From a critical review of four metaphors of learning (implicitly referred to or explicitly adopted by CL researchers) and identification of their limitations, Strijbos (2011) identified three challenges for CL assessment and proposed the *group experience metaphor* (explained in detail within Strijbos, 2011) as the underlying conceptualization in response to the three challenges. These challenges are whether (a) assessment should focus on the individual level or on the group level; (b) cognitive outcomes should be operationalized in terms of students' having the same knowledge (i.e., convergence in CL), similar knowledge, and/or even divergent knowledge; and (c) assessment of CL should focus solely on cognitive outcomes or also on social and motivational outcomes.

Challenge 1: Individual Versus Group Level

There has been much debate as to whether the individual or the group should be assessed (i.e., scores or grades for individuals versus the group) (Boud, Cohen, & Sampson, 1999) or whether a combination of individual and group scores or grades should be generated (Ross & Rolheiser, 2003; Slavin, 1995). Obviously, this is connected to CL mechanisms of individual accountability (emphasis on the individual level) and positive interdependence (emphasis on the group level). Furthermore, Webb (1993) concluded early on that "students' competence may be misestimated in group assessment, but some groups may produce more misestimation than others" (p. 147) and that

> scores on work submitted from group assessment should not be used to make inferences about the competence of individual students. Without data on group processes, scores from group assessment are better interpreted as what students can produce when working with others.
>
> (p. 149)

Finally, whether the emphasis is on the individual and/or group level, it is important to consider that in educational settings, most groups are ad hoc, established in relation to and for the duration of a specific task, series of tasks, or course. To some degree, their group product will be codified in an artifact (e.g., group report, dialogue, etc.), but each individual's experience of that CL event will be transferred to future CL events. Thus, although group-level interaction is the engine for CL, the individual level cannot be dismissed.

Challenge 2: Convergence Versus Similarity

Whereas early CL approaches assumed that all students should achieve (at least move towards) a common knowledge standard (Slavin, 1995), CL approaches in the 1990s introduced 'convergence.' The more knowledge students have in common during or after a CL event, the more they have 'converged' and the more it can be assumed that interaction resulted in cognitive benefits (Fischer & Mandl, 2005; Jeong & Chi, 2007; Weinberger, Stegmann, & Fischer, 2007). Although technically independent of a standard, the construct of convergence, operationalized as 'held in common,' reflects the assumption that individuals should learn the same things.

However, it is much more likely that what individuals learn from CL is 'similar rather than the same.' In fact, Fischer and Mandl (2005) concluded that, given each participant's individual knowledge, much less convergence in terms of shared knowledge was observed in comparison to the potential for convergence. Hence, 'similarity' appears more appropriate because it does not imply equality in the result or achievement (Strijbos, 2011). Moreover, divergent processes are in operation (Jeong & Chi, 2007), meaning each individual may develop an internal cognitive representation different from that achieved as a group (Hatano & Inagaki, 1991; Miyake, 2008). In other words, knowledge emerging from a CL event is internalized differently; thus, individual students' knowledge may become more similar due to CL, but may simultaneously differ due to each participant's prior perspective (Miyake, 2007; Strijbos, 2011). In sum, convergence can best be construed as the pinnacle of CL. Assessment of CL, then, should determine when an observed degree of similarity can be attributed to CL and establish a minimum (threshold) for the similarity induced by a specific CL event.

Challenge 3: It Is Not All About Cognition

Cognitive outcomes are clearly central to the assessment of learning in CL studies (Gress, Fior, Hadwin, & Winne, 2010), but cognitive outcomes are not the only outcomes of CL. Slavin (1996) identified three perspectives: motivational, social (cohesion), and cognitive. He stated that these three perspectives "may be seen as complementary, not contradictory" (p. 52). Social aspects, such as intergroup relations, are emphasized in the 'Learning Together' (Johnson & Johnson, 1994) and 'Group Investigation' approaches (Sharan & Sharan, 1992). The latter approach also has positive effects on intrinsic motivation (Sharan & Sharan, 1992; Sharan, Sharan, & Tan, 2013).

The social dimension and outcomes are considered in recent CL literature to some degree (Gillies, 2007; Janssen & Bodemer, 2013; Kreijns, 2004; Volet, Summers, & Thurman, 2009). Tolmie et al. (2010) studied social effects among 575 primary schools students (aged 9–12), revealing that CL led to a dual impact in terms of cognitive and social gains and that "cognitive and social gains would appear to be interlinked, if distinguishable outcomes" (p. 188). Yet, in the context of CL, social interaction is still often taken for granted or restricted to cognitive processes (Kreijns, Kirschner, & Jochems, 2003). The motivational dimension and outcomes are increasingly being considered (Boekaerts & Minnaert, 2006; Hijzen, Boekaerts, & Vedder, 2007; Järvelä & Hadwin, 2013; Järvelä, Volet, & Järvenoja, 2010). Students have multiple (i.e., individual and group) goals and motivations in the context of CL (Hijzen et al., 2007; Johnson & Johnson, 2003), and, in effective CL groups, students appear more aware of their goals compared to those in ineffective groups (Hijzen et al., 2007).

Consideration of outcomes other than cognition has direct implications for the design of CL assessment (Boud et al., 1999): "If the emphasis is on using peer learning to improve subject-matter learning, it will lead to one kind of assessment design. If the emphasis is on promoting teamwork then design for assessment will need to be quite different" (p. 419). In fact, Strijbos, Kirschner et al. (2004b) argue that CL assessment should not solely focus on "the specific learning goal X, but X' and X" or even some unforeseen 'U' are equally probable collaboration outcomes that signal learning—intended or not" (p. 247). The unforeseen outcome(s) could be cognitive, social, or motivational. Moreover, the quality and quantity of cognitive, social, and motivational processes and outcomes can be considered as concurrent nonlinear dynamic strands that develop differently over time (Fischer & Granott, 1995), implying that their assessment requires different timescales. Finally, researchers who investigate CL within communities often do assume predefined outcomes; they stress 'value' (be it cognitive, social, or motivational) experienced by the community members (Dingyloudi & Strijbos, 2015; Wenger, Trayner, & De Laat, 2011).

CURRENT CL ASSESSMENT PRACTICES

Discussion of approaches to and issues with CL assessment started in the 1990s (Goldfinch, 1994; Kagan, 1995; Webb, 1993, 1997) and gained attention in the past decade in face-to-face (Cohen, Lotan, Abram, Scarloss, & Schultz, 2002; Gillies, 2007; Gillies & Boyle, 2010; Ross & Rolheiser, 2003) and online contexts (Gress et al., 2010; McConnell, 2006; Oosterhof, Conrad, & Ely, 2008; Rummel, Deiglmayer, Spada, Kahrimanis, & Avouris, 2011; Strijbos, 2011; Swan, Shen, & Hiltz, 2006; Van Aalst, 2013).

Ideally, any course involving CL should use assessment that (1) targets the individual and group level by assessing the collaborative process and product (Frykedal & Chiriac, 2011; Gillies, 2007; Macdonald, 2003; Prins, Sluijsmans, Kirschner, & Strijbos, 2005; Strijbos, 2011; Van Aalst, 2013: Webb, 1997), (2) is conducted before, during, and after a CL event, and (3) identifies and/or promotes students' cognitive, social, and motivational processes and outcomes. However, despite consensus on individual accountability and positive interdependence as core mechanisms for effective and efficient CL, these are not systematically considered when deciding if, and how, (a) data from the group level and/or individual level will be used separately or in combination and (b) student agency and involvement will be included via peer and/or self-assessment (i.e., aligning interactive assessment practices with the interactive nature of CL as per Biggs's [1996] principle of 'constructive alignment').

Juggling Group-level and Individual-level Assessment Information

It can be problematic practically and theoretically if the final grade is completely or partially based on the score or grade on a group task and/or on a mix of scores or grades on group and individual tasks. Kagan (1995) gave four reasons that grades solely based on the group score should never be used, despite the appeal for grading efficiency. First, it violates individual accountability by inviting free-riding behaviour and/or encouraging the most able group member(s) to perform most (or all) of the shared task ('sucker effect'; Kerr, 1983; Salomon & Globerson, 1989). Second, an individual student typically has little influence on group formation and due to the coincidental presence of high- or low-achieving students or a free-rider, a group score or grade over- or underspecifies an individual student's competence, and equally active students may receive different scores or grades merely because of group formation processes outside their control. Third, low- and medium-ability students generally profit more from group scores or grades than their high-ability counterparts (Ross & Rolheiser, 2003). Last, unsatisfactory experiences with group scores or grades often result in reluctance toward CL among students (and parents).

Combining or supplementing a score or grade on a group task with the score or grade from one or more individual tasks is a common practice in CL assessment (Boud et al., 1999; Gillies & Boyle, 2010; Hoffman & Rogelberg, 2001). This approach uses individual tasks to 'correct' group scores or grades for potential social loafing and free-riding (Hoffman & Rogelberg, 2001). However, this becomes problematic when the final grade consists of the average of group and individual scores with a 'weighting factor' applied. This approach assumes that the performance on individual tasks (a) directly reflects that individuals' contribution to the group task and (b) validly compensates for a possible lack of individual effort and quality of contributions during the group task. Further, approaches to weighting components vary and no clear guidelines exist. In fact, the percentage of the final grade contributed by the group or individual score or grade can each range from 10% to 90%. Theoretically, if the group component is only 10% of the final grade, then CL is devalued and students are prompted to give it very little consideration (Boud et al., 1999), whereas if the group component makes up 90%, free-riding is invited and a group member who invested more effort in the shared task is not rewarded. Irrespective of the two extremes, it is debatable whether even a 50–50 format could be considered acceptable, because the extent to which a group score or grade contributes to the final grade affects students' CL preferences (Hoffman & Rogelberg, 2001), with low-ability students being more prone to prefer a course where the score or grade on a group task contributes more to their final grade compared to scores or grades on individual tasks.

Apart from combining scores and grades on group and individual tasks, the literature contains various other suggestions as to how the group and individual level can be dealt with when assessing CL. Ross and Rolheiser (2003) explicitly refer to the approach by Slavin (i.e., group scores or grades are based on the individual improvement of all group members) as the fair assessment procedure, which could work when the prior and current performance by each member can be measured reliably and validly. Ross and Rolheiser (2003) also mention practices like "randomly selecting one member's paper to score, or totalling/averaging members' individual scores" (p. 125). Another approach is to determine 'transactivity,' which is the extent to which students (a) refer to and build on each other's contributions (Weinberger et al., 2007) as part of interaction or in individual products, or (b) the extent to which students transform a shared artifact (e.g., a group report). To date, data on reliability and validity of these practices is sparse and limited to research contexts, rather than teaching and classroom contexts.

Finally, several rating schemes have been developed to assess CL through individual self-report on their CL experiences. The 10-item Quality of Working in Groups Instrument (QWIGI) has been used to measure students' CL situational interest, competence, autonomy, and social relatedness (Boekaerts & Minnaert, 2006). The QWIGI has an acceptable profile reliability with good confirmatory factor fit indices. Wang, MacCann, Zhuang, Liu, and Roberts (2009) developed the 30-item Self-report Teamwork Scale (STS) to measure CL in terms of 'cooperate,' 'advocate/guide,' and 'negotiate.' Confirmatory factor analysis supported a three-factor structure. Pauli, Mohiyeddini, Bray, Michie, and Street (2012) developed the 21-item Negative Group Work Experiences (NGWE) questionnaire to measure perceived lack of commitment, task disorganisation, storming group (e.g., falling out, shouting, inflexibility), and fractioned group (e.g., exclusion, unclear roles, factions). The four subscales and the overall scale had good reliability, with good fit to the data in confirmatory factor analysis. Instruments like QWIGI, STS, or NGWE facilitate group reflection or what Johnson and Johnson (1994) referred to as 'group processing,' which is essentially equivalent to 'group monitoring' to foster shared regulation (Järvelä & Hadwin, 2013; Järvelä et al., 2010). Law and Wong (2003) developed a 10-item rubric to assess knowledge building in small groups within a larger community. The rubric blends cognitive (e.g., idea generation, knowledge refinement, etc.) and social aspects (e.g., democratizing knowledge is defined as 'no one dominates discussion'). Although it was applied to assess CL of 250 students in 43 groups, information on reliability is not available. Finally, a rating scheme by Rummel et al. (2011) measures five CL aspects (i.e., communication, joint information processing, coordination, interpersonal relationship, and motivation) with seven dimensions (one to two for each aspect) to determine the quality of CL and had good reliability for these dimensions.

Teachers' CL Assessment Practices

The challenges for CL assessment and variability in CL assessment are underlined by a couple of studies on teachers' actual practices of CL assessment. Ross, Rol-heiser, and Hogaboam-Gray (1998) interviewed 13 teachers (five from primary schools; eight from secondary school) and found that the teachers were uncertain about their capability in CL assessment literacy and expressed a need for professional development on and more resources relating to CL assessment practices. Gillies and Boyle (2010) interviewed 10 teachers who taught Grades 6–8 (11- to 14-year-old students) and they considered assessment of CL a difficult task. The teachers' concerns covered establishing the purpose of CL assessment, understanding degrees of student agency and involvement, and addressing the group level and individual level. Frykedal and Chiriac (2011) conducted three focus groups (11 teachers; three–four teachers each from three schools) and found that teachers (a) mostly used informal CL assessments, (b) focused on students' collaboration skills, and (c) assessed the process and product at the individual and group levels, both by the teacher and students. However, teacher descriptions of what was to be assessed were very vague, a finding mirrored in a follow-up study in which students expressed a lack of transparency and criteria for CL assessment (Chiriac & Granström, 2012). Finally, De Hei, Strijbos, Sjoer, and Admiraal (2015) interviewed 100 lecturers in higher education, of whom 84 used CL as part of the course grade. Of these 84 lecturers, 42 used formative assessment and 21 combined summative and formative assessment. When asked about interactive assessment practices, 69 out of 96 respondents replied they used peer assessment and/or peer feedback.

Student Agency and Involvement via Peer Assessment of Collaborative Learning

Peer assessment (PA) is an interpersonal process where students judge a performance of a peer (or multiple peers) quantitatively (scores or grades) and/or qualitatively (written or oral feedback) (Strijbos & Sluijsmans, 2010; Topping 1998; Van Gennip, Segers, & Tillema, 2009) and aims to stimulate students to share responsibility for learning, reflection, discussion, and collaboration (Panadero, this volume). With respect to the assessment of CL, PA can cover the part of collaboration that a teacher has difficulty assessing (i.e., the collaborative process) (Strijbos, Ochoa, Sluijsmans, Segers, & Tillema, 2009). In essence, PA is a specific form of collaboration (Kollar & Fischer, 2010; Strijbos et al., 2009), it aligns quite naturally with CL (as Johnson & Johnson, 1994 note), and it can enhance positive interdependence (by confirming and/ or enabling (re)alignment with the shared goal) and individual accountability (by making members' below, mean, or above average contribution to CL visible) to help a group to accomplish its shared goal(s).

In general, PA of both the collaborative process and product is recommended (De Wever, Van Keer, Schellens, & Valcke, 2011; Frykedal & Chiriac, 2011; Lee, Chan, & Van Aalst, 2006; Prins et al., 2005). However, this depends on the assessment constellation. With respect to PA of CL, it is important to distinguish between *intragroup PA* and *intergroup PA* (Sivan, 2000). Intragroup PA is an assessment where each individual group member assesses all fellow group members, and sometimes themselves.

Intergroup PA is the procedure by which a group, or individual members of that group, assesses the product of another group. Intragroup PA can make students more aware of their internal group dynamics and of the individual contributions to the shared goal, whereas intergroup PA provides the group an external reference about the quality of their product. Intragroup PA can be product-oriented (i.e., focused on the group product and/or individual contributions to that group product), process-oriented (i.e., focused on group processes and/or individual contributions to those group processes) or a combination of the two.

Although PA has a clear potential for making CL assessment more interactive and for increasing student involvement in CL, PA can simultaneously be an additional source of bias. Interpersonal variables (e.g., trust in the other, psychological safety, cooperativeness, reliability, etc.) and interpersonal relations (e.g., friendship, anonymity, etc.) (McConnell, 2006; Panadero, this volume; Phielix, Prins, & Kirschner, 2010; Van Gennip, Segers, & Tillema, 2010) can (a) mediate/moderate the CL processes, and thereby (b) act as another source of bias and reduce reliability and validity.

PA of CL recently regained interest in CL research (Chen, Looi, Xie, & Wen, 2013; De Wever et al., 2011; Gillies, 2007; Strijbos et al., 2009), whereas it has been prevalent in assessment research since the early 1990s. Most assessment studies involve the use of PA to moderate a group score or grade into individual scores or grades (Bushell, 2006; Cheng & Warren, 2000; Freeman & McKenzie, 2002; Goldfinch, 1994; Johnston & Miles, 2004; Kench, Field, Agudera, & Gill, 2009; Lejk & Wyvill, 2001a, 2001b; Li, 2001; Nepal, 2012; Neus, 2011; Sharp, 2006; Wu, Chanda, & Willison, 2014). Typically a rating format is used (as opposed to a ranking or distribution format; Lejk, Wyvill, & Farrow, 1996), but these studies also differ as to whether a self-assessment should be included (Goldfinch, 1994; Johnston & Miles, 2004; Wu et al., 2014) or excluded (Cheng & Warren, 2000; Kench et al., 2009; Neus, 2011) as part of score moderation, and whether group members are assessed holistically (single criterion 'contribution') (Kench et al., 2009; Lejk & Wyvill, 2001b; Neus, 2011) or on multiple criteria addressing various aspects of the collaborative processes and/or the product (Cheng & Warren, 2000; Johnston & Miles, 2004; Lejk & Wyvil, 2001a). Corrections have been proposed to control for (a) subjectivity and dishonesty of PA scores (Li, 2001), (b) assessing oneself higher or lower than fellow group members (Bushell, 2006), and (c) large variations in individual scores due to formulas for moderation (Nepal, 2012; Neus, 2011; Sharp, 2006). Currently there are no agreed upon practices or formulas to convert a group score or grade into individual scores or grades with the help of PA, similar to the issues in combining scores or grades on group and individual tasks.

Although the majority of studies on PA of CL use a rating scale (either a single holistic criterion or multiple criteria), rubrics or matrices can be an alternative (Lee et al., 2006; Van Aalst & Chan, 2007). Lee et al. (2006) and Van Aalst and Chan (2007) used a rubric to assess students' portfolios of community knowledge building. They asked students to identify the four best contribution-clusters, including others' as well as their own contributions, with explanations for their selection. Regrettably, Lee et al. (2006) and Van Aalst and Chan (2007) transformed their rubric to a rating scale and the informative portfolio rubric was not used to stimulate discussion amongst students as to what constituted a good or poor contribution. Thus, information important for monitoring collaboration and determining whether criteria and standards were met was lost to the community and individual students.

Finally, similar to the need for reliable and valid PA of individual performance (Panadero, this volume), reliability and validity are pertinent for PA of CL, but few studies have investigated these issues. Zhang, Johnston, and Kilic (2008) used generalizability theory to disentangle variances at the person, rater, and group level in two studies. They found in one study that the group level accounted for about one-third of the total variance, while in a second study the group level accounted for about one-quarter of the variance. They also reported moderate to good reliability for holistic criteria group effort and academic contribution; however, when split into the six constituent criteria, reliabilities were different for each of the three classes in the study. The inclusion of self-assessment had weakly positive and larger negative impact on reliability depending on the study. De Wever et al. (2011) determined rater reliability with intraclass correlation (ICC) and found that by criterion (four in all), values ranged from medium to intermediate effect sizes, but when combined into an overall score, ICCs ranged from intermediate to high effect sizes. Magin (2001) proposed and illustrated an approach that enabled comparison of intragroup PA with the rating of a single teacher by calculating the reliability as a function of the F-ratio for intragroup PA with and without the teacher rating. Another open issue is whether the comparison with teacher scores is a prerequisite for determining the reliability of intragroup PA of CL.

COMPUTER SUPPORT FOR ASSESSMENT OF COLLABORATIVE LEARNING

Advances in computer technology over the past 15 years have expanded the possibilities of CL assessment. Among the earliest systems was the Self and Peer Assessment Resource Kit (SPARK; Freeman & McKenzie, 2002; Wu et al., 2014) that used PA to moderate a group score or grade into individual scores or grades. Yet, SPARK and its successor, SPARK[PLUS] (Willey & Gardner, 2009), are subject to the same criticisms as the formulas used for PA moderation of group scores or grades. Other systems for PA of CL are the Web-based Self and Peer Assessment System (Web-SPA; Sung, Chang, Chiou, & Hou, 2005) and Collaborative e-learning Structures (CeLS; Kali & Ronen, 2008) systems. These systems differ in their features, but allow (to a certain degree) flexible selection of criteria, type of rating scale, and length of rating scale. Web-SPA and CeLS also offer the possibility of written comments and both intragroup and intergroup PA. Nevertheless, regardless of the system, students are encouraged to reflect and/or discuss their scores, and/or they receive teacher feedback on their scores.

Recent advances in intelligent technologies increasingly enable the use of interaction data such as log files (state data) and periodical digests (change reports) for the visualization of recorded interactions during and/or after CL to students, and dynamic tracking of interactions (Kumar, Gress, Hadwin, & Winne, 2010). Intelligent technology will be especially useful for assessment of CL in large-scale settings (e.g., PA in massive open online courses (MOOCs); Piech et al., 2013) to handle the huge amount of available CL data and to assist in decisions about whether or not to intervene in a group or address an individual group member, perhaps because of free-riding. However, critical issues for CL assessment are determination of (1) what information to collect, (2) how to analyse the information, and (3) how to make the information accessible to the teacher and students (i.e., CL mining, CL analysis, and CL display) (Strijbos, 2011).

CL mining is related to the field of (educational) data mining and involves gathering information about (a) students' access of system objects (e.g., discussion forum, chat, and whiteboard) and student artifacts (e.g., group reports, wikis, blogs), (b) student discourse and actions (e.g., text, video, digital and/or transcribed audio, movement/gestures), and (c) system or instructional scripts or agents (e.g., a collaboration script specifying student roles and annotating discourse according to these roles) (Reimann, Yacef, & Kay, 2011; Romero & Ventura, 2010).

CL analysis is related to the field of learning analytics and involves (a) the integrated analysis of multiple parallel data sources (e.g., cognitive, social and motivational outcomes and/or processes) in addition to system objects and student artifacts (Petropoulou, Vassilikopoulou, & Retalis, 2011); (b) analysis of multiple levels simultaneously (i.e., analysis of individual and group-level data, as well as relations between both levels), using common techniques like social network analysis and multilevel analysis and CL specific techniques such as 'epistemic network analysis' (Shaffer et al., 2009); and (c) analysis of sequentiality and transformation over time in terms of cognitive, social, and motivational processes (e.g., common techniques like latent growth curves, dynamic multilevel analysis, and CL-specific techniques like 'statistical discourse analysis' (Chiu, 2008; Wise & Chiu, 2011). Automated coding and natural language processing are rapidly becoming more feasible for CL analysis (Mu, Stegmann, Mayfield, Rosé, & Fischer, 2012), for example, to determine (aspects of) transactivity such as other-orientated CL contributions (Gweon, Jain, McDonough, Raj, & Rosé, 2013). Puntambekar, Erkens and Hmelo-Silver (2011) provide additional detail on advances in measures to analyse CL.

CL display is related to the field of information visualisation (Janssen & Bodemer, 2013) and involves displays that provide information in terms of social awareness (*Who is around?*), activity awareness (*Who has done what?*), group performance (*How have individual members contributed to the group?*), knowledge awareness (*Who knows what?*) (visualization of PA scores of CL as Radar Diagrams; Phielix et al., 2010; Willey & Gardner, 2009) or visualisation of annotations (Zottmann et al., 2013). CL display also has clear potential for dynamic assessment (e.g., displaying relevant CL assessment information to teachers, screening out well-functioning groups that do not need intervention) and being user group adaptable (e.g., a separate display for teacher and students and/or displays for specific education levels, or information fit for a summative or formative purpose of CL assessment).

DIRECTIONS FOR PRACTICE, POLICY, AND RESEARCH

Over the past decades, assessment of CL has remained a practical problem rather than a research problem. Although CL assessment practices vary widely across educational levels, they can be summarised as (a) a mix of both formative and summative purposes, (b) typically designed and conducted by the teacher, although, at some educational levels, the students can be included in the design, (c) comprised of scores or grades on a group task, individual tasks, and/or a combination of group and individual tasks, (d) focused on the cognitive and social outcomes, and (e) typically conducted during and after CL in face-to-face contexts, and after CL in online contexts. Common CL assessment practices have differing strengths and weaknesses; assessment practices that are counterproductive and/or suspect with respect to reliability and validity must be identified, with alternatives developed and validated.

Directions for Practice

In general, it is crucial that assessment of CL acknowledges individual accountability and positive interdependence to counteract social loafing and free-riding. However, teachers experience the design of CL assessment as a daunting task. The literature reveals three issues for practice.

First, teachers need to be more specific in describing the expected CL processes, products, and criteria used for CL assessment (Cohen et al., 2002; Frykedal & Chiriac, 2011; Gillies & Boyle, 2010). However, simultaneously, they need (and deserve) more support when designing and implementing assessment of CL (De Hei et al., 2015; De Hei et al., 2016; Gillies & Boyle, 2010; Strijbos, Martens et al., 2004). It should be kept in mind that criteria can highlight and produce undesired effects in the sense that students can become more active in the CL process simply because participation is assessed, whereas increased participation may not always be conducive to high(er) group performance (Webb, 1997). Akin to test construction, teachers could be supported in mapping the anticipated or expected knowledge and skill(s) improvement in order to develop appropriate assessments.

Second, when feasible, teachers should be supplied with, and encouraged to use, methodologically (formulas, algorithms) and technologically sound tools for assessment of CL processes and products. When available, the information collected by these tools (e.g., most systems collect log files) is typically not used in CL assessment. Despite technological opportunities, teachers and researchers should remain critical and "let technology show us what can be done, and let educational considerations determine what will be done" (Salomon, 2000, last paragraph). Furthermore, the apparent ease of computer-supported PA of CL might be misleading and result in overly simplistic implementations, leading students to question its fairness (Wu et al., 2014). For the same reasons, anonymous computer-supported PA of CL can decrease peer pressure and fear of disapproval in a secondary school context (Vanderhoven, Raes, Montrieux, Rotsaert, & Schellens, 2015), but such use should be carefully balanced against the non-anonymous future work places (Strijbos et al., 2009) and sustainable long-term learning (Boud & Falchikov, 2006).

Third, central to the assessment of CL are the teacher's assessment design decisions in terms of the purpose of assessment (summative, formative), format (PA, portfolios), scoring (rating scales, rubrics, feedback), focus (cognitive, social, and/or motivational outcomes and/or processes), and degree of student involvement (e.g., self-, peer, co-, or teacher assessment). Practical examples of CL assessment can be found in Johnson and Johnson (2004), Belfer and Wakkary (2005), and Gillies (2007).

Directions for Policy

In general, an increased use and exploration of computer support for assessment of CL is needed and feasible (Katz & Gorin, this volume). The PISA 2015 study includes the measurement of CL problem solving at the individual level in a collaborative problem solving context, in which an individual student interacts with "enhanced menu-based chat interfaces, interactive simulations . . . and other web-like applications" (p. 21) that simulate a collaboration partner (OECD, 2013). Rosen and Foltz (2014) compared such human-human and human-computer collaboration in a sample of 179 students aged 14 from three countries (i.e., U.S., Singapore, and Israel) and found that students collaborating with a computer partner showed at least the skill level of students collaborating with a human partner. PISA 2015 focuses specifically on the cognitive and social competencies of: "establishing and maintaining shared understanding," "taking appropriate action to solve the problem," and "establishing and maintaining team organization" (OECD, 2013, p. 13). This approach has potential to uncover cultural differences in collaborative problem solving as operationalized, but care is needed to inform teachers that differences in collaborative context, and motivational and affective processes, have not been accounted for in the PISA measurement model.

Whereas the advent of computer technology enables the large-scale assessment of CL, with an increase in computational power and online archives (e.g., cloud computing) also comes a responsibility for data privacy and data protection, which should not be left to individual teachers or schools (Tierney & Koch, this volume). Given the potential long-term persistent existence of digital 'results,' the development of adequate policies for any type of electronic assessment is a must.

Directions for Research

In general, research on assessment of CL should focus more intensively on the actual CL assessment practices of teachers. Such research will reveal what teachers already do and do well, as well as their challenges and needs. The literature reveals four issues for research.

First, there is currently no generic set of agreed-upon CL indicators that can be used for the assessment of CL. Research studies show a wide variety of holistic and specific criteria for assessment of CL, and identification of a core set of 'indicators' can guide teacher implementation of CL assessment and development of tools for CL assessment.

Second, there seems to be a research-practice mismatch when it comes to CL assessment. Where research emphasizes cognitive benefits (e.g., increased domain knowledge), the initial evidence on teachers' CL assessment practices shows that they emphasize social benefits, like increased team-working skills (Frykedal & Chiriac, 2011). It is unclear whether teachers' practices are shaped by lack of assessment tools or whether their assessment literacy and competency needs to be developed.

Third, both Zhang et al. (2008) and De Wever et al. (2011) showed robust reliability of PA of CL, but they also addressed areas that need more research, such as the inclusion or not of self-assessment and the validity of PA of CL, notwithstanding the single validity study by Magin (2001). Likewise, more research is needed on reliability and validity of combining a group task and individual tasks. Do they lead to more accurate assessment? Is such mixing of practices valid? What ratio of group and individual task scores or grades is defensible?

Finally, more research is needed on teacher and student uses of technologies for assessment of CL. Specifically, we need more sophisticated approaches and formulas to derive individual scores or grades from group scores of grades (via evidence-based and valid weighting of performance on group and individual tasks or via PA of CL). This is especially important when there are serious concerns about the summative use of individual scores or grades inferred via PA-moderated group scores or grades with the help of systems such as SPARK[PLUS] (Wu et al., 2014).

CONCLUSION

Assessment of CL is very challenging. It involves multiple concurrent processes and outcomes at multiple levels by multiple agents. This chapter has identified the challenges and, given the complexity of the field, its contribution might be somewhat slight. Nevertheless, CL assessment is an important daily and demanding part of the learning environment for teachers and students. There are many available, yet often unused, tools, with others waiting to be discovered. As a research community (from cooperative learning, collaborative learning, assessment, learning sciences, and computer sciences) we can make the assessment of CL less complex, less demanding, and more worthwhile for teachers and students. We have the rudimentary methods and tools; all that is left is to figure out how these can be applied, adapted, and further developed to better meet the needs of teachers and students while still providing psychometrically valid and reliable judgements about learning and performance!

ACKNOWLEDGEMENTS

Many thanks to Miranda de Hei, Filitsa Dingyloudi, Karsten Stegmann and further members of the Chair of Education and Educational Psychology for their suggestions and discussion of early drafts of the definition of collaborative learning. I also thank the editors, Gavin Brown and Lois Harris for their endless patience, suggestions, and prompting me to write this definition of collaborative learning.

REFERENCES

Barfield, R. L. (2003). Students' perceptions of and satisfaction with group grades and the group experience in the college classroom. *Assessment & Evaluation in Higher Education, 28*(4), 355–370.

Belfer, K., & Wakkary, R. (2005). Team assessment guidelines: A case study of collaborative learning in design. In P. Comeaux (Ed.), *Assessing online learning* (pp. 34–54). San Francisco, CA: Jossey-Bass.

Biggs, J. (1996). Enhancing teaching through constructive alignment. *Higher Education, 32*(3), 347–364.

Boekaerts, M., & Minnaert, A. (2006). Affective and motivational outcomes of working in collaborative groups. *Educational Psychology, 26*(2), 187–208.

Boud, D., Cohen, R., & Sampson, J. (1999). Peer learning and assessment. *Assessment & Evaluation in Higher Education, 24*(4), 413–426.

Boud, D., & Falchikov, N. (2006). Aligning assessment with long-term learning. *Assessment & Evaluation in Higher Education, 31*(4), 399–413.

Bushell, G. (2006). Moderation of peer assessment in group projects. *Assessment & Evaluation in Higher Education, 31*(1), 91–108.

Chen, W., Looi, C. K., Xie, W., & Wen, Y. (2013). Empowering argumentation in the science classroom with a complex CSCL environment. In L. H. Wong, C.-C. Lui, T. Hirashima, P. Sumedi, & M. Lukman (Eds.), *Proceedings of the 21st International Conference on Computers in Education* (pp. 348–357). Bali: Asia-Pacific Society for Computers in Education.

Cheng, W., & Warren, M. (2000). Making a difference: Using peers to assess individual students' contributions to a group project. *Teaching in Higher Education, 5*(2), 243–255.

Chiriac, E. H., & Granström, K. (2012). Teachers' leadership and students' experience of group work. *Teachers and Teaching: Theory and Practice, 18*(3), 345–363.

Chiu, M. M. (2008). Flowing toward correct contributions during group problem solving: A statistical discourse analysis. *The Journal of the Learning Sciences, 17*(3), 415–463.

Cohen, E. G. (1994). Restructuring the classroom: Conditions for productive small groups. *Review of Educational Research, 64*(1), 1–35.

Cohen, E. G., Lotan, R. A., Abram, P. L., Scarloss, B. A., & Schultz, S. E. (2002). Can groups learn? *Teachers College Record, 104*(6), 1045–1068.

De Hei, M. S. A., Strijbos, J. W., Sjoer, E., & Admiraal, W. (2015). Collaborative learning in higher education: Lecturers' practices and beliefs. *Research Papers in Education, 30*(2), 232–247.

De Hei, M., Strijbos, J.-W., Sjoer, E., & Admiraal, W. (2016). Thematic review of approaches to design group learning activities in higher education: The development of a comprehensive framework. *Educational Research Review, 18*, 33–45. doi: 10.1016/j.edurev.2016.01.001

De Wever, B., Van Keer, H., Schellens, T., & Valcke, M. (2011). Assessing collaboration in a wiki: The reliability of university students' peer assessment. *The Internet and Higher Education, 14*(4), 201–206.

Dingyloudi, F., & Strijbos, J. W. (2015). Examining value creation in a community of learning practice: Methodological reflections on story-telling and story-reading. *Seminar.net: International Journal of Media, Technology & Lifelong Leaning, 11*(3), 209–222.

Fischer, K. W., & Granott, N. (1995). Beyond one-dimensional change: Parallel concurrent, socially distributed processes in learning and development. *Human Development, 38*(6), 302–314.

Fischer, F., & Mandl, H. (2005). Knowledge convergence in computer-supported collaborative learning: The role of external representation tools. *The Journal of the Learning Sciences, 14*(3), 405–441.

Frederiksen, N. (1984). The real test bias: Influences of testing on teaching and learning. *American Psychologist, 3*, 193–202.

Freeman, M., & McKenzie, J. (2002). SPARK, a confidential web-based template for self and peer assessment of team work: Benefits of evaluating across different subjects. *British Journal of Educational Technology, 33*(5), 551–569.

Frykedal, K. F., & Chiriac, E. H. (2011). Assessment of students' learning when working in groups. *Educational Research, 53*(3), 331–345.

Gillies, R. M. (2007). *Cooperative learning: Integrating theory and practice.* Los Angeles, CA: Sage.

Gillies, R. M., & Ashman, A. F. (2003). An historical overview of the use of groups to promote socialization and learning. In R. M. Gillies & A. F. Ashman (Eds.), *Co-operative learning: The social and intellectual outcomes of learning in groups* (pp. 1–18). London: Routledge.

Gillies, R. M., & Boyle, M. (2010). Teachers' reflections on cooperative learning: Issues of implementation. *Teaching and Teacher Education, 26*(4), 933–940.

Goldfinch, J. (1994). Further developments in peer assessment of group projects. *Assessment & Evaluation in Higher Education, 19*(1), 29–35.

Gress, C. L. Z., Fior, M., Hadwin, A. F., & Winne, P. H. (2010). Measurement and assessment in computer-supported collaborative learning. *Computers in Human Behavior, 26*(5), 806–814.

Gweon, G., Jain, M., McDonough, J., Raj, B., & Rosé, C. P. (2013). Measuring prevalence of other-oriented transactive contributions using an automated measure of speech style accommodation. *International Journal of Computer-Supported Collaborative Learning, 8*(2), 245–265.

Harlen, W., & James, M. (1996 April). *Creating a positive impact of assessment on learning.* Paper presented at AERA 1996 annual meeting, New York, NY.

Hatano, G, & Inagaki, K. (1991). Sharing cognition through collective comprehension activity. In L. B. Resnick, J. M. Levine, & S. D. Teasley (Eds.), *Perspectives on socially shared cognition* (pp. 331–348). Washington, DC: American Psychological Association.

Hijzen, D., Boekaerts, M., & Vedder, P. (2007). Exploring the links between students' engagement in cooperative learning, their goal preferences and appraisals of instruction conditions in the classroom. *Learning and Instruction, 17*(6), 673–687.

Hoffman, J. R., & Rogelberg, S. G. (2001). All together now? College students' preferred project group grading procedures. *Group Dynamics: Theory, Research, and Practice, 5*(1), 33–40.

Janssen, J., & Bodemer, D. (2013). Coordinated computer-supported collaborative learning: Awareness and awareness tools. *Educational Psychologist, 48*(1), 40–55.

Järvelä, S., & Hadwin, A. (2013). New frontiers: Regulating learning in CSCL. *Educational Psychologist, 48*(1), 25–39.

Järvelä, S., Volet, S., & Järvenoja, H. (2010). Research on motivation in collaborative learning: Moving beyond the cognitive-situative divide and combining individual and social processes. *Educational Psychologist, 45*(1), 15–27.

Jeong, H., & Chi, M. T. H. (2007). Knowledge convergence and collaborative learning. *Instructional Science, 35*(4), 287–315.

Johnson, D. W. (1981). Student-student interaction: The neglected variable in education. *Educational Researcher, 10*, 5–10.

Johnson, D. W., & Johnson, R. T. (1994). *Learning together and alone: Cooperative, competitive and individualistic learning* (4th ed.). Needham Heights, MA: Allyn & Bacon.

Johnson, D. W., & Johnson, R. T. (2003). Student motivation in co-operative groups: social interdependence theory. In R. M. Gillies & A. F. Ashman (Eds.), *Co-operative learning: The social and intellectual outcomes of learning in groups* (pp. 136–176). London, UK: Routledge.

Johnson, D. W., & Johnson, R. T. (2004). *Assessing students in groups: Promoting group responsibility and individual accountability.* Thousand Oaks, CA: Corwin Press.

Johnston, L., & Miles, L. (2004). Assessing contributions to group assignments. *Assessment & Evaluation in Higher Education, 29*(6), 751–768.

Kagan, S. (1995). Group grades miss the mark. *Educational Leadership, 52*(8), 68–71.

Kali, Y., & Ronen, M. (2008). Assessing the assessors: Added value in web-based multi-cycle peer assessment in higher education. *Research and Practice in Technology Enhanced Learning, 3*(1), 3–32.

Kench, P. L., Field, N., Agudera, M., & Gill, M. (2009). Peer assessment of individual contributions to a group project: Student perceptions. *Radiography, 15*(2), 158–165.

Kerr, N. L. (1983). Motivation losses in small groups: A social dilemma analysis. *Journal of Personality and Social Psychology, 45*(4), 819–828.

Kerr, N. L., & Bruun, S. E. (1983). Dispensability of member effort and group motivation losses: Free rider effects. *Journal of Personality and Social Psychology, 44*(1), 78–94.

Kollar, I., & Fischer, F. (2010). Peer assessment as collaborative learning: A cognitive perspective. *Learning and Instruction, 20*(4), 344–348.

Kreijns, K. (2004). *Sociable CSCL environments: Social affordances, sociability and social presence.* Unpublished doctoral dissertation, Open University of the Netherlands, Heerlen, The Netherlands.

Kreijns, K., Kirschner, P. A., & Jochems, W. M. G. (2003). Identifying the pitfalls for social interaction in computer-supported collaborative learning: A review of the research. *Computers in Human Behavior, 19*(3), 335–353.

Kumar, V. S., Gress, C. L. Z., Hadwin, A. F., & Winne, P. H. (2010). Assessing process in CSCL: An ontological approach. *Computers in Human Behavior, 26*(5), 825–834.

Law, N., & Wong, E. (2003). Developmental trajectory in knowledge building: An investigation. In B. Wasson, S. Ludvigsen, & U. Hoppe (Eds.), *Designing for change in networked learning environments* (pp. 57–66). Dordrecht, the Netherlands: Kluwer/ Springer.

Lee, E.Y.C., Chan, C.K.K., & Van Aalst, J. (2006). Students assessing their own collaborative knowledge building. *International Journal of Computer-Supported Collaborative Learning, 1*(1), 57–87.

Lejk, M., & Wyvill, M. (2001a). The effect of inclusion of self-assessment with peer-assessment of contributions to a group project: A quantitative study of secret and agreed assessments. *Assessment & Evaluation in Higher Education, 26*(6), 551–561.

Lejk, M., & Wyvill, M. (2001b). Peer assessment of contributions to a group project: A comparison of holistic and category-based approaches. *Assessment & Evaluation in Higher Education, 26*(1), 61–72.

Lejk, M., Wyvill, M., & Farrow, S. (1996). A survey of methods of deriving individual grades from group assessments. *Assessment & Evaluation in Higher Education, 21*(3), 267–280.

Li, L. (2001). Some refinements on peer assessment of group projects. *Assessment & Evaluation in Higher Education, 26*(1), 5–18.

Lipponen, L., Hakkarainen, K., & Paavola, S. (2004). Practices and orientations of CSCL. In J. W. Strijbos, P. A. Kirschner, & R. L. Martens (Eds.), *What we know about CSCL: And implementing it in higher education* (pp. 31–50). Boston, MA: Kluwer/ Springer.

Macdonald, J. (2003). Assessing online collaborative learning: Process and product. *Computers & Education, 40*(4), 377–391.

Magin, D. J. (2001). A novel technique for comparing the reliability of multiple peer assessments with that of single teacher assessments of group process work. *Assessment & Evaluation in Higher Education, 26*(2), 139–152.

McConnell, D. (2006). *E-learning groups and communities.* Berkshire, UK: The Society for Research into Higher Education & The Open University Press.

Miyake, N. (2007). Computer supported collaborative learning. In R. Andrews & C. Haythornthwaite (Eds.), *The Sage handbook of e-learning research* (pp. 248–265). London, UK: Sage.

Miyake, N. (2008). Conceptual change through collaboration. In S. Vosniadou (Ed.), *International handbook of conceptual change* (pp. 453–478). New York: Routledge.

Mu, J., Stegmann, K., Mayfield, E., Rosé, C., Fischer, F. (2012). The ACODEA framework: Developing segmentation and classification schemes for fully automatic analysis of online discussions. *International Journal of Computer-Supported Collaborative Learning, 7*(2), 285–305.

Nepal, K. P. (2012). An approach to assign individual marks from a team mark: The case of Australian grading system at universities. *Assessment & Evaluation in Higher Education, 37*(5), 555–562.

Neus, J. N. (2011). Peer assessment accounting for student agreement. *Assessment & Evaluation in Higher Education, 36*(3), 301–314.

OECD. (2013). *PISA 2015 draft collaborative problem solving framework.* Retrieved from http://www.oecd.org/pisa/pisaproducts/Draft%20PISA%202015%20Collaborative%20Problem%20Solving%20Framework%20.pdf

Oosterhof, A., Conrad, R. M., & Ely, D. P. (2008). *Assessing learners online.* Upper Saddle River, NJ: Pearson.

Pauli, R., Mohiyeddini, C., Bray, D., Michie, F., & Street, B. (2012). Individual differences in negative group work experiences in collaborative learning. *Educational Psychology, 28*(1), 47–58.

Petropoulou, O., Vassilikopoulou, M., & Retalis, S. (2011). Enriched assessment rubrics: A new medium for enabling teachers to easily assess student's performance when participating in complex interactive learning scenarios. *Operational Research, 11*(2), 171–186.

Phielix, C., Prins, F. J., & Kirschner, P. A. (2010). Awareness of group performance in a CSCL environment: Effects of peer feedback and reflection. *Computers in Human Behavior, 26*(2), 151–161.

Piech, C., Huang, J., Chen, Z., Do, C., Ng, A., & Koller, D. (2013). Tuned models of peer assessment in MOOCs. In S. K. D'Mello, R. A. Calvo, & A. Olney (Eds.), *Proceedings of The 6th International Conference on Educational Data Mining (EDM 2013)* (pp. 153–160). Memphis, TN: International Educational Data Mining Society.

Prins, F. J., Sluijsmans, D.M.A., Kirschner, P. A., & Strijbos, J. W. (2005). Formative peer assessment in a CSCL environment. *Assessment & Evaluation in Higher Education, 30*(4), 417–444.

Puntambekar, S., Erkens, G., & Hmelo-Silver, C. (Eds.). (2011). *Analyzing interactions in CSCL: Methods, approaches and issues.* New York: Springer.

Reimann, P., Yacef, K., & Kay, J. (2011). Analyzing collaborative interactions with data mining methods for the benefit for learning. In S. Puntambekar, G. Erkens, & C. Hmelo-Silver (Eds.), *Analyzing interactions in CSCL: Methods, approaches and issues* (pp. 161–185). New York: Springer.

Romero, C., & Ventura, S. (2010). Educational data mining: A review of the state-of-the-art. *IEEE transactions on Systems, Man and Cybernetics, Part C: Applications and Reviews, 40*(6), 601–618.

Rosen, Y., & Foltz, P. W. (2014). Assessing collaborative problem solving through automated technologies. *Research and Practice in Technology Enhanced Learning, 9*(3), 389–410.

Ross, J. A., & Rolheiser, C. (2003). Student assessment practices in co-operative learning. In R. M. Gillies & A. F. Ashman (Eds.), *Co-operative learning: The social and intellectual outcomes of learning in groups* (pp. 119–135). London, UK: Routledge.

Ross, J. A., Rolheiser, C., & Hogaboam-Gray, A. (1998). Student evaluation in co-operative learning: Teacher cognitions. *Teachers and Teaching: Theory and Practice, 4*(2), 299–316.

Rummel, N., Deiglmayer, A., Spada, H., Kahrimanis, G., & Avouris, N. (2011). Analyzing collaborative interactions across domains and settings: An adaptable rating scheme. In S. Puntambekar, G. Erkens, & C. Hmelo-Silver (Eds.), *Analyzing interactions in CSCL: Methods, approaches and issues* (pp. 367–390). New York: Springer.

Salomon, G. (2000, June 28). *It's not just the tool, but the educational rationale that counts.* Invited keynote address at the 2000 ED-MEDIA Meeting, Montreal, Canada.

Salomon, G., & Globerson, T. (1989). When teams do not function the way they ought to. *International Journal of Educational Research, 13*(1), 89–99.

Scriven, M. (1967). The methodology of evaluation. In R. E. Stake (Ed.), *Perspectives of curriculum evaluation* (Vol. 1, pp. 39–55). Chicago: Rand McNally.

Shaffer, D. W., Hatfield, D., Svarovsky, G. N., Nash, P., Nulty, A., Bagley, E., Frank, K., Rupp, A. A., & Mislevy, R. (2009). Epistemic network analysis: A prototype for 21st century assessment of learning. *International Journal of Learning and Media, 1*(2), 33–53.

Sharan, Y., & Sharan, S. (1992). *Expanding cooperative learning through group investigation.* New York: Teachers College Press.

Sharan, S., Sharan, Y., & Tan, I. G.-C. (2013). The group investigation approach to cooperative learning. In C. E. Hmelo-Silver, C. A. Chinn, C.K.K. Chan, & A. O'Donnell (Eds.), *The international handbook of collaborative learning* (pp. 351–369). New York: Routledge.

Sharp, S. (2006). Deriving individual student marks from a tutor's assessment of group work. *Assessment & Evaluation in Higher Education, 31*(3), 329–343.

Sivan, A. (2000). The implementation of peer assessment: An action research approach. *Assessment in Education: Principles, Policy & Practice, 7*(2), 193–213.

Slavin, R. E. (1980). Cooperative learning in teams: State of the art. *Educational Psychologist, 15*(2), 93–111.

Slavin, R. E. (1995). *Cooperative learning: Theory, research and practice* (2nd ed.). Needham Heights: Allyn & Bacon.

Slavin, R. E. (1996). Research on cooperative learning and achievement: What we know, what we need to know. *Contemporary Educational Psychology, 21*(1), 43–69.

Stahl, G., Koschmann, T., & Suthers, D. (2006). Computer-supported collaborative learning: A historical perspective. In R. K. Sawyer (Ed.), *Cambridge handbook of the learning sciences* (pp. 409–426). Cambridge, UK: Cambridge University Press.

Strijbos, J. W. (2011). Assessment of (computer-supported) collaborative learning. *IEEE Transactions on Learning Technologies, 4*(1), 59–73.

Strijbos, J. W., & Fischer, F. (2007). Methodological challenges for collaborative learning research. *Learning and Instruction, 17*(4), 389–394.

Strijbos, J. W., Kirschner, P. A., & Martens, R. L. (Eds.). (2004a). *What we know about CSCL: And implementing it in higher education.* Boston, MA: Kluwer Academic/ Springer.

Strijbos, J. W., Kirschner, P. A., & Martens, R. L. (2004b). What we know about CSCL: And what we do not (but need to know) about CSCL. In J. W. Strijbos, P. A. Kirschner, & R. L. Martens (Eds.), *What we know about CSCL: And implementing it in higher education* (pp. 245–259). Boston, MA: Kluwer/ Springer.

Strijbos, J. W., Martens, R. L., & Jochems, W.M.G. (2004). Designing for interaction: Six steps to designing computer-supported collaborative learning. *Computers & Education, 42*(4), 403–424.

Strijbos, J. W., Martens, R. L., Jochems, W.M.G., & Broers, N. J. (2007). The effect of functional roles on perceived group efficiency during computer-supported collaborative learning: A matter of triangulation. *Computers in Human Behavior, 23*(1), 353–380.

Strijbos, J. W., Ochoa, T. A., Sluijsmans, D.M.A., Segers, M.S.R., & Tillema, H. H. (2009). Fostering interactivity through formative peer assessment in (web-based) collaborative learning environments. In C. Mourlas, N. Tsianos, & P. Germanakos (Eds.), *Cognitive and emotional processes in web-based education: Integrating human factors and personalization* (pp. 375–395). Hershey, PA: IGI Global.

Strijbos, J. W., & Sluijsmans, D.M.A. (2010). Unravelling peer assessment through (quasi) experimental research. *Learning and Instruction, 20*(4), 265–269.

Stuart, M. A. (1994). Effects of group grading on cooperation and achievement in two fourth-grade math classes. *The Elementary School Journal, 95*(1), 11–21.

Sung, Y. T., Chang, K. E., Chiou, S. K., & Hou, H. T. (2005). The design and application of a web-based self- and peer-assessment system. *Computers & Education, 45*(2), 187–202.

Swan, K., Shen, J., & Hiltz, S. R. (2006). Assessment and collaboration in online learning. *Journal of Asynchronous Learning Networks, 10*(1), 45–61.

Tolmie, A. K., Topping, K. J., Christie, D., Donaldson, C., Howe, C., Jessiman, E., Livingston, K., & Thurston, A. (2010). Social effects of collaborative learning in primary schools. *Learning and Instruction, 20*(3), 177–191.

Topping, K. (1998). Peer assessment between students in colleges and universities. *Review of Educational Research, 68*(3), 249–276.

Van Aalst, J. (2013). Assessment in collaborative learning. In C. E. Hmelo-Silver, C. A. Chinn, C.K.K. Chan, & A. O'Donnell (Eds.), *The international handbook of collaborative learning* (pp. 280–296). New York: Routledge.

Van Aalst, J., & Chan, C.K.K. (2007). Student-directed assessment of knowledge building using electronic portfolios. *The Journal of the Learning Sciences, 16*(2), 175–220.

Van Gennip, N.A.E., Segers, M.S.R., & Tillema, H. H. (2009). Peer assessment for learning from a social perspective: The influence of interpersonal variables and structural features. *Educational Research Review, 4*(1), 41–54.

Van Gennip, N.A.E., Segers, M.S.R., & Tillema, H. H. (2010). Peer assessment as a collaborative learning activity: The role of interpersonal variables and conceptions. *Learning and Instruction, 20*(4), 280–290.

Vanderhoven, E., Raes, A., Montrieux, H., Rotsaert, T,, Schellens, T. (2015). What if pupils can assess their peers anonymously? A quasi-experimental study. *Computer & Education, 81*, 123–132.

Volet, S., Summers, M., & Thurman, J. (2009). High-level co-regulation in collaborative learning: How does it emerge and how is it sustained? *Learning and Instruction, 19*(2), 128–143.

Wang, L., MacCann, C., Zhuang, X., Liu, O. L., & Roberts, R. D. (2009). Assessing teamwork and collaboration in high school students: A multimethod approach. *Canadian Journal of School Psychology, 24*(2), 108–124.

Webb, N. M. (1993). Collaborative group versus individual assessment in mathematics: Processes and outcomes. *Educational Assessment, 1*(2), 131–152.

Webb, N. M. (1997). Assessing students in small collaborative groups. *Theory into Practice, 36*(4), 205–213.

Weinberger, A., Stegmann, K., & Fischer, F. (2007). Knowledge convergence in collaborative learning: Concepts and assessment. *Learning and Instruction, 17*(4), 416–426.

Wenger, E., Trayner, B., & De Laat, M. (2011). *Promoting and assessing value creation in communities and networks: A conceptual framework.* Heerlen, the Netherlands: Ruud de Moor Centrum.

Willey, K., & Gardner, A. (2009). Improving self- and peer assessment processes with technology. *Campus-Wide Information Systems, 26*(5), 379–399.

Williams, K. D., & Karau, S. J. (1991). Social loafing and social compensation: The effects of expectations of co-worker performance. *Journal of Personality and Social Psychology, 61*(4), 570–581.

Wise, A. F., & Chiu, M. M. (2011). Analyzing temporal patterns of knowledge construction in a role-based online discussion. *International Journal of Computer-Supported Collaborative Learning, 6*(3), 445–470.

Wu, C., Chanda, E., & Willison, J. (2014). Implementation and outcomes of online self and peer assessment on group based honours research projects. *Assessment & Evaluation of Higher Education, 39*(1), 21–37.

Zhang, B., Johnston, L., & Kilic, G. B. (2008). Assessing the reliability of self- and peer rating in student group work. *Assessment & Evaluation in Higher Education, 33*(3), 329–340.

Zottmann, J. M., Stegmann, K., Strijbos, J. W., Vogel, F., Wecker, C., & Fischer, F. (2013). Computer-supported collaborative learning with digital video cases in teacher education: The impact of teaching experience on knowledge convergence. *Computers in Human Behavior, 29*(5), 2100–2108.

18

STUDENT SELF-ASSESSMENT IN THE CLASSROOM

Heidi L. Andrade and Gavin T. L. Brown

Self-assessment is an entirely human process; no machines or statistics can take the place of the learner's own self-awareness. The student's context, personal life, values, ideas, personality, abilities, and traits all filter, guide, and even warp the judgments he or she makes about learning and performance on academic tasks. This chapter examines the individual and social influences on student self-assessment, including (a) intra-individual competence and confidence in self-assessment, (b) interpersonal relations with teachers/instructors who require students to conduct and perhaps share their self-assessments, (c) interpersonal relations with peers, in front of whom students are sometimes required to carry out self-assessments, and (d) the students' cultural contexts. We suggest that the power of self-assessment is dependent upon the conditions under which it is implemented.

This chapter begins with a discussion of the difficulties in defining self-assessment, followed by reviews of the literature on the effects of the intra- and interpersonal factors on the usefulness of self-assessment. The chapter concludes with implications for the implementation of self-assessment, as well as recommendations for ensuring validity and reliability, for research and reporting, and for policy and teacher education.

DEFINITIONS OF SELF-ASSESSMENT

Self-assessment is something of a misnomer, since it is not an evaluation of the self but rather of the work or learning done by oneself (Kasanen & Räty, 2002). In the broadest sense, self-assessment is a description and/or evaluation of one's own academic products and processes (Brown & Harris, 2013). This expansive definition includes several terms that are often used interchangeably in the literature, including self-evaluation, self-grading, self-rating, self-assessment, and judgment of learning. For the sake of clarity, we would like to impose a distinction between summative and formative self-assessment processes. Summative self-assessment processes involve the process of attributing value, worth, or merit to one's own work, and include self-grading, self-rating, and judgments of learning. Self-grading involves marking, scoring, or grading one's own work. Similarly, self-rating refers to the process of using a rating scale (e.g., smiley faces; number of stars or points) to assign a quality or value to one's performance or learning. Much of the research on the accuracy of self-evaluation or assessment involves self-rating (e.g., Baxter & Norman, 2011; Sung, Chang, Chang, & Yu, 2010). Judgment of learning involves estimating, usually on a percentage correct basis, how accurately one has remembered (postdiction) or will remember (prediction) learning objects (e.g., translated word pairs) (Nelson & Narens, 1990).

Formative self-assessment refers to formative judgments that occur during the learning process and can therefore inform revision and relearning (Andrade, 2010). Formative self-assessment tends to necessitate more complex, and possibly multidimensional, descriptions of and reflections on work quality than summative self-evaluations, which are often reduced to holistic judgments. The formative approach to self-assessment emphasizes pedagogical effects (i.e., informing subsequent learning actions), while the summative approach emphasizes the terminal evaluative component (i.e., the quality or worth judgment of completed work).

It has been suggested that summative self-marking, -grading, or -rating might not be self-assessment at all (Panadero, Brown, & Strijbos, 2014). This perspective has been espoused by Boud (1995a, b), who identified two defining characteristics of self-assessment: (1) standards or criteria for student work, and (2) judgments about the extent to which the work meets those standards or criteria. Self-assessment processes that are used formatively, summatively, or in both ways can include these characteristics (i.e., standards and judgments), but Boud noted that many self-assessment processes undermine learning by rushing students to judgment, thereby failing to engage students with the standards or criteria. Nonetheless, the process of making a judgment about one's own learning and performance is likely to have an impact (positive or negative) on that learning, regardless of its timing or whether it involves numeric values or narrative descriptions. Hence, both summative and formative uses of self-assessment are within the scope of this chapter, as well as processes that combine formative and summative uses.

Unfortunately, it is not always possible to discern from a published study which type of self-assessment was implemented—formative or summative—or even if the focus is on feedback or grades. Ideally, any discussion of the effects of and influences on classroom-based self-assessment would make clear distinctions between the two. Since the extant literature does not yet lend itself to such a precise analysis, in this chapter we combine the types, use the generic term *self-assessment*, and call for clearer distinctions in future.

Types of Self-assessment

A second problem in self-assessment research is that a wide variety of tools and practices are classified as self-assessment, each of which can be used formatively, summatively, or in both ways. Types of self-assessment range from very simple and holistic techniques to more complex, multidimensional analyses. Simple, holistic techniques include rating one's work with a series of smiley faces, rating one's understanding showing a traffic light (i.e., green = understood; yellow = unsure; red = not understood) (Black & Harrison, 2001; Clarke, 2005), or estimating the number of times an action could be completed successfully (Powel & Gray, 1995). Other simple self-assessments include retrospective reporting of previous performance on a test (Baars, Vink, van Gog, de Bruin, & Paas, 2014), and estimating future performance on a test (Baxter & Norman, 2011; Dunlosky & Nelson, 1994; Nelson & Dunlosky, 1991).

More complex tools include structured, hierarchical rubrics or scripts. Rubrics are descriptions of the characteristics of student work with different levels of performance, from strong to weak, for each characteristic (Brookhart, 2013; Brown, Irving, & Keegan, 2014). Other terms for a rubric include marking scheme, progress indicator, and progress map or matrix. Rubrics typically describe the products of student work. Scripts, in contrast, focus students' attention on the adequacy of the processes they use during learning, as compared to expert-like steps for performing a task. Scripts have assessment criteria in the form of questions but, unlike rubrics, do not have a scoring feature (Panadero, Alonso-Tapia, & Reche, 2013).

In their review of K–12 self-assessment practices, Brown and Harris (2013) concluded that greater learning effects were associated with the use of more complex judgments, if the techniques were supported by guided instruction. However, because self-assessments take place in many different ways, competence in one method may have no relationship to how well students use another (Bol & Hacker, 2012; Maki, Shields, Wheller, & Zacchilli, 2005). The disparity and diversity of behaviors considered to be student self-assessment, as well as the purposes that the self-assessments are intended to serve, make it difficult to precisely analyze the ways in which social and human factors interact with self-assessment processes.

Whatever it is called, and however it is done, a number of psychological and social processes conspire to modify the self's judgment of the self's work. Since self-assessment is an evaluation of work carried out by the worker herself, it is important to appreciate that it can suffer from many of the same validity threats as self-reports, including socially desirable responding (Duckworth & Yeager, 2015; Paulhus, 1991), particularly for females (Dalton & Ortegren, 2011). Social response bias reflects both internal psychological traits and processes, as well as the effects of the social environment of classrooms. Because trust and respect are essential qualities of a classroom in which students are willing to disclose their knowledge and engage in assessment for learning (Tierney, 2013), the quality of self-assessments will be affected by classroom climate and relations with teachers and peers (Harris & Brown, 2013).

INTRAPERSONAL FACTORS IN STUDENT SELF-ASSESSMENT

The accuracy or consistency of student self-assessments is one of the most studied topics in the field. There is still considerable doubt about the benefits and costs of accuracy, especially as compared to positive bias (Butler, 2011). As pointed out elsewhere (Brown, Andrade, & Chen, 2015), however, some of this doubt could be related to the fact that evaluating the value of self-assessment is a thorny matter because it is difficult to establish the degree to which students' self-assessments of their own work are truthful. This is so because there is no absolute standard by which to judge student perceptions of their work. The use of test scores, teacher judgments, or peer evaluations as standards against which to test the consistency of self-assessments is imperfect, in part because the sources of information used by students themselves, their teachers, or their peers can be quite different (Marsh, Smith, & Barnes, 1983). For example, Chang and colleagues (Chang, Tseng, & Lou, 2012; Chang, Liang, & Chen, 2013) report that five of seven correlations between student self-assessments and teacher-assessments of Web-based portfolio work were statistically not significant, indicating the two groups had different bases for evaluation. Furthermore, because teacher grading is marked by considerable inconsistency (Brown, 2009; Falchikov, 2005; Heldsinger & Humphry, 2013; Kirby & Downs, 2007), the expectation that there should be alignment between self- and teacher assessments may not be well-founded (Leach, 2010).

Recent research addresses the problem of estimating accuracy by anchoring judgments of student work and learning to criteria. For example, the self-criterion residual strategy, which is used in research on self-appraisal bias, involves either calculating a difference score by subtracting a criterion (e.g., actual math or language grades) from the self-evaluation measure (e.g., a self-report of self-efficacy for math or language), or regressing the self-evaluation data on the external criterion and using the residual as the self-evaluation bias index (Bouffard & Narciss, 2011). This approach does not eliminate bias, but it can help researchers manage it better than approaches that rely on social comparison (asking learners to evaluate their academic competence in comparison to the average academic competence of their class or peers) or social consensus (comparing self-assessments with the evaluations of parents, teachers, or peers). Other researchers argue that self-assessments should be evaluated by what students themselves believe to be valuable when engaging in learning, rather than determining the realism of a self-assessment by reference to an external source (Bourke, 2014; Tan, 2009; Taras, 2008).

However measured, the correlations between student self-assessments and other measures tend to be positive (Blanch-Hartigan, 2011; Boud & Falchikov, 1989). In Brown and Harris's (2013) review of K–12 studies, the values ranged from weak to moderate ($r \approx .20$ to .80, median $r = .45$), with few studies reporting correlations greater than $r = .60$. Yet there are cases of self-assessments that are inconsistent with external measures. For example, Baxter and Norman (2011) suggested that, because 15 of the 16 correlations between nursing students' self-ratings and objective clinical examination scores were negative, self-assessment might be better considered to be self-deception.

Dunning, Heath, and Suls (2004) identified many reasons self-assessment can be unverifiable through other means; these include the human tendency to (a) be unrealistically optimistic about one's own abilities, (b) believe that one is above average, (c) neglect crucial information, and (d) have deficits in information. Students have also been found to consider their own effort, which ought to be independent of a quality evaluation of work products, when assessing their work (Ross, Rolheiser, & Hogaboam-Gray, 1998). A number of intrapersonal characteristics influence self-assessments, including self-concept, self-efficacy, outcome expectations, locus of control, and self-esteem (Boekaerts, 1991). The personal factors that have received the most attention from researchers focused on the consistency of self-assessments with other measures, however, include academic ability, age and experience, and the inclination or disinclination to self-judge.

Ability

In general, higher performing students tend to produce either more consistent or more humble self-assessment than lower performing students (Barnett & Hixon, 1997; Blatchford, 1997a, 1997b; Boekaerts, 1991; Claes & Salame, 1975; Eccles, Wigfield, Harold, & Blumenfeld, 1993; Frey & Ruble, 1987; Jackson, 2014; Kaderavek, Gillam, Ukrainetz, Justice, & Eisenberg, 2004; Karnilowicz, 2012; Kasanen, Räty, & Eklund, 2009; Kostons, van Gog, & Paas, 2010; Kwok & Lai, 1993; Laveault & Miles, 2002; Lew, Alwis, & Schmidt, 2010; Mitman & Lash, 1988; Ng & Earl, 2008; Ross, Hogaboam-Gray, & Rolheiser, 2002; Stipek, 1981; Stipek & Tannatt, 1984; Sung, et al., 2010; Wall, Singh, Whitehouse, Hassell, & Howes, 2012; Watt, 2000; Wilson & Wright, 1993). As an example of the relationship between ability and consistency, higher performing French-speaking students in Grades 7 and 8 in Montreal (i.e., the first two grades of secondary schooling) were more accurate in their self-ratings than lower performing students ($d = 0.84$; Claes & Salame, 1975).

More common, however, are studies that show that high performing students tend to underestimate. For instance, Sung et al. (2010) reported two studies of self-scoring with Taiwanese middle school students (Grade 7 recorder playing and Grade 8 group multimedia Web page projects) that found a tendency for high achievers to underrate, particularly on the recorder playing, and low achievers to overrate. Similarly, in a study of Australian final-year high school students (average age 17 years, 8 months), Ng and Earl (2008) found higher performing students underestimated their performance on a school-based trial examination of English compared to their final examination scores in the same subject.

Cowie's (2009) study of middle school students might shed light on this issue. Cowie described students deliberately underestimating their proficiency relative to what they thought the teacher would give so as to avoid the disappointment of being awarded a lower grade by the teacher. Hence, some inaccuracy may be deliberate, and not explained simply in terms of ability or the lack thereof. In addition, Nowell and Alston (2007) point out that underrating may simply occur for high proficiency students because "students who earn a grade of A do not have the opportunity to be overconfident" (p. 134).

Overestimation by low proficiency students seems consistent with the notion of double-handicapping, which means that lower ability students are both more lenient on themselves and less aware of their lower ability (Dunning et al., 2004). However, recent studies (Bouffard, Vezeau, Roy, & Lengele, 2011; Gonida & Leonardi, 2011) have shown that students who overestimated their academic competence tended to have performance goals and the need for approval from others, which "challenges proposals that people who show chronic positive biases do so in large part because of deficits in general cognitive abilities" (Butler, 2011, p. 254).

Age and Experience

The age of the student or her experience within a system of schooling also seems to contribute to the comparability and realism of student self-assessments. High school and university students seem to be able to judge how well they have done on formal tests and assessments (Alsaker, 1989; Dunlosky & Nelson, 1994; Ikeguchi, 1996; Wilson & Wright, 1993), or performances (Hewitt, 2005). Falchikov (2005) found that, in most studies of university students, "greater numbers of student marks agreed than disagreed with teacher marks" (p. 179).

In contrast, many recent studies with primary to middle school students suggest that overrating is more common than underrating (Bradshaw, 2001; Elder, 2010; LaVoie & Hodapp, 1987; Sadler & Good, 2006). As students age, improvements in realism seem to occur. Kaderavek et al. (2004) found that Grade 5 American students were more accurate in estimating their test performance than Grade 3 and 4 students. Butler (1990) found that the difference between self and teachers' evaluations of drawings was much larger for kindergarten students than for Grade 5 students. In general, it may be the case that, among younger children, over-optimism is a function of insufficient negative feedback through formal assessment systems (e.g., failing test scores or extensive red ink corrections by teachers), which may discourage optimism.

Studies reviewed in Boekaerts (1991) have shown that unrealistic and overly optimistic self-assessments occurred less in children who had normative feedback. Similarly, consistency with teacher ratings was observed by Higgins, Harris, and Kuehn (1994), who reported that 54% of American Grade 1 and 2 student self-ratings of social studies projects exactly matched the teacher ratings, and that the teachers tended to rate students' work higher than the students did. The authors attributed these results in part to the students' involvement in generating the assessment criteria, which included criteria of great importance to them, such as effort and respectful group interactions.

Inclination to Self-assess

Another significant intrapersonal characteristic that impacts the quality of student self-assessment is willingness. Leach (2010) notes that some students are reluctant to self-assess, perhaps because they feel they lack the necessary skills to judge their own work, are afraid of being wrong, do not understand the benefit of self-assessment, or simply prefer and expect to be assessed by experts. For an example of the latter, a sample of New Zealand high school students suggested that self-assessment was irrelevant since parents "care more about what my teacher would have to say about me, not what I would have to say about me" (Peterson & Irving, 2008, p. 245). Some students in a Hong Kong high school class also resented doing what they saw as the teacher's work (Gao, 2009). Cowie's (2009) investigations of teacher-directed self-assessment activities in New Zealand middle school science classes showed that students doubted the authenticity of the process. These students questioned the reason for recording a self-rating, since it was tantamount to telling themselves what they already knew.

In contrast, the undergraduates in Andrade and Du's (2007) study appreciated the self-assessment exercises they had done for a semester-long course, in part because self-assessment helped them understand the expectations for their assignments, identify weaknesses in their work, and plan revisions. Students in that study had been engaged in formative self-assessment that was explicitly intended to promote learning and achievement. We speculate that students are generally more willing to engage in formative self-assessment that is followed by opportunities to improve than in summative approaches that label or categorize their work and lack opportunities to revise based on identified weaknesses.

INTERPERSONAL RELATIONS WITH THE TEACHER

Unsurprisingly, much of the research on student self-assessment is conducted as a formal classroom activity initiated by the teacher. This raises issues of identity, power, and trust (Leach, 2010). These issues are most visible in higher education research, where students are expected to attain autonomy and focus on learning for personal reasons and goals. In any context, however, self-assessment "can be seen in a sinister light, interpreted as a way of making students discipline themselves with values that are effectively imposed upon them" (Brown & Knight, 2004, p. 57) in such a way that self-assessment becomes "linked to notions of surveillance and social control" (Brown, Bull, & Pendlebury, 1997, p. 185). Tan (2004) argues that self-assessment can be "part of the self-policing machinery of normalization that sustains compliant identities in students. . . . The students' self-assessment practice subjects the students to self-surveillance over what prevailing discourses dictate knowledge should (be assessed to) be" (p. 659). Taras (2010), also referring to higher education contexts, prefers self-assessment in which the students are empowered to decide for themselves what the learning goals are, and whether or not their own work meets those expectations.

Higher education students themselves have expressed similar concerns about power and trust. Some of the undergraduates interviewed by Andrade and Du (2007) identified a tension between teachers' expectations and their own standards of quality. Those students spoke of needing to give the teacher what he or she wanted, while regularly rejecting their own assessments of their work in favor of guesses about how their teacher or professor would grade it.

The power of the teacher to compel students to conduct self-assessment and compulsorily disclose it to either the teacher or class is noteworthy. Raider-Roth (2005) reported that American Grade 6 students carefully selected what they would disclose to teachers, and their decisions about disclosure depended on trust. For example, one girl told of not admitting to being good at writing paragraphs because she did not want the teacher to talk about it in front of the whole room of students, while another stressed the need to get the self-assessment work 'right,' meaning what the teacher expected. In a study of middle school students in New Zealand, one girl indicated, "I don't really care what I think about what I've done. I just think about what Mrs. Cooper thinks and what my friends think" (Harris & Brown, 2013, p. 12). In the same class, a boy went so far as to say he made things up in order to meet teacher requests for more detail in self-assessment.

While student self-assessments written in their own school books may seem to be private (i.e., a personal diary), they are normally accessible to teachers without any special permission. Thus, as Cowie (2009) describes, students may become uncomfortable and be less than fully forthcoming when teachers are able to see what they write about their own proficiency. Cowie describes student shame at having their task-oriented questions, which were clearly based on a self-assessed need, being publicly answered without their consent. Self-assessment disclosed by the teacher to the class is no longer private, and this influences student willingness to disclose a realistic self-assessment in future learning interactions.

It is likely that the way self-evaluation or self-assessment is implemented determines, at least in part, whether it is empowering to students or an imposition on them (Bourke, 2014; Falchikov, 2005; Tan, 2009; Taras, 2008). It is easy to imagine that self-assessments which require independent and autonomous judgments of the quality of work in light of relevant standards and goals would lead to the most sophisticated self-assessments (Brew, 1999). However, as students require training in evaluating their work against socially validated criteria, their self-assessments will need to be disclosed. This disclosure may not have to be to the teacher, but rather with someone the student trusts (Andrade, 2010; Brown & Harris, 2014). This could create a dilemma for teachers, however, since one of the reasons self-assessment is conducted is to allow the teacher insights into his or her own students' state of learning.

INTERPERSONAL RELATIONS WITH PEERS

Student self-assessments that are disclosed to others are also affected by peer relations. Students have differing and highly personal reactions to disclosure (Cowie, 2009; Harris, Harnett, & Brown, 2009). Some students have raised concerns about their own psychological safety when their self-assessments are made public to peers, as is inevitable with techniques such as traffic lights or answering questions out loud (Cowie, 2009; Harris & Brown, 2013; Raider-Roth, 2005; Ross et al., 1998, 2002). Where students sense pressure to enhance or even protect their self-worth (Duckworth & Yeager, 2015), they may overestimate their ability (Saavedra & Kwun, 1993) or inaccurately self-report their level of understanding or grades or test scores (Kuncel, Credé, & Thomas, 2005). Examples of deliberate overestimation include a New Zealand middle school student who reported giving an elevated traffic light, which was visible to the teacher and class, to avoid being shamed by a classmate who was clearly not a friend (Harris & Brown, 2013). Deliberate underestimation is done when students want to avoid negative social stigmas associated with being smart or being a minority student acting 'white' (Tyson, Darity, & Castellino, 2005). Even calling on students to ask questions in class about what they do not understand may generate the possibility of being seen as stupid or slow by classmates, leading some to more silent and passive learning practices (Cowie, 2009).

If lack of trust in the classroom is widespread, self-assessments disclosed in class are likely to produce counterfeit data. Thus, it cannot be assumed that students are honest in self-assessments that are disclosed to others; nor can it be assumed that inaccurate self-assessments indicate a lack of accurate self-awareness on the part of the student. For an example of the latter, one girl in Raider-Roth's (2005) study noted that although "she might selectively tell all the truth to the outside world, she does not avoid confronting the whole truth inside herself" (p. 128). Creating a safe, constructive way to disclose self-assessments to teachers and peers might be important, however, since justifying one's analysis of one's work to a trusted person or receiving feedback on it might help students calibrate their self-assessments and, thereby, increase realism (Dunning et al., 2004).

CULTURE

Culture is another social influence on students' willingness or ability to self-judge in a verifiable fashion. In some societies, giving oneself a good assessment can be viewed as inappropriate boasting (Brown & Harris, 2013; Leach, 2010). For instance, in Confucian heritage cultures, people are much more constrained from making positive self-assessments by social modesty norms than those from individualistic societies (Kim, Chiu, Peng, Cai, & Tov, 2010; Kwok & Lai, 1993). Being highly confident in oneself is encouraged in other societies (e.g., the United States particularly) and can lead to self-promotion or overrating. In contrast, societies that prioritize equality (e.g., Sweden) or which actively resent genuinely superior performance (e.g., the 'tall poppy syndrome' in the United Kingdom, New Zealand, and Australia) may discourage realistic self-assessment of superior performance or proficiency (Brooks, 2002). The potential effect of cultural and societal norms on student self-assessment seems obvious, but is largely unexamined.

IMPLICATIONS FOR RESEARCH, PRACTICE, TEACHER EDUCATION, AND POLICY

This review has identified the effects of internal psychological factors, interpersonal relations with teachers and peers, and culture on the accuracy and potential usefulness of student self-assessment. The findings from research have many implications for research, policy, and practice, some of which create interesting tensions. In this section, we make suggestions for future research, introduce relatively uncontroversial practical implications, and also discuss the tension between the value of nondisclosure and of feedback about the consistency of a self-assessment with external measures. Following that is a brief discussion of the implications of this review for teacher education and for policy.

Implications for Research

Given the social and interpersonal nature of student self-assessment in classroom contexts, and the great variation in culturally preferred classroom climates and practices, more work needs to be done to understand whether self-assessment is equally effective in all societies. It is possible that in Confucian heritage cultures, for example, the importance placed on high performance and the need to avoid low ranks, combined with the pressure from teachers and parents to continually do better (Brown & Wang, 2013), would discourage or even prevent realistic evaluations. In systems that are highly selective, it is difficult to expect the weakest students in a highly proficient class to realize that their work has some merit. Likewise, students in systems or schools that provide relatively positive and inflated reports of proficiency (e.g., Hattie and Peddie's (2003) description of New Zealand primary school report cards) are unlikely to develop a realistic sense of the quality of their work. The cultural context of self-assessment must be understood by researchers and practitioners.

Wherever self-assessment is being studied, we strongly recommend that researchers clearly define the type of self-assessment they implement as formative or summative, and describe the processes and outcomes of students' self-assessments. We also urge researchers to carefully track and report their efforts to optimize students' honest, evidence-based assessments. Issues related to reliability should be addressed by maximizing the psychometric quality of any criterion used to judge the validity of student self-assessments (e.g., a test, teacher rating, etc.). By taking these steps, our understanding of self-assessment can become much more nuanced and informative.

Practical Implications

The challenges related to accurate, useful student self-assessment in the classroom are complex and not easily resolved. As we continue to develop an understanding of the nature of self-assessment, we must attempt to create the optimal conditions for realism in self-assessment. Problems related to grading and trust/respect can be managed by implementing self-assessment in a context likely to promote accuracy—or at least *not* promote inaccuracy—meaning that self-assessments should not count toward grades, and perhaps, should be private. Social response bias and response style can be managed to some degree by encouraging students to be honest and accurate. If feedback on consistency is given, it must be done in a supportive, constructive manner. Perhaps, consistent with our other work (Andrade, 2010; Brown & Harris, 2014), any attempt to treat student self-assessment as a formal assessment should be eschewed, given the social and psychological reasons for over- or underestimation.

Scaffolding for Self-assessment

There is at least one overarching principle about which most researchers agree: accurate, useful self-assessment demands scaffolding that promotes thoughtful consideration of one's own work and learning. As Epley and Gilovich (2005) put it, when people are overconfident in the accuracy of their assessments, it is because they think too little about the ways in which they might be wrong; errors in assessment are reduced when people "pause for a moment and think a bit harder" (p. 200). Thinking a bit harder about self-assessment can be supported in the classroom in many ways: through how-to instruction, authentic engagement, and practice with feedback in an environment of trust.

More specifically, high quality, verifiable self-assessments are more likely when students (a) are taught how to self-assess (Brown & Harris, 2013; Konopasek, Kelly, Bylund, Wenderoth, & Storey-Johnson, 2014; McDonald, 2013; Ross, 2006), (b) discuss and agree on criteria (which exclude effort) (Brookhart, 2013; Falchikov & Boud, 1989), (c) have experience with the subject (Hu et al., 2015; Morrison, Ross, Sample, & Butler, 2014), and (d) have opportunities to practice self-assessment (Brookhart, Andolina, Zuza, & Furman, 2004; Fastre, van der Klink, & van Merrienboer, 2010; Lopez & Kossack, 2007). Further, we speculate that self-assessments which are used formatively are likely to be accurate and useful because students understand that these are being done in order to support them in deepening their learning and improving their performance.

It is important to note that practice and feedback by themselves are not sufficient to increase accuracy of low achieving students (Hacker, Bol, Horgan, & Rakow, 2000; Nietfeld, Cao, & Osborne, 2005). According to Bol and Hacker (2012), low achieving students tend to need to (a) be helped to reflect, (b) get instruction in or guidelines for monitoring, (c) receive feedback on any initial adjustments, (d) engage in group discussion and evaluation of their understandings with their peers, and (e) receive incentives for improved realism in self-assessments. Miller and Geraci (2011) examined the relation between the accuracy of 81 undergraduate students' predictions of their performance on four exams and (1) extra credit incentives and (2) explicit, concrete feedback. They found that the incentives and feedback were related to improved accuracy for low performing students (but not for higher scores on exams). Because this study did not distinguish between the effects of incentives and feedback, and the effects of incentives on accuracy tend to be mixed (Hacker, Bol, & Bahbahani, 2008), concrete rewards for accuracy should be employed with caution.

Samples of target performances, particularly exemplars, might enhance accuracy if the models are used as benchmarks (Dunning et al., 2004). Exemplification of benchmark performances has been shown to align student self-assessments with expert raters (Hawkins, Osborne, Schofield, Pournaras, & Chester, 2012). Additionally, aspects of the product or performance being evaluated affect student self-assessments: The simpler and more concrete the task (Barnett & Hixon, 1997; Bradshaw, 2001; Hewitt, 2005), and the more specific and concrete the reference criteria (Claes & Salame, 1975), the more similarly students estimated their own performance relative to teachers or tests.

Formative Self-assessment as Self-regulated Learning (SRL)

Another overarching principle for accurate, useful self-assessment is that it should be formative. Including student self-assessments as part of summative course grades introduces high-stakes consequences for honest, accurate evaluations. When a self-evaluation counts toward a total grade or mark, there can be a strong temptation to inflate, especially if there are serious consequences for performance. As we have argued elsewhere (Andrade & Brookhart, 2014; Brown & Harris, 2014) treating self-assessment as a self-regulatory competence is better than using self-evaluations for evaluation or grading purposes.

Self-regulated learners evaluate their own performance and make adaptive attributions linked to deeper processing, better learning and achievement, positive affect, positive efficacy and expectancy judgments, persistence, and effort (Pintrich, 2000). Self-assessment is a core element of self-regulation because it involves focusing student awareness on a task's goals and having students check their progress toward them (Andrade & Brookhart, in press; Boekaerts, 1991). Brown and Harris's (2013) survey of research on self-assessment led them to conclude that there is evidence of a link between self-assessment and better self-regulation skills, "provided such self-evaluation involves deep engagement with the processes affiliated with self-regulation (i.e., goal setting, self-monitoring, and evaluation against valid, objective standards)" (p. 386).

For example, Panadero and his colleagues have explored the relationship between both task-level and process-level self-assessment and SRL in secondary students (Panadero, Alonso-Tapia, & Huertas, 2012) and undergraduates (Panadero et al., 2013; Panadero, Alonso-Tapia, & Huertas, 2014; Panadero & Romero, 2014). They used rubrics to scaffold self-generated task-level feedback, and scripts (i.e., guides to the processes required by a task) for process-level feedback. The results suggest that, in general, students who engaged in self-assessment of their learning were more self-regulated, as measured by self-report questionnaires and/or think aloud protocols, than were students in the comparison groups. Effect sizes were very small but statistically significant.

Process-level self-assessment tended to be more closely associated with SRL than task-level self-assessment. This is probably the case because process-level self-assessment engages students in the processes affiliated with self-regulation (Brown & Harris, 2013). Thus, when we structure self-assessment as formative feedback for students from themselves, we are likely to see enhancements to both their academic performance and self-regulation (Andrade & Brookhart, in press).

Privacy Versus Feedback

An implication of the research on self-assessment that creates a tension is related to disclosure. On the one hand, there are findings from studies that suggest students report dishonest self-ratings when required to disclose them to others (Cowie, 2009; Harris & Brown, 2013; Raider-Roth, 2005). These results strongly imply that self-assessments should be kept private, or students should be assured of anonymity (e.g., handing in their self-assessments with no identifying information attached). The latter approach assumes that the primary benefit of self-assessment is to students, not to teachers, and so could be difficult to implement in a classroom context.

One the other hand, there is some evidence that feedback on the consistency of self-assessments with other measures can improve alignment (Bol & Hacker, 2012; Miller & Geraci, 2011; Dunning et al., 2004; Taylor, 2014). For example, in a study of 82 high school science students, Bol, Hacker, Walck, and Nunnery (2012) found that students who practiced calibration in groups using guidelines showed the greatest accuracy in their predictions and postdictions. Getting feedback requires disclosure, of course; hence the tension with the need for anonymity.

A middle-ground approach involves minimizing socially desirable responding by giving students sufficient time to engage in a task (in this case, self-assessment), avoiding emotional arousal by not associating the task with high stakes (e.g., grades), and minimizing distractions (Paulhus, 1991). Paulhus also recommended that researchers estimate the degree of socially desirable responding with a faking scale (i.e., scales that reveal degrees of self-deceptive positivity, or impression management). Given what we know about the powerful role of feedback in learning (Hattie & Timperley, 2007), it seems wise to find ways to create environments of trust in which students can use non-evaluative, constructive feedback on the usefulness of their self-assessments.

Implications for Teacher Education and for Policy

An obvious implication of this review for teacher education is the need for explicit attention to psychosocial influences on self-assessment. Teachers should be aware of the differences between formative and summative self-assessment, the tensions related to disclosure, and the need for thoughtful scaffolding of self-assessment processes. Preservice teachers should have opportunities to implement student self-assessment practices and reflect on the effectiveness of those practices on different types of students (e.g., high- and low-achievers), adjusting practice accordingly. In addition, preservice teachers are likely to develop an understanding of and appreciation for self-assessment if they experience it as learners themselves.

Although we would love to know that all teachers everywhere are skillfully engaging their charges in accurate, formative self-assessment that deepens learning, increases achievement, and supports self-regulated learning, we stop short of recommending policy that mandates it. While self-assessment should be encouraged, the many issues identified in this review regarding the importance of context, including and especially teacher-student and student-student relationships, suggest that the decision to implement self-assessment should be a local one; there are some classrooms where self-assessment may not be advisable due to the classroom climate.

The consequences of student self-assessment are likely to be positive if it is implemented with consideration of the conditions outlined in this chapter. Under less than optimal conditions, the threats to validity outlined in this chapter will come to bear and might invalidate the construct-relevance of self-assessment. Self-assessment, being highly personal, must be supported and taught so that honest self-reflection and analysis contribute to learning.

REFERENCES

Alsaker, F. D. (1989). School achievement, perceived academic competence and global self-esteem. *School Psychology International, 10*(2), 147–158. doi:10.1177/0143034389102009

Andrade, H. (2010). Students as the definitive source of formative assessment: Academic self-assessment and the self-regulation of learning. In H. Andrade & G. Cizek (Eds.), *Handbook of formative assessment* (pp. 90–105). New York: Routledge.

Andrade, H., & Brookhart, S. (2014). *Toward a theory of assessment as the regulation of learning.* Symposium presentation at the annual meeting of the American Educational Research Association. Philadelphia, PA.

Andrade, H., & Brookhart, S. (in press). The role of classroom assessment in supporting self-regulated learning. In D. Levault & L. Allal (Eds.), *Assessment for learning: Overcoming the challenge of implementation.* Zug, Switzerland: Springer.

Andrade, H., & Du, Y. (2007). Student responses to criteria-referenced self-assessment. *Assessment and Evaluation in Higher Education, 32*(2), 159–181.

Baars, M., Vink, S., van Gog, T., de Bruin, A., & Paas, F. (2014). Effects of training self-assessment and using assessment standards on retrospective and prospective monitoring of problem solving. *Learning & Instruction, 33,* 92–107. doi:10.1016/j.learninstruc.2014.04.004

Barnett, J. E., & Hixon, J. E. (1997). Effects of grade level and subject on student test score predictions. *Journal of Educational Research, 90*(3), 170–174.

Baxter, P., & Norman, G. (2011). Self-assessment or self-deception? A lack of association between nursing students' self-assessment and performance. *Journal of Advanced Nursing, 67*(11), 2406–2413.

Black, P., & Harrison, C. (2001). Self- and peer-assessment and taking responsibility: The science student's role in formative assessment. *School Science Review, 83*(302), 43–49.

Blanch-Hartigan, D. (2011). Medical students' self-assessment of performance: Results from three meta-analyses. *Patient Education and Counseling, 84*(1), 3–9.

Blatchford, P. (1997a). Pupils' self assessments of academic attainment at 7, 11 and 16 years: Effects of sex and ethnic group. *British Journal of Educational Psychology, 67*(2), 169–184.

Blatchford, P. (1997b). Students' self-assessment of academic attainment: Accuracy and stability from 7 to 16 years and influence of domain and social comparison group. *Educational Psychology, 17*(3), 345–359. doi:10.1080/0144341970170308

Boekaerts, M. (1991). Subjective competence, appraisals and self-assessment. *Learning and Instruction, 1,* 1–17.

Bol, L., & Hacker, D. (2012). Calibration research: Where do we go from here? *Frontiers in Psychology, 3,* 229 (Article 29). doi:10.3389/fpsyg.2012.00229

Bol, L., Hacker, D. J., Walck, C., & Nunnery, J. (2012). The effect of individual or group guidelines on the calibration accuracy and achievement of high school biology students. *Contemporary Educational Psychology, 37*(4), 280–287.

Boud, D. (1995a). *Implementing student self-assessment* (2nd ed.). Australian Capital Territory: Higher Education Research and Development Society of Australasia.

Boud, D. (1995b). *Enhancing learning through self-assessment.* London: Kogan Page.

Boud, D., & Falchikov, N. (1989). Quantitative studies of student self-assessment in higher education: A critical analysis of findings. *Higher Education, 18*(5), 529–549.

Bouffard, T., & Narciss, S. (2011). Benefits and risks of positive biases in self-evaluation of academic competence: Introduction. *International Journal of Educational Research, 50*(4), 205–208.

Bouffard, T., Vezeau, C., Roy, M., & Lengele, E. (2011). Stability of biases in self-evaluation and relations to well-being among elementary school children. *International Journal of Educational Research, 50*(4), 221–229.

Bourke, R. (2014). Self-assessment in professional programmes within tertiary institutions. *Teaching in Higher Education, 19*(8), 908–918. doi:10.1080/13562517.2014.934353

Bradshaw, B. K. (2001). Do students effectively monitor their comprehension? *Reading Horizons, 41*(3), 143–154.

Brew, A. (1999). Towards autonomous assessment: Using self-assessment and peer assessment. In S. Brown & A. Glasner (Eds.), *Assessment matters in higher education: Choosing and using diverse approaches* (pp. 159–171). Buckingham, UK: The Society for Research into Higher Education and Open University Press.

Brookhart, S. M. (2013). *How to create and use rubrics for formative assessment and grading.* Alexandria, VA: Association for Supervision & Curriculum Development.

Brookhart, S. M., Andolina, M., Zuza, M., & Furman, R. (2004). Minute math: An action research study of student self-assessment. *Educational Studies in Mathematics, 57*(2), 213–227.

Brooks, V. (2002). *Assessment in secondary schools: The new teacher's guide to monitoring, assessment, recording, reporting and accountability.* Buckingham, UK: Open University Press.

Brown, G., Bull, J., & Pendlebury, M. (1997). *Assessing student learning in higher education.* London: Routledge.

Brown, G.T.L. (2009). The reliability of essay scores: The necessity of rubrics and moderation. In L. H. Meyer, S. Davidson, H. Anderson, R. Fletcher, P. M. Johnston, & M. Rees (Eds.), *Tertiary assessment and higher education student outcomes: Policy, practice and research* (pp. 40–48). Wellington, NZ: Ako Aotearoa.

Brown, G.T.L., Andrade, H., & Chen, F. (2015). Accuracy in student self-assessment: directions and cautions for research. *Assessment in Education: Principles, Policy & Practice, 22*(4), 444–457. doi:10.1080/0969594X.2014.996523

Brown, G.T.L., & Harris, L. R. (2013). Student self-assessment. In J. H. McMillan (Ed.), *The Sage handbook of research on classroom assessment* (pp. 367–393). Thousand Oaks, CA: Sage.

Brown, G.T.L., & Harris, L. R. (2014). The future of self-assessment in classroom practice: Reframing self-assessment as a core competency. *Frontline Learning Research, 3*, 22–30. doi:10.14786/flr.v2i1.24

Brown, G.T.L., Irving, S. E., & Keegan, P. J. (2014). *An introduction to educational assessment, measurement and evaluation: Improving the quality of teacher-based assessment* (3rd ed.). Auckland, NZ: Dunmore Publishing.

Brown, G.T.L., & Wang, Z. (2013). Illustrating assessment: How Hong Kong university students conceive of the purposes of assessment. *Studies in Higher Education, 38*(7), 1037–1057. doi:10.1080/03075079.2011.616955

Brown, S., & Knight, P. (2004). *Assessing learners in higher education.* London: Kogan Page.

Butler, R. (1990). The effects of mastery and competitive conditions on self-assessment at different ages. *Child Development, 61*(1), 201–210.

Butler, R. (2011). Are positive illusions about academic competence always adaptive, under all circumstances: New results and future directions. *International Journal of Educational Research, 50*(4), 251–256. doi:10.1016/j.ijer.2011.08.006

Chang, C.-C., Liang, C., & Chen, Y.-H. (2013). Is learner self-assessment reliable and valid in a Web-based portfolio environment for high school students? *Computers & Education, 60*(1), 325–334.

Chang, C.-C., Tseng, K.-H., & Lou, S.-J. (2012). A comparative analysis of the consistency and difference among teacher-assessment, student self-assessment and peer-assessment in a Web-based portfolio assessment environment for high school students. *Computers & Education, 58*(1), 303–320.

Claes, M., & Salame, R. (1975). Motivation toward accomplishment and the self-evaluation of performances in relation to school achievement. *Canadian Journal of Behavioural Science/Revue canadienne des sciences du comportement, 7*(4), 397–410. doi:10.1037/h0081924

Clarke, S. (2005). *Formative assessment in the secondary classroom.* Abingdon, UK: Hodder Murray.

Cowie, B. (2009). My teacher and my friends helped me learn: Student perceptions and experiences of classroom assessment. In D. M. McInerney, G.T.L. Brown, & G. A. D. Liem (Eds.), *Student perspectives on assessment: What students can tell us about assessment for learning* (pp. 85–105). Charlotte, NC: Information Age Publishing.

Dalton, D., & Ortegren, M. (2011). Gender differences in ethics research: The importance of controlling for the social desirability response bias. *Journal of Business Ethics, 103*, 73–93. doi:10.1007/s10551-011-0843-8

Duckworth, A., & Yeager, D. (2015). Measurement matters: Assessing personal qualities other than cognitive ability for educational purposes. *Educational Researcher, 44*(4), 237–251.

Dunlosky, J., & Nelson, T. O. (1994). Does the sensitivity of Judgments of Learning (JOL) to the effects of various study activities depend on when the JOLs occur? *Journal of Memory and Language, 33*, 545–565.

Dunning, D., Heath, C., & Suls, J. M. (2004). Flawed self-assessment: Implications for health, education, and the workplace. *Psychological Science in the Public Interest, 5*(3), 69–106.

Eccles, J., Wigfield, A., Harold, R. D., & Blumenfeld, P. (1993). Age and gender differences in children's self- and task perceptions during elementary school. *Child Development, 64*(3), 830–847.

Elder, A. D. (2010). Children's self-assessment of their school work in elementary school. *Education 3–13, 38*(1), 5–11.

Epley, N., & Gilovich, T. (2005). When effortful thinking influences judgmental anchoring: Differential effects of forewarning and incentives on self-generated and externally provided anchors. *Journal of Behavioral Decision Making, 18*(3), 199–212.

Falchikov, N. (2005). *Improving assessment through student involvement: Practical solutions for aiding learning in higher and further education.* London: Routledge Falmer.

Falchikov, N., & Boud, D. (1989). Student self-assessment in higher education: A meta-analysis. *Review of Educational Research, 59*(4), 395–430.

Fastre, G. M. J., van der Klink, M. R., & van Merrienboer, J. J. (2010). The effects of performance-based assessment criteria on student performance and self-assessment skills. *Advances in Health Sciences Education, 15*(4), 517–532.

Frey, K. S., & Ruble, D. N. (1987). What children say about classroom performance: Sex and grade differences in perceived competence. *Child Development, 58*(4), 1066–1078.

Gao, M. (2009). Students' voices in school-based assessment of Hong Kong: A case study. In D. M. McInerney, G.T.L. Brown, & G.A.D. Liem (Eds.), *Student perspectives on assessment: What students can tell us about assessment for learning* (pp. 107–130). Charlotte, NC: Information Age Publishing.

Gonida, E., & Leonardi, A. (2011). Patterns of motivation among adolescents with biased and accurate self-efficacy beliefs. *International Journal of Educational Research, 50*(4), 209–220.

Hacker, D. J., Bol, L., & Bahbahani, K. (2008). Explaining calibration accuracy in classroom contexts: the effects of incentives, reflection, and explanatory style. *Metacognition and Learning, 3*, 101–121.

Hacker, D. J., Bol, L., Horgan, D., & Rakow, E. (2000).Test prediction and performance in a classroom context. *Journal of Educational Psychology, 92*(1), 160–170.

Harris, L. R., & Brown, G.T.L. (2013). Opportunities and obstacles to consider when using peer- and self-assessment to improve student learning: Case studies into teachers' implementation. *Teaching and Teacher Education, 36*, 101–111. doi:10.1016/j.tate.2013.07.008

Harris, L. R., Harnett, J., & Brown, G.T.L. (2009). "Drawing" out student conceptions of assessment: Using pupils' pictures to examine their conceptions of assessment. In D. M. McInerney, G.T.L. Brown, & G.A.D. Liem (Eds.), *Student perspectives on assessment: What students can tell us about assessment for learning* (pp. 53–83). Charlotte, NC: Information Age Publishing.

Hattie, J., & Peddie, R. (2003). School reports: "Praising with faint damns". *Set: Research Information for Teachers, 3*, 4–9.

Hattie, J., & Timperley, H. (2007). The power of feedback. *Review of Educational Research, 77*(1), 81–112.

Hawkins, S., Osborne, A., Schofield, S., Pournaras, D., & Chester, J. (2012). Improving the accuracy of self-assessment of practical clinical skills using video feedback: The importance of including benchmarks. *Medical Teacher, 34*(4), 279–284.

Heldsinger, S. A., & Humphry, S. M. (2013). Using calibrated exemplars in the teacher-assessment of writing: An empirical study. *Educational Research, 55*(3), 219–235.

Hewitt, M. P. (2005). Self-evaluation accuracy among high school and middle school instrumentalists. *Journal of Research in Music Education, 53*(2), 148–161.

Higgins, K. M., Harris, N. A., & Kuehn, L. L. (1994). Placing assessment into the hands of young children: A study of student-generated criteria and self-assessment. *Educational Assessment, 2*(4), 309–324. doi:10.1207/s15326977ea0204_3

Hu, Y., Kim, H., Mahmutovic, A., Choi, J., Le, I., & Rasmussen, S. (2015). Verification of accurate technical insight: A prerequisite for self-directed surgical training. *Advances in Health Sciences Education, 20*, 181–191. doi:10.1007/s10459–014–9519–3

Ikeguchi, C. B. (1996). *Self-assessment and ESL competence of Japanese returnees.* Retrieved March 23, 2016 from http://eric.ed.gov/PDFS/ED399798.pdf

Jackson, D. (2014). Self-assessment of employability skill outcomes among undergraduates and alignment with academic ratings. *Assessment & Evaluation in Higher Education, 39*(1), 53–72.

Kaderavek, J. N., Gillam, R. B., Ukrainetz, T. A., Justice, L. M., & Eisenberg, S. N. (2004). School-age children's self-assessment of oral narrative production. *Communication Disorders Quarterly, 26*(1), 37–48. doi:10.1177/15257401040260010401

Karnilowicz, W. (2012). A comparison of self-assessment and tutor assessment of undergraduate psychology students. *Social Behavior and Personality, 40*(4), 591–604.

Kasanen, K., & Räty, H. (2002). "You be sure now to be honest in your assessment": Teaching and learning self-assessment. *Social Psychology of Education, 5*(4), 313–328. doi:10.1023/A:1020993427849

Kasanen, K., Räty, H., & Eklund, A.-L. (2009). Elementary school pupils' evaluations of the malleability of their academic abilities. *Educational Research, 51*(1), 27–38.

Kim, Y. H., Chiu, C. Y., Peng, S., Cai, H., & Tov, W. (2010). Explaining East-West differences in the likelihood of making favorable self-evaluations: The role of evaluation apprehension and directness of expression. *Journal of Cross-Cultural Psychology, 41*(1), 62–75. doi:10.1177/0022022109348921

Kirby, N., & Downs, C. (2007). Self-assessment and the disadvantaged student: Potential for encouraging self-regulated learning? *Assessment and Evaluation in Higher Education, 32*(4), 475–494.

Konopasek, L., Kelly, K. V., Bylund, C. L., Wenderoth, S., & Storey-Johnson, C. (2014). The group objective structured clinical experience: Building communication skills in the clinical reasoning context. *Patient Education and Counseling, 96*, 79–85. doi:10.1016/j.pec.2014.04.003

Kostons, D., van Gog, T., & Paas, F. (2010). Self-assessment and task selection in learner-controlled instruction: Differences between effective and ineffective learners. *Computers & Education, 54*(4), 932–940.

Kuncel, N. R., Credé, M., & Thomas, L. L. (2005). The validity of self-reported grade point averages, class ranks, and test scores: A meta-analysis and review of the literature. *Review of Educational Research, 75*(1), 63–82.

Kwok, D. C., & Lai, D. W. (1993, May). *The self-perception of competence by Canadian and Chinese children.* Paper presented at the annual convention of the Canadian Psychological Association, Montreal, QC.

Laveault, D., & Miles, C. (2002, April). *The study of individual differences in the utility and validity of rubrics in the learning of writing ability.* Paper presented at the annual meeting of the American Educational Research Association, New Orleans, LA.

LaVoie, J. C., & Hodapp, A. F. (1987). Children's subjective ratings of their performance on a standardized achievement test. *Journal of School Psychology, 25*(1), 73–80. doi:10.1016/0022–4405%2887%2990062–8

Leach, L. (2010). Optional self-assessment: Some tensions and dilemmas. *Assessment and Evaluation in Higher Education, 37*(2), 137–147. doi:10.1080/02602938.2010.515013

Lew, M. D., Alwis, W., & Schmidt, H. G. (2010). Accuracy of students' self-assessment and their beliefs about its utility. *Assessment & Evaluation in Higher Education, 35*(2), 135–156.

Lopez, R., & Kossack, S. (2007). Effects of recurring use of self-assessment in university courses. *International Journal of Learning, 14*(4), 203–216.

Maki, R. H., Shields, M., Wheller, A. E., & Zacchilli, T. L. (2005). Individual differences in absolute and relative metacomprehension accuracy. *Journal of Educational Psychology, 97*, 723–731.

Marsh, H. W., Smith, I. D., & Barnes, J. (1983). Multi-trait multi-method analyses of the self-description questionnaire: Student-teacher agreement on multidimensional ratings of student self-concept. *American Educational Research Journal, 20*(3), 333–357.

McDonald, B. (2013). Mentoring and tutoring your students through self-assessment. *Innovations in Education and Teaching International, 50*(1), 62–71.

Miller, T. M., & Geraci, L. (2011). Training metacognition in the classroom: the influence of incentives and feedback on exam predictions. *Metacognition and Learning, 6*(3), 303–314. doi:10.1007/s11409–011–9083–7

Mitman, A. L., & Lash, A. A. (1988). Student's perceptions of their academic standing and classroom behavior. *Elementary School Journal, 89*(1), 55–68.

Morrison, C. A., Ross, L. P., Sample, L., & Butler, A. (2014). Relationship between performance on the NBME comprehensive clinical science self-assessment and USMLE Step 2 Clinical Knowledge for USMGs and IMGs. *Teaching and Learning in Medicine, 26*(4), 373–378.

Nelson, T. O., & Dunlosky, J. (1991). When people's Judgments of Learning (JOLs) are extremely accurate at predicting subsequent recall: The "Delayed-JOL Effect". *Psychological Science, 2*(4), 267–270.

Nelson, T. O., & Narens, L. (1990). Metamemory: A theoretical framework and new findings. *The Psychology of Learning and Motivation, 26*, 125–141.

Ng, J. R., & Earl, J. K. (2008). Accuracy in self-assessment: The role of ability, feedback, self-efficacy and goal orientation. *Australian Journal of Career Development, 17*(3), 39–50.

Nietfeld, J. L., Cao, L., & Osborne, J. W. (2005). Metacognitive monitoring accuracy and student performance in the postsecondary classroom. *The Journal of Experimental Education, 74*(1), 7–28.

Nowell, C., & Alston, R. (2007). I thought I got an A! Overconfidence across the economics curriculum. *Research in Economic Education, 38*(2), 131–142.

Panadero, E., Alonso-Tapia, J., & Huertas, J. A. (2012). Rubrics and self-assessment scripts effects on self-regulation, learning and self-efficacy in secondary education. *Learning and Individual Differences, 22*(6), 806–813. doi.org/10.1016/j.lin- dif.2012.04.007

Panadero, E., Alonso-Tapia, J., & Huertas, J. A. (2014). Rubrics vs. self-assessment scripts: Effects on first year university students' self-regulation and performance. *Journal for the Study of Education and Development, 3*(7), 149–183. doi:0.1080/02103702.2014.881655

Panadero, E., Alonso-Tapia, J., & Reche, E. (2013). Rubrics vs. self-assessment scripts effect on self-regulation, performance and self-efficacy in pre-service teachers. *Studies in Educational Evaluation, 39*(3), 125–132. doi:10.1016/j.stueduc.2013.04.001

Panadero, E., Brown, G.T.L., & Strijbos, J-W. (2014, August). *The future of student self-assessment: Known unknowns and probable directions.* Paper presented at the biennial conference of the Assessment & Evaluation SIG, EARLI, Madrid, Spain.

Panadero, E., & Romero, M. (2014). To rubric or not to rubric? The effects of self-assessment on self-regulation, performance and self-efficacy. *Assessment in Education: Principles, Policy & Practice, 21*(2), 133–148. doi:10 .1080/0969594X.2013.877872

Paulhus, D. L. (1991). Measurement and control of response bias. In J. Robinson, P. Shaver, & L. Wrightsman (Eds.), *Measures of personality and social psychological attitudes: Vol. 1* (pp. 17–59). New York: Academic Press.

Peterson, E. R., & Irving, S. E. (2008). Secondary school students' conceptions of assessment and feedback. *Learning and Instruction, 18*(3), 238–250.

Pintrich, P. R. (2000). Multiple goals, multiple pathways: The role of goal orientation in learning and achievement. *Journal of Educational Psychology, 92,* 544–555.

Powel, W. D., & Gray, R. (1995). Improving performance predictions by collaboration with peers and rewarding accuracy. *Child Study Journal, 25*(2), 141–154.

Raider-Roth, M. B. (2005). Trusting what you know: Negotiating the relational context of classroom life. *Teachers College Record, 107*(4), 587–628.

Ross, J. A. (2006). The reliability, validity, and utility of self-assessment. *Practical Assessment Research & Evaluation, 11*(10). Retrieved March 16, 2007 from http://pareonline.net/getvn.asp?v=11&n=10

Ross, J. A., Hogaboam-Gray, A., & Rolheiser, C. (2002). Student self-evaluation in Grade 5–6 mathematics: Effects on problem-solving achievement. *Educational Assessment, 8*(1), 43–59.

Ross, J. A., Rolheiser, C., & Hogaboam-Gray, A. (1998). Skills training versus action research in-service: Impact on student attitudes to self-evaluation. *Teaching and Teacher Education, 14*(5), 463–477.

Ross, J. A., Rolheiser, C., & Hogaboam-Gray, A. (2002). Influences on Student Cognitions about Evaluation. *Assessment in Education: Principles, Policy & Practice, 9*(1), 81–95.

Saavedra, R., & Kwun, S. K. (1993). Peer evaluation in self-managing work groups. *Journal of Applied Psychology, 78*(3), 450–462. doi:10.1037/0021–9010.78.3.450

Sadler, P. M., & Good, E. (2006). The impact of self- and peer-grading on student learning. *Educational Assessment, 11*(1), 1–31.

Stipek, D. J. (1981). Children's perceptions of their own and their classmates' ability. *Journal of Educational Psychology, 73*(3), 404–410. doi:10.1037/0022–0663.73.3.404

Stipek, D. J., & Tannatt, L. M. (1984). Children's judgments of their own and their peers' academic competence. *Journal of Educational Psychology, 76*(1), 75–84. doi:10.1037/0022–0663.76.1.75

Sung, Y.-T., Chang, K.-E., Chang, T.-H., & Yu, W.-C. (2010). How many heads are better than one? The reliability and validity of teenagers' self- and peer assessments. *Journal of Adolescence, 33*(1), 135–145.

Tan, K. (2004). Does student self-assessment empower or discipline students? *Assessment & Evaluation in Higher Education, 29*(6), 651–662.

Tan, K. (2009). Meanings and practices of power in academics' conceptions of student self-assessment. *Teaching in Higher Education, 14*(4), 361–373.

Taras, M. (2008). Issues of power and equity in two models of self-assessment. *Teaching in Higher Education, 13*(1), 81–92.

Taras, M. (2010). Student self-assessment: Processes and consequences. *Teaching in Higher Education, 15*(2), 199–209. doi:10.1080/13562511003620027

Taylor, S. N. (2014). Student self-assessment and multisource feedback assessment: Exploring benefits, limitations, and remedies. *Journal of Management Education, 38*(3), 359–383.

Tierney, R. D. (2013). Fairness in classroom assessment. In J. H. McMillan (Ed.), *Sage handbook of research on classroom assessment* (pp. 125–144). Thousand Oaks, CA: Sage.

Tyson, K., Darity, W., & Castellino, D. R. (2005). It's not "a Black Thing": Understanding the burden of acting white and other dilemmas of high achievement. *American Sociological Review, 70*(4), 582–605. doi:10.1177/000312240507000403

Wall, D., Singh, D., Whitehouse, A., Hassell, A., & Howes, J. (2012). Self-assessment by trainees using self-TAB as part of the team assessment of behaviour multisource feedback tool. *Medical Teacher, 34*(2), 165–167.

Watt, H. M. (2000). Measuring attitudinal change in mathematics and English over the 1st year of junior high school: A multidimensional analysis. *Journal of Experimental Education, 68*(4), 331–361. doi:http://dx.doi.org/10.1080/00220970009600642

Wilson, J., & Wright, C. R. (1993). The predictive validity of student self-evaluations, teachers' assessments, and grades for performance on the verbal reasoning and numerical ability scales of the differential aptitude test for a sample of secondary school students attending rural Appalachia schools. *Educational and Psychological Measurement, 53*(1), 259–270. doi:10.1177/0013164493053001029

19

CLASSROOM PROCESSES THAT SUPPORT EFFECTIVE ASSESSMENT

Bronwen Cowie and Christine Harrison

INTRODUCTION

Assessment "does not objectively measure what is already there, but rather creates and shapes what is measured—it is capable of 'making up people'" (Stobart, 2008, p. 1). While Stobart was referring to the impact of testing, including national testing, the same is true of the formal and informal assessment practices that are embedded in and accomplished through everyday classroom routines, activities, and interactions. Classroom assessment makes up people (i.e., what it means to be a teacher or a student) and constructs and measures curriculum (i.e., what counts as valued knowledge and ways of expressing and representing this). Curriculum, pedagogy, and evaluation (assessment) act as message systems (Bernstein, 1971), collectively shaping students' understandings of schooling and of themselves as learners and members of society. While it is not possible to disentangle curriculum, pedagogy, and assessment, the relationships among them can be productive and synergetic or characterised by tensions and contradictions. In this chapter, we focus on how classroom assessment practices, both formal and informal, can effectively benefit student learning and learner motivation. We acknowledge that classroom assessment can be used to inform, evaluate, and credential student learning and teacher and school practice, but our focus is on its formative function in learning. The goal of formative assessment is not just to support and motivate student learning, but also to ensure that students develop identities where they see themselves as capable learners (Shepard, 2000).

Within this chapter, classroom assessment includes all activities within the classroom that involve the interpretation of and action on evidence of student learning. Students modify their learning and how they identify themselves as learners using evidence drawn from formal displays of knowing and informal acknowledgments of achievement. This evidence can shape a student's sense of self in ways that are affirming or it can lead to situations where students ignore their own learning purposes in favour of artificial targets embedded in assessments. The difficulty here is the public nature of classroom assessment, where students respond not only to the feedback they receive from their teacher, but also to how they perceive teachers' feedback to peers and feedback among peers.

Irrespective of the source of evidence, judgments and actions based on this information have social, emotional, and intellectual consequences for students.

ESTABLISHING THE PARAMETERS FOR CLASSROOM ASSESSMENT

Typically, classroom assessment encompasses both summative uses and diverse formative practices that include teachers specifying learning goals and criteria for quality, questioning, engaging in dialogue and feedback, and facilitating peer and self-assessment (Black & Wiliam, 1998). It is also likely to include regular tests, quizzes, and exercises to inform teacher reporting of student achievement and progress to others. Additionally, various activities to prepare students for written or oral examinations used for qualifications purposes may be considered classroom assessment. In practice, teachers can spend from a quarter to a third of their professional time engaged in assessment related activities (Stiggins, 2008). If this assessment is done well, then students prosper, but if it is done badly, then this can affect students' prospects, aspirations, and attitudes to learning.

Assessment cannot, and should not, stand alone in the education system (Pellegrino, 2010); at all levels (classroom, school, district/state/nation) it needs to align with curriculum and instruction so that these three message systems are directed toward the same ends and mutually reinforce each other. Only when curriculum goals and aims are clearly defined, recognized, and valued is it then possible to produce an assessment system that supports and augments the curriculum. In many cases however, curricula are ill-defined and teachers, therefore, use the confines of the assessment system to determine their teaching approach and focus. This approach to assessment can constrain how curricula are enacted and experienced (Crooks, 1988), all the more so because assessment issues are complex and testing practices are products of historical and societal contexts and expectations (Black, Harrison, Lee, Marshall, & William, 2003). At the same time, teachers' own views of assessment and of its demands on them have profound effects on their teaching, even to the extent of making them feel obliged to teach in ways they do not value (Bonner, this volume), which may in turn distort their students' experience of curriculum. Similarly, students are not passive consumers in assessment. Learning may not be the only, or even the most important, goal they pursue at any given time. Their understanding of likely teacher assessment purposes and consequences has been shown to shape what they are willing to disclose, how they interpret teacher feedback, and the value they accord to this feedback (Cowie, 2005).

ELABORATING A FORMATIVE APPROACH TO CLASSROOM ASSESSMENT

Black and Wiliam's (1998) survey of evidence linking assessment with improved learning has significantly influenced how educators and policy makers have conceptualised assessment over the last two decades. Black & Wiliam drew on Sadler's (1989) emphasis on the importance of feedback to assist student self-monitoring to close the gap between current and desired performance. Inherent in Sadler's conception of classroom assessment is that both teachers and students must understand and act upon data. This led Black and Wiliam to highlight the teacher's role in feedback and student actions in response to guidance. In doing so, they shifted the focus to how assessment is part of the dynamic interaction between teachers and students whereby teachers learn about their students and their own teaching, while students learn about the viability of their ideas. Thus understood, action on assessment data either by way of feedback or more informed decision-making and action is fundamental to formative assessment (Andrade & Cizek, 2010; Black & Wiliam, 1998, 2009; Sadler, 1989).

Scholars have continued to debate the definition and value of formative assessment and assessment for learning (Bennett, 2011; Black & Wiliam, 2009; Kingston & Nash, 2011; Klenowski, 2009; Swaffield, 2011). There has been an increasing emphasis on students taking an active role in their own learning and assessment processes and recognition that formative assessment needs to enable and empower students to learn how to learn and to motivate them to keep on learning. In this view, assessment is considered sustainable only if it "meets the needs of the present without compromising the ability of students to meet their own future learning needs" (Boud, 2000, p. 151), where this includes affiliation with a discipline and the capacity and motivation to continue to learn and use its ideas (Cowie & Moreland, 2015; Willis, 2011). Hence, assessment activities must address immediate student needs (e.g., certification or feedback on their current learning status) while also contributing to their future learning.

The recent focus on students engaging in inquiry and understanding how knowledge is generated and legitimated adds another layer to the meaning of the gap Sadler (1989) described in his definition of formative assessment. Simultaneously, this focus has the potential to enhance the role classroom assessment plays in student learning over the long term. Indeed, inquiry and formative assessment are natural partners (Harlen, 2013). Inquiry offers new and different opportunities and imperatives for students to exercise agency and authority in learning, assessment, and feedback. For their next inquiry steps to be informed and strategic, students need to monitor their progress towards their goals. Teachers need to monitor where students are in relation to learning goals in order to provide useful guidance. In technology education, for example, product specifications double as success criteria (Cowie, Moreland, & Otrel-Cass, 2013). Within this dynamic, student understanding of how and why different disciplines generate knowledge can serve as both a means and an end for learning and assessment.

FORMATIVE ASSESSMENT STRATEGIES AND TECHNIQUES

The Assessment Reform Group (ARG) in the U.K. has been at the forefront of challenging thinking about assessment for learning and formative practice by ensuring that research-based principles guide classroom practice. The ARG (2002) suggested that there are ten principles of AfL, which suggest assessment should be:

- part of effective planning,
- focusing on how students learn,
- central to classroom practice,
- a key professional skill,
- generated in sensitive and constructive ways,
- able to foster motivation,
- promoting understanding of goals and criteria,
- helping learners know how to improve,
- developing capacity for self-assessment, and
- recognizing all educational achievement

What is important to note in relation to this list is that while all assessment requires some way of collecting evidence of learning, followed by analysis and judgments of that evidence, realisation of the formative potential of classroom assessment relies on the synergistic interaction of these principles. Activities that offer opportunity for formative assessment involve a mosaic of tools, routines, and practices that are often embedded within one another and occur as a linked sequence (Cowie & Moreland, 2015; Riggan & Oláh, 2011; Torrance & Pryor, 2001). For example, a teacher might plan probing questions and then organise students to discuss answers in pairs, so that s/he might listen in to the conversations to collect evidence of learning. More specifically, whether or not assessment practice in a classroom is formative depends on the extent that evidence is used by teachers, students, and their peers to make decisions and take actions to enhance learning (Black & Wiliam, 2009). A teacher's formative action may be to continue as planned, to change course immediately or at some later time, or to seek more information. What is important is that teacher actions and subsequent activities are responsive to the complexity of the factors underlying variations in student interests, understanding, and achievement. We review a number of learning techniques that have been studied somewhat more extensively.

Role of the Teacher

Teachers need to plan assessment opportunities into their lessons so that both they and their students can check their understandings as learning is taking place. While some teachers might use diagnostic tests and quizzes at key points, others structure classroom activities to provide interactive assessment opportunities (Cowie & Bell, 1999). More formal and planned activities have the advantage of enabling teachers to step back at key points during instruction to check student understanding against their intended curriculum. Formative assessment possibilities also arise within the run of normal classroom interactions and activities in a less formal way (Cowie & Bell, 1999; Ruiz-Primo, 2011). Informal formative interactions (e.g., listening in to conversations or one-to-one discussions) tend to be contingent, personalised, and quick cycle with information generated and used in the same context, drawing on immediate resources (e.g., available physical resources or student-peer ideas). Teacher responsiveness in this case depends to a considerable extent on his or her pedagogical content knowledge (Cowie et al., 2013; Harris, 2015). On the other hand, if teachers have rehearsed possible student ideas and actions, they can anticipate and prepare for at least some of the actions and feedback that they might productively use (Cowie & Bell, 1999). In practice, teachers need to establish a balance between planned formative assessment and contingent responsive assessment because they each create different assessment situations and opportunities for teacher and student learning and action.

We agree with Heritage (2010) when she advocates for investment in teachers rather than tools. Teachers need time and support to think through the principles of formative assessment, and to re/consider their role in the learning process and how to empower their students (Hawe & Parr, 2014; James & Pedder, 2006; Webb & Jones, 2009). Formative assessment, especially when carried out on the fly, places substantial demands on teachers' knowledge of curriculum, subject content, pedagogy, and their students (Bell & Cowie, 2001). Teachers face the dilemma of what to pay attention to within the dynamics of classroom activity; how to make sense of the information they notice; what, if any, relevance a particular idea or action has for students' short- and long-term learning; and how to respond in a manner that will be understood, valued, and acted upon by students. Such sense-making is a complex process that entails detecting relevant cues, attributing retrospective meaning, and integrating this in a plausible narrative that allows understanding of a situation and sets the stage for action. At the same time, it is important to recognise that each of these activities is a socially situated and emotionally charged process embedded in and accomplished through interactions between teachers and students where these interactions are shaped by the resources and features of the immediate cultural, material, and organisational setting (Cowie et al., 2013; Hermansen & Nerland, 2014; Weick, Sutcliffe, & Obstfeld, 2005). Thus, it is not surprising that it is often only after 18 months or more of teacher professional learning that there is a significant shift in student achievement; students as well as teachers need time to change and this needs to be taken into account (Hayward & Hedge, 2005; Lai & Schildkamp, this volume; McNaughton, Lai, & Hsiao, 2012; Wiliam, Lee, Harrison & Black, 2004).

Teachers need to have an understanding of how learning in a specific area progresses. *Learning progressions* aim to provide such an overview. While the notion of progression has long been embedded in curriculum learning objectives, researchers recently have expended considerable energy in developing and investigating the efficacy of progressions derived from empirical studies of learning and from an interpretation of growing complexity within a topic (Black, Wilson, & Yao, 2011). While there is still considerable research to be done to ensure that learning progressions provide a comprehensive and useful framework to aid formative judgment and action, they are being promoted as a promising approach to aligning standards, curriculum, and assessment (Shea & Duncan, 2013). The argument is that by linking classroom assessments to learning progressions, teachers will have access to resources to elicit student understanding and for interpreting and taking instructional action on the basis of what students know. In considering these possible benefits, it is important that the notion of learning progressions is not conflated with 'standards' that mandate what students should know and be able to do at times in their schooling. It is also important to keep in mind that teacher interpretation of student responses to classroom assessments linked to a learning progression can be problematic. Teachers still need to know what action to take (Brown, 2013; Furtak, Morrison, & Kroog, 2014). These studies also illustrate the challenge in finding a useful grain size; what length and depth of a progression is useful to teachers on a moment-to-moment and day-to-day basis? At this time, it appears that professional development that attends to teacher understanding of student thinking and how students learn is needed to realize the potential learning progressions have to offer.

Shared Criteria and Goals

To enable students to take charge of their learning progress, it is essential that teachers share their goals for student learning alongside criteria describing quality performance, as these help students begin to understand teacher expectations. However, the level of specificity and the ways these are introduced, co-constructed, and/or negotiated (i.e., "social construction of judgment" [Torrance, 2012, p. 338]) has potential to narrow down or open up the curriculum. A weakness in many approaches to formative assessment, in practice, has been an overreliance on checking attainment against a set of predetermined objectives and the use of a tightly sequenced set of criteria or learning objectives (Swaffield, 2011). In this case, success can default to criteria compliance and what Torrance and Pryor (1998) refer to as convergent assessment; this contrasts with divergent assessment, where the focus is on finding out what a student actually understands and can do. This latter approach opens up space for new learning goals and criteria to emerge and/ or to be introduced and developed as they become salient (Sadler, 1989; Torrance, 2012). This said, Pryor and Crossouard (2008) emphasise that both forms have their place in a classroom when a teacher is working to develop student curricular learning *and* to assist students to appreciate the wider relevance of what they are learning (Willis, 2011). Managing this dynamic is not easy and requires pedagogy that gives careful attention to the interplay of assessment, curriculum, and student learning.

Questioning

Teacher questioning is a key strategy in eliciting evidence of learning and supporting students to construct meaning and apply knowledge (Black et al., 2003; Dekker-Groen, Van der Schaaf, & Stokking, 2015). The 'to and fro' of classroom talk provides the vehicle for shared understanding and feedback that can drive learning. To be effective in guiding learning, teacher questions need to tap into students' thinking and emerging understanding (Chinn, 2007), rather than simply check recognition of key terms. Wait time, after posing a question, is essential in supporting student thinking (Rowe, 1986): when teachers provide wait time, students give longer responses and provide more evidence for their ideas and conclusions (Black et al., 2003). Students also ask more questions and talk more to other students when teachers show interest in their replies.

Careful preparation of questions is recommended as part of teacher planning for learning and assessment (Black et al., 2003). Productive questions are strategic in that they focus on 'big' ideas and foster dialogue that stimulates students to question their own thinking (Harrison, 2006). Wiliam (2011) advocates the use of 'hinge point' questions as a structured approach to eliciting student ideas related to intended learning goals. Hinge point questions use multiple-choice format and provide a quick check on the understanding within a class. Constructing these questions is challenging because the answers and distractors must allow teachers to ensure that the correct answer was given for the correct underlying reasoning. This is quite a high expectation of a teacher's assessment capabilities. Recognising this, and in response to the value accorded to formative assessment as a lever for school improvement (Clarke, 2012; OCED, 2013), a number of publishers have produced banks of assessment items. These formalized formative assessment systems allow for the assessment of student progress and the production of reports that identify students, or particular aspects of the curriculum, that require special attention (Brown, 2013). They can also incorporate the provision of automated feedback (Wilson, Olinghouse, & Andrada, 2014). These formalized tools hold the potential to be educative and supportive of teachers and students. However, there is also the potential of disconnect between what is taught and what they measure and the possibility that they can be used to position learning gaps as problems rather than opportunities. Consequently, their merits are currently a subject of debate (Bennett, 2011).

Pedder, James, and MacBeath (2005) stress that student autonomy, assessment for learning's goal, relies on student initiative. Students' questions, resulting from their realization of a gap in their knowledge and/or their desire to extend their knowledge, are one example of such initiative taking. The act of questioning requires students to engage in critical reflection and action on their current understanding (Chin & Osborne, 2008). Students taking the initiative to ask a question can be considered a student formative self-assessment action. At the same time, student questions provide evidence to teachers about student interests and areas of confusion and need. A series of student questions on the same idea can alert a teacher to the likely depth and breadth of understanding and knowledge in a class (Chinn, 2007). This said, student willingness to pose questions depends on teachers establishing a classroom culture where student ideas are respected and questioning is viewed as integral to learning. It may also be seen as inappropriate in some cultures.

Across a number of nations, evidence is emerging that students make a conscious decision about whether it is worth the effort or the risk of answering or asking a question (Cowie, 2005; Raider-Roth, 2005; Stiggins, 2008). Students are aware that teachers question them for a variety of purposes, making them only able to know their teacher's purpose through her response to their answer (Cowie, 2005; Smith & Higgins, 2006). Problematically for students, teacher responses can affirm their sense of self as a learner, contributing to their learning, or embarrass and undermine them in front of their peers. On the other hand, and problematic for teachers, students juggle multiple, often contradictory, agendas and goals, among which the learning their teacher intended is only one. Hence, student questions may not be reflective of student ideas or a desire to progress their learning (Brown & Harris, 2013; Cowie, 2005; Raider-Roth, 2005).

Feedback

While the teacher role in deciding when and how to assess matters, it is the feedback that students receive that drives learning. A number of reviews have elaborated on the nature of effective teacher feedback (Hattie & Timperley, 2007; Nicol & Macfarlane, 2006; Shute, 2008). These studies highlight that students are aware of the different kinds of feedback their teachers provide and point to the benefits of teacher feedback that is descriptive (i.e., specific to the task and focused on constructing and/or negotiating achievement and ways forward) (Tunstall & Gipps, 1996). Ideally, feedback is a dialogue that generates ideas for improvement (rather than praise or directives), as such ideas are more likely to be accepted and acted upon by students (Cowie, 2005; Hargreaves, 2013). When teacher feedback is embedded in informal interaction, the processes of assessment and feedback are often conflated and indistinguishable (Moss, Pullin, Haertel, Gee, & Young, 2008). Regardless, teachers need to allow time for students to reflect and act on any feedback, otherwise students will fail to see its value or realise its benefit (Gamlem & Smith, 2013).

Student action in response to feedback information is fundamental, and the impact of feedback depends just as much on how students perceive and act on it as it does on what it includes and when and how it is provided (Andrade & Cizek, 2010; Cowie, 2005; Dann, 2014; Gamlem & Smith, 2013; Hattie & Gan, 2011; Lipnevich, Berg, & Smith, this volume; Perrenoud, 1998). Indeed, feedback can be accepted, rejected, or modified by learners for a variety of reasons, both personal and situational; each of these student responses has different consequences for future learning (Kluger & DeNisi, 1996). Thus, the challenge for teachers is not just to provide feedback, but around how to provide it in ways that their students understand, value, and respond to (Torrance, 2012).

Recent research demonstrates that oral and written feedback that scaffolds students by providing the structure needed for independence is generally more effective than simple outcome feedback (Hattie & Gan, 2011; Shute 2008). There are many overlaps between scaffolding and formative assessment; in both teachers strategically provide various forms of material, social, linguistic, or conceptual assistance aimed at supporting students' reasoning, participation, and learning (Sawyer, 2006). A critical component of scaffolding is 'fading,' in which teachers gradually withdraw their support and hand over control to students as they develop their understanding and capabilities (Murtagh, 2014; Pea, 2004). Kangu, Thompson, and Windschitl (2014) demonstrated that factors such as when and how to remove support is crucially important in shaping student learning and self-regulation. Hence, scaffolding can be seen to support the principles of student empowerment and autonomy.

Students interpret and take action on feedback for a variety of reasons that include their beliefs about a subject area, their goals at the time, and their understanding of the task/context (Andrade, 2010). Students may, for example, lack the requisite domain knowledge and understanding to act on feedback. Students who focus on learning goals are more likely to view feedback as a joint teacher-student responsibility and to prefer teacher feedback in the form of suggestions. Students with performance goals tend to view assessment as the teacher's responsibility and see no role for themselves in seeking help to extend their understanding (Cowie, 2005). This, coupled with the widely acknowledged impact of feedback on student motivation (Stiggins, 2008), sense of self as a successful or unsuccessful learner, and relationships with peers and the subject area (Cowie, 2005), underpins moves to argue that feedback needs to encompass a careful consideration of the epistemological, ontological, and practical aspects (Sutton, 2012). This would seem to be a priority area for further development.

Sharing Power

Assessment that fosters student capacity to independently monitor and progress their own learning requires the renegotiation of teacher and student roles (Harrison, 2005; Webb & Jones, 2009). Several studies have foregrounded the influence of teacher understandings of learning as a social process and collective responsibility. For instance, Marshall and Drummond (2006) distinguished between classrooms where the 'letter' of formative assessment was put in place (teachers used the recommended strategies) and classrooms consistent with the 'spirit' of formative assessment (students were empowered to take and share responsibility for their learning and assessment as social processes). They found that when learning was regarded as the responsibility of the individual learner, failure to develop autonomy was blamed on the student's lack of readiness. When learning was seen as the shared responsibility of the teacher and the student, teachers enacted the strategies in ways that generated classroom cultures where challenge, reflection, and making mistakes were viewed as part of learning and autonomy was more often seen as an outcome.

While teachers sharing control of the learning has been recognised as essential in developing student self-assessment and autonomy (Gipps, 2002; Webb & Jones, 2009), it is something many teachers seem to struggle with. Marshall and Drummond (2006) found around 80% of the teachers in their study fell into this category. To date, however, only limited research has sought to understand the emotional aspect of assessment for teachers as they move to share power in the classroom (Cowie, Otrel-Cass, Glynn, & Kara, 2011; Pryor & Crossouard, 2008) and when they are faced with the need to manage potentially conflicting demands on their time and assessment priorities (Harrison, 2005; Steinberg, 2008). Unfortunately, as the external demands on teachers to give an account of and account for student achievement increase, teachers will likely have more difficulty promoting learning through assessment (Brown, 2004). This, coupled with the demands of high-stakes assessment, has the potential to overshadow and refocus teachers away from the formative potential of classroom assessment (OECD, 2013; Ratnam-Lim & Tan, 2015).

Peer Assessment

Peer assessment has been shown to have positive effects on student motivation and engagement in learning (Topping, 2013) and more regular use can also foster better attitudes towards collaborative work (Falchikov, 2001). In these classroom situations, peers use one another as a resource, both sharing their ideas and evaluating the ideas of others. Peer discussion potentially provides a safe environment for learners to reveal their thinking and allows it to be challenged by others. Peers can provide useful feedback because of their familiarity with the context, the language they use, and the immediacy of the feedback they are able to provide. Students can use peer feedback to reflect on their initial understanding and, if they consider it necessary, adapt their explanations before they submit it to more public scrutiny by the whole class or to expert diagnosis by their teacher. One innovative example of this approach is through the use of concept cartoons (Keogh & Naylor, 1999), where learners are presented with a cartoon depicting the reactions of several children to a problem-solving situation or a scientific phenomenon, and the learners are asked to discuss their *own* thinking about the situation and the responses provided. Through the ensuing discussion, ideas can be tried out and evaluated, alternative conceptions considered, and mistakes recognised and dealt with. While such resources are useful at eliciting pre-knowledge, they are equally useful in determining learner competence later in a teaching sequence. However, this iterative approach to classroom assessment requires teachers to hone their listening skills and to carefully consider when and when not to intervene as they evaluate student discussion. It also requires them to conceptualize their role as guiding and supporting, rather than simply correcting student ideas.

At the same time, peer assessment is a complex social and emotional interactional process (Brown & Harris, 2013; Panadero, this volume; Topping, 2013; van Gennip, Segers, & Tillema, 2009). Students' interpersonal and academic perceptions and relations can influence their learning from peer assessment (van Gennip et al., 2009). For example, students may consider their friendship with peers, the fairness of peer scoring (Kaufman & Schunn, 2011), and the potential negative effects of remarks to peers (Cowie, 2005) when providing feedback. They may also have limited trust in themselves or peers as assessors (Liu & Carless, 2006).

Social and Cultural Settings of the Classroom

Studies focused on student classroom experiences have highlighted the need to develop assessment as part of the classroom learning culture (Shepard, 2000; Stobart, 2008), including consideration of the social-emotional milieu of the classroom. Specifically, it is necessary to have a classroom climate of trust and respect from and between the teacher and peers as this influences student participation in assessment practices, including their response to feedback (Brown, Andrade, & Chen, 2015; Carless, 2009; Cowie, 2005). In seeking to make sense of student and teacher expectations for and experiences of assessment, we also need to remember these are shaped by schools as social institutions; formative assessment practices challenge conventional understanding of teacher and student roles, responsibilities, and authority.

The teacher's stance and actions are critical in developing a classroom culture that supports the sharing and debate of ideas and explanations in a manner that is accepting of individual differences. For this to work effectively in the classroom, the social rules of a classroom (Pryor & Crossouard, 2008) need to include the expectation that students will exercise some critical agency by contributing their experiences, instigating inquiries, and/or providing constructive feedback. When this is the case, students have an opportunity to contribute to the classroom curriculum, which can enhance their affiliation with the learning area and learning (Cowie, 2013). However, because students are differently positioned with respect to these rules of the game, a 'meta-social' element in classroom dialogue is needed to support students' awareness of social aspects, such as the obligation to provide only constructive feedback to peers (Pryor & Crossouard, 2008).

SUMMATIVE ASSESSMENT AS PART OF
CLASSROOM ASSESSMENT

The increased emphasis on the formative potential of classroom assessment has in no way diminished teachers' responsibility to report on students' overall progress and achievement in a specific area of learning at a particular time (i.e., summative assessment). Indeed, the increased demand on teachers to provide an account of and for student learning has focused attention on teacher capacity to summarise student achievement. Given that summative assessment practices and results are often high-stakes, it is important that teacher summative classroom practices have a positive impact on teaching, as well as student learning and motivation. Teachers need to be able to select or design valid and reliable assessment tasks that align with curriculum goals and instructional practices and balance the needs of learners and learning with accountability and reporting aspects (Colbert, Wyatt-Smith, & Klenowski, 2012; Stobart, 2008). Tensions arising from their dual responsibility for formative and summative assessment mean that classroom assessment can be demanding for teachers (Black et al., 2003; Hume & Coll, 2009). In part, this is because summative assessment works on the premise that students are responsible for their own results and teachers are expected to maintain an emotional distance between themselves as assessor and students as the ones being assessed. By way of contrast, formative assessment generally assumes teachers are jointly responsible with students for their progress.

Studies in a number of countries have found teacher moderation practices are generally underdeveloped or absent (Allal, 2013; Hay & Macdonald, 2008). With regard to judging student achievement, it seems that teachers often use idiosyncratic and flexible criteria when making summative judgments (Allal, 2013; Friedman & Frisbie, 1995), with these criteria including student effort and attitude. However, even individual acts of judgment carried out in isolation and with autonomy are shaped by the collective practices of a professional community (Allal, 2013). Wyatt-Smith, Klenowski, and Gunn (2010) have suggested that having standards alone is insufficient in accounting for how the teachers ascribe value and award grades to student work. This indicates that social moderation processes have an important role in developing shared assessment understandings and practices amongst a group of teachers, although this can take time (Hermansen & Nerland, 2014).

Improved teacher summative assessment practice requires sustained commitment over several years (Black et al., 2011; Lai & Schildkamp, this volume). Black et al. (2011) suggest that teachers begin by auditing their existing practices and then sharing, reflecting on, and developing their summative assessment practices through the use of portfolios and/or social moderation exercises. What is important here is that teachers not only consider the reliability of their judgements, but also the validity of the assessments they administer, considering how closely individual assessment activities and overall assessment processes fit with the intended goals of learning (Newton & Shaw, 2014). Classroom assessment needs to make visible and valuable the full breadth of what students know and can do, and it needs to do this for all students, preferably in a way that supports productive action on this information (Moss et al., 2008)

Interestingly, marked differences between English and mathematics teachers have been reported during moderation of student work (Black et al., 2011). Mathematics teachers had concerns about variation in the support given to students as tasks were introduced and while students were completing them. English teachers, conversely, accepted that teacher input and support would and should vary and trusted their colleagues to rationalise this as part of their judgment of work quality. English teachers believed that classroom contextual factors were key to understanding the demands and students' subsequent performances. They refused to 'blind mark' students' work as part of the moderation process. Instead, they preferred to examine marked work and decide if they agreed or disagreed with the final holistic teacher judgment. By doing this, they validated the judgments made, trusting that the teacher who undertook the assessment factored in the support given during the process. What is evident here is that the way assessment practices are taken up by one subject community may be very different, and not understood, by a different subject community.

Classroom Assessment Responding to Change

Teachers implementing classroom assessment practices need to take into account many factors to ensure their assessments are validly enacted to support of learning (Bonner, 2013). These include consideration of student characteristics (e.g., culture, disabilities, language proficiency), the emotional dynamics of assessment, and the needs of diverse stakeholders within the education system, including parents. Student backgrounds, values, and agendas influence what and how they learn, and assessment needs to take account of this (Gipps & Murphy, 1994; Moon, this volume; Stobart, 2005). There is compelling evidence that we need to move beyond a focus on variation in student ideas and capabilities as an obstacle to be overcome to a stance whereby diversity becomes a resource enriching the curricular learning of all students and of teachers (Cowie, 2013). Such a move requires teachers to refocus their pedagogy on encouraging learners to share, elaborate, and illustrate their ideas on a particular issue so that they become more aware not only of their own experiences and interpretations, but also those of their peers. Hence, classroom assessment is "complex and ripe with tensions, implicating deeply held epistemologies and craft theories" (Crossouard, 2011, p. 62), relying on a dynamic balancing between convergent and divergent assessment (Torrance, 2012) to support equitable instruction and assessment for and of student learning and success.

The use of multiple modes and media is one way to help ensure every child has an opportunity to demonstrate what they know and can do, thereby making the assessment process fairer and more equitable (Stobart, 2005; Tierney, 2013). Promising formative assessment practices to better support English second language learners are currently being developed (Heritage, Walqui, & Linquanti, 2013). Similarly, we are beginning to appreciate the implications of cultural norms such as those that socialize students to listen rather than to question or offer ideas (Hang & Bell, 2013). Simultaneously, the mainstreaming of students with special needs and disabilities challenges what counts as knowledge and progress (Bourke & Mentis, 2014).

Increasingly, teachers and policy makers are recognising the affective dimension of student assessment experience and the implications of these for student opportunities to learn (The Gordon Commission, 2013). Stiggins (2008) argues for closer attention to the emotional dynamics of classroom assessment. The degree of trust and respect that exists between students and teachers influences student willingness to disclose honest self-assessment as part of routine classroom assessment (Cowie, 2005; Harris & Brown, 2013; Raider-Roth, 2005). Unsurprisingly, there is compelling evidence that high-stakes classroom-based testing regimes can narrow the curriculum and lead to students feeling worthless if they do not reach expected standards (Dutro & Selland, 2012; Nichols & Harris, this volume; Reay & Wiliam, 1999). Combined, these studies serve to remind us that classroom assessment is a situated social and relational process, one that can be an intensely subjective and emotional experience (Falchikov & Boud, 2007). While not all negative emotions need to be avoided, the emotional and relational dimensions and consequences of even informal classroom assessment need careful consideration (see Vogl & Pekrun, this volume).

Advocacy for parent and family engagement in their children's education is being incorporated into assessment policy (OECD, 2013; Swaffield, 2011). This requires teachers to give parents data that can be used to support their children's learning (Wood & Warin, 2014). Many parents want 'concrete' data, often restricted to information generated through a narrowly focused assessment regime, that proves their child is 'doing okay' (Harris, 2015). However, some parents want school assessment that provides a more holistic view of their child's accomplishments (Thrupp & White, 2013). Overall, it would seem more attention must be given to assisting teachers in how to educate parents about school assessment systems (Cowie & Mitchell, 2015), particularly those with a strong focus on formative assessment and student agency, or risk having parents misunderstand the information they are given (Harris, 2015).

CONCLUSION

There is clearly a need to consider classroom assessment in relation to curriculum, pedagogy, and classroom culture in order to enact classroom assessment in ways that are responsive, formative, and foundational for quality learning. At one level, this framing represents an attempt to see educational assessment in terms of its connectedness to issues of meaning, knowing, learning, teaching, and empowerment. At another level, we hope it might be a provocation to consider divergent assessment priorities and the implications of longer term and more expansive learning goals. How might complex learning goals coexist with the pressure to follow short-term imperatives and quickly deliver 'improved' results? Deep learning and improvement take time. They also involve new conversations around what is to be valued in the classroom, by learners, families, schools, communities, and government policy and practice. The educational community needs to endorse assessment initiatives that focus on providing support for the long-term professional development teachers need to support the breadth of outcomes we now value within society. As teachers know only too well, assessment procedures and instruments, in and of themselves, do not necessarily lead to improvement. Instead, teachers' professional knowledge, implementation, and judgment practices are central if we are serious about improving learning and engagement for all. Teachers will need time and support to develop, discuss, and debate the merits of different assessment approaches and to hone their assessment practices. Given that teacher assessment is both situated and social in nature, professional development needs to involve teachers in collegial groups from the same and differing schools. At the same time, the social, emotional, and identity-making (Stobart, 2008) aspects of classroom assessment for students need to be given more consideration. More work is needed to better understand the dynamics of classroom assessments that genuinely put students and their learning, individually and collectively, at the center. Importantly, this work needs to simultaneously engage governments, communities, schools, teachers, and students.

REFERENCES

Allal, L. (2013). Teachers' professional judgment in assessment: A cognitive act and a socially situated practice, *Assessment in Education: Principles, Policy & Practice, 20*(1), 20–34, doi:10.1080/0969594X.2012.736364

Andrade, H., & Cizek, G. (Eds.). (2010). *Handbook of formative assessment*. New York: Routledge.

Assessment Reform Group. (2002). *Assessment for Learning: 10 principles research-based principles to guide classroom practice*. London, UK: Assessment Reform Group.

Bell, B., & Cowie, B. (2001). *Formative assessment in science education.* Dordrecht: Kluwer.

Bennett, R. E. (2011). Formative assessment: A critical review. *Assessment in Education: Principles, Policy and Practice, 18,* 5–25. doi:10.1080/0969594X

Bernstein, B. (1971). On the classification and framing of educational knowledge. In M. F. D. Young (Ed.), *Knowledge and control: New directions for the sociology of education* (pp. 47–69). London: Collier Macmillan.

Black, P., Harrison, C., Hodgen, J., Marshall, M., & Serret, N. (2011). Can teachers' summative assessments produce dependable results and also enhance classroom learning? *Assessment in Education, 18*(4), 451–469. doi:10.1080/0969594X.2011.557020

Black, P., Harrison, C., Lee, C., Marshall, B., & William, D. (2003). *Assessment for learning: Putting it into practice.* Buckingham, UK: Open University Press.

Black, P., & Wiliam, D. (1998). Assessment and classroom learning. *Assessment in Education: Principles Policy and Practice, 5*(1), 7–73. doi:0.1080/0969595980050102

Black, P., & Wiliam, D. (2009). Developing the theory of formative assessment. *Educational Assessment, Evaluation and Accountability, 21*(1), 5–31. doi:10.1007/s11092–008–9068–5

Black, P., Wilson, M., & Yao, S-Y. (2011). Road maps for learning: A guide to the navigation of learning progressions. *Measurement: Interdisciplinary Research and Perspectives, 9*(2–3), 71–123. doi:10.1080/15366367.2011.591654

Bonner, S. (2013). Validity in classroom assessment: Purposes, properties, and principles. In J. McMillan (Ed.), *Sage handbook of research on classroom assessment* (pp. 87–106). doi:10.4135/9781452218649.n6

Boud, D. (2000). Sustainable assessment: Rethinking assessment for the learning society. *Studies in Continuing Education, 22,*151–167. doi:10.1080/713695728

Bourke, R., & Mentis, M. (2014). An assessment framework for inclusive education: integrating assessment approaches. *Assessment in Education, 21*(4), 384–397. doi:10.1080/0969594X.2014.888332

Brown, G. (2013). asTTle—A national testing system for formative assessment: How the national testing policy ended up helping schools and teachers. In M. Lai & S. Kushner (Eds.), *A national developmental and negotiated approach to school and curriculum evaluation* (pp. 39–56). London: Emerald Group Publishing. doi:10.1108/S1474–7863(2013)0000014003

Brown, G., Andrade, H., & Chen, F. (2015). Accuracy in student self-assessment: Directions and cautions for research. *Assessment in Education, 22*(4), 444–457. doi:10.1080/0969594X.2014.996523

Brown, G., & Harris, L. (2013). Student self-assessment. In J. McMillan (Ed.), *Sage handbook of research on classroom assessment* (pp. 367–393). Los Angeles: Sage. doi:10.4135/9781452218649

Brown, G.T.L. (2004). Teachers' conceptions of assessment: Implications for policy and professional development. *Assessment in Education, 11*(3), 301–318. doi:10.1080/0969594042000304609

Carless, D. 2009. Trust, distrust and their impact on assessment reform. *Assessment & Evaluation in Higher Education, 34*(1), 79–89. doi:10.1080/02602930801895786

Chin, C., & Osborne, J. (2008). Students' questions: A potential resource for teaching and learning science. *Studies in Science Education, 44,* 1–39. doi:10.1080/03057260701828101

Chinn, P. (2007). Teacher questioning in science classrooms: Approaches that stimulate productive thinking. *Journal of Research in Science Teaching, 44*(6), 815–843. doi:10.1002/tea.20171

Clarke, M. (2012). *What matters most for student assessment systems: A framework paper.* The International Bank for Reconstruction and Development. The World Bank.

Colbert, P., Wyatt-Smith, C., & Klenowski, V. (2012). A systems-level approach to building sustainable assessment cultures: Moderation, quality task design and dependability of judgment. *Policy Futures in Education, 10*(4), 386–401. doi:10.2304/pfie.2012.10.4.386

Cowie, B. (2005). Pupil commentary on assessment for learning. *Curriculum Journal, 16,* 137–151. doi:10.1080/09585170500135921

Cowie, B. (2013). Classroom assessment: Making space for diversity. In D. Corrigan, R. Gunstone, & A. Jones (Eds.), *Valuing assessment in science education: Pedagogy, curriculum, policy* (pp. 249–265). Rotterdam: Springer. doi:10.1007/978–94–007–6668–6_13

Cowie, B., & Bell, B. (1999). A model of formative assessment in science education. *Assessment in Education, 6,* 101–16. doi:10.1080/09695949993026

Cowie, B., & Mitchell, L. (2015). Equity as family/whānau opportunities to contribute to formative assessment. *Assessment Matters, 8,* 119–141.

Cowie, B., & Moreland, J. (2015). Leveraging disciplinary practices to support students' active participation in formative assessment. *Assessment in Education, 22*(2), 247–264. doi:10.1080/0969594X.2015.1015960

Cowie, B., Moreland, J., & Otrel-Cass, K. (2013). *Expanding notions of assessment for learning.* Rotterdam, The Netherlands: Sense. doi:10.1007/978–94–6209–061–3

Cowie, B., Otrel-Cass, K., Glynn, T., & Kara, H. (2011). *Culturally responsive pedagogy and assessment in primary science classrooms: Whakamana tamariki.* Wellington, NZ: TLRI.

Crooks, T. (1988). The impact of classroom evaluation practices on students. *Review of Educational Research, 58*(4), 438–481. doi:10.3102/00346543058004438

Crossouard, B. (2011). Using formative assessment to support complex learning in conditions of social adversity. *Assessment in Education, 18*, 59–72. doi:10.1080/0969594X.2011.536034

Dann, R. (2014). Assessment as learning: Blurring the boundaries of assessment and learning for theory, policy and practice. *Assessment in Education, 21*(2), 149–166. doi:10.1080/0969594X.2014.898128

Dekker-Groen, A., Van der Schaaf, M., & Stokking, K. (2015). Teachers' questions and responses during teacher-student feedback dialogues. *Scandinavian Journal of Educational Research, 59*(2), 231–254. doi:10.1080/00 313831.2014.937359

Dutro, E., & Selland, M. (2012). "I like to read, but I know I'm not good at it": Children's perspectives on high-stakes testing in a high-poverty school. *Curriculum Inquiry, 42*(3), 340–367. doi:10.1111/j.1467–873X.2012.00597.x

Falchikov, N. (2001). *Learning together: Peer tutoring in higher education.* London: Routledge Falmer. doi:10.4324/9780203451496

Falchikov, N., & Boud. D. (2007). Assessment and emotion. The impact of being assessed. In D. Boud & N. Falchikov (Eds.), *Rethinking assessment in higher education* (pp. 144–156). London: Routledge.

Friedman, S. J., & Frisbie, D. A. (1995). The influence of report cards on the validity of grades reported to parents. *Educational and Psychological Measurement, 55*(1), 5–26. doi:10.1177/0013164495055001001

Furtak, E., Morrison, D., & Kroog, H. (2014). Investigating the link between learning progressions and classroom assessment. *Science Education, 98*, 640–673.doi:10.1002/sce.21122

Gamlem, S., & Smith, K. (2013). Student perceptions of classroom feedback. *Assessment in Education, 20*(2), 150–169, doi:10.1080/0969594X.2012.749212

Gipps, C. (2002). Sociocultural perspectives on assessment. In G. Wells & G. Claxton (Eds.), *Learning for life in the 21st century* (pp. 73–83). Oxford: Blackwell publishers. doi:10.1002/9780470753545.ch6

Gipps, C., & Murphy, P. (1994). *A fair test? Assessment, achievement and equity.* Buckingham, UK: Open University Press.

Gordon Commission on the Future of Assessment in Education. (2013). *To assess, to teach, to learn: a vision for the future of assessment. Executive summary.* Princeton, NJ: Educational Testing Service.

Hang, D., & Bell, B. (2013). Formative assessment as a cultural practice: The use of written formative assessment in Samoan science classrooms. In D. Corrigan, R. Gunstone, & A. Jones (Eds.), *Valuing assessment in science education: Pedagogy, curriculum, policy* (pp. 267–284). Rotterdam: Springer. doi:10.1007/978–94–007–6668–6_14

Hargreaves, E. (2013). Inquiring into children's experiences of teacher feedback: Reconceptualising assessment for learning, *Oxford Review of Education, 39*(2), 229–246. doi:10.1080/03054985.2013.787922

Harlen, W. (2013). *Assessment & inquiry-based science education: Issues in policy and practice.* Global Network of Science Academies (IAP) Science Education Programme (SEP), Trieste, Italy.

Harris, L. R. (2015, April 16–20). Reviewing research on parent attitudes towards school assessment: Implications for classroom assessment practices. Paper presented at the American Educational Research Association Annual Meeting, Chicago, IL.

Harris, L., & Brown, G. (2013). Opportunities and obstacles to consider when using peer- and self-assessment to improve student learning: Case studies into teachers' implementation. *Teaching and Teaching Education, 35*, 101–111. doi:10.1016/j.tate.2013.07.008

Harrison, C. (2005). Teachers developing assessment for learning: Mapping teacher change. Teacher Development: *An International Journal of Teachers' Professional Development, 9*(2), 255–263. doi:10.1080/13664530500200264

Harrison, C. (2006). Banishing the quiet classroom, *Education Review, 19*(2), 67–77.

Hattie, J., & Gan, M. (2011). Instruction based on feedback. In R. E. Mayer & P. A. Alexander (Eds.), *Handbook of research on learning* (pp. 249–271). New York: Routledge.

Hattie, J., & Timperley, H. (2007). The power of feedback. *Review of Educational Research, 77*(1), 81–112. doi:10.3102/003465430298487

Hawe, E., & Parr, J. (2014). Assessment for learning in the writing classroom: An incomplete realisation. *The Curriculum Journal, 25*(2), 210–237. doi:10.1080/09585176.2013.862172

Hay, P., & Macdonald, D. (2008). (Mis)appropriations of criteria and standards-referenced assessment in a performance-based subject. *Assessment in Education, 15*(2), 153–168. doi:10.1080/09695940802164184

Hayward, L., & Hedge, N. (2005). Travelling towards change in assessment: Policy, practice and research in education. *Assessment in Education, 12*(1), 55–75. doi:10.1080/0969594042000333913

Heritage, M. (2010). *Formative assessment and next-generation assessment systems: Are we losing an opportunity?* Washington, DC: Council of Chief State School Officers.

Heritage, M., Walqui, A., & Linquanti, R. (2013). *Formative assessment as contingent teaching and learning: Perspectives on assessment as and for language learning in the content areas.* Palo Alto, CA: Stanford University Understanding Language Initiative.

Hermansen, H., & Nerland, M. (2014). Reworking practice through an AfL project: an analysis of teachers' collaborative engagement with new assessment guidelines. *British Educational Research Journal, 40*(1), 187–206. doi:10.1002/berj.3037

Hume, A., & Coll, R. K. (2009). Assessment of learning, for learning, and as learning: New Zealand case studies. *Assessment in Education, 16*(3), 269–290. doi:10.1080/09695940903319661

James, M., & Pedder, D. (2006). Beyond method: Assessment and learning practices and values. *The Curriculum Journal, 17*(2), 109–138. doi:10.1080/09585170600792712

Kangu, H., Thompson, J., & Windschitl, M. (2014). Creating opportunities for students to show what they know: The role of scaffolding in assessment tasks. *Science Education, 98*, 674–704. doi:10.1002/sce.21123

Kaufman, J. H., & Schunn, C. D. (2011). Students' perceptions about peer assessment for writing: Their origin and impact on revision work. *Instructional Science, 39*(3), 387–406. doi:10.1007/s11251–010–9133–6

Keogh, B., & Naylor, S. (1999). Concept cartoons, teaching and learning in science: An evaluation. *International Journal of Science Education, 21*(4), 431–446. doi:10.1080/095006999290642

Kingston, N., & Nash, B. (2011). Formative assessment: A meta-analysis and a call for research. *Educational Measurement: Issues and Practice, 30*(4), 28–37. doi:10.1111/j.1745–3992.2011.00220.x

Klenowski, V. (2009). Assessment for learning revisited : An Asia-Pacific perspective. *Assessment in Education: Principles, Policy and Practice, 16*(3), 263–268. doi:10.1080/09695940903319646

Kluger, A., DeNisi, A. (1996). The effects of feedback interventions on performance: A historical review, a meta-analysis, and a preliminary feedback intervention theory. *Psychological Bulletin, 119*(2), 254–284. doi:10.1037/0033–2909.119.2.254

Liu, N., & Carless, D. (2006). Peer feedback: The learning element of peer assessment. *Teaching in Higher Education, 11*(3), 279–290. doi:10.1080/13562510600680582

Marshall, B., & Drummond, M. (2006). How teachers engage with assessment for learning: Lessons from the classroom. *Research Papers in Education, 21*(2), 133–149. doi:10.1080/02671520600615638

McNaughton, S., Lai, M. K., & Hsiao, S. (2012). Testing the effectiveness of an intervention model based on data use: A replication series across clusters of schools. *School Effectiveness and School Improvement, 23*(2), 203–228. doi:10.1080/09243453.2011.652126

Moss, P., Pullin, D., Haertel, E. H., Gee, J., & Young, L. (Eds.). (2008). *Assessment, equity, and opportunity to learn.* New York: Cambridge University Press. doi:10.1017/CBO9780511802157

Murtagh, L. (2014). The motivational paradox of feedback: Teacher and student perceptions. *The Curriculum Journal, 25*(4), 516–541. doi:10.1080/09585176.2014.944197

Newton, P., & Shaw, S. (2014). *Validity in educational and psychological assessment.* London: Sage. doi:10.4135/9781446288856

Nicol, D., & Macfarlane, D. (2006). Formative assessment and self-regulated learning: A model and seven principles of good feedback practice. *Studies in Higher Education, 31*, 199–218. doi:10.1080/03075070600572090

OECD. (2013). *Synergies for better learning: An international perspective on evaluation and assessment. OECD reviews and assessment in education.* Paris, France: OECD Publishing. doi:10.1787/9789264190658-en

Pea, R. (2004). The social and technological dimensions of scaffolding and related theoretical concepts for learning, education and human activity. *The Journal of the Learning Sciences, 13*(3), 423–451. doi:10.1207/s15327809jls1303_6

Pedder, D., James, M., & MacBeath, J. (2005). How teachers value and practise professional learning. *Research Papers in Education, 20*(3), 209–243. doi:10.1080/02671520500192985

Pellegrino, J. W. (2010). *The design of an assessment system for the Race to the Top: A learning sciences perspective on issues of growth and measurement.* Paper presented at the Exploratory Seminar: Measurement Challenges within the Race to the Top Agenda, Princeton, NJ.

Perrenoud, P. (1998). From formative evaluation to a controlled regulation of learning processes. Towards a wider conceptual field. *Assessment in Education, 5*(1), 85–102. doi:10.1080/0969595980050105

Pryor, J., & Crossouard. P. (2008). A socio-cultural theorisation of formative assessment. *Oxford Review of Education, 34*(1), 1–20. doi:10.1080/03054980701476386

Raider-Roth, M. (2005). Trusting what you know: Negotiating the relational context of classroom life. *Teachers College Record, 107*(4), 587–628.

Ratnam-Lim, C., & Tan, K. (2015). Large-scale implementation of formative assessment practices in an examination-oriented culture. *Assessment in Education, 22*(1), 61–78. doi:10.1080/0969594x.2014.1001319

Reay, D., & Wiliam, D. (1999). 'I'll be a nothing': Structure, agency and the construction of identity through assessment. *British Educational Research Journal, 25*(3), 343–354. doi:10.1080/0141192990250305

Riggan, M., & Oláh, N. (2011). Locating interim assessments within teachers' assessment practice. *Educational Assessment, 16*(1), 1–14. doi:10.1080/10627197.2011.551085

Rowe, M. (1986). Wait-time: slowing down may be a way of speeding up. *Journal of Teacher Education, 37*, 43–50. doi:10.1177/002248718603700110

Ruiz-Primo, M. (2011). Informal formative assessment: The role of instructional dialogues in assessing students' learning. *Studies in Educational Evaluation, 37*, 15–24. doi:10.1016/j.stueduc.2011.04.003

Sadler, D. R. (1989). Formative assessment and the design of instructional systems. *Instructional Science, 18*, 119–144. doi:10.1007/BF00117714

Sawyer, K. (2006). Introduction: The new science of learning. In R. Keith Sawyer (Ed.), *The Cambridge handbook of the learning sciences* (2nd ed., pp. 1–16). Cambridge, UK: Cambridge University Press.

Shea, N., & and Duncan, R. (2013). From theory to data: The process of refining learning progressions. *The Journal of the Learning Sciences, 22*, 7–32. doi:10.1080/10508406.2012.691924

Shepard, L. A. (2000). The role of assessment in a learning culture. *Educational Researcher, 29*(7), 4–14. doi:10.3102/0013189X029007004

Shute, V. J. (2008). Focus on formative feedback. *Review of Educational Research, 78*(1), 153–189. doi:10.3102/0034654307313795

Smith, H., & Higgins. S. (2006). Opening classroom interaction: The importance of feedback. *Cambridge Journal of Education, 36*(4), 485–502. doi:10.1080/030576406010483

Steinberg, C. (2008). Assessment as an "emotional practice". *English Teaching: Practice and Critique, 7*(3), 42–64.

Stiggins, R. (2008). *A manifesto: Call for the development of balanced assessment systems*. ETS Assessment Training Institute, Portland, OR.

Stobart, G. (2005). Fairness in multicultural assessment systems. *Assessment in Education, 12*(3), 275–287. doi:10.1080/09695940500337249

Stobart, G. (2008). *Testing times: The uses and abuses of assessment*. Abingdon, Oxon: Routledge.

Sutton, P. (2012). Conceptualizing feedback literacy: Knowing, being, and acting. *Innovations in Education and Teaching International, 49*(1), 31–40. doi:10.1080/14703297.2012.647781

Swaffield, S. (2011). Getting to the heart of authentic assessment for learning. *Assessment in Education: Principles, Policy & Practice, 18*(4), 433–449. doi:10.1080/0969594X.2011.582838

Thrupp, M., & White, M. (2013). *National standards and the damage done*. Hamilton, NZ: WMIER.

Tierney, R. (2013). Fairness in classroom assessment. In J. McMillan (Ed.), *Sage handbook of research on classroom assessment* (pp. 124–145). Thousand Oaks, CA: Sage Publications. doi:10.4135/ 9781452218649.n8

Topping, K. (2013). Peers as a source of formative and summative assessment. In J. H. McMillan (Ed.), *Sage handbook of research on classroom assessment* (pp. 395–412). London: Sage, doi:10.4135/9781452218649.n22

Torrance, H. (2012). Formative assessment at the crossroads: Conformative, deformative and transformative assessment. *Oxford Review of Education, 38*(3), 323–342. doi:10.1080/03054985.2012.689693

Torrance, H., & Pryor, J. (1998). *Investigating formative assessment: Teaching, learning and assessment in the classroom*. Buckingham, UK: Open University Press.

Torrance, H., & Pryor, J. (2001). Developing formative assessment in the classroom: Using action research to explore and modify theory. *British Educational Research Journal, 27*(5), 615–631, doi:10.1080/01411920120095780

Tunstall, P., & Gipps, C. (1996). Teacher feedback to young children in formative assessment: A typology. *British Educational Research Journal, 22*(4), 389–404. doi:10.1080/0141192960220402

Van Gennip, N., Segers, M., & Tillema, H. (2009). Peer assessment for learning: The influence of interpersonal variables and structural features. *Educational Research Review, 4*(1) 41–54. doi:10.1016/j.edurev.2008.11.002

Webb, M., & Jones, J. (2009). Exploring tensions in developing assessment for learning. *Assessment in Education, 16*(2), 165–184, doi:10.1080/09695940903075925

Weick, K. E., Sutcliffe, K. M., & Obstfeld, D. (2005). Organizing and the process of sense-making and organizing. *Organization Science, 16*(4), 409–421. doi:10.1287/orsc.1050.0133

Wiliam, D. (2011). *Embedded formative assessment*. Bloomington, IN: Solution Tree.

Wiliam, D., Lee, C., Harrison, C., & Black, P. (2004). Teachers developing assessment for learning: impact on student achievement. *Assessment in Education: Principles Policy and Practice, 11*(1), 49–65. doi:10.1080/0969594042000208994

Willis, J. (2011). Affiliation, autonomy and assessment for learning. *Assessment in Education, 18*(4) 399–415. doi:10.1080/0969594x.2011.604305

Wilson, J., Olinghouse, N., & Andrada, G. (2014). Does automated feedback improve writing quality? *Learning Disabilities—A Contemporary Journal, 12*(1), 93–118.

Wood, P., & Warin, J. (2014). Social and emotional aspects of learning: Complementing, compensating and countering parental practices. *British Educational Research Journal, 40*(6), 937–951. doi:10.1002/berj.3122

Wyatt-Smith, C., Klenowski, V., & Gunn, S. (2010). The centrality of teachers' judgment practice in assessment: A study of standards in moderation. *Assessment in Education, 17*(1), 59–75. doi:10.1080/09695940903565610

20

SECTION DISCUSSION: BUILDING ASSESSMENTS THAT WORK IN CLASSROOMS

Susan M. Brookhart

This set of chapters on classroom conditions highlights the fact that assessment (and learning, for that matter) is a human and social activity. Section chapters have reviewed research on classroom processes such as collaboration, peer and self-assessment, and on issues such as privacy, diversity, and equity. The research shows the classroom context has an effect on assessment and on student learning and motivation. Actually, there is a two-way effect. Different classroom practices in assessment and instruction help create the classroom context as well. This chapter uses a co-regulation of learning framework to help us understand some of the relationships between classroom context and cognition and motivation.

CO-REGULATION OF LEARNING

Allal (2011, p. 332) defines co-regulation of learning as "the joint influence of student self-regulation and regulation from other sources (teachers, peers, curriculum materials, assessment instruments, etc.) on student learning." This section focuses on classroom conditions and contexts that affect, and are affected by, assessment. Therefore, this section ostensibly is concerned with characteristics of those other sources. However, as Allal points out, teaching and learning are inextricably linked in a situated and social environment. Effective pedagogies (teaching) are only effective if they are accompanied by student achievement (learning), and theory about the regulation of learning forms the conceptual underpinnings that link the two (Allal, 2011).

The chapters in this section have described aspects of some of those other sources that affect learning in the classroom, specifically: the amount and nature of privacy in the classroom, issues of power and trust, issues of diversity and equity, the amount and nature of collaborative work, and the amount and nature of peer assessment and self-assessment in the classroom. These classroom conditions foster certain kinds of student responses. They signal for students what it means to learn, what it means to be 'intelligent,' and what counts as knowledge (Dweck, 2000). They also identify who owns the learning and what their role is as learners (Perry, 1998).

Ultimately, however, it is the students who learn. Classroom conditions do not *make* students learn; rather, they create the circumstances within which students are more or less likely to learn what was intended. Conversely, because the classroom is a social environment, the manner in which students learn and how they go about learning contribute to those classroom conditions. Using the lens of co-regulation of learning, any discussion of classroom conditions—those other sources of regulation of learning—would not be complete without a consideration of student self-regulation of learning.

Self-regulation of learning is a process students engage in as they set learning goals, implement strategies to reach those goals, monitor and assess their progress toward those goals, establish a productive learning environment, and maintain a sense of self-efficacy (Zimmerman & Schunk, 2011). Differences in self-regulation of learning are an important source of achievement differences among students (Zimmerman & Schunk, 2011). Developing self-regulation of learning is an effective strategy for improving achievement among students who vary widely in achievement level (Schunk, 1981, 1984), including students with disabilities (Butler & Schnellert, 2015).

Most theories of self-regulation of learning describe a series of phases through which students move, beginning with task definition and moving through setting goals and planning, acting on those study plans (and monitoring and adjusting one's work), then reflecting on the results and adapting accordingly (Pintrich & Zusho, 2002; Winne & Hadwin, 1998). Pintrich and Zusho's (2002) model of the phases and areas for self-regulated learning crosses four phases (i.e., forethought, planning, and activation; monitoring; control; reaction and reflection) and four areas (i.e., cognition, motivation/affect, behavior, and context), thus giving context an important role in the self-regulation of learning.

Self-regulation processes are manifest in assessment processes. Andrade and Brookhart (2014) show how classroom assessment has a central role in the self-regulation of learning, and conversely the self-regulation of learning is a major impetus for students' gathering and using assessment information. Assessment, especially classroom formative assessment, is involved in each phase of self-regulation. For example, students' forethought, planning, and activation are influenced by the learning goals and success criteria shared by a teacher. Students' monitoring and control are affected by feedback provided via formative and summative assessments. Students' reaction and reflection are affected by opportunities teachers give students to use feedback and decisions students make based on that feedback. Thus, assessment supports the self-regulation of learning in classroom settings.

Self-regulation also affects the use of assessment in classroom settings; the self-regulation/classroom assessment relationship is reciprocal. For example, Pintrich and Zusho (2002) point out students' perceptions of the learning task and context affect their forethought and planning. Thus, the context affects the learner's goal setting and strategy selection. However, one of the options available to the learner through the self-regulation process is changing the context. Thus, for example, a learner might choose to change a task or even leave the context altogether (i.e., quit working), depending on how he perceives the learning is going. Thus, the learner also affects the context.

Co-regulation theory, applied to the findings in the chapters, makes it possible to synthesize the elements of the classroom assessment context described in the chapters in this section into a broader and more coherent description of how classroom conditions affect student's self-regulation of learning than self-regulation theory alone. The specific model of co-regulation that will guide this synthesis is Andrade's (2013) model, presented in Figure 20.1. It shares many features with other models of co-regulation of learning (Allal, 2011; Butler, Schnellert, & Cartier, 2013), explicitly includes student self-regulation, and is specific to assessment.

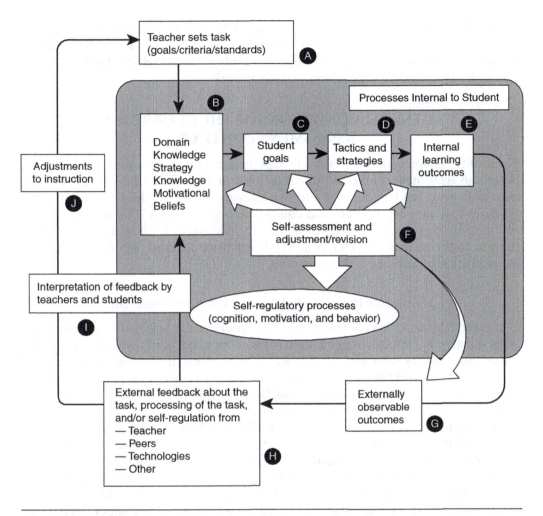

Figure 20.1 Model of Assessment as the Regulation of Learning by Oneself and Others

In this model, processes internal to the student (that is, self-regulatory processes) are shown in the gray area. When a teacher sets an assessment task (A), students respond. Or sometimes, students collaborate with teachers to set tasks and criteria; nevertheless, the teacher is still the ultimate arbiter of what happens in the classroom. In responding to a task, the student calls up background knowledge and beliefs (B) and uses the phases of self-regulation of learning (C, D, E, and F). Internal learning outcomes are represented in externally observable outcomes (G), for example, student work on the assessment. Feedback comes from various sources (H), and is interpreted by both teachers and students (I). These results may affect teachers' future instruction (J) and assessment (A), and they also become part of the student background (B) that informs the next self-regulatory cycle. This cycle is not completely linear, but rather is recursive (Winne, 2011). The phases of self-regulation of learning are very compatible with the formative assessment questions, "Where am I going? Where am I now? Where to next?" (Brookhart, 2013a).

As students move through a self-regulatory cycle, so do teachers (Butler, Schnellert, & Cartier, 2013). The classroom conditions that are the subject of this section have opportunities to affect student learning through any of the external elements in the model (G, H, I, J, and A) and through any background influences on these events, which are not depicted in the model but which are real nonetheless. For example, teacher background knowledge and beliefs partially affect the selection of tasks, provision of feedback, and interpretation of student work.

GENERAL CONDITIONS OF THE CLASSROOM ASSESSMENT CONTEXT

Three of the chapters in this section discussed classroom processes that help form the classroom assessment context for learning. Cowie and Harrison (this volume) describe classroom processes that support effective assessment. Moon (this volume) describes practices that support diversity and equity. Tierney and Koch (this volume) discuss privacy and the processes that can support or undermine it. All of these have something in common; they are other factors (other than student self-regulation) that affect the regulation of learning in the classroom.

Classroom Processes that Support Effective Assessment

Cowie and Harrison (this volume) write, "Classroom assessment makes up people (i.e., what it means to be a teacher or a student) and constructs and measures curriculum (i.e., what counts as valued knowledge and ways of expressing and representing this)." Both the content and format of an assessment are powerful signals to the student and teacher about what should be learned and, by extension, what is important to learn. In terms of co-regulation of learning, these are aspects of the other things that students must take into consideration as they plan what and how to study and that teachers must take into consideration as they plan what and how to teach. That is, what is to be assessed becomes part of the domain knowledge; indeed, it helps define the domain to be known, for both student and teacher. Practitioners have known this for a long time, without reference to theory about the co-regulation of learning. As the saying goes, "What is inspected becomes what is expected," or what is tested becomes what is taught (Resnick & Resnick, 1989).

Cowie and Harrison (this volume) spend some time comparing definitions of formative assessment, agreeing with many other authors it is the act of judgment—even if the judgment is to continue on with teaching and learning as planned—based on assessment information that makes an assessment formative. This definition, then, asserts that formative assessment is intentional participation in the co-regulation of learning. Judgments by the teacher about what she should do next are part of the regulation of learning from outside the student (area J in the model in Figure 20.1). Judgments by the student about what he should do next are part of the regulation of learning internal to the student (area F in the model). As Allal (2011) points out, the co-regulation of learning is the theory that connects the two. The same formative assessment strategy, yielding information about a student's thinking in relation to a learning goal, can support both internal and external regulation of learning. If the interpretations of the student and the teacher are compatible, the results for learning are likely to be enhanced. If the student and teacher see things differently, the results for learning are likely to be diminished as the student works toward a different goal than his teacher wishes or becomes confused.

Cowie and Harrison (this volume) discuss ways in which the practice of formative assessment is not the exercise of a set of strategies but rather a way of approaching learning. They argue that the purpose of formative assessment is to set up a learning situation in which students are active learners, that is, self-regulated learners. The job of the teacher is not to engage in certain particular strategies, but to set up learning opportunities in which students can actually *be* their own learners.

Stated differently, the formative assessment process requires teachers to be co-regulators of student learning by supporting student self-regulation of learning. Indeed, effective pedagogy in general, not just assessment practice, requires supporting learner autonomy (James & Pollard, 2011). Since assessment is a particularly powerful aspect of pedagogy, especially in light of defining what it is that should be learned and who is in charge of deciding what students are learning, it is one of, if not the, most important aspect of this co-regulation. Marshall and Drummond (2006) noted a teacher-centered, didactic use of formative assessment 'strategies' that does not support student self-regulation of learning does not conform to the 'spirit' of formative assessment but only to the 'letter'. In terms of the model of co-regulation, the more directive the regulation of learning from other sources—the teacher, the textbook, assessments that create a reified view of knowledge as something decided on by others—the less there is room for student goal setting (B) and the more constrained the self-regulatory processes (F).

This is a particularly difficult message to convey to practitioners who are used to taking a teacher-centered approach to instruction. Many lesson plan models and many teacher education paradigms instill in teachers a view of their job that can be summed up as "I decide on a learning objective; I decide on some instructional activities that I think will be helpful to students. Afterwards, I assess how much they learned." If professional training and internships inculcate this model into teachers' beliefs and actions, and if a culture of teaching exists in a school that supports this view, making a change to viewing assessment as supportive of student self-regulation of learning requires a dramatic 180 degree shift in perspective that is difficult for many teachers to conceptualize, much less accomplish. Teachers must move from thinking "what do I have to teach today?" to "what will I help the students try to learn?" This really is a sea change for many teachers. The magnitude and difficulty of such a change is the reason why a teacher-centered use of classroom formative assessment persists, even though it may not yield learning benefits (Furtak et al., 2008; Jonsson, Lundahl, & Holmgren, 2015). Cowie and Harrison (this volume) talk about students reconceptualizing their role. For that to happen, teachers also need to reconceptualize their role and move from regulating student learning to co-regulation that supports student self-regulation. Carless (2011) found that diagnostic analysis of summative testing can be an effective first step toward moving teachers in historically exam-driven educational systems toward a more formative approach to assessment.

Differentiating Assessment

Moon (this volume) addresses implementing assessment practices that acknowledge student diversity and treat all learners with equity. She describes Tomlinson and colleagues' vision of differentiated instruction as based on the premise that students learn best when curriculum, instruction, and assessment address learners' differences in readiness levels, interests, and learning profiles. She describes this approach as comparable to the National Research Council's (Bransford, Brown, & Cocking, 2000) four attributes of an effective classroom, all of which point to the centrality of students making meaning individually and together. This approach is also compatible with the Teaching and Learning Research Programme's 10 principles for effective pedagogy (James & Pollard, 2011), which are based on a view of learning that recognizes the need for learner autonomy and student self-regulation.

Moon (this volume) describes using pre-assessment, ongoing assessment, and summative assessment in service of diversity and equity. In most cases, this means 'what' the assessment is intended to measure does not change, but the process by which the student shows what he knows may be adapted for different learners. These adaptations are based on student prior knowledge, student learning needs during ongoing assessment and instruction, and student needs for accommodations during summative assessment. In terms of the model of co-regulation, teachers should be mindful of student domain knowledge, strategy knowledge, and beliefs as they set tasks for students, and give students the support they need to engage in self-regulatory processes. Similarly, feedback and adjustments to instruction should be based on student learning needs. The aim is for each student to be able to maximize his or her learning of important content, which implies one cannot treat all students the same during the learning. After all, when students differ in a myriad of ways, applying homogeneous assessment and instructional practices are guaranteed to lead to heterogeneous outcomes; the way to strive for standards is, ironically, to treat students differently (Katz, 2009).

Privacy

Tierney and Koch (this volume) present privacy as a human right necessary for human dignity. They cite evidence that privacy has a role in human development and autonomy in a democratic society. After reviewing privacy issues in classroom assessment, they suggest three implications for improvement: improving the quality of classroom assessment, raising awareness of privacy rights, and broadening the policy conversation beyond avoiding litigation. All three are relevant to the co-regulation of learning.

Regarding raising awareness of privacy rights, Tierney and Koch (this volume) point out that AfL practices result in students' sharing their thinking and learning from their mistakes in a collaborative learning context. Therefore, privacy concerns about assessment information may not be confined to official records, because instructional episodes are shot through with assessment information. Indeed, to the extent that the self-regulation of learning functions as a formative assessment cycle (Andrade & Brookhart, 2014), unofficial, often informal assessment information plays a more important role in learning than do official records.

In terms of the model of co-regulation, a student's trust that information about his or her learning will be handled in confidence and with respect will affect his or her motivational beliefs (B in the model), how far he or she is willing to stretch when he or she sets goals (C), and the learning tactics and strategies he or she uses (D). For example, students who believe their performance might not be good sometimes choose not to do the work rather than risk doing it, believing that it is better to fail because one didn't try, than to try and be found out as a failure by the teacher or by peers (Covington, 1992).

Students use evidence from the area of external regulation to develop trust that information about their learning will be handled in confidence and with respect. For example, the ways teachers (and sometimes peers) give feedback send messages to students. In classrooms where whole group instruction is the norm and where there is little student choice and frequent summative grading, students tend to develop a view of intelligence as fixed and to evaluate themselves as 'smart' or 'dumb' (Rosenholtz & Rosenholtz, 1981). In such classrooms, students may perceive even feedback that is intended as helpful for learning as another act of evaluation. In such classrooms, the main goal of students taking assessments is to get things right. In contrast, in classrooms where instruction is more individualized and there is more student choice and less frequent grading, as described in Moon (this volume), students are more likely to perceive that ability is learned and that they are in school to get smarter (Rosenholtz & Rosenholtz, 1981). In such classrooms, students may perceive even corrective feedback as constructive criticism that will help them learn.

This phenomenon can be observed in classrooms where teachers struggle to move from teacher-centered pedagogy focused on summative assessment to a more student-centered pedagogy using strategies, including more formative assessment, intended to increase student ownership of learning. A popular formative assessment strategy for having all students, not just one, answer questions is called 'thumbs up, thumbs down.' The teacher poses a question and asks students to indicate with a hand gesture, for example, "Thumbs up if you think the cork will float and thumbs down if you think it will sink." The intention of this strategy and others like it is to give all students a chance to engage with the content and monitor their progress and simultaneously to give the teacher access to assessment information from all students, not just one. The thumbs strategy is a good informal gauge of the extent to which students feel comfortable having assessment information available to others in the particular classroom. In some classrooms, instead of answering the question themselves, many students will look toward a smart kid and copy what she does. In others, students will enthusiastically punch the air with their own thumb vote. Hence, it is clear that the amount of privacy learners perceive they need may be highly dependent on how safe they feel within the classroom environment.

This author has also observed a compromise strategy that seemed an excellent example of the kind of quality classroom assessment Tierney and Koch (this volume) called for. Third grade students sat on a mat in front of a bulletin board displaying writing examples, from poor through good, which formed a kind of illustrated rubric for writing quality. The teacher asked students how confident they were that they understood the success criteria: thumbs up for confident, thumbs sideways for not sure, and thumbs down for not confident. Since the students were sitting on a mat and facing the teacher, she asked them to make their hand gestures close to their bodies, so "Nobody else can see, just me." The teacher got the information she needed about student understanding, and the students got the opportunity they needed to self-reflect, and privacy was maintained. This is quite a different approach than the 'traffic lights' method where students lay red, yellow, or green cups or markers on their desks and students' confidence in their work is made public.

In more general terms, the model of co-regulation suggests that, as Tierney and Koch (this volume) propose, if teachers create a classroom environment where all students are respected and use assessment information in the service of students, instead of against them, students are more likely to participate openly (D in the model) and to interpret feedback as supportive of learning (I) because they have come to believe that the classroom is set up to support their learning (B).

Student Controlled Processes in Assessment

Chapters in this section also discuss peer assessment (Panadero, this volume) and self-assessment (Andrade & Brown, this volume), respectively. While these are sometimes listed as equally valuable formative assessment strategies (e.g., Heritage, 2010; Wiliam, 2011), they are not, as the two chapters make clear. Theory about the co-regulation of learning helps to explain why the two chapters, and other literature reviews on self- and peer assessment, respectively, reach different conclusions about the effects of these strategies on student learning, motivation, and perceptions. Despite sharing a spot in the model of co-regulation (H), these two strategies are not simply equivalent feedback with two different agents.

Strijbos (this volume) discusses the assessment of collaborative learning, which fits in this section for two reasons. One, both Panadero (this volume) and Strijbos (this volume) review evidence and theory to support the conception of peer assessment as a collaborative learning activity. Two, Strijbos (this volume) points out that peer assessment is a logical strategy to assess the group functioning and teamwork aspects of collaborative learning, because peers have a perspective which teachers would not.

Peer Assessment

Panadero (this volume) shows peer assessment has recently been conceptualized as a collaborative learning activity. Panadero reviews traditional research on peer assessment, which is mostly concerned with the reliability and validity of summative scores, and then discusses more recent research about the human and social factors involved in peer assessment. He found students have some concerns about peer assessment, and that a friendship bias exists in peer assessment scoring. Psychological safety and trust are not easy to build into peer assessment. The relationship of motivation and emotion to peer assessment is mixed, and students may perceive peer assessment as unfair because the assessors—their peers—are not the knowledgeable evaluators they perceive their teachers to be.

In Pintrich and Zusho's (2002) self-regulation of learning framework, most aspects of peer assessment would be part of the classroom context area. Students would be concerned about disclosure, trusting others, how one will be treated, and what others think is good to know. As far as cognitive outcomes, it may help clarify the learning target to look at another person's example. But assessing another person's work does not directly help students improve their own work.

The model of co-regulation is more helpful for interpreting Panadero's (this volume) findings, because it allows for weaving together factors internal and external to the student. A student's work (G in the model) is assessed by a peer (H), who is external to the student. The results of peer assessment must be interpreted, and the results fed back into the student's—the learner's—learning, filtered through the learner's domain knowledge and motivational beliefs (B). Only after that does it affect the phases of self-regulation of learning (C, D, E, and F). Thus, if a peer criticizes a students' paper, for example, the results of that peer assessment are filtered through beliefs that may vary from negative (e.g., this peer doesn't like me, this peer doesn't know much about what we are trying to learn) through to positive (e.g., this peer is a good friend and is trying to help, this peer is very good at what we are trying to learn), resulting in very different messages with very different levels of accuracy and helpfulness for learning.

Research on peer assessment in higher education has been reviewed thoroughly (Falchikov & Goldfinch, 2000). Much of the research has been about peer-teacher scoring agreement (Falchikov & Goldfinch, 2000; van Zundert, Sliujsmans, & van Merriënboer, 2010). However, the learning, performance, and interpersonal aspects of peer assessment in higher education have also been studied (Topping, 1998; van Gennip, Segers, & Tillema, 2009; van Zundert et al., 2010). Peer assessment skill does not come naturally; training in how to do peer assessment improves its outcomes (van Zundert et al., 2010). Students who receive better feedback derive more learning benefits from peer feedback (van Gennip et al., 2009). Social embarrassment and peer qualifications as evaluators are potential issues (Topping, 1998).

Besides Panadero (this volume), however, only one other review of literature on K–12 peer assessment was found (Topping, 2013). Topping used Piagetian and Vygotskian perspectives in a model of peer assessment; his model coordinates well with the view of co-regulation of learning used in this chapter and recognizes the important roles of affect and communication, as well as cognition, in peer assessment. Topping found the research base for peer assessment as a support of learning to be weak; there was little evidence suggesting peer assessment supported learning at the elementary level, although there was some evidence at the secondary level. Secondary students questioned the value of peer assessment and noted that the feedback from peer assessment may not be accurate. Affirming and suggestive peer feedback has positive effects on learning, but didactic and corrective feedback has negative effects.

Panadero (this volume) concludes that, despite the difficulties, peer assessment should be pursued as a collaborative learning strategy. Similarly, Topping (2013, p. 410), despite drawing similar conclusions, wrote that peer assessment "shows promise." Panadero (this volume) counsels a move away from superficial approaches to peer assessment, for example, peer grading, and points out that the more intensive peer assessment interventions produced better outcomes. Similarly, Topping (2013) counsels more investment in formative peer assessment and a move away from summative peer assessment.

This is excellent advice, to which this author would add one more step. Peer assessment should be seen as an episode of learning for the assessor. Panadero (this volume) came close in his realization that peer assessment was closer to a collaborative learning activity than a pure assessment strategy. When done well, peer assessment imposes a deeper understanding of the learning goal that is so important to formative assessment ("Where am I going?") as well as to the self-regulation of learning more generally (Pintrich & Zusho, 2002; Zimmerman & Schunk, 2011) because it obliges students to work deeply with criteria and with an example of student work, both of which are known to clarify a student's understanding of what is to be learned (Andrade, 2013; Heritage, 2010; Wiliam, 2011).

Collaborative Learning

Strijbos (this volume) reviews the panorama of literature on assessment of collaborative learning, identifying many strengths and weaknesses with existing practices. Building from a discussion of individual accountability and positive interdependence and different kinds of collaborative learning, Strijbos (this volume) identifies three challenges for the assessment of collaboration before discussing examples of current CL assessment practice. He answers his own challenges by arguing for assessment of collaborative learning that is two-level (individual and group), multistage (before, during, and after learning), and multidimensional (measuring cognitive, social, and motivational outcomes). However, he suggests that there is need for more work to be done to determine what is the most appropriate and valid way to apportion results to these different components and dimensions. He suggests peer assessment as a method for assessing collaboration skills, identifying that peers have a perspective on the conduct of group work that the teacher does not. This multiple-measures approach resonates with current thinking about assessing complex learning and is well supported by the research cited.

The question of what should be assessed is still pending, however. Citing Boud et al., (1999), Strijbos (this volume) reminds readers that collaborative learning can be used for two broad purposes, improving subject-matter learning and promoting teamwork.

These are two different kinds of constructs, based in two different instructional purposes, and requiring two different types of assessment methods and strategies. Furthermore, sometimes collaborative learning is used to promote both subject-matter learning *and* teamwork.

The model of co-regulation offers a way to understand both subject-matter learning and collaborative skills together. Teachers usually set tasks (A in the model) that are intended to have students reach standards or curricular goals—that is, subject-matter learning. They usually need individual measures of subject-matter learning for the individual reporting required in schools. Teachers may also want to teach 21st-century skills such as collaboration, as an ancillary goal, for which they may need only group-level measures because they will be using the information primarily for classroom instructional planning. Teachers do not (or at least, should not) report collaboration skills in students' academic grades; if teachers do need individual measures of students' collaboration skills, it is for a learning skills or citizenship rating on a report card, not for the academic grade (Guskey, 1996; McMillan, 2001).

Students can set goals (C in the model) regarding both subject-matter learning and collaborative teamwork skills, pursue them with varying tactics and strategies (D), and monitor and adjust their work (F) using self-regulatory processes. The externally observable outcomes (G) for subject-matter learning and collaborative skills usually, although not always, are separate. Excluding true cooperative learning where the learning outcomes are gauged by individual test scores, the subject-matter outcomes for group work are academic products or performances, for example a report or a presentation. These are amenable to formative feedback (H) or summative grades. However, if there is one product for the group, the unit of analysis is the group, and this is not what is required for individual reporting of student achievement of standards or curricular outcomes.

In contrast, the externally observable outcomes (G) for collaborative skills are often observations of group functioning. These are amenable to formative feedback, although as Strijbos (this volume) describes, they are often assessed with rating scales. The unit of analysis for collaborative skills is properly the group, so at least the measure is at the proper level. However, Strijbos (this volume) uncovers a troubling phenomenon. In an effort to solve the unit of analysis problem for subject matter learning (i.e., how to give individual grades when the learning product was a group effort), much of the literature on peer assessment of collaborative learning has created an even bigger problem. Many of the studies reported have confounded the two constructs (i.e., subject-matter learning and collaboration skills) by adjusting a group assessment of subject matter achievement by using peer ratings of collaborative skills. The result is an individual grade that is a mixture of both apples and oranges that solves neither problem.

Several authors (Brookhart, 2013b; O'Connor, 2009) have offered practical suggestions to teachers about grading practices that separate the two constructs. These recommendations are efforts to counter what many teachers do in practice, which is to mix the two constructs into a measure that is a clear indicator of neither, similar to the research programs that Strijbos (this volume) cites. Indeed, many teachers would say they assess group projects to develop both subject matter knowledge and collaborative teamwork skills. The model of co-regulation refers to goals in the plural, acknowledging that teachers intend many tasks to address several goals at one time and that students self-regulate with respect to several goals at once. Certainly, students can attend to their subject-matter learning and teamwork at the same time—and probably should.

What is problematic about the formative assessment of collaborative learning is that the feedback effective for subject matter learning and collaborative skills is bound to be very different. So, whether the task separates the two or not, teachers and students must separate the two goals and associated criteria in their minds. From a student's point of view, for example, aiming to understand mass and volume is very different from aiming to be a better listener during group work. What is problematic about the summative assessment of collaborative learning is that subject-matter and team-work goals have different relationships to the written, taught, and learned curricula (Glatthorn, 2000) and, thus, must be reported and accounted for differently. A 'group grade' is not valid because only part of the grade is an indicator of achievement of curricular goals. Individual measures of learning are needed, even if that learning happened in collaborative groups, for valid reporting of individual achievement, which is the purpose of school report cards.

Self-assessment

Andrade and Brown (this volume) argue that "self-assessment is entirely a human process; no machines or statistics can take the place of the learner's own self-awareness." They review literature to determine how accurate that self-awareness is. Greater self-assessment competency is associated with more humble self-evaluation. High achievers tend to underestimate, while low achievers tend to overestimate their performance as compared with teacher ratings. In general, most students are accurate in their evaluation of how well they have done on tests. Factors contributing to consistency in self-assessment include training and practice in self-assessment, opportunities to discuss criteria, the nature of the task and criteria (simple and concrete tasks work best), experience with the subject, age, and ability.

These findings resonate with other reviews of the self-assessment literature (Andrade & Valtcheva, 2009; Brown, Andrade, & Chen, 2015; Brown & Harris, 2013; Falchikov & Boud, 1989; Ross, 2006). In contrast to the reviews of the peer assessment literature, only one of these reviews (Falchikov & Boud, 1989) was restricted to higher education, and that review mostly dealt with reliability of marking in summative self-assessment. Andrade and Valtcheva (2009) argued that self-assessment can increase both achievement (learning) and learner autonomy, creating more self-regulated learners.

As for peer assessment, the criteria play a central role in the functioning of self-assessment. Andrade and Valtcheva (2009) found students' attitudes toward self-assessment were generally positive, but this positive feeling did not transfer to other courses, which supports the contention that the specific criteria, rather than a general sense of autonomy, are important. They also found that students' attitudes toward self-assessment were only negative when the self-assessment was used for grading (i.e., summative assessment). This finding, also, supports the idea that one of the main functions of self-assessment is to engage students at a deep level with their learning goals and the criteria for success, a foundational principle in formative assessment. That is, what is effective about self-assessment is that it fosters student engagement with the formative assessment cycle (i.e., Where am I going? Where am I now? Where to next?), giving students a tool for self-regulation of learning (setting goals, monitoring, adjusting, and reflecting). Ross (2006) and Brown and Harris (2013) also emphasize the intimate connection between self-assessment and self-regulation of learning. Brown and Harris (2013) reviewed literature that specifically connected these two, finding that self-assessment enhances an internal locus of control, supports self-referencing over norm-referencing, and leads to improved self-efficacy, engagement, behavior, and student-teacher relationships.

The model of co-regulation of learning suggests some reasons why the literature on self-assessment is more sanguine than the literature on peer assessment. While both begin with the teacher setting tasks (A in the model), self-assessment invokes more self-regulatory processes internal to the learner. During self-assessment, a student engages with the goals and criteria for learning (C), increasing the likelihood that the student makes those learning goals her own. The student mediates her own learning during self-assessment (F), leading to adjustment and revision in her own work (G). In contrast, peer assessment gives external feedback (H) that, as discussed above, must be drawn back into the learner through the filter of the learner's knowledge and beliefs (B), meaning that the peer feedback can be distrusted as inexpert. Thus, self-assessment is in the warp and woof of self-regulated learning. Self-assessment has the same boundaries of meaning as the phases of self-regulated learning (i.e., goals, monitoring, adjusting, and reflecting). The assessment is conducted by the same self who exhibits the relevant cognition, motivation, and behavior. Assessment information from self-assessments directly helps students improve their work.

So the functions of peer and self-assessment are different. Peer assessment is part of the classroom context, requires trust, and a certain view of learning (beliefs and attitudes). It is best seen as a collaborative learning activity rather than purely an assessment (Panadero, this volume; Strijbos, this volume). In contrast, self-assessment is part of the student's own self-regulatory process and leads more directly to learning. The conclusion is clear; use student self-assessment often, teaching students how to evaluate their own work using criteria. Self-assessment should be used for formative purposes rather than summative (Andrade & Valtcheva, 2009), and be taught as a core curricular competence that helps students self-regulate and improve their learning (Brown & Harris, 2014). Use peer assessment when a lesson calls for a collaborative learning activity that emphasizes clarifying learning goals and criteria for success, that is, as an instructional activity more than an assessment. Note that summative assessment is not an effective use in either case; neither self- nor peer assessment is reliable enough or seen by students as sufficiently valid for grading purposes.

All of this is easier said than done. Wylie and Lyon (2015) studied 202 mathematics and science teachers participating in a two-year, school-based professional development program in formative assessment. Teachers' use of self-assessment and peer assessment both changed little over the two years, and although teachers used peer assessment somewhat more than self-assessment, most of the descriptions were of peer collaboration more than peer assessment. In short, they found that for these practices teachers needed even more support than the two-year intervention they investigated.

BUILDING ASSESSMENTS THAT WORK IN CLASSROOMS

As the model of co-regulation of learning suggests, assessment strategies and tools are part of the classroom conditions—part of the other sources of influence (Allal, 2011) on learning. All of the chapter authors, and many of the authors of additional literature reviews, have emphasized the importance of formative assessment, as opposed to summative, in order to build assessments that work—in the sense of furthering learning—in classrooms. In some ways that is not surprising, because it is the nature of formative assessment to support learning. Table 20.1 summarizes the assessment strategies that can be recommended as grounded in the literature reviewed in this section

Table 20.1 Compendium of Recommendations for Classroom Assessment from Chapter Authors and Other Literature Reviews

---

Increase the quality of classroom assessment (M, S, TK)

Increase awareness of students' safety, dignity, and privacy rights and needs (AB, BH, CH, R, TK)

Use self-assessment and peer assessment for formative purposes (AB, AV, CH, P)

Use and share clear criteria with students, involving them in criteria development where possible (AB, AV, BH, CH, R, T)

Use models (examples, exemplars) of student work (AB, S)

Teach students to be competent self- and peer assessors (AB, AV, BH, CH, R, T)

Give students feedback on the quality of their assessment skills, the accuracy of their assessment judgments, and their use of assessment results, providing enough time for each (AB, AV, BH, R, T)

Situate assessments in learning progressions (CH)

Do not use external rewards; rather, let students develop internal rewards as they grow in assessment competence (AB)

Be mindful of response styles of students from different cultures and backgrounds (AB, CH, M)

Improve assessment policies (TK)

Note: Recommendations are summarized from chapters in this section (AB = Andrade & Brown; CH = Cowie & Harrison; M = Moon; P = Panadero; S = Strijbos; TK = Tierney & Koch) and related literature reviews (AV = Andrade & Valtcheva, 2009; BH = Brown & Harris, 2013; R = Ross, 2006; T = Topping, 1998)

on classroom conditions. Recommendations in the table were developed by grouping together recommendations from each of the chapters in this section, as well as other cited literature reviews, into categories. The degree of convergence is remarkable.

On balance, the compendium of recommendations is compatible with a view of teaching and learning that acknowledges the co-regulation of learning. On the student side, assessment needs to support students as they become assessment-capable, self-regulating learners, or what has been called 'learning how to learn' (James & Pollard, 2011). This is the reason why many of the recommendations espouse a formative view of assessment. While not discounting summative assessment, which clearly has a place in the conduct of schooling and, especially, in the policy arena (Tierney & Koch, this volume), formative assessment supports learning (Cowie & Harrison, this volume).

On the side of regulation from other sources besides the student himself or herself (Allal, 2011), teachers need to use assessment to create a climate where students can generate evidence of their progress in a safe environment, where both teacher and students interpret mistakes as opportunities for learning and interpret learning itself as an ongoing process. Students and teachers must be co-assessors, operating under a shared vision that there is always something more to learn, that teachers and students and peers are 'in it together', and that accurate information based on assessing students' performance of worthwhile tasks against relevant criteria helps everyone learn.

While all of the recommendations in Table 20.1 are based on research evidence, several require further research, mostly in regard to the specifics of how to accomplish them. What general strategies, for example, could a teacher use to situate assessments within learning progressions? What strategies should a teacher use to assess that take into account response styles of students with different backgrounds? The recommendations are rooted in research but the range of classroom practices that supports them needs further investigation.

There is also the question of preparation. For teachers and teacher candidates to learn to follow these recommendations, some habits will need to change. The history of self- and peer assessment, for example, suggests that the first inclination of many teachers is to use these assessment methods in a summative fashion, for grading. A mindset shift in assessment practices, to privilege learning over grading and to devote more time and energy to assessment for learning than assessment of learning, would be a good place to start. This brings us back to the topic of this section, classroom conditions that affect assessment. All of the chapters, including this commentary, have suggested that a shift in classroom culture toward a learning-centered classroom climate or context will improve learning by supporting the self- and co-regulation of learning. A change in the nature of classroom assessment and an increase in its quality will go a long way toward this shift.

REFERENCES

Allal, L. (2011). Pedagogy, didactics and the co-regulation of learning: A perspective from the French-language world of educational research, *Research Papers in Education, 26*(3), 329–336.

Andrade, H. L. (2013). Classroom assessment in the context of learning theory and research. In J. H. McMillan (Ed.), *Sage handbook of research on classroom assessment* (pp. 17–34). Los Angeles: Sage.

Andrade, H. L., & Brookhart, S. M. (2014, April). *Assessment as the regulation of learning.* Paper presented at the annual meeting of the American Educational Research Association, Philadelphia, PA.

Andrade, H. L., & Valtcheva, A. (2009). Promoting learning and achievement through self-assessment. *Theory Into Practice, 48*, 12–19.

Boud, D., Cohen, R., & Sampson, J. (1999). Peer learning and assessment. *Assessment & Evaluation in Higher Education, 24*(4), 413–426.

Bransford, J. D., Brown, A. L., & Cocking, R. R. (Eds.). (2000). *How people learn: Brain, mind, experience, and school.* Washington, DC: National Academy Press.

Brookhart, S. M. (2013a). Classroom assessment in the context of motivation theory and research. J. H. McMillan (Ed.), *Sage handbook of research on classroom assessment* (pp. 35–54). Los Angeles: Sage.

Brookhart, S. M. (2013b). *Grading and group work.* Alexandria, VA: ASCD.

Brown, G.T.L., Andrade, H., & Chen, F. (2015). Accuracy in student self-assessment: directions and cautions for research. *Assessment in Education: Principles, Policy & Practice, 22*(4), 444–457. doi:10.1080/09695 94X.2014.996523

Brown, G.T.L., & Harris, L. R. (2013). Student self-assessment. In. J. H. McMillan (Ed.), *Sage handbook of research on classroom assessment* (pp. 367–393). Los Angeles: Sage.

Brown, G.T.L., & Harris, L. R. (2014). The future of self-assessment in classroom practice: Reframing self-assessment as a core competency. *Frontline Learning Research, 3*, 22–30. doi:10.14786/flr.v2i1.24

Butler, D. L., & Schnellert, L. (2015). Success for students with learning disabilities: What does self-regulation have to do with it? In T. Cleary (Ed.), *Self-regulated learning interventions with at-risk youth: Enhancing adaptability, performance, and well-being* (pp. 89–111). Washington DC: APA Press.

Butler, D. L., Schnellert, L., & Cartier, S. C. (2013). Layers of self- and co-regulation: Teachers working collaboratively to support adolescents' self-regulated learning through reading. *Education Research International, 845694.* doi:10.1155/2013/845694

Carless, D. (2011). *From testing to productive student learning: Implementing formative assessment in Confucian-Heritage settings.* London: Routledge.

Covington, M. V. (1992). *Making the grade: A self-worth perspective on motivation and school reform.* Cambridge: Cambridge University Press.

Dweck, C. S. (2000). *Self-theories: Their role in motivation, personality, and development.* New York: Psychology Press.

Falchikov, N., & Boud, D. (1989). Student self-assessment in higher education: A meta-analysis. *Review of Educational Research, 59*(4), 395–430.

Falchikov, N., & Goldfinch, J. (2000). Student peer assessment in higher education: A meta-analysis comparing peer and teacher marks. *Review of Educational Research, 70*(3), 287–322.

Furtak, E., Ruiz-Primo, M. A., Shemwell, J. T., Ayala, C. C., Brandon, P. R., Shavelson, R. J., & Yin, Y. (2008). On the fidelity of implementing embedded formative assessments and its relation to student learning. *Applied Measurement in Education, 21*(4), 360–389.

Glatthorn, A. A. (2000). *The principal as curriculum leader: Shaping what is taught and tested* (2nd ed.). Thousand Oaks, CA: Corwin.

Guskey, T. R. (1996). Reporting on student learning: Lessons from the past-prescriptions for the future. In T. R. Guskey (Ed.), *Communicating student learning* (pp. 13–24). Alexandria, VA: Association for Supervision and Curriculum Development.

Heritage, M. (2010). *Formative assessment: Making it happen in the classroom.* Thousand Oaks, CA: Corwin.

James, M., & Pollard, A. (2011). TLRP's ten principles for effective pedagogy: Rationale, development, evidence, argument and impact. *Research Papers in Education, 26*(3), 275–328.

Jonsson, A., Lundahl, C., & Holmgren, A. (2015). Evaluating a large-scale implementation of assessment for learning in Sweden. *Assessment in Education, 22*(1), 104–121.

Katz, L. G. (2009). Where I stand on standardization. *Educational Researcher, 38*(1), 52–58.

Marshall, B., & Drummond, M. J. (2006): How teachers engage with assessment for learning: lessons from the classroom. *Research Papers in Education, 21*(2), 133–149.

McMillan, J. H. (2001). *Classroom assessment: Principles and practice for effective instruction* (2nd ed.). Boston, MA: Allyn & Bacon.

O'Connor, K. (2009). *How to grade for learning K–12* (3rd ed.). Thousand Oaks, CA: Corwin.

Perry, N. E. (1998). Young children's self-regulated learning and context that support it. *Journal of Educational Psychology, 90,* 715–729.

Pintrich, P. R., & Zusho, A. (2002). The development of academic self-regulation: The role of cognitive and motivational factors. In A. Wigfield & J. S. Eccles (Eds.), *Development of achievement motivation* (pp. 249–284). San Diego: Academic Press.

Resnick, L. B., & Resnick, D. P. (1989). *Assessing the thinking curriculum: New tools for educational reform.* Washington, DC: National Commission on Testing and Public Policy.

Rosenholtz, S. J., & Rosenholtz, S. H. (1981). Classroom organization and the perception of ability. *Sociology of Education, 54,* 132–140.

Ross, J. A. (2006). The reliability, validity, and utility of self-assessment. *Practical Assessment Research & Evaluation, 11*(10). Retrieved March 16, 2007 from http://pareonline.net/getvn.asp?v=11&n=10

Schunk, D. H. (1981). Modeling and attributional feedback effects on children's achievement: A self-efficacy analysis. *Journal of Educational Psychology, 73,* 93–105.

Schunk, D. H. (1984). Sequential attributional feedback and children's achievement behaviors. *Journal of Educational Psychology, 76,* 1159–1169.

Topping, K. J. (1998). Peer assessment between students in colleges and universities. *Review of Educational Research, 68*(3), 249–276.

Topping, K. J. (2013). Peers as a source of formative and summative assessment. In. J. H. McMillan (Ed.), *Sage handbook of research on classroom assessment* (pp. 395–412). Los Angeles: Sage.

van Gennip, N.A.E., Segers, M.S.R., & Tillema, H. H. (2009). Peer assessment for learning from a social perspective: The influence of interpersonal variables and structural features. *Educational Research Review, 4,* 41–54.

van Zundert, M., Sluijsmans, D., & van Merriënboer, J. (2010). Effective peer assessment processes: Research findings and future directions. *Learning and Instruction, 20,* 270–279.

Wiliam, D. (2011). *Embedded formative assessment.* Bloomington, IN: Solution Tree Press.

Winne, P. H. (2011). A cognitive and metacognitive analysis of self-regulated learning. In B. J. Zimmerman & D. H. Schunk (Eds.), *Handbook of self-regulation of learning and performance* (pp. 15–32). New York: Routledge.

Winne, P. H., & Hadwin, A. F. (1998). Studying as self-regulated learning. In D. J. Hacker, J. Dunlosky, & A. C. Graesser (Eds.), *Metacognition in educational theory and practice* (pp. 277–304). Mahwah, NJ: Lawrence Erlbaum.

Wylie, E. C., & Lyon, C. J. (2015). The fidelity of formative assessment implementation: Issues of breadth and quality. *Assessment in Education, 22*(1), 140–160.

Zimmerman, B. J., & Schunk, D. H. (2011). Self-regulated learning and performance: An introduction and overview. In B. J. Zimmerman & D. H. Schunk (Eds.), *Handbook of self-regulation of learning and performance* (pp. 1–12). New York: Routledge.

Section 4

Cultural and Social Contexts

21

THE IMPACT OF INTERNATIONAL TESTING PROJECTS ON POLICY AND PRACTICE

Janna Teltemann and Eckhard Klieme

INTRODUCTION

For knowledge-based economies competing with each other worldwide, the production of human capital is deemed to be an important growth factor. The growing importance of education as a means of productivity involves an increasing need for effectiveness within national education systems. Consequently, standardized international student assessments have become more frequent during the last decades and have raised considerable interest in politics, media, and academia. Prominent examples of these testing projects include the OECD's Programme for International Student Assessment (PISA), and the International Association for the Evaluation of Educational Achievement's (IEA) Trends in International Mathematics and Science Study (TIMSS) and the Progress in International Reading Literacy Study (PIRLS). Associated with the rise of international testing projects is a substantial change in the modes of policy making in education. The assessments are not only used to identify good and weak performers, but rather they are used as a central instrument for prescribing reforms of national education policies (Feniger & Lefstein, 2014).

In fact, educational reform as a response to results of international assessments can be observed in many countries (Breakspear, 2012; Knodel, Martens, Olano, & Popp, 2010; Lingard & Grek, 2006; Martens, Nagel, Windzio, & Weymann, 2010). Currently, the implications of these policy trends are highly controversial among educational scientists, politicians, and other stakeholders in education. Particularly the PISA study is criticized for being a vehicle for a model of education that is solely driven by economic demands (Han, 2008; Uljens, 2007). While there is considerable research devoted to how PISA influences national education systems, most look only at the level of formal policies, without taking practices and outcomes into account. In this chapter, we aim to evaluate the scope of effects of international assessments and to judge their capacity to influence the ways education is organized. We take the OECD PISA study as an example, as it is the most prominent and biggest endeavor in this respect. We argue that the current debate lacks robust empirical findings of the real effects and consequences of international testing projects on practices as well as on learning outcomes. One reason for this research gap is that the analytical potential of the data provided by international assessments is not yet exploited. This holds for the analyses of effects of assessments on policies, practices, and outcomes as well as for possibilities of providing alternative policy recommendations derived from assessment results.

We first briefly summarize general changes in national and international educational governance and illustrate central features of the OECD PISA study. The third section presents theoretical accounts explaining changes—or resistance to change—in education policies and practice. In the fourth section, we review previous case studies on policy effects of international assessment. We take a closer look at Germany as an example where PISA has had considerable impact on the education system. Further, we present our own empirical analyses with PISA data to illustrate changes in assessment and accountability practices in OECD countries between 2000 and 2012. In our conclusion, we argue that future research should focus on exploiting the potential of the data generated by international assessments. This would promote a better understanding of effects of assessments on practices and outcomes and open up possibilities to formulate alternative policy recommendations based on solid research.

THE INTERNATIONALIZATION OF EDUCATIONAL GOVERNANCE AND THE CHANGING FACE OF ACCOUNTABILITY

International testing projects are the most salient feature of processes of internationalization in education. However, changes in international educational governance began much earlier than the heyday of international testing projects and have been extensively described from different angles (Davis, Kingsbury, & Merry, 2012; Green, 1997; Kamens & McNeely, 2010; Lawn, 2013; Ozga, 2013). In many accounts, the diverse changes are framed as reactions to the competitive pressures arising from 'globalization.' In order to increase the overall means of economic productivity, the role of *human capital* (Becker, 1993) in the so-called 'knowledge-based economy' is emphasized. Consequently, the demand for an effective provision of education has increased since the 1980s. Nation states, which traditionally have a strong interest in securing mass education, conceived themselves as less and less able to manage the new challenges alone (Leuze, Martens, & Rusconi, 2007, p. 5). As a result, the modes of policy making in education gradually became more and more *international*. This is reflected in an expanded impact of international organizations such as the OECD and the perceived necessity of comparing performance with other countries. A second consequence was an increasing *marketization* of education, meaning that formerly public institutions became more and more privatized. By default, marketization creates a growing need for objective assessments and measures of quality assurance and transparency, because 'customers' of education want to know that their investments pay off (Dolin, 2007).

The International Association for the Evaluation of Educational Achievement (IEA) developed a framework for large scale international studies in the 1950s (Normand, 2008; Owens, 2013); the First International Tests in Mathematics (FIMS) in 1964 was the result. The OECD, usually dealing in the narrowest sense with economic policies, increased its engagement in education only since the 1980s. Encouraged by its member states, it quickly developed a remarkable capacity in testing and comparison in education (Lingard & Lewis, this volume; Lingard & Rawolle, 2011; Martens & Weymann, 2007; Martens, 2007).

The new 'faith' in international assessments implies that institutions and policies are perceived to be at least to some extent transferable, or in other words borrowable and lendable (Steiner-Khamsi, 2004). The new power of assessments for education policy is not undisputed; however, one major argument against a simple transfer of policies between countries is the importance of cultural and societal factors for educational success (Feniger & Lefstein, 2014; Meyer & Schiller, 2013). Other arguments criticize the economization and standardization of education and learning and the neglect of holistic ideas about 'good education' (Connell, 2013; Han, 2008; Uljens, 2007). This particularly refers to the OECD's PISA study—although PISA undoubtedly has helped to raise awareness of old and new inequalities in education.

So far, PISA is the most comprehensive standardized achievement survey at the secondary education level. Its research design seeks to compare the competences of 15-year-old students and determinants of these competences at different levels in a broad international perspective. The Programme was explicitly administered by the OECD in order to foster reform and the improvement of secondary education (Anderson, Chiu, & Yore, 2010).

Since its first publication in 2001, PISA has generated considerable attention among policy makers, scholars, and media and seems to have successfully effectuated its explicit policy orientation. Particularly the first two studies triggered education policy changes in a number of participating countries. PISA is not the first standardized international student assessment and, although the OECD—unlike, for instance, the IEA—has no genuine capacity in education, it successfully framed education as an economic issue. Yet, numerous academic works have expressed severe concerns, challenging the cross-national comparability of competence measures and questioning the OECD's ability to provide evidence that meets scientific standards (Goldstein, 2004a; Prais, 2004). Some scholars try to explain the impact of the study by pointing to the "simplicity and presumed clarity" (Meyer & Benavot, 2013, p. 17) of the PISA country rankings. Further, the OECD's financial, social, and symbolic resources to disseminate PISA results are greater than those of the IEA for TIMSS/PIRLS and other studies (e.g., Civics).

THE POWER OF INTERNATIONAL ASSESSMENTS— THEORETICAL ACCOUNTS

Why Assessments (Do Not) Change Policies

International organizations and their policy projects—such as international school assessments—are likely to promote *convergence* (Drezner, 2001), since they disseminate coherent norms and policy models among their member states. Processes of convergence (in education) have theoretically been analyzed by the Stanford School of Sociological Institutionalism (Meyer, Ramirez, & Soysal, 1992; Powell & DiMaggio, 1991). One of their central assumptions is that the global proliferation of mass education is a means to achieve general societal aims such as democracy, human rights, and welfare. The common belief that education is a societal and economic necessity promoted the expansion of modern education systems during the second half of the twentieth century (Ramirez & Boli, 1987). Education systems of politically and economically powerful countries serve as role models in this respect, and international organizations help to disseminate these models (Meyer & Ramirez, 2009). This educational 'isomorphism' (i.e., copying from powerful countries) results in globally standardized and universal ideas about the organization of education. National idiosyncrasies become less relevant because they gradually converge into a 'world polity.' Thus, from the perspective of the Stanford School of Sociological Institutionalism, it is likely that education policies would become more similar over time.

However, despite internationalization, contemporary education systems differ across countries, raising doubts about the linear and deterministic mechanism of convergence. When it comes to non-convergence of policies, the theory of institutional differentiation (Lepsius, 1995) is useful, as it illuminates how conflicts between different spheres induce or impede change. This approach emphasizes the relevance of national idiosyncrasies and of power struggles between institutional contexts, which affect whether and how external influences shape national policies. According to Lepsius (1997), institutions are defined as social groups in behavioral contexts that establish rationality criteria according to which behavior can be evaluated. However, following the rationality criterion (e.g., policies that seek to increase test performance) can have effects for actors in other behavioral contexts or 'externalities.' Consequently, the process of institutionalization is dynamic because permanent conflicts arise over the extent to which various rationality criteria create which kinds of externalities. If we think of the education system, policy makers do not act independently. To remain in power, their actions have to be legitimized. Therefore, it is important that policies are in line with the general discourse of 'good education,' however that is understood. However, educational researchers and academics generally follow a different rationale than politicians. For example, they are rarely involved in (political) decision-making and rather seek for 'true' evidence. Further, other stakeholders in education (e.g., teachers or parents), in turn, follow their own rationales and might variously oppose or support reform ideas of policy makers. The theory of institutional differentiation further elucidates the role of political opportunity structures in a country (Knodel, Windzio, & Martens, 2014). Political opportunity structures define the accessibility of a political system for the strategic actions of collective actors (e.g., decentralized states often provide multiple access points). These opportunity structures potentially increase conflicts that arise between actors, inhibiting effective policy reforms.

Why Policies (Do Not) Change Practices and Outcomes

According to the Stanford School of Sociological Institutionalism, education policies around the world become more similar (i.e., isomorphic) and this is independent from national testing projects, which merely are one aspect of the process of isomorphism. Following Lepsius (1995), assessments can affect education policies if policy makers and other stakeholders in education agree on a new rationality criterion (i.e., high performance in assessments). However, change is not deterministic if it raises negative externalities and conflicts, which may derail expected consequences from the pursuit of a specific rational criterion.

However, education systems are not just about formal *policies*; the overall aim is to provide learning opportunities and to train students according to their interests and talents. These learning opportunities (as well as the sorting of students with its far-reaching consequences), are only indirectly influenced by formal policies. Thus, outcomes of education systems, such as average competence levels or social gradients, might differ across countries even though policies have converged. This would mean that reforms are not effective, in that they do not yield the desired *outcomes*. Education policies seek to set the *conditions* of learning processes in educational institutions; they structure opportunities and incentives for the behavior of teachers, school-heads, parents, and students (Knodel et al., 2014). Thus, the target of policies is the level of *practice* and the school as an organization.

As organizational sociology has shown, governing organizations is complex (Cohen et al., 1972). There are multiple sources of potential problems resulting, for example, from idiosyncratic considerations and strategies of members in the organization. Teachers and school-heads might be much more concerned about their personal situations, about power struggles within the staff room, or about their working hours than about a recent educational reform or results of international assessments. This means that learning in schools is often distorted by factors that are not always predictable. As a result, many actual tasks may not be solved adequately within the organization and efficiency may actually decrease after a reform is implemented, because the changes disrupt an already fragile system (Windzio, 2013, p. 10).

Finally, as Meyer and Rowan (1977) argue, organizations in modern societies tend to decouple their formal structures and their actual activities. If there are well-established norms in a society (e.g., to protect nature, to promote gender equality, or to participate in international assessments), organizations that formally follow these norms have a higher chance of success. Consequently, schools might adapt to increased testing (e.g., through 'teaching to the test'). In a best case scenario, external criteria and internal needs match, but often, the institutionalized external rules are costly for the organization (Meyer & Rowan, 1977). These arguments show that policy changes are not necessarily reflected in change of practice and, thus, are not always effective in having an impact on actual outcomes, such as learning or decreasing inequality. Internationalization of education is mediated through a range of institutions and evaluating the impact of testing has to take this complexity into account.

EMPIRICAL FINDINGS ON EFFECTS OF INTERNATIONAL TESTING PROJECTS ON POLICIES AND PRACTICES

Effects on Policies and Practice

Since the publication of the first PISA results in 2001, a considerable body of research, mostly country case studies dealing with effects of international assessments, has emerged. In Switzerland (Bieber, 2010, 2014; Bieber & Martens, 2011; Criblez, 2008), a federalist and multiculturalist state, education had been relatively stable for a long time before the first PISA round. The fact that Switzerland only reached rank 18 in reading in PISA 2000 triggered debates about the quality of the education system and finally led to major changes through the project HarmoS (Bieber, 2010). Bieber (2010, p. 121) concluded that PISA was considered a salvation because it illustrated weaknesses and reform potential and provided policy recommendations.

The USA has a long tradition of national assessments and its experiences served as a template for the design of international assessments. When assessing effects of international studies, the strongly decentralized structure of the education sector in the USA has to be taken into account. Experience with assessments, a decentralized system, and the circumstance that "US educators and policymakers are perpetually pessimistic about the quality of American education" (Wiseman, 2013, p. 305) might explain why PISA did not trigger any shocks, despite the fact that the USA only performed average in 2000 and below average in 2003. Only from 2009 onwards does there seem to be any reaction towards PISA data, especially in comparison to Asian countries and their high performances (Bieber, Martens, Niemann, & Windzio, 2014; Lee & Park, 2014; see more in Buckendahl, this volume).

Similarly, England had a long tradition of testing systems, and so PISA did not appear as something completely new, but rather as another burden (Knodel & Walkenhorst, 2010). Although it scored rather low in the first PISA studies, the results did not change policies or institutions in England. In New Zealand, a traditionally internationalized country, PISA results served as an argument to reconsider support strategies for weaker students, which however had been well established before (Dobbins, 2010).

Egelund (2008) traced the impact of PISA in Denmark, where the first PISA results raised debates as to why the highly funded Danish system had produced only moderate outcomes and social inequality remained high. Substantial changes towards increased national assessment procedures and support for disadvantaged students, however, were implemented only after an international in-depth review. Dolin (2007) shows that the Danish government introduced, with direct reference to the poor results in PISA 2003, a number of school tests, causing strong protest from the teachers' organizations and education researchers.

Popp (2014) illustrated how PISA raised attention to weaknesses in the education system of Spain, where students had performed below average in the first PISA rounds. Here too, PISA served as a source of legitimacy for reform. This worked even for very diverse and opposing policy ideas that were raised by the conservative and socialist parties, respectively (Bonal & Tarabini, 2013).

Another way of employing PISA as a policy tool has been described in Canada where the implementation of international assessments promoted an alignment of internal assessment programs with PISA and a harmonization of national indicators with OECD Education Indicators (Froese-Germain, 2010).

Further country case studies show how PISA results are used to legitimize previously intended reforms, for example Afonso and Costa (2009) for Portugal, Takayama (2008) for Japan, Rautalin and Alasuutari (2009) for Finland, and Gür, Çelik, & Özouglu (2012) for Turkey. Other works (e.g., Simola et al. [2013] with their study on Finland or Dobbins and Martens [2012] for France) analyze how PISA and its implications interact with national peculiarities and path dependencies. In a similar vein, a number of studies trace how PISA results and rhetoric are translated and reformulated according to preexisting national discourses (Berényi & Neumann, 2009; Mons & Pons, 2009; E. Neumann et al., 2012). Again others (e.g., Starr [2014] for Australia, and Mangez & Cattonar [2009] for Belgium) take a critical perspective against PISA and try to show negative aspects of increased competition and control.

In addition to these case studies, other research, which is not limited to developed countries and not restricted to the effects of PISA, provides overviews about policy effects of international student assessments (Best et al., 2013; Breakspear, 2012; Heyneman & Lee, 2014; Lockheed, 2013; Robitaille & Beaton, 2002; Schwippert, 2012; Wiseman, 2010, 2013). For example, Heyneman and Lee (2014) report changes in teaching practices after TIMSS 1995 and 1999 in England and in selected developing countries. They also summarize findings observing that Romania, Slovak Republic, Latvia, and Japan added new topics, mainly devoted to applicable competences and sciences, to their national curricula. Canada and New Zealand developed new instructional material as a reaction to TIMSS. By contrast, Macedonia, Israel, and Malaysia changed aspects of teacher training. As Heyneman and Lee further point out, other countries, such as Iceland, used test results as a trigger for reforms that had already been planned. Another aspect of change was the introduction of educational standards, which could be observed in, among others, Russia.

Breakspear (2012) conducted a standardized expert questionnaire among PISA Governing Board members and national experts of 37 PISA participating countries. The results revealed that 17 countries judged that PISA had been very influential and respondents from a further 11 countries evaluated PISA as moderately influential. In England, Denmark, and Japan, PISA was perceived as extremely influential (partly contradicted by other studies, Knodel [2014]). By contrast, respondents from Finland,

France, Indonesia, Luxembourg, and Turkey found PISA 'not very' influential (Breakspear, 2012). While the broad international perspective and the standardized survey is a strength, one has to keep in mind that the choice of respondents might inhibit objective and valid results.

Taken together, the diverse existing studies illustrate different ways countries have dealt with PISA and other testing projects. Some scholars have suggested typologies of reactions towards international assessments (Ozga, 2012). For example, Steiner-Khamsi distinguishes glorification, scandalisation, and indifference (Steiner-Khamsi, 2003). Grek (2009) identifies three different responses to PISA: surprise (e.g., Finland, where the good results in PISA 2000 were not expected), shock (e.g., Germany), and promotion (e.g., the U.K. where PISA is used for self-assurance). In countries where reactions to PISA were strong, actors typically adopted policy recommendations selectively and in an instrumental fashion (Bonal & Tarabini, 2013). Results and recommendations were chosen and reinterpreted deliberately to 'fit' the political agenda, often to legitimize and justify planned reforms (Feniger & Lefstein, 2014; Heyneman & Lee, 2014; Lingard & Lewis, this volume; Ozga, 2013; Sellar & Lingard, 2013). This means that any effects of PISA depend on pre-established opinions in a country (Pons, 2012). The idiosyncratic intentions of national actors, institutions, and cognitions should, thus, not be underestimated (Grek, 2012).

What is notable, however, is that the majority of the previous studies have only looked at the level of formal policies or of media and political discourse. What is neglected so far is the level of the enactment of such policies within the classroom and the outcomes of education systems. Although there is a vivid debate of how standards-based accountability and data-driven assessments distort the educational process (Froese-Germain, 2010), actual consequences are rarely analyzed. First steps in comparatively analyzing actors' reactions towards changes in policies exist (Martens, Knodel, & Windzio, 2014), but knowledge about the actual scope of policy effects is still limited.

The Case of Germany

Whenever the impact of international assessments is discussed, Germany is mentioned as an example where PISA results induced considerable changes in policies, practice, and even in the academic infrastructure of education research (Ertl, 2006; Hartong, 2012; Neumann, Fischer, & Kauertz, 2010). Traditionally, education policy making in Germany was strongly nationally organized, input-oriented, and mainly about budget allocation; very different from the view of education promoted by the OECD. Policy making in education was primarily shaped by strong federalism, granting exclusive policy-making competences to the *Länder* (i.e., state) level. The general understanding of education in Germany was traditionally shaped by humanistic ideas (Pepin, 1999). Furthermore, secondary schooling in Germany is tripartite in that students are separated after four years of primary schooling into one of three kinds of secondary schooling designed to cater for students according to their academic potential (i.e., *Hauptschule, Realschule,* and *Gymnasium;* lowest to highest potential respectively). The tripartite secondary school system can be understood as a generic feature of the overall German conservative welfare regime. This means that there are complementary institutions (e.g., vocational training), rendering the system relatively stable and resistant towards ad hoc changes. Accordingly, the comparison of educational performance or policies with other countries was uncommon.

In the early 1990s, Germany participated in the International Reading Literacy Study (IRLS). The results, although indicating rather mediocre reading abilities and a significant degree of educational inequality, did not attract the attention of policy makers. Likewise, the results of TIMSS in 1997 only motivated a small group of experts to develop reform plans. However, after the German 'PISA shock' in 2001 (Germany scored lower than Italy in reading), immense reforms were launched.

Consequently, PISA became a symbol in the German discourse and triggered a heated debate about the content and meaning of *Bildung* (i.e., education). It brought about a new understanding of school performance, as measurable and standardized competencies, as well as of teacher training (Klieme et al., 2003). Overall, policy making changed to output-based steering; economic ideas and evidence-based policy making superseded philosophical ideas of how education should be organized (Bieber et al., 2014). Consequently, traditional school settings were transformed, through an expansion of all-day schools and the introduction of different learning cultures regarding 'dealing with heterogeneity' and 'individualization of learning' (Fischer & Klieme, 2013). Further, school autonomy was expanded in all 16 states.

These structural changes were accompanied by the introduction of binding education standards that formulated the aims of education and provided the basis for the evaluation of school performances (Klieme et al., 2003). Education standards for mathematics, German, and foreign language were introduced in December 2003 and became effective for all states from 2004/2005 onwards (Niemann, 2014). The process of standardization was continuously expanded to subjects such as biology, chemistry, and physics. In 2004, a centralized organization, the Institute for Quality Development in the Education System (IQB) was founded to provide assistance to the states to monitor these standards. In 2006, the Standing Conference of the Ministers of Education and Cultural Affairs agreed on an overall strategy of educational monitoring (*Gesamtstrategie Bildungsmonitoring*; Kuhn [2014]) that comprised four central aspects: (1) participation in international assessments (i.e., PISA, TIMSS, and IGLU/PIRLS), (2) the centralized evaluation of education standards, (3) national tests, and (4) a national monitoring system (Niemann 2014).

Many of these changes were in line with OECD recommendations (Niemann, 2014); for example, the focus on early education, support for lower status students and quality assurance, all-day services, and a general shift of attention towards output measures. However, a major feature of the education systems remained untouched: the selective tripartite secondary education system. This is remarkable, because the PISA results indicate that early tracking and schooling in homogeneous classes is related to higher degrees of educational inequality and does not necessarily result in higher overall achievement. The adherence to the German selective school system reflects the principle that PISA recommendations are mediated according to long established national structures and perceptions.

As discussed earlier, implementation and effectiveness of reforms depend on diverse factors including what is happening in schools and teachers' stances towards the reforms. Although there was a clear cleavage between the OECD's economic approach and the traditional German holistic understanding of education, the teacher unions were already in favor of education reforms before the first PISA results were published. Thus, they could and did not criticize the reforms recommended by PISA. In general, the new output orientation was supported by teachers as long as it was accompanied by sufficient resource measures to target low outcomes (Niemann, 2014). Further, the reforms were subsequently supported by steadily rising PISA results (in the ranking of OECD countries, Germany ranked twenty-second in PISA 2000 and thirteenth in 2012, reflected in an absolute increase of 24 points on the reading scale). This was accompanied by a decreasing effect of socioeconomic status on reading performance (the respective indicator of 2012 amounted to less than 80% of the same indicator measured in 2000). Overall, the reactions of teachers were "not that severe" (Niemann, 2014, p. 100) since the need for reforms was undisputed.

Findings From Inside: What Does PISA Tell Us?

Other than Breakspear (2012), standardized surveys across several countries to evaluate the effects of assessments are rare. The question arises, whether data produced by international testing projects could actually be used to assess changes in policies and practices. PISA collects detailed information at the school level, covering a variety of aspects of school organization. Particularly, questions directed towards funding, school autonomy, admission policies, ability grouping, and assessment procedures are regularly included in the questionnaires. The resulting school level variables in the data sets can be aggregated at the country level and serve as indicators describing features of education systems. If there are comparable indicators available over time (as in the case of PISA, every three years), they can be used for trend analyses of convergence or divergence across countries or groups of countries. An advantage of such an approach is that information is collected at the school level and, thus, reflects the level of actual practice as compared to formal policy statements.

However, with PISA, a main difficulty arises from the fact that wording and coding of questions change substantially between study rounds. Accordingly, so far there are only very few attempts to use PISA data as a source for analyzing time trends in policies and practices (e.g., OECD 2014; Teltemann, 2014). Nevertheless, the first five PISA rounds available allow for comparisons of selected variables, such as school funding, school autonomy, and certain assessment and accountability practices at the school level. Since changes in accountability measures and in the usage of assessments are a typical policy response to PISA results (Wiseman, 2013), we present examples for changes in assessment practices at the school level. Within the PISA studies between 2000 and 2012, there are four different accountability-related questions that have been included in at least three of the five rounds. They relate to (a) the *frequency* of different forms of assessments, including standardized tests, assignments, and teacher-developed tests; (b) the *usage* of assessments, distinguishing among others between "used to inform parents," "used to group students for instructional purposes," and "used to compare the school to district or national performance"; (c) to *specific assessment measures* (e.g., "observation of classes by inspectors or other external persons") that have been used during the last year in a school, and (d) towards the usage of assessments, asking if assessment data are used for *specific accountability procedures*, for publication in the media, or for tracking by an administrative authority. For these four questions, we evaluate one item respectively, namely (1) assessment by standardized tests (at least one time per year), (2) use of assessments to compare to district or national performance, (3) observation of classes by inspectors or other external persons during the last year, and (4) tracking of achievement data. For each of these four items, we present aggregated mean values at the country level. These figures have to be read as: "X% of students in country Y attend schools where assessment practice Z is implemented." Bear in mind that the generalizability of the statement depends on the national sampling being sufficiently large and representative to support such claims. The analysis is restricted to OECD countries which have participated in all PISA studies.

Figure 21.1 presents findings for the prevalence of standardized assessments in schools. The darker bars depict 'change scores'; that is, the difference between the most recent available measurement (i.e., PISA 2009) and the first measurement (i.e., PISA 2000).

The graph shows that the number of students at schools using standardized assessments has increased in most OECD countries, most dramatically in Luxemburg, where 100% of all respondents in 2000 indicated never using standardized assessments. It is not clear however, if the values of 2000 result from a measurement error. The average across countries increased from 59% to 73%; at the same time the standard deviation decreased from 25% to 22%. Thus, there seems to be a trend towards more standardized tests over time, as well as towards more homogeneity across countries (in other words, greater isomorphism).

Figure 21.2 shows the proportion of 15-years-old students enrolled in schools that used assessments for comparison with district or national scores per country. This feature has been surveyed in 2000, 2003, 2009, and 2012. Again, the darker bars show changes between the first and the last measurement in a country, the lighter bars absolute values in 2012. Figure 21.2 illustrates that the practice of accountability increased considerably in many countries, corroborating the impression from Figure 21.1. Interestingly, PISA 2000 top performer Finland reduced the number of students attending schools using this accountability practice. Overall, there is still considerable variation across countries; the average proportion of students going to schools using assessments for national comparisons is 62%. However, the standard deviation is relatively high, but decreasing (from 27% in 2000 to 22% in 2012). Thus, we can again conclude that norm-referenced assessment practices have become more prevalent and OECD countries more similar over time.

Figure 21.3 illustrates the prevalence of an accountability procedure that is more elaborate and less standardized than the test practices presented above, namely school and class inspections by external experts. Not surprisingly, the overall implementation

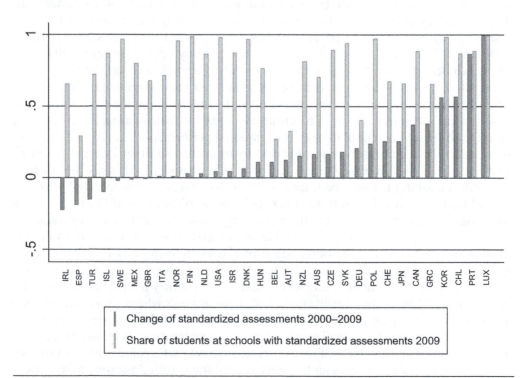

Figure 21.1 Proportion of Students Attending Schools Using Standardized Assessments

Source: OECD PISA databases 2000, 2003, 2009; own calculations

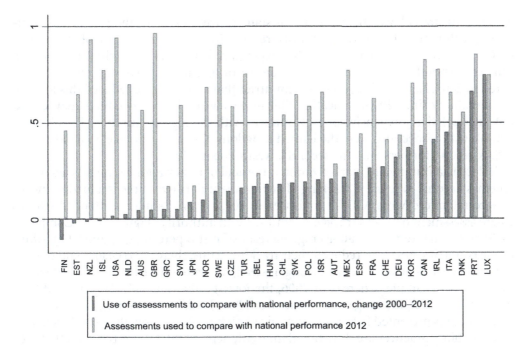

Figure 21.2 Proportion of Students Attending Schools Using Assessments to Compare With National or District Performance

Source: OECD PISA databases 2000, 2003, 2009, 2012; own calculations. See also Bieber, Martens, Niemann, & Teltemann (2015).

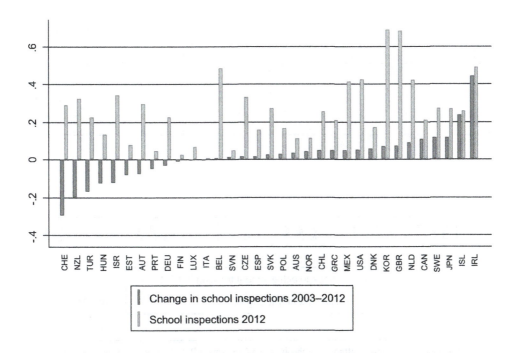

Figure 21.3 Proportion of Students Attending Schools Observed by External Inspectors

Source: OECD PISA databases 2003, 2009, 2012; own calculations. See also Bieber, Martens, Niemann, & Teltemann (2015).

of this measure is lower than the use of standardized tests and the practice of comparing with national performance measures. In 2012, on average, 27% of students in OECD countries attended schools that experienced inspections during the last year. This corresponds to a small average increase of about 2.3 percentage points compared to 2003. Nevertheless, there are countries that seem to have reduced this form of accountability since 2003, indicating that more standardized procedures may 'crowd out' such relatively expensive ones. Countries with the highest number of students at schools with inspections were the United Kingdom, Korea, and France. Finland, one of PISA's best performers, had the second lowest value in 2012.

If decentralization and marketization is the goal of policy reforms, quality assurance schemes become necessary. Tracking of achievement data over time is a further means of accountability. Across OECD countries, in 2012, 72% of students attended schools where assessment data was tracked over time by an authority (Figure 21.4). Compared to 2006, this figure reflects an average increase of just 6 percentage points. One-third of the countries, however, reduced their tracking. Thus, there is no clear trend of convergence towards achievement tracking; instead, the values have become slightly more extreme. For example, whereas in 2006, the lowest value was 16% (Japan) and 97% the highest (USA), the range took values from 7% (Japan) to 98% in the USA in 2012.

The figures presented here provide a mixed picture. They show that assessment and accountability practices are distributed unevenly across OECD countries and that they are dynamic. With the exception of external school observations, a rather specific measure, there is a tendency to expand standardized testing for accountability purposes.

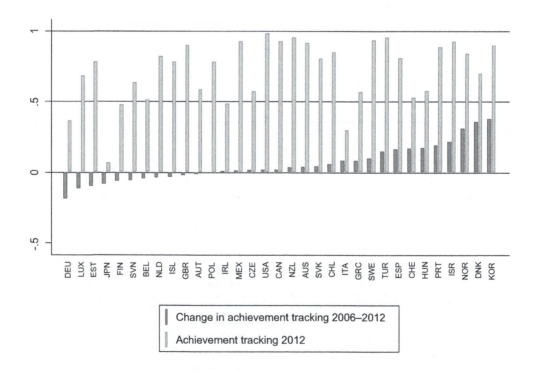

Figure 21.4 Proportion of Students Attending Schools Where Assessment Data Is Used by National or District Authority to Track Achievement

Source: OECD PISA databases 2006, 2009, 2012; own calculations. See also Bieber, Martens, Niemann, & Teltemann (2015).

The distinction between different measures of accountability might conceal a general trend since the different measures often serve a very similar purpose and, thus, not every practice is implemented everywhere. Rather, countries are likely to choose practices that are cost-effective and most accepted among the affected actors; hence, a greater probability of using standardized testing.

CONCLUSION

It seems undisputed that international testing projects, especially the OECD PISA study, have the potential to influence national policy making. PISA reflects a soft governance mechanism generating recommendations based on use and interpretation of comparative test results. However, the impact of the PISA system depends on being deliberately accepted by national actors, who exploit (Hanberger, 2014) results of assessments according to their own goals. This puts the assumption of an independent influence of the PISA testing project into perspective. According to the Stanford School of Sociological Institutionalism, assessments are only a concomitant feature of a world polity. While previous research has acknowledged the importance of existing national institutions and discourses, it has barely been asked in what ways and with which outcomes recent formal policy changes affected the education process. According to Lepsius's (1995) theory of institutional differentiation and organizational sociology, formal policy changes do not necessarily lead to the intended effects. Our descriptive analyses based on data from five PISA surveys showed how assessment practices at the school level have changed since the year 2000. Apart from the fact that new assessment practices might affect teaching practices ('teaching to the test'), more assessments often lead to a greater amount of data that has to be processed. Sometimes, authorities do this; in other cases teachers themselves may be urged to adjust their teaching and grading according to the generated data. Thus, there is a growing demand for a new qualification for teaching staff, namely the ability to handle assessment data in a responsible and autonomous way.

But overlooking the impact of PISA on practices and outcomes is not the only flaw in previous research. Particularly, the PISA study is often criticized for its economic, utilitarian idea of education and for a reductionist presentation of results (Connell, 2013; Dohn, 2007; Goldstein, 2004b; Prais, 2004; Uljens, 2007). What is most often ignored is the potential that the PISA data have in themselves. The data generated by PISA and comparable projects have considerable strength for educational effectiveness research as they cover multiple sources of variation in the determinants of educational outcomes (Hanushek & Wößmann, 2014). Unfortunately, there are relatively few primary or secondary analyses of the data by national researchers (Kanes, Morgan, & Tsatsaroni, 2014). Researchers should take responsibility to develop independent policy recommendations based on methodologically sound analyses. Methodological concerns regarding the validity of large scale international assessments can be put into perspective when understanding that the data they produce is suitable for high-level inferences, or in other words is dealing with "climate" and not with "weather" (Gustafsson & Rosen, 2014, p. 26)

Lastly, common research designs are often too constrained to gather solid findings on the interplay between international assessments, educational reform, practices, and learning outcomes. Traditionally, disciplinary oriented analyses are not able to capture the complex dynamics. Interdisciplinary approaches that focus simultaneously at different levels and processes in education (i.e., on formal policies, on discourses, on practices, and on outcomes) are required to illuminate the open question of effects of international school assessments. In addition to the necessary interdisciplinary approach, the elaboration of the longitudinal issue is crucial. The cross-sectional character of most testing projects prevents reliable findings on determinants of learning outcomes, as well as on causes of policy outcomes. Panel studies that are costly and effortful are not the only solution in this regard; the repeated character of testing projects such as PISA provides at least some possibilities for longitudinal analyses (Hanushek, Link, & Woessmann, 2011; Teltemann, 2014). Future research on effects of testing projects should focus on overcoming existing methodological and disciplinary limitations—the topic at stake is important enough.

REFERENCES

Afonso, N., & Costa, E. (2009). The influence of the Programme for International Student Assessment (PISA) on policy decision in Portugal: The education policies of the 17th Portuguese Constitutional Government. *Sísifo. Educational Sciences Journal, 10*, 53–64.

Anderson, J. O., Chiu, M.-H., & Yore, L. D. (2010). First cycle of PISA (2000–2006)-international perspectives on successes and challenges: Research and policy directions. *International Journal of Science And Mathematics Education, 8*(3), 373–388.

Becker, G. S. (1993). *Human capital: A theoretical and empirical analysis, with special reference to education.* Chicago, IL: The University of Chicago Press.

Berényi, E., & Neumann, E. (2009). Grappling with PISA—Reception and translation in the Hungarian policy discourse. *Sísifo. Educational Sciences Journal, 10*, 41–52.

Best, M., Knight, P., Lietz, P., Lockwood, C., Nugroho, D., & Tobin, M. (2013). *The impact of national and international assessment programmes on education policy, particularly policies regarding resource allocation and teaching and learning practices in developing countries.* Final report. London: EPPI-Centre, Social Science Research Unit, Institute of Education, University of London.

Bieber, T. (2010). Playing the multilevel game in education—The PISA study and the Bologna process triggering Swiss harmonization. In K. Martens, A. K. Nagel, M. Windzio, & A. Weymann (Eds.), *Transformation of education policy* (pp. 105–131). Basingstoke, UK: Palgrave Macmillan.

Bieber, T. (2014). Cooperation or conflict? Education policy in Switzerland after the PISA study and the Bologna process. In K. Martens, P. Knodel, & M. Windzio (Eds.), *Internationalization of education policy* (pp. 179–201). New York: Palgrave Macmillan.

Bieber, T., & Martens, K. (2011). The OECD PISA study as a soft power in education? Lessons from Switzerland and the US. *European Journal of Education, 46*(1), 101–116. doi:10.1111/j.1465–3435.2010.01462.x

Bieber, T., Martens, K., Niemann, D., & Teltemann, J. (2015). Towards a global model in education? International student literacy assessments and their impact on policies and institutions. In M. Hamilton, B. Maddox, & C. Addey (Eds.), *Literacy as Numbers. Researching the politics and practices of international literacy assessment* (pp. 165–186). Cambridge: Cambridge University Press.

Bieber, T., Martens, K., Niemann, D., & Windzio, M. (2014). Grenzenlose Bildungspolitik? Empirische Evidenz für PISA als weltweites Leitbild für nationale Bildungsreformen. *Zeitschrift Für Erziehungswissenschaft, 17*(S4), 141–166. doi:10.1007/s11618–014–0513–6

Bonal, X., & Tarabini, A. (2013). The role of PISA in shaping hegemonic educational discourses, policies and practices: The case of Spain. *Research in Comparative and International Education, 8*(3), 335–341. doi:10.2304/rcie.2013.8.3.335

Breakspear, S. (2012). The policy impact of PISA: An exploration of the normative effects of international benchmarking in school system performance. *OECD Education Working Paper Number 71*.

Cohen, M. D., March, J. G., & Olsen, J. P. (1972). A garbage can model of organizational choice. *Administrative Science Quarterly, 17*(1), 1–25.

Connell, R. (2013). The neoliberal cascade and education: An essay on the market agenda and its consequences. *Critical Studies in Education, 54*(2), 99–112. doi:10.1080/17508487.2013.776990

Criblez, L. (2008). Die neue Bildungsverfassung und die Harmonisierung des Bildungswesens. In L. Criblez (Ed.), *Bildungsraum Schweiz* (pp. 277–299). Bern, CH: Haupt.

Davis, K. E., Kingsbury, B., & Merry, S. E. (2012). Indicators as a technology of global governance. *Law & Society Review, 46*(1), 71–104. doi:10.1111/j.1540–5893.2012.00473.x

Dobbins, M. (2010). Education policy in New Zealand—Successfully navigating the international market for education. In K. Martens, A. K. Nagel, M. Windzio, & A. Weymann (Eds.), *Transformation of education policy* (pp. 153–178). Basingstoke, UK: Palgrave Macmillan.

Dobbins, M., & Martens, K. (2012). Towards an education approach à la finlandaise? French education policy after PISA. *Journal of Education Policy, 27*(1), 23–43. doi:10.1080/02680939.2011.622413

Dohn, N. B. (2007). Knowledge and skills for PISA? Assessing the assessment. *Journal of Philosophy of Education, 41*(1), 1–16. doi:10.1111/j.1467–9752.2007.00542.x

Dolin, J. (2007). PISA—An example of the use and misuse of large-scale comparative tests. In S. T. Hopmann, G. Brinek, & M. Retzl (Eds.), *PISA zufolge PISA—PISA according to PISA: Hält PISA, was es verspricht?— Does PISA keep, what it promises?* (pp. 93–125). Berlin, DE: LIT-Verlag.

Drezner, D. W. (2001). Globalization and policy convergence. *International Studies Review, 3*(1), 53–78. doi:10.1111/1521–9488.00225

Egelund, N. (2008). The value of international comparative studies of achievement—A Danish perspective. *Assessment in Education: Principles, Policy & Practice, 15*(3), 245–251. doi:10.1080/09695940802417400

Ertl, H. (2006). Educational standards and the changing discourse on education: The reception and consequences of the PISA study in Germany. *Oxford Review of Education, 32*(5), 619–634. doi:10.2307/4618685

Feniger, Y., & Lefstein, A. (2014). How not to reason with PISA data: An ironic investigation. *Journal of Education Policy, 29*(6), 845–855. doi:10.1080/02680939.2014.892156

Fischer, N. & Klieme, E. (2013). Quality and effectiveness of German all-day-schools: Results of the study on the development of all-day schools in Germany. In J. Ecarius, E. Klieme, L. Stecher, & J. Woods (Eds.), *Extended education–an international perspective: Proceedings of the International Conference on Extracurricular and Out-of-School-Time Educational Research* (pp. 27–52). Opladen: Budrich.

Froese-Germain, B. (2010). The OECD, PISA and the impacts on educational policy. *Virtual Research Centre (VRC),* (September).

Goldstein, H. (2004a). International comparisons of student attainment: Some issues arising from the PISA study. *Assessment in Education: Principles, Policy & Practice, 11*(3), 319–330. doi:10.1080/0969594042000304618

Goldstein, H. (2004b). International comparisons of student attainment: Some issues arising from the PISA study. *Assessment in Education: Principles, Policy & Practice, 11*(3), 319–330. doi:10.1080/0969594042000304618

Green, A. (1997). *Education, globalization and the Nation State.* Basingstoke: Palgrave Macmillan. doi:10.1057/9780230371132

Grek, S. (2009). Governing by numbers: The PISA "effect" in Europe. *Journal of Education Policy, 24*(1), 23–37. doi:10.1080/02680930802412669

Grek, S. (2012). What PISA knows and can do: Studying the role of national actors in the making of PISA. *European Educational Research Journal, 11*(2), 243–254. doi:10.2304/eerj.2012.11.2.243

Gür, B. S., Çelik, Z., & Özouglu, M. (2012). Policy options for Turkey: A critique of the interpretation and utilization of PISA results in Turkey. *Journal of Education Policy, 27*(1), 1–21. doi:10.1080/02680939.2011.595509

Gustafsson, J.-E., & Rosen, M. (2014). Quality and credibility of international studies. In R. Strietholt, W. Bos, J.-E. Gustafsson, & M. Rosén (Eds.), *Educational policy evaluation through international comparative assessments* (pp. 19–32). Münster, DE: Waxmann.

Han, S. (2008). Competence: Commodification of human ability. *Asia Pacific Education Review, 9*(1), 31–39. doi:10.1007/BF03025823

Hanberger, A. (2014). What PISA intends to and can possibly achieve: A critical programme theory analysis. *European Educational Research Journal, 13*(2), 167–180. doi:10.2304/eerj.2014.13.2.167

Hanushek, E. A., Link, S., & Woessmann, L. (2011). *Does school autonomy make sense everywhere? Panel estimates from PISA* (Vol. 3648: Eco). Munich, DE: University, Center for Economic Studies.

Hanushek, E. A., & Wößmann, L. (2014). Institutional structures of the education system and student achievement: A review of cross-country economic research. In R. Strietholt, W. Bos, J.-E. Gustafsson, & M. Rosen (Eds.), *Educational policy evaluation through international comparative assessments* (pp. 145–176). Münster: Waxmann.

Hartong, S. (2012). Overcoming resistance to change: PISA, school reform in Germany and the example of Lower Saxony. *Journal of Education Policy, 27*(6), 747–760. doi:10.1080/02680939.2012.672657

Heyneman, S. P., & Lee, B. (2014). The impact of international studies of academic achievement on policy and research. In L. Rutkowski, M. von Davier, & D. Rutkowski (Eds.), *Handbook of international large-scale assessment* (pp. 37–75). Boca Raton, FL: CRC Press.

Kamens, D. H., & McNeely, C. L. (2010). Globalization and the growth of international educational testing and national assessment. *Comparative Education Review, 54*(1), 5–25. doi:10.1086/648471

Kanes, C., Morgan, C., & Tsatsaroni, A. (2014). The PISA mathematics regime: Knowledge structures and practices of the self. *Educational Studies in Mathematics, 87*(2), 145–165. http://doi.org/10.1007/s10649–014–9542–6

Klieme, E., Avenarius, H., Blum, W., Döbrich, P., Gruber, H., Prenzel, M., Reiss, K., Riquarts, K., Rost, J., Tenorth, H.E. & Vollmer, J. (2003). Zur Entwicklung nationaler Bildungsstandards. Eine Expertise. [The Development of National Educational Standards. An Expertise]. Bonn: Bundesministerium für Bildung und Forschung. Reihe Bildungsreform, Band 1. (English version published 2004)

Knodel, P. (2014). On silent wings—PISA, Bologna, and the debate about internationalization in England. In K. Martens, P. Knodel, & M. Windzio (Eds.), *Internationalization of education policy* (pp. 142–162). New York: Palgrave Macmillan.

Knodel, P., Martens, K., Olano, D. de, & Popp, M. (Eds.). (2010). *Das PISA-Echo: Internationale Reaktionen auf die Bildungsstudie* (Vol. 16). Frankfurt am Main, DE: Campus-Verl.

Knodel, P., & Walkenhorst, H. (2010). What's England got to do with It?~British underestimation of international initiatives in education policy. In K. Martens, A. K. Nagel, M. Windzio, & A. Weymann (Eds.), *Transformation of education policy* (pp. 132–152). Basingstoke: Palgrave Macmillan.

Knodel, P., Windzio, M., & Martens, K. (2014). Outcomes and actors' reactions on internationalization in education policy—A theoretical approach. In K. Martens, P. Knodel, & M. Windzio (Eds.), *Internationalization of education policy* (pp. 1–34). New York: Palgrave Macmillan.

Kuhn, H.-J. (2014). Anspruch, Wirklichkeit und Perspektiven der Gesamtstrategie der KMK zum Bildungsmonitoring/Claim, reality and perspectives of the overall strategy of the KMK—ProQuest. *Die Deutsche Schule*, *106*(4), 414–426.

Lawn, M. (2013). *The rise of data in education systems : Collection, visualization and use.* Oxford: Symposium Books.

Lee, J., & Park, D. (2014). Do American and Korean education systems converge? Tracking school reform policies and outcomes in Korea and the USA. *Asia Pacific Education Review*, *15*(3), 391–399. doi:10.1007/s12564-014-9325-x

Lepsius, M. R. (1995). Institutionenanalyse und Institutionenpolitik. In B. Nedelmann (Ed.), *Politische Institutionen im Wandel* (Vol. 35, pp. 392–403). Opladen: Westdt. Verl.

Lepsius, M. R. (1997). Institutionalisierung und Deinstitutionalisierung von Rationalitätskriterien. In G. Göhler (Ed.), *Institutionenwandel* (pp. 57–69). Opladen: Westdt. Verl.

Leuze, K., Martens, K., & Rusconi, A. (2007). Introduction: New arenas of education governance : The impact of international organizations and markets on educational policy making. In K. Martens, A. Rusconi, & K. Leuze (Eds.), *New arenas of education governance : The impact of international organizations and markets on educational policy making* (pp. 3–15). Basingstoke, UK: Palgrave Macmillan.

Lingard, B., & Grek, S. (2006). The OECD, indicators and PISA: An exploration of events and theoretical perspectives. *ESRC/ESF Research Project on Fabricating Quality in Education Working Paper 2*(2003), 1–44.

Lingard, B., & Rawolle, S. (2011). New scalar politics: Implications for education policy. *Comparative Education*, *47*(4), 489–502. doi:10.1080/03050068.2011.555941

Lockheed, M. (2013). Causes and consequences of international assessments in developing countries. In H.-D. Meyer & A. Benavot (Eds.), *PISA, power, and policy: Oxford studies in comparative education* (pp. 163–184). Oxford: Symposium Books.

Mangez, E., & Cattonar, B. (2009). The status of PISA in the relationship between civil society and the educational sector in French-speaking Belgium. *Sísifo. Educational Sciences Journal*, *10*, 15–26.

Martens, K. (2007). How to become an influential actor—The 'Comparative Turn' in OECD education policy. In K. Martens, A. Rusconi, & K. Leuze (Eds.), *New arenas of education governance* (pp. 40–56). Basingstoke and Hampshire: Palgrave Macmillan.

Martens, K., Knodel, P., & Windzio, M. (Eds.). (2014). *Internationalization of education policy: A new constellation of statehood in education?* New York: Palgrave Macmillan.

Martens, K., Nagel, A. K., Windzio, M., & Weymann, A. (Eds.). (2010). *Transformation of education policy.* Basingstoke: Palgrave Macmillan.

Martens, K., & Weymann, A. (2007). The Internationalization of education policy—Towards convergence of national paths? In A. Hurrelmann (Ed.), *Transforming the golden-age nation state* (pp. 152–172). Basingstoke: Palgrave Macmillan.

Meyer, H.-D., & Benavot, A. (2013). PISA and the globalization of education governance: some puzzles and problems. In H.-D. Meyer & A. Benavot (Eds.), *PISA, power, and policy: Oxford studies in comparative education* (pp. 7–26). Oxford: Symposium Books.

Meyer, H.-D., & Schiller, K. (2013). Gauging the role of non-educational effects in large-scale assessments: Socio-economics, culture and PISA outcomes. In H.-D. Meyer & A. Benavot (Eds.), *PISA, power, and policy: Oxford studies in comparative education* (pp. 207–224). Oxford: Symposium Books.

Meyer, J. W., & Ramirez, F. O. (2009). The world institutionalization of education. In J. Schriewer (Ed.), *Discourse formation in comparative education* (Vol. 10, pp. 111–132). Frankfurt and M.; Berlin; Bern; Bruxelles; New York; Oxford and Wien: Lang.

Meyer, J. W., Ramirez, F. O., & Soysal, Y. N. (1992). World expansion of mass education, 1870–1980. *Sociology of Education*, *65*(2), 128. doi:10.2307/2112679

Meyer, J. W., & Rowan, B. (1977). Institutionalized organizations: Formal structure as myth and ceremony. *American Journal of Sociology*, *83*(2), 340–363.

Mons, N., & Pons, X. (2009). The reception of PISA in France—A cognitive approach of institutional debate (2001–2008). *Sísifo. Educational Sciences Journal, 10,* 27–40.

Neumann, E., Kiss, A., Fejes, I., Bajomi, I., Berényi, E., Biró, Z. A., & Vida, J. (2012). The hard work of interpretation: The national politics of PISA reception in Hungary and Romania. *European Educational Research Journal, 11*(2), 227. doi:10.2304/eerj.2012.11.2.227

Neumann, K., Fischer, H. E., & Kauertz, A. (2010). From Pisa to educational standards: The impact of large-scale assessments on science education in Germany. *International Journal of Science and Mathematics Education, 8*(3), 545–563. doi:10.1007/s10763–010–9206–7

Niemann, D. (2014). After the big bang: German education policy in the wake of the PISA study and the Bologna process. In K. Martens, P. Knodel, & M. Windzio (Eds.), *Internationalization of education policy. A new constellation of statehood in education?* (pp. 91–114). London, UK: Palgrave Macmillan.

Normand, R. (2008). School effectiveness or the horizon of the world as a laboratory. *British Journal of Sociology of Education, 29*(6), 665–676. doi:10.1080/01425690802423346

OECD. (2014). *Measuring innovation in education: A new perspective.* Paris, France: OECD Publishing.

Owens, T. L. (2013). Thinking beyond league tables: A review of key PISA research questions. In H.-D. Meyer & A. Benavot (Eds.), *PISA, power, and policy: Oxford studies in comparative education* (pp. 27–50). Oxford: Symposium Books.

Ozga, J. (2012). Assessing PISA. *European Educational Research Journal, 11*(2), 166–171. doi:10.2304/eerj.2012.11.2.166

Ozga, J. (2013). Accountability as a policy technology: Accounting for education performance in Europe. *International Review of Administrative Sciences, 79*(2), 292–309. doi:10.1177/0020852313477763

Pepin, B. (1999). The influence of national cultural traditions on pedagogy: Classroom practice in England, France and Germany. In J. Leach & B. Moon (Eds.), *Learners & pedagogy* (pp. 124–136). London: Sage Publications.

Pons, X. (2012). Going beyond the "PISA Shock" discourse: An analysis of the cognitive reception of PISA in six European countries, 2001–2008. *European Educational Research Journal, 11*(2), 206–226. doi:10.2304/eerj.2012.11.2.206

Popp, M. (2014). New culture, old system—Reactions to internationalization in Spanish education policy. In K. Martens, P. Knodel, & M. Windzio (Eds.), *Internationalization of education policy* (pp. 163–178). New York: Palgrave Macmillan.

Powell, W. W., & DiMaggio, P. (1991). *The New institutionalism in organizational analysis.* Chicago, IL: University of Chicago Press.

Prais, S. J. (2004). Cautions on OECD's recent educational survey (PISA): Rejoinder to OECD's response. *Oxford Review of Education, 30*(4), 569–573. doi:10.2307/4127166

Ramirez, F. O., & Boli, J. (1987). The political construction of mass schooling: European origins and worldwide institutionalization. *Sociology of Education, 60*(1), 2–17. doi:10.2307/2112615

Rautalin, M., & Alasuutari, P. (2009). The uses of the national PISA results by Finnish officials in central government. *Journal of Education Policy, 24*(5), 539–556.

Robitaille, D. F., & Beaton, A. E. (2002). *Secondary analysis of the TIMSS data.* Dordrecht and Boston: Kluwer Academic Publishers.

Schwippert, K. (2012). *Progress in reading literacy in national and international context: The impact of PIRLS 2006 in 12 countries* (Vol. 13). Münster: Waxmann.

Sellar, S., & Lingard, B. (2013). PISA and the expanding role of the OECD in global educational governance. In H.-D. Meyer & A. Benavot (Eds.), *PISA, power, and policy: Oxford studies in comparative education* (pp. 185–206). Oxford: Symposium Books.

Simola, H., Rinne, R., Varjo, J., & Kauko, J. (2013). The paradox of the education race: How to win the ranking game by sailing to headwind. *Journal of Education Policy, 28*(5), 612–633. doi:10.1080/02680939.2012.758832

Starr, K. (2014). The influences and implications of PISA: An Australian perspective. *AASA Journal of Scholarship and Practice, 10*(4), 19–30.

Steiner-Khamsi, G. (2003). The politics of league tables. *Journal of Social Science Education,* (December 2004), 1. Retrieved December 15, 2004 from http://www.jsse. org/index.php/jsse/article/view/470/386. doi: 10.4119/UNIBI/jsse-v2-i1-470

Steiner-Khamsi, G. (2004). *The global politics of educational borrowing and lending.* New York: Teachers College Press.

Takayama, K. (2008). The politics of international league tables: PISA in Japan's achievement crisis debate. *Comparative Education, 44*(4), 387–407. doi:10.1080/03050060802481413

Teltemann, J. (2014). Achievement vs. Equality—What determines PISA performance? In K. Martens, P. Knodel, & M. Windzio (Eds.), *Internationalization of education policy. A new constellation of statehood in education?* Basingstoke: Palgrave Macmillan.

Uljens, M. (2007). The hidden curriculum of PISA—The promotion of neo-liberal policy by educational assessment. In S. Hopmann, G. Brinek, & M. Retzl (Eds.), *PISA zufolge PISA* (Vol. 6, pp. 295–303). Wien: Lit.

Windzio, M. (2013). Integration and inequality in educational institutions: An institutional perspective. In M. Windzio (Ed.), *Integration and inequality in educational institutions* (pp. 3–20). Dordrecht and New York: Springer.

Wiseman, A. W. (2010). *The impact of international achievement studies on national education policymaking.* Bingley: Emerald.

Wiseman, A. W. (2013). Policy responses to PISA in comparative perspective. In H.-D. Meyer & A. Benavot (Eds.), *PISA, power, and policy: Oxford studies in comparative education* (pp. 303–322). Oxford: Symposium Books.

22

GLOBALIZATION OF THE ANGLO-AMERICAN APPROACH TO TOP-DOWN, TEST-BASED EDUCATIONAL ACCOUNTABILITY

Bob Lingard and Steven Lewis

INTRODUCTION

This chapter deals with the globalization of the Anglo-American approach to educational accountability that first emerged in the early 1980s. This top-down, test-based mode of accountability developed in the USA in incremental ways from the time of President Reagan's influential and critical report on schooling, *A Nation at Risk* (1983), which argued for school reform and the raising of standards in a policy domain over which the federal government had, historically and constitutionally, limited jurisdiction. There were also parallel developments in England from the time of Thatcher's prime ministership (1979–1990) following the 1988 *Education Reform Act*, which witnessed the first national curriculum in England and the introduction of standardized testing for all students in all schools. We refer here to England, rather than the U.K., given different developments in schooling in Scotland, Wales, and Northern Ireland.

Top-down, test-based accountability in education gathered pace in the USA following President George W. Bush's federal legislation in the *No Child Left Behind Act* ("No Child Left Behind (NCLB) Act of 2001," 2002), and was firmly institutionalized under the Obama presidency through *Race to the Top* (RTTT) (US Department of Education, 2009) and agreement by the majority of states to a common core for curriculum. The latter has witnessed a huge growth in policy and funding based on test results, with this situation opening up spaces for edu-businesses to develop, manage, and administer testing, as the State itself has been downsized and some of its functions outsourced (Burch, 2009). A requirement for states to win federal RTTT funding (a good example of a funding/compliance trade-off) is that they have relevant test performance data and create the required data infrastructure (Anagnostopoulos, Rutledge, & Jacobsen, 2013). This has complemented the push for even more testing linked to the implementation of the common core.

Similarly, top-down, test-based accountability was introduced in England during Thatcher's period of government, entrenched under the New Labour governments of Blair and Brown, and strengthened further under both Coalition and Conservative governments through to the present. The effect has been a strengthening of the hand of the Westminster government in schooling in England and a weakening of the role of local government, with the system constructed through test data and related account-ability measures (Lawn, 2013; Ozga, 2009).

The title of this chapter suggests that the Anglo-American model of accountability has become globalized, and we argue this reflects what de Sousa Santos (2006) calls a globalized localism, or the ways in which this local Anglo-American development has spread globally. Sahlberg (2011) proposes a similarly global spread of schooling policy in his talk of the Global Educational Reform Movement (GERM), which he suggests is infecting schooling systems in negative ways, across both developing and developed nations. We would contend that GERM is, in fact, the globalization of more local Anglo-American developments. GERM emphasizes several related measures, includ-ing: high-stakes testing; educational accountability based on testing; national curricula (e.g., England and Australia); an emphasis on literacy and numeracy (e.g., Ontario and Australia) and standards; new managerialism; and marketization and privatization of various kinds (Ball, 2012; Ball & Youdell, 2008). This regime includes school choice policies and competition between schools as a putative means to drive up standards.

From the late 1990s, the USA pressured the OECD to develop comparative inter-national measures of school system performance (Henry, Lingard, Rizvi, & Taylor, 2001). The OECD response created what has become the annual report *Education at a Glance*, which provides comparative input/outcome measures of school system performance across the 34 OECD member countries. The substantive move, however, came with the OECD's creation of the *Programme for International Student Assess-ment* (PISA), first administered in 2000 and then every three years subsequently. The numbers participating have grown so that in 2012, for example, 65 countries and economies participated, with almost as many non-members as member nations participating. Although nations or economies pay to participate, it is expected that PISA 2015 will measure the performance of more than 70 national (and subnational) schooling systems (OECD, 2015).

What we have today then is a complementarity between these global measures of national system performance and testing within nations (Lingard, Martino, & Rezai-Rashti, 2013). Nóvoa and Yariv-Mashal (2003) actually speak of the 'global eye' and the 'national eye' governing together: a politics of mutual global accountability related to comparison as central to new modes of governance. PISA has also become a prototype inside the OECD for other related policy developments, such as the *Programme for International Assessment of Adult Competencies* (PIAAC), *Assessment of Higher Educa-tion Learning Outcomes* (AHELO), *PISA for Schools*, and *PISA for Development*. In this sense, we consider the OECD's education policy work as expanding the *scope* (what is measured), *scale* (number of nations and systems participating), and *explanatory power* of PISA (e.g., attempting to link classroom practices with test scores) (Sel-lar & Lingard, 2014). The International Association for the Evaluation of Educational Achievement's (IEA) *Trends in International Science and Maths Study* (TIMSS) and *Progress in International Reading Literacy Study* (PIRLS) also contribute, with PISA and related developments, to making the globe a commensurate space of measurement and governance.

We, thus, see two emergent realities of education policy making globally: (1) it is no longer the sole purview of national governments, involving instead a diverse and ever-changing array of actors and organizations from the public, private, intergov-ernmental, and voluntary sectors, including edu-businesses; and (2) processes of development and enactment are no longer confined within the traditional territorial boundaries of the nation-state. Instead, networked connections between these policy actors and agencies help constitute the very spaces in which processes of policy making and implementation occur, with issues of *relation* perhaps being of greater influence than issues of *location* (Allen, 2011).

In what follows, we contextualize this policy assemblage and elaborate the relationships it has to new modes of educational governance associated with State restructuring, before documenting specific developments in top-down, test-based accountability in the USA. We, then, provide an account of the ways in which the Anglo-American model has been localized in Australia, before documenting somewhat alternative developments in Finland. We conclude with a discussion of these matters and the costs of top-down, test-based accountability, and call for the development of alternative educational accountabilities.

CONTEXTUALIZING NEW MODES OF ACCOUNTABILITIES: FROM GOVERNMENT TO GOVERNANCE

Since the end of the Cold War, neoliberalism has arguably become the dominant political ideology on a global scale. Neoliberalism prioritizes (a) the market over the State and (b) the individual over the common good, manifesting in different nations in decidedly vernacular ways (Appadurai, 1996). Neoliberalism has also been accompanied by the restructuring of the State bureaucracy under the principles of New Public Management (NPM), which has in turn influenced public sector reform and governance (Hood, 1990). These processes of reform have occurred with varying intensities in England and the USA from the late 1970s, and more recently in countries including Canada, Australia, and New Zealand (Jessop, 2002).

NPM advocates the replacement of traditional bureaucratic modes of governing with managerial values and tenets derived from the private sector. In particular, the control of outputs, performance, and efficiency is afforded much greater significance than focusing on inputs or processes, a feature endemic to traditional bureaucracies (Rizvi & Lingard, 2010). These methods include: devolving the responsibility for policy enactment to local actors and practitioners; the use of (largely quantitative) indicators to measure outputs and performance, and to hold local sites accountable; a readiness to respond to 'customer needs'; and a focus upon entrepreneurialism in organizational culture (Ball & Junemann, 2012). Adopting such sensibilities into governing helps avoid the (alleged) inherent 'failings' of bureaucracy, with power and responsibility reallocated to a diverse range of policy actors and agencies supposedly 'better suited' to the provision of public services.

Neoliberalism has, thus, seen government develop a somewhat paradoxical 'big-small' nature, with the withdrawal of service provision from the social sector accompanying an increasing regulatory stance, and with government effectively setting the rules of the (market) game. As individuals are positioned to take greater responsibility for their own economic and social development and well-being, the hand of government has become less visible but arguably more palpable through indirect modes of steering. We believe schooling has taken on a central role in this move. Here we can see how contemporary governance discourses and practices, in particular NPM and (subsequently) networked, or *heterarchical*, governance, have emerged through the neoliberal redefining of the State upon market principles. In this instance, network governance involves the inclusion of horizontal relationships and new non-State actors into the work of the State, while heterarchy refers to the combination of these new horizontal and older vertical relationships, and modes of organization, through which the State now functions (Ball & Junemann, 2012). For example, heterarchical modes of governance see governments outsource test development, management, and analysis to edu-businesses, and/or to international and intergovernmental organizations (e.g., the OECD), and also involve them in policy processes. This results in the displacement of government as the sole provider and site of public policy production, enactment, and evaluation, with education policy now effectively "being 'thought', influenced and done, locally and nationally, in many different sites by an increasing number and diverse set of actors and organizations" (Ball & Junemann, 2012, p. 9).

Whereas the power of governing was previously, and in many respects solely, wielded by the hierarchical government bureaucracies of nation-states under the direction of elected politicians, neoliberalism has produced a move from *government* to *governance* (Ball & Junemann, 2012; Rhodes, 1997). Central to this move to governance are processes of comparison of performance, the development of associated data infrastructures, and the involvement of non-State actors in the work of the State. Here we can see policy heterarchies and networked modes of governance that bring together a diverse range of government and non-government actors and that stretch beyond both the nation-state and traditional divisions between the public and private sectors. Indeed, the contemporary governance of schooling includes intergovernmental organizations (e.g., the OECD) and various non-governmental bodies, including transnational edu-businesses, philanthropic foundations, and not-for-profit agencies, in processes of policy production, enactment, and evaluation. Indeed, proponents of such networked modes of governance argue that it provides the flexibility, innovation, and external orientation necessary to adjust to changing economic and social conditions, and in ways largely unavailable to top-down bureaucratic government (Eggers, 2008; Scharpf, 1994).

While this new arrangement sees government relinquish some of its 'privileged' position, it must be emphasized that "the [S]tate does not 'go away'" (Ozga, 2009, p. 158), but rather that it still possesses the ability to "indirectly and imperfectly steer networks" (Rhodes, 1997, p. 53). This steering may occur via such mechanisms as accountability regimes driven by government legislation (e.g., NCLB in the USA), the provision of funding associated with performance targets established by government (e.g., RTTT in the USA), the collection and management of performance data such as Australia's *National Assessment Program—Literacy and Numeracy* (NAPLAN) (ACARA, 2011), or the OECD's PISA and PISA for Schools.

Collectively, these developments have complemented the global ascendance of what has been described as a "neoliberal imaginary" (Rizvi & Lingard, 2010), in which social domains and practices are increasingly viewed through an economistic framework, leading to the economization of social life (Ball, 2012). In short, more market and less State; more individual responsibility and less welfare provision; and more focus on the individual and less on the common good. Schooling accountability, and hence assessment policy, is now increasingly framed by this neoliberalism, while schooling itself is, at the same time, restructured to produce such self-responsibilizing individuals (Rose, 1999).

THE EDUCATIONAL IMPACTS OF NETWORKS, NPM, AND NEOLIBERALISM

Top-down, test-driven modes of accountability generate large amounts of data, in schools and at the system level, for the purposes of measuring and governing performance. In the context of educational accountability and governance, these developments also reflect the relevance of numbers (Lingard, 2011) and data (Ozga, 2009), and a growing sense of policy and governance by numbers (Grek, 2009; Rose, 1999).

For instance, enumerations of education performance—notably PISA on a global scale, but also various national articulations (e.g., NAPLAN in Australia)—produce commensurable spaces of measurement, in which different schools and/or schooling systems can be putatively 'known,' compared, and evaluated by reference to a common metric. While this assumed comparability largely elides local contexts, histories, and cultures, there is also the added danger that what matters in education becomes restricted to what is measured (Wilson, Croxson, & Atkinson, 2006), meaning that the complex intricacies of schooling and pedagogy are reduced to the readily quantifiable. As policy has been constituted through numbers and metrics, edu-businesses have also taken on an increasing role in network governance and policy (Au & Ferrare, 2015; Ball, 2012; Burch, 2009).

In this context, edu-businesses not only carry out government policy, but are also active in making that very policy (Mahony, Hextall, & Menter, 2004), effectively opening up new, and often profitable, policy spaces and opportunities for corporate involvement in the networked governance of education. Ball (2012) notes that this now involves:

> the production by education and consultancy companies of policy "texts" and policy ideas *for* and *within* the state, that is, the export of "statework" to private providers and "agencies", and the formation and dissemination of new policy discourses arising out of the participation of these companies in report writing, evaluations, advice, consultancy and recommendations.
>
> (p. 99; emphasis original)

Two recent examples in the USA of edu-businesses, and other non-government organizations, proffering (or, more accurately, *selling*) private 'solutions' to the notionally public 'problem' of education may be particularly illustrative. We consider the recent development and administration of the OECD's PISA for Schools test in the USA as occurring in the context of such moves toward networked forms of educational governance (Lewis, Sellar, & Lingard, in press). Here, a range of non-government and intergovernmental organizations has collaborated to sponsor and fund policy, and provide testing services to U.S. schools and districts. Although officially overseen by the OECD, PISA for Schools has been funded by a series of major American philanthropic trusts and is managed, in practice, in the USA by the edu-business CTB McGraw-Hill and the not-for-profit agency America Achieves. This makes available new opportunities for the export of statework to a variety of private providers (Ball, 2012), enabling schools to engage with global discourses and comparative benchmarking that make available new possibilities for local policy and practice (Lewis et al., in press). The local uptake of PISA for Schools in the USA can also be viewed as developing out of existing national and state-level data infrastructures (Sellar, 2014), and from rationales of accountability facilitated by government legislation, such as RTTT (Mintrop & Sunderman, 2013). In both instances, data—and attendant processes of 'datafication' (Mayer-Schönberger & Cukier, 2013)—are given an increasingly prominent position in how schooling is known and governed.

While not wishing to critique schools and districts that voluntarily employ such data to inform local policy making and decision-making (Lai & Schildkamp, this volume), we would suggest that an overwhelming focus on 'improving' performance data as an end in itself creates potentially corruptible situations. As Charles Goodhart (1984) presciently noted, "Any statistical regularity will tend to collapse once pressure is placed upon it for control purposes" (p. 96). We would also draw attention to the fact that employing such data in 'evidence-based' policy making is never a purely objective or 'scientific' practice, as it is necessarily mediated, to a greater or lesser extent, by political and ideological judgments and prioritization, as well as by professional values at the moment of enactment (Head, 2008).

As a further example, Pearson plc, the world's largest edu-business, accrued approximately US$6 billion in sales globally in 2014, making more than half of its profits in the USA. Ravitch (2012) has aptly described this situation as the 'Pearsonization' of U.S. education. For example, Pearson has contracts in New York State for the PARCC (*Partnership for Assessment of Readiness for College and Careers*) tests, teacher certification and evaluation, and language arts and mathematics tests for all students from Grades 3 to 8, constituting a US$32 million contract over five years. A strategic business goal of Pearson is also to help set global educational policy agendas, through meta-analyses like *The Learning Curve* (Hogan, Sellar, & Lingard, 2015), which arguably privileges access of such edu-businesses to politicians and policy makers. Indeed, the Center for Media and Democracy in Wisconsin has noted how the four companies with the largest share of student testing in the USA—Pearson, Educational Testing Service, Houghton Mifflin Harcourt, and CTB/McGraw-Hill—expended US$20 million during the period 2009–2014 lobbying state and federal governments on the need for mandated student assessments (Harrer, 2015).

Of course, our purpose here is not to (un)reflexively position all private involvement in education as necessarily bad or harmful simply by virtue of it being private, and we would note the long-established (and legitimate) role that edu-businesses have played in the production and provision of textbooks for decades in the USA. Rather, we draw attention to the potential dangers arising when unelected private interests and motives, including *profit*, become deeply embedded in the public domain of education policy making, and where the provision of schooling is construed more as a 'business opportunity' (Ball, 2012).

GLOBALIZED LOCALISM: ANGLO-AMERICAN MODES OF EDUCATIONAL ACCOUNTABILITY AND GERMS

It is important here not to conflate the apparent material (e.g., tests, infrastructures) and discursive convergence of education policy (Rutkowski, 2007) with a deterministic notion of globalization. Globalized educational policy discourses such as GERM are always, to a greater or lesser degree, locally inflected by the historical and political specificities of a given nation or context. As noted by de Sousa Santos (2006), "there is no originally global position; what we call globalization is always *the successive globalization of a particular localism*" (p. 396; emphasis added). We can see how such complementarity arises between Anglo-American modes of accountability (i.e., test-based, top-down, evidence-based, marketized) and other more 'global' developments, with the features of GERM enacted in vernacular ways within different nations and systems, and always mediated by local histories, politics, and cultures. Hence, we think we ought to speak of *GERMs*, instead of an essentialized GERM.

This mediation is what is referred to as path dependency for policy in specific systems (Simola, Rinne, Varjo, & Kauko, 2013; Takayama, 2015), vernacular globalization (Appadurai, 1996), or localized globalisms (de Sousa Santos, 2006). The take-up in various nations of an Anglo-American model of accountability might, thus, be seen as an example of localized globalism—a globalism that itself emerged from the globalization of a local Anglo-American approach. Rather than considering the national scale as subordinate to the international and global, and, thus, positioning U.S. schooling accountability solely as a local articulation of international discourses and processes, we propose an alternative rendering in which local Anglo-American accountabilities have informed more global developments. In this way, global convergences in education policy such as GERM can be seen more as the successive globalization of American and English policies and practices, rather than somehow appearing spontaneously and irreversibly *ex nihilo* around the world.

Globalized localisms and localized globalisms are both integral parts of top-down multiscalar globalization, where the nation-state is but one scale overlapped by, and overlapping, many supranational and subnational territorial spaces (Brenner, 2004; Jessop, 2008; Sassen, 2006). They also create new 'topological' spatialities of globalization based on relations (discursive and/or material) between individuals and organizations (Amin, 2002), such as when the OECD 'reaches' into school level spaces through PISA for Schools (Lewis et al., in press). These topological spatialities framed around relations can be contrasted with more 'topographical' relations, which are framed around geography and location. However, local sites are not straightforwardly amenable to the one-way import of discursive and material flows, as reflected by the varied use and uptake of PISA in various national spaces (Carvalho & Costa, 2014). Thus, while Anglo-American approaches to educational accountability are currently ascendant and prevalent within circulating global discourses, we would stress that such developments are far from universal, and are instead highly contingent on the local conditions where such accountabilities may be deployed.

U.S. DEVELOPMENTS IN EDUCATIONAL ACCOUNTABILITY

We have spoken about the Anglo-American approach to educational accountability. Here we will document a longer history of the specific U.S. example, a particular localism, because it represents the most developed instance of top-down, test-driven modes of accountability, and the expression of a strong privatization agenda. This particular policy assemblage can be traced back to growing concerns about falling U.S. educational standards that first became prevalent from the early 1980s, and the purported national 'crisis' that would follow in its wake (Slater, 2014).

Externalization (Schriewer, 1990) is a process whereby national and other systems of schooling use comparative test performance as a justification for reform that needs political legitimation, rather than as a genuine means for learning from a reference society (Schriewer & Martinez, 2004). After World War II, the USA looked purposefully abroad (i.e., 'externalized') to international reference societies, supposedly for learning purposes and for the purpose of legitimating domestic educational reforms (Takayama, 2008). For example, the launch of *Sputnik* by the Soviet Union in 1957 catalyzed increased U.S. funding and focus towards the militarily and economically critical subjects of science, technology, engineering, and mathematics (STEM) (Tröhler, 2013). *A Nation at Risk* (1983) justified an extensive reform agenda by comparing a stagnating U.S. school system against its supposedly high performing global competitors, such as Germany and Japan (Takayama, 2007). Amongst the many recommendations, the foremost consideration was the development of standardized tests of student achievement at major transition phases during K–12 schooling. This was notionally to verify learning outcomes and to identify instances where remedial or advanced tuition was required to achieve more rigorous and measurable standards. Here we see the gradual dominant positioning of student performance testing in the USA, and the commensurate development of state and national regimes to effect such measurements.

It is noteworthy that referencing U.S. student performance to the performance of other national systems has been a continuing justification for educational reforms.

For example, the unprecedented (and unexpected) stellar performance of Shanghai, China, on PISA 2009 and 2012 was a watershed in U.S. education (Sellar & Lingard, 2013). President Obama noted it was a contemporary *Sputnik* moment during a speech to a North Carolina college audience, which was subsequently reprinted in *The New York Times*: "Fifty years later, our generation's *Sputnik* moment is back. As it stands right now, America is in danger of falling behind" (Dillon, 2010, para. 22). We note too that the U.S. reaction to comparative PISA performance is not unfamiliar to other nations. For example, there have been similar 'PISA shocks' in Germany, following its poor comparative performance on PISA 2000, and Japan, with respect to its declining math performance on PISA 2006. Such shocks resulted in the institution of numerous policy reforms, including new forms of standardized student testing and changes to curriculum in both countries (Ertl, 2006; Grek, 2009; Takayama, 2008, 2010; Teltemann & Klieme, this volume). Shanghai's unprecedented PISA performance also precipitated high levels of political and policy consternation in Australia, resulting in a target to be back in the 'top five' of PISA by 2025 being written into federal government legislation (Australian Government, 2012). This demonstrates how international test-based accountabilities can exert a disproportionately significant influence on local education reforms, including schooling systems implementing their own standardized national measures of school performance that are often modeled on PISA testing.

Following the reforms instigated by *A Nation at Risk*, high-stakes, test-based accountabilities in the USA have since undergone numerous permutations (e.g., NCLB and RTTT); Nichols and Harris (this volume) provide a description of these federal and state government initiatives. State-based accountability systems founded on student testing have long predated such recent responses to accountability and are therefore not in themselves unique (Smith & Fey, 2000; Smith, Heinecke, & Noble, 1999). However, evident here is the assumption that testing, *ipso facto*, improves learning and performance (Linn, 2000), while the evidence would suggest that an emphasis on testing largely improves test-taking and strengthens teaching to the test (Nichols & Berliner, 2007; Stobart, 2008).

It is perhaps unsurprising, then, that 'perverse effects,' at both the local and systemic level, have arisen in response to standardized testing. This includes the intentional gaming of performance targets (Lee, 2010), and narrowing of curricula and pedagogy (Berliner, 2011; Supovitz, 2009) by schools and states that seek to maximize the appearance of success. We have seen the classic 'teaching to the test' as one common response from schooling systems structured and run around high-stakes testing (Lingard, Martino, Rezai-Rashti, & Sellar, 2016; Nichols, Glass, & Berliner, 2012). The much publicized recent exposure of grade manipulation at Atlanta Public Schools (APS) in the U.S. state of Georgia, where 11 public education officials and teachers were found guilty in 2015 of cheating on state standardized tests to inflate perceptions of student performance (Cooper & Jackson, 2015; Noguera, 2015) is arguably but one example of many. While not in any way condoning the actions of the accused teachers and education officials, this clearly demonstrates how the pressure to continually improve standardized student test scores, and indeed the assumption that such test scores are the most valid representation of student learning and teacher effectiveness, exert considerable pressure on schools and schooling systems. However, we openly concede that 'teaching to the test' would not be such a concern if test items accurately represented the full breadth of the curriculum, which they rarely do.

However, there is considerable (and growing) opposition to these developments. Hursh (2013, 2016), for example, has documented a granular narrative of these developments in New York State and the multiple modes of resistance to them, including a parent 'opt-out' movement that is supported by the teacher unions and the work of investigative journalists. Other resistance to test-based teacher evaluation and related privatization of various kinds in U.S. schooling can be seen in blogs by anti-accountability writers, such as Diane Ravitch (2012) and Alan Singer (2014), and strong opposition by the national teachers' union (e.g., The American Federation of Teachers). Such movements appear to be gathering strength, with over 200,000 students in New York State opting out of mathematics and English standardized exams in April 2015, a fourfold increase on the previous year (Singer, 2015).

These developments are not only present in New York. Indeed, Zeichner (2013) has drawn attention to similar teacher boycotts and 'opt-outs' in relation to the implementation of Measures of Academic Progress (MAP) testing in Seattle during January 2013, in which eight high schools refused to administer the standardized test, while teachers at 10 other campuses signed written statements supporting the action. The basis of these boycotts stemmed from teacher concerns over the misalignment of MAP testing with curricula standards, lost teaching time, and the attribution of teacher ratings on the basis of student performance on such standardized testing. These Seattle teachers instead called for the introduction of accountabilities that considered (and valued) teacher input, and which reflected, and could inform, authentic classroom practices—an assessment *as* and *for* learning, rather than merely being an assessment *of* learning (Lewis & Hardy, 2015).

Both examples of local resistance here demonstrate how accountability policy uptake is far from straightforward and homogeneous, even when it is undergirded by dominant political and ideational discourses, and even when situated within a heavily test-dependent U.S. schooling system. Instead, the top-down implementation of federal government programs like NCLB and RTTT are necessarily mediated by local contexts and conditions at system, school, teacher, and community levels, constituting more agentic, and contested, forms of policy enactment rather than uncontested implementation (Ball, Maguire, & Braun, 2012). As we shall see in the remaining sections of this chapter, the Finnish and Australian schooling systems have also responded to the Anglo-American approach to accountability in a variety of vernacular (Appadurai, 1996) ways. These processes and examples lead us to reject any notion of a uniform global uptake, or indeed of straightforward policy convergence.

THE CASES OF AUSTRALIA AND FINLAND: A LOCALIZED GLOBALISM AND THE REJECTION OF GERM

We would like to turn our attention now to specific examples of the Anglo-American approach to accountability being taken up in two distinct national settings, namely Australia and Finland. This is not to suggest that these schooling systems represent all possible local inflections of the Anglo-American approach. Rather, these instances of vernacularization reflect how local contexts, and the broader mediating effects of political and ideological judgements and prioritization, influence how 'global' discourses and processes are enacted in a decidedly contingent manner. In de Sousa Santos's (2006) terms, this is the play between globalized localisms and localized globalisms.

Case Study One: Australia

Although Australia is a federal system in which authority for education policy is constitutionally devolved to the states, the Rudd-Gillard federal Labor Government in Australia (2007–2013) introduced national census testing of literacy and numeracy (NAPLAN) for all students in Years 3, 5, 7, and 9. This was part of a broader educational reform agenda that included the introduction of a national curriculum and the publication of NAPLAN performance data, for all government and private schools, on the public *MySchool* website. The distribution of school funding via the federal government's 'National Partnerships' scheme was also intricately linked with standardized NAPLAN testing, as the receipt of this funding by schools was to some extent contingent upon demonstrating continuing year-to-year improvements in student performance on NAPLAN.

In turn, NAPLAN has exerted a significant influence upon pedagogy and curriculum in Australia, becoming, arguably, the dominant means of accounting for school, teacher, and state and territory schooling system performance (Lewis & Hardy, 2015; Lingard, Thompson, & Sellar, 2016). In this way, NAPLAN is a clear example of how the Anglo-American mode of test-based educational accountability has been localized within the Australian context, constituting GERMs that have 'infected' many schooling systems across the globe, albeit with decidedly local pathologies. Julia Gillard, the then education minister of the federal Labor government, actually observed how policy developments around testing in New York City, led by schools chancellor Joel Klein, had been formative in her introduction of this agenda (Gorur & Koyama, 2013).

However, this is not to say that the Anglo-American approach was implemented wholesale, or unopposed, in the Australian context. Just as Anglo-American developments built on the path-dependent specificities of the history of testing in both England and the USA, so too did the 2008 implementation of NAPLAN build on earlier sample-based literacy testing conducted by all Australian states and territories. This testing had first commenced in 1989 with the emergence of the Basic Skills Test in New South Wales and had been used to inform the collation of national comparative schooling data from 1999 (Education, Employment and Workplace Relations References Committee, 2010). The Gillard Labor government also had an equity element in this policy regime that linked to national policies around equity funding (National Partnerships), as well as the use of socioeconomically 'like schools' comparisons of school NAPLAN performance on the *MySchool* website. These policies sought to acknowledge how socioeconomic differences influenced school performance.

There has also been some resistance to NAPLAN testing in Australia from a variety of stakeholders, including teachers' unions, parent groups, and education researchers. This includes the prominent "Say no to NAPLAN" campaign of the Literacy Educators Coalition, an advocacy organization composed of teachers, principals, and university educators (Literacy Educators Coalition, 2015). Such activism has since seen the opt-out rate of Year 3 students from NAPLAN approach 2.7% in 2014, the highest level in the history of the assessment and more than a 50% increase from 2013 (Milman, 2014). Interestingly, opt out is highest among professional families in affluent inner-city communities in Melbourne and Sydney. These developments have been largely due to fears that the perceived 'high-stakes' nature of NAPLAN testing was placing undue pressure on teachers and students alike (Milman, 2014).

It is also worth noting how the introduction of NAPLAN in 2008 was a substantive departure from existing means of schooling accountability and testing in some Australian jurisdictions, a situation that reflects the federal nature of the Australian polity. For instance, the state of Queensland had separately developed Queensland Common Assessment Tasks (QCATs) in parallel to federal NAPLAN testing, being implemented in Queensland primary and secondary schools between 2009–2012. QCATs were annual standards-based assessments for students in Years 4, 6, and 9 across the subjects of English, mathematics, and science, providing models of high-quality assessment tasks and enabling teachers throughout the state to assess student learning by reference to common tasks and metrics (Queensland Curriculum and Assessment Authority, 2015). Furthermore, teachers moderated and evaluated QCATs on the basis of exemplars, and extensive professional development was provided to ensure teachers could appropriately judge student work according to standards. Indeed, QCATs could be considered to have emerged from a long history of school-based, teacher-moderated assessment in Queensland secondary schooling from 1972, in which senior secondary teachers are notionally responsible for developing, administering, and evaluating student assessment programs (QCAA, 2014).

However, the election of a Conservative Queensland state government in 2012 saw the abolishment of QCATs, meaning that NAPLAN is (currently) the sole means by which the performance of Queensland students can be compared within the state. In this way, we can see an interesting intermingling between global flows around GERM, both discursive and material, and prevailing local conditions and politics, resulting in a contingent and mediated uptake of the Anglo-American approach to accountability in Australia (and, more specifically, the state of Queensland).

Case Study Two: Finland

By contrast, Finland has adopted an alternative approach to schooling accountability that largely eschews the characteristics of GERM and the Anglo-American model. Sahlberg (2011) has juxtaposed the idiosyncrasies of Finnish education policies since the early 1990s with the characteristics of GERM more generally. He suggests that while GERM emphasizes standardized teaching and learning with a focus on literacy and numeracy, a prescribed curriculum framed by test-based accountability and control in a system restructured around neoliberal ideas, marketization, and NPM, this can be starkly contrasted with the 'Finnish way.' This Finnish way customizes teaching and learning, with a focus on creativity, risk taking, and learning from the past, within a culture of responsibility and trust for teachers across the entire schooling system, and in the absence of standardized testing.

We also draw attention to the fact that Finland has a universal public schooling system and a low Gini coefficient of social inequality (Sahlberg, 2011). It is worth noting that Finland's education success, in terms of high quality and high equity, was achieved not through short-term, politically expedient reform measures that were normatively 'borrowed' from abroad. Instead, it arose from decades of systemic, and mostly intentional, education policy developments that were directed to the specific needs of the Finnish society, while paying (relatively) little attention to the dominant education policy trends of market-oriented reforms and standardization (Sahlberg, 2007).

Sahlberg (2011) has also documented the features of Finnish schooling that he sees as being the basis of the success of Finnish schools, and in so doing stresses that GERM has not (as yet) infected Finnish school policy and practice. There is no census, high-stakes testing. Schools tend to collaborate rather than compete with each other. Finland basically only has government schools, which are attended by the vast majority of students. There is much trust of teachers and principals based on an historical reverence for them and their, in turn, high academic and social standing, which provides space for professional judgement with reduced political oversight. These trusted teachers largely have a free hand with regards to curriculum, thereby recontextualizing national requirements locally through professional judgement. There is early intervention for students with learning difficulties, while all school funding has a redistributive focus. Sahlberg (2011) has also adumbrated the increased interdependencies across public sector policies (i.e., economic, employment, social, and education) from the 1970s onwards. As such, there is political recognition and consensus across political divides (i.e., conservative, progressive) that accepts the necessity of maintaining a more equal society, the necessity of more equitable distribution of resources within schooling, and the importance of addressing inequality across the broader ensemble of public policies as collectively being central to the effectiveness of Finnish schooling.

What is interesting to us is that, since the first PISA in 2000, Finland has been an education 'poster child' globally because of its outstanding performance. Although much 'education tourism' takes place through visits of international educators and policy makers to Finland, the lessons that might be learnt from the Finnish way have not been taken up in the face of the dominant Anglo-American model of schooling accountability. We think an explanation of this failure to learn from the Finnish way lies in processes of externalization, where reference societies are used largely to justify reforms rather than inform meaningful, and contextually aware, policy learning. As Condron (2011) has demonstrated, poverty and societal inequality, along with inequitable funding of schools, are major contributing factors to poor outcomes in U.S. schooling, yet the resulting policy responses have seemed to focus on yet more testing and the blaming, and accountability, of teachers.

We would suggest as well that the OECD's use of PISA underplays historical and cultural factors and structural inequalities in societies and schooling systems, and overplays policy and in-school factors (Feniger & Lefstein, 2014; Meyer & Schiller, 2013), thus reinforcing externalization rather than productive policy learning. This stems from the policy focus of the OECD's education work, and the context indifference in the representation of performance on both quality and equity dimensions as measured by PISA. Clearly, context, culture, and history *do* matter in respect to the performance of schooling systems, yet they cannot be borrowed, as might be the case with policies and practices.

DISCUSSION AND CONCLUSION

We have argued that the top-down, test-based modes of educational accountability that typify the Anglo-American approach have become a globalized localism, with uptake in vernacular, path-dependent ways in many schooling systems around the globe. This move has been complemented by the strengthening influence of the OECD's PISA, both inside the OECD itself as a prototype for other policy developments and more globally. The OECD is strengthening the scope, scale, and explanatory power of PISA, which has become an exceptionally influential education policy tool, used by nations for accountability and reform purposes. The latter has most often been through externalization to justify national reforms already under way. For example, Finland's stellar performance on PISA over time has not been used by nations to put in place elements of Finland's system of schooling, where there is no high-stakes testing, or to seek to confront structural inequality. Rather, as with Shanghai's performance on PISA 2009, Finland has been used by nations as a justification to push reforms already under way, instead of meaningfully learning from the features of the Finnish system.

There is a large literature documenting the negative and perverse impact of this policy regime of top-down, test-based accountability on the width of curriculum, pedagogies, and the schooling experience of young people (Nichols & Berliner, 2007; Stobart, 2008). Despite being a key instigator of NCLB, Ravitch (2010) has made the following observations around the test-driven U.S. schooling system:

> What once was an effort to improve the quality of education turned into an accounting strategy: Measure, then punish or reward. No education experience was needed

to administer such a program. Anyone who loved data could do it. *The strategy produced fear and obedience among educators; it often generated higher test scores. But it had nothing to do with education.*

(pp. 15–16; emphasis added)

Data have thus become an important element of the functioning of schooling systems, with notions of social justice often reduced to comparative performance on tests (Lingard, Sellar, & Savage, 2014). In the USA, teacher accountability has also been constructed around the test performance of their students, with all of these developments pressuring schools in particular ways that exert considerable negative impacts on teacher professionalism and student learning. As already noted, there has been significant teacher union opposition to over-testing and the use of tests for teacher evaluation in the USA, as well as in many other jurisdictions.

We have also documented how testing and the enhanced involvement of edu-businesses in schooling systems are now part of the restructured State, reflecting the move more broadly from NPM to heterarchical modes of governance. This raises some important issues about public policy and schooling, especially as edu-businesses (e.g., Pearson) use test data paid for from the public purse to pursue its own strategic business purposes, including profit. There are also questions about the involvement of edu-businesses in the policy cycle in education, given they have no democratic constituencies and that their bottom line is largely financial.

In conclusion, we need to reiterate that we are not opposed to testing per se or to school systems using such data for policy making purposes; indeed, decisions about substantive public issues, like education, should be made in the context of informative and meaningful data. Rather, we are opposed to the *misuse* of such data by politicians and policy makers, particularly when that brings about reductive effects on the width of school curriculum, the democratic and citizenship purposes of schooling, teacher professionalism, and the schooling experience of students. We have pointed out how most high-stakes testing in the USA, for example, is multiple choice, demonstrating that debate is needed about other more educative modes of testing that better align with the higher-order learning purposes of schooling, and which are as much about learning (assessment *as* and *for* learning) as they are about measuring learning outcomes (assessment *of* learning). This critique should serve as a warning, then, about the real limitations of Anglo-American model of educational accountability based on multiple-choice, high-stakes testing. We are also concerned at the enhanced role of edu-businesses, particularly in the USA, but also globally, in ways that appear to challenge the democratic control over public policy making with respect to schooling.

In response, we argue for the necessary development of different modes of educational accountability that only partially rely on test data and that reflect the broader societal purposes of schooling outside of constituting stocks of human capital, both individually and collectively (Brown & Hattie, 2012; Hattie & Brown, 2007). Such a reconstitution of educational accountability would also function bottom-up in an 'opportunity to learn' way (Darling-Hammond, 2010), giving schools and their communities the capacity to demand of the system and policy makers that schools and their communities are provided with the necessary resources, both human and otherwise, to achieve what is demanded of them. We also see the need to complement such a mode of accountability with two-way horizontal relationships between schools and their communities, recognizing the funds of knowledge in all communities and how these might foster what could perhaps be described as more authentic, intelligent, and ethical modes of educational accountability (Biesta, 2004).

Outright opposition to accountability is not a justifiable position. Rather, we need a progressive reconceptualization of accountability that acknowledges the broader societal purposes for schooling, and which holds systems, schools, and communities to account, in both bottom-up and top-down ways. This should help to alleviate the perverse and distorting effects that often accompany exclusively top-down, test-based modes of accountability.

REFERENCES

ACARA. (2011). *National assessment program*. Retrieved March 23, 2016 from http://www.nap.edu.au

Allen, J. (2011). Topological twists: Power's shifting geographies. *Dialogues in Human Geography, 1*(3), 283–298. doi:10.1177/2043820611421546

Amin, A. (2002). Spatialities of globalization. *Environment and Planning A, 34*(3), 385–399. doi:10.1068/a3439

Anagnostopoulos, D., Rutledge, S. A., & Jacobsen, R. (Eds.). (2013). *The infrastructure of accountability: Data use and the transformation of American education*. Cambridge: Harvard Education Press.

Appadurai, A. (1996). *Modernity at large: Cultural dimensions of globalization*. Minneapolis: University of Minnesota Press.

Au, W., & Ferrare, J. J. (Eds.). (2015). *Mapping corporate education reform: Power and policy networks in the neoliberal state*. New York: Routledge.

Australian Government. (2012). *Better schools: A national plan for school improvement: The Australian Education Bill 2012*. Canberra: Australian Government.

Ball, S. (2012). *Global education inc.: New policy networks and the neo-liberal imaginary*. New York: Routledge.

Ball, S., & Junemann, C. (2012). *Networks, new governance and education*. Bristol: Policy Press.

Ball, S., Maguire, M., & Braun, A. (2012). *How schools do policy: Policy enactments in secondary schools*. London: Routledge.

Ball, S., & Youdell, D. (2008). *Hidden privatization in public education*. Brussels: Education International.

Berliner, D. C. (2011). Rational responses to high-stakes testing: The case of curriculum narrowing and the harm that follows. *Cambridge Journal of Education, 41*(3), 287–302. doi:10.1080/0305764x.2011.607151

Biesta, G. (2004). Education, accountability and the ethical demand: Can the democratic potential of accountability be regained? *Educational Theory, 54*(3), 233–250. doi:10.1111/j.0013–2004.2004.00017.x

Brenner, N. (2004). *New state spaces: Urban governance and the rescaling of statehood*. Oxford: Oxford University Press.

Brown, G.T.L., & Hattie, J. A. (2012). The benefits of regular standardized assessment in childhood education: Guiding improved instruction and learning. In S. Suggate & E. Reese (Eds.) *Contemporary educational debates in childhood education and development* (pp. 287–292). London: Routledge.

Burch, P. (2009). *Hidden markets: The new education privatization*. New York: Routledge.

Carvalho, L. M., & Costa, E. (2014). Seeing education with one's own eyes and through PISA lenses: Considerations of the reception of PISA in European countries. *Discourse: Studies in the Cultural Politics of Education, 36*(5), 638–646. doi:10.1080/01596306.2013.871449

Condron, D. J. (2011). Egalitarianism and educational excellence: Compatible goals for affluent societies? *Educational Researcher, 40*(2), 47–55. doi:10.3102/0013189x11401021

Cooper, E., & Jackson, P. (2015, 19 May). The Atlanta cheating scandal: Students were the victims but the school system suffers too. *The Huffington Post*. Retrieved from http://www.huffingtonpost.com/eric-cooper/the-atlanta-cheating-scan_b_7309084.html

Darling-Hammond, L. (2010). *The flat world and education: How America's commitment to equity will determine our future*. New York: Teachers College Press.

de Sousa Santos, B. (2006). Globalizations. *Theory, Culture & Society, 23*(2–3), 393–399. doi:10.1177/026327640 602300268

Dillon, S. (2010, December 7). Top test scores from Shanghai stun educators. *The New York Times*. Retrieved from http://www.nytimes.com/2010/12/07/education/07education.html?_r=0

Education, Employment and Workplace Relations References Committee (The Senate). (2010). *Administration and reporting of NAPLAN testing*. Canberra: Commonwealth of Australia.

Eggers, W. D. (2008). The changing nature of government: Network governance. In J. O'Flynn & J. Wanna (Eds.), *Collaborative governance: A new era of public policy in Australia?* (pp. 23–28). Canberra: ANU E Press.

Ertl, H. (2006). Educational standards and the changing discourse on education: The reception and consequences of the PISA study in Germany. *Oxford Review of Education, 32*(5), 619–634. doi:10.1080/03054980600976320

Feniger, Y., & Lefstein, A. (2014). How not to reason with PISA data: An ironic investigation. *Journal of Education Policy, 29*(6), 845–855. doi:10.1080/02680939.2014.892156

Goodhart, C.A.E. 1984. Monetary Theory and Practice. The UK Experience. London: Macmillan.

Gorur, R., & Koyama, J. P. (2013). The struggle to technicize in education policy. *The Australian Educational Researcher, 40*(5), 633–648. doi:10.1007/s13384–013–0125–9

Grek, S. (2009). Governing by numbers: The PISA "effect" in Europe. *Journal of Education Policy, 24*(1), 23–37. doi:10.1080/02680930802412669

Harrer, A. (2015, March 30). Big education firms spend millions lobbying for pro-testing policies. *The Washington Post*. Retrieved from http://www.washingtonpost.com/blogs/answer-sheet/wp/2015/03/30/report-big-education-firms-spend-millions-lobbying-for-pro-testing-policies/

Hattie, J.A.C., & Brown, G.T.L. (2007). Technology for school-based assessment and assessment for learning: Development principles from New Zealand. *Journal of Educational Technology Systems, 36*(2), 189–201. doi:10.2190/ET.36.2.g

Head, B. W. (2008). Three lenses of evidence-based policy. *Australian Journal of Public Administration, 67*(1), 1–11. doi:10.1111/j.1467-8500.2007.00564.x

Henry, M., Lingard, B., Rizvi, F., & Taylor, S. (2001). *The OECD, globalization and education policy*. Oxford: IAU Press.

Hogan, A., Sellar, S., & Lingard, B. (2015). Network restructuring of global edu-business: The case of Pearson's Efficacy Framework. In W. Au & J. J. Ferrare (Eds.), *Mapping corporate education reform: Power and policy networks in the neoliberal state* (pp. 43–62). New York: Routledge.

Hood, C. (1990). *Beyond the public bureaucracy state: Public administration in the 1990s*. London: London School of Economics.

Hursh, D. (2013). Raising the stakes: High-stakes testing and the attack on public education in New York. *Journal of Education Policy, 28*(5), 574–588. doi:10.1080/02680939.2012.758829

Hursh, D. (2016) *The end of public schools: The corporate reform agenda to privatize public education*. New York: Routledge.

Jessop, B. (2002). Liberalism, neoliberalism, and urban governance: A state-theoretical perspective. *Antipode, 34*(3), 452–472. doi:10.1111/1467–8330.00250

Jessop, B. (2008). *State power*. Cambridge: Polity Press.

Lawn, M. (Ed.). (2013). *The rise of data in education systems: Collection, visualization and use*. Wallingford: Symposium Books.

Lee, J. (2010). Trick or treat: New ecology of education accountability system in the USA. *Journal of Education Policy, 25*(1), 73–93. doi:10.1080/02680930903377423

Lewis, S., & Hardy, I. (2015). Funding, reputation and targets: The discursive logics of high-stakes testing. *Cambridge Journal of Education, 45*(2), 245–264. doi:10.1080/0305764x.2014.936826

Lewis, S., Sellar, S., & Lingard, B. (2015). "PISA for Schools": Topological rationality and new spaces of the OECD's global educational governance. *Comparative Education Review, 60*(1), 27–57. doi: 10.1086/684458

Lingard, B. (2011). Policy as numbers: Ac/counting for educational research. *The Australian Educational Researcher, 38*(4), 355–382. doi:10.1007/s13384–011–0041–9

Lingard, B., Martino, W., & Rezai-Rashti, G. (2013). Testing regimes, accountabilities and education policy: Commensurate global and national developments. *Journal of Education Policy, 28*(5), 539–556. doi:10.1080/02680939.2013.820042

Lingard, B., Martino, W., Rezai-Rashti, G., & Sellar, S. (2016). *Globalizing educational accountabilities*. New York: Routledge.

Lingard, B., Sellar, S., & Savage, G. C. (2014). Re-articulating social justice as equity in schooling policy: The effects of testing and data infrastructures. *British Journal of Sociology of Education, 35*(5), 710–730. doi:10.1080/01425692.2014.919846

Lingard, B., Thompson, G., & Sellar, S. (Eds.). (2016) *National testing in schools: An Australian assessment*. London: Routledge.

Linn, R. L. (2000). Assessments and accountability. *Educational Researcher, 29*(2), 4–16. doi:10.3102/0013189X029002004

Literacy Educators Coalition. (2015). *Say no to NAPLAN*. Retrieved from http://www.literacyeducators.com.au/naplan/naplan-articles/

Mahony, P., Hextall, I., & Menter, I. (2004). Building dams in Jordan, assessing teachers in England: A case study in edu-business. *Globalization, Societies and Education, 2*(2), 277–296. doi:10.1080/1476772041000 01733674

Mayer-Schönberger, V., & Cukier, K. (2013). *Big data: A revolution that will transform how we live, work and think*. New York: Houghton Mifflin Harcourt.

Meyer, H.-D., & Schiller, K. (2013). Gauging the role of non-educational effects in large-scale assessments: Socio-economics, culture and PISA outcomes. In H.-D. Meyer & A. Benavot (Eds.), *The emergence of global educational governance* (pp. 207–224). Oxford: Symposium Books.

Milman, O. (2014, 10 December). NAPLAN: Number of children opting out of national tests hits all-time high. *The Guardian Australia*. Retrieved from http://www.theguardian.com/australia-news/2014/dec/10/naplan-number-of-children-opting-out-tests-hits-high

Mintrop, H., & Sunderman, G. L. (2013). The paradoxes of data-driven school reform: Learning from two generations of centralized accountability systems in the United States In D. Anagnostopoulos, S. A. Rutledge, & R. Jacobsen (Eds.), *The infrastructure of accountability: Data use and the transformation of American education* (pp. 23–39). Cambridge, MA: Harvard Education Press.

The National Commission on Excellence in Education. (1983). *A Nation at Risk: The imperative for educational reform* Retrieved from http://www2.ed.gov/pubs/NatAtRisk/index.html

Nichols, S. L., & Berliner, D. (2007). *Collateral damage: How high-stakes testing corrupts America's schools*. Cambridge, MA: Harvard Education Press.

Nichols, S. L., Glass, G. V., & Berliner, D. C. (2012). High-stakes testing and student achievement: Updated analyses with NAEP data. *Education Policy Analysis Archives, 20*(20), 1–35. doi:10.14507/epaa.v20n20.2012

No Child Left Behind (NCLB) Act of 2001, Pub. L. No. 107–110 § 115, 1425 Stat. (2002).

Noguera, P. (2015, 15 April). Accountability for whom? *The Huffington Post*. Retrieved from http://www.huffingtonpost.com/pedro-noguera/atlanta-teachers-convicted_b_7069000.html

Nóvoa, A., & Yariv-Mashal, T. (2003). Comparative research in education: A mode of governance or a historical journey? *Comparative Education, 39*(4), 423–438. doi:10.1080/0305006032000162002

OECD. (2015). *Programme for international student assessment: About PISA*. Retrieved from http://www.oecd.org/pisa/aboutpisa/

Ozga, J. (2009). Governing education through data in England: From regulation to self-evaluation. *Journal of Education Policy, 24*(2), 149–162. doi:10.1080/02680930902733121

QCAA. (2014). *School-based assessment: The Queensland system*. Brisbane: Queensland Curriculum and Assessment Authority.

Queensland Curriculum and Assessment Authority. (2015). *Queensland Comparable Assessment Tasks (QCATs 2009–2012)*. Retrieved from https://www.qcaa.qld.edu.au/3163.html

Ravitch, D. (2010). *The death and life of the great American school system: How testing and choice are undermining education*. New York: Basic Books.

Ravitch, D. (2012, 7 June). Pearsonizing our children [Web log message]. *Diane Ravitch's blog*. Retrieved from http://dianeravitch.net/2012/06/07/pearsonization/

Rhodes, R. (1997). *Understanding governance: Policy networks, governance, reflexivity and accountability*. Buckingham, UK: Open University Press.

Rizvi, F., & Lingard, B. (2010). *Globalizing education policy*. New York: Routledge.

Rose, N. (1999). *Powers of freedom: Reframing political thought*. Cambridge: Cambridge University Press.

Rutkowski, D. (2007). Converging us softly: How intergovernmental organizations promote neoliberal educational policy. *Critical Studies in Education, 48*(2), 229–247. doi:10.1080/17508480701494259

Sahlberg, P. (2007). Education policies for raising student learning: The Finnish approach. *Journal of Education Policy, 22*(2), 147–171. doi:10.1080/02680930601158919

Sahlberg, P. (2011). *Finnish lessons: What can the world learn from educational change in Finland?* New York: Teachers College Press.

Sassen, S. (2006). *Territory, authority, rights: From medieval to global assemblages*. Princeton, NJ: Princeton University Press.

Scharpf, F. W. (1994). Games real actors could play: Positive and negative coordination in embedded negotiations. *Journal of Theoretical Politics, 6*(1), 27–53. doi:10.1177/0951692894006001002

Schriewer, J. (1990). The method of comparison and the need for externalization: Methodological criteria and sociological concepts. In J. Schriewer & B. Holmes (Eds.), *Theories and methods in comparative education* (2nd ed., pp. 25–83). Frankfurt am Main: Peter Lang.

Schriewer, J., & Martinez, C. (2004). Constructions of internationality in education. In G. Steiner-Khamsi (Ed.), *The global politics of educational borrowing and lending* (pp. 29–53). New York: Teachers College Press.

Sellar, S. (2014). Data infrastructure: A review of expanding accountability systems and large-scale assessments in education. *Discourse: Studies in the Cultural Politics of Education, 36*(5), 765–777. doi:10.1080/01596306.2014.931117

Sellar, S., & Lingard, B. (2013). Looking East: Shanghai, PISA 2009 and the reconstitution of reference societies in the global education policy field. *Comparative Education, 49*(4), 464–485. doi:10.1080/03050068.2013.770943

Sellar, S., & Lingard, B. (2014). The OECD and the expansion of PISA: New global modes of governance in education. *British Educational Research Journal, 40*(6), 917–936. doi:10.1002/berj.3120

Simola, H., Rinne, R., Varjo, J., & Kauko, J. (2013). The paradox of the education race: How to win the ranking game by sailing to headwind. *Journal of Education Policy, 28*(5), 612–633. doi:10.1080/02680939.2012.758832

Singer, A. (2014). *Education flashpoints: Fighting for America's schools.* New York: Routledge.

Singer, A. (2015, 16 August). Big win for opt-out. *The Huffington Post.* Retrieved from http://www.huffington post.com/alan-singer/big-win-for-opt-out_b_7994054.html

Slater, G. B. (2014). Education as recovery: Neoliberalism, school reform, and the politics of crisis. *Journal of Education Policy, 30*(1), 1–20. doi:10.1080/02680939.2014.904930

Smith, M. L., & Fey, P. (2000). Validity and accountability in high-stakes testing. *Journal of Teacher Education, 51*(5), 334–344. doi:10.1177/0022487100051005002

Smith, M. L., Heinecke, W., & Noble, A., J. (1999). Assessment policy and political spectacle. *Teachers College Record, 101*(2), 157–191.

Stobart, G. (2008). *Testing times: The uses and abuses of assessment.* Oxon: Routledge.

Supovitz, J. (2009). Can high-stakes testing leverage educational improvement? Prospects from the last decade of testing and accountability reform. *Journal of Educational Change, 10*(2), 211–227. doi:10.1007/s10833-009-9105-2

Takayama, K. (2007). *A Nation at Risk* crosses the Pacific: Borrowing of the U.S. crisis discourse in the debate on education reform in Japan. *Comparative Education Review, 51*(4), 423–446. doi:10.1086/520864

Takayama, K. (2008). The politics of international league tables: PISA in Japan's achievement crisis debate. *Comparative Education, 44*(4), 387–407. doi:10.1080/03050060802481413

Takayama, K. (2010). Politics of externalization in reflexive times: Reinventing Japanese educational reform discourse through "Finnish PISA success". *Comparative Education Review, 54*(1), 51–75. doi:10.1086/644838

Takayama, K. (2015). Provincializing the world culture theory debate: Critical insights from a margin. *Globalization, Societies and Education, 13*(1), 34–57. doi:10.1080/14767724.2014.967485

Tröhler, D. (2013). The OECD and cold war culture: Thinking historically about PISA. In H.-D. Meyer & A. Benavot (Eds.), *PISA, power and policy: The emergence of global educational governance* (pp. 141–161). Oxford: Symposium Books.

US Department of Education. (2009). *Race to the Top program: Executive summary.* Washington, DC. Retrieved from http://www2.ed.gov/programs/racetothetop/executive-summary.pdf

Wilson, D., Croxson, B., & Atkinson, A. (2006). "What gets measured gets done". *Policy Studies, 27*(2), 153–171. doi:10.1080/01442870600637995

Zeichner, N. (2013). Mapping a teacher boycott in Seattle. *Phi Delta Kappa, 92*(5), 52–58. doi:10.1177/003172171309500212

23

EXPLORING THE INFLUENCE OF CULTURE ON ASSESSMENT

The Case of Teachers' Conceptions of Assessment in Confucian Heritage Cultures

Kerry J. Kennedy

Cooper and Denner (1998, p. 2) have made the point that:

> The concept of culture has come to the forefront of social-science and social policy to address issues of human diversity in psychological processes and performance. Debates about the role of culture in psychological processes have sparked a movement towards research that is directly applicable to social problems. A key challenge lies in how to reconcile community-specific applications with broader theories that guide research.

It is against this background that Confucian heritage cultural (CHC) contexts have exerted an impact on research in educational psychology in general and assessment in particular. Geographically, CHC contexts are associated with the North Asian countries of Korea, Japan, China (taking in Macau and Hong Kong), and Taiwan, and also including Vietnam and Singapore. It is also the case that CHC influences extend to the diasporic communities of these countries. The focus on CHC has been a popular theme over the past two decades, especially since the appearance of *The Chinese Learner* (Watkins & Biggs, 1996) and its successors *Teaching the Chinese Learner* (Watkins & Biggs, 2001a) and *Revisiting the Chinese Learner* (Chan & Rao, 2009). The issue of culture and learning is not new. It had been raised especially in relation to the increased mobility of Chinese university students and clashes between the assumed learning styles of these students and the more open learning styles claimed to be characteristic of Western higher education (Ho, 1994; Ho & Crookall, 1995; Littlewood, 1999).

This focus on culture is also reflected in a broader cross-cultural psychology research agenda that seeks to understand better the effects of culture on constructs such as self-efficacy (Oettingen & Zosuls, 2006) and learning motivation (McInerney & Ali, 2006). Neuroscientists have also recognized the importance of culture and learning as it relates to brain functioning (Ansari, 2011). Goh & Park (2009), for example, used brain imaging techniques to show differences between Westerners (i.e., U.S. subjects) and East Asians (i.e., Chinese subjects) in their perception of contexts and visual environments. As Cooper and Denner (1998, p. 63) have argued, "bringing concepts of culture into psychological theories is an abstract, disputed, and inherently irresolvable process, yet . . . doing so is crucial to both social science and policy in multicultural societies, particularly democracies."

Culture can be conceived in different ways. It can include, among other things, shared values, material and technological characteristics, cognitive orientations, and systems of morality (Cooper & Denner, 1998). For positivists, these cultural characteristics are often viewed monolithically as independent variables that can influence different kinds of outcomes. For poststructuralists, on the other hand, these same characteristics are more likely to be seen, at best, as individual characteristics exerting influences in unknown and immeasurable ways. In the review that follows, both views of cultural influence will be referred to since the literature on the influence of CHC does not speak with a single voice.

The particular emphasis taken with regard to the influence of CHC in the area of education was on learning, and this led naturally to a more specific emphasis on student assessment (Brown, Kennedy, Fok, Chan, & Yu 2009; Carless, 2011; Kennedy, Chan, Yu, & Fok, 2006). The success of East Asian students in international assessments in particular has often featured as an issue in research on 'the Chinese learner.' As other countries have sought to understand the reasons for such success, the 'culture' issue has been given special attention (Mason, 2014):

> The latest PISA results (2012) might be a good place to start. The top seven performers in mathematics were Shanghai, Singapore, Hong Kong, Taiwan, South Korea, Macau, and Japan. The top five in reading: Shanghai, Hong Kong, Singapore, Japan, and South Korea, with Taiwan coming in eighth place. The top four in science: Shanghai, Hong Kong, Singapore, and Japan, with South Korea and Vietnam in seventh and eighth place respectively. These are all territories described as "Confucian heritage cultures", and it is highly probable that there is a culturally related explanation for these excellent performances.

The attempt to link learning, assessment, and CHCs, therefore, is now well established and can be found as both a significant research agenda, as well as a folk explanation, of the success of East Asian students. The countries mentioned by Mason (2014) above are most often seen as those that have fallen under the influence of CHC because of the historical influence of Confucianism across East Asia. There is also some evidence that East Asian diaspora communities retain CHC values and attitudes in new locations, thus contributing to the diffusion of these values (e.g., Madsen & Riemenschnitter, 2009). While the influence of culture among CHC diaspora communities deserves further study, the topic is outside this chapter's scope.

Yet the research using CHC as a causal explanation for achievement has been contested, with challenges from a range of critics (Gieve & Clark, 2005; Ryan & Louie, 2007; Ryan & Slethaug 2010; Wang, 2013). These challenges will be discussed later in this chapter. Nevertheless, it is important to understand why a particular cultural perspective has so frequently been used to explain assessment perspectives and results, and evaluate its utility. Hence, this chapter addresses the following questions:

- Why has 'Confucian heritage culture' (CHC) achieved such prominence in the discourse of learning and assessment?

- What are the lessons from current research on assessment in Confucian heritage cultures?
- What opposing discourses are present within the literature?
- How should policy makers understand CHC research, and what might a future research agenda be?

CONFUCIAN HERITAGE CULTURE WITHIN LEARNING AND ASSESSMENT DISCOURSE

CHC as an explanation for learning success was first raised in a systematic way with a focus on 'the paradox of the Chinese learner' (Biggs, 1996 a,b). The paradox, simply stated, was that the perceived conditions of teaching and learning in Asian classrooms did not appear to match with the success of many Asian students in international large scale assessments. How could conditions such as large classes, didactic teaching, passive students, and low level cognitive learning produce such results? The paradox became even more intriguing with the assertion that "when hard data are examined . . . Asian students are more likely than Westerners to report that they use meaning-oriented approaches to learning, and they perform not only at a high cognitive level, but better than Western students" (Biggs, 1996a, pp. 180–181). It was this double set of paradoxes that set off an ongoing line of research that has attempted to insert culture in its broadest sense into debates and discussion, initially around learning in general, but eventually with specific reference to assessment practices. This has been and remains an ambitious research agenda at the centre of which is an assumed relationship between CHC and learning. Table 23.1 summarises research by Watkins and Biggs (2001b) that sought to resolve the 'paradox of the Chinese learner,' largely derived from the fields of learning and motivational psychology, with many of these features also discussed by other authors (e.g., Peterson, Brown, & Hamilton, 2013; Purdie & Hattie, 2002).

The psychological emphasis is not surprising given that the two leaders of the initial research agenda, John Biggs and David Watkins, were psychologists! As important as these insights from psychology were to understanding the distinctive features of CHC, they alone were not enough for a complete understanding of that culture. This was recognized by the psychologists, and other contributions were sought from philosophers and sociologists (Lee, 1996; Li, 2009).

Lee's (1996) essay appeared in the original collection on *The Chinese Learner* (Watkins & Biggs, 1996). It stands out from the other psychology-oriented contributions because of its philosophical perspective, drawing heavily on Confucius's *Analects*, as well as the work of Mencius and Xunzi, scholars interpreting different aspects of the Confucian tradition. There is agreement amongst these scholars, as well as neo-Confucian scholars such as Tu (1979), that education plays a central role in the Confucian tradition, irrespective of class, origins, or status. In a Confucian context, individuals are not weighed down by the Christian doctrine of 'original sin,' so that human perfectibility is possible, and education is a key process that can lead to perfection. Even Xunzi, who held a strong view about human imperfection, believed that education was the process that could overcome it. Lee (1996, p. 32) provided one of Xunzi's very telling quotations:

Sincerely put forth your efforts, and finally you will progress. Study until death and do not stop before. For the art of study occupies the whole of life; to arrive at its purpose, you cannot stop for an instant. To do that is to be a man [sic], to stop is to be a bird or a beast.

Table 23.1 Features of Confucian Culture Facilitating Learning as Proposed by Watkins and Biggs (2001b)

Features of Confucian Culture	How Cultural Features Facilitate Learning
Memorising and understanding	Chinese students use memorisation not just to learn by rote but rather to understand what they are learning and to discover new meaning.
Effort versus ability attribution	Understanding comes through working hard rather than through ability. For Chinese students, the only barrier to success is lack of application.
Intrinsic versus extrinsic motivation	Chinese students are more likely to be motivated by external influences such as family, peers, or even material rewards.
General patterns of socialisation	Respect for hierarchy and obedience are important aspects of childhood socialization, thus preparing Chinese students for school.
Achievement motivation: ego versus social	Success for Chinese students is often seen as meeting obligations related to the group (e.g., the family) rather than an individual pursuit.
Collective versus individual orientation	Chinese students often prefer a more collaborative learning environment.

This focus on effort is seen as the driving force to perfectibility. Lee (1996, p. 32) commented "human perfectibility, learning, rationality, effort, and will power are discussed in the Confucian tradition in close relation. They are so closely interrelated that they are sometimes inseparable."

An important point to note here is that the link between human perfectibility and learning provides a moral dimension to the learning process (Li, 2001). Western conceptions of learning in general usually have a secular purpose: simply to know, do, and understand more. As Li (2005, p. 190) commented, "the best learner [in the Socratic tradition] is one who develops and uses his or her mind well to inquire into the world"; whereas, in the Confucian tradition "to become a better (i.e., more virtuous) person— is still believed . . . to be the most essential quality for any learner (Li, 2005, p. 190). The picture she paints of the Chinese learner therefore is distinctive:

> For Chinese students, the purposes of learning are mainly to perfect themselves morally and socially, to achieve mastery of the material, and to contribute to society. To accomplish these aims, the learner needs to develop the virtues of resolve, diligence, endurance of hardship, perseverance, and concentration. These virtues are not task-specific but are viewed as enduring personal dispositions that are more essential than actual learning activities (e.g., reading), and they are believed applicable to all learning activities and processes.
>
> (Li, 2005, p.191)

But how is this approach to learning related to the assessment of learning? Li (2009) made the important point that the two need to be considered separately. The examination systems, so characteristic of Confucian societies, are not a product of social attitudes to the assessment of student learning. Rather, according to Li (2009), examinations historically and currently are a response to the value placed by Confucian societies on education and the necessity to treat all students equally and fairly (another Confucian principle). A common examination, therefore, is the means to achieve this goal free from family and other social influences. Wang (2013) reported that there may not be as much faith in the *gao kao* (the Chinese National College Entrance Exam) as there once was, but for many students it remained the only hope of upward social mobility. As one of the students she interviewed commented:

> We can't choose our family background; this is not our parent's fault but the system's. What we can do is strengthen ourselves. Don't wildly wish for this social system [to] be changed one day; no one else is your savior in this world but yourself. Study hard. Though the Gaokao is not the only way out, it is the safest and fastest way out of poverty.
>
> (Wang, 2013)

Examinations, therefore, are seen as mechanisms to assess learning in an objective and, therefore, equitable manner. In a rapidly changing world, this belief may not be as strong as it once was, but it has been shown that when alternatives are considered, such as school based assessment, community concerns are raised in Confucian societies (Kennedy, 2013). Examinations, rightly or wrongly, are seen as guarantees of fairness in contexts where further education is rationed and where there is a considerable population striving to obtain a share of those opportunities.

A helpful approach to a better understanding of how issues related to CHCs might best be considered can be found in Park's (2010, p. 3) distinction between "thin" and "thick" discourses related to Confucian heritage cultures. The former "bears lighter forms of Confucian cultural values with only meagre to modest resemblance to classic Confucianism," while the latter "uphold[s] some clearly distinct Confucian elements . . . that exist across more than one geographical region . . . (and) elements can be traced back to textual Classics of Confucius or widely recognized Confucian school." A related, although not identical, idea is that of 'vernacular Confucianism' (Chang, 2000), which is "Confucianism as it may be relevant and interpreted by ordinary Chinese people today" (Watkins & Biggs, 2001a, p. 4). Chan and Rao (2009, p. 16) also gave the reminder that "there is much controversy about the nature and interpretation of Confucianism." Thus, it is well to remember that current psychological research has in all likelihood dealt with a socially constructed view of Confucianism that fits with psychological theory rather than with deep aspects of the culture as described by philosophers over time. This view is reinforced with reference to Table 23.1, where psychological theory is loosely linked to aspects of Confucianism. This is best regarded as a 'thin' version of Confucianism, rather than one deeply embedded in Confucian philosophical principles.

CURRENT RESEARCH ON ASSESSMENT IN CHCs

Assessment, or more specifically examination, has a long history in Confucian heritage countries as evidenced by the Chinese Civil Service Examinations (*keju*) that can be traced back at least to the Han Dynasty (206 BC–220 AD) (Têng, 1943). Modern assessment scholars, seeking an explanation for current attitudes to assessment in Confucian contexts, have drawn a link between this assessment history and the current emphasis on examinations in countries such as China, Japan, Taiwan, and Singapore (Brown, Kennedy, Fok, Chan, & Yu, 2009; Carless & Lam, 2014).

As Lee (2006), however, has pointed out, this linkage is not strictly accurate. Today's examinations are basically about selection, and in this they share a function with the keju. Importantly, however, the keju were also concerned with promoting a political ideology steeped in classical Confucianism, the purpose of which was to provide a loyal scholar class that would serve the interests of the Emperor. This is an important point to understand. For political reasons, key texts of Confucianism provided the content for the keju and this meant that both successful and unsuccessful examinees (Elman, 2009) became the spokesmen (not spokeswomen since women were not allowed to sit for the keju) for Confucian values and principles at both the level of the Imperial government as well as in the community. Confucianism, thus, provided the basis for stability and loyalty across dynasties until the keju outlived its usefulness in the wake of reforms and was abolished in 1904 (Elman, 2009). This political function of the keju is clearly not the function of modern examinations, although it is this function itself that accounts for the longevity of the system. Yet as Elman (2009, p. 410) has pointed out, "the ghost of the civil service examinations lived on in Chinese public school and college entrance examinations, which have now become universal and are no longer unique to imperial China."

This 'ghost' is best seen in the selection function of the keju that is still reflected in today's postmodern world where competition, the quest for social mobility, and the increasing value placed on education are as salient as they ever were in dynastic China, or indeed Korea, Japan, Taiwan, or Singapore. Lee's (2006, p. 6) graphic description of the influence of the keju on community values may well be describing what is commonly referred to as 'examination hell' in many modern Confucian societies:

> Since the struggle for "success" was always so competitive and the number who achieved it extremely limited, most Chinese must have regarded life as an endless process of predictable failures; in a non-pluralist society such as Ming or Qing China, success was definitely a rarity. A person could thus be easily convinced of the imperative of living a perfect moral life of constant self-examination and ceaseless merit accumulation, so as to safeguard the little that he had in hand.

Apart from their political function, the essence of the keju, as with modern examinations, was their rationing function—limited places and unlimited expectations. The struggle across time has been to succeed in what undoubtedly remains a competition in which further education can mean the difference between access to a better life and maintaining the social and economic status quo. This 'better life,' of course, includes a better life not just for the individual but for the whole family, since it is families rather than individuals that form the basis of Confucian societies. Add to this the further Confucian gloss of education's role in the development of human perfectibility, and the importance of examinations and examination success can be better understood.

Yet how relevant are these Confucian values in today's modern world? Wang and Brown (2014) conducted focus group interviews with a sample of Hong Kong students in order to understand better students' attitudes to assessment. Part of their results indicated that:

> Assessment was seen predominantly as examinations with high-stake consequences, beginning early in life, and lasting throughout the life course. From a personal and familial perspective, assessment results determined one's personal value or worth,

and achievement was an obligation one had toward one's family in order to please, show respect to, or build reputation for the family. From a societal perspective, assessment was a legitimate tool for selecting the best candidates for educational and career opportunities. Assessment provided upward social mobility; but also served the function of monitoring and surveillance to shape people's behaviour according to societal expectations.

(Wang & Brown, 2014, p. 1073)

The links between these findings and Lee's (2006) quote above are unmistakeable. While it is not possible to be more precise about the persistence of Confucian values in modern societies, Wang and Brown's (2014) study has provided some face validity for the idea that these values have stretched across time, continuing to orient successive generations towards family, learning, and social and economic progress. This view is also consistent with emerging empirical research that has found the success of East Asian students in international assessments can be traced "to traditional Confucian and family values and to a view of education as the basis for national development" (Pajares & Urdan, 2006, p. xii).

Enhancing the salience of the above discussion have been educational reforms that influenced many Confucian heritage societies in the late twentieth and early twenty-first centuries (Kennedy & Lee, 2008), including a push for greater reliance on formative assessment (OECD, 2005). Researchers over the past five years have been interested in whether the social construction of assessment and assessment systems in Confucian heritage societies influences teachers and students' beliefs about assessment to the extent that they are unable to respond to the reform agendas. Or put another way, are teachers' conceptions of assessment in Confucian heritage classrooms so strongly developed that they are impervious to change?

Hence, this research agenda has been characterised by investigations into whether teachers' conceptions of assessment differed across cultural contexts. An initial study using a sample of Hong Kong teachers responding to a translated version of the Teachers Conception of Assessment Inventory (TCoA-IIIA) (Brown, 2006) did not produce configural invariance between Hong Kong teachers' conceptions of assessment and those of samples from New Zealand and Australia (Brown et al., 2009). Nevertheless, there were considerable conceptual similarities in the cross-cultural samples, although these could not be compared directly (because of the lack of invariance). One striking result, for Hong Kong teachers, however, was the relationship between their conception of assessment as 'improvement' and their conception of assessment as 'student accountability,' evidenced by a very high correlation ($r = .91$). It is almost as though improvement and accountability were the same things in the minds of the teachers: helping students to improve, improving teacher assessments, and/or making assessments more valid enabled students to do better, achieve more, and, perhaps, even work harder. In this way, students could be held to account for their achievement (or lack of it). Improvement, therefore, was seen as an instrumental value for assessment, keeping students engaged and enabling them to do what was expected of them by their families and society.

This finding was not part of earlier research in two Western countries (Australia and New Zealand) and it seemed to suggest that Hong Kong teachers' conceptions of assessment were distinctive, but in line with Confucian principles that expected students to be accountable for their learning through effort and application and out of concern for the collective rather than for themselves as individuals. While this study indicated in a tentative way that Hong Kong teachers' conceptions of assessment, or at least the relationship between them, differed from those in Western contexts, its general direction was supported by an earlier study using TCoA (III) (Li & Hui, 2007). Like the previous study, there was a lack of configural invariance with the same inventory used with Western samples of teachers and a strong focus on assessment as accountability. What seemed clear from both of these studies was that teachers' conceptions of assessment in Chinese contexts might not be fully tapped by an instrument developed in another cultural context. More work was needed to understand this different context.

Brown, Hui, Yu, and Kennedy (2011) undertook this work by redeveloping TCoA (III), taking into account qualitative data collected from Hong Kong teachers and reported in Hui (2012) and Wang (2010). From this process there emerged a new questionnaire—a Chinese version of Teachers' Conception of Assessment (C-TCoA). While there was some overlap with the original TCoA questionnaire, three new factors emerged from the analysis of data with teacher samples from Hong Kong and Southern China: "student development," "examinations," and "teacher and school control," leading to the conclusion that, for Chinese teachers, it seems that "a powerful way to improve student learning is to examine them" (Brown et al., 2011, pp. 313–314). This view was reinforced (as with the original version of the TCoA) with a strong correlation between 'improvement' and 'accountability' ($r = .80$). Yet these constructs were not exactly the same as in the original TCoA. 'Improvement' included more of a student development focus both in terms of improving learning and personal development (p. 315) and this accorded with Gao and Kennedy (2011) and Brown and Gao's (2015) results with broader samples of mainland Chinese teachers—learning in Chinese contexts is more than skills acquisition. 'Accountability' was more about schools and teachers than individuals, a conception also supported by Brown and Gao's (2015) identification of 'management' and 'institutional targets' as part of Chinese teachers' conceptions of assessment. Thus, assessment supports students by helping them to achieve, and this student achievement is the means of making schools and teachers accountable. This rationale is less aligned with assessment *for* learning than assessment *for* accountability, focusing on accountability for students, as well as their teachers and schools.

Despite the desire to portray Chinese teachers as a homogenous group in relation to their beliefs, there are nevertheless variations that must be acknowledged. Brown et al.'s (2011) development of the C-TCoA involved two groups of teachers, 1,014 from Hong Kong and 898 from Guangzhou in Southern China (p. 311). Multigroup confirmatory factor analysis demonstrated equivalent factor residuals between the two groups of teachers, indicating that their scores on the related factors could be compared with some confidence. There were large differences, however, on the 'assessment as helping' factor, with Hong Kong teachers endorsing this more strongly than the other group. There were moderate differences on the 'examinations' factor, with Hong Kong teachers again endorsing it more strongly. Guangzhou teachers showed greater concern for the 'irrelevance' factor than Hong Kong teachers, although the differences were small. What this indicates is that even within what might be considered a single cultural group (i.e., Chinese teachers), there will be differences, perhaps caused by local context, values, or personal dispositions. Culture is always subject to social and other contexts that can modify and influence the way people think and act in relation to the values they hold.

When examining preservice teachers' conceptions of assessment and excellent teaching, the preservice teachers surveyed, not unexpectedly, strongly endorsed 'control' as a major purpose of assessment that controlled teachers' work (Chen & Brown, 2013). At the same time, 'examination preparation' emerged as an important conception of excellent teaching. Interestingly, 'diagnosis' as a conception of assessment negatively predicted 'control.' This suggests that in the minds of these preservice teachers, the diagnostic function of assessment militated against assessment as 'control,' perhaps because it took up time that otherwise might be used for exam preparation. Importantly, 'diagnosis' also negatively predicted assessment as being concerned with 'life character,' again suggesting that the students' main consideration when it came to assessment was the extent to which it controlled their lives as teachers and even that of their students.

This research in societies characterized as CHCs supports several conclusions. First, it is clear that teachers' conceptions of assessment in these societies do differ from teachers' conceptions in Western societies. This can be seen by the configural non-invariance in teachers' conceptions across studies. Second, there is a dominant concern in the CHC studies with the accountability function of assessment so that student results in either school assessments or larger scale assessments seem to be attributed to teachers and schools. Examinations were often seen as part of this accountability orientation to assessment. Third, the improvement function of assessment was usually strongly endorsed, except by the preservice teachers in the Chen and Brown (2013) study. This improvement, however, is also linked to personal development, as well as skills and knowledge, thus giving assessment a moral and social purpose. Fourth, despite these similarities, it cannot be argued from the data presented in these studies that teachers in the sampled CHCs are all influenced in the same way. There are configural similarities in the conceptions of assessment held by teachers in Hong Kong and Guangzhou, but they endorse these conceptions differentially. Social and cultural contexts appear to interact, resulting in these differences. Fifth, as with the 'Chinese learner' research in general, research on the conceptions of assessment held by teachers in Chinese contexts has been limited to Hong Kong and mainland China, although there is a growing body of research in Singapore (Leong, 2014a, b, c). Generalisations to other CHC-oriented societies such as Japan, Korea, or Vietnam cannot be readily made without further research in these specific contexts.

OPPOSING DISCOURSES—A CAUTIONARY NOTE

While there has been a great deal of enthusiasm for CHC-oriented research and its impact on learning and assessment, it has not been shared by all researchers. It is important, therefore, to be aware of a body of literature that regards culture as neither monolithic nor deterministic. These views have important implications for teaching and learning.

Gieve and Clark (2005) trialled self-directed learning strategies with a mixed group of international undergraduate students from either mainland China or continental Europe. They reported that Chinese students were as enthusiastic about these autonomous strategies as were the European students. They concluded from this that cultural dispositions towards learning should be treated cautiously and that they should not be regarded as deterministic. Given appropriate conditions of learning, Chinese students were open to alternative ways to learn.

In a subsequent paper, Clark and Gieve (2006) provided a theoretical framework for their work, drawing on poststructural theory to downplay what they referred to as 'large culture' (in this case, Confucian heritage culture) and focusing on the everyday experiences of students that can create alternative instructional cultures. They portrayed reliance on a single cultural characteristic as a deficit view "that offer(s) individual learners a restrictive social identity as a homogenised representative of a national culture" (p. 56). This poststructural critique is by no means new and, in the context of this chapter, it needs to be seen as a paradigm clash between scientific psychology and postmodern sociology. As shown in Gieve and Clark (2005), the empirical evidence for the postmodern sociological view is somewhat weak, but the theoretical framing in Clark and Gieve (2006) is very strong.

Ryan and Louie (2007) followed a similar line of argument to that of Clark and Gieve (2006), although the poststructural framing was not as strong. Their focus was on the stereotyping of Chinese students undertaking higher education outside of China by assuming that a common cultural background meant common approaches and attitudes to learning. They argued that "rather than taking either a 'deficit' or 'surplus' view of either Western or Confucian education, teachers need to recognise this diversity and complexity within not only other cultures, but their own" (p. 414). In other words, culture in this view is not monolithic, and Chinese students, or Asian students in general, should not be regarded simply as passive consumers of such a culture. The arguments here are philosophical in nature rather than empirical and implications are identified for teaching and learning.

Wang (2013) argued that there was too much reliance on Confucian values (for example those outlined in Table 23.1) in attempting to explain the Chinese learner. He further argued that this has resulted in neglecting the influence of the examination system that has characterised Chinese education for thousands of years, including the recent Republican and Communist periods. According to Wang (2013), it is this "examination heritage" that has been more influential on Chinese learning styles so that "government control over the examination system as well as the outside influences all have contributed to Chinese learners' strategic choice of learning approaches to respond to the cultural heritage of the examination" (p. 111). In this view, Chinese learning styles are more a product of the pragmatics of negotiating a competitive high-stakes examination system, rather than culturally determined learning dispositions. A similar point has been made by Brown and Wang (2016).

Taken together, these critiques are a caution about both theorizing the culture concept and overgeneralising its effects. The arguments are broadly philosophical in nature rather than empirical, but there is evidence that they have had some influence on psychologically oriented research that has also questioned homogenised views of the so-called Chinese learner (Mok, Kennedy, Moore, Shan, & Leung, 2008). The lesson for this current chapter is that extravagant claims of links between Confucian values and assessment policy and practice need to be avoided. Rather, the body of conceptual and empirical research that has been generated in relation to assessment in CHC contexts requires careful scrutiny and review in order to determine the appropriateness of cultural explanations in a growing body of research.

A positive outcome from this cautionary literature is that it shows how teachers outside of CHC contexts have attempted to provide challenging learning environments for CHC students. This is important because the alternative is to regard such students as incapable of learning in any other way than that endorsed by their cultural experiences. Teaching can transcend these experiences, as shown in the studies cited above, and this can only be positive for students as they negotiate new cultural norms and new learning expectations.

IMPLICATIONS FOR ASSESSMENT POLICY

As mentioned earlier, one of the drivers of this research agenda was the changing policy landscape, both internationally and regionally, where more emphasis was being advocated for formative assessment with the hope that less emphasis would be placed on summative assessment. Thus the key question was whether teachers in Confucian heritage societies could respond positively to this policy agenda or if it clashed with fundamental beliefs they might have about the purpose of assessment.

If there was ever a view that examinations might eventually be replaced by formative assessments in contexts such as Hong Kong or mainland China, then the research reviewed here clearly indicates that this would be highly problematic. Assessment in Confucian heritage contexts is about results, with students, teachers, and schools being held accountable for those results ('assessment as accountability'). It might be argued that there is a moral purpose to these results—they demonstrate the character of students, their capacity for hard work, and their perseverance ('assessment as personal development or life character'). Thus, trying to replace summative assessment in the form of examinations, regarded as accurate and objective, with assessments perceived to be less rigorous and more idiosyncratic, runs counter to long-held and well-understood beliefs.

There is some additional evidence for this view in the implementation of school based assessment (SBA) in Hong Kong. As part of its reform of senior secondary education, the Hong Kong Examinations and Assessment Authority introduced elements of SBA into some subjects that were part of the newly developed Hong Kong Diploma of Secondary Education (Kennedy, 2013). SBA became a hotly contested subject both with teachers and the community. Teachers were happy to accept the results of externally developed examinations as accurate reflections of students' capacity and their own teaching, but were much less willing to insert themselves into the assessment process in the form of SBA that would contribute towards to final examination result. Additionally, the community showed signs of scepticism about such assessment processes, even though the SBA results themselves were statistically moderated by the results of the public examination. Over time, SBA has been delayed in many subjects, and timelines for implementation have been extended. It was quite clear from the ongoing public and professional debates that attempts to modify the externally developed examination system were bound to meet with resistance from difference sources and for different reasons. Strictly speaking, SBA was not formative in nature, but it did represent an attempt to make terminal examinations less important and teacher judgments more important, and it was for these reasons that it encountered so much resistance.

For policy makers, the issue is whether teacher beliefs can be changed. The broad assumption of the research reviewed above was that teacher beliefs about assessment reflected their attitudes and these attitudes would lead to action in practice, a more general issue that has been reviewed extensively (Fives & Buehl, 2012). While the attitude-action link has not been explored in current studies relating to CHCs and assessment beliefs, it seems clear that any reform agenda designed to change assessment practices would first have to take teacher beliefs about assessment into consideration. This means that reforms are not just about 'doing things differently,' but, more importantly, 'thinking about things differently.' This latter is a much more difficult challenge for any change agenda and there is evidence from the studies in Hong Kong and mainland China reviewed here that assessment reform processes did not go far enough to make a clean break with the previous assessment landscape.

In Hong Kong, for example, while the reform agendas in both basic and senior secondary education espoused more liberal approaches to assessment, an end of schooling examination remained as the mechanism for university selection (approximately 18% of the age cohort eventually receive a university place). As long as examinations play such a fundamental social role in CHCs, it seems unlikely that teachers can be convinced to change their beliefs about assessment. The same can be said for mainland China. While there has been some attempt to promote alternative forms of assessment, the National College Entrance Examination has remained in place so that, for teachers, this life-influencing examination will likely continue to dominate their thinking about assessment. Also, as long as schools and teachers are judged by their success in examinations, it seems unrealistic to expect them to change their beliefs about assessment. Certainly, Chen and Brown (2013) demonstrated that young teachers about to enter the profession saw examinations and their control function as governing their beliefs about the role and function of assessment in the schools where they would end up teaching. Reform agendas that send mixed messages about assessment are likely to encounter difficulties if old values and beliefs continue to hold sway alongside new expectations. In this context, teachers' beliefs are unlikely to change.

One approach to the particular context of CHCs has been suggested by Carless (2011). He argued that summative assessments could be given more formative characteristics so that teachers do not need to make wholesale changes to their practice but could provide more feedback as part of the summative assessment process. This idea has some support in the literature on formative assessment that increasingly is becoming a priority in CHC contexts (Ratnam-Lim & Tan, 2015). It is an attempt to accommodate teacher beliefs rather than change them, and to make change and innovation more achievable in contexts where radical change is likely to encounter considerable resistance.

Overall, policy makers ought to take note of the results reviewed earlier, because they indicate that changing assessment modes and practices in CHCs are likely to present considerable challenges. Changing beliefs is more difficult than changing practices and, until the beliefs are well understood, it is unlikely that traditional change processes will be successful. What is more, policy makers need to think carefully about the ways different forms of assessment can be accommodated both at system and classroom level. Going directly in one step from an examination based system to one in which assessments are more school based and formative in nature will not be the way to go. Getting the best out of different forms of assessment will be more productive and more consistent with local values than attempting to replace one system with another.

IMPLICATIONS FOR FUTURE RESEARCH

Only two CHC societies were studied in the reviews reported above. For the research to be more inclusive, it needs to cover other CHC societies (e.g., Korea, Japan, Taiwan, and Vietnam). Within these societies, large representative samples of teachers would need to be recruited. These two processes would provide greater confidence about the generalizability of the results. It would also provide the opportunity to explore in more depth the interaction between cultural and social contexts in these different societies.

A key issue in broadening the scope of the research in this way would be to take into account local issues and contexts that might affect teachers' beliefs about assessment. While the focus of the research to date has been on statistical modelling, in the later stages, the research was informed by identifying the views of local teachers and feeding these in to the instrument development process. This is an important process to continue in an expanded research agenda. It means that such an agenda is not just about testing statistical models—it is about creating valid and reliable models based, when possible, on locally collected data.

The methods of cross-cultural psychology require invariant structures before results from different samples can be validly compared. Psychometrically, this is an acceptable requirement. Yet it is often taken further to mean that unless structures are invariant they are not valid. Put another way, psychometricians regard invariant structures as evidence of enduring traits and latent constructs. To date, however, research in the area reviewed earlier has produced multiple structures within the same, or at least similar, cultural context. This may be a reflection of the impact of social context in the different research locations or it may be that the structures identified so far are not sufficiently theoretically informed. It is generally accepted that data can fit multiple structures and that fit itself is not a substitute for considering the theoretical adequacy of a particular model. In an ongoing research agenda, attention needs to be paid to the structure of teachers' conceptions of assessment in CHCs, the extent to which they need to be seen as invariant and, if they are not invariant, then attention needs to be brought to the possible explanations and the extent to which they might undermine the 'culture thesis' that underlies the research agenda.

A further measurement issue is concerned with whether structures might be more reliably and validly determined if less error was associated with them. The research conducted so far in this area is paradigmatically a reflection of Classical Test Theory (CTT), and it might be useful as a comparative approach to explore how results might be influenced using the Rasch model. This is not to suggest that one analytic method is better than another, but rather to highlight the importance of identifying valid and reliable scales. Increasingly, studies are using both methods in order to benefit from the insights that can be gained from multiple approaches to analysis. When latent constructs are being identified, it is important to understand how different items contribute to these, whether there are misfitting items, and whether measurement can be made more accurate.

Finally, there is a need to track teacher beliefs to assess the extent to which they translate into practice. This is a fundamental assumption of the research conducted to date based on health related models such as the theory of planned change (TPC) (Ajzen, 2005). Are teacher beliefs about assessments really proxies for their classroom practice? TPC has accommodated a range of research that is not health related and it would be possible to follow up teachers with additional surveys about their attitudes, self-efficacy, behavioural intentions, subjective norms, and actual behaviours to explore how their beliefs translate into action and, in so doing, to understand why they hold the beliefs that they do. In addition, observational studies could be undertaken to document teachers' assessment practices in real classroom environments. All of this suggests a more longitudinal approach to the research agenda is needed to extend and enhance what to date has been exclusively cross-sectional in nature. This would also enable teachers' conceptions of assessment to be monitored over time in order to determine the stability of such conceptions, as well as their influence.

There is little doubt that the kind of research agenda outlined here has multiple benefits. It would enhance the theoretical dimensions of the research, focusing on both theoretical and statistical adequacy. It would also provide further insights into teacher beliefs and teacher practice and the link between them. Given the importance of assessment to the educational aspirations of individuals and societies, it is clearly a worthwhile agenda to explore.

CONCLUSION

A very promising research agenda has been initiated exploring how CHC might have an effect on the way teachers think about assessment and carry it out in their classrooms. While the agenda is not uncontested, in the sense that questions have been raised about the advisability of treating culture as monolithic and deterministic, the results never-theless suggest that samples of teachers in several CHCs do appear to have conceptions of assessment that differ from those in Western societies. Putting measurement issues aside, the characteristics of these conceptions suggest that improvement, control, and accountability are salient for the teachers surveyed, as well as the contribution assess-ment can make to the personal development of students. In this context, assessment takes on important social and, indeed, moral purposes. This expands considerably the purely evaluative nature of assessment that characterises the views of teachers in West-ern contexts, so that assessment takes on larger social purposes. It is these purposes that could be profitably explored further in both CHCs and in other contexts, and these purposes could inform future instrument development.

Are the dispositions and conceptions about assessment reviewed here clearly influenced by Confucian values? The evidence so far points in this direction, but it is indicative rather than conclusive. More work is needed with larger samples, adding a longitudinal element to the research, and finding out more about how teachers' beliefs are developed and enacted. It is a promising research agenda with considerable poten-tial to expand knowledge about assessment and the impact culture can exert on a pro-cess so important to modern societies and the individuals within them. The cultural contexts of assessment should clearly be on any future assessment research agenda. Current work as analysed here provides a sound basis for such an agenda that can build, extend, and theorise further cultures' impact on assessment and learning.

REFERENCES

Ajzen, I. (2005). *Attitudes, personality and behavior* (2nd ed.). New York: Open University Press.

Ansari, D. (2011). Culture and education: New frontiers in brain plasticity. *Trends in Cognitive Sciences, 16*, (2), 93–95.

Biggs, J. (1996a). Approaches to learning of Asian students: A multiple paradox. In Janak Pandey, Durganand Sunha & Dham P.S. Bhawuk (Eds.), *Asian Contributions to Cross Cultural Psychology* (pp. 180–199). New Delhi: SAGE.

Biggs, J. (1996b). Western misconceptions of the Confucian-heritage learning culture. In D. Watkins & J. Biggs (Eds.), *The Chinese learner: Cultural, psychological and contextual influences* (pp. 45–68). Hong Kong and Melbourne: Comparative Education Research Centre and Australian Council for Educational Research.

Brown, G.T.L. (2006). Teachers' conceptions of assessment: Validation of an abridged instrument. *Psychological Reports, 99*, 166–117.

Brown, G.T.L., & Gao, L. B. (2015). Chinese teachers' conceptions of assessment for and of learning: Six com-peting and complementary purposes. *Cogent Education, 2*(1), 993836. doi:10.1080/2331186X.2014.993836

Brown, G.T.L., Hui, S.K.F., Yu, W. M., & Kennedy, K. (2011). Teachers' conceptions of assessment in Chinese contexts: A tripartite model of accountability, improvement, and irrelevance. *International Journal of Edu-cational Research, 50*, 307–320.

Brown, G.T.L., Kennedy, K., Fok, P. K., Chan, J.K.S, & Yu, W. M. (2009). Assessment for improvement: Under-standing Hong Kong teachers' conceptions and practices of assessment. *Assessment in Education: Principles, Policy and Practice, 16*(3), 347–363.

Brown, G.T.L., & Wang, Z. (2016). Understanding Chinese university student conceptions of assessment: Cul-tural similarities and jurisdictional differences between Hong Kong and China. *Social Psychology of Educa-tion, 19*(1), 151–173. doi:10.1007/s11218–015–9322-x

Carless, D. (2011). From testing to productive student learning: Implementing formative assessment in Confucian-heritage settings. New York: Routledge.

Carless, D., & Lam, R. (2014). Developing assessment for productive learning in Confucian-influenced settings. In Claire Wyatt-Smith, Valentina Klenowski, & Peta Colbert (Eds.), *Designing Assessment for Quality Learn-ing: The Enabling Power of Assessment* (pp. 167–179). Heidelberg: Springer.

Chan, C.K.K., & Rao, N. (Eds.). (2009). *Revisiting the Chinese learner: Changing contexts, changing education.* Hong Kong: Comparative Education Research Centre.

Chang, W. C. (2000). In search of the Chinese in all the wrong places. *Journal of Psychology in Chinese Societies, 1*(1), 125–142.

Chen, J. J & Brown, G.T.L. (2013). High-stakes examination preparation that controls teaching: Chinese prospective teachers' conceptions of excellent teaching and assessment. *Journal of Education for Teaching, 39*(5), 541–556.

Clark, R. and Gieve, S. (2006). On the discursive construction of 'The Chinese Learner'. *Language, Culture and Curriculum, 19*(1), 54–73.

Cooper, C., & Denner, J. (1998). Theories linking culture and psychology: Universal and community-specific processes. *Annual Review of Psychology, 49*, 559–84.

Elman, B. (2009). Civic service examinations. In L. Cheng (Ed.), *Berkshire Encyclopedia of China* (pp. 405–410). Retrieved January 1, 2015 from https://www.princeton.edu/~elman/documents/ Civil%20Service%20 Examinations.pdf

Fives, H., & Buehl, M. M. (2012). Spring cleaning for the "messy" construct of teachers' beliefs: What are they? Which have been examined? What can they tell us? In K. R. Harris, S. Graham, & T. Urdan (Eds.), *APA educational psychology handbook: Individual differences and cultural and contextual factors* (Vol. 2, pp. 471–499). Washington, DC: APA.

Gao, L. B., & Kennedy. K. (2011). Teachers' conception of assessment in Mainland China: Categories, characteristics and implications [中国内地教师的考评观:类型、特点与启 示]. *Journal of Educational Studies* [教育学报], *7*(1), 39–47.

Gieve, S. and Clark, R. (2005). 'The Chinese approach to learning': Cultural trait or situated response? *System, 33* (2), 261–276.

Goh, J & Park, C. (2009). Culture sculpts the perceptual brain. In J. Y. Chiao (Ed.), *Progress in Brain Research, 178*, 95–111.

Ho, D.Y.F. (1994). Cognitive socialization in Confucian Heritage cultures. In P. M. Greenfield & R. R. Cocking (Eds.), *Cross-cultural roots of minority child development* (pp. 285–314). Hillsdale, NJ: L. Erlbaum Associates.

Ho, J., & Crookall, D. (1995. Breaking with Chinese cultural traditions: Learner autonomy in English language teaching. *System, 23*(2), 235–242.

Hui, S.K.F. (2012). Missing conceptions of assessment: Qualitative studies with Hong Kong curriculum leaders. *Asia-Pacific Education Researcher, 21*(2), 375–383.

Kennedy, K. (2013). High stakes school based assessment and cultural values: Beyond issues of validity. Key note address, Cambridge Horizon's seminar, 'School based assessment: Prospects and realities in Asian contexts', 3 June, Kuala Lumpur, Malaysia. Retrieved January 3, 2015 from http://www.cambridgeassessment.org.uk/ Images/139719-sba-seminar-papers.pdf

Kennedy, K., & Lee. J.C.K. (2008). *The changing role of schools in Asian societies—Schools for the knowledge society.* London: Routledge.

Kennedy, K. J., Chan, J.K.S., Yu, F.W.M., & Fok, P. K. (2006). *Assessment for productive learning: forms of assessment and their potential for enhancing learning.* Paper presented at the 32nd Annual Conference of the International Association for Educational Assessment, Singapore, May, 21–26. Retrieved January 5, 2015 from https://www.ied.edu.hk/fpece_project/QEF/Download%20area/1_Assess%20for%20productive%20 learning%20(Kerrypaper).pdf

Lee, T.H.C. (2006). Review. *China Review International, 13*(1), 1–12.

Lee, W. O. (1996). The cultural context for Chinese learners: Conceptions of learning in the Confucian tradition. In David Watkins & John Biggs (Eds.), *The Chinese learner: Cultural, psychological and contextual influences* (pp. 25–42). Hong Kong and Melbourne: Comparative Education Research Centre and Australian Council for Educational Research.

Leong, W. S. (2014a). Singaporean teachers' views of classroom assessment: Findings from using Q-Methodology. *Assessment Matters, 6*, 34–64.

Leong, W. S. (2014b). Understanding classroom assessment in dilemmatic spaces: Case studies of Singaporean music teachers' conceptions of classroom assessment. *Music Education Research, 16*(4), 454–470.

Leong, W. S. (2014c). Knowing the intentions, meaning and context of classroom assessment: A case study of Singaporean teacher's conception and practice. *Studies in Educational Evaluation, 43*, 70–78.

Li,. J. (2001). Chinese conceptualization of learning. *Ethos, 29*(2), 111–137.

Li, J. (2005). Mind or virtue—Western and Chinese beliefs about learning. *Current Directions in Psychological Science, 14*(4), 190–194.

Li, J. (2009). Learning to self-perfect: Chinese beliefs about learning. In C. K. K. Chan & N. Rao (Eds.), *Revisiting the Chinese learner: Changing contexts, changing education* (pp. 35–70). Hong Kong: Comparative Education Research Centre.

Li, W. S., & Hui, S.K.F. (2007). Conceptions of assessment of mainland China college lecturers: A technical paper analyzing the Chinese version of CoA-III. *Asia Pacific Education Researcher, 16*(2), 185–198.

Littlewood, W. (1999). Defining and developing autonomy in East Asian contexts. *Applied Linguistics, 20*(1), 71–94.

Madsen, D., & Riemenschnitter, A. (2009). *Diasporic histories—Cultural archives of Chinese transnationalism.* Hong Kong: Hong Kong: University Press.

Mason, M. (2014). Culture and educational outcomes in "Confucian heritage" societies. In Asia (Ed.), Revue internationale d'éducation de Sèvre. Colloque: L'éducation en Asie en 2014: Quels enjeux mondiaux? Retrieved January 2, 2014 from http://ries.revues.org/3812

McInerney, D., & Ali, J. (2006). Multidimensional and hierarchical assessment of school motivation: Cross-cultural validation. *Educational Psychology, 26* (6), 717–734.

Mok, M.M.C., Kennedy, K., Moore, P., Shan, P.W.J., & Leung,. S. O. (2008). The use of help-seeking by Chinese secondary school students: Challenging the myth of 'the Chinese learner'. *Evaluation and Research in Education, 21*(3), 188–213.

OECD. (2005). *Formative assessment: Improving learning in secondary classrooms.* Paris: OECD.

Oettingen, G., & Zosuls, K. (2006). Culture and self-efficacy in adolescents. In F. Pajares & T. Urdan (Eds.), *Self-efficacy beliefs in adolescents* (pp. 245–266). Greenwich, CT: Information Age Publishing.

Pajares, F., & Urdan, T. (2006). Foreword. In F. Pajares & T. Urdan (Eds.), *Self-efficacy beliefs in adolescents* (pp. ix–xii). Greenwich, CT: Information Age Publishing.

Park, J. (2010). *Metamorphosis of Confucian heritage culture and the possibility of an Asian education research methodology.* Paper presented at the 7th Annual Ethics Conference: The Ethics of Sustainable Development, Strathmore University, Nairobi, Kenya, October, 28–30. Retrieved December 7, 2014 from http://hub.hku. hk/handle/10722/127130

Peterson, E. R., Brown, G.T.L., & Hamilton, R. J. (2013). Cultural differences in tertiary students' conceptions of learning as a duty and student achievement. *The International Journal of Quantitative Research in Education, 1*(2), 167–181.

Purdie, N., & Hattie, J. (2002). Assessing students' conceptions of learning. *Australian Journal of Educational & Developmental Psychology, 2*, 17–32.

Ratnam-Lim, C.T.L., & Tan, K.H.K. (2015). Large-scale implementation of formative assessment practices in an examination-oriented culture. *Assessment in Education: Principles, Policy & Practice, 22*(1), 61–78. doi:10.1 080/0969594x.2014.1001319

Ryan, J., & Louie, K. (2007). False dichotomy? 'Western' and 'Confucian' concepts of scholarship and learning. *Educational Philosophy and Theory, 39*(4), 404–417.

Ryan, J., & Slethaug, G. (Eds.). (2010). International education and the Chinese learner. Hong Kong: Hong Kong University Press.

Têng, S. Y. (1943). Influence on the Western examination system: I. Introduction. *Harvard Journal of Asiatic Studies, 7*(4), 267–312.

Tu, W. M. (1979. *Humanity and self cultivation: Essays in Confucian thought.* Berkeley: Asian Humanities Press.

Wang, P. (2010). *Research on Chinese teachers' conceptions and practice of assessment* [in Chinese]. Unpublished doctoral dissertation. China: South China Normal University Guangzhou.

Wang, R. (2013). *A test of faith: Chinese students' changing views on the national college entrance examination.* Retrieved December 7, 2014 from http://www.tealeafnation.com/2013/06/a-test-of-faith-chinese-students-changing-views-on-the-national-college-entrance-examination/

Wang, Z., & Brown, G. (2014). Hong Kong tertiary students' conceptions of assessment of academic ability. *Higher Education Research and Development, 33*(5), 1063–1077.

Watkins, D., & Biggs, J. (Eds.). (1996). *The Chinese learner: Cultural, psychological and contextual influences.* Hong Kong and Melbourne: Comparative Education Research Centre and Australian Council for Educational Research.

Watkins, D., & Biggs, J. (Eds.). (2001a). *Teaching the Chinese Learner: Psychological and Pedagogical Perspectives.* Hong Kong: Comparative Education Research Centre.

Watkins, D., & Biggs, J. (2001b). The paradox of the Chinese learner and beyond. In David Watkins & John Biggs (Eds.), *Teaching the Chinese learner: Psychological and pedagogical perspectives* (pp. 3–26). Hong Kong: Comparative Education Research Centre.

24

EDUCATIONAL ASSESSMENT IN MUSLIM COUNTRIES

Values, Policies, and Practices

Atta Gebril

INTRODUCTION

There has been an increasing worldwide interest in Islamic and Arab culture during the last century. This interest could be due to a number of reasons, the first of which has to do with the strategic location of this region, stretching across three continents. This is also an area where the three largest monotheistic religions started: Judaism, Christianity, and Islam. The discovery of huge reserves of natural resources, especially oil, in many of its countries is a third reason for this growing attention. Recently, there have been unfortunate claims about the connection between terrorism and Islam, which have urged people from other countries to read more about this religion (Jackson, 2014). A final reason has to do with the fact that Islam is the fastest growing religion in the world and the Muslim countries are also among the fastest growing populations worldwide (Jenkins, 2015). According to Thobani (2011), " no subject has raised more questions than Islam in the past decade, provoking suspicions, controversies, and polarized debates across a range of contexts" (p. 1).

The Islamic world includes those countries in which Muslims make up a majority of the total population. Muslim countries are mainly located in Asia and Africa. The population of Muslims worldwide is around 1.6 billion people, constituting almost 23% of the world's population. If current trends stay the same, the number of Muslims by 2050 will be almost equal to Christians (Pew Research Center, 2015). The Islamic world is extremely diverse, including a wide range of ethnic groups, linguistic backgrounds, and cultural norms. In terms of economy, Muslim countries have a huge amount of natural resources, especially oil reserves, of which they possess around 75% of the world's total (Chossudovsky, 2007). These huge reserves have made the oil-producing Muslim countries among the richest worldwide. Some other Muslim countries, such as Turkey and Malaysia, have rapidly growing economies. However, most Muslim countries are considered developing or emerging economies. As for literacy rates, around 71% of the population in Muslim counties are literate, leaving 29% of the population in urgent need of learning how to read and write (Organization for Islamic Countries, 2012).

Education in Muslim societies is also of great interest since a number of concerns have been raised about how Islamic schools prepare future generations of Muslims.

The same concern has been raised about the way Muslim families educate their children in Western societies (Hefner, 2014). Education in Islam has always been part and parcel of the daily activities of Muslims for the last 14 centuries. The first word revealed to Prophet Muhammad is اقْرَأ, which means 'read.' According to Kadi (2006, p. 312), education is "one of the cornerstones of Islamic civilization and its backbone."

One of the main motives of education in the early era of Islam was to enable reading of the Qur'an[1] and to know more about religious instructions and laws. With the establishment of Islamic civilization, Muslims expanded their interest in education beyond religious knowledge to other fields, including, but not limited to, mathematics, physics, medicine, and chemistry. Examples of Muslim scientists who have substantially contributed to our knowledge include Algoritmi (780–850), who introduced the concept of algebra; Thebit (826–901), who is considered the founder of mechanical statics; Geber (722–804), whose work influenced chemistry, specifically alchemy and metallurgy; and Alhazen (965–1040), for his influential work on the principles of optics and principles of scientific experiments (Morgan, 2007; Scientist, 2015). An impressive aspect of these contributions is the fact that they were introduced over 1,000 years ago, when Europe was still in the Dark Ages.

It is important to clarify two common misconceptions about Islam and Muslims. Islam started as a religion in the Middle East, specifically in Saudi Arabia, and the Qur'an was revealed to Prophet Muhammad in Arabic. However, Islam is not restricted to the Middle East. It is safe to say that the most populated Muslim country, Indonesia, is not part of the Arab world. Many of the largest Muslim countries are located in regions outside the Middle East. This chapter focuses on assessment practices in the Arab countries, but also discusses these issues, when relevant and possible, as they apply to other Muslim countries. The second misconception has to do with the language spoken in Muslim countries. The majority of Muslims do not speak Arabic as a native language, but many of them learn it for religious purposes. For these reasons, the current synthesis within this chapter is a relatively difficult undertaking given the geographical, cultural, and linguistic diversity of the Islamic world. The chapter focuses mainly on Muslim countries in the Middle East, but also refers to some examples from other areas, especially in the South Asia region.

Discussing how Islam has affected educational practices is always a tricky and problematic issue for a number of reasons. People usually confuse Islam with Muslims, while in fact this is not exactly the case. Educational contexts in Muslim countries have been shaped by a wide network of complex factors (e.g., local culture, socioeconomic variables, linguistic and ethnic diversity) and, therefore, it is not possible to argue that a specific practice is due to the influence of Islamic religious teachings. In fact, many Muslim countries follow a secular public school system that detaches itself, at least partially, from religious instructions—good examples are Turkey and Tunisia. Many practices, whether educational or even religious, are sometimes shaped by the local culture, rather than a macro-culture of Islam or the Arabic world (McLoughlin, 2007). For this reason, it is always recommended to understand the social, economic, historical, and political settings in which an educational institution operates when interpreting certain instructional practices and decisions.

HISTORICAL BACKGROUND ON EDUCATION IN MUSLIM COUNTRIES

Different educational institutions have evolved in Muslim countries over time, including the mosque, *kuttab*, and madrasa. The mosque, which is a place of worship for Muslims, is the oldest educational institution in Islam. The pedagogical experience was usually offered by a sheik شيخ who shared his knowledge with students in what is called to this day *Halaqa*, literally meaning study circles. Examples of topics typically discussed in these study circles included memorization and interpretation of the Qur'an, the teachings of Prophet Muhammad (Sunnah سنة), jurisprudence فقه, and other theological issues. By the 9th century, the mosques expanded their educational experience to include secular fields, such as mathematics, science, and medicine (Kadi, 2006). A good example of how a mosque developed into an educational institution is Al-Azhar University in Egypt, which was built as a mosque over 1,000 years ago. Now Al-Azhar has thousands of schools and many higher education institutions in Egypt and worldwide where both religious and secular subjects are taught (Gesink, 2006, 2014).

The second type of Islamic educational institution is the kuttab, which is a room or a building usually attached to a mosque. According to Kadi (2006), the kuttab appeared in the 1st Islamic century (the 7th century) and initially focused largely on memorization and recitation of the Qur'an. It expanded at a later stage and started to provide instruction in reading, writing, and arithmetic. Parents used to send their children to learn religious texts and literacy skills in return for a sum of money paid to the teacher. The kuttab is still visible in some Muslim countries, such as Egypt and Sudan, but it has become less common with the introduction of public education.

During the 4th century of the Islamic calendar (around 1000 CE), a third institution appeared, the madrasa. According to Kadi (2006), "madrasas were built by members of the ruling elite and soon became the ubiquitous colleges of Islam" (p. 314). Madrasas helped turn Islamic education into a formal process, with a regular schedule, staff, and curriculum. Funding for madrasas was mainly based on philanthropy in the form of endowments, usually by a ruling family or a rich Muslim. These forms of education continued in Muslim countries throughout the centuries, even during the colonial era, since they were the main source of religious and secular education to the masses, who could not afford private or colonial schools.

During the colonial era, most Muslim countries were occupied by either Great Britain or France. The British occupied many parts of Egypt, Sudan, the Gulf area, and Iraq, while the French controlled most of North Africa and Lebanon. Muslim countries in South Asia were targeted by colonial powers including the Portuguese, Dutch, British, and French. The indigenous educational systems in these countries substantially suffered during the colonial era. For example, the British attempted to restrict access to education; in a 1902 report, Lord Cromer, the British Consul-General in Egypt, referred to the practice of discouraging Egyptian children from joining schools by raising fees (Morsy & Aly, 1980). Morsy and Aly (1980) also pointed out that the British used exams to terrorize and intimidate students to further restrict access to education. While exams had been present before the British occupation of Egypt, they had been used as part of the learning process and for making it more 'fun,' as described in a document written by an Egyptian education officer in the 19th century (Aly, 2015). Mansfield (1971, p. 139) indicated that, "no aspect of the British occupation of Egypt is more open to criticism than its effect on education."

After obtaining their independence in the 20th century, Muslim countries were generally left with an elitist private education system that primarily served the very small segment of the society that could afford the relatively high cost of education. Students graduating from these schools were hired predominantly to fill posts in different government offices, replacing displaced colonial bureaucrats and policy makers. People who could not afford these private schools usually sent their children to a kuttab where they learned literacy and numeracy skills and Qur'an. The rest of the population was involved in manual labor (especially agriculture) that did not need any level of education.

After the colonial era, Muslim countries embarked on educational policies aimed at reaching the whole population, especially the disadvantaged majority who could not afford to pay school fees for private schooling during the colonial period. The policies that Egypt introduced after the 1952 revolution are a good example; the country offered free education for all students in public schools and higher education institutions (Ramadan, 1993). The same policy was introduced in most other Arab and Muslim countries. While offering great opportunities for a large group of citizens who had been left out for a very long time, the expansion of schools resulted in a wide range of challenges that needed prompt action from governments and the public at large. For example, governments moved in the direction of building new schools and hiring teachers to meet the expansion requirements.

It is important to consider the multifaceted purposes of education after decolonization. Since many Muslim countries were inhabited at that time, and until this day, by citizens from diverse cultural and linguistic backgrounds, it was important to implement an educational policy that would unify citizens around one national identity and move beyond ethnic and regional differences. Hence, government-funded education was about preparing citizens who could contribute to the building of the nation, and, more importantly, develop a national identity (Morsy & Aly, 1980). To achieve this purpose, Muslim governments attempted to follow a centralized system of education especially because of the many advantages of this system (Gebril & Brown, 2014). First, it was easier (at least as believed then) for governments to achieve national educational goals through this centralized system since decisions could be made by one person and disseminated to officials in different parts of the country. Second, educational institutions in different regions did not have skilled staff who could be trusted and/or were capable of managing schools in a decentralized system. More importantly, it was a necessity to have control over the content taught in schools to help achieve national cohesion.

CHARACTERISTICS OF ASSESSMENT IN MUSLIM COUNTRIES

The main issue in this section is how assessment is perceived in the Arab and Islamic world. There appears to be a negative legacy when it comes to assessment, especially in the Arab culture. This negative perception of assessment can be observed even in the terminology used in schools. For example, the Arabic word used for evaluation is التقويم which literally means 'fixing something.' The assumption here is that something is wrong with the students and needs to be fixed. The English form does not share the same connotation, and one may argue 'evaluation' is relatively neutral, at least in the way native speakers currently use it in their daily activities. Another example is the way teachers and students use the verb يصحح (to correct): يصحح الاختبار (literally, to correct the test) and يصحح الواجب (literally, to correct homework). While in English, a verb like 'grade' or 'score' is commonly used to refer to these processes and carries a sense of determining the quality of something, this is not the case in Arabic. Through using the verb 'correct,' teachers and students are likely to assume that the purpose of grading an assignment or a test is to look for and fix mistakes. Such language substantially affects the way assessment functions are perceived by different stakeholders inside and outside schools (Gebril & Taha-Thomure, 2014).

Another issue that has often been perceived negatively and, possibly, misinterpreted by Western scholars is rote memorization in Islamic schools and schools in Muslim countries in general. Memorization has always been associated with the learning of religious texts, especially Qur'an, in these schools. Memorization has also been widely adopted in general education classes with other school subjects. This practice, as argued by some researchers, has usually resulted in assessment tools that favor memorization and rote learning. Hargreaves (1997, 2001) looked into memorization and rote learning in the assessment context in Egypt. She argued that memorization and rote learning are prevalent in Egyptian schools:

> The assessment goals of selection and accountability also made formal, written examinations, based on rote memorisation, the easiest instrument of assessment; especially since pupil outcomes from examinations are numerical and so are straightforward to use, even with vast numbers of pupils. Examinations traditionally motivated children to learn by heart in order to achieve high marks in written examinations. The objective of these examinations had never been for individual learning in any other sense. Their objective had been the instrumental one of the government to select a useful elite and the objective of the people was to be selected into that ruling elite.
>
> (Hargreaves, 2001, p. 259)

However, memorization is perceived differently in Islamic education, as argued by Boyle (2006):

> Memorization and understanding are often considered to be opposites. Memorization without comprehension is mindless rote learning, and comprehension is not automatically associated with prior memorization. However, in Islamic education memorization of the Qur'an is generally considered the first step in understanding (not a substitute for it), as its general purpose was to ensure that sacred knowledge was passed on in proper form so that it could be understood later. Daniel A. Wagner quotes the most influential Muslim jurist, theologian, and Sufi al-Ghazali who pointed out almost a millennium ago that memorization of the Qur'an, as a first step to learning, did not necessarily preclude comprehension later on: "The creed ought to be taught to a boy in the earliest childhood, so that he may hold it absolutely in memory. Thereafter, the meaning of it will keep gradually unfolding itself to him, point by point, as he grows older.
>
> (p. 488)

Hence, memorization in Islam is perceived as a first step in understanding a specific issue. This view is actually compatible with current theories of learning (Anderson & Krathwohl, 2001) that have the process of remembering as a first step in cognitive processing. Added to that, Islam and the Qur'an themselves always encourage Muslims to exercise *ijtihad* اجتهاد an Arabic word which means independent reasoning (Khan & Ramadan, 2011).

The question remains, why is memorization prevalent in assessment practices in Muslim countries? There are some historical events that should be considered in order to understand current practices. With the decline of the 'golden age' of Islamic civilization in the late 13th century and the neglect of ijtihad, memorization by itself became more common. The same method was prevalent in Muslim countries during the post-colonial era partly because the expansion of education placed more emphasis on quantity than on quality. Added to that, the impact of autocratic regimes in some Muslim countries (e.g., Bashar Al Assad in Syria, Ben Ali in Tunisia, Mubarak in Egypt, and Suharto in Indonesia) at certain periods was a critical factor in this issue. It was in the interest of these regimes to have an educational system that promoted obedience and fear, instead of reasoning and challenging the status quo. These variables, among others, have resulted in memorization-oriented educational practices in various Muslim countries at various times (Boyle, 2006).

Nonetheless, efforts to move away from memorization and rote learning, at least in Egypt, have been documented (Hargreaves, 1997, 2001). Strategies used by the Ministry of Education included preparing specifications for exams that emphasized higher-order thinking skills and also developing new textbooks fostering critical thinking. However, Hargreaves (1997, 2001) argued that the suggested reform policies were not successful mainly because they did not follow a gradual process. This may always be the case with top-down policies imposed by a central entity. Ministries often develop policies that are not sensitive to the local contexts in which teachers and students work. As a result, these policies failed basically because they were not compatible with realities on the ground.

The UAE is another country that has recently transitioned to a formative assessment framework. Abu Dhabi Education Council (ADEC) introduced an English Continuous Assessment Rich Task (ECART), which is a framework that promotes ongoing and alternative assessment (AlAlili, 2014). In her study, AlAlili showed a number of benefits from the ECART framework; however, she reported some discrepancies between teachers' beliefs and the underlying principles of reform. AlAlili attributed these discrepancies to teachers' inadequate understanding of reform principles. She also referred to the lack of professional development opportunities for teachers as another reason. She calls for education officials and policy makers to provide support and training for teachers as part of the reform process.

The centralized system of education adopted in the post-colonial era in most Muslim countries affected almost every aspect of the school curriculum, especially assessment policies. For example, schools usually used the same textbook nationwide at each and every grade. In addition, teachers adhered to the same curriculum guidelines suggested by the ministry of education. This is a common practice until this day in many Muslim Arab countries including Egypt, Saudi Arabia, Kuwait, Syria, and Bahrain. An assessment policy was needed to measure learning outcomes and also to measure the quality of both teachers and schools. Governments in a centralized system of education usually prefer an accountability-oriented policy since it lends itself to the prevalent mindset in such a context. As Kamens and Benavot (2011) argue, "countries receive material support for conducting these assessments as well as increased credibility as 'good citizens' and 'proper' nation states" (p. 293). For this reason, accountability-oriented policies have been a common phenomenon in different Muslim countries. The National Examination (NE) that was introduced in its current form in Indonesia in 2005 is a good example of a high-stakes exam. This assessment is used as a school-leaving exam and consequently exit decisions are made based on its results. According to Sukyadi and Mardiani (2011), the test "has a strong effect and determines everything [that] happened in the classroom, and lead[s] all teachers to teach in the same way toward the examination" (p. 107). Similar results of teaching only for the examinations have been reported in other contexts, including Egypt (Gebril & Brown, 2014), Yemen (Tayeb, Aziz, Ismail, & Khan, 2014), Iran (Salehi & Yunus, 2012), and Jordan (Al-Jamal & Ghadi, 2008).

Evaluating Assessment Systems in Muslim Contexts

Within an assessment system, it is always helpful to look into the effectiveness of policies by using a host of quality indicators. Generally, there are three main indicators of information quality within an assessment system (AERA, APA, & NCME, 2014; Darling-Hammond & Wentworth, 2010): enabling context, system alignment, and assessment quality. These three indicators will be used to examine the effectiveness of assessment systems in Muslim countries.

The context in which assessment information is gathered concerns whether the setting in which assessment takes place is conducive to learning. This aspect covers areas such as assessment policies, the availability of resources, and staff competency (Clarke, 2011). According to Averett and McLennan (2004), developing countries, many of which are in the Muslim world, "are often still dealing with the tradeoff between increasing access to education and improving the quality of existing education" (p. 239). The expansion of education has caused strains related to availability of financial resources required for developing quality assessment tools. In addition, teachers working in many Muslim countries do not have the assessment literacy (i.e., "the level of knowledge, skills, and understanding of assessment principles and practice that is increasingly required by . . . test stakeholder groups, depending on their needs and context" [Taylor, 2009, p. 24]) needed to develop assessment tools or adequately use assessment results.

On a related note, many of the assessment policies endorsed by governments may be in conflict with current assessment practices and also with teachers' beliefs about the purposes of assessment. In an Egyptian study (Gebril & Brown, 2014), teachers endorsed an accountability-oriented function of assessment that was in conflict with a new national assessment policy that aimed to introduce more formative activities. As a result, the new policy failed to achieve its objectives and was eventually abandoned by the Ministry of Education.

The second indicator, system alignment, focuses on the following aspects:

- the extent to which assessment activities provide information on student learning and achievement in relation to the curriculum in general and key knowledge, skills, and competencies in particular (domain coverage);
- the extent to which assessment activities provide information on all students at all grades (population/system coverage); and
- the extent to which assessment activities are consistent with, and useful/usable in relation to, stakeholder learning goals and priorities (utility). (Clarke, 2011, p. 17)

There has been a move recently to use different indicators to look into these issues, which goes beyond checking the alignment between test content and content of a curriculum. Examples of these indicators include adopting standards-based assessment and also participation in international assessments, such as TIMSS and PIRLS. A number of Muslim countries have participated in these international exams. As shown in Table 24.1, most of the Muslim countries achieved below the international average ($M = 500$) on the TIMSS (Trends in International Mathematics and Science Study) tests.

These disappointing results show an urgent need for Muslim countries to develop better educational policies comparable to those in developed nations. These attempts should also be accompanied with developing better educational funding in order to effectively reach out to different segments of the society. This call for change is not new: a UNESCO report published almost 25 years ago showed that the expansion of education in developing countries in the 1960s and 1970 was associated with a decline in the quality of educational outcomes (Grisay & Mahlck, 1991).

Assessment quality focuses on the psychometric qualities of assessment tools (AERA, APA, & NCME, 2014). The main factor in ensuring assessment quality is whether

Table 24.1 TIMSS Results for Participating Muslim Countries in 2011

Country	Mathematics		Science	
	Grade 4	Grade 8	Grade 4	Grade 8
Turkey	469	452	463	483
Malaysia		440		426
Bahrain	436	409	449	452
UAE	434	456	428	465
Lebanon		449		406
Iran	431	415	453	474
Qatar	413	410	493	419
Saudi Arabia	410	394	429	436
Jordan		406		449
Indonesia		386		406
Oman	385	366	377	420
Syria		380		426
Tunisia	359	425	346	439
Palestine			404	420
Kuwait	342		347	
Morocco	335	371	264	376
Yemen	248		209	

Note: Information from Martin, Mullis, Foy, & Stanco, 2012; Mullis, Martin, Foy, & Arora, 2012; scores not reported for missing cells; international mean = 500

different stakeholders have adequate assessment literacy and also whether there are independent testing entities that oversee the development and validation of assessment tools at the national level. In terms of institutions and centers overseeing assessment development and validation, there is some encouraging news, with different countries establishing assessment and evaluation centers that are involved in developing and validating educational tests. Examples of these centers include:

- The National Center for Evaluation and Examinations—Egypt
- Qiyas: National Center for Assessment in Higher Education—Kingdom of Saudi Arabia
- Common Educational Proficiency Assessment (CEPA) Center developed by the United Arab Emirates Ministry of Higher Education and Scientific Research
- High Committee for Examinations (HCE)—Yemen

While establishing these testing entities is a good first step towards creating a quality mechanism, little information about the validation of assessment tools by these programs is available to the public.

CURRENT RESEARCH ON ASSESSMENT IN MUSLIM COUNTRIES

One strand of research on assessment in Muslim countries has looked into the role of assessment within educational systems and its impact on instructional practices. In the Arab region, research has shown that educational practices tend to endorse a summative accountability-oriented approach to assessment (Gebril & Taha-Thomure, 2014).

In addition, many Muslim countries suffer from what Dore (1976) called the 'diploma disease,' where education focuses on earning a qualification rather than developing skills. In his reflections on his own work after 25 years since writing on the diploma disease, Dore (1997) still believed that exam-oriented schooling has turned "what ought to be an educational experience into mere qualification-earning, ritualistic, tedious, suffused with anxiety and boredom, destructive of curiosity and imagination" (pp. 198–199). The high-stakes nature of exams in Muslim countries, especially university entrance exams, has caused a wide range of negative effects on teaching and learning in schools (Gebril & Hozayin, 2014; Ghorbani, 2008; Tayeb et al., 2014).

A considerable body of assessment literature in the Muslim world has investigated the washback of exams on instructional practices (Al-Jamal & Ghadi, 2008; Al Jawabreh, 2009; Al Sheraiqi, 2010; Ghorbani, 2008; Haddadin, Dweik, & Sheir, 2008; Salehi & Yunus, 2012; Tayeb et al., 2014). For example, a study in Yemen (Tayeb et al., 2014) that investigated the washback effects of general secondary school exam (GSSE) on teaching and learning provided clear evidence of the negative effects of GSSE on both teaching and learning. Tayeb et al. (2014) noted that "[T]eachers are not concerned about the real classroom learning and whether their students have learned the language. They only think of how to help students pass the exam and therefore, there is no real language teaching and learning" (p. 91). Given the high-stakes nature of the tests, teachers reported widespread test-oriented teaching practices (i.e., teaching to the test), which resulted in narrowing the curriculum scope by focusing on skills targeted by the test. Tayeb et al. (2014) reported similar results in students' attitudes towards the test, with 93% of the Yemeni students indicating that their main priority was to pass the test. Comparable results were obtained in other countries, including Iran (Ghorbani, 2008), Egypt (Gebril, forthcoming; Gebril & Brown, 2014; Hargreaves, 2001), Indonesia (Maniruzzaman & Hoque, 2010), UAE (Al Sheraiqi, 2010), Bahrain (Janahi, 2013), and Jordan (Al-Jamal & Ghadi, 2008; Haddadin et al., 2008).

Research has also looked into the test methods used in classroom-based assessment in Muslim countries. Gebril (in press) asked groups of preservice and in-service teachers about their preference for types of assessment tasks. The majority of the teachers (76%, 59% respectively) selected *teacher-made tests* (mainly objective items in this context) as their first choice. Most of the alternative assessment types received a relatively low ranking: *oral questions* (34%, 35% respectively), *essay tests* (30%), *portfolio assessment* (1.5%, 4% respectively), and *unplanned observation* (4%, 8% respectively). The findings showed that both groups of teachers generally preferred traditional assessment tools. In Turkey, Vardar (2010) looked into the same issue with a group of sixth, seventh, and eighth grade teachers and found that teachers preferred traditional objective items over constructed-response question types. These results are not surprising given the long tradition in both countries related to the use of formal tests to assess learning outcomes. It is expected that the views expressed by these teachers conform to the formal policy imposed by the governments in these countries.

A considerable body of literature in Muslim countries has looked into how teachers conceive of assessment, mainly through using the Teachers' Conceptions of Assessment (TCoA) inventory (Gebril & Brown, 2014; Pishghadam, Adamson, Sadafian, & Kan, 2014; Pishghadam & Shayesteh, 2012; Vardar, 2010). For example, Gebril and Brown (2014) showed that teachers from the southern part of Egypt perceived assessment as a strong indicator of school quality and student learning (i.e., endorsing the accountability function of assessment). The surveyed teachers also perceived a strong relationship between school accountability and improvement, in which student accountability was a sub-factor under the improvement meta-factor, rather than an independent factor as found in Western jurisdictions. This finding indicated that "teachers believe a high quality school improves student learning and teaching which shows in high scores on examinations; judge us by our student exam results" (Gebril & Brown, 2014, p. 26). This study was consistent with Hargreaves's (1997, 2001) research in the Egyptian context that demonstrated how educational activities are dominated by the common use of examinations to make a wide range of decisions, including selection, certification, and hiring.

In other Muslim countries, the educational context of assessment is relatively similar to that in Egypt. For example, in Iran, summative assessment is dominant and plays a considerable role in instructional decisions (Pishghadam et al., 2014). In their study, Pishghadam and Shayesteh (2012) surveyed 103 teachers of English in Iran with the TCoA inventory. The teachers strongly endorsed the student accountability function of assessment. As in the Egyptian study, the researchers found a strong relationship between both student accountability and improvement. Additionally, many of the participating teachers in that study perceived assessment as bad and irrelevant. This result may be due to the negative consequences of tests, such as narrowing the curriculum scope and teaching to the test practices (Alderson & Hamp-Lyons, 1996; Crocker, 2005). It could also be due to the mounting pressures on teachers in this context from parents, students, and administrators to prepare students for exams (Gebril & Eid, forthcoming; Hargreaves, 2001).

In a related study, Khan (2011) investigated the conceptions of assessment with a sample of Pakistani secondary school teachers. The study showed that teachers had a high level of agreement on three conceptions of assessment: school accountability, improvement, and student accountability. In Turkey, Vardar (2010) found a strong positive correlation between improvement and both student and school accountability. Hence, it seems that across the Islamic societies studied so far, teachers associate assessment with examinations used for student accountability and that this use is strongly related to using assessment for improved outcomes.

It has been suggested earlier that teachers in Islamic societies do not have the required assessment literacy needed to effectively implement national and local policies. Alkharusi conducted a series of studies looking into teacher assessment literacy in Oman (Alkharusi, 2011a, 2011b; Alkharusi, Aldhafri, Alnabhani, & Alkalbani, 2012). For example, Alkharusi (2011a) found that, while the teachers self-reported high competency in assessment literacy, they demonstrated a low level of knowledge of appropriate assessment practices. Similar results were obtained with a sample of Iranian teachers (Kiomrs, Abdolmehdi, & Naser, 2011). Kimors et al. (2011) concluded that Iranian teachers tend to exhibit poor knowledge of assessment fundamentals, such as validity, reliability, score use, and interpretation. These findings are consistent with those in other parts of the world showing relatively little emphasis on assessment issues in teacher training (Stiggins, 2002; Taylor, 2009). For example, a recent report conducted by the U.S. National Council on Teacher Quality (NCTQ, 2012) showed that teacher education programs are not adequately preparing teachers to effectively use assessment data to make professionally sound decisions.

Generally, the assessment literacy literature worldwide suffers from a number of shortcomings. At the conceptual level, a consensus over what constitutes assessment literacy, for what purposes, and in which context is missing. What makes it more difficult is the lack of assessment literacy measures that could be used in different contexts. As Kahl, Hofman, and Bryant (2013) argue, the available measures "promote shallow knowledge and simplistic awareness of concepts, many of which have inherent complexities" and "overlook portions of the assessment literacy domain we think are essential" (p. 16). Given this evident shortcoming, Muslim countries might benefit from research attempts that focus on developing assessment literacy measures that are sensitive to teachers' needs and the uniqueness of local contexts.

IMPLICATIONS FOR VALID AND RELIABLE IMPLEMENTATION OF ASSESSMENT

The current educational scene in Muslim countries is changing, with the opening of more private schools and universities as well as the continuing expansion of public education. While the purpose of tests in the past was to help rationally distribute limited opportunities in universities and schools, the need for this rationalization is decreasing. Consequently, assessment policies should shift attention from mainly making selection or admission decisions to other areas of interest. A promising area in this respect is diagnostic assessment, which is principally envisioned as a developmental approach to student learning. Resources should be invested in making sure that assessment effectively informs learning and teaching. This process entails endorsing a formative assessment or assessment for learning paradigm (Black & Wiliam, 2005, 2010). While this paradigm has been strongly advocated, its implementation is not without challenges in many developing countries, such as Egypt (Gebril, forthcoming). These challenges include tensions between accountability-oriented traditions and practices and formative policies. Teachers may also lack assessment skills and beliefs needed to successfully implement such policies.

Implementing learning-oriented assessment practices requires a number of considerations to ensure its success. A first step is to assign a lower weight to end-of-year exams and consequently lower their stakes. In some grades, especially at lower levels of the system, formal exams could be avoided by focusing mainly on formative activities. This policy has proved to be successful in a number of countries including Finland and New Zealand (Brown & Harris, 2009; Brown, Irving, Peterson, & Hirschfeld, 2009; Gebril & Brown, 2014; Harris & Brown, 2009). A number of teacher-related variables should also be considered in this context. First, before introducing any policy change, training should be provided to teachers to help them meet the demanding nature of assessment for learning activities. Without acquiring such skills, teachers will not be able to successfully implement the new policy. The training should go beyond providing assessment knowledge by also targeting their belief systems. The literature has shown that teachers in Muslim countries strongly endorse the accountability function of assessment, with the improvement function receiving relatively weaker agreement. Without convincing teachers of the importance of learning-oriented assessment, any assessment reform will not achieve its goals. Another variable that should also be addressed in school contexts is teacher workload. Within a learning-oriented assessment paradigm, teachers are usually involved in a wide range of activities, including providing regular feedback to students, developing materials, and monitoring student progress. Such activities take time, and this must be given full consideration when assigning teacher workloads. A final issue has to do with the high teacher/student ratio in many Muslim countries. Since formative assessment requires one-on-one interaction between teachers and students, large classes can make this process difficult. Teachers need to come up with innovative strategies to overcome this hurdle, including the use of peer and self-assessment and perhaps the utilization of information technology as well. A good example of using technology would be automated online feedback in writing classes where students obtain immediate, diagnostic feedback. This online feedback might not be customized to the needs of each student, but is at least better than waiting for a long time for teacher feedback, which is not expected to be extensive in large classes.

Resources and funding for assessment is a factor that should be revisited in Muslim countries. Budgetary constraints could affect the quality of assessment outcomes and education in general. Many Muslim countries, such as Pakistan, Mauritania, and Bangladesh, allocate less than 2% of their gross national income to public education (The World Bank, 2008). In contrast, this percentage reaches to more than 5% in middle- and high-income countries (e.g., France, Denmark), not to mention the high GDP in rich countries, which will probably make assessment-related budgets more generous in these contexts. What adds to the problem, according to the World Bank data, is the greatest part of education budgets in these countries is allocated to non-technical expenses (e.g., school construction, teacher training, and provision of educational materials) rather than monitoring educational achievement. For this reason, it is hard to invest resources in areas related to developing technical expertise and capacity building.

Methodological rigor in national assessment is sometimes missing in many Muslim countries. While many of these countries have established national centers for developing and managing national assessment tools, the process of developing these exams is not transparent. Many of these centers do not provide enough information about the validation procedures of tests and their psychometric qualities. Qiyas in Saudi Arabia is an exception in terms of the test validation projects within the center. However, many of the validation documents are not usually shared with the public. Another concern in Muslim countries is the absence of a research arm for the national assessment centers. As is the case with many state assessment agencies, such as the Koran Institute for Curriculum and Evaluation (KICE), a research program that aims at conducting validation research should be established. Part of this validation work could be carried out by researchers who do not work at these centers, and this could be made possible through external grants awarded on a competitive basis.

With the increasing stakes of national tests used to make important decisions about one's future, teachers and students alike are sometimes involved in unhealthy, and sometimes unethical, test preparation practices (Crocker, 2005, 2006; Lai & Waltman, 2008). As argued by Crocker (2006), "[N]o activity in educational assessment raises more instructional, ethical and validity issues than test preparation for large-scale, high-stakes tests" (p. 115). Such practices have a number of negative effects on both teaching and learning. When teachers and students are involved in *teaching to the test* practices, this behavior harms the learning process. The focus in these contexts shifts from real learning to inflating test scores. As a result, long-term learning objectives are sacrificed for short-sighted, score-oriented goals. Another related issue has to do with score validity; inflated scores do not usually reflect actual ability. Inappropriate high-stakes decisions are made based on these inaccurate scores which could lead to a number of expensive consequences. This dilemma has apparently cut across national boundaries in Muslim countries and it should be urgently addressed (Gebril & Eid, forthcoming; Sukyadi & Mardiani, 2011; Tayeb et al., 2014). Measures taken to address this concern include minimizing the pressure on teachers and students by lowering test stakes, providing training for teachers on how to conduct appropriate test preparation sessions, and also improving communications with the parents and the public in general.

The concept of teacher assessment literacy needs to be investigated within local contexts. While there are many common competencies that cut across different countries and contexts, the local setting in which assessment is used should be the focus of future research efforts. As indicated earlier, there are a number of shortcomings in the current measures used to investigate teacher assessment literacy. Many of them tend

to focus on large-scale testing and do not pay enough attention to classroom assessment whereas others do the opposite. For example, Brookhart (2011) argues that most
of the assessment literacy standards, such as the *Standards for Teacher Competence in
Educational Assessment of Students* developed by the American Federation of Teachers (1990), focus on issues related to standardized testing rather on classroom-based
activities. Given the generic nature of many of these measures, they usually do not tap
into many of the assessment activities in local contexts. Another concern has to do
with the quantitative approaches to designing these measures, which essentially use
objective-response items. Future measures should follow a mixed methods paradigm that uses both qualitative and quantitative approaches. Examples of qualitative
approaches may include interviews, classroom observation, and analysis of assessment
documents. Such information could provide much richer data that may contribute to
better understanding of competences teachers have mastered and it could also help in
identifying their future training needs.

While memorization is not totally harmful, both teaching and assessment practices need to shift attention to higher order skills. Students and teachers alike need to
experiment with new tasks and skills. Examples of these skills include critical thinking,
argumentation, and reflection. Without such skills, we cannot produce citizens able to
succeed in a competitive international job market and able to navigate their journey
in a world full of extremist views. Integrating such skills in educational practices is not
an easy undertaking. Such change will not happen in one day and this process requires
much patience and experimentation since it is not easy to push policy makers, teachers,
parents, and students out of their comfort zones. Boyle (2006) shares some good news
with us by indicating that many school leaders in Muslim countries "seemed intent on
both memorizing the Qur'an while also working toward future advancement, public
school success, career achievement, and economic prosperity" (p. 495). If these intentions are genuine, educational leaders in Muslim countries should push for an agenda
that promotes higher order skills.

A final implication is actually directed to teacher educators and teacher education
programs. Teachers in Muslim countries work in a context where there is a great tension
between assessment and instruction. This issue is caused primarily by the accountability-
oriented school setting. Teachers are torn between both meeting accountability requirements and investing in learning activities. Anecdotal evidence from teachers in these countries shows that teacher education does not provide them with the tools necessary for taking
on the competing priorities. Teacher training programs are sometimes accused of providing
a rather idealistic image of a school context (Darling-Hammond, 2000). Without addressing these concerns and challenges, teachers in these countries, and worldwide, might lose
confidence in what we do in these programs. We have to listen to our customers, otherwise
teachers and policy makers will be looking for other providers.

CONCLUSION

Investigating assessment policies and practices in Islamic countries is a thorny undertaking given diverse linguistic, cultural, and ethnic backgrounds. Further, this issue
cannot be studied without addressing the historical, political, and social factors affecting educational policies and practices. Economic and nationalistic priorities have
always been the main driver behind most educational policy initiatives in Muslim
countries and have, consequently, affected assessment practices and values. Preserving/
re-creating national identity and rationalizing the distribution of limited opportunities in schools and universities have helped in promoting the gatekeeping function of

assessment in these countries. Most policies in Muslim countries have also promoted the accountability function of assessment. Within such a high-stakes assessment setting, unhealthy instructional activities thrive. Muslim countries need to address these challenges by developing learning-oriented assessment policies that foster real learning rather than test-oriented practices. Teachers should also be provided with the support needed to work within this context. Finally, there is a need for improving communication about assessment results and their meaning among different stakeholders to make sure that those stakeholders understand issues similarly.

ACKNOWLEDGMENT

The author would like to thank the editors of the current volume, Gavin Brown and Lois Harris, for their invaluable comments on multiple drafts of this chapter. Their comments were instrumental in improving the overall quality of the manuscript. My thanks are extended to Nourhan Sorour for her constructive feedback on an early draft of the chapter. My appreciation also goes to many colleagues who provided me with materials and data related to educational assessment in Muslim countries; this chapter would not have been possible without their help, collegiality, and generosity.

NOTE

1 The author is using English terminology for key religious terms throughout the document and the original Arabic term is consulted when possible for accuracy purposes.

REFERENCES

AlAlili, S. (2014). *Reforming English curriculum in United Arab Emirates: An examination of Emirate teachers' beliefs and practices regarding the adoption of "English Continuous Assessment Rich Task" (ECART)*. Doctoral dissertation. East Lansing, MI: Michigan State University.

Alderson, J. C., & Hamp-Lyons, L. (1996). TOEFL preparation courses: A study of washback. *Language Testing, 13*(3), 280.

Al-Jamal, D., & Ghadi, N. (2008). English language general secondary certificate examination washback in Jordan. *The Asian EFL Journal Quarterly, 10*(3), 158–186.

Al Jawabreh, H. (2009). *Cheating by students in English tests in private schools in the UAE: Cheating techniques and teacher/administrator responses.* MA thesis. Sharjah, United Arab Emirates: American University of Sharjah.

Al Sheraiqi, K. R. (2010). *Washback effect of the CEPA English test on teaching in an educational zone in the UAE.* MA thesis. Sharjah, United Arab Emirates: American University of Sharjah.

Alkharusi, H. (2011a). An analysis of the internal and external structure of the teacher assessment literacy questionnaire. *International Journal of Learning, 18*(1), 515–528.

Alkharusi, H. (2011b). Psychometric properties of the teacher assessment literacy questionnaire for preservice teachers in Oman. *Procedia-Social and Behavioral Sciences, 29*, 1614–1624.

Alkharusi, H., Aldhafri, S., Alnabhani, H., & Alkalbani, M. (2012). Educational assessment attitudes, competence, knowledge, and practices: An exploratory study of Muscat teachers in the Sultanate of Oman. *Journal of Education and Learning, 1*(2), 217–232.

Aly, S. E. (2015, May 25). Examinations system: The day when a person is either dignified or humiliated. *Al-Ahram Newspaper.* Retrieved from http://www.ahram.org.eg/News/111551/4/NewsPrint/398181.aspx

American Educational Research Association, American Psychological Association, & National Council on Measurement in Education. (2014). *Standards for educational and psychological testing.* Washington, DC: American Educational Research Association.

American Federation of Teachers (AFT), National Council on Measurement in Education (NCME), & National Education Association (NEA). (1990). Standards for teacher competence in educational assessment of students. *Educational Measurement: Issues and Practice, 9*(4), 30–32.

Anderson, L. W., & Krathwohl, D. R. (2001). *A Taxonomy for learning, teaching, and assessing: A revision of bloom's taxonomy of educational objectives.* New York: Longman.

Averett, S. L., & McLennan, M. C. (2004). Exploring the effect of class size on student achievement: What have we learned over the past two decades? In Geraint Johnes & Jill Johnes (Eds.), *International handbook on the economics of education* (pp. 329–367).Cheltenham, UK: Edward Elgar Publishing Ltd.

Black, P., & Wiliam, D. (2005). Lessons from around the world: How policies, politics and cultures constrain and afford assessment practices. *Curriculum Journal, 16*(2), 249–261.

Black, P., & Wiliam, D. (2010). Inside the black box: Raising standards through classroom assessment. *Phi Delta Kappan, 92*(1), 81–90.

Boyle, H. N. (2006). Memorization and learning in Islamic schools. *Comparative Education Review, 50*(3), 478–495.

Brookhart, S. M. (2011). Educational assessment knowledge and skills for teachers. *Educational Measurement: Issues and Practice, 30*(1), 3–12.

Brown, G.T.L., & Harris, L. R. (2009). Unintended consequences of using tests to improve learning: How improvement-oriented resources engender heightened conceptions of assessment as school accountability. *Journal of Multi-Disciplinary Evaluation, 6*(12), 68–91.

Brown, G.T.L., Irving, S. E., Peterson, E. R., & Hirschfeld, G.H.F. (2009). Use of informal-interactive assessment practices: New Zealand secondary students' conceptions of assessment. *Learning and Instruction, 19*(2), 97–111.

Chossudovsky, M. (2007). *The "Demonization" of Muslims and the battle for oil.* Retrieved from http://www.globalresearch.ca/the-demonization-of-muslims-and-the-battle-for-oil/4347.

Clarke, M. (2011). *Framework for building an effective student assessment system.* London: The World Bank.

Crocker, L. (2005). Teaching for the test: How and why test preparation is appropriate. In R. Phelps (Ed.), *Defending standardized testing* (pp. 159–174). Mahwah, NJ: Lawrence Erlbaum.

Crocker, L. (2006). Preparing examinees for test taking: Guidelines for test developers and test users. In S. Downing & T. Haladyna (Eds.), *Handbook of test development* (pp. 115–128). Mahwah, NJ: Lawrence Erlbaum.

Darling-Hammond, L. (2000). How teacher education matters. *Journal of Teacher Education, 51*(3), 166–173.

Darling-Hammond, L., & Wentworth, L. (2010). *Benchmarking learning systems: Student performance assessment in international context.* Retrieved from http://ncee.org/wp-content/uploads/2010/11/BenchmarkingLearn ingSystemHAMMOND.pdf

Dore, R. (1976). *The diploma disease: Education, qualification and development.* London: Allen & Unwin.

Dore, R. (1997). Reflections on the diploma disease twenty years later. *Assessment in Education, 4*(1), 189–206.

Gebril, A. (forthcoming). Arabic language teachers' conceptions of assessment. In A. Benmamoun & R. Bassiouney (Eds.), *The Routledge handbook of Arabic linguistics.* New York: Routledge.

Gebril, A. (in press). Language teachers' conceptions of assessment: An Egyptian perspective. *Teacher Development.*

Gebril, A., & Brown, G. T. (2014). The effect of high-stakes examination systems on teacher beliefs: Egyptian teachers' conceptions of assessment. *Assessment in Education: Principles, Policy & Practice, 21*(1), 16–33.

Gebril, A., & Eid, M. (forthcoming). Test preparation beliefs and practices: a teacher's perspective. *Language Assessment Quarterly.*

Gebril, A., & Hozayin, R. (2014). Assessing English in the Middle East and North Africa. In A. Kunnan (Ed.), *The companion to language assessment.* Malden, MA: Wiley-Blackwell. doi: 10.1002/9781118411360.wbcla077

Gebril, A., & Taha-Thomure, H. (2014). Assessing Arabic. In A. Kunnan (Ed.), *The companion to language assessment.* Malden, MA: Wiley-Blackwell. doi: 10.1002/9781118411360.wbcla065

Gesink, I. F. (2006). Islamic reformation: A history of Madrasa reform and legal change in Egypt. *Comparative Education Review, 50*(3), 325–345.

Gesink, I. F. (2014). *Islamic reform and conservatism: Al-Azhar and the evolution of modern Sunni Islam.* London: I. B. Tauris.

Ghorbani, M. R. (2008). *Washback effect of the university entrance examination on Iranian pre-university English language teachers' curriculum planning and instruction.* PhD dissertation. Selangor, Malaysia: Universiti Putra Malaysia.

Grisay, A., & Mahlck, L. (1991). *The quality of education in developing countries: A review of some research studies and policy documents.* Paris: UNESCO.

Haddadin, A., Dweik, B., & Sheir, A. (2008). Teachers' and students' perceptions of the effect of public examinations on English instruction at the secondary stage in Jordan. *Jordanian Journal of Applied Sciences, 11*(2), 331–344.

Hargreaves, E. (1997). The diploma disease in Egypt: Learning, teaching and the monster of the secondary leaving certificate. *Assessment in Education: Principles, Policy & Practice, 4*, 161–176.

Hargreaves, E. (2001). Assessment in Egypt. *Assessment in Education: Principles, Policy & Practice, 8*(2), 247–260.

Harris, L. R., & Brown, G. T. (2009). The complexity of teachers' conceptions of assessment: Tensions between the needs of schools and students. *Assessment in Education: Principles, Policy & Practice, 16*(3), 365–381.

Hefner, R. W. (2014). Modern Muslims and the challenge of plurality. *Society, 51*(2), 131–139.

Jackson, L. (2014). *Muslims and Islam in US education: Reconsidering multiculturalism.* New York: Routledge.

Janahi, S. (2013). *Bahraini university students' conception of assessment within different educational cultures.* MA thesis. Auckland, NZ: The University of Auckland.

Jenkins, P. (2015). The world's fastest growing religion: Comparing Christian and Muslim expansion in the modern era. In S. Brunn (Ed.), *The changing world religion map* (pp. 1767–1779). New York: Springer.

Kadi, W. (2006). Education in Islam—Myths and truths. *Comparative Education Review, 50*(3), 311–324.

Kahl, S. R., Hofman, P., & Bryant, S. (2013). *Assessment literacy standards and performance measures for teacher candidates and practicing teachers.* Retrieved from https://www.measuredprogress.org/caep-paper

Kamens, D. H., & Benavot, A. (2011). National, regional and international learning assessments: Trends among developing countries, 1960–2009. *Globalisation, Societies and Education, 9*(2), 285–300.

Khan, A. A. (2011). *Secondary school mathematics teachers conceptions regarding assessment.* MA thesis. Karachi, Pakistan: The Aga Khan University.

Khan, L. A., & Ramadan, H. M. (2011). *Contemporary ijtihad: Limits and controversies.* Edinburgh: Edinburgh University Press.

Kiomrs, R., Abdolmehdi, R., & Naser, R. (2011). On the interaction of test washback and teacher assessment literacy: The case of Iranian EFL secondary school teachers. *English Language Teaching, 4*(1), 156–161.

Lai, E. R., & Waltman, K. (2008). Test preparation: Examining teacher perceptions and practices. *Educational Measurement: Issues and Practice, 27*(2), 28–45.

Maniruzzaman, M., & Hoque, M. E. (2010). How does washback work on the EFL syllabus and curriculum? A case study at the HSC level in Bangladesh. *Language in India, 10*(12), 49–88.

Mansfield, P. (1971). *The British in Egypt.* London: Cox & Wyman.

Martin, M. O., Mullis, I. V., Foy, P., & Stanco, G. M. (2012). *TIMSS 2011 international results in science.* Boston: TIMSS & PIRLS International Study Center.

McLoughlin, S. (2007). Islam (s) in context: Orientalism and the anthropology of Muslim societies and cultures. *Journal of Beliefs & Values, 28*(3), 273–296.

Morgan, M. H. (2007). *Lost history: The enduring legacy of Muslim scientists, thinkers, and artists.* Washington, DC: National Geographic Books.

Morsy, M. S. and Aly, S. E. (1980). *History of education and instruction in Egypt.* Cairo: Alam Alkotob. (in Arabic)

Mullis, I. V., Martin, M. O., Foy, P., & Arora, A. (2012). *TIMSS 2011 international result in mathematics.* Boston: TIMSS & PIRLS International Study Center.

National Council on Teacher Quality. (2012). *What teacher preparation programs teach about assessment.* Washington, DC: Author.

Organization for Islamic Countries. (2012). *Education and scientific development in the OIC member countries.* Ankara: Statistical, Economic and Social Research and Training Centre for Islamic Countries (SESRIC)

Pew Research Center. (2015). *The future of world religions: Population growth projections, 2010–2050.* Retrieved from http://www.pewforum.org/files/2015/03/PF_15.04.02_ProjectionsFullReport.pdf

Pishghadam, R., Adamson, B., Sadafian, S. S., & Kan, F. L. (2014). Conceptions of assessment and teacher burn-out. *Assessment in Education: Principles, Policy & Practice, 21*(1), 34–51.

Pishghadam, R., & Shayesteh, S. (2012). Conceptions of assessment among Iranian EFL teachers. *Iranian EFL Journal, 8*(3), 9–23.

Ramadan, M. (1993). *History of reform in Al-Azhar in the modern era from 1872–1961.* Cairo: Dar Al-Wafa'. (In Arabic).

Salehi, H., & Yunus, M. M. (2012). The wash-back effect of the Iranian universities entrance exam: Teachers' insights. *GEMA Online Journal of Language Studies, 12*(2), 609–628.

Scientist. (2015). *15 Famous Muslim (Arab & Persian) scientists and their inventions. Famous scientists: The art of genius.* Retrieved August 26, 2015 from http://www.famousscientists.org/famous-muslim-arab-persian-scientists-and-their-inventions

Stiggins, R. J. (2002). Assessment crisis: The absence of assessment for learning. *Phi Delta Kappan, 83*(10), 758–765.

Sukyadi, D., & Mardiani, R. (2011). The washback effect of the English national examination (ENE) on English teachers' classroom teaching and students' learning. *K@Ta, 13*(1), 96–111.

Tayeb, Y. A., Aziz, M.S.A., Ismail, K., & Khan, A.B.M.A. (2014). The washback effect of the General Secondary English Examination (GSEE) on teaching and learning. *GEMA Online Journal of Language Studies, 14*(3), 83–103.

Taylor, L. (2009). Developing assessment literacy. *Annual Review of Applied Linguistics, 29*(1), 21–36.

Thobani, S. (2011). *Islam in the school curriculum: Symbolic pedagogy and cultural claims.* New York: Bloomsbury Academic.

Vardar, E. (2010). *Sixth, seventh, and eights grade teachers' conception of assessment.* MA thesis. Ankara, Turkey: Middle East Technical University.

The World Bank. (2008). *The road not traveled: Education reform in the Middle East and North Africa.* Washington, DC: Author.

25

ASSESSMENT IN EDUCATION IN MULTICULTURAL POPULATIONS

Fons J. R. van de Vijver

SETTING THE STAGE

Student populations are becoming increasingly multicultural. However, many educational systems were originally set up for monocultural populations in which the medium of instruction was the mother tongue for students. Catering for a multicultural population can require adjustments at various levels, ranging from changes in curriculum to staff composition. In this chapter, I focus on assessment issues in education concerning multicultural student populations. The central argument of the chapter is that if we want to achieve evidence-based assessment, we should reconceptualize the problem and adapt our procedures in multicultural assessment. An adequate assessment of students in multicultural populations often requires a culture-informed, multidisciplinary approach, whereas there is an emphasis on monodisciplinary approaches in much psychological and educational assessment. We need to go beyond a piecemeal approach and try to integrate our efforts, combining insights and evidence about multicultural assessment from education, psychology, linguistics, and ethnography.

The first section presents an overview of problems in multicultural assessment from different perspectives (test design, validity, and use of test scores). In the second section, I review the concepts of bias and equivalence as an integrative framework to issues in multicultural assessment. The third section deals with an often neglected topic in multicultural assessment: acculturation. I give an overview of theoretical models of acculturation, studies of school adjustment, and ways of accounting for acculturation in assessment. The fourth section describes ways toward best practices. The last section is devoted to conclusions and recommendations.

WHAT IS THE PROBLEM IN MULTICULTURAL ASSESSMENT?

Some 25 years ago, we conducted a study involving the assessment of intelligence of both immigrant and mainstream Dutch primary school children (Van de Vijver, Willemse, & Van de Rijt, 1993). One of the vocabulary items asked: "What is bacon?" The item showed a mean score difference that was larger than the difference found for the other items in the subtest. We attributed the difference to the cultural background of the pupils. Most immigrant children had a Muslim background. As a consequence, there is less pork meat in their homes than in the homes of mainstream Dutch children, which is presumably the context where most children learn the word. Despite its simplicity, this example illustrates an important aspect of multicultural assessment: in order to assess and understand the nature of problems in multicultural assessment, a multidisciplinary approach is needed. A psychometric perspective is needed to appreciate that the performance difference on this item is larger than on the other items, whereas a cultural and ethnographic perspective is needed to appreciate the background of the cross-cultural performance difference.

Three related perspectives on problems in multicultural assessment in education are described here. The first is the issue of the *tacit culture in assessment procedures*. Psychological and educational tests contain both explicit and implicit references to culture. The most obvious explicit references involve the language being used. However, there are also implicit references, as exemplified in the item about bacon. In the past, many attempts have been made to remove cultural elements as much as possible from psychological assessment. The idea was that by a careful selection of stimuli, it would be possible to create a level playing field for pupils from many different cultural groups, an approach championed by Raymond Cattell (1940). He argued that by choosing abstract geometric stimuli and other materials that were very common across cultures, it would be possible to compile so-called culture-free tests. This assumption was later relaxed by arguing that such geometric stimuli are equally familiar to individuals from many different cultural groups, thereby making tests culture-fair (e.g., Cattell & Cattell, 1963). Requirements for culture-fairness amounted to equal exposure to (or opportunity to learn) relevant skills and knowledge, and equal familiarity with item format. The condition was assumed to be supported by observing equal test score distributions. In a later stage, Jensen (1980) referred to 'culture-reduced tests' to indicate that it is possible to design tests that are minimally influenced by cultural factors. Performance differences on these tests reflect genuine cross-cultural differences.

In my reading, there are two important lessons to be learned from this influential tradition in assessment. First, it is difficult to see, in retrospect, why the idea that cultural factors would not (or would not differentially) affect test performance remained so popular. In the course of assessment history, it has become increasingly clear that cultural and linguistic factors are closely related to test performance (Frijda & Jahoda, 1966). Most psychological and educational tests have been developed in a Western context; the use of such tests in multicultural or non-Western populations can be problematic. Exporting cognitive tests to a non-Western context can imply a cultural imposition, or in the words of Wober (1969): "How well can they do our tricks?" (p. 488). Nonetheless, tests that are not differentially affected by cultural characteristics are the Holy Grail of cross-cultural cognitive assessment. Second, even if attempts to develop instruments that are not differentially affected by cultural factors are futile, work by Cattell and Jensen has helped to increase awareness of the essential role of cultural factors in multicultural assessment. Their work has been instrumental in developing standards for the adequacy of tests to be used in cross-cultural studies. Statistical procedures that have been developed in the last decades have helped clarify that some instruments are more suitable for cross-cultural comparisons than other instruments. Clearly, notions like culture-free, -fair, and -reduced have been instrumental in putting instrument quality on the agenda in cross-cultural assessment.

A second perspective on multicultural assessment comes from work on *internal validity* (Shadish, Cook, & Campbell, 2002). Work in this tradition, further discussed in the next section, deals with the question of whether constructs gauged by a test and, if applicable, test scores carry the same meaning across different cultural groups (Poortinga, 1989). This assumption can usually be readily made in applications of instruments within homogeneous groups. An educational achievement test that is administered at the end of a curriculum unit to a group of pupils with a homogeneous cultural and linguistic background will most likely have the same psychological meaning for all pupils. However, the assumption cannot be taken for granted when applied with multicultural groups. For example, if there are substantial differences in the level of mastery of the testing language among the pupils, test performance can be moderated by this mastery. As a consequence, individual differences may reflect both differences in educational achievement and language proficiency. As documented below, the extensive work on internal validity has led to a wide variety of statistical procedures aimed at establishing similarity of constructs and scores.

A third perspective on multicultural assessment refers to *external validity*, also labeled predictive bias. This is a field that is no longer as vibrant as the other fields. The issue of predictive bias plays an important role in the assessment procedures in education that are used to formulate a recommendation for further curricula or courses. Examples can be found in nationwide assessment procedures employed in many countries at the end of primary school. Such tests show predictive bias if persons from different ethnic groups with the same score on the educational achievement instrument do not show the same performance in their further curricula or courses (e.g., children from different groups who have the same score on an instrument used for school selection but do not show the same educational achievement after being admitted to the same school). In such a case, the educational instrument would discriminate against the group whose performance is underpredicted. The topic of predictive bias has been extensively studied within the context of industrial–organizational psychology in the U.S.; in the literature, the topic has become known as validity generalization (e.g., Schmidt & Hunter, 1998). Based on an impressive amount of empirical data, integrated in meta-analyses, these authors provide ample evidence that regression lines for different ethnic groups in the U.S. are not substantially different. A regression line links the test performance to the school performance. If the line is identical for two ethnic groups, this means that the test works equally well for both groups and that applicants with the same test scores are expected to perform equally well later in the job. Therefore, the authors concluded that there is no predictive bias if well-established and validated instruments are used to assess applicants.

More recently, this line of evidence has been challenged (Van de Vijver & Poortinga, 2015). Recent work has found that there may have been methodological artifacts in studies of predictive bias. More specifically, many of these studies may suffer from power problems and may not have been well suited to identify differences in regression lines between the groups (Aguinis, Culpepper, & Pierce, 2010). These authors concluded that Monte Carlo simulations revealed that both slopes and intercepts could be affected. In addition, doubts have been expressed whether criterion scores are always unbiased, especially criterion scores assigned by supervisors. Also, doubts have been expressed whether in societies that are segregated along ethnic lines and in which discrimination is common, it is realistic to take identity of regression lines as prerequisite for comparability. Bias may be more subtle than that picked up by differences in regression lines. For example, identity of regression lines in developing and emerging countries, which show huge variations in educational quality, is difficult to defend as talent and skill is confounded with quality of educational background.

BIAS AND EQUIVALENCE

The Concepts of Bias and Equivalence

Bias and equivalence are key terms in the methodology of cross-cultural studies and both have been defined in multiple ways in the literature (Johnson, 1998). Rather than integrating these various definitions, I choose definitions here that have the advantage of enabling an integrative framework.

Bias

Bias refers to differences in what an instrument measures in different cultural groups or to differences in what scores mean across cultural groups (Poortinga, 1989). Scores obtained in different cultures show bias if differences in measurement outcomes are not reflective of the construct targeted by the instrument but are due to other differences. For example, it has been found in mathematics achievement tests in the Netherlands that performance differences between immigrants and mainstreamers are larger when items call more on linguistic abilities. So, it could be expected that an item "$3 \times 8 =$" would show less bias than the item asking the same in a more indirect way using more words (e.g., "Three children have eight toys each. How many toys do the children have together?").

Bias, thus, refers to the presence of nuisance factors (Poortinga, 1989; Van de Vijver & Leung, 1997) or construct-irrelevance variance (Messick, 1989). If scores are biased, their psychological meaning is culture/group dependent and group differences in assessment outcomes need to be accounted for, partly or wholly, by auxiliary psychological constructs or measurement artifacts. Bias is not an inherent characteristic of an instrument, but arises in the application of an instrument in at least two cultural groups. As a consequence, an instrument is not inherently biased, but may become so when scores from specific cultural groups are compared.

Construct Bias

This kind of bias leads to construct non-equivalence. Construct bias can be caused by incomplete overlap of construct-relevant behaviors. An empirical example can be found in Ho's (1996) work on filial piety (defined as a psychological characteristic associated with being a good son or daughter). The Chinese conception, which includes the expectation that children should assume the role of caretaker of elderly parents, is broader than the corresponding Western notion. An inventory of filial piety based on the Chinese conceptualization covers aspects unrelated to the Western notion, whereas a Western-based inventory will leave important Chinese aspects uncovered (Hofstede, 2007).

Construct bias can be caused by differential appropriateness of the behaviors associated with the construct in the different cultures. Studies in various non-Western countries (Azuma & Kashiwagi, 1987; Grigorenko et al., 2001) show that descriptions of an intelligent person go beyond the school-oriented domain and involve social aspects such as obedience; however, the domain covered by Western intelligence tests is usually restricted to school-related intelligence. Another example comes from the discussion of Asian learners in which there is a popular conception that they emphasize rote learning and engage less in deep learning. If this would be the case, the concept of a 'learner' would be context dependent and measures of learning could then easily be misguided.

However, Watkins, Reghi, and Astilla (1991) compared Filipino, Nepalese, Australian, and Hong Kong students, finding similar types of learning across the groups, thereby invalidating the presumed construct bias in their measure of learning. Interestingly, Peterson, Brown, and Hamilton (2013) did not find invariance in a measure of duty for learning that was administered to Asian and Caucasian students in New Zealand.

Method Bias

Method bias is used here as a label for all sources of bias due to factors often described in the method section of empirical papers. Three types of method bias are distinguished here, depending on whether the bias comes from the sample, administration, or instrument. First, sample bias is more likely to jeopardize cross-cultural comparisons when the cultures examined differ in many respects. A large cultural distance often increases the number of alternative explanations that need to be considered. Fernández and Marcopulos (2008) describe how incomparability of norm samples made international comparisons of the Trail Making Test (an instrument to assess attention and cognitive flexibility) impossible. In the personality and social domain, recurrent rival explanations include cross-cultural differences in social desirability and stimulus familiarity (i.e., testwiseness). The main problem with both social desirability and testwiseness is their relationship with country characteristics, in particular affluence; more affluent countries tend to show lower scores on social desirability (Van Hemert, Van de Vijver, Poortinga, & Georgas, 2002). Second, administration method bias can be caused by differences in the procedures or mode used to administer an instrument. For example, when interviews are held in respondents' homes, physical conditions (e.g., ambient noise, presence of others) are difficult to control. Respondents are more prepared to answer sensitive questions in a self-completion mode than in a face-to-face interview (e.g., Van Der Heijden, Bouts, & Hox, 2000). A final source of administration bias is constituted by communication problems between the respondent and the tester/interviewer. For example, interventions by interpreters may influence the measurement outcome. Communication problems are not restricted to working with translators. Language problems are particularly salient when an interview or test is administered in the second or third language of interviewers or respondents or when working in diglossic countries where the official national language ('the high-status variant') is the medium of instruction, but the main language in everyday life is a local dialect ('the low-status variant').

Third, instrument bias is a common source of bias in cognitive tests. An example can be found in Piswanger's (1975) application of the Viennese Matrices Test (Formann & Piswanger 1979). A Raven-like figural inductive reasoning test was administered to high school students in Austria, Nigeria, and Togo (educated in Arabic). The most striking findings were the cross-cultural differences in item difficulties related to identifying and applying rules in a horizontal direction (i.e., left to right). This was interpreted as bias in terms of the different directions in writing Latin-based languages as opposed to Arabic.

Item Bias

This type of bias refers to anomalies at the item level and is called *item bias* or *differential item functioning* (Camilli & Shepard, 1994). According to a definition that is widely used, an item is biased if pupils with the same construct propensity (e.g., they are equally intelligent) do not have the same mean score on the item because of different cultural origins. Item bias has been extensively studied; various psychometric techniques are available to identify item bias (Zumbo, 1999). Item bias can arise in various ways; an important source in multicultural assessment can be differential familiarity/appropriateness of the item content across cultural groups. Suppose that a general knowledge test (crystallized intelligence) is administered in the U.S. and the Netherlands and that one of the items asks the name of the Dutch prime minister. Dutch pupils can be expected to show higher scores on the item than U.S. students. However, what makes the item biased is that this even holds for pupils from the two countries with the same level of general knowledge.

Equivalence

Equivalence refers to comparability of measurement outcomes. For example, do diagnostic categories have the same meaning across cultures? Do persons from different cultures with the same diagnosis of ADHD show the same symptoms? Do cross-cultural differences in working memory scores have the same meaning across cultural groups? Bias and equivalence are closely related. Full equivalence assumes the absence of any bias. The seamless transition of scores across cultures (the full comparability of concepts or scores across cultural groups) presupposes the absence of bias.

Taxonomies of equivalence in psychological tests often use hierarchical levels of equivalence (e.g., Poortinga, 1989). This tradition is followed here; four hierarchically nested types of equivalence are described below: construct, structural or functional, metric or measurement unit, and scalar or full score equivalence.

Construct Non-equivalence

Constructs that are non-equivalent lack a shared meaning, which precludes any cross-cultural comparison. In the literature, claims of construct non-equivalence can be grouped into three broad types, which differ in the degree of non-equivalence (partial or total).

The first and strongest claim of non-equivalence is found in studies that opt for a completely emic, relativistic viewpoint, which argues that psychological constructs are inextricably tied up to their natural context and cannot be studied outside this context. Any cross-cultural comparison is, then, erroneous as psychological constructs are cross-culturally non-equivalent.

The second type is exemplified by psychological constructs that are associated with specific cultural groups. Good examples are culture-bound syndromes. A good example is Amok, which occurs among males in Asian countries, such as Indonesia and Malaysia. It is characterized by a brief period of violent, aggressive behavior. The period is often preceded by an insult and the patient shows persecutory ideas and automatic behaviors. After the period, the patient is usually exhausted and has no recollection of the event (Azhar & Varma, 2000). The combination of triggering events, symptoms, and lack of recollection is culture-specific. Such a combination of universal and culture-specific aspects is characteristic for all culture-bound syndromes. Another example is the Japanese Taijin Kyofusho (Suzuki, Takei, Kawai, Minabe, & Mori, 2003; Tanaka-Matsumi & Draguns, 1997), which is characterized by an intense fear that one's body is discomforting or insulting to others by its appearance, smell, or movements. The description of the symptoms suggests a strong form of a social phobia (a universal), which finds culturally unique expressions in a country in which conformity is a widely shared norm. Suzuki et al. (2003) argue that most symptoms of Taijin Kyofusho can be readily classified as social phobia, which (again) illustrates that culture-bound syndromes involve both universal and culture-specific aspects that do not co-occur in other cultures.

The third type of non-equivalence is empirically based and found in comparative studies in which the data do not show any evidence for comparability of construct; non-equivalence is the consequence of statistical tests that indicate a lack of cross-cultural comparability. Van Leest (1997) administered a standard personality questionnaire to mainstream Dutch and Dutch immigrants. The instrument showed various problems, such as the frequent use of colloquialisms. The structure found in the Dutch mainstream group could not be replicated in the immigrant group. It was concluded, therefore, that the constructs measured in both groups by this instrument were non-equivalent.

Structural or Functional Equivalence

An instrument administered to different cultural groups shows structural equivalence if it measures the same construct(s) in all of them. In operational terms, this condition requires identity of underlying dimensions (factors) in all groups: the instrument should have the same factor structure in all groups. Structural equivalence has been examined for personality models (Barrett, Petrides, Eysenck, & Eysenck, 1998; McCrae & Allik, 2002; McCrae et al., 2005); similarly, numerous studies have shown that both the educational achievement and student background variables (such as motivation and self-esteem) in the Programme for International Student Assessment (PISA) often show similar factor loadings in all participating countries (Täht & Must, 2013). Functional equivalence, as a specific type of structural equivalence, refers to identity of nomological networks. A questionnaire that measures, say, openness to new cultures, shows functional equivalence if it measures the same psychological constructs in each culture, as manifested in a similar pattern of convergent and divergent validity (i.e., non-zero correlations with presumably related measures and zero correlations with presumably unrelated measures). Tests of structural equivalence are applied more often than tests of functional equivalence. The reason is not statistical-technical. With advances in statistical modeling (notably path analysis as part of structural equation modeling), tests of the cross-cultural similarity of nomological networks are straightforward. However, nomological networks are often based on a combination of psychological scales and background variables, such as socioeconomic status, education, and sex. In the absence of a guiding theoretical framework, the use of psychological scales to validate other psychological scales can easily lead to an endless regression in which each scale used for validation has itself to be validated.

Metric or Measurement Unit Equivalence

Instruments show metric (or measurement unit) equivalence if their measurement scales have the same units of measurement, but a different origin (such as the Celsius and Kelvin scales in temperature measurement). This type of equivalence assumes interval- or ratio-level scores (with the same measurement units in each culture). Measurement unit equivalence applies when a source of bias shifts the scores of cultural groups differentially, but does not affect the relative scores of individuals within each cultural group. For example, social desirability and stimulus familiarity influence questionnaire scores more in some cultures than in others, but they may influence individuals within a given cultural group in a similar way. When the relative contribution of both bias sources cannot be estimated, the interpretation of group comparisons of mean scores remains ambiguous.

Scalar or Full Score Equivalence

Scalar equivalence assumes both an identical interval or ratio scale and an identical scale origin across cultural groups. Only in the case of scalar (or full score) equivalence can direct cross-cultural comparisons be made; this is the only type of equivalence that allows for the conclusion that average scores obtained in two cultures are different or equal. Large-scale educational studies, such as PISA and TALIS, typically do not find evidence for scalar equivalence, which is tested using confirmatory factor analysis, and metric equivalence is the highest level of invariance obtained.

ACCULTURATION

There are various reasons why we should bother to assess acculturation in multicultural school populations (Van de Vijver & Phalet, 2004). The first reason is that problems in the school career of students may be related to acculturation issues. This is particularly true for students from immigrant groups that are disadvantaged in school settings. Insight in the acculturation status of a pupil can help to understand, among other things, how the pupil combines or does not combine heritage and mainstream culture and how much acculturative stress the pupil experiences. Clearly, the way in which a pupil handles the acculturation process can have a bearing on what happens with him or her in school, including assessment processes.

Before presenting the theoretical model, a caveat is needed. The model below was not developed to include marginalized Indigenous groups such as Aboriginals in Australia, Māori in New Zealand (Keegan, Brown, & Hattie, 2013), and Roma in various European countries, even if some aspects of the model may be applicable to these groups. Acculturation models in such extreme conditions have their own dynamics. For example, we found that discrimination and segregation needed to be factored in heavily to understand acculturation and identity processes among Roma living in Bulgaria as well as the role of education in these communities (Dimitrova, Chasiotis, Bender, & Van de Vijver, 2013).

Theoretical Model

Acculturation is defined as "the process of cultural change that occurs when individuals from different cultural backgrounds come into prolonged, continuous, first-hand contact with each other" (Redfield, Linton, & Herskovits, 1936, p. 146). The acculturation process can be taken to comprise three components: antecedent factors (acculturation conditions), mediators (acculturation orientations), and consequences (acculturation outcomes) (see Figure 25.1; Celenk & Van de Vijver, 2011).

Acculturation conditions are individual- and group-level factors, such as the characteristics of the receiving society (e.g., perceived or objective discrimination), characteristics of the society of origin (e.g., political context), characteristics of the immigrant group (e.g., ethnic vitality), and personal characteristics (e.g., expectations, norms, and personality). These conditions define the context in which the process of acculturation takes place. Important factors within the school context are the multicultural climate in the school, discrimination, and heterogeneity of the cultural and linguistic make-up of the school population.

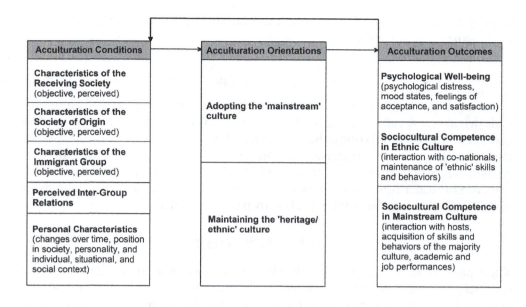

Figure 25.1 Framework of Acculturation (Celenk & Van de Vijver, 2011)

The second dimension of the process, acculturation orientations (also referred to in the literature as acculturation strategies, styles, and attitudes), involves the way pupils prefer to relate to the society of settlement (cultural adoption) and country of origin of the ancestors (cultural maintenance). Acculturation orientations are often taken to be the core of the acculturation process. It is the component of acculturation that has been most frequently studied. Many countries have multiculturalism policies that imply a certain preference for how immigrants should deal with the two cultures (Huddleston, Niessen, Chaoimh, & White, 2011), usually ranging from more inclusive perspectives that leave room for multiple cultures in the classroom (e.g., Canada) to a more restrictive policy emphasizing the assimilation to the mainstream (e.g., the emphasis in France on language assimilation of immigrants).

Different models dealing with the relationship between adoption and maintenance have been proposed. These models mainly differ in their dimensionality. A unidimensional model describes cultural maintenance and adoption as bipolar opposites. An individual can either maintain the culture of origin or adapt to the culture of settlement. A major critique of the unidimensional model was leveled at the main assumption that the acculturation process varies along a single continuum from identification with the country of origin to the country of settlement (Berry, 1997). Unlike unidimensional models, bidimensional models treat cultural maintenance and adoption as two distinct dimensions which are conceptually, though not necessarily empirically, unrelated. Our work on preferences of immigrants in the Netherlands clearly suggests that most pupils prefer to maintain their ethnic ties as well as to adopt the mainstream culture (Van de Vijver, Helms-Lorenz, & Feltzer, 1999). In the literature this is called integration (Berry, 1997), which is not to be confused with the everyday concept of integration that often refers to adjustment to the new context (e.g., an integrated immigrant is then a fully adjusted immigrant; whereas, in cross-cultural psychology an integrated immigrant has both an immigrant and a majority group identity). The common preference for strong ties with both cultures indicates the deficit of acculturation models that treat the dimensions of maintenance and adoption as mutually exclusive.

The final component of the acculturation process refers to acculturation outcomes. A distinction has been made between psychological outcomes (i.e., mental, internal adjustment) and behavioral adaptation (i.e., social, external adjustment) (Ward, Leong, & Low, 2004). Internal adjustment refers to the question of how well the immigrant feels in the new cultural context; it refers to emotional and affective acculturation outcomes. It is usually assessed by measures of well-being, mental health, and satisfaction with life. The second acculturation outcome, external adjustment, refers to the question of how well the immigrant does in the new cultural context; it comprises culturally appropriate knowledge and skills, which result in success in interacting with the mainstream culture and in dealing with stressors.

Celenk and van de Vijver (2011) argued that in addition to social adjustment to the mainstream culture, sociocultural competence in ethnic culture needs to be addressed as it is an essential outcome of acculturation. Maintenance in the sociocultural domain (e.g., ethnic language proficiency and cultural maintenance) is less frequently studied than sociocultural adjustment (e.g., friendships with members of the mainstream culture and mainstream language proficiency). Notably within the school context, sociocultural adjustment usually refers to the mainstream dimension and is measured by school performance and measures of friendship and support networks in the mainstream group.

Another reason to measure acculturation is its pervasive influence on behavior. Acculturative changes have been documented in various psychological domains, including psychological health and well-being (Phinney, Horenczyk, Liebkind, & Vedder, 2001), value orientations (Marín & Gamba, 2003), and competence and skills (Sue, 2006). Notably if a pupil has not yet been exposed to schooling for a long time in the new cultural context and does not speak the language of testing very well, information about the acculturation status of the pupil could help to determine whether a test administration with this specific pupil is meaningful (Cummins, 1979, 1989).

It can be concluded that assessment of acculturation is important because acculturation can moderate test performance. Prior to an assessment procedure, we need to establish whether a pupil has sufficient knowledge of the language and culture that will be used in the tests. The need to establish the 'testability' of a pupil also involves the applicability of test norms. If an instrument is used for assessment in multicultural populations, norms developed for the mainstream group may not be adequate for other groups. Applicability of the norms will depend on the level of adjustment of the immigrant group to the mainstream society. Such norms can only be applied in groups that can be taken to belong (psychologically and linguistically) to the mainstream group.

Accounting for Acculturation

The most common, yet inadequate, and rarely discussed approach to deal with acculturation in assessment is to simply ignore the influence of acculturation. Various more adequate ways can be envisaged (Van de Vijver & Phalet, 2004). The first approach uses *cut-off scores* on an acculturation instrument to assess the testability of a pupil on other educational and psychological instruments. Values below (or above) a critical threshold indicate that the scores on the target instrument cannot be interpreted in the standard way. This follows a practice that is often employed in personality assessment, such as the Lie Scale (measuring social desirability) of the Eysenck Personality Questionnaire (Eysenck & Eysenck, 1975). This measure gives a score above which outcomes on the other questionnaire scales (extraversion, neuroticism, and psychoticism) are no longer interpreted because of their presumed distortion by social desirability. Analogously, it is easy to imagine an approach in which an acculturation questionnaire is administered that focuses on knowledge of the language and culture in a target test, such as an intelligence test. Insufficient knowledge of the language or culture of the intelligence test (i.e., scores lower than a threshold value) is then taken as an indication that the intelligence test cannot be adequately administered or that test scores should be interpreted with caution, taking the limited applicability of the instrument into account.

The second approach uses acculturation scores as a *covariate or moderator*. The most elaborate approach was developed by Cuéllar (2000). Acculturation is measured by means of a questionnaire of cultural orientation ('soft' acculturation data are used here). The scores on the acculturation instrument are correlated with the scores on the target instrument. A regression approach is then used to correct the score on the target instrument for acculturation.

The third way uses biographical acculturation data, such as length of stay in the host country, to establish *differential norms*. Mercer (1979) designed a system for 'correcting' test scores of an immigrant child (such as scores on the WISC) based on information of the socioeconomic and ethnic background; the correction factor is based on norm data in which observed differences in mean scores of cultural groups are eliminated. Such a procedure typically leads to an upward correction of immigrant pupils' scores. Policies based on differential norms, positive discrimination, and other procedures that treat test scores of migrants and non-migrants in a differential manner are relatively straightforward from a psychometric perspective, but often meet with resistance in society.

A fourth way of dealing with multiculturalism is the application of some form of *standardization or centering* (i.e., taking the deviation scores from the individual or group mean). The main purpose is to eliminate group differences due to confounding variables, such as response styles. In practice, such reference data are often absent and it is difficult to decide whether or not to standardize data (Fischer, 2004). In case of doubt, it may be instructive to carry out data analyses both for raw and standardized data in order to evaluate the influence of the data transformation.

The fifth approach employs statistical procedures that do not require items to be identical across all groups involved in study, such as *item response theory*. If data meet the assumptions of item response theory both among migrants and hosts and show the same parameter values for a number of items in these groups (Thomas, 2011), comparisons on the latent-trait scale can then be carried out, which allows for a comparison of scores across cultural groups even when not all items have been identical.

The final approach is based on the so-called *person fit tradition* (Karabatsos, 2003). Conceptually, this approach is related to the use of acculturation instruments to assess testability (the first approach described here). Data obtained in a mainstream group serve as reference. Using sophisticated psychometric modeling, such as item response theory, it is possible to establish the likelihood that the immigrant belongs to the reference group, given his or her response pattern. The procedure yields an outcome indicating whether or not the immigrant can be taken to belong to the reference group. Scores on the target instrument are interpreted only if the immigrant shows an adequate person fit.

TOWARDS BEST PRACTICES

Design Approaches

The most interesting developments in the area of design approaches can be found in the work on test adaptations (Hambleton, Merenda, & Spielberger, 2005). I present here a taxonomy of five types of adaptation (see also Malda et al., 2008). *Construct-driven adaptations* are related to differences in definitions of psychological concepts across cultures. For example, there are various non-Western studies of everyday conceptions of children's intelligence in which obedience and rule compliance are part of intelligence (Goodnow, 2002), which are not typically addressed in Western instruments. Adding instruments to assess these concepts would increase the ecological validity of an intelligence instrument. *Language-driven adaptations* result from the unavailability of synonyms or similar concepts across languages. For example, the Dutch common word "gezellig" [phonetically: xə'zɛləx] can be translated as cozy, snug, homey, sociable (agreeable), and convivial. However, the Dutch word can be used to refer to a wide variety of objects and persons, such as a party, a house, the design of a house, a partner, and a phone call (Van de Vijver, 2015). The translation to English will require knowledge of the context in which the word is used and may even require a word that was not among the above translations. *Culture-driven adaptations* result from different cultural norms, values, communication styles, customs, or practices. The translation of the English "you" requires cultural knowledge about appropriate modes of address in tests in languages that have a distinction between an informal and formal mode address, such as "je" and "u" in Dutch, "du" and "Sie" in German, and "tu" and "vous" in French. Interestingly, norms as to when the formal and informal modes are used are not entirely identical across these languages. *Theory-driven adaptations* involve changes based on underlying conceptualization or theory. For example, digit span items should ideally have digit names that are all of similar length. However, similarity in digit length may be lost when the items are translated into another language. Finally, *familiarity/ recognizability-driven adaptations* are based on differential familiarity with task or item characteristics. Cognitive tests using stimuli drawn from one cultural group may show low familiarity for other cultural groups. Malda, van de Vijver, and Temane (2010), in a study in South Africa comparing children of Setswana and Afrikaans origin, observed that children from both cultural groups performed significantly better in tasks that involved items, vocabulary, and experiences drawn directly from their own cultural settings.

Statistical Approaches

Three commonly applied procedures for testing the cross-cultural equivalence of data are described. The first addresses *structural equivalence* and uses *exploratory factor analysis*. The analysis answers the question whether an instrument that has been applied in two or more cultures measures the same underlying constructs in each of these. The procedure starts with conducting a factor analysis for each country separately. There is structural equivalence if the factors identified are similar across the countries. In exploratory factor analysis, factor loadings can be rotated arbitrarily. As a consequence, factor structures found in different countries should be rotated toward each other before their congruence is assessed. Standard procedures for these target rotations are available (Van de Vijver & Leung, 1997). If the number of cultures involved is not very large, the factor structures found in each of these cultures can be compared in a pairwise manner. If many countries are involved, the number of pairwise comparisons becomes prohibitively large. In such cases, a factor analysis can be conducted on pooled data (Leung & Bond, 2004). Factor solutions obtained in the separate countries are then compared to this pooled factor structure. Extensive experience with the use of exploratory factor analysis in assessing structural equivalence has shown that the procedure often yields valuable information and is quite sensitive in detecting major cultural differences in a factor structure. Its main shortcoming is its relatively low power to detect minor cultural differences in factor structure. An additional disadvantage of the procedure is the focus on factor loadings and the absence of any test of identity of other parameters, such as factor correlations and unique variances.

The second procedure is based on *confirmatory factor analysis*. This technique is much more flexible than exploratory factor analysis and can address various levels of equivalence (or invariance in the terminology of structural equation modeling) (Byrne, 2013). Three levels of invariance are tested: configural invariance, metric invariance, and scalar invariance (more details can be found in Vandenberg & Lance, 2000; see also Brown, Harris, O'Quin, & Lane, in press).

The main strengths of confirmatory factor analysis in testing cross-cultural equivalence are its flexibility in testing various kinds (levels) of equivalence and the possibility of testing hierarchically nested models. The use of confirmatory factor analysis in testing equivalence is hampered by problems with fit statistics. Sensitivity to large sample sizes of the incremental chi square statistic is one problem; the lack of widely accepted rules for determining a significant and meaningful difference when other statistics flag a non-trivial increase or decrease in fit is another one. Applications of confirmatory factor analysis in testing equivalence in data involving many cultural groups suffer from additional problems. If a poor fit is found, it is often not clear whether the problem is due to misspecifications of the underlying model or to minor cross-cultural differences that are psychologically trivial. Nye and Drasgow (2011) proposed using effect sizes to deal with such problems (for an example, see Asil & Brown, 2016).

A great variety of statistical techniques has been proposed to deal with *item bias* or *differential item functioning* (Camilli & Shepard, 1994). In terms of confirmatory factor analysis, item bias refers to a test of intercept invariance. So, item bias analysis is employed to establish scalar equivalence. In the beginning of the item bias tradition, there was an emphasis on statistical procedures that are based on observed variables (i.e., that do not use latent variables), such as analysis of variance, loglinear analyses, and logistic regression (see Van de Vijver & Leung, 1997, for an overview). In the last decades, the preference has shifted to latent variable models, such as confirmatory factor analysis and item response theory. Item response theory is often applied for educational and achievement data where the item responses are dichotomously scored (as right or wrong).

A strong argument can be made that the analysis of bias and equivalence should always precede substantive analyses of cross-cultural similarities and differences, in very much the same way as an analysis of the internal consistency of an instrument is conducted prior to further analyses. The replicability of findings in cross-cultural research would improve if the issue of bias were dealt with more consistently. Unfortunately, experience shows that the application of bias and equivalence analyses is not without problems. Three problems that are shared by all the analyses discussed above are mentioned here. It should be emphasized that these are not inherent problems of the techniques, but problems with the way these techniques are usually implemented. First, criteria for bias and equivalence are often applied in a mechanical manner. An item with a significance value just above 0.05 in an item bias analysis is retained, while an item with a significance value just below 0.05 is eliminated. Clearly, decisions about bias and equivalence should be based on a combination of statistical and substantive considerations. The finding that a latent factor challenges the metric equivalence of a confirmatory factor analytic model in two cultures may provide interesting information about cross-cultural differences. Mechanically removing this factor from the analysis may save the metric equivalence of the remaining factors of the instrument, but it may also mask genuine cross-cultural differences. So, the differences may be based on a combination of bias and real differences (or bias and impact, as the split is also called in the literature; see Zumbo, 1999). Second, the techniques seem to favor short instruments, which often show high levels of equivalence and few biased items. The question of whether such short instruments provide an adequate representation of the underlying construct is hardly ever asked, let alone answered. From a substantive point of view, short instruments may not adequately cover the underlying construct because they restrict the assessment to a small set of items with presumably universal applicability. Third, the focus on item bias may have detracted the attention from method bias, which is often at least as problematic. Various sources of method bias cannot be identified with these techniques, such as cross-cultural differences in response styles, social desirability, and educational background, and the difficulty in equating administration conditions across cultures (e.g., an interviewer has a higher status in one culture than in another culture).

Mixed Approaches

Decades of item bias research have not led to cumulative insights as to which items tend to be biased. Consequently, insights and recommendations as to how items should be written in a multicultural context so as to minimize the likelihood of item bias are missing. In the area of educational testing, Linn (1993) argued that out of the many item features studied, item difficulty was the only characteristic that was more or less systematically associated with bias. One of the ways forward to overcome this problem may be the implementation of mixed methods in which qualitative methods seek explanations for observed quantitatively identified bias (Tashakkori & Teddlie, 2003).

For example, Van Schilt-Mol (2007) identified item bias in nationwide administered educational tests (i.e., CITO tests) in Dutch primary schools, using psychometric procedures. She then attempted to identify the source of the item bias, using a content analysis of the items and interviews with teachers and immigrant pupils. Based on this analysis, she changed the original items. Causes for item bias tended to be very specific, such as the use of figures that were not easily recognizable or the use of words not widely known among immigrant children. After a few iterations (of changing, applying the new items, and analyzing the new data), the instrument showed little or no bias, indicating that she had successfully identified and removed the bias. Her study illustrates an effective, yet laborious way to deal with item bias.

CONCLUSION AND RECOMMENDATIONS

Advances in multicultural assessment have been described in this chapter. A central theme in the chapter was that we need to take stock of past efforts. Many different approaches have been developed to deal with methodological issues. These range from applying more scrutiny to language issues in items to statistical analyses of item-level data. There have been qualitative approaches aimed to improve instruments, combining expertise about cultures and languages involved, and quantitative approaches to identify, estimate, and (statistically) eliminate bias. We are now at the crossroads where we can integrate different approaches. If we want to go beyond implicit culture in our instruments, we need to integrate approaches. There is a rich tradition of models and empirical studies to support us in these endeavors. Much educational assessment is based on the mainstream culture and assumes a full-fledged knowledge of the language and culture of this group. Cummins observed already in the 1970s that a monocultural focus in education does not do justice to the multiplicity of cultures in many modern classrooms. Some countries implemented procedures to accommodate such differences; for example, admissions tests to higher education in Israel can be taken in multiple languages (Beller, 2001). Other countries like the U.S. employ bias tests on such instruments (Holland & Wainer, 1993). However, we are still far from educational test design that incorporates its future usage in a multicultural population and test application that considers this diversity.

Recommendations

It is important to increase awareness of assessment issues among professionals who work with assessment in education, such as teachers, teacher training students, and psychologists. These professionals need to be aware of implicit culture in educational assessment and how to write items that avoid this cultural bias as much as possible. It is important to note that knowledge of specific cultures is often only possible to a limited extent in schools with many cultures represented in the student population. However, sensitivity to cultural issues in general should be part and parcel of teachers' professional skills. When groups of teachers discuss assignments given to students and provide feedback on each others' assignments from the perspective of suitability of the instrument for a multicultural student population (possibly facilitated by assessment specialists such as psychologists), they may become quickly aware of the cultural pitfalls of item writing in multicultural contexts. Thus, it may be relatively easy for them to focus in their assessments on the aspects of the curriculum that they want to address in their educational assessment, while avoiding unwanted, confounding features such as strong cultural loadings in their tests. Recommendations as to how to adapt items and how to write items that do not show much cultural loading are often easy to give. For example, it is relatively easy to understand how items can be written that do not heavily depend on reading competence when reading is not the target of the assessment. To the best of my knowledge, such a topic is hardly ever addressed in teacher education.

Furthermore, much more systematic research of bias in educational testing is needed. Much research is now closely related to academia and does not find its way to users. Much research into differential item functioning is technical in nature and difficult to translate into everyday practice. Studies of differential item functioning just do not produce enough replicable results to be easily translated into practice. The practical value of studies of cultural bias would probably increase by focusing less on specific items and more on cross-cultural differences in assessment-related factors, such as response styles, the minimum level of language proficiency required for writing educational tests, and the development of new testing formats (e.g., display of skills taught in everyday situations).

Finally, it is important to realize the limitations of assessment. Educational testing always takes place in a wider societal context. If a society is deeply segregated and access to educational resources differs across ethnic groups (examples of groups with limited access to education include Blacks in South Africa, Roma in various European countries, and Indigenous groups in various countries), adequate assessment is important in education. However, even good assessment cannot undo the consequences of differential access. Adequate multicultural assessment can help to identify talent in groups with limited access to education, but identification is only one step in a long process required to achieve equal opportunities.

REFERENCES

Aguinis, H., Culpepper, S. A., & Pierce, C. A. (2010). Revival of test bias research in preemployment testing. *Journal of Applied Psychology, 95*, 648–680.

Asil, M., & Brown, G.T.L. (2016). Comparing OECD PISA reading in English to other languages: Identifying potential sources of non-invariance. *International Journal of Testing, 16*(1), 71–93. doi: 10.1080/15305058.2015.1064431

Azhar, M. Z., & Varma, S. L. (2000). Mental illness and its treatment in Malaysia. In I. Al-Issa (Ed.), *Al-Junun: Mental illness in the Islamic world* (pp. 163–185). Madison, CT: International Universities Press.

Azuma, H., & Kashiwagi, K. (1987). Descriptors for an intelligent person: A Japanese study. *Japanese Psychological Research, 29*, 17–26.

Barrett, P. T., Petrides, K. V., Eysenck, S.B.G., & Eysenck, H. J. (1998). The Eysenck personality questionnaire: An examination of the factorial similarity of P, E, N, and L across 34 countries. *Personality and Individual Differences, 25*, 805–819.

Beller, M. (2001). Admission to higher education in Israel and the role of the Psychometric Entrance Test: Educational and political dilemmas. *Assessment in Education: Principles, Policy & Practice, 8*, 315–337.

Berry, J. W. (1997). Immigration, acculturation and adaptation. *Applied Psychology: An International Review, 46*, 5–68.

Brown, G.T.L., Harris, L. R., O'Quin, C. R., & Lane, K. (in press). Using multi-group confirmatory factor analysis to evaluate cross-cultural research: Identifying and understanding non-invariance. *International Journal of Research and Method in Education.* Advance online publication. doi:10.1080/1743727X.2015.1070823

Byrne, B. M. (2013). *Structural equation modeling with AMOS: Basic concepts, applications, and programming* (2nd ed.). New York: Routledge.

Camilli, G., & Shepard, L. A. (1994). *Methods for identifying biased test items.* Thousand Oaks, CA: Sage.

Cattell, R. B. (1940). A culture free intelligence test, I. *Journal of Educational Psychology, 31*, 176–199.

Cattell, R. B., & Cattell, A.K.S. (1963). *Culture fair intelligence test.* Champaign, IL: Institute for Personality and Ability Testing.

Celenk, O., & Van de Vijver, F.J.R. (2011). Assessment of acculturation: Issues and overview of measures. *Online Readings in Psychology and Culture, Unit 1.* Retrieved from http://scholarworks.gvsu.edu/orpc/vol8/iss1/10

Cuéllar, I. (2000). Acculturation and mental health: Ecological transactional relations of adjustment. In I. Cuéllar & F. A. Paniagua (Eds.), *Handbook of multicultural mental health: Assessment and treatment of diverse populations* (pp. 45–62). New York: Academic Press.

Cummins, J. (1979). Linguistic Interdependence and the educational development of bilingual children. *Review of Educational Research, 49*, 222–251.

Cummins, J. (1989). Institutionalized racism and the assessment of minority children: A comparison of policies and programs in the United States and Canada. In R. J. Samuda, S. L. Kong, J. Cummins, J. Pascual-Leone, & J. Lewis (Eds.), *Assessment and placement of minority students* (pp. 94–107). Toronto, ON: Hogrefe.

Dimitrova, R., Chasiotis, A., Bender, M., & Van de Vijver, F.J.R. (2013). Collective identity and well-being of Roma minority adolescents in Bulgaria. *International Journal of Psychology, 48*, 502–513.

Eysenck, H. J., & Eysenck, S.B.G. (1975). *Manual of the Eysenck personality questionnaire (junior and adult).* London: Hodder and Stoughton.

Fernández, A. L., & Marcopulos, B. A. (2008). A comparison of normative data for the Trail Making Test from several countries: Equivalence of norms and considerations for interpretation. *Scandinavian Journal of Psychology, 49*, 239–246.

Fischer, R. (2004). Standardization to account for cross-cultural response bias: A classification of score adjustment procedures and review of research in JCCP. *Journal of Cross-Cultural Psychology, 35*, 263–282.

Formann, A. K., & Piswanger, K. (1979). *Wiener Matrizen-Test. Ein Rasch-skalierter sprachfreier Intelligenztest* [The Viennese matrices test. A Rasch-calibrated non-verbal intelligence test]. Weinheim, Germany: Beltz Test.

Frijda, N. H., & Jahoda, G. (1966). On the scope and methods of cross-cultural research. *International Journal of Psychology, 1*, 109–127.

Goodnow, J. J. (2002). Parents' knowledge and expectations: Using what we know. In M. H. Bornstein (Ed.), *Handbook of parenting* (Vol. 3, Being and becoming a parent, pp. 439–460). Mahwah, NJ: Erlbaum.

Grigorenko, E. L., Geissler, P. W., Prince, R., Okatcha, F., Nokes, C., Kenny, D. A., et al. (2001). The organisation of Luo conceptions of intelligence: A study of implicit theories in a Kenyan village. *International Journal of Behavioral Development, 25*, 367–378.

Hambleton, R. K., Merenda, P. F., & Spielberger, C. D. (Eds.). (2005). *Adapting educational tests and psychological tests for cross-cultural assessment.* Mahwah, NJ: Erlbaum.

Ho, D. Y. F. (1996). Filial piety and its psychological consequences. In M. H. Bond (Ed.), *Handbook of Chinese psychology* (pp. 155–165). Hong Kong, SAR: Oxford University Press.

Hofstede, G. (2007). A European in Asia. *Asian Journal of Social Psychology, 10,* 16–21.

Holland, P. W., & Wainer, H. (1993). *Differential item functioning.* Hillsdale, NJ: Lawrence Erlbaum.

Huddleston, T., Niessen, J. Chaoimh, E. N., & White, E. (2011). *Migrant Integration Policy Index III.* Brussels, Belgium: British Council and Migration Policy Group.

Jensen, A. R. (1980). *Bias in mental testing.* New York, NY: Free Press.

Johnson, T. P. (1998). Approaches to equivalence in cross-cultural and cross-national survey research. *ZUMA-Nachrichten Spezial, 3,* 1–40.

Karabatsos, G. (2003). Comparing the aberrant response detection performance of thirty-six person-fit statistics. *Applied Measurement in Education, 16,* 277–298.

Keegan, P. J., Brown, G.T.L., & Hattie, J.A.C. (2013). A psychometric view of sociocultural factors in test validity: The development of standardised test materials for Māori medium schools in New Zealand/Aotearoa. In S. Phillipson, K. Ku, & S. N. Phillipson (Eds.), *Constructing educational achievement: A sociocultural perspective* (pp. 42–54). London: Routledge.

Leung, K., & Bond, M. H. (2004). Social axioms: A model for social beliefs in multicultural perspective. In M. P. Zanna (Ed.), *Advances in experimental social psychology* (Vol. 36. pp. 119–197). San Diego, CA: Elsevier Academic Press.

Linn, R. L. (1993). The use of differential item functioning statistics: A discussion of current practice and future implications. In P. W. Holland & H. Wainer (Eds.), *Differential item functioning* (pp. 349–364). Hillsdale, NJ: Erlbaum.

Malda, M., Van de Vijver, F.J.R., Srinivasan, K., Transler, C., Sukumar, P., & Rao, K. (2008). Adapting a cognitive test for a different culture: An illustration of qualitative procedures. *Psychology Science Quarterly, 50,* 451–468.

Malda, M., Van de Vijver, F.J.R., & Temane, M. Q. (2010). Rugby versus soccer in South Africa: Content familiarity explains most cross-cultural differences in cognitive test scores. *Intelligence, 38,* 582–595.

Marín, G., & Gamba, R. J. (2003). Acculturation and changes in cultural values. In K. Chun, O. P. Balls, & G. Marín (Eds.), *Acculturation: Advances in theory, measurement, and applied research* (pp. 83–93). Washington, DC: American Psychological Association.

McCrae, R. R., & Allik, J. (Eds.). (2002). *The five-factor model of personality across cultures.* New York: Kluwer Academic/Plenum.

McCrae, R. R., Terracciano, A., & 78 Members of the Personality Profiles of Cultures Project. (2005). Universal features of personality traits from the observer's perspective: Data from 50 cultures. *Journal of Personality and Social Psychology, 88,* 547–561.

Mercer, J. R. (1979). *Technical manual. System of multicultural pluralistic assessment.* New York: Psychological Corporation.

Messick, S. (1989). Validity. In R. L. Linn (Ed.), *Educational measurement* (3rd ed., pp. 13–103). New York: Macmillan.

Nye, C. D., & Drasgow, F. (2011). Effect size indices for analysis of measurement equivalence: Understanding the practical importance of difference between groups. *Journal of Applied Psychology, 96,* 966–980.

Peterson, E. R., Brown, G.T.L., & Hamilton, R. J. (2013). Cultural differences in tertiary students' conceptions of learning as a duty and student achievement. *The International Journal of Quantitative Research in Education, 1*(2), 167–181.

Phinney, J. S., Horenczyk, G., Liebkind, K., & Vedder, P. (2001). Ethnic identity, immigration, and well-being: An interactional perspective. *Journal of Social Issues, 57,* 493–510.

Piswanger, K. (1975). *Interkulturelle Vergleiche mit dem Matrizentest von Formann* [Cross-cultural comparisons with Formann's Matrices Test]. Unpublished doctoral dissertation. Vienna: University of Vienna.

Poortinga, Y. H. (1989). Equivalence of cross-cultural data: An overview of basic issues. *International Journal of Psychology, 24,* 737–756.

Redfield, R., Linton, R., & Herskovits, M. H. (1936). Memorandum on the study of acculturation. *American Anthropologist, 38,* 149–152.

Schmidt, F. L., & Hunter, J. E. (1998). The validity and utility of selection methods in personnel psychology: Practical and theoretical implications of 85 years of research findings. *Psychological Bulletin, 124,* 262–274.

Shadish, W. R., Cook, T. D., & Campbell, D. T. (2002). *Experimental and quasi-experimental designs for generalized causal inference.* Boston, MA: Houghton Mifflin Co.

Sue, S. (2006). Cultural competency: From philosophy to research and practice. *Journal of Community Psychology, 34,* 237–245.

Suzuki, K., Takei, N., Kawai, M., Minabe, Y., & Mori, N. (2003). Is Taijin Kyofusho a culture-bound syndrome? *American Journal of Psychiatry, 160,* 1358.

Täht, K., & Must, O. (2013). Comparability of educational achievement and learning attitudes across nations. *Educational Research and Evaluation, 19,* 19–38.

Tanaka-Matsumi, J., & Draguns, J. G. (1997). Culture and psychotherapy. In J. W. Berry, M. H. Segall, & C. Kagitcibasi (Eds.), *Handbook of cross-cultural psychology* (Vol. 3, pp. 449–491). Needham Heights, MA: Allyn and Bacon.

Tashakkori, A., & Teddlie, C. (Eds.). (2003). *Handbook on mixed methods in the behavioral and social sciences.* Thousand Oaks, CA: Sage Publications.

Thomas, M. L. (2011). The value of item response theory in clinical assessment: A review. *Assessment, 18,* 291–307.

Van de Vijver, F.J.R. (2015). Methodological aspects of cross-cultural research. In M. Gelfand, Y. Hong, & C. Y. Chiu (Eds.), *Handbook of advances in culture & psychology* (Vol. 5, pp. 101–160). New York: Oxford University Press.

Van de Vijver, F.J.R., Helms-Lorenz, M., & Feltzer, M. F. (1999). Acculturation and cognitive performance of migrant children in the Netherlands. *International Journal of Psychology, 34,* 149–162.

Van de Vijver, F.J.R., & Leung, K. (1997). *Methods and data analysis for cross-cultural research.* Newbury Park, CA: Sage.

Van de Vijver, F.J.R., & Phalet, K. (2004). Assessment in multicultural groups: The role of acculturation. *Applied Psychology: An International Review, 53,* 215–236.

Van de Vijver, F.J.R., & Poortinga, Y. H. (2015). On item pools, swimming pools, birds with webbed feet, and the professionalization of multilingual assessment. In C. S. Wells & M. Faulkner-Bond (Eds.), *Educational measurement: From foundations to future* (pp. 273–290). New York: Guildford Press.

Van de Vijver, F.J.R., Willemse, G.R.C.M., & Van de Rijt, B.A.M. (1993). Het testen van cognitieve vaardigheden van allochtone leerlingen [The assessment of cognitive skills of immigrant pupils]. *De Psycholoog, 28,* 152–159.

Van Der Heijden, P. G., Bouts, J., & Hox, J. J. (2000). A comparison of randomized response, computer-assisted self-interview, and face-to-face direct questioning eliciting sensitive information in the context of welfare and unemployment benefit. *Sociological Methods & Research, 28,* 505–537.

Van Hemert, D. A., Van de Vijver, F.J.R., Poortinga, Y. H., & Georgas, J. (2002). Structural and functional equivalence of the Eysenck Personality Questionnaire within and between countries. *Personality and Individual Differences, 33,* 1229–1249.

Van Leest, P. F. (1997). Bias and equivalence research in the Netherlands. *European Review of Applied Psychology, 47,* 319–329.

Van Schilt-Mol, T. M. M. L. (2007). *Differential item functioning en itembias in de Cito-Eindtoets Basisonderwijs* [Differential item functioning and item bias in the Cito-Eindtoets Basisonderwijs]. Amsterdam, the Netherlands: Aksant.

Vandenberg, R. J., & Lance, C. E. (2000). A review and synthesis of the measurement invariance literature: Suggestions, practices, and recommendations for organizational research. *Organizational Research Methods, 3,* 4–70.

Ward, C., Leong, C. H., & Low, M. (2004). Personality and sojourner adjustment: An exploration of the Big Five and the cultural fit proposition. *Journal of Cross-Cultural Psychology, 35,* 137–151.

Watkins, D., Reghi, M., & Astilla, E. (1991). The-Asian-learner-as-a-rote-learner Stereotype: myth or reality? *Educational Psychology, 11,* 21–34.

Wober, M. (1969). Distinguishing centri-cultural from cross-cultural tests and research. *Perceptual and Motor Skills, 28,* 488.

Zumbo, B. D. (1999). *A handbook on the theory and methods of differential item functioning (DIF): Logistic regression modeling as a unitary framework for binary and Likert-type (ordinal) item scores.* Ottawa, ON: Directorate of Human Resources Research and Evaluation, Department of National Defense.

26

PUBLIC PERCEPTIONS ABOUT ASSESSMENT IN EDUCATION

Chad W. Buckendahl

INTRODUCTION

In partnership with curriculum and instruction, assessment represents an important component in closing the educational feedback loop. Information collected through formal and informal assessment has the potential to provide multiple sources of evidence about opportunity to learn, learning progress, student achievement, and effectiveness of instruction. Stakeholders with an interest in the results of assessment are numerous. Students, educators, parents, policy makers, and the public will each have varying degrees of interest in what is assessed, how it is assessed, and the outcomes of those assessments. This breadth of interest is only natural given the public funding of education in many countries.

Clearly, students are the most proximate consumers of assessment information. Their interactions with cognitive measurements provide the information that yields evidence of their learning, leading to formative and summative uses of the information. Educators also represent an important stakeholder group because they generally have the skills and responsibility to provide interventions through adapting instruction in response to students' strengths and weaknesses. The public represents an umbrella characterization of multiple stakeholder groups with an interest in assessment results. Among members of the public, parents are the primary consumers of assessment information that contributes to a better understanding of where their children need to further explore or focus. There is also a system of policy makers, at multiple jurisdictional levels (e.g., local, regional, national), who have responsibility for resource development, allocation, and implementation. As a significant public funding commitment, policy makers are held accountable through assessments for decisions made about educational performance. Because of the diverse roles members of the public play in educational systems, it is difficult to characterize a unifying perspective of the public and their perceptions of assessment.

Because other chapters in this volume discuss student and educator perceptions, this chapter focuses on the public as defined above. Their perceptions of assessments are approached through a discussion of historical information along with attention on more contemporary education policies involving assessment intended to reflect public goals. Last, how educators can play a key role in helping to inform the broader public about assessment is discussed.

When attempting to consider public perceptions about assessment in education, it is important to recognize at the outset that the average person has probably taken multiple assessments at some point or other in his or her life. These experiences may have initially occurred in a school classroom or more formally for course placement or admissions. More experiences with assessment could have occurred as part of workforce or career development activities. This range of personal experiences may encourage individuals to form opinions about assessments for these different purposes, and in general. As in any technical field, active engagement in taking an assessment does not suggest that an individual understands the stages of development and validation needed to generate and evaluate evidence that supports intended uses and interpretations of scores.

Braun and Mislevy (2005) characterized this phenomenon as 'intuitive test theory,' meaning that anyone who has taken an assessment develops a schema and belief structure about how the test was developed, how items were chosen, and how the passing score was established. They argue that someone with an intuitive understanding of physics would not be in a position to build a rocket ship in his or her backyard that could reach the moon, even if he or she understood some of the basic concepts of aerodynamics and propulsion. In contrast, many adults would claim not finding it hard to create a test, administer it, score it, and set a passing grade. Although it might be satisfying for researchers and practitioners to know that their expertise in the area of assessment exceeds that of the general public, we should not simply be content with that knowledge. In reality, there are more members of the public than there are experts in education and assessment, so continual outreach is needed to help convey the processes and practices of assessment development and validation. This is particularly critical because most policy makers have not had training in educational measurement principles. For example, the 113th U.S. Congress included 44 representatives and seven senators with formal training in education, less than 10% of the 538 members of the two houses (Cillizza, 2013). As a result, policy makers are part of the group whose understanding is largely based on intuitive perceptions, yet they are in a position to define and fund education assessment and accountability initiatives.

HISTORICAL PERSPECTIVES

Understanding how systems have evolved to their current status involves exploring some of the historical foundations on which these systems were built. Some of the earliest records of formalized assessment systems can be traced to China and the civil service examinations that served the utilitarian purpose of identifying individuals for positions in the government (DuBois, 1970) (see more on function of assessment in Confucian societies in Kennedy, this volume). With a large number of examinees compared to few positions, these examinations were highly competitive with similarly high failure rates. Success on these examinations offered individuals an opportunity to move beyond agrarian employment. The content of the examinations was based on multiple domains and was measured using written and performance tasks. Some of these domains included measuring examinees' abilities in ceremonial rites and horsemanship. Further, the administration and scoring processes were also quite formal in that examinees took their examinations under proctored conditions with judges responsible for evaluating examinees' performance on a given examination.

Although there is evidence that these examination programs were developed, at least, by approximately 2200 BC (DuBois, 1970), there were core elements of the test development process that will look familiar to practitioners today. Domains were developed based on defined expectations with decision rules about acceptable and unacceptable performance. In addition, the number of separate decisions suggested that there were concerns about representation of the construct and dimensionality, even if more contemporary views about validity were not articulated. There have been significant advances in sophistication of empirical evaluation of assessment information and the technologies used to develop and administer tests. However, had there also been evidence in the archives about statistical estimates of item or judge performance, we might be hard-pressed to distinguish the test development activities of this earlier era from the core of our current processes.

The resilience of this civil service exam system over centuries illustrates how testing can be not only accepted, but endorsed, as a useful tool for making important decisions. However, the lasting credibility relies on important assumptions. One key factor in the use of these formal examination processes rests on a philosophy of fairness among the examinee population. The concept of aptitude or ability being a primary determinant of future opportunities is promoted through this model. The standardization of content, administration, scoring, and decision-making represents a laudable effort to reduce subjectivity in the measurement. That these particular systems continued to evolve and expand provides some evidence of how testing can be adopted by the public as a necessary component in defining how its society functions. These observations, though, are not limited to the workforce or this particular geographic region.

Comparatively, DuBois (1970) indicated that efforts to reduce subjectivity in European higher education assessment and decision-making began to appear in the 1200s. A key advance at this time was the transition to formal oral examinations where students were assessed by faculty members via a combination of private and public demonstrations of their competence. Although scoring expectations were likely still more variable than we would expect today, establishing greater commonality provided students with equivalent opportunities to demonstrate their knowledge. Similarly, when some scoring changes were implemented at the University of Louvain, students' performances were categorized into four categories, one of which was labeled *charity passes* (DuBois, 1970). Written examinations developed concurrently with the transition to paper in the 1400s as a common medium for communication. The shift in practice in European universities was influenced, in part, by perceptions among students and the public that historical factors such as heredity and social standing may have previously played a larger role than competence. These transitions during the late medieval period in testing to methods that were viewed as more egalitarian began at the same time as other major changes were transpiring. For example, the signing of the Magna Carta in June 1215 served as an early attempt in Western society to codify and more broadly define individual liberties (Howard, 1998). Concurrent changes in other segments of society were slower to evolve, but may have been a natural progression of these efforts.

Formal and informal assessments have long been a part of the education process at the primary, secondary, and higher education levels. These assessments may be used to identify students for particular educational pathways, schools, or universities. The introduction of mass public schooling in the industrial era expanded experience with educational assessment and, thus, the public's understanding of its role is a relatively recent phenomenon relative to the history of assessment. Formal educational assessment developed in the United States in the 1830s–40s through initiatives advanced by Horace Mann (Hayes, 2006). That Mann pressed for universal schooling and required a common curriculum may not be that remarkable. However, his attempts to eval-uate students through a common assessment were an effort to provide evidence to the public that funding universal schooling was worthwhile. The Boston Survey was a standardized assessment initially administered to approximately 7,000 students across the schools in 1845 to evaluate what the students had learned during the academic year (Crocker, 2003). To communicate to the public about how the students did, results of the assessment were published in the newspaper. Mann's vision was that the results of these assessments should be used to improve the quality of education and to also pro-vide a mechanism for educator accountability (Parsons, et al., 1845). Similar to some of the core elements of the civil service examinations in China, some of the policy elements observed at the beginning of public education in the United States have been seemingly resurrected in some of the more recent federal education policies (more in Nichols & Harris, this volume).

United States Assessment Policy History

While mass schooling and assessment are nearly universal around the world, research about public perceptions of assessment is not systematic. Unsurprisingly, most infor-mation about this topic resides in research conducted in the United States, partly as a consequence of the long tradition of public opinion polling on a wide variety of polit-ical topics, including education. Hence, the focus of subsequent discussions of policy and practice in this chapter is the American case, with implications offered as cautions for other societies. It is important to consider the context of the results reported in this chapter. Within the United States, federal (i.e., national) involvement in educational assessment and accountability is a relatively recent and controversial component of educational reform when compared to many other countries where national involve-ment in education is more the norm.

In the United States, education is largely viewed as a locally controlled enterprise with respect to curriculum, instruction, assessment, and perhaps most important, funding. As opposed to being driven by the federal government, individual states are responsi-ble for education, with many of them delegating responsibility to local municipalities. The strength of such a system is the opportunity to engage communities in defining local education needs and taking ownership for implementation and outcomes. How-ever, like most programs in the public sector, the funding mechanism will significantly influence the design and implementation of education systems. This is particularly evi-dent when communities are not equivalent with respect to their resources and capacity to provide equivalent opportunities for children.

For many countries that have national or other pooled funding mechanisms for education, these differences may not appear to be important. However, because public education in the United States is generally funded by revenues collected through prop-erty taxes and, potentially, supplemented through other sources, differences in com-munity resources can create large discrepancies if additional efforts are not undertaken to attempt to counterbalance the effects. The public recognition of such differences led to national education reform policies that (a) intended to provide more equitable support and (b) emphasized efforts to educate all students.

Elementary and Secondary Education Act of 1965

National concerns about equity in educational opportunities and funding emerged concurrently with societal changes in the United States. The *Elementary and Secondary*

Education Act of 1965 (ESEA [U.S. Congress, 1965]) was passed at the national level, marking the beginning of a shift in control of education policy. This particular legislation was one component of a national 'War on Poverty' initiative advanced by President Lyndon Johnson intended to provide funding for more equitable education practices and reduce achievement gaps among student groups (Califano, 1991). At the outset, the primary focus was on schools that had large populations of economically disadvantaged students, providing funds to support educational interventions in exchange for meeting eligibility requirements and demonstrating compliance with expectations for participation.

Assessment became a component of the compliance aspect of the program where students in programs receiving funds were required to participate in assessments aligned to the interventions. The purpose of these assessments was to collect outcomes data that could be used to evaluate the success of the law's implementation. However, these assessments did not extend to all students. Rather, only schools identified under the legislation participated, begging the question of whether additional information about student achievement might be valuable at the national level to inform education policy discussions.

Because public education had been historically overseen by states or local municipalities, national information about student achievement was not easily available. Therefore, soon after the ESEA legislation was enacted, the *National Assessment of Educational Progress* (NAEP) was launched in 1969 as an attempt to provide, for the first time, information about student achievement on a national basis (Jones & Olkin, 2004). An interesting challenge when interpreting the results of NAEP—both at its inception and since—is that there is no guaranteed alignment in a given jurisdiction between NAEP and curriculum because the federal government in the United States is precluded from mandating a national curriculum; this creates a confound that cannot be easily overcome.

Because the assessment component of the ESEA legislation was only required for schools that received funding, widespread public awareness was relatively limited even though the purpose of the Act was in response to public perceptions about inequality. Further, even though it was designed as a national survey, even NAEP had limited exposure, let alone understanding among the public. However, that perception began to change with the publication of Cannell's (1988) lay observations of how students in his state were out-performing the national norms on commercially available achievement tests. Cannell characterized this inflated performance as the 'Lake Wobegon' effect, where all children were above average and raised doubts about the quality of instructional and assessment practices within the state. This concept received widespread attention, raising public concerns about the quality of assessments (Smith & Rottenberg, 1991).

Similarly, prior to Cannell's observations, the public's increased concerns about student achievement in the United States can be traced to *A Nation at Risk* (National Commission on Excellence in Education, 1983) that highlighted increased competition from developed and emerging markets as threatening continued economic growth (for more see Lingard & Lewis, this volume). As the global economy has become more integrated, a greater focus on education and workforce development in an international context has been part of American conversations about school quality.

At the national level, the variability of these state level programs led to complementary concerns about the credibility of results, as well as the ongoing inequity of educational funding. In response, there was an attempt to develop a voluntary national testing program (Wise et al., 1998). The initiative was short-lived, but a variation of the concept can be seen in the development and implementation of subsequent policies that have sought to increase expectations, along with the capacity to compare student performance.

No Child Left Behind Act of 2001

Although gradual expansion of the legislation occurred during multiple reauthorizations of the ESEA, it was not until the 2002 iteration that the public became more aware of the role of assessment in education policy. Specifically, the *No Child Left Behind Act of 2001* (NCLB [U.S. Congress, 2002]) expanded the expectations of the ESEA by requiring states to develop academic content standards and assessments for all students. Because the proportion of funding from state, federal, and sometimes other sources (e.g., private sector, foundations) had increased, most local education agencies were not in a position to protest against the requirements or reject the financial support. As a result, states began to develop academic content standards, achievement standards, and assessments designed to measure student achievement relative to these standards. In addition, states were required to submit information about their state level systems to the national Department of Education for external evaluation of compliance and quality. Though uneven in its implementation, the federal peer review process that evaluated technical characteristics of assessment systems developed by states was an attempt to provide some evidence that would help to mitigate interpretation of seemingly disparate results observed across states (Davis & Buckendahl, 2007).

Another artifact of the implementation of this law was heightened public awareness of assessment as part of education policy and accountability. Within the law, there were accountability provisions that expected all students across grade levels to achieve proficiency in reading and mathematics by 2014 (U.S. Congress, 2002). Though states had different strategies for meeting expectations for adequate yearly progress (AYP), the conjunctive nature of the requirements meant that each year more schools would be categorized as needing improvement. Although reaching proficiency for all students was commendable from a policy perspective and politically necessary, full proficiency was an aspirational expectation that was comingled with an accountability expectation (Linn, 2003). Linn (2003) highlights the problem that the expectations of NCLB were designed in such a way as to be unattainable without compromising the intent of the law. Because of the important role that student assessment played in implementation of this policy and a backlash by stakeholder groups (e.g., teacher unions, parents, testing experts, politicians) surrounding the policy expectations, the public's exposure to assessment in education was restricted primarily to measurement for summative purposes under these accountability systems (Broder, 2007; Layton, 2014). Based on these policy missteps, one would expect that efforts would be made to correct some of the untenable expectations and assumptions. If only policies were constructed without the influence of politics.

Race to the Top

In an effort to respond to growing criticisms from educators and the public about the design and implementation of the NCLB legislation, the national Department of Education promoted a change to policy that was characterized as *Race to the Top* (RTTT) and funded as part of the American Recovery and Reinvestment Act of 2009 (U.S. Congress, 2009). One of the key features of this shift in policy was the recognition that, from an accountability perspective, schools with high scores were as effective as schools with growing scores. In providing flexibility for accountability systems to reduce some of the conjunctive elements that NCLB had previously required, systems were permitted to consider additional indicators and in different combinations. Thus, state departments of education that sought to remove some of the burdens of the NCLB policy, could apply for a waiver with a requirement that they would need to agree to certain new terms in order to modify their systems. Unfortunately, many states have recently begun to recognize some unintended consequences of moving from NCLB regulations to RTTT. Specifically, two of the more contentious aspects of the RTTT policy were an adoption of the Common Core State Standards (CCSS; de facto national academic content standards) and the implementation of teacher evaluation systems that are based at least 50% on student achievement measures.

As a concurrent activity during the development of curricula and accountability systems around these new academic expectations, national funding created opportunities for two consortia (i.e., PARCC, SBAC) to develop assessments for college and career readiness that could be used across states (Howard, 2015). Although these consortia took different approaches to assessment development and validation, both engaged in activities with a focus on measuring the CCSS in compliance with federal requirements. The public's awareness of these assessments is still emerging, but the reaction by stakeholders in a number of jurisdictions suggests dissatisfaction. Specifically, some states have chosen to drop or not to adopt the CCSS and, instead, have opted for development of their own academic content and achievement standards, and taken responsibility for their own assessment systems (Timm, 2014). Similarly, the arbitrary policy requirement that at least 50% of teachers' evaluation be derived from student outcome measures has created tensions among educator organizations, local communities, and policy makers (Jennings, 2012). Although the public may not understand why, bolstered by increased caution recommended by educators, parents, and testing experts, there appears to be public understanding that the RTTT policy is going beyond the capacity of many of these measurement tools to confidently contribute to such important decisions (Maxwell, 2015).

RATIONALE FOR PUBLIC PERCEPTIONS

The public's love-hate relationship with many systems of measurement, educational assessment included, may begin with an expectation of what Rawls (1971) characterized in political philosophy as a 'fair opportunity of equality.' That is, decisions made about a student's academic ability or achievement are intended to be independent of the relationship the student has with the teacher, the effort the student puts forth, familial relationships, or demographic characteristics such as sex, race, ethnicity, or socioeconomic status. It does not suggest equal outcomes. Revisiting the civil service examinations noted earlier, in Western societies, the concept of social mobility being influenced through meritocratic as opposed to hereditary factors is still relatively novel. For example, civil service examination processes that had been evident in China for centuries were not introduced in France until 1791, in the United Kingdom until the 1830s, and in the United State until 1883 (DuBois, 1970). Although these were not perfect tools, as noted earlier, the expansion of formal measurement systems has contributed to a public belief that some of the subjectivity evident in previous selection systems has been reduced. This expectation extends to educational assessments.

Public Opinion Polls

One of the strategies to elicit feedback from diverse constituencies is the use of questionnaires to survey a sample of a targeted population. The Gallup name has been synonymous in the United States with political opinion polling survey research. Perhaps not as well known, the organization has also been involved in partnership with Phi Delta Kappa (PDK) for many years in education survey research (Elam, 1995). When considering results from such surveys, it is important to consider the proximity of the individual forming the opinion to the phenomenon. For example, a questionnaire about the use of assessments for making decisions about the quality of their local school as opposed to using assessments for evaluating school quality in general may elicit differing perspectives.

As described earlier, national policies in the United States over the past few decades have increased the role of formal assessment in education reform efforts. Because public opinion polls are designed to ascertain the perspectives of intended populations on topics that may or may not be salient to them, it makes sense that the topic of assessment would be part of the questionnaire. Elam (1995) summarizes some of the key findings and trends collected in the 1970s and 1980s at a time when there was limited national involvement in education policy and practice, and when there were even efforts to eliminate the federal Department of Education (White, 1981). Topics about assessment (or testing) included questions about educators and students. Table 26.1 summarizes the percentage of respondents who favored versus opposed the respective statement.

As shown in Table 26.1, results from these studies suggest consistent public support for testing requirements for educators. These results are not surprising, because the teacher certification process is similar to credentialing for other professions. There is a public interest served in the establishment of a credentialing process for professionals

Table 26.1 Respondents' Support for or Opposition of Statements Related to Educational Assessment or Testing in the PDK/Gallup Poll 1969–1994 (Elam, 1995)

Change considered	Year	Favor %	Oppose %
Educator testing			
State board exams for teacher certification	1979	85	9
	1981	84	11
	1984	89	7
	1986	85	11
Periodic testing for teachers to retain certification	1979	85	10
	1988	86	11
National standards for teacher certification	1988	86	9
Test school principals periodically	1979	85	10
Student testing			
National tests to compare academic achievement among schools	1970	75	16
	1971	70	21
	1983	75	17
	1986	77	16
	1988	81	14
Required national achievement standards and goals	1989	70	19
	1991	81	12
Standardized national tests for high school graduation	1976	65	31
	1981	69	26
	1984	65	29
	1988	73	22

that protect health, safety, and welfare. There was also general support among the public for testing students as part of school accountability and for purposes of high school graduation. Related to this public support was an increase in support for national academic achievement standards even though, at the time and currently, the United States does not have national curriculum.

With respect to support for student testing, these results were similar to what Gilmore (1998) observed in a study conducted in New Zealand. Brookhart's (2013) findings also suggest that the American public's support for assessment is perhaps built on a belief in using common measurement approaches that are perceived to be objective and permit comparability. As a consequence of the trends illustrated in Table 26.1, it seems the American public would be generally supportive of increased national involvement in assessment and education policy in general through the NCLB and RTTT initiatives. That the federal policies and funding which has supported development of the PARCC and SBAC consortia assessments were designed to permit comparability across states appears to reinforce these findings (Howard, 2015). However, as policies change, it is important to evaluate whether these changes have a consequential effect on public perceptions about the process and outcomes of these policies.

As illustrated in results from Bushaw and Calderon's (2014) PDK/Gallup Poll study and shown in Table 26.2, although the overall majority of respondents did not think that standardized tests were helpful, the public appeared to be at least somewhat supportive of common assessments that would be characterized as standardized. The use of the word *standardized* has become almost pejorative within educational assessment, perhaps because of its connotations with commercially available assessments that members of the public may have taken themselves at one point in time (Fairtest, 2007), yet this understanding is not universal (Phelps, 2009). However, had the questionnaire asked respondents whether they supported common assessments, administered under similar conditions, and that were developed to be fair for all students, the responses may have been different. Although the general perception about the value of assessment suggests that there are less favorable views of assessment than observed in the historical data (see Table 26.1), the additional questions about specific uses of tests (e.g., college entrance, promotion, college credit, high school diploma) suggested continued support for important interpretations and uses. Even with some of the perceived backlash, the support for tests related to graduation shown in Table 26.2 (78% very and somewhat supportive) remain surprisingly consistent compared with the levels of endorsement shown in Table 26.1.

In contrast to support for standardized testing, Bushaw and Calderon's (2014) data suggest that there was greater skepticism in the United States about the value of international comparative tests. However, it is uncertain whether resistance arises from concerns for test quality, a dislike for the relatively poor performance of the United States, influence on federal assessment and accountability policies, or other factors. Nonetheless, respondents supported understanding education in other countries as a way to improve local schools. In 1991, the support for national achievement standards and goals was 81% (Elam, 1995); however, in 2014, the support for national achievement standards, in the guise of the expectations of the CCSS, had declined to 33% (Bushaw & Calderon, 2014). The changing perspective may be a function of how the aspirational NCLB goals of AYP could be supported theoretically, but become less desirable once accountability consequences impacted education systems.

It is important for readers to understand that the results of these longitudinal PDK/Gallup Polls and other surveys targeting these topics have yielded fairly convergent results. Harris (2015) synthesized international literature from a series of

Table 26.2 National Total Respondents' Responses to Statements Related to Educational Assessment or Testing in the PDK/Gallup Poll 2014 (Bushaw & Calderon, 2014) in Percentages

Topic Area	Agreement		Level of Support				Level of Agreement				
	Yes	No	Very supportive	Somewhat	Not very	Not at all	Strongly Agree	4	3	2	Strongly Disagree
Student assessment using standardized tests											
Standardized tests are helpful	45	54									
Supportive of											
College entrance tests, such as SAT or ACT			29	51	15	5					
Tests that determine if the student should be promoted from one grade to the next			35	42	14	7					
Tests used to award high school students college credit, such as Advanced Placement (i.e., AP) exams			53	38	5	2					
Tests used to determine whether a student can be awarded a high school diploma			38	40	16	5					
International Comparisons of Student Achievement											
International comparison tests such as PISA accurately measure student achievement across nations							8	21	43	16	11
Understanding how students are taught in other countries could help improve schools in my community							40	34	15	5	5
International test comparisons are critical to helping improve schools in this country							17	29	29	13	11
Favor or oppose having teachers in your community use the Common Core State Standards to guide what they teach	33	60									

qualitative and quantitative studies about parents' perceptions about assessment that suggested continued trust in this evidence along with teachers' use of the results. Phelps (1998) summarized the results of more than 50 public opinion polls on topics related to educational assessment and testing, and concluded that the general public, civic leaders, state administrators, parents, and students generally thought that education would improve if there were more testing. Local administrators and principals generally thought that the current amount of testing was about right. Interestingly, results for teachers were inconclusive, with some teachers thinking that education would improve if there was less testing, some thinking that the current amount was about right, and some thinking, like the general public, that more testing was needed in education. Phelps (1998) also reported that the general public, civic leaders, parents, students, and teachers believed that education would improve if there were higher student stakes in testing, with only principals indicating that the current level of stakes was fine. Phelps (2005) indicated the public's attitudes about testing in education have remained generally stable, even though some of the political messaging has changed over time.

INFLUENCING PERCEPTIONS

As noted at the outset of this chapter, public perceptions about assessment are largely driven by individuals' own experiences with assessment and intuitive test theory (Braun & Mislevy, 2005). Changing those perceptions requires a concerted effort to develop assessment literacy about the benefits and limitations of using assessment information for various purposes. Although a multifaceted approach is needed, there is potentially a greater cost-benefit opportunity to influence public perceptions by prioritizing future members of the public (i.e., schoolchildren) while supplementing these efforts with outreach to adult stakeholder groups.

Educator Assessment Literacy as a Lever

Students' experiences with educational assessments represent both early-in-life and frequent opportunities to support positive, appropriate uses of assessment. Educators play a critical role for transferring knowledge and developing learning habits. Specifically, teachers engage with students and parents; administrators engage with teachers, policy makers, and the public. Therefore, educators serve as key collaborators in helping to communicate and support appropriate assessment practices to the public through their interaction with students. On a long-term basis, informing public perceptions of assessment depends on ensuring teachers have appropriate perceptions and practices themselves, so that students have appropriate experiences to counteract intuitive theories of assessment. With assessment being an integrated component of an educational system, it is important that educators contribute to outreach efforts because we expect that the public's knowledge will be even more limited.

However, to be able to engage educators, it is important to know what professional expectations form the basis of assessment literacy and evidence of where these needs may be greatest. Within the measurement community, the primary set of guidelines for practice are found in the *Standards for Educational and Psychological Testing* (American Educational Research Association, American Psychological Association, & National Council on Measurement in Education, 2014). Having been updated periodically for decades, these expectations for test developers, test takers, and test users provide guidance about test development and validation activities. The extension of these expectations to classroom educators, though, has been less widely disseminated with respect to raising awareness of measurement principles.

Earlier efforts to respond to the perceived gap between the testing industry standards and educators involved a collaboration that produced the *Standards for Teacher Competence in Educational Assessment of Students* (American Federation of Teachers, National Council on Measurement in Education, & National Education Association, 1990). The goals of the organizations in producing this document were to (a) provide guidance for teacher education programs, (b) serve as a self-assessment guide for teachers, (c) serve as a guide for workshop instructors, and (d) act as a call to think about student assessment more broadly than its historical treatment. Although not widely known, these recommendations continue to provide a concise summary of expectations for educators as they relate to student assessment. The seven standards are:

1. Teachers should be skilled in *choosing* assessment methods appropriate for instructional decisions.
2. Teachers should be skilled in *developing* assessment methods appropriate for instructional decisions.
3. The teacher should be skilled in administering, scoring, and interpreting the results of both externally produced and teacher-produced assessment methods.
4. Teachers should be skilled in using assessment results when making decisions about individual students, planning teaching, developing curriculum, and school improvement.
5. Teachers should be skilled in developing valid pupil grading procedures that use pupil assessments.
6. Teachers should be skilled in communicating assessment results to students, parents, other lay audiences, and other educators.
7. Teachers should be skilled in recognizing unethical, illegal, and otherwise inappropriate assessment methods and uses of assessment information.

The application of formal measurement principles to classroom assessment has also been discussed along with some innovative strategies to apply them in ways that are more reasonable for the intended population of users. Specifically, as part of a special issue on the topic, Brookhart (2003) suggested rethinking the thought processes that had begun with psychometric theory and then attempting to modify or transfer such principles into the classroom. Rather, she suggested starting with assessment development in the classroom itself, focusing on how information is dynamically used as part of instruction. Under this model, some of the core principles of validity and reliability still have meaning, but how they manifest and are interpreted will appear unfamiliar to researchers and practitioners who may not be as comprehensive in their thinking about the practice. Similarly, Smith's (2003) discussion of how we may reform interpretation of reliability in the classroom is particularly interesting because many of the psychometric calculations and statistics that the field uses to evaluate assessment characteristics have limited use for a classroom teacher. He suggested instead a concept of sufficiency of information as a reasonable proxy for more traditional calculations of reliability.

More recently, the Joint Committee on Standards for Educational Evaluation (2003) developed classroom-level expectations for student assessment, and this has done more to integrate classroom practice with measurement principles. Specifically, these *Classroom Assessment Standards for PreK–12 Teachers* (Klinger et al., 2015) bring the concepts of validity, reliability, and fairness into a classroom setting with a focus on foundational measurement principles and appropriate assessment use.

Although it is convenient to suggest that the general public does not have a sufficient understanding of assessment, unfortunately this dearth of knowledge often extends to educators themselves (Wainer et al., 1999; Hambleton & Slater, 1997; Linn & Dunbar, 1992; Impara et al., 1991). Observing a trend, educator preparation programs have consistently focused on developing content and pedagogical abilities, but have fallen short in the incubation of knowledge about assessment (see more in Hill & Eyers, this volume). For example, Plake et al. (1993) discussed levels of training and experience with assessment among teachers, reporting that administrators tended to have more knowledge about characteristics of assessment and that they generally received more training on the topic. In response to these findings, Impara and Plake (1996) suggested a training framework for student assessment for administrators. A review of the matrix of knowledge, skills, and abilities in this framework suggests that many of the expectations could be extended to teachers, too.

The purpose of highlighting these challenges to assessment literacy among educators is to reinforce the importance of their role as key outreach messengers for informing public perceptions about appropriate assessment practices. As highlighted in this chapter, members of the public often rely on their past experiences to intuitively form perceptions about assessment and related policy. Therefore, it is important that additional outreach efforts occur to help the public understand fundamentals of measurement. With an opportunity to engage with a large segment of the population over a period of time, teachers are a logical option for (a) helping better explain assessments to students and parents and (b) helping students and parents interpret and use results. However, literature suggests that many teachers struggle to do this because they lack the training and support to understand and implement this in practice (Brown, 2004). Complicating our ability to evaluate and respond to the challenge, Gotch and French (2014) explored the availability of instruments and resources that could be used to measure assessment literacy among educators and concluded that evidence to support the use of any of the 36 instruments was weak. Further, they recommended additional efforts to define and evaluate effective measures given the connection of teacher effectiveness to student achievement, especially intertwined in the RTTT education policy. Clearly, if we expect teachers to be more effective in their efforts, we should be able to appropriately define the underlying constructs that contribute to the meaning of effectiveness.

Influence of Assessment Literacy on Public Perceptions

Given the American devolution of control of education to the local level within states, efforts have been made to systematically support the development of assessment literacy among educators and administrators. This is normally done through higher education and in-service training programs (Roschewski, 2004; Roschewski et al., 2001). As part of this devolved system, local school districts assume responsibility for development of assessment systems that are used locally, but reported at the state level. Due to the variability of the assessments across districts, one state sought to develop a strategy that would provide some evidence about the technical quality of the assessments to mitigate interpretation of the results. Buckendahl et al. (2004) described how this information was incorporated into the resulting accountability system. This system represented an attempt to communicate basic measurement principles to the public as they evaluated the performance of their local assessment system.

The technical quality that districts were asked to demonstrate is described in greater detail in Plake et al. (2004). However, at a summary level, districts were required to provide evidence of how their assessments aligned with the state's academic content standards; gave students opportunity to learn prior to assessment; reviewed bias and sensitivity; leveled appropriate, determined reliability of scores and/or scorers; and based achievement levels on appropriate practice. These factors were included in district reports made available publicly in online and print versions to provide the public some assurance of external quality control of the local systems that were being developed and used to report student performance.

Because most of these topics were not part of preservice education for most educators, different strategies were implemented to facilitate the development of necessary assessment literacy for teacher and administrators over multiple years. Some of these efforts are described in Lukin et al. (2004), along with evaluation research suggesting that there was a relationship between professional development in assessment literacy and improvement in student achievement. Brookhart (2005) also conducted an external evaluation of this assessment and accountability system, concluding that the combination of activities contributed to generally raising the level of assessment literacy in the state. Further, it spurred conversations about additional professional development activities related to assessment development and validation. One of the outcomes of these efforts on public perceptions was that teachers and administrators were better able to communicate to members of their local constituencies (e.g., parents, school board members, public) about assessment concepts and how they aligned with local curriculum and instructional efforts.

Role of the Media as a Lever

The measurement community, along with media sources, plays a key role in helping to communicate appropriate information to the public. Assessment information can be communicated through a variety of sources. Students receive formal and informal feedback from teachers; parents may receive similar feedback from teachers and administrators. However, the public may receive more information from popular media sources that also influences their perceptions. Media has become a more competitive environment with the advent of the Internet as additional outlets are available to consumers. As a result, traditional sources such as newspapers, periodicals, and television are being supplemented and in some instances supplanted through digital sources and social media. This can increase the challenge of accurately communicating information because there are more sources that yield competing information without uniform quality control mechanisms.

Murphy (2013) highlighted this idea as part of a special issue on public understanding of assessment. Specifically, he discussed how the media in the United Kingdom reported the national examination results for secondary students and, in particular, how changes to technical aspects were interpreted and reported. In response to this coverage, he suggested strategies that practitioners and educators might be able to use in helping media outlets understand some of these assessment literacy principles and, thus, assist with communication. Similarly, Chamberlain (2013) also offered recommendations for communicating assessment information, drawing from disciplines that have also been challenged in transferring technical concepts into lay language.

Further illustrating this point, one of the more contentious topics over the last couple of decades in the United States is the use of achievement levels for purposes of communicating students' abilities. Buckendahl et al. (2009), through a series of studies, explored the use of achievement levels on the NAEP in the United States. In these studies, evaluators explored how achievement levels were developed relative to industry standards, the value to the public, and how the use of such levels was analogous to numerous policy decisions that were widely developed and used. Given the diversity of the audience, a focus on developing some modicum of assessment literacy was inherent in the effort to produce a report that could be valuable to policy makers.

Another recent example that highlights how the media represents assessment can be found in Foley et al. (2013). In this short documentary of compiled video clips about testing, they highlighted how movies and television have portrayed tests and aspects of testing over the past few decades. Common themes observed in these popular sources of media were the consequences of testing, test anxiety, criticisms of testing, test preparation, and cheating. The author-producers used these examples to highlight what the public will be most aware of and as a starting point for further discussion about appropriate practice.

Role of Psychometric Community as a Lever

I am concerned about the increasing gap between theoreticians and practitioners in terms of fundamental understanding of how to communicate principles of assessment literacy to lay audiences. Hattie and Brown (2010) reinforce this point in the context of educational systems. This work illustrates a broader perspective of communicating assessment results that also considers much of the work about stakeholders', including educators', understandings of score reports (Hambleton & Slater, 1997; Hattie, 2010; Wainer et al., 1999; Zenisky et al. 2014; Zenisky & Hambleton, 2012).

Paraphrasing Robert Louis Stevenson, we are reminded that there are no foreign lands, only travelers who are foreign. It is naïve to expect the public to somehow become interested in technical aspects of assessment to the breadth and depth of psychometricians. However, because the public does care about education, particularly for their own children, if we want them to care at least a little more about what we are communicating, it will take concerted outreach that uses language that is familiar to a broader constituency. As such, I am recommending that outreach efforts for communicating assessment literacy concepts to the public be framed around the following three core principles: accuracy, consistency, and fairness. Each of these is briefly defined here using language that may be more palatable to the public and could be used as a starting point.

- *Accuracy*—assessment questions, tasks, and scoring expectations target the breadth and depth of the learning objectives.
- *Consistency*—assessment scores and decisions have an acceptably low margin of error.
- *Fairness*—students have equivalent opportunities to learn and demonstrate their abilities.

Although simplistic, when explaining assessment to the public, it is reasonable to think that we could characterize key phases of development and validation in these areas. Some readers may interpret this suggested framework as nuanced semantics in that one may be tempted to substitute the more technical language of validity and reliability for accuracy and consistency. However, in using the language of the profession, we will then be obligated to translate it into more accessible terminology. Newton (2013) highlights this point by illustrating how the myriad of ways the profession characterizes validity (e.g., content, criterion, face, procedural) has been less than helpful in appropriately communicating a concept that is central to assessment. While the profession continues to work to get its house in order, the public continues to move forward as consumers, critics, and policy makers who will continue to co-opt assessment information for appropriate, and frequently inappropriate, uses.

CONCLUSION

As noted throughout this chapter, the public have been exposed to assessment as part of educational and workforce systems for many years and have been generally supportive of the use of assessments to inform decisions when they believe that the systems are fair in comparison with alternative models. However, these perceptions are based on an intuitive understanding of basic measurement principles that may not be based on the science of testing. As a result, the opportunity for misperceptions and misinterpretation is high. Further, when communicated in the media, there can be more instances where intuitive perceptions of the public are reinforced, rather than corrected. Therefore, we can see growing opportunities for developing assessment literacy among members of the public.

In responding to this need, the measurement community will need to take a multilevel approach. There is a current population of stakeholders who would benefit from some of the proactive strategies discussed in the literature regarding framing arguments and evidence using terminology that is more accessible to a broader audience. Concurrently, there is an opportunity for self-assessment within the field to ensure that there is reasonable consensus on what concepts are important and how we can better demonstrate value to the public, beyond a theoretical need. Although we can include current members of the public in outreach efforts, it is the future generations of the public that would seemingly benefit from assessment literacy development.

From an efficiency perspective, educators arguably have the best opportunity to effect change in assessment literacy knowledge through their widespread interactions with students, parents, and communities. To help the public move beyond intuitive perceptions about assessments, we need to engage with members of the public earlier than we currently do at present.

REFERENCES

American Educational Research Association, American Psychological Association, & National Council on Measurement in Education. (2014). *Standards for educational and psychological testing.* Washington, DC: American Educational Research Association.

American Federation of Teachers, National Council on Measurement in Education, and National Education Association. (1990). *Standards for teacher competence in educational assessment of students.* Washington, DC: Authors.

Braun, H., & Mislevy, R. (2005). Intuitive test theory. *Phil Delta Kappan, 86,* 488–497.

Broder, D. S. (2007, March 22). Battling the 'No Child' backlash. *The Washington Post.* Retrieved from http://www.washingtonpost.com/wp-dyn/content/article/2007/03/21/AR2007032101785.html

Brookhart, S. M. (2003). Development measurement theory for classroom assessment purposes and uses. *Educational Measurement: Issues and Practice, 22*(4), 5–12.

Brookhart, S. M. (2005). The quality of local district assessments used in Nebraska's school-based teacher-led assessment and reporting system (STARS). *Educational Measurement: Issues and Practice, 24*(2), 14–21.

Brookhart, S. M. (2013). The public understanding of assessment in educational reform in the United States. *Oxford Review of Education, 39*(1), 52–71.

Brown, G.T.L. (2004). Teachers' conceptions of assessment: Implications for policy and professional development. *Assessment in Education, 11*(3), 301–318.

Buckendahl, C. W., Davis, S. L., Plake, B. S., Sireci, S. G., Zenisky, A., Hambleton, R. K., Wells, C. S., & Keller, L. (2009). *Evaluation of the National Assessment of Educational Progress: Final Report.* Washington, DC: U.S. Department of Education.

Buckendahl, C. W., Plake, B. S., & Impara, J. C. (2004). A strategy for evaluating district developed assessment for state accountability. *Educational Measurement: Issues and Practice, 23*(2), 17–25.

Bushaw, W. J., & Calderon, V. J. (2014). Try it again, Uncle Sam: The 46th annual PDK/Gallup Poll of the public's attitudes toward the public schools. *Kappan, 96*, 9–20.

Califano, Jr. J. A. (1991). *The triumph and tragedy of Lyndon Johnson: The white house years.* New York: Simon & Schuster.

Cannell, J. J. (1988). *How public educators cheat on standardized achievement tests: The "Lake Wobegon" report.* Albuquerque, NM: Friends for Education.

Chamberlain, S. (2013). Communication strategies for enhancing qualification users' understanding of educational assessment: Recommendations from other public interest fields. *Oxford Review of Education, 39*(1), 114–127.

Cillizza, C. (2013, January 17). A cool diagram of the 113th Congress. *The Washington Post.* Retrieved from http://www.washingtonpost.com/blogs/the-fix/wp/2013/01/17/an-awesome-diagram-of-the-113th-congress

Crocker, L. (2003). Teaching for the test: Validity, fairness, and moral action. *Educational Measurement: Issues and Practice, 22*(3), 5–11.

Davis, S. L., & Buckendahl, C. W. (April, 2007). *Evaluating NCLB's peer review process: A comparison of state compliance decisions.* Paper presented at that annual meeting of the National Council on Measurement in Education. Chicago, IL.

DuBois, P. H. (1970). *A history of psychological testing.* Boston, MA: Allyn & Bacon.

Elam, S. (1995). *How America views its schools: The PDK/Gallup Polls, 1969–1994.* Bloomington, IN: Phi Delta Kappa Educational Foundation.

Fairtest (2007, August 28). How standardized testing damages education. Retrieved June 13, 2015 from http://fairtest.org/how-standardized-testing-damages-education-pdf

Foley, B. P., Dwyer, A. C., Chuah, D., & Rawls, A. (2013). Testing in the movies and on the internet. Retrieved from https://www.youtube.com/watch?v=4hDEbVE_-Yc

Gilmore, A. (1998). *Assessment for success in primary schools: Report of the submissions to the green paper (Report for the Ministry of Education).* Christchurch, NZ: University of Canterbury.

Gotch, C., & French, B. (2014). A systematic review of assessment literacy measures. *Educational Measurement: Issues and Practice, 33*(2), 14–18.

Hambleton, R. K., & Slater, S. C. (1997). *Are NAEP executive summary reports understandable to policy makers and educators?* Los Angeles, CA: National Center for Research on Evaluation, Standards, and Student Testing. Graduate School of Education & Information Studies, University of California.

Harris, L. (April, 2015). *Reviewing research on parent attitudes towards school assessment: Implications for classroom assessment practices.* Paper presented at the annual meeting of the American Educational Research Association. Chicago, IL.

Hattie, J.A.C. (2010). Visibly learning from reports: The validity of score reports. *Online Educational Research Journal,* 1–15. Retrieved from http://www.oerj.org/View?action=viewPaper&paper=6.

Hattie, J. A., & Brown, G.T.L. (2010). Assessment and evaluation. In C. Rubie-Davies (Ed.), *Educational psychology: Concepts, research and challenges* (pp. 102–117). Abingdon, UK: Routledge.

Hayes, W. (2006). *Horace Mann's vision of the public schools: Is it still relevant?* Lanham, MD: Rowman & Littlefield Education.

Howard, A. (2015, April 3). What is the big difference between PARCC and Smarter Balanced? Retrieved from: http://blog.wowzers.com/what-is-the-big-difference-between-parcc-and-smarter-balanced.

Howard, A.E.D. (1998). *Magna Carta: Text and commentary.* Charlottesville, VA: The University of Virginia Press.

Impara, J. C., Divine, K. P., Bruce, F. A., Liverman, M. R., & Gay, A. (1991). Does interpretive test score information help teachers? *Educational Measurement: Issues and Practice, 10*(4), 16–18.

Impara, J. C., & Plake, B. S. (1996). Professional development in student assessment for educational administrators: An instructional framework. *Educational Measurement: Issues and Practice, 15*(2), 14–19.

Jennings, J. (2012, December 23). The fundamental flaws of 'value added' teacher evaluation. *The Washington Post.* Retrieved from http://www.washingtonpost.com/blogs/answer-sheet/wp/2012/12/23/the-fundamental-flaws-of-value-added-teacher-evaluation/.

Joint Committee on Standards for Educational Evaluation. (2003). *The student evaluation standards: How to improve evaluations of students.* Thousand Oaks, CA: Corwin Press.

Jones, L. V., & Olkin, I. (2004). *The nation's report card: Evolution and perspectives.* Bloomington, IN: Phi Delta Kappa Educational Foundation and American Educational Research Association.

Klinger, D., McDivitt, P., Howard, B., Munoz, M., Rodgers, T., & Wylie, C. (2015). *Classroom assessment standards for PreK-12 teachers.* Joint Committee on Standards for Educational Evaluation.

Layton, L. (2014, October 15). School standardized testing is under growing attack, leaders pledge change. *The Washington Post.* Retrieved from https://www.washingtonpost.com/local/education/school-standard ized-testing-is-under-growing-attack-leaders-pledge-changes/2014/10/15/bd1201b8–549b-11e4-ba4b-f6333e2c0453_story.html?wprss=rss_education

Linn, R. L. (2003). Accountability: Responsibility and reasonable expectations. *Educational Researcher, 32*(7), 3–13.

Linn, R. L., & Dunbar, S. B. (1992). Issues in the design and reporting of the National Assessment of Educational Progress. *Journal of Educational Measurement, 29*(2), 177–194.

Lukin, L. E., Bandalos, D. L., Eckhout, T., & Mickelson, K. (2004). Facilitating the development of assessment literacy. *Educational Measurement: Issues and Practice, 23*(2), 26–32.

Maxwell, L. A. (2015, June 27). Test experts wary on 'Race to the Top' rules. *Education Week.* Retrieved from http://www.edweek.org/ew/articles/2009/10/08/07academies.h29.html

Murphy, R. (2013). Media roles in influencing the public understanding of educational assessment issues. *Oxford Review in Education, 39*(1), 139–150.

National Commission on Excellence in Education. (1983). *A nation at risk: The imperative for educational reform.* Washington, DC: United States Department of Education.

Newton, P. E. (February 4, 2013). Does it matter what 'validity' means? Seminar presented at the University of Oxford, Department of Education. Oxford, U.K.

Parsons, T., Howe, S. G., & Neale, R. H. (1845). Reports of the annual examining committee of the Boston grammar and writing schools. *The Common School Journal, 8,* 287–306.

Phelps. R. (1998). The demand for standardized student testing. *Educational Measurement: Issues and Practice, 17*(3), 5–23.

Phelps, R. (2005). Persistently positive: Forty years of public opinion on standardized testing. In R. Phelps (Ed.), *Defending standardized testing* (pp. 1–22). Mahwah, NJ: Erlbaum.

Phelps, R. P. (2009). Educational achievement testing: Critiques and rebuttals. In R. P. Phelps (Ed.), *Correcting fallacies about educational and psychological testing* (pp. 89–146). Washington, DC: American Psychological Association.

Plake, B. S., Impara, J. C., & Buckendahl, C. W. (2004). Technical quality criteria for evaluating district assessment portfolios used in the Nebraska STARS. *Educational Measurement: Issues and Practice, 23*(2), 12–16.

Plake, B. S., Impara, J. C., & Fager, J. J. (1993). Assessment competencies of teachers: A national survey. *Educational Measurement: Issues and Practice, 12*(4), 10–12.

Rawls, J. (1971). *A theory of justice.* Cambridge, MA: President and Fellows of Harvard College.

Roschewski, P. (2004). History and background of Nebraska's school-based teacher-led assessment and reporting system (STARS). *Educational Measurement: Issues and Practice, 23*(2), 9–11.

Roschewski, P., Gallagher, C., & Isernhagen, J. (2001). Nebraskans reach for the STARS. *Phi Delta Kappan, 82,* 611–615.

Smith, J. K. (2003). Reconsidering reliability in classroom assessment. *Educational Measurement: Issues and Practice, 22*(4), 26–33.

Smith, M. L., & Rottenberg, C. (1991). Unintended consequences of external testing in elementary schools. *Educational Measurement: Issues and Practice, 10,* 7–11.

Timm, J. C. (2014, April 4). *States mull dropping Common Core.* Retrieved June 19, 2015 from http://www.msnbc.com/morning-joe/states-mull-dropping-common-core.

United States Congress. (1965). *Elementary and Secondary Education Act of 1965.* Pub. L. 89–10.

United States Congress. (2002). *No Child Left Behind Act of 2001.* Pub. L. 107–110.

United States Congress. (2009). *American Recovery and Reinvestment Act of 2009.* Pub. L. 111–5.

Wainer, H., Hambleton, R. K., & Meara, K. (1999). Alternative displays for communicating NAEP results: A redesign and validity study. *Journal of Educational Measurement, 36*(4), 301–335.

White, E. (1981, September 28). Reagan weighing much deeper education cuts and faster dismantling of federal department. *Education Week.* Retrieved from http://www.edweek.org/ew/articles/1981/09/28/01040069.h01.html

Wise, L. L., Hauser, R. M., Mitchell, K. J., & Feuer, M. J. (1998). *Evaluation of the voluntary national tests: Phase I.* Washington, DC: Washington Academy Press.

Zenisky, A. L., & Hambleton, R. K. (2012). Developing test score reports that work: The process and best practices for effective communication. *Educational Measurement: Issues and Practice, 31*(2), 21–26.

Zenisky, A. L., van den Heuvel, J. R., Davis-Becker, S., & Buckendahl, C. W. (July, 2014). *International perspectives on score reporting in credentialing: Best practices for providing meaningful feedback to examinees.* Paper presented at the bi-annual meeting of the International Test Commission. San Sebastian, Spain.

27

COMPUTERISING ASSESSMENT

Impacts on Education Stakeholders

Irvin R. Katz and Joanna S. Gorin

In any review of the literature on technology and assessment, it becomes clear that the primary perspective represented has been that of the test maker rather than the test taker. Around the turn of the 21st century, multiple papers were published that documented the growing presence of technology in educational measurement and predicted many of the impacts that we see today (Bennett, 2002; Embretson & Hershberger, 1999; Frederiksen, Mislevy, & Bejar, 1993; Mislevy, 1997). In looking at large-scale testing programs across the globe, it is difficult to identify steps in the assessment development, delivery, and scoring process that have not been affected by computers, to a greater or lesser extent. Bartram and Hambleton (2006) highlighted four test-maker-oriented themes that defined the role of computer-based testing: new test designs, item selection algorithms, exposure control issues and methods, and new tests that leverage the unique capabilities of the technology. These authors' works provide ample evidence that technology has impacted both practical (e.g., cost, logistics, scaling) and psychometric concerns, but there is less information on the effects of new technologies on examinees', and other stakeholders', experiences with computerised assessment.

This focus on stakeholders is a key validity concern. Technology introduced into assessment may affect some examinees differently than others owing to their experiences with technology. Technology may impact the nature of the inferences that stakeholders may draw about examinees. Thus, the field must also consider issues concerning the human element of technology introduction: What are the reactions of examinees or other education stakeholders? Do new assessment technologies affect all examinees equally? To what extent do the new technologies affect the construct being assessed and the inferences that can be made about examinees based on the assessment? These types of questions move the focus of research about technology and assessment toward the people who take assessments (e.g., students) and those who use assessment results.

In this chapter, we explore the evolving impact of technology on educational assessment. Such a broad topic requires some scoping, and consistent with the goals of this handbook and the questions outlined above, we focus on the influences of digital technology that are most visible to education stakeholders—students and other examinees, parents, teachers, and administrators. We take a somewhat chronological approach to discussing the growing presence of technology in assessment, focusing primarily, although not exclusively, on the trends apparent in compulsory and university assessment in the United States. We begin in the 1960s, when technology changed the nature of the scores that could be reported for traditional, dichotomously scored (e.g., multiple choice) paper-and-pencil tests as a result of advances in computationally intensive psychometric models. These models allowed for efficient estimation of abilities (and shorter test-taking time) through computer-adaptive testing. The larger political movement toward performance assessment in the 1990s brought increased use of automatic scoring of essays and, in the 2000s, interactive performance assessments that allowed content and interactions not feasible without digital technology (e.g., viewing the inside of a volcano), and automated scoring that incorporated evidence of solution procedures. We conclude with a look toward the future, discussing examples of current research on assessment technology that expands (a) the range of assessment contexts (games, conversations) experienced by examinees and (b) the types of evidence collected (interactive action logs) about examinees' knowledge and skills.

PSYCHOMETRIC MODELLING

One might be surprised that the impact of technology on educational assessment was most profound prior to any test being administered via computer. Even when tests were still administered via paper and pencil, technology enhanced measurement via the scoring of test responses with new, computationally demanding statistical models.

Classical test theory (CTT), the dominant measurement theory for most of the 20th century, used relatively simple mathematics to estimate test statistics, including item statistics, reliability coefficients, and individual examinee scores (Lord, Novick, & Birnbaum, 1968). With increased computational capacity in the 1970s, new possibilities arose for item response theory (IRT), also called latent trait theory, which offered an (albeit computationally demanding) alternative to CTT for issues such as examining (a) the relationship of item responses with the underlying construct, (b) the information provided by items about the construct, and (c) the presence of group differences in item responses (Steinberg & Thissen, 1996).

From the perspective of an examinee or other stakeholder reading a score report, the movement away from CTT—and 'number correct' scoring—must have been confusing. Some stakeholders have difficulty understanding fundamental testing concepts (e.g., score distribution, measurement error) represented in score reports (Hambleton & Slater, 1997; Jaeger, 2003; Zapata-River & Katz, 2014), let alone the complexity inherent in IRT-based scoring. A test score under IRT depends on the statistical qualities of the constituent items. As such, there is not a straightforward (from a lay perspective) relationship between performance on a test and one's score. While IRT improved measurement and evidence by moving from scores reflecting performance on a particular test to a scale meant to reflect underlying ability, it might have done so at the cost of transparency in how easily stakeholders, who are not testing professionals, understand test performance in test scores.

On the other hand, IRT was only the first of many computation-intensive psychometric models that are in use today and that provide education stakeholders with assessment information beyond test scores. These models allow for diagnostic assessment and modelling, providing finer-grained estimates of ability at the subskill level rather than scores on a one-dimensional scale. Approaches such as Tatsuoka's RuleSpace model (Tatsuoka, 1990), Leighton and Gierl's Attribute Hierarchy Method (Leighton, Gierl, & Hunka, 2004), and other cognitive diagnostic assessment approaches (see Leighton & Gierl, 2007) give feedback to examinees on specific strengths and weaknesses within a construct, such as misconceptions in solving linear equations (Birenbaum, Kelly, & Tatsuoka, 1992) or difficulties in responding to analytic versus design-oriented architectural figural response tasks (Katz, Martinez, Sheehan, & Tatsuoka, 1998). More recently, the NetPass assessment of CISCO Systems uses Bayesian Inference Networks to score the actions taken (and results obtained) as candidates design networks or troubleshoot provided networks (Williamson, Bauer, Steinberg, Mislevy, Behrens, & DeMark, 2004). Although these models might be just as impenetrable as IRT to most education stakeholders, they have the benefit of changing the nature of the assessment information given to education stakeholders, providing a stronger evidentiary basis for drawing inferences about examinee abilities.

EARLY COMPUTER-BASED TESTING

While the increased computational power had the greatest impact on psychometric modelling and scoring, it is examinees' increased access to computers that has allowed for computer-based test administration. In its earliest form, computer-based tests were merely digital versions of the same multiple-choice (or simple constructed response) tests administered on paper. Nevertheless, one cannot assume that even a 'simple' multiple-choice test can be put onto computer without impact on examinees. For example, people differ in their familiarity and comfort with using computers, perhaps owing to differences in their experience with computers (both positive and negative) and opportunities to use digital technology (McDonald, 2002). Although people throughout the world, from a greater variety of backgrounds and circumstances, are increasingly familiar with technology (Organisation for Economic Cooperation and Development [OECD], 2013), there exist persistent differences in technology familiarity based on demographic factors such as age and socioeconomic background. For example, although 59% of U.S. citizens aged 65 and older reported going online in 2013, an increase from 14% in 2000, that number still lags the 86% of all adults in the U.S. who reported going online in 2013 (Pew Research Center, 2014). Because of these differences in familiarity with computers, some examinees might experience difficulties, confusion, or anxiety (McDonald, 2002) when completing computer-based assessments compared with the more familiar paper-and-pencil assessments.

There are many 'comparability studies' comparing paper and computer versions of traditional assessments; see meta-analyses by Mead and Drasgow (1993) and Wang, Jiao, Young, Brooks, and Olson (2008) and reviews by Leeson (2006), Lottridge, Nicewander, Schulz, and Mitzel (2010), Noyes and Garland (2008), and Paek (2005). Research has demonstrated few consistent differences in examinees' performance between paper and computer versions of traditional assessments. The most consistent mode effects (differences between paper and computer versions) are for speeded tests and for tests having long reading passages that require scrolling on computer. Interestingly, both of these results relate to differences in the *user interface* of the computer test (i.e., what examinees see on the computer and how they interact with it). For example, regarding possible reasons for mode effects on speeded tests, Mead and Drasgow (1993) suggest that these effects occur because "Reading from a piece of paper and using a pencil to fill a bubble on another piece of paper evidently constitute different motor activities than reading from a monitor and pressing a key" (Mead & Drasgow, 1993, p. 453). In other work, user interface issues such as screen size or resolution, the need to scroll through reading comprehension passages, and characteristics of text led to difficulties for some examinees (Bridgeman, Lennon, & Jackenthal, 2003; Leeson, 2006; Noyes & Garland, 2008).

Thus, beyond coarse-grain comparisons of paper versus computer assessments, it is important to consider the examinees' likely reaction to and skill with using the computer-based assessment. A few researchers address this issue by investigating whether mode effects are moderated by measures of computer familiarity (Powers & O'Neill, 1993; Taylor et al., 1999). For multiple-choice tests, computer familiarity is only an inconsistent moderator of mode effects, possibly due to the wide range of computer-familiarity measures used. For example, Taylor, Kirsch, Jamieson, and Eignor (1999) systematically created a computer familiarity measure, first investigating its validity before using it as a moderator. In contrast, Powers and O'Neill (1993) used a few self-report questions to gauge computer familiarity. Interestingly, even examinees with less computer familiarity appear to adapt quickly to the computer-based testing mode after some tutorials (Powers & O'Neill, 1993).

COMPUTER ADAPTIVE TESTING

With the feasibility of IRT estimation offered by increased computational power, as well as advances in other computational systems, it became possible to move away from straightforward adaptations of paper tests to computer delivery. Instead of linear testing, it became possible to adapt the items presented in a test based on the examinee's performance. Computer adaptive testing (CAT) improved the quality of the evidence collected. This advance not only helped strengthen the reliability and validity of education stakeholders' score interpretations, but also changed the testing experience for the examinee.

In general, CAT works as follows. After an examinee responds to an item, an estimation algorithm calculates the ability estimate for that individual. Based on that estimate, an item is selected that provides maximal discrimination at the examinee's ability level (i.e., an item that would best help refine the ability estimate, one that is neither too difficult nor too easy for examinees at this ability level). This process continues until an estimate is reached with a prescribed level of accuracy or a pre-specified number of items have been administered. Computerised adaptive tests yield highly accurate examinee ability estimates with relative efficiency (van der Linden, 2005); CAT allows for an accurate ability estimate after administering only a small number of items.

How does CAT affect examinees? CAT may increase examinee engagement in testing. There is reason to believe that when students are given test questions that are either too hard or too easy their engagement decreases, as does their effort, resulting in performance that reflects effort as opposed to ability (Wise & DeMars, 2006). Further, the shortened testing time allowed by CAT can help to avoid fatigue or other unintended sources of variance that may reduce the validity of score interpretations. To date, the adaptation to examinees is primarily based on the match between item difficulty and examinee ability (i.e., maximise statistical information). However, increases in the amount and type of information gathered in real time (during assessment administration), such as variables reflecting student engagement and interest, might allow for a greater range of adaptations.

PERFORMANCE ASSESSMENT USING ESSAYS

Around the 1990s, there was significant concern that assessments composed solely of forced-choice item types (i.e., multiple-choice questions) were limited in their ability to measure more complex cognitive processes. A movement towards more 'performance assessment' began, for which the use of extended constructed responses in the form of essays (or other types of performances as discussed later in this chapter) became increasingly demanded for large scale assessment. The rationale for essay items was that they provided better evidence of the writing skills and complex reasoning that were the focus of many assessment claims.

No doubt students' reactions to taking an essay assessment on computer have changed significantly over the years, as word processing and other software have become familiar even to students at the primary school level (Paek, 2005). When such computer-based tests were first introduced, composing on computer was rare and many students did not have any experience with word processing software, grammar or spelling checkers, and other support that technology can bring to writing. The novelty of writing on computer, along with the availability of spell checkers, was sometimes viewed favourably by students (Wolfe, Bolton, Feltovich, & Welch, 1993). Nevertheless, often students performed better on paper (Yu, Livingston, Larkin, & Bonett, 2004) than on computer. However, some of those results might have been due to a bias of human raters to assign higher scores to handwritten essays compared with typed essays (Powers, Fowles, Farnum, & Ramsey, 1994). Unless rater training counteracts these effects, raters sometimes give higher scores to handwritten essays because (a) the handwritten essays appear longer, (b) the raters are more likely to excuse handwritten spelling or punctuation errors, or (c) the typed essays appear more polished and so are (inadvertently) held to a higher standard (Way, Vickers, & Nichols, 2008).

As noted earlier, comparability studies differ in the care taken in measuring examinee factors such as computer familiarity or technical skill. For example, in a large ($N \approx 400$) international study of International English Language Testing System (IELTS) essay tasks, students responded to essay prompts on paper and on computer. No discernible differences were observed between essays written on paper and essays written on computer. The researchers included a set of questions about computer familiarity, and only two of the questions appeared to interact with testing mode (Wier, O'Sullivan, Yan, & Bax, 2007). On the other hand, Horkay, Bennett, Allen, Kaplan, and Yan (2006) used a direct measure of computer skill, asking students to complete a set of typing and editing tasks. The researchers compared performance on the computer task as a function of typing and editing skill, after controlling for performance on the writing task, and observed that students with better computer skills performed better on the computer-based writing tasks.

AUTOMATED SCORING OF ESSAYS

No matter how well defined the construct, or well-constructed the task, if the scoring is not reliable, valid, cost-effective, and sufficiently rapid, the instructional utility of the assessment scores is limited. Currently, however, in the United States, most (if not all) state writing and reading assessments now include various types of constructed response items. This condition has been facilitated by technological advances that support automated scoring of essays (Shermis & Burstein, 2013) by systems such as *e-rater*® (Burstein, Tetreault, & Madnani, 2013), Intelligent Essay Assessor™ (Foltz, Laham, & Landauer, 1999), and LightSIDE (Mayfield & Rosé, 2013). A growing literature (Shermis & Burstein [2013] provide an overview) and recent controlled evaluations of automated scoring systems from leading vendors (Shermis & Hamner, 2012) have documented that automated scoring systems often achieve comparable reliability to human raters for extended constructed response items, such as essays, although the automated systems may not yet fully cover all aspects of the construct targeted by the assessment.

Automated scoring offers a cost-effective, time-saving solution to several of the challenges associated with scoring extended reading and writing constructed-responses. Though the focus on much of their use has been on summative assessment, where the demands on precision and accuracy are the priority, they potentially offer more utility in lower-stakes contexts, such as classroom and formative assessments, where the emphasis is on instructionally relevant feedback on process rather than status. Through the use of automated tutoring systems, computer-based classroom reading and writing exercises, and possibly simulation-based assessment, automated scoring engines can be used to provide meaningful feedback to students about their writing and to teachers about their instructional effectiveness (Graesser, Hu, & Person, 2001; McNamara, Levinstein, & Boonthum, 2004). However, there are still limits to the types of writing features that can be reliably captured and scored. For example, automated scoring systems are challenged to score the factual accuracy, content appropriateness, and argument quality of essays. Further, automated scoring tools have been limited primarily to the essay, which is not the dominant writing activity outside of K–12 settings. Additional research is needed to improve these systems and to examine differences in automated scoring approaches, their relationship to human scoring, and the impact of unintended sources of variance on both approaches (Bejar, 2012).

PERFORMANCE ASSESSMENTS BEYOND ESSAYS

The 1990s call for performance assessment extended beyond essays to the desire for a wide variety of 'authentic' assessment tasks (Wiggins, 1993), particularly in the United States where multiple-choice testing had been the dominant approach for decades. Through a performance assessment, an examinee "communicates his or her understanding of content, of process and strategy, and of the results obtained" (Baker & O'Neill, 1996, p. 186). Examinees create their responses (sometimes involving extended activities) rather than selecting from a set of responses as in the traditional multiple-choice item. For example, instead of reading about an experiment and selecting from possible outcomes, an examinee would actually conduct that experiment and describe the outcomes.

Performance assessments often are designed to mimic the types of experiences that examinees have in their classrooms, work environments, or personal lives. The implicit belief is that such assessments allow for an authenticity of performance that both results in more accurate measurement and also feels more natural to the examinee. Quellmalz and Pellegrino (2009) have argued that performance assessments using digital technology are required to assess students in ways that align with the ways they are being taught. This is because the pervasive impact of digital technology in the classroom has greatly extended (a) the range of learning opportunities for students and (b) the complexity of the tasks that students are asked to do during learning.

Performance assessments implemented using technology, which we will refer to as 'digital performance assessments,' engage the examinee in some type of interaction with the computer (whether via desktop computer, laptop, tablet, smartphone, or other technology). There are a wide variety of digital performance assessments in use today ranging from school-level implementations (Quellmalz & Pellegrino, 2009) to national licensure programs (e.g., Architecture Registration Exam [Braun, 1994; Katz, 1994]) to large, multinational testing programs, such as the Programme for International Student Assessment (PISA [Lennon, Kirsch, von Davier, Wagner, & Yamamoto, 2003]) and the Programme for the International Assessment of Adult Competencies (PIAAC [OECD, 2013]). While the actual nature of the interactions and other aspects of the user interface of these types of assessments differ not only from assessment to assessment, but even within an assessment, the consistent goal is that the examinee is being asked to perform tasks to demonstrate his or her knowledge and skills. See, for example, those discussed at a research symposium on Technology-Enhanced Assessment (K-12 Center for Assessment, 2012).

One example of this type of interactive performance assessment was demonstrated in the National Assessment of Educational Progress (NAEP) Problem-Solving in Technology Rich Environments (TRE) feasibility study (Bennett, Persky, Weiss, & Jenkins, 2010). This study was intended to demonstrate how a psychometrically sound digital performance assessment could be administered in a logistically feasible way on a large scale (nationally). Although the tasks developed were never intended to be used directly within NAEP assessments, the work served as the basis for several new efforts within NAEP that incorporated digital performance assessments in several domains, including science and technology, and engineering literacy.

The study created two performance tasks, aimed at eighth graders, based on the scenario of understanding about how helium balloons are used by scientists: Search and Simulation. The Search task asked students to conduct background research via a simulated Internet search; students were scored based on their approach to conducting the search (e.g., the keywords used) as well as the relevance and quality of the search results obtained. The conclusion of this task was a short-essay type of constructed-response question. The Simulation tasks asked students to conduct simulated experiments with the goal of explaining the relationship between key variables (i.e., payload mass and amount of helium in the balloon) and the resulting altitude of the balloon. In all three experimental tasks, students conduct simulated experiments, selecting values for different variables, then 'releasing' the resulting balloon; an animation showed the speed and eventual altitude of the balloon. For each Simulation task, students completed a short-answer constructed-response question to explain the relationship between two of the variables and also completed some multiple-choice questions about their inquiry process.

Several other digital performance assessments have been developed and used since the NAEP TRE study. For example, at the classroom level, the SimScientist assessments (described by Quellmalz & Pellegrino, 2009) involve tasks concerning simulations of fish in a specific ecology. In one set of tasks, students draw the food chain based on information about the ecology. In another simulation, students are asked to run 'experiments' that simulate the introduction of other or new fish species into the ecology and their effect on the number of competing fish species. Internationally, PIAAC (OEDC, 2013) included an assessment of problem solving in technology-rich environments. Adults were given tasks in which they interacted with simulated software and other technology to solve information-related problems. For example, one task "involves managing requests to reserve a meeting room on a particular date using a reservation system. Upon discovering that one of the reservation requests cannot be accommodated, the test-taker has to send an e-mail message declining the request" (OECD, 2013, p. 89).

What are examinees' reactions to these types of interactive, digital technology assessments? This is a difficult question to address. A frequent approach is to ask examinees about their reactions to these new types of assessments. For example, after a field trial ($N \approx 5,000$) of an interactive assessment of digital literacy skills, Katz (2007) administered an opinion survey asking the extent to which examinees agreed with statements such as "I enjoyed taking this test" and "The tasks reflect activities I have done at school, work, or home." Although somewhat informative, opinion surveys of examinees' reactions to the assessments may overrepresent acceptance of these assessments simply because the tasks are novel or because the performance tasks reported represent revised versions of earlier (sometimes not reported) pilot studies. That is, because of their complexity, performance assessments are often developed through a process of iterative design (Hix & Hartson, 1993), whereby earlier versions are tried out with smaller samples of students, errors noted and corrected, tried again with other students, and so forth until a larger sample is used, with only the larger sample study, using the revised performance tasks, being reported in the literature. More on this matter is available in Struyven and Devesa (this volume).

Unlike multiple-choice or essay assessments, comparability studies of paper versus computer versions are rarer for performance assessments. This rarity might be because many digital performance assessments do not represent a reimplementation of an existing assessment (allowing for direct comparison); rather they are a reconceptualisation of the assessment and the associated construct, such as in the case when a multiple-choice test is replaced by a digital performance assessment. Even if non-digital performance assessments existed, due to the complexity of performances, the creation of the digital versions might have required so many changes to be implemented on computer that a direct comparison would be difficult. For example, NAEP implemented 'hands-on tasks' (i.e., physical performance assessments) in which students worked with physical materials to demonstrate scientific concepts and processes (National Research Council, 1996). Although the current NAEP Science test now includes interactive computer tasks (National Center for Educational Statistics, 2012), thus far, none of these new tasks directly implement the existing hands-on tasks. Instead, the digital technology allowed the creation of new tasks that went beyond what would have been feasible in a physical task (e.g., the balloon task described earlier; A. Oranje, personal communication, 18 June 2015).

Missing from most discussions of digital performance assessments are considerations of the *user interface* of the performance assessment. For computerized multiple-choice, simple constructed response, and essay assessments, the user interface (i.e., how the examinee interacts with the assessment system) is relatively straightforward: clicking on a button to indicate a selected response or typing into a text box as well as navigating from one test question to another. Nevertheless, some consistent differences in performance on these simple implementations were observed, as discussed earlier. Digital performance assessments, such as the simulations described above, often simplify their real-world counterpart tasks by relying on keyboard, mouse, or touch tablet rather than hands-on interactions. Thus, each performance assessment essentially represents a new software application for the examinee to learn. In this way, the very complexity in performance that defines performance assessment also potentially leads to a complex digital environment (i.e., the user interface) that may disrupt measurement and cause difficulties for the examinee.

ASSESSMENT OF TECHNOLOGY-RELATED CONSTRUCTS

In addition to technology being used to deliver and score assessments, as described above, technology has also impacted the nature of the constructs assessed. Since the turn of the century, a great deal has been written about the growing presence of technology in everyday lives. A particular focus has been the technology of the Internet and related devices, often referred to as information and communication technology (ICT). Whether accessing the Internet (or the virtual applications and storage referred to as 'the cloud') via desktop, laptop, tablet, smartphone, GPS, or other devices, this form of technology pervades everyday life for an increasing proportion of the world's population (World Bank, 2015). Of course, ICT pervades the classroom as well, not only in support of traditional instructional topics, but also as a topic of learning itself.

It is not surprising, then, that there has been a growing focus on assessing the cognitive and technological skills associated with information and communication technology. For example, many discussions of '21st century skills' (International ICT Literacy Panel, 2002; Partnership for 21st Century skills, 2003) include the researching and communication skills that, in the past, primarily occurred in a library (cf., information literacy [Association of College and Research Libraries, 2000; Australian and New Zealand Institute for Information Literacy & Council of Australian University Librarians, 2004]), but now are part of everyday activities in school, work, and home. These skills include strategies to locate particular pieces of digital information to answer a question or to build knowledge about a topic, evaluating the relevance and quality of digital information, synthesising material from different digital sources to draw conclusions, and communicating effectively via digital media (e.g., email, texting, PowerPoint).

Over the past decade, several assessments have been developed to assess the cognitive skills associated with use of information and communication technology. One of the earliest assessments of this type was investigated as part of a feasibility study for the international PISA system (Lennon, Kirsch, von Davier, Wagner, & Yamamoto, 2003). The tasks in this computerised assessment had stimuli that looked like common software tools (email, browser), although there was minimal interactive behaviour; instead, examinees would answer questions by selecting materials on the screen or typing their answers to constructed-response questions. One of the more real-world assessments of ICT skills was pilot tested by the U.K. Qualifications and Curriculum Authority (Ripley, 2009), in which students used specially designed software tools (e.g., word processing, spreadsheets, presentations) to create artefacts that were human scored.

An example of a digital performance assessment in current usage is the iSkills assessment. This assessment was designed to assess upper-level high school (ages 16–18) and university students' digital literacy skills (i.e., researching, managing, synthesising, and communicating digital information [Katz, 2005, 2007]). The assessment is composed of 14 scenario-based performance tasks in which examinees interact with simulated software as they solve problems having to do with the handling of digital information. The assessment focuses on the cognitive, rather than technical, skills associated with digital literacy, and so is meant to be more general than the usage of any single software application. As a result, the software tools that examinees interact with are generic versions of common office applications, incorporating only the most general features found in most software.

Some tasks target skills at accessing digital information via Internet search. Students enter search terms to simulate a search to address a class assignment and may be scored on the keywords used, the number of searches done, and the relevance and other characteristics (e.g., authority, credibility, timeliness) of any material selected by the student for further use in the assignment. Other tasks target skills at interpreting digital information, such as by explicitly judging the credibility of a particular website, deciding the appropriate categories for information (e.g., files, emails) to be organised, or creating tables that summarise provided digital materials.

Technology-related constructs have also been assessed within the context of other academic domains. As presented earlier, the NAEP TRE (Bennett et al., 2010) had examinees conduct simulated Internet searches, just as in iSkills, but for the purposes of assessing science inquiry skills. The skill of reading online is argued to involve skills beyond the typical assessment of reading (Coiro, 2009) and has motivated assessments that present technology-related contexts for reading (Leu et al., 2013; Sabatini, O'Reilly, & Deane, 2013). Interestingly, despite some claims that primary and secondary students have sufficient and consistent technology familiarity (Paek, 2005), skills at reading online and processing online information still show an achievement gap between students with more academic online opportunities compared with those who have had fewer opportunities (Leu, Forzani, Rhoads, Maykel, Kennedy, & Timbrell, 2015).

THE FORESEEABLE FUTURE OF TECHNOLOGY AND ASSESSMENT

Educational systems are increasingly pressed to refocus instruction toward newly defined 21st century skills; that is, the knowledge and skills individuals need to be successful in a changing workplace and modern global economy. Assessments must also change. Needed are new types of assessments that generate multiple evidence sources of varied types across numerous contexts to provide robust arguments about what students have learned, what they still need to learn, and what will lead them to contribute productively to society. These assessments will increasingly use innovative, interactive tasks, framed in engaging and meaningful contexts, to gather the evidence of students' knowledge, skills, and other attributes that education stakeholders need. In turn, this evidence will increasingly rely on analyses of examinees' moment-by-moment interactions with the tasks, providing new insights into examinee performance. When considering the impact of these new types of tests on examinees, new issues are raised because these innovations may not be perceived as assessments in the traditional sense.

Two recent types of digital performance assessments that are emerging as the next generation of assessment include conversation-based assessment and game-based assessment. These innovations represent advances that could conceivably be part of operational assessments in the next one–three years.

CONVERSATION-BASED ASSESSMENT

Conversation-based assessment engages examinees in interactive dialogs with one or more virtual agents. There has been more than a decade of research in the area of intelligent tutoring systems (ITSs) that involve conversations between a student and virtual characters (e.g., a virtual peer or teacher [Chan & Baskin, 1990; Graesser, Person, Harter, & Tutoring Research Group, 2001; Johnson, Rickel, & Lester, 2000]). Recent research applies this approach to assessment (e.g., OperationARIES [Millis et al., 2011; Zapata-Rivera et al., 2014]). Conversation-based assessment allows assessment developers an innovative avenue for exploring new techniques that adapt to individual users and include response data not found in traditional measures (i.e., conversational responses related to current cognitive processing).

A challenge for conversation-based assessment is to create sufficiently rich situations for conversations in which examinees' language provides evidence of deep cognition, while also constraining the task to allow for reliable scoring. For example, Figure 27.1 shows a section of a conversation-based assessment for scientific inquiry in Earth Science. Examinees interact with the computer agents (i.e., a scientist and a fellow student) to demonstrate their understanding of how information from seismometers may be interpreted to predict the likelihood of a volcanic eruptions.

In conversation-based assessment, the system evaluates the response from an examinee and probes further if more information would provide greater insight into examinee knowledge and skills. For example, if an initial response to a question is

Figure 27.1 Conversation-based Assessment. © 2015 Educational Testing Service. All Rights Reserved.

recognised by the system as incomplete in some way, additional prompts may elicit a more complete response. Compared with similarly worded constructed response items on a test, the use of simulated conversations allows the system to adapt to the individual student's responses and act accordingly.

What is the experience of taking a conversation-based assessment for an examinee? Early work suggests that conversation-based assessments result in a more engaging experience for the student and a more complete set of evidence to be scored and reported (Zapata-Rivera, Jackson, Liu, Bertling, Vezzu, & Katz, 2014). However, some examinees recognise the artificiality of the onscreen avatars, and so do not treat them as people even when they engage in 'discussions' (Forsyth et al., 2015; Johnson, Gardner, & Wiles, 2004). For example, in a study using a conversation-based assessment for English language learners, Forsyth et al. (2015) compared middle-school students' summaries of a story to either a human experimenter or the onscreen avatar. Although students used more words in their summary to the humans than to the avatars, the quality of the summaries, as scored by independent raters, were equivalent, suggesting that the additional words might not have been functional.

GAME-BASED ASSESSMENT

Another future direction for digital performance assessment is game-based assessment. While games have been used in education for many years, games specifically used for assessment are a relatively recent research area. The idea is to engage students in the content area, and the problem solving needed for that area, while motivating students by using aspects of games that make them so appealing.

Through game-based assessment, examinees can engage in real-world, extended tasks that elicit a wide range of behaviours that might serve as evidence of knowledge and skills of interest. Epistemic games, for example, present real-world challenges to test takers that mimic activities in a profession; for example, in *Urban Planner* (Rupp, Gushta, Mislevy, & Shaffer, 2010), the 'players' design parks, commercial centers, and other urban areas, receiving feedback on such aspects as cost and usage. Rupp et al. (2010) discuss how epistemic games may be adapted for use as assessments of complex skills such as systems thinking.

A recent example of game-based assessment is SimCityEDU (Mislevy et al., 2014). This assessment was built from the original SimCity game in which players construct and modify the specifications for a city (e.g., residential, industrial, and commercial zones, locations of roads, location of power plants) on a map, into which the simulated residents move, commute, work at jobs, spend money in business, and otherwise 'live' their lives. The game-based assessment was designed to assess systems thinking skills such as "identifying, investigating, and operating on multiple independent variables in complex economic and environmental systems" (GLASSLab, 2014, p. 1). Reliable assessment flows from the careful identification of game actions that provide evidence of growing systems thinking skills.

In SimCityEDU, game play continues just as in the original game, but the challenges present more focused goals that involve modifying a preexisting city. For example, students are asked to promote the growth of the city, while increasing jobs and maintaining low pollution rates. In some cases, the city is a new city that needs to grow. In other challenges, the city is large and successful, but has too much pollution. Building power plants helps power the city, encourages growth, and also creates jobs. However, some power plants increase pollution (e.g., coal) while others keep pollution lower (e.g., solar), but might not produce as much energy. The student must consider the balance among these different variables to achieve the desired outcomes.

While game-based assessment represents a potential way to leverage the excitement and engagement of video games in an assessment, it might be the case that not all students have the same motivation or interest in video games. For example, in a survey of more than 1,000 U.S. teens (Lenhart, 2015), 91% of boys report having access to a gaming console compared with 70% of girls, suggesting a gender-based difference in gaming experience. On the other hand, research has also demonstrated a lack of effect from experience or gender on learning from educational games (using computer game self-efficacy as a proxy for familiarity or experience [Bergey, Ketelhut, Liang, Natarajan, & Karakus, 2015]). Further research is needed to investigate the experience of a wide range of students with game-based assessments to determine ways of avoiding (or at least detecting) negative reactions or off-task behaviours.

PROCESS DATA

Interactive assessment tasks, such as those in conversation- and game-based assessments, as well as other digital performance assessment, allow the collection of data in the time-course of examinee interactions with the task, or 'process data.' These data potentially reveal information as to the processes by which examinees solve a problem, communicate with a virtual agent, or reach a solution to a game-based challenge. If such process data can be effectively interpreted and incorporated into examinee scores, or even more descriptive reports of their performance, it would provide examinees and other education stakeholders with information about examinees' performance and suggestions for improvement (Keehner & Smith, 2013). Recent approaches to large-scale use of process data combine computational tools from computer science, such as machine learning and data mining, with more theoretically driven psychometric and cognitive modelling (Keehner, Agard, Berger, Bertling, & Shu, 2014; Kerr, 2014; Kerr & Chung, 2012).

In addition to collecting moment-by-moment evidence of cognitive skill, some researchers have investigated the affective component of student performance

(D'Mello & Kory, 2012 provide a review). In some cases, facial recognition or physiological measures are used to track students' emotional states during learning, such as the automatic detection of boredom or other disengagement, which can lead to off-task behaviour. For assessment, automated detection of emotional states suggests the intriguing possibility of adapting test content based on those states (see Vogl & Pekrun, this volume, for more on achievement emotions). The simplest example would be to discount performance that could be tied to disengagement or boredom, suggesting the examinee might not have been taking the assessment seriously (see Wise & Smith, this volume, for more on examinee effort during assessment), which reduces the value of the evidence obtained of the student's knowledge and skill. Alternatively, visual or auditory feedback could be provided to examinees who appear disengaged to help bring them back on track.

CONCLUSIONS

In reflecting on the research reviewed in this chapter, it is clear that the effect of technology on assessment has been both positive and negative for examinees and the stakeholders who use assessment information. On the one hand, compared with traditional assessments, technology has enabled more authentic, complex, and interactive assessments that more closely mimic real-world performances in ways that many examinees have come to expect. These assessments produce more detailed evidence of examinee knowledge and skills, allowing the people who use assessment results a wider range of inferences that can be made about examinees (Gorin, 2012). On the other hand, although researchers typically have investigated psychometric characteristics of computerised assessments, less is known about the effects of new technology on diverse examinees (e.g., different genders or cultural backgrounds [Gallagher, Bridgeman, & Cahalan, 2002]) who might differ widely in their familiarity, comfort, and ways in which they engage with technology.

We have tried to convey an optimistic view of the potential for new forms of technology-based assessment for education stakeholders, both in terms of improved examinee experience as well as an enhanced basis for educational decision-making. However, we simultaneously acknowledge that care is needed in deploying these types of innovations for assessments in classrooms or for large-scale assessments.

For interactive technology-based assessments in the classroom, teachers must understand how assessment results might be used as part of instruction. Digital performance assessments may generate data and information that differ significantly from the more commonly used percent correct or scale scores, challenging teachers to understand how the assessments connect to their learning objectives. Teacher training on the use of these new types of assessment data will be critical if the potential positive impact of the technologies is to be realised. To the extent that similar technologies and activities appear in both learning and assessment contexts during teacher preparation, the linkages between the two may become more visible to prospective teachers.

Outside of the classroom, there is the issue of examinee motivation. Large-scale assessments may be used for high-stakes decision-making by institutions or governments, but may be low-stakes (i.e., have few direct consequences) for examinees. Engagement and the resulting motivation to perform well are important for sound measurement (Liu, Bridgeman, & Adler, 2012). If an examinee does not try his or her best on an assessment, it calls into question the score resulting from such a half-hearted performance (Wise & DeMars, 2006). With enough unmotivated examinees, stakeholders might (incorrectly) conclude, for example, that fewer students have achieved the proficient performance expected of them. As mentioned earlier, technology may detect, and correct for, examinee lack of effort. Further, digital performance assessments might improve motivation by being more engaging for students, by giving them a sense of agency (Podolefsky, Moore, & Perkins, 2013), and by better reflecting familiar classroom activities. When evaluating assessments for large-scale use, policy makers, and other users of large-scale assessments results, should include considerations of possible examinee motivation, in addition to traditional psychometric concerns.

As the research reviewed in this chapter suggests, technology impacts examinees differently depending on their familiarity and other variables, and further work is needed so that the motivating aspects of technology could provide benefits for all test takers. For continued research in this area, we offer the following suggestions.

Align Measures of Computer Familiarity With the Assessment Tasks

When investigating the influence of examinees' computer experience on their performance, care should be taken to include measures that are guided by theories of performance. Measures of computer experience should *directly* reflect the specific types of actions and performances demanded by the computer-based test. The Horkay et al. (2006) study is an excellent example of this approach in their use of a computer typing and editing task. The researchers measured precisely those computing skills that come into play when composing essays on computers. Similar considerations of the user interface requirements for digital performance assessments and other interactive assessments may suggest more consistently useful measures of examinees' familiarity with technology.

Consider the Tasks and Examinees' Interaction With Them, Not Just the Testing Mode

Research should move beyond coarse-grain comparisons of different testing modes, whether paper versus computer or alternative technologies such as desktop versus laptop versus tablet. As mentioned earlier, rarely considered by researchers are the specific user interface characteristics of the performance task. The same performance task might be implemented on the screen in many different ways—through the screen layout, the interface functions available (drop-down menus, radio buttons), and the actions that examinees use to complete the task. Depending on the particular design elements, an examinee might approach a computer-based task in the same way as a paper task (or a task implemented on a different technology platform), or the computer interface may lead the examinee to take a very different approach. Unfortunately, most research reports about digital performance tasks provide only few examples of what the tasks look like to examinees, and do not report on the role played by specific design elements of the task on examinee performance. Future research on the impact of technology on assessment and examinees might incorporate results from other fields, especially ergonomics, human factors, and human-computer interaction to consider how examinees of different computing skills may respond to alternative versions of computer-based tests.

Ultimately, there is a real tension between the desire to move assessment into the digital age and the reality that we know little about the impact of such a move on the validity of our scores for their intended uses and the intended impact of assessments on education. The suggested research strategies should help guide the design and deployment of computerised assessments that provide solid measurement across a range of examinee backgrounds and experiences. At the very least, they will provide an empirical basis for making policy and practical decisions regarding computerised assessment in education.

REFERENCES

Association of College and Research Libraries. (2000). *Information literacy standards for higher education.* Washington, DC: American Library Association.

Australian and New Zealand Institute for Information Literacy & Council of Australian University Librarians. (2004). *Australian and New Zealand information literacy framework: Principles, standards, and practice.* Adelaide: Author.

Baker, E. L., & O'Neill, H. F., Jr. (1996). Performance assessment and equity. In M. B. Kane & R. Mitchell (Eds.), *Performance assessment: Problems, promises, and challenges* (pp. 183–199). Washington, DC: American Institutes for Research.

Bartram, D., & Hambleton, R. K. (2006). *Computer-based testing and the Internet: Issues and advances.* New York: John Wiley & Sons Ltd.

Bejar, I. I. (2012). Rater cognition: Implications for validity. *Educational Measurement: Issues and Practice, 31*(3), 2–9.

Bennett, R. E. (2002). Inexorable and inevitable: The continuing story of technology and assessment. *Journal of Technology, Learning, and Assessment, 1*(1), 1–23.

Bennett, R. E., Persky, H. R., Weiss, A., & Jenkins, F. (2010). Measuring problem solving with technology: A demonstration study for NAEP. *The Journal of Technology, Learning, and Assessment, 8*(8), 1–44.

Bergey, B. W., Ketelhut, D. J., Liang, S., Natarajan, U., & Karakus, M. (2015). Scientific inquiry self-efficacy and computer game self-efficacy as predictors and outcomes of middle school boys' and girls' performance in a science assessment in a virtual environment. *Journal of Science Education and Technology, 24*, 696–708.

Birenbaum, M., Kelly, A. E., & Tatsuoka, K. K. (1992). *Diagnosing knowledge states in algebra using the Rule Space model* (ETS Research Report No. RR-92–57-ONR). Princeton, NJ: Educational Testing Service.

Braun, H. I. (1994). Assessing technology in assessment. In E. Baker & H. O'Neill, Jr. (Eds.), *Technology assessment in education and training: Volume 1* (pp. 231–246). New York: Routledge.

Bridgeman, B., Lennon, M. L., & Jackenthal, A. (2003). Effects of screen size, screen resolution, and display rate on computer-based test performance. *Applied Measurement in Education, 16*, 191–205.

Burstein, J., Tetreault, J., & Madnani, N. (2013). The E-rater® automated essay scoring system. In M. D. Shermis & J. Burstein (Eds.), *Handbook of automated essay scoring: Current applications and future directions* (pp. 55–67). New York: Routledge.

Chan, T. W., & Baskin, A. B. (1990). Learning companion systems. In C. Frasson & G. Gauthier (Eds.), *Intelligent tutoring systems: At the crossroads of artificial intelligence and education* (pp. 6–33). Norwood, NY: Ablex Publishing.

Coiro, J. (2009). Rethinking online reading assessment: How is reading comprehension different and where do we turn now. *Educational Leadership, 66*, 59–63.

D'Mello, S., & Kory, J. (2012). Consistent but modest: A meta-analysis of unimodal and multimodal affect detection accuracies from 30 studies. In L.-P. Morency, D. Bohus, & H. Aghajan (Eds.), *Proceedings of the 14th ACM International Conference on Multimodal Interaction* (pp. 31–38). New York: ACM.

Embretson, S. E., & Hershberger, S. L. (1999). *The new rules of measurement: What every psychologist and educator should know.* New York: Psychology Press.

Foltz, P. W., Laham, D., & Landauer, T. K. (1999). Automated essay scoring: Applications to educational technology. In B. Collis & R. Oliver (Eds.), *Proceedings of World Conference on Educational Media and Technology 1999* (pp. 939–944). Waynesville, NC: Association for the Advancement of Computing in Education (AACE). Retrieved from http://www.editlib.org/p/6607

Forsyth, C., So, Y., Luce, C., Battistini, L., Evanini, K., Zapata-Rivera, D., Tao, Jidong, & Jackson, G. T. (2015, April). *Man vs. machine: Analyzing human responses to other humans vs. artificial agents in conversation-based assessments.* Poster presented at the 2015 annual meeting of the American Education Research Association, Chicago, IL.

Frederiksen, N., Mislevy, R. J., & Bejar, I. I. (1993). *Test theory for a new generation of tests.* New York: Routledge.

Gallagher, A., Bridgeman, B., & Cahalan, C. (2002). The effect of computer-based tests on racial-ethnic and gender groups. *Journal of Educational Measurement, 39*, 133–147.

GLASSLab. (2014). *Students playing SimCityEDU made statistically significant gains in systems thinking.* Retrieved from http://about.glasslabgames.org/downloads/SCE_ResearchShortV2.pdf

Gorin, J. S. (2012). *Assessment as evidential reasoning.* White paper commissioned by The Gordon Commission on the Future of Educational Assessment. Retrieved from http://gordoncommission.org/rsc/pdfs/gorin_assessment_evidential_reasoning.pdf

Graesser, A. C., Hu, X., & Person, N. K. (2001). Teaching with the help of talking heads. *Proceedings of the IEEE International Conference on Advanced Learning Technologies,* (pp. 460–461). Los Alamitos, CA: IEEE Computer Society.

Graesser, A. C., Person, N., Harter, D., & Tutoring Research Group. (2001). Teaching tactics and dialog in AutoTutor. *International Journal of Artificial Intelligence in Education, 12,* 257–279.

Hambleton, R. K., & Slater, S. (1997). *Are NAEP executive summary reports understandable to policy makers and educators?* (CSE Technical Report 430). Los Angeles, CA: National Center for Research on Evaluation, Standards, and Student Testing.

Hix, D., & Hartson, H. R. (1993). *Developing user interfaces: Ensuring usability through product & process.* Hoboken, NJ: John Wiley & Sons, Inc.

Horkay, N., Bennett, R. E., Allen, N., Kaplan, B., & Yan, F. (2006). Does it matter if I take my writing test on computer? An empirical study of mode effects in NAEP. *Journal of Technology, Learning, and Assessment, 5*(2), 1–49.

International ICT Literacy Panel. (2002). *Digital transformation: A framework for ICT literacy.* Princeton, NJ: Educational Testing Service. Retrieved from http://www.ets.org/Media/Tests/Information_and_Communication_Technology_Literacy/ictreport.pdf

Jaeger, R. M. (2003). *NAEP validity studies: Reporting the results of the National Assessment of Educational Progress.* Washington, DC: National Center for Education Statistics.

Johnson, D., Gardner, J., & Wiles, J. (2004). Experience as a moderator of the media equation: the impact of flattery and praise. *International Journal of Human-Computer Studies, 63,* 237–258.

Johnson, W. L., Rickel, J. W., & Lester, J. C. (2000). Animated pedagogical agents: Face-to-face interaction in interactive learning environments. *International Journal of Artificial Intelligence in Education, 11,* 47–78.

K-12 Center at ETS. (2012). Invitational research symposium on technology enhanced assessments. *Driving Advances in K–12 Assessment.* Retrieved August 29, 2015 from http://k12center.org/events/research_meetings/tea.html

Katz, I. R. (1994). Coping with the complexity of design: Avoiding conflicts and prioritizing constraints. In A. Ram & K. Eiselt (Eds.), *Proceedings of the Sixteenth Annual Conference of the Cognitive Science Society* (pp. 485–489). Hillsdale, NJ: Lawrence Erlbaum Associates.

Katz, I. R. (2005). Beyond technical competence: Literacy in information and communication technology. *Educational Technology Magazine, 45*(6), 44–47.

Katz, I. R. (2007). Testing information literacy in digital environments: ETS's iSkills Assessment. *Information Technology and Libraries, 26*(3), 3–12.

Katz, I. R., Martinez, M. E., Sheehan, K., & Tatsuoka, K. K. (1998). Extending the Rule Space methodology to a semantically-rich domain: Diagnostic assessment in architecture. *Journal of Educational and Behavioral Statistics, 23,* 254–278.

Keehner, M., Agard, C., Berger, M., Bertling, J., and Shu, Z. (2014). *Analyzing interactivity, performance, and background data from the NAEP TEL Wells Task.* Federal Research Memorandum on NAEP Task Component, U.S. Dept. of Education, Contract Award No. ED-IES-13-C-0015.

Keehner, M. and Smith, L. (2013, April). *Connecting actions, cognitions, and measurement: The role of cognitive science in NAEP TEL Task Development.* San Francisco, CA: NCME Annual Meeting.

Kerr, D. (2014). *Identifying common mathematical misconceptions from actions in educational video games* (CRESST Report 838). Los Angeles, CA: University of California, National Center for Research on Evaluation, Standards, and Student Testing (CRESST).

Kerr, D., & Chung, G.K.W.K. (2012). Identifying key features of student performance in educational video games and simulations through cluster analysis. *Journal of Educational Data Mining, 4,* 144–182.

Leeson, H. V. (2006). The mode effect: A literature review of human and technological issues in computerized testing. *International Journal of Testing, 6*(1), 1–24.

Leighton, J., & Gierl, M. (Eds.). (2007). *Cognitive diagnostic assessment for education: Theory and applications.* New York: Cambridge University Press.

Leighton, J. P., Gierl, M. J., & Hunka, S. M. (2004). The attribute hierarchy method for cognitive assessment: A variation on Tatsuoka's rule-space approach. *Journal of Educational Measurement, 41,* 205–237.

Lenhart, A. (2015). *Teens, social media, and technology overview.* Pew Research Center. Retrieved from http://www.pewinternet.org/files/2015/04/PI_TeensandTech_Update2015_0409151.pdf

Lennon, M., Kirsch, I., von Davier, M., Wagner, M., & Yamamoto, K. (2003). *Feasibility study for the PISA ICT literacy assessment.* Retrieved from http://www.oecd.org/education/school/programmeforinternationalstudentassessmentpisa/33699866.pdf

Leu, D. J., Forzani, E., Burlingame, C., Kulikowich, J., Sedransk, N., Coiro, J., & Kennedy, C. (2013). The new literacies of online research and comprehension: Assessing and preparing students for the 21st century with common core state standards. In S. B. Neuman & L. B. Gambrell (Eds.), Massey, C. (Assoc. Ed.), *Reading instruction in the age of common core standards.* (pp. 219–236). Newark, DE: International Reading Association.

Leu, D. J., Forzani, E., Rhoads, C., Maykel, C., Kennedy, C., & Timbrell, N. (2015). The new literacies of online research and comprehension: Rethinking the reading achievement gap. *Reading Research Quarterly, 50,* 37–59.

Liu, O. L., Bridgeman, B., & Adler, R. M. (2012). Measuring outcomes in higher education: Motivation matters. *Educational Researcher, 41,* 352–362.

Lord, F. M., Novick, M. R., & Birnbaum, A. (1968). *Statistical theories of mental test scores.* Reading, MA: Addison-Wesley.

Lottridge, S. M., Nicewander, W. A., Schulz, E. M., & Mitzel, H. C. (2010). Comparability of paper-based and computer-based tests: A review of the methodology. In P. C. Winter (Ed.), *Evaluating the comparability of scores from achievement test variations* (pp. 119–152). Washington, DC: Council of Chief State School Officers.

Mayfield, E., & Rosé, C. P. (2013). LightSIDE: Open source machine learning for text. In M. D. Shermis & J. Burstein (Eds.), *Handbook of automated essay scoring: Current applications and future directions* (pp. 124–135). New York: Routledge.

McDonald, A. (2002). The impact of individual differences on the equivalence of computer-based and paper-and-pencil educational assessments. *Computers & Education, 39,* 299–312.

McNamara, D. S., Levinstein, I. B., & Boonthum, C. (2004). iSTART: Interactive strategy trainer for active reading and thinking. *Behavioral Research Methods, Instruments, and Computers, 36,* 222–233.

Mead, A. D., & Drasgow, F. (1993). Equivalence of computerized and paper cognitive ability tests: A meta-analysis. *Psychological Bulletin, 114,* 449–458.

Millis, K., Forsyth, C., Butler, H., Wallace, P., Graesser, A. C., & Halpern, D. (2011). Operation ARIES! A serious game for teaching scientific inquiry. In M. Ma, A. Oikonomou, & J. Lakhmi (Eds.), *Serious games and edutainment applications* (pp.169–196). London: Springer-Verlag.

Mislevy, R. J. (1997). Postmodern test theory. In A. Lesgold, M. J. Feuer, & A. M. Black (Eds.), *Transitions in work and learning: Implications for assessment* (pp. 180–199). Washington DC: National Academies Press.

Mislevy, R. J., Oranje, A., Bauer, M. I., von Davier, A., Hao, J., Corrigan, S., Hoffman, E., DiCerbo, K., & John, M. (2014). *Psychometric considerations in game-based assessment.* Retrieved from http://www.instituteofplay.org/wp-content/uploads/2014/02/GlassLab_GBA1_WhitePaperFull.pdf

National Center for Educational Statistics. (2012). *The nation's report card: Science in action: Hands-on and interactive computer tasks from the 2009 science assessment* (NCES 2012–468). Washington, DC: Institute of Education Sciences, U.S. Department of Education.

National Research Council. (1996). *National science education standards.* Coordinating Council for Education, National Committee on Science Education Standards and Assessment. Washington, DC: National Academy Press.

Noyes, J. M., & Garland, K. J. (2008). Computer- vs. paper-based tasks: Are they equivalent? *Ergonomics, 51,* 1352–1375.

Organisation for Economic Cooperation and Development (OECD) (2013). *OECD skills outlook 2013: First results from the survey of adult skills.* Paris, France: OECD Publishing. doi: 10.1787/9789264204256-en

Paek, P. (2005). Recent trends in comparability studies. *Pearson Educational Measurement.* Retrieved from http://images.pearsonassessments.com/images/tmrs/tmrs_rg/TrendsCompStudies.pdf

Partnership for 21st Century Skills. (2003). *Learning for the 21st century: A report and mile guide for 21st century skills.* Washington, DC: Author.

Pew Research Center. (2014). *Older adults and technology use.* Retrieved from http://www.pewinternet.org/2014/04/03/older-adults-and-technology-use/

Podolefsky, N. S., Moore, E. B., & Perkins, K. K. (2013). *Implicit scaffolding in interactive simulations: Design strategies to support multiple educational goals.* Retrieved from http://arxiv.org/ftp/arxiv/papers/1306/1306.6544.pdf

Powers, D. E., Fowles, M. E., Farnum, M., & Ramsey, P. (1994). Will they think less of my handwritten essay if others word process theirs? Effects on essay scores on intermingling handwritten and word-processed essays. *Journal of Educational Measurement, 31,* 220–233.

Powers, D. E., & O'Neill, K. (1993). Inexperienced and anxious computer users: Coping with a computer-administered test of academic skills. *Educational Assessment, 1,* 153–173.

Quellmalz, E. S., & Pellegrino, J. W. (2009). Technology and testing. *Science, 323,* 75–79.

Ripley, M. (2009). Technology in the service of 21st century learning and assessment. In F. Scheuermann & A. G. Pereira (Eds.), *Towards a research agenda on computer-based assessment: Challenges and needs for European educational measurement* (pp. 22–29). Ispra, Italy: European Commission Joint Research Centre. Retrieved from http://www.k-link.it/klinkwiki/images/6/63/EU-Report-CBA.pdf

Rupp, A. A., Gushta, M., Mislevy, R. J., & Shaffer, D. W. (2010). Evidence-centered design of epistemic games: Measurement principles for complex learning environments. *Journal of Technology, Learning, and Assessment, 8*(4), 1–47.

Sabatini, J., O'Reilly, T., & Deane, P. (2013). *Preliminary reading literacy assessment framework: Foundation and rationale for assessment and system design* (ETS Research Report No. RR-13–30). Princeton, NJ: Educational Testing Service.

Shermis, M. D., & Burstein, J. (2013). *Handbook of automated essay evaluation: Current applications and new directions.* New York: Routledge Academic.

Shermis, M. D., & Hamner, B. (2012, April). *Contrasting state-of-the-art automated scoring of essays: Analysis.* Paper presented at the National Council of Measurement in Education, Vancouver, BC, Canada.

Steinberg, L., & Thissen, D. (1996). Uses of item response theory and the testlet concept in the measurement of psychopathology. *Psychological Methods, 1,* 81–97.

Tatsuoka, K. K. (1990). Toward an integration of item-response theory and cognitive error diagnosis. In N. Frederiksen, R. L. Glaser, A. M. Lesgold, & M. G. Shafto (Eds.), *Diagnostic monitoring of skills and knowledge acquisition* (pp. 453–488). Hillsdale, NJ: Erlbaum.

Taylor, C., Kirsch, I., Jamieson, J., & Eignor, D. (1999). Examining the relationship between computer familiarity and performance on computer-based language tasks. *Language Learning, 49*(2), 219–274.

van der Linden, W. J. (2005). *Linear models of optimal test design.* New York: Springer.

Wang, S., Jiao, H., Young, M. J., Brooks, T., and Olson, J. (2008). Comparability of computer-based and paper-based testing in K–12 reading assessments: A meta-analysis of testing mode effects. *Educational and Psychological Measurement, 68,* 5–24.

Way, W. D., Vickers, D., & Nichols, P. (2008, April). *Effects of different training and scoring approaches on human constructed response scores.* Paper presented at the annual meeting of the National Council on Measurement in Education, New York. Retrieved from http://images.pearsonassessments.com/images/tmrs/tmrs_rg/TrainingandScoringApproachesonHumanConstructedResponseScoring.pdf?WT.mc_id=TMRS_Effects_of_Different_Training_and_Scoring

Wier, C., O'Sullivan, B., Yan, J., & Bax, S. (2007). Does the computer make a difference? The reaction of candidates to a computer-based versus a traditional hand-written form of the IELTS Writing component: Effects and impact. *IELTS Research Reports Volume 7.* Retrieved from https://www.ielts.org/pdf/Vol7,Report6.pdf

Wiggins, G. (1993, November). Assessment: Authenticity, context, and validity. *Phi Delta Kappan,* 200–214.

Williamson, D. M., Bauer, M. I., Steinberg, L.S, Mislevy, R. J., Behrens, J. T., & DeMark, S. (2004). Design rationale for a complex performance assessment. *International Journal of Testing, 4,* 303–332.

Wise, S., & DeMars, C. (2006). An application of item response item: The effort-moderated IRT model. *Journal of Educational Measurement, 43,* 19–38.

Wolfe, E., Bolton, S., Feltovich, B., & Welch, C. (1993). *A comparison of word-processed and handwritten essays from a standardized writing assessment* (ACT Research Report No. 93–8). Iowa City, IA: American College Testing.

World Bank. (2015). *Internet users (per 100 people).* Retrieved data table from http://data.worldbank.org/indicator/IT.NET.USER.P2.

Yu, L., Livingston, S. A., Larkin, K. C., & Bonett, J. (2004). *Investigating differences in examinee performance between computer-based and handwritten essays* (ETS Research Report RR-04–18). Princeton, NJ: Educational Testing Service.

Zapata-Rivera, D., Jackson, G. T., Liu, L., Bertling, M., Vezzu, M., and Katz, I. R. (2014). Assessing science inquiry skills using trialogues. In S. Trausan-Matu, K. Boyer, M. Crosby, & K. Panourgia (Eds.), *Proceedings of the 12th International Conference on Intelligence Tutoring Systems* (pp. 625–626). Cham, CH: Springer International Publishing AG.

Zapata-Rivera, J. D., & Katz, I. R. (2014). Keeping your audience in mind: Applying audience analysis to the design of interactive score reports. *Assessment in Education: Principles, Policy, & Practice, 21,* 442–463.

28

SECTION DISCUSSION: ASSESSMENT AND SOCIOCULTURAL CONTEXT

A Bidirectional Relationship

Kadriye Ercikan and Guillermo Solano-Flores

INTRODUCTION

The six chapters in this section discuss multiple aspects of the relationship between educational assessment and social and cultural contexts. Each details the design of assessments and their interpretive use, spanning educational contexts from classroom practices to international assessments. These chapters make valuable contributions to the field, highlighting many conceptual and practical issues relevant to designing, conducting, validating, and using assessments.

Our discussion is divided into four parts. First, we offer a conceptual framework for discussing two aspects of the dynamic relationship between assessment and sociocultural context. The conceptual framework lays out the groundwork for discussing the six chapters in this section. Second, we discuss the influence of culture and society on assessment; and third, the influence of assessment on society. Finally, we make concluding comments about the bidirectional relationship between assessment and cultural and societal contexts.

CONCEPTUAL FRAMEWORK

Assessment systems and instruments have come to play an important role in educational systems around the world as tools and means for obtaining, documenting, monitoring, and communicating information about educational outcomes. This process involves not only students and educators, but also parents, stakeholders and, more broadly, societies. Assessment results are used (at least in principle) to evaluate individual student learning and the effectiveness of teachers, schools, and districts; for accountability purposes; and to inform policy and practice about several aspects of education systems. Provided they are used in appropriate ways, assessments can be catalysts for significant changes in education and society. For example, they can be used to document achievement gaps and guide policy to reduce those gaps. In the United States, milestone efforts intended to narrow these achievement gaps, such as the Elementary and Secondary Education Act (ESEA) of 1965 (U.S. Congress, 1965), the Head Start program (Cooke, 1965), and No Child Left Behind (NCLB, 2001) have been tied to educational assessment. The influence of assessment programs such as the National Assessment of Educational Progress (NAEP) and the two state assessment consortia funded by the Race to the Top program (i.e., Smarter Balanced and Partnership for Assessment of Readiness for College and Careers [PARCC])—cannot be understated. For example, NAEP has become a model for assessment design (Vinovskis, 1998) and Smarter Balanced and PARCC are intended to be a major force for improving the teaching and learning of skills deemed relevant to access and success in higher education (U.S. Department of Education, 2014).

The conceptual framework guiding our discussion of the chapters in this section postulates that the relationship between assessment and sociocultural context is a two-way relationship. On the one hand, society influences assessment. Culture and the characteristics of a society (mainly its history, social structure, priorities, values, technological development, legislation, communication styles, and ways of doing things and viewing the world) shape assessment content, who is to be assessed, how, and to what end. On the other hand, assessment influences society: the information produced by assessment instruments and systems shape decisions made about individuals, institutions, and policy. These mutual influences operate at different levels, including test item, assessment program, country, and international test comparisons.

THE INFLUENCE OF CULTURE AND SOCIETY ON ASSESSMENT

As with any activity or object created or developed by human beings, assessment instruments are cultural products (Cole, 1999). How assessments are created and used is a reflection of the societies and cultures that generate them. For example, the types of items (e.g., multiple choice, open ended) and the form of language (e.g., standard dialect, idiomatic expressions) used in an assessment and the contexts provided by the items in that assessment (e.g., a baseball game used as a context to pose a statistical problem), assume test takers' familiarity with a given set of everyday life experiences and a shared set of epistemologies, views, and communication styles (Lakin, 2014; Martinez, 1999; Solano-Flores, 2006; Solano-Flores & Nelson-Barber, 2001). Even if such familiarity is not assumed, the complexity of these influences may be beyond total control (Solano-Flores, Backhoff, & Contreras-Niño, 2009). Due to this complexity, the actions taken by assessment systems may be limited in their effectiveness to address these cultural influences.

Assessment systems are also cultural products. The content assessed by tests reflects the needs, knowledge, and skills valued in that society or the trends of a society (including a global society). One example is the intended emphasis of PISA, NAEP, PARCC, and Smarter Balanced on critical inquiry and other higher-order-thinking-related constructs (e.g., collaborative problem solving, and technology and engineering literacy). As cultural products, assessment systems and the practices they institutionalize, combined with the weight of accountability as a driving force, greatly influence the participation of educators in the process of assessment development (Black & Wiliam, 2005). In this process, reason and evidence-based knowledge are not necessarily the only agents dictating assessment policy and practice. The role of politics and power in education cannot be underestimated (Crawford, 2000; Cummins, 2000). Ultimately, the purposes of assessment and the procedures used by assessment systems to obtain and process information on and make inferences and decisions about students are shaped by a country's social organization and culture, including its institutions, legislation, and structure of power.

The role of culture as a factor that shapes validity in testing has been recognized for a long time, probably since popular instruments used in large-scale assessment began to be adapted and translated (Becker, 2003; Ercikan, 1998; Ercikan & Roth, 2011). Yet test development practices have focused on ensuring sound translation and adaptation of tests originally developed with a specific cultural or linguistic group in mind. Also, analytical approaches (e.g., differential item functioning analysis) have focused on examining differences across cultural groups based on the psychometric properties of items (Camilli, 2013; Hambleton, Merenda, & Spielberger, 2005). In this tradition, cultural differences are examined basically at the item level and using a specific group (typically, the predominant cultural or linguistic group in a society) as a reference or benchmark.

In cross-cultural assessment, considerations of cultural influences on assessment primarily focus on how cultural contexts and students' cultural background affect their performance on assessments. Van de Vijver (this volume) discusses several issues critical to assessing individuals from multicultural contexts. He emphasizes three challenges: (1) cultural factors affecting performance; (2) threats to internal validity due to limited language proficiency in the language of testing; and (3) differential predictive validity of assessments for individuals from different cultural groups. He discusses different approaches to addressing these challenges, including assessment design and statistical approaches. While these approaches are needed, they are not sufficient to address validity in assessment in a global economy. When culture and social context are considered beyond score differences between cultural groups, a more complex picture of the relationship between culture and validity emerges. Box 28.1 shows examples that illustrate how cultural differences need to be properly understood and taken into consideration. The examples originate from different national and international projects (Solano-Flores & Nelson-Barber, 2001). The identity of the cultural groups and countries are not disclosed to ensure confidentiality.

BOX 28.1 EXAMPLES OF THE RELATION BETWEEN ASSESSMENT AND SOCIOCULTURAL CONTEXT: ASSESSMENT DEVELOPMENT, TRANSLATION, AND REVIEW

Case 1: Collectivism, Social Structure, and Assessment Development Procedures

As part of a research project on the assessment of Indigenous populations, a test developer working in a small, remote community asks a teacher to review the draft of a mathematics test to make sure that the characteristics of its items are consistent with the ways in which the content is taught by the teachers in the school of her community. Before making any comment, the teacher consults with the elder of her community—the most respectable figure in the community. The elder, in turn, consults with other elders from other communities who happen to be visiting.

Case 2: Working Styles, Communication, and Test Translation Review

A team of researchers organize a series of panels in two countries that share the same language and are in the same geographical region. The panels (including educators, content specialists, and linguists) are in charge of reviewing the adequacy of the translation of an international test into their language. Each item is reviewed using a procedure where each panel member completes three initial activities individually: 1) read the item in the target language; 2) respond to the item; and 3) take note of any concerns. Then, with the researchers' facilitation, panel members take turns sharing their notes and discussing their observations and concerns.

The procedure is implemented with ease in one of the countries. In contrast, in the second country, it is extremely difficult to have the panelists work individually, as they exchange ideas and work collaboratively as soon as they are given the items, regardless of the directions provided and repeated by the researchers. The research team realizes that, although the two countries share the same language and have related histories and cultures, each country has a different set of forms of communication and working styles. The team also realizes that while the panels in the second country could be pushed to implement the review procedure as intended, this would have a cost—the information provided by the panels might not be rich.

Case 3: Human Resources and Test Translation

A researcher visits a country to give a workshop on the procedures authorized by an international assessment program to translate its tests. The country has a long large-scale testing tradition and a long history of participation in international tests for comparison purposes. The country's participation in each international test provides the grounds for several doctoral students to conduct investigations for their dissertations. The organization representing the country in the assessment program has a team of educational researchers with ample experience in test translation.

Given this level of experience, there is some skepticism among the team members about the extent to which the team should change their practices to adopt a new translation procedure. In the end, the team decides to slightly adapt their procedures to incorporate aspects of the new procedure that it considers relevant to improving their work. While it cannot be said that the translation team implements the new procedure with fidelity, given its qualifications, it is likely to produce an optimal translation.

Case 4: Cultural Sensitivity and Task Equivalence

An international test includes a task consisting of a scenario in which accidents have occurred in a public park with an unusually high frequency. As part of the task, students need to examine multiple sources of information (e.g., hypothetical newspaper clips, email exchanges between city officials, technical reports from engineers). Each source contains information that is relevant or irrelevant to making appropriate inferences about the frequency with which accidents in that particular park and other parks have occurred in the past. Also as part of the task, students need to write a letter to the city mayor, letting her know the probable causes of the problem and the actions the city should take to solve the problem.

> The translation teams from different participating countries raise different concerns regarding the degree to which the task reflects their own social contexts. For example, in one country, it would be impossible to have a female occupying a public office. In another, it would be unthinkable to have access to communications between top-ranked city officials. In another, making comments on government actions or indicating actions for local governments to take might not be in accord with appropriate political styles. It becomes evident that a series of substantial changes are needed in each country's version of the task—to the extent that task may end up varying considerably across countries. Yet not making these changes would be antithetical to the rationale for using scenarios—assessing students' skills in meaningful, realistic contexts.

Used to obtaining feedback from teachers individually, the test developer finds it difficult to obtain information from the teacher, who avoids expressing personal opinions. Soon the test developer realizes that no meaningful information will be obtained about the extent to which the task is sensitive to the enacted curriculum unless the procedure used to collect information on the test is consistent with the social structure of the community and the collective style in which decisions are made and opinions are expressed. At the same time, this alternative procedure is extremely time-consuming and deviates from the assessment development procedures typically used by many test developers when they work with teachers.

The four cases described in Box 1 involve activities in the process of assessment development other than comparing the performance of different cultural groups. They illustrate how validity issues concern the entire process of development (Basterra, Trumbull, & Solano-Flores, 2011). Also, the four cases involve dilemmas. On the one hand, if test developers or researchers apply existing procedures created in a predominant society (or for a mainstream cultural or linguistic group), they may fail to obtain important information about new, different groups. On the other hand, being flexible and sensitive to the values, characteristics, and styles of different cultural groups comes with a cost—violating currently accepted practice regarding standardization and comparability. Ultimately, these dilemmas have implications concerning the validity of score interpretations, which may be challenged due to lack of adherence to existing procedures or for their failure to reflect the characteristic of cultural groups.

Not all countries have policies in place for properly recognizing cultural and linguistic diversity (Ercikan & Lyons-Thomas, 2013). Self-recognition as a multilingual society (as is the case of two and 11 official languages, respectively, in Canada and South Africa) may be a desirable condition for implementing practices intended to ensure fair, valid assessment of multiple cultural and linguistic groups. Yet, while necessary, that condition is not sufficient to ensure fair, valid testing. For example, in South Africa, the number of students' home languages spoken at home is much greater than the number of official languages (Setati & Adler, 2001). Moreover, in practice, due to language loss, curriculum may be extremely difficult to enact in the languages of linguistic minority communities if those languages have social stigma attached to them or if the number of educators who are native users of those languages are below critical numbers (Oliveri, Ercikan, & Simon, 2015; Solano-Flores, Backhoff, Contreras-Niño, & Vázquez-Muñoz, 2015).

Five chapters in Section IV provide examples of how societal changes and factors have influenced changes in assessment. Teltemann and Klieme (this volume) provide several examples of societal contexts. In many cases, those contexts are defined by challenges countries face regarding the effectiveness of their education systems. Such challenges, they argue, led to joint efforts in building international assessments of educational outcomes such as the Trends in International Mathematics and Science Study (TIMSS) and the Programme for International Student Assessment (PISA). Accordingly, international assessments are an outcome of changes in national and international educational governance leading to internationalization in education. Teltemann and Klieme illustrate how international assessments, especially PISA, have become a powerful tool for educational reform. But the processes by which outcomes are interpreted and translated into policy are complex and not necessarily sound. These processes may be difficult to understand and they may vary tremendously across countries. Also, it can be argued that, given the variety and complexity of challenges faced by different societies, the influences should not be assumed to be beneficial or optimal when countries lack the resources needed to properly interpret and use results from international comparisons according to their own social and cultural contexts. Comparability issues critical to properly interpreting international assessment results are often overlooked (Ercikan, Roth, & Asil, 2015). The misinterpretation, misuse, and abuse of international test comparison rankings are special sources of concern and alarm (Ercikan, Roth, & Asil, 2015; Figazzolo, 2009; Tatto, 2006).

A historical perspective is presented in the Buckendahl (this volume) chapter on how public recognition of discrepancies in educational funding and achievement across districts in the U.S. led to education reform policies such as ESEA, NAEP, NCLB, and Race to the Top. To a large extent, the rationale for these reform initiatives was based on the goal of providing equitable financial support and addressing inequities in educational outcomes. For example, NCLB legislation (U.S. Congress, 2002) required states to develop academic content standards and assessments for all students. NCLB requirements have had significant impact on educational assessments in the U.S., including what is assessed (focusing primarily on reading and mathematics), how students are assessed (primarily with multiple-choice items), and how performance is evaluated (mainly through comparisons against a level of proficiency). Race to the Top was proposed in reaction to growing criticisms from educators and the public about the design and implementation of NCLB legislation. Central to this change is the shift from a focus on adequate yearly progress based on meeting the 'proficient' performance criterion to a focus on growth from year to year.

A societal development that is transforming assessment, along with education, is advances in information technology and increased computation power as discussed in Katz and Gorin (this volume). These developments make it possible to create large-scale assessments drawing on a wide range of assessment types, using psychometric models that would be impossible to imagine a decade ago. Further, changes include automated scoring of performance tasks, essays, or constructed-response tasks, which make the use of open-ended questions feasible in large-scale assessments. New information technology also makes it possible to create multistage tests or computer-adaptive test administration models that are sensitive to individual examinees' ability levels. Perhaps more significantly, these developments are changing not only *how* assessments occur, but also *what* constructs can now be assessed. Unsurprisingly, it is now feasible to assess interactive communication and collaborative problem-solving—constructs whose assessment implies the violation of the assumption of item and examinee independence.

Culture and societal contexts can have multifaceted influences on assessment. Kennedy (this volume) describes the Confucian heritage culture context for learning and assessment and its potential contribution to high achievement levels in East Asian student populations. This focus allows examination of what appears to be a paradox. Traditional, lecture-based teaching, large classes, and expectations of students' passive learning based on memorization (among other features of such systems) in these cultural contexts do not appear to be conditions that account for the high academic achievement levels observed in these populations. Instead, how assessments are viewed by students, educators, and the public seems to be a relevant factor. In the Confucian cultural context, examinations are viewed as a mechanism for treating all students equally and fairly and free from family and other social influences. This view contrasts with the view that such tests are unfair, a major reason for criticism of large-scale testing in the U.S. While this belief in East Asian countries may not be as strong as it used to be in the past, examinations are still seen as the basis of meritocracy. Kennedy implies that, when students view examinations as fair and important mechanisms for upward mobility and success, they are more motivated to perform better on tests.

This connection between culture and academic success, as operationalized by international assessments, has been contested (Gieve & Clark, 2005; Ryan & Louie, 2007; Wang, 2013) on the grounds that it overemphasizes culture and stereotypes East Asian students. However, a growing body of research in the U.S. on the reverse side of this relationship argues that stereotype threat (fear of confirming a negative stereotype of one's social or ethnic group) may have an adverse effect on the performance of racial minorities in tests (see Steele, Spencer, & Aronson, 2002). It has to be said that the construct of stereotype threat carries its own burden of controversy (Cullen, Hardison, & Sackett, 2004; Sackett, Hardison, & Cullen, 2004). Yet an important lesson from this chapter is the attention to the fact that fairness and the perception of fairness in testing is shaped by culture. A large body of research has examined how assessments may underestimate academic proficiency for students whose home language is different than the language of schooling and assessment (Abedi, 2004; Abedi, Hofstetter, & Lord, 2004; Abedi & Lord, 2001; Butler, Bailey, Stevens, Huang, & Lord, 2004; Ercikan, et al., 2015; Penfield & Lee, 2010). Another research corpus has examined the role that cultural differences play as a source of unfair testing (Kopriva, Gabel, & Cameron, 2011; Luykx et al., 2007; Noble, Rosebery, Suarez, Warren, & O'Connor, 2015; Solano-Flores & Trumbull, 2003). In contrast, relatively little attention has been paid to the psychological or social mechanisms by which students' perceptions of examinations may influence performance, one of the reasons for the current volume.

Another factor that affects how assessment is conducted is assessment capacity within countries. Gebril (this volume) discusses the cultural context of assessment in Muslim countries, and points to the link between assessment capacity (including assessment literacy, expertise, and resources) and assessment quality. An incipient assessment literacy and the lack of independent institutions that oversee the development and validation of assessment instruments ultimately affect assessment quality. We argue that unequal assessment capacities among countries that participate in comparative international testing is a matter of validity that is yet to be examined. Ironically, since its inception, in 1961, the International Association for the Evaluation of Educational Achievement (IEA) recognized countries' adequate human and institutional resources as critical to properly participating in international comparisons (Husén, 1983).

Moving assessment in directions that support learning and improve education, such as incorporating formative assessment in learning contexts, is inevitably affected by educational context and teacher assessment capacity. Both Kennedy (this volume) and Gebril (this volume) describe resistance to incorporating formative assessment practices into Confucian and Muslim cultural contexts, where summative objective tests are widely used. Gebril argues that centralized education systems in Muslim countries favor summative assessment-based accountability systems. Even though the great majority of teachers prefer using teacher-made assessments, these assessments are primarily multiple-choice question tests; they do not include constructed-response tasks. This should not be a surprise. Assessment, and especially formative assessment, is a process of communication and social interaction (Ruiz-Primo, Solano-Flores, & Li, 2014). To a large extent, the social structure in a given culture will favor some forms of assessment over others because they involve forms of social interaction that are more acceptable or more familiar.

Societal contexts not only affect assessments but they also affect perceptions of assessments. Buckendahl (this volume) and Kennedy (this volume) provide contrasting examples of how social contexts affect perceptions of assessment. Buckendahl reports that the perception of assessment as valuable has decreased significantly during the last 30 years in the U.S. Most notably, in a Gallup survey, only 45% of the respondents described standardized tests as useful and only 33% indicated support for teachers to follow the Common Core Standards in their teaching. This public opinion clearly contrasts with what Kennedy (this volume) describes in Confucian heritage societies, likely due to their long history of assessment being used as an equalizer and a tool for fairness. In surveys of Hong Kong teachers, assessment was seen as a powerful way for promoting student learning (Brown, Hui, Yu, & Kennedy, 2011). According to Kennedy, there are clear differences between teachers in Western societies and teachers in Confucian historical cultural contexts. In the former, student assessment results are consistently attributed to teachers and schools; in the latter, teachers view examinations as resources for assessing learning in an objective, equitable manner. Clearly, cultural differences in the functions and values attributed to assessments are a reflection of the forms of learning valued by different societies and who is held accountable for student learning.

THE INFLUENCE OF ASSESSMENT ON SOCIETY

Educational assessment has become the focal point of educational practice, guiding curriculum and instruction. This influence on society has been positive, as well as negative. On one hand, assessment has been the key source of information in education policy for informing decisions about the effectiveness of education. On the other hand, unfortunately, assessment also has been used as a gatekeeper of access to higher education or for sometimes unfair or inappropriate accountability purposes. In many cases, it has unintentionally contributed to the perpetuation of educational inequities. These influences include providing comparative information about educational outcomes for dozens of countries and, thereby, having an impact on educational policy at national levels in numerous countries. They also include their use in high-stakes accountability for rewarding or penalizing schools and teachers, and for allocating resources.

The same sociocultural contexts that affect student performance on tests play an important role in how assessments are perceived and used in the society. These include whether they are viewed as fair sources of information about outcomes and whether and how they are valued. In the U.S., the Scholastic Aptitude Test (SAT) was once perceived as a key instrument of the merit-based system, reducing inequities in the U.S. higher education system (Lemann, 2000; Zwick, 2002). Currently, perceptions of the

SAT do not include one of being an equalizer. First, it is often criticized as not measuring academic potential, not assessing creativity and motivation, and not assessing non-cognitive variables which are considered as relevant to academic success (Atkinson & Geiser, 2009). The second criticism concerns fairness based on its alleged bias against ethnic and language minority groups and because it spurs test preparation and coaching that not everyone can afford (Allalouf & Ben Shankhar, 1998; Atkinson, 2001; Powers, 2012). Other examples can be cited of how culture and social contexts affect perceptions of assessments and how these perceptions are functions of the roles they fulfill in different societies. Thus, for example in North America and Australia, assessments are considered as central to accountability models. In contrast, in Nordic countries, assessments are not considered the dominant mechanism for accountability (Sahlberg, 2007). In Finland, for example, trust, shared responsibility, and equality, among others, take precedence over accountability as factors that explain high performance in international test comparisons (Sahlberg, 2011).

Of utmost importance in the analysis of the impact of assessment on society is the extent to which societies are prepared to make effective use of assessment information. One aspect that shapes this impact is the abuse of tests and the use of tests in ways not intended by test developers or education systems (Shepard, 1992). As experience shows, a long history of large-scale assessment is not necessarily a guarantee that assessment systems operate solely based on informed decisions; they are strongly influenced by political forces and social pressures. Experiences from the United States are very illustrative. One is the California Learning Assessment System, which was discontinued because of pressure from conservative groups, which challenged its content and its emphasis on performance tasks (Kirst & Mazzeo, 1996). Another is the inclusion in large-scale assessment programs of English language learners who are at early stages in their development of English as a second language in spite of evidence that questions the validity of interpretations of measures of academic achievement for those students (Hakuta & Beatty, 2000).

Another aspect that shapes the impact of assessment on society is the extent to which societies are prepared to benefit from assessments. For example, assessment programs cannot have a substantial, positive impact in education in the absence of long-term, coordinated efforts that include long-term support for educators (Valdés, Menken, & Castro, 2015). An important aspect of this readiness is assessment capacity. We can think of assessment capacity as the extent to which a country is able to develop and use sound assessment instruments and create and sustain effective assessment systems. Limited financial resources and limited experience with large-scale assessment projects; an incipient or non-existing culture of assessment, evaluation, and accountability; and a limited number of professionals with training in assessment and educational measurement limit a country's assessment capacity (Solano-Flores, 2008). While evaluating countries' assessment capacity is a matter for a whole research project, certain simple indicators may suggest that countries vary tremendously in their assessment capacity. For instance, 24 of the 59 countries that participated in TIMSS 2007 did not have any representation from individuals or organizations with membership in the International Test Commission, an indication that a significant number of countries that participate in international test comparisons do not have adequate numbers of assessment experts. Of these 24 countries, 17 are ranked by the World Bank as low- or middle-income level, and 23 were non-Western countries (D. Illescu, personal communication to Tamara L. Milbourn, November 11, 2012).

Table 28.1 shows a list of conditions needed for the viability and success of national assessment systems (Solano-Flores, 2008). Perhaps the table should be considered as an

Table 28.1 Assessment Capacity Dimensions

Human resources:
Sufficient numbers of qualified professionals in the field of assessment and related areas.

Infrastructure:
Appropriate resources, facilities, equipment, materials, software, logistics, and social and institutional networks needed to develop and sustain assessment activities.

Conceptual preparedness:
Ability to generate assessment frameworks, instruments, item banks, and analytical tools for developing assessments and processing information from tests.

Theoretical and methodological soundness:
Ability to use diverse psychometric theories and methodological approaches.

Operationality:
Existence of a set of procedures for the systematic completion of multiple activities of the assessment process, such as population sampling, test administration, score reporting, and test security.

Planning:
Existence of a well-articulated design and a long-term assessment program.

Social equity and professional development:
Fairness, social participation, multidisciplinary work in testing practices; integration of assessment activities and the development of human resources related to assessment.

Sustainability, stability, and continuity:
Ability to sustain long-term assessment efforts systematically; resilience to financial and political uncertainty.

Systemic congruence:
Coordinated efforts with other components in the educational system; impact of assessment on policy and decision-making.

Research and practice agenda:
Systematic efforts oriented to generating knowledge and improving practice in areas of social relevance in the country according to assessment outcomes.

initial attempt to evaluate inequality in assessment in different countries. More dimensions could be added to the table. Based on these dimensions, it is possible to examine the extent to which a country can derive a substantial benefit from its participation in an international test comparison, for example, by making informed educational policy decisions based on results from these comparisons, beyond simply interpreting international rankings as evidence of failure or success.

Clearly, these dimensions are relevant to examining consequential validity as critical to examining the use of tests. Messick (1989) defines consequential validity as the "integrated evaluative judgment of the degree to which empirical evidence and theoretical rationales support the adequacy and *appropriateness* of *inferences* and the *actions* based on test scores or other modes of assessment" (p. 13, italics in the original). Accordingly, in order to properly evaluate an assessment, it is of utmost importance to examine not only what the assessment is supposed to measure, but also how the information it produces is interpreted and used to serve certain national goals.

Five of the chapters provide rich examples of how assessment may impact societies. Teltemann and Klieme (this volume) review research on the impact of international assessments on education systems around the world. While cultural validity or validity in general do not play a central role in their review, the authors do point to criticisms raised about the comparability of assessment results and the meaning of scores across countries. Despite these criticisms, results from international assessments are widely used to compare countries as to effectiveness in education. The authors describe how international assessments have impacted education systems and governance of education more broadly. PISA, one of the international assessments considered as having had the greatest impact on education policy worldwide, is the primary focus of the discussion in this chapter. The review includes observations that the growing reliance on international assessments implies that institutions and policies are perceived to be, at least to some extent, transferable. A consequence of that perceived transference is a promotion of *convergence* (Drezner, 2001) towards each other and towards an international convention of institutions and policies, with the merits of this trend a matter of some debate.

An important component of the reported impact of international assessments has been the shift of the discussion about education policy at country levels from 'input oriented' to 'output oriented.' A further implication is described as a shift from decision-making based on ideas or principles to 'reactive' evidence- and knowledge-based governance (Grek, 2012). In fact, several examples of significant change in educational governance internationally are described in which assessment results are used to motivate or provide rationales for education reform (Feniger & Lefstein, 2014). In Canada, the implementation of international assessments promoted an alignment of within-country assessment programs with PISA and the harmonization of national indicators with OECD Education at a Glance indicators (Froese-Germain, 2010). Based on TIMSS 1995 and 1999 results, England and some developing countries changed teaching practices, teacher training, instructional materials, educational standards, and curricula (Heyneman & Lee, 2014).

In a survey of countries that participated in PISA, when asked about the impact of international assessments on their education systems, more than half of the 37 countries reported that PISA had been 'extremely' or 'very' influential (Breakspear, 2012). One impact PISA made on a great majority of these countries has been the development of new elements of a national/federal assessment strategy (Breakspear, 2012). The review makes distinctions between countries such as the USA and England, which have a long tradition of large-scale assessment and in which the results from international assessments did not reveal shocking results and, therefore, did not lead to significant policy changes. In contrast, in Germany, the initial PISA results shocked the country and prompted considerable changes in education policies and practice (Ertl, 2006; Hartong, 2012; Neumann, Fischer, & Kauertz, 2010). In particular, output- and evidence-based policy making replaced philosophical ideas about how education should be organized (Bieber et al., 2014).

There has not been a comprehensive investigation of impact of international assessments on education policy and practice. In fact, Teltemann and Klieme (this volume) convincingly argue that, even when changes in policy have been observed, these changes are not necessarily reflected in changes of practices. Therefore, assessments are not always effective in having an impact on actual outcomes such as learning or inequality. However, the analysis Teltemann and Klieme conducted of surveys from international assessments during the last two decades pointed to an increase, from 59% to 73%, of student standardized testing practices and a decrease in standard deviation, which they interpret as a clear indication of a trend towards more standardized tests and more homogeneity across countries as an impact of international assessment. Arguments supporting these findings are presented by Lingard and Lewis (this volume). These authors focus on the globalization of U.S.-based, large-scale assessment models and the use of education indicators for monitoring education. Lingard and Lewis argue that international assessments such as PISA (which was modeled after U.S.-based assessments) are, in turn, affecting how national assessments are conducted. They argue that the assessment models in international assessments are replicated by national assessment programs in the participating countries. Within the U.S. context, they raise several negative consequences of high-stakes accountability assessments, including an adverse impact on the width of countries' curricula, the variety of pedagogies, and the schooling experience of young people.

CONCLUDING COMMENTS

The chapters in Section IV provide multiple examples of the strong bidirectional relationship between assessment and sociocultural context. Sociocultural context influences the content, forms, and modes of assessment and the ways in which assessment results are interpreted and used. Correspondingly, assessment influences a society, from individual students, to teachers, to schools, to education systems. Based on the arguments and evidence offered, we draw three conclusions that should contribute to enhanced assessment practices based on a comprehensive view of assessment.

First, while bidirectional, the relationship between assessment and sociocultural context is not necessarily synergistic. For example, the set of public perceptions of assessment instruments and programs are heavily influenced by the role assessment fulfills in a society. This role is not necessarily limited to providing information about learning outcomes. Often, it is tightly embedded in complex political contexts. The popularity of international assessments speaks to the willingness of countries to adopt assessments, in many cases under the assumption that the information these assessments generate will contribute to the enhancement of their education systems. Unfortunately, the mechanisms by which this information is translated into policy and implemented in practice are complex. In fact, only a small proportion of countries have developed policies intended to address results from international test comparisons. While outcomes from international assessments are often invoked in the debate about education reform, they may actually be used as part of the rhetoric intended to justify reforms that are motivated by political, financial, or ideological agendas.

Second, both within a country and in international test comparisons, standardization does not necessarily ensure equity. While it is guided by scientific reasoning and methods, assessment is not used and understood in the same ways by different cultures or different segments of a society. Even in the context of international comparisons, in which cultural equivalence and comparability issues are more evident, the participation of countries and the ways in which countries use the results from those comparisons are shaped by the characteristics of their societies. What counts as objective, fair assessment, and even as assessment, is shaped by culture. In particular, appropriate use of assessment results greatly depends on assessment capacity.

Third, ignoring the relationship between assessment and sociocultural context leads to wrong expectations about the ways in which assessment can contribute to fair education reform. As an example, the use of computer-administered tests in large-scale assessment programs is a reflection of the increasing influence of technology in education; a great deal of students' learning takes place in technology-based environments.

But, is this true for all countries participating in international comparisons or for all segments of the society within a country? In addition, several types of knowledge and competencies identified as critical for life and work in the 21st century (e.g., communication, collaboration, and problem solving) assume certain technological skills. Frameworks that follow these trends in the society with regards to technology are likely to strengthen the alignment of assessment and learning according to constructs of increasing complexity. However, differences between economic and cultural groups in the levels of access to and engagement with technology pose a serious threat to the validity of score interpretations in multicultural societies and in a global economy marked by tremendous inequalities. Ultimately, proper consideration of the relationship between assessment and sociocultural context is critical to validity. Underestimating the importance of this relationship may contribute to perpetuating unfair assessment practices. Also, it can lead to erroneous interpretations and misinformed uses of assessment outcomes.

Both the assessments and perceptions of assessments are critically tied to the purposes and uses they serve. Educators interested in using assessment as effective tools for improving education and reducing inequities in opportunities need to pay close attention to the sociocultural context of assessments. This includes how assessments are designed, with diverse students and educational contexts in mind, how assessment results are used, and their functions in the society. In particular, this means avoiding the use of assessment results for unfair decisions such as penalizing teachers and schools and using assessments as gatekeepers when students from different cultural and social backgrounds do not have equal opportunities to succeed. It also means developing capabilities among educators and policy makers for effective and proper uses of assessment results. These considerations need to be taken into account continuously, particularly with new assessment modes, new constructs, and new uses of assessment results.

REFERENCES

Abedi, J. (2004). The no child left behind act and English language learners: Assessment and accountability issues. *Educational Researcher, 33*(1), 4–14.

Abedi, J., Hofstetter, C., & Lord, C. (2004). Assessment accommodations for English language learners: Implications for policy-based empirical research. *Review of Educational Research, 74*(1), 1–28.

Abedi, J., & Lord, C. (2001). The language factor in mathematics tests. *Applied Measurement in Education, 14*(3), 219–234.

Allalouf, A., & Ben-Shankhar, G. (1998). The effect of coaching on the predictive validity of scholastic aptitude tests. *Journal of Educational Measurement, 35*(1), 31–47.

Atkinson, R. C. (2001, February 18). *Standardized tests and access to American universities* (2001 Robert H. Atwell Distinguished Lecture). Paper presented to the 83rd Annual Meeting of the American Council on Education, Washington, DC. Retrieved from http://works.bepress.com/richard_atkinson/36/

Atkinson, R. C., & Geiser, S. (2009). Reflections on a century of college admissions tests. *Educational Researcher, 38*(9), 665–676.

Basterra, M. R., Trumbull, E., & Solano-Flores, G. (Eds.). (2011). *Cultural validity in assessment: Addressing linguistic and cultural diversity.* New York: Routledge.

Becker, K. A. (2003). *History of the Stanford-Binet intelligence scales: Content and psychometrics.* Itasca, IL: Riverside.

Bieber, T., Martens, K., Niemann, D., & Windzio, M. (2014). Grenzenlose Bildungspolitik? Empirische Evidenz für PISA als weltweites Leitbild für nationale Bildungsreformen. *Zeitschrift Für Erziehungswissenschaft, 17*(S4), 141–166. doi:10.1007/s11618–014–0513–6

Black, P., & Wiliam, D. (2005). Lessons from around the world: how policies, politics and cultures constrain and afford assessment practices. *The Curriculum Journal, 16* (2), 249–261.

Breakspear, S. (2012). *The policy impact of PISA: An exploration of the normative effects of international benchmarking in school system performance* (OECD Education Working Paper Number 71). Paris, France: OECD Publishing. doi:10.1787/5k9fdfqffr28-en

Butler, F. A., Bailey, A. L., Stevens, R., Huang, B., & Lord, C. (2004). *Academic English in fifth-grade mathematics, science, and social studies textbooks* (CSE Report No. 642). Los Angeles, CA: University of California, National Center for Research on Evaluation, Standards, and Student Testing (CRESST).

Brown, G., Hui, S. K. F., Yu, W. M., & Kennedy, K. (2011). Teachers' conceptions of assessment in Chinese contexts: A tripartite model of accountability, improvement, and irrelevance. *International Journal of Educational Research, 50,* 307–320.

Camilli, G. (2013): Ongoing issues in test fairness. *Educational Research and Evaluation: An International Journal on Theory and Practice, 19*(2–3), 104–120.

Cole, M. (1999). Culture-free versus culture-based measures of cognition. In R. J. Sternberg (Ed.), *The nature of cognition* (pp. 645–664). Cambridge, MA: The MIT Press.

Cooke, R. (1965). *Recommendations for a head start program.* Washington, DC: U.S. Department of Health, Education, and Welfare, Office of Child Development.

Crawford, J. (2000). *At war with diversity: US language policy in an age of anxiety.* Clevedon, UK: Multilingual Matters.

Cullen, M. J., Hardison, C. M., & Sackett, P. R. (2004). Using SAT-grade and ability-job performance relationships to test predictions derived from stereotype threat theory. *Journal of Applied Psychology, 89*(2), 220–230.

Cummins, J. (2000). *Language, power, and pedagogy: Bilingual children in the crossfire.* Clevedon, UK: Multilingual Matters Ltd.

Drezner, D. W. (2001). Globalization and policy convergence. *International Studies Review, 3*(1), 53–78. doi:10.1111/1521–9488.00225

Ercikan, K. (1998). Methodological issues in international assessments. *International Journal of Education, 29,* 487–489.

Ercikan, K., & Lyons-Thomas, J. (2013). Adapting tests for use in other languages and cultures. In K. Geisinger (Ed.), *APA Handbook of testing and assessment in psychology* (Vol. 3, pp. 545–569). Washington, DC: American Psychological Association.

Ercikan, K., & Roth, W-M. (2011). Constructing data. In C. Conrad & R. Serlin (Eds.), *Sage handbook for research in education* (2nd ed., pp. 219–245). Thousand Oaks, CA: Sage Publications.

Ercikan, K., Roth, W-M., & Asil, M. (2015). Cautions about uses of international assessments. *Teachers College Record, 117*(1), 1–28.

Ercikan, K., Yue, M., Lyons-Thomas, J., Sandilands, D., Roth, W-M., & Simon, M. (2015). Reading proficiency and comparability of mathematics and science scores for students from English and non-English backgrounds: An international perspective. *International Journal of Testing, 15,* 153–175.

Ertl, H. (2006). Educational standards and the changing discourse on education: The reception and consequences of the PISA study in Germany. *Oxford Review of Education, 32*(5), 619–634. doi:10.2307/4618685

Feniger, Y., & Lefstein, A. (2014). How not to reason with PISA data: An ironic investigation. *Journal of Education Policy, 29*(6), 845–855. doi:10.1080/02680939.2014.892156

Figazzolo, L. (2009). *Impact of PISA 2006 on the education policy debate.* Report published by Education International. Retrieved December 12, 2012 from http://ei-ie.org/en/websections/content_detail/3272

Froese-Germain, B. (2010, September). The OECD, PISA and the Impacts on Educational Policy. *Virtual Research Centre (VRC).*

Gieve, S. and Clark, R. (2005) 'The Chinese approach to learning': Cultural trait or situated response? *System, 33* (2), 261–276.

Grek, S. (2012). What PISA knows and can do: Studying the role of national actors in the making of PISA. *European Educational Research Journal, 11*(2), 243–254. doi:10.2304/eerj.2012.11.2.243

Hakuta, K., & Beatty, A. (Eds.). (2000). *Testing English-language learners in U.S. schools: Report and workshop summary.* Washington, DC: National Academy Press.

Hambleton, R. K., Merenda, P. F., & Spielberger, C. D. (2005). *Adapting educational and psychological tests for cross-cultural assessment.* Mahwah, NJ: Lawrence Erlbaum Associates, Publishers.

Hartong, S. (2012). Overcoming resistance to change: PISA, school reform in Germany and the example of Lower Saxony. *Journal of Education Policy, 27*(6), 747–760. doi:10.1080/02680939.2012.672657

Heyneman, S. P., & Lee, B. (2014). The impact of international studies of academic achievement on policy and research. In L. Rutkowski, M. von Davier, & D. Rutkowski (Eds.), *Handbook of international large-scale assessment* (pp. 37–75). Boca Raton, FL: CRC Press.

Husén, T. (1983). *An incurable academic; Memoirs of a professor.* Oxford, UK: Pergamon Press.

Kirst, M. W., & Mazzeo, C. (1996). The rise, fall, and rise of state assessment in California, 1993–1996. *Phi, Delta, Kappan, 78*(4), 319–323.

Kopriva, R., Gabel, D., & Cameron, C. (2011). *Designing dynamic and interactive assessments for English learners that directly measure targeted science constructs.* Paper presented at the Society for Research on Educational Effectiveness Fall 2011 Conference, Washington, DC.

Lakin, J. M. (2014). Test directions as a critical component of test design: Best practices and the impact of examinee characteristics. *Educational Assessment, 19*(1), 17–34.

Lemann, N. (2000). *The big test: The secret history of the American meritocracy*. New York, NY: Farrar, Straus and Giroux.

Luykx, A., Lee, O., Mahotiere, M., Lester, B., Hart, J., & Deaktor, R. (2007). Cultural and home language influences on children's responses to science assessments. *The Teachers College Record, 109*(4), 897–926.

Martinez, M. E. (1999). Cognition and the question of test item format. *Educational Psychologist, 34*, 207–218.

Messick, S. (1989). Validity. In R. L. Linn (Ed.), *Educational measurement* (3rd ed., pp. 13–103). New York: American Council on Education and Macmillan.

Neumann, K., Fischer, H. E., & Kauertz, A. (2010). From PISA to educational standards: The impact of large-scale assessments on science education in Germany. *International Journal of Science and Mathematics Education, 8*(3), 545–563. doi:10.1007/s10763–010–9206–7

No Child Left Behind (NCLB) Act of 2001, 20 U.S.C.A. § 6301 *et seq.*

Noble, T., Rosebery, A., Suarez, C., Warren, B., & O'Connor, C. (2015). Science assessments and English language learners: Validity evidence based on response processes. *Applied Measurement in Education, 27*(4), 248–260.

Oliveri, M. E., Ercikan, K., & Simon, M. (2015). A Framework for developing comparable multi-lingual assessments for minority populations: Why context matters. *International Journal of Testing, 15*, 94–113.

Penfield, R. D., & Lee, O. (2010). Test-based accountability: Potential benefits and pitfalls of science assessment with student diversity. *Journal of Research in Science Teaching, 47*(1), 6–24.

Powers, D. E. (2012). Understanding the impact of special preparation for admissions tests. *ETS Research Report Series, 1*, i–15.

Ruiz-Primo, M. A., Solano-Flores, G., & Li, M. (2014). Formative assessment as a process of interaction through language: A framework for the inclusion of English language learners. In C. Wyatt-Smith, V. Klenowski, & P. Colbert (Eds.), *Developing assessment for quality learning: The enabling power of assessment* (Vol. 1, pp. 265–282). Dordrecht: Springer.

Ryan, J., & Louie, K. (2007). False dichotomy? 'Western' and 'Confucian' concepts of scholarship and learning. *Educational Philosophy and Theory, 39*(4), 404–417.

Sackett, P. R., Hardison, C. M., & Cullen, M. J. (2004). On interpreting stereotype threat as accounting for African American-White differences on cognitive tests. *American Psychologist, 59*(1), 7.

Sahlberg, P. (2007). Education policies for raising student learning: The Finnish approach. *Journal of Education Policy, 22*(2), 147–171.

Sahlberg, P. (2011). *Finnish lessons: What can the world learn from educational change in Finland?* New York: Teachers College Press.

Setati, M., & Adler, J. (2001). Between languages and discourses: Language practices in primary multilingual mathematics classrooms in South Africa. *Educational Studies in Mathematics, 43*, 243–269.

Shepard, L. A. (1992). Uses and abuses of testing. In Marvin C. Alkin (Ed.), *Encyclopedia of educational research* (6th ed., pp. 1477–1485). New York: MacMillan.

Solano-Flores, G. (2006). Language, dialect, and register: Sociolinguistics and the estimation of measurement error in the testing of English-language learners. *Teachers College Record, 108*(11), 2354–2379.

Solano-Flores, G. (2008). *A conceptual framework for examining the assessment capacity of countries in an era of globalization, accountability, and international test comparisons*. Paper presented at the 6th Conference of the International Test Commission. Liverpool, UK, July 16–18, 2008.

Solano-Flores, G., Backhoff, E., & Contreras-Niño, L. A. (2009). Theory of test translation error. *International Journal of Testing, 9*, 78–91.

Solano-Flores, G., Backhoff, E., Contreras-Niño, L. A., & Vázquez-Muñoz, M. (2015). Language shift and the inclusion of indigenous populations in large-scale assessment programs. *International Journal of Testing, 15*(2), 136–152.

Solano-Flores, G., & Nelson-Barber, S. (2001). On the cultural validity of science assessments. *Journal of Research in Science Teaching, 38*(5), 553–573.

Solano-Flores, G., & Trumbull, E. (2003). Examining language in context: The need for new research and practice paradigms in the testing of English-language learners. *Educational Researcher, 32*(2), 3–13.

Steele, C. M., Spencer, S. J., & Aronson, J. (2002). Contending with group image: The psychology of stereotype and social identity threat. *Advances in Experimental Social Psychology, 34*, 379–440.

Tatto, M. T. (2006). Education reform and the global regulation of teachers' education, development and work: A cross-cultural analysis. *International Journal of Educational Research, 45*, 231–241.

United States Congress. (1965). *Elementary and Secondary Education Act of 1965*. Pub. L. 89–10.

United States Congress. (2002). No Child Left Behind Act, 10 U.S.C. 6301.

U.S. Department of Education. (2014). Race to the top assessment program. Retrieved September 3, 2015 from http://www2.ed.gov/programs/racetothetop-assessment/index.html

Valdés, G., Menken, K., & Castro, M. (Eds.). (2015). *Common core, Bilingual and English language learners: A resource for educators.* Philadelphia, PA: Caslon, Inc.

Vinovskis, M. A. (1998). *Overseeing the nation's report card: The creation and evolution of the National Assessment Governing Board (NAGB).* Washington, DC: National Assessment Governing Board, U.S. Department of Education.

Wang, K. (2013). *A test of faith: Chinese students' changing views on the National College Entrance Examination.* Retrieved December 7, 2014 from http://www.tealeafnation.com/2013/06/a-test-of-faith-chinese-students-changing-views-on-the-national-college-entrance-examination/

Zwick, R. (2002). *Fair game?: The use of standardized admission tests in higher education.* New York: Psychology Press.

29

VOLUME CONCLUSION: THE FUTURE OF ASSESSMENT AS A HUMAN AND SOCIAL ENDEAVOUR

Gavin T. L. Brown and Lois R. Harris

Tests and assessments are valued in society, especially when the cost of getting it right matters, for example, when they are used to certify people we need to trust in order to assure public safety and well-being (e.g., engineers, doctors, pilots, train drivers, electricians, teachers, etc.). Without such formal assessments, we would need to rely solely on the attestation of some individual who may well be subject to the influences of collusion, corruption, and cheating (which is why tests were devised in the first place). Alternatively, we might have to rely on free market processes which would take time to weed out incompetents; we know that deficient practitioners (e.g., peddlers of quackery, pseudo-medicine, or health fraud) may well harm unsuspecting and naïve citizens (e.g., Gerald Shirtcliff's engineering work, produced under false engineering credentials, may have contributed to a building collapse in the 2011 Christchurch earthquake with significant loss of life; Howe, 2014). Hence, society needs confidence that learners and professionals can perform satisfactorily the responsibilities we assign them and we rely on validated evidence of those competencies before opportunities are given.

While members of the public generally perceive assessment as a useful and necessary mechanism (Buckendahl, this volume; Brookhart, 2013), do the current ways we conduct formative and summative evaluation merit this support? Furthermore, are the data generated from such assessments being interpreted and used in ways which actually are legitimate? As Buckendahl (this volume) reminds us, many rely on intuitive test theory (Braun & Mislevy, 2005) to comprehend assessments; this approach reduces the complexity of psychometric theory (i.e., all measures contain error and uncertainty and the validity of test-based claims must be argued and evidenced) to a few simple heuristics. For example, in relation to tests, people in society find it easy, perhaps because of the scoring objectivity of multiple-choice tests and the standardised administration, to believe that: (a) a test fairly measures the domain, (b) the test score is an accurate indicator of competence, (c) a high test score equals high personal competence, and (d) high average student test scores are proof of competent schools and teachers. These intuitive heuristics reflect a type of System I fast thinking used to replace thoughtful System II slow thinking; however, it is only via System II thinking where the complexities and variabilities of the social world can be properly considered (Kahneman, 2011).

The appeal of System I thinking around educational assessments is great as it can make complex decisions seem simple to justify. For example, parenting choices can be resolved by reference to the latest report card or test score (e.g., bad grades = grounding or removal of other privileges); mandates around educational policy (e.g., introduction of charter schools or a new curriculum) can be justified and defended by referencing 'problems' detected by tests scores or concerns over 'falling' or stagnant scores (Linn, 2000); and complex decisions around the quality of personnel in schools can be made by reference to absolute and value-added test scores. In contrast, System II thinking, based on expertise in what may be considered arcane arts like item response theory score calculation, standard setting, test equating, value-added measurement, and so on takes a much more careful and considered position concerning the meaning of scores and changes in those scores. Experts consider the reliability of a score, its stability as a correlated measure with other variables, its nature as a sample of both a domain and a population, its power to appropriately define a domain, and so on before reaching a tentative conclusion about teaching, schools, students, curriculum, or innovations. This last point, 'tentative,' is crucial; measurement experts will never consider a score to be absolute or certain as they acknowledge the error component, a very different stance to the newspaper headline which declares outright that a school or student group is 'failing' based on the latest round of test scores.

However, these System II complex processes and tentative conclusions do not lend themselves easily to the decisions that parents, policy makers, media, and educators have to and want to make. As mentioned in Chapter 1, the innovative California Learning Assessment System, which was adequately reliable, was abandoned because politicians and media deemed it to have failed, due in part to public misunderstandings around measurement statistics. Experts tend to display the more subtle and nuanced thinking that needs to take place around tests and assessments; however, their voices are often missing, misinterpreted, or overshadowed within educational debates. Chapters in this book provide examples of the necessary nuanced thinking; that is, they have introduced knowledge about the complex interrelationships between and among teachers, students, and policy makers around educational tests and assessments. Perhaps unsurprisingly, even System II thinking around statistical models of test scores comes under question when the human and social conditions of assessment are taken into consideration, given that they introduce variables which are not adequately accounted for in statistical models or most teachers' evaluation frameworks.

ERROR IN SITU CONDITIONS

In reflecting upon the substantive messages of this handbook, it becomes apparent that much of what we now know about how assessment affects teachers and students on a personal and emotional level has classically been treated as the error component within statistical models of test scores (Traub, 1994). As is well established (Feldt & Brennan, 1989; Haertel, 2006), the error component in a test score consists of both systematic and random error. It is generally accepted that systematic error threatens the validity of test scores and attempts should be made to mitigate such known sources (e.g., marker tiredness, distracting test environments, and inadequate teaching). In contrast, random and unpredictable errors (e.g., momentary lapses in attention, motivation, or transient negative thoughts) are considered to be exactly that, and cannot be accounted for in a statistical model. The assumption is that random errors impact all test takers equally and, with sufficient data collection, the influence of random errors is mitigated. Hence, random error exists, but can be safely ignored. This assumption itself is a kind of intuitive thinking that is belied by the complexities of test takers, who do learn and change from being assessed. While error in test theory has at least been identified, it is worth noting that few models of Assessment for Learning admit that formative classroom assessment processes (e.g., setting learning intentions and criteria; carrying out classroom discussions and questioning; providing feedback; involving students in peer and self-assessment [Leahy, Lyon, Thompson, & Wiliam, 2005]) have the potential for inaccuracy, unreliability, or invalidity.

While emotional variability around assessment events may seem relatively random, Vogl and Pekrun (this volume) have shown that there are regularities in how students emotionally react to and interact with various stages of the assessment process. Hence, not even students' achievement feelings can be treated as purely random. Similarly, student willingness to cheat (Murdock, Stephens, & Groteweil, this volume) or not try (Wise & Smith, this volume) are characterised by both random and systematic elements. These are just three characteristics easily identified as impacting the validity of standardized testing, but which also impact on other forms of assessment.

The complexity of assessment in a classroom situation where most educational assessment data is collected and used by teachers to make decisions about student learning is quite different to that of a formal standardised test. The most informal assessment data is gathered in the middle of public pedagogical interactions between a teacher and a student or group; thus, it happens on the fly and in the moment, with no independent quality assurance mechanisms in place to evaluate whether the student has expressed his or her knowledge as intended or whether the teacher has interpreted and responded appropriately. More formally, teachers might evaluate homework samples or assignments submitted by students who may or may not have had help at home or from the Internet, introducing possible construct-irrelevant factors in each child's demonstration of their learning. Because classroom assessment takes place in classes (face-to-face and cyber, or in vivo and in silico), it is public and thus subject to the pressures and challenges of social relationships which colour the quality and nature of the demonstrations students make of their learning. Thus, classroom assessment data are characterised by much noise, chaos, distraction, and emotion. Unfortunately for statistical models of student responding, the impact of cheating (Murdock et al., this volume), effort (Wise & Smith, this volume), emotion (Vogl & Pekrun, this volume), peer interactions (Panadero, this volume; Strijbos, this volume), or even self-directed evaluation (Andrade & Brown, this volume; Dinsmore & Wilson, this volume) is not trivial, nor can these variables be safely ignored. While we might be most concerned around important high-stakes decisions (e.g., promotion, graduation, selection for awards, etc.), the cumulative effect of 'garbage in, garbage out' factors on the many low-stakes decisions implemented in classrooms (e.g., placement in an inappropriate within-class reading group, assignment of class work which is too easy/difficult, etc.) may have serious impacts on learners' motivation, effort, progress, and desire to learn.

These realities might lead us to conclude that error is not construct irrelevant; it is the construct. Those pesky interfering factors (e.g., cheating, emotions, effort, relationships, motivations, etc.) constitute the substance of human life and cannot be readily ignored for the sake of a concrete but unreal or inaccurate score or grade. Random error is tightly bundled and highly unpredictable in the individual, but this handbook reveals that we do understand somewhat the processes and mechanisms involved in participating in assessment. What we are trying to do in educational assessment is multidimensional and impacts all dimensions simultaneously. Assessment affects emotions; thinking; behaving; interrelationships with peers, parents, and teachers; and intrarelationships with self—and all this across time, knowledge domains, methods, contexts, cultures, and societies. Thus, in-the-moment and on-the-fly assessment may be impossible to model mathematically; however, perhaps with greater research, we can reach a comprehensive ability, especially through the application of computerised assessment technologies, to detect and account in assessment for anything that looks like error but which reflects the real-world uncertainties of the human and social condition.

This complexity taps into what is known in biological research as the difference between in vivo (i.e., within the living) and in vitro (i.e., within the glass) research. In vivo refers to studies with living organisms, while in vitro refers to controlled laboratory environments. Indeed, in vitro studies might lead to false conclusions when applied to living animals because "they fail to replicate the precise cellular conditions of an organism" (Autoimmunity Research Foundation, 2012). As Zumbo (2015) points out, in vitro and in vivo concepts help us understand the differences addressed by psychometric approaches to testing and formative approaches to classroom assessment. Formal assessments administered under controlled conditions (both in pilot and norming phases) function as in vitro experiments in which the learner responds (usually alone, but increasingly in groups [Strijbos, this volume]) to the task (whether paper or computer-based), uninfluenced by other factors, while exercising peak and continuous effort, attention, and integrity. In contrast, assessments conducted in classroom or educational settings are social, interactive processes mediated by the many factors identified in this handbook (e.g., emotions, relationships, psychological concerns, personal and socially shared beliefs, attitudes, etc.) and function as the in vivo organism.

It is clear that our current approach to statistical modelling of tests and examinations fits assessment in vitro, but the chapters of this handbook raise serious concerns about their adequacy for in vivo assessment. Additionally, there has been little effort to even attempt to model or moderate summative classroom assessment, except for efforts to socially moderate school-based student certification systems (e.g., Queensland, Australia [Wyatt-Smith, Klenowski, & Gunn, 2010] and New Zealand [Crooks, 2010]). Without systematic efforts to account for these concerns, each teacher/assessor has to handle these confounding variables within their professional judgment of student work. Nonetheless, validity is threatened because teachers often have very different perceptions of explicit, latent, and meta-criteria, even when working within the same set of standards or criteria (Wyatt-Smith & Klenowski, 2012).

THE TEACHER IN SITU

Classroom assessment conditions require high levels of teacher assessment capability (Hill & Eyers, this volume) and as Parr and Timperley (this volume) note, context really matters in relation to teachers' assessment decisions and actions. In an extreme approach to Assessment for Learning, formative assessment only occurs during informal student processes, perhaps facilitated by teachers (Swaffield, 2011), while other approaches require the teacher to be the professional facilitator, using both informal and formal methods of assessment (Cowie & Harrison, this volume). Nonetheless, classroom implementation of assessment is enacted by teachers. Consequently, many of the chapters in this volume have identified significant responsibilities in classroom assessment that teachers need to deal with. These include:

- developing positive attitudes to and understandings of Assessment for Learning (Bonner, this volume);
- using assessment data for improved schooling effectiveness (Lai & Schildkamp, this volume);

- learning to use assessment to fulfill a teacher's responsibilities (Hill & Eyers, this volume);
- assessing all students fairly and appropriately regardless of their differences in skill, background, or abilities (Moon, this volume);
- protecting children's privacy in the open space of the classroom and also in regards to digital information (Tierney & Koch, this volume);
- giving useful and timely feedback that empowers learning (Lipnevich, Berg, & Smith, this volume);
- using assessment processes to develop students' own self-regulatory processes and ambitions (Dinsmore & Wilson, this volume);
- ensuring students have adequate preparation and skill to participate in assessment (Andrade & Brown, this volume; Panadero, this volume; Strijbos, this volume; Vogl & Pekrun, this volume).

All these aspects highlight the very challenging nature of the tasks we give to teachers when we ask them to conduct assessment (Cowie & Harrison, this volume). In the face of the myriad of responsibilities of a teacher and immediacy of classroom pressures, it is not surprising that so many teachers rely on their intuition, as well as practices they learned when they too were students (Hill & Eyers, this volume).

Placing students in classrooms with peers of a similar age and ability is a cost-efficient solution of long standing (Cole, 2010), ensuring the maximum number of children attain socially expected levels of competence. Yet, expecting that children within a classroom will be automatically immune to social fear, criticism, attack, or any other form of negative interaction smacks of incredible naïveté and wishful thinking. Hence, without having to resort to pre-industrial one-on-one tutoring as the dominant form of educational practice, we need to somehow reconcile the ideals of Assessment for Learning with the real-world experiences of humans who are required to interact with each other by social policy.

THE KNOTTY PROBLEM OF ASSESSMENT FOR ACCOUNTABILITY

Further complicating the teacher's classroom life are external accountability pressures in policies that use student test scores as a basis for judging the quality of teachers and schools (Nichols & Harris, this volume). Even those used to making high-stakes decisions about students independent of teacher input (e.g., graduation, higher education entry, or mandatory retention within grade level) can elicit negative evaluations. Teachers generally believe that assessing teacher and student performance solely through student test results is invalid as the scores do not adequately reflect the richness of what students know and the progress they have made (Nichols & Berliner, 2007). Most teachers appear to prefer using more teacher-controlled assessment methods (e.g., performance assessments, oral presentations, peer and self-assessment, group and individual projects) because they consider that external assessments (a) tend to facilitate surface learning outcomes and unfair blaming of the student, (b) are often disconnected from students' classroom learning, and (c) damage student self-esteem via invidious comparisons to peers and somewhat arbitrary 'proficiency' cut-offs (Brown, 2009; Irving, Harris, & Peterson, 2011). Ensuring that schooling, including assessment, does no harm to the child is perhaps a paramount value in child-centered pedagogy; hence, many teachers experience discomfort due to the dual obligation of being facilitator and evaluator of learning (Bonner, this volume; Harris & Brown, 2009).

Unfortunately, the intuitive test theory assumptions parents and community members make about assessments (e.g., test scores are fair and objective and help detect good schools; Brookhart, 2013; Buckendahl, this volume) lend support to policy pressures to use tests to evaluate schools and teachers. Government departments or ministries of education, despite often being staffed by education and teaching experts, are subject to many political winds, especially those that seek to change education into a private benefit instead of a social good (Lingard & Lewis, this volume). Use of international test scores (e.g., OECD, PISA) to justify significant changes to how assessments are used are hard for educators or education-oriented policy makers to resist (Teltemann & Klieme, this volume). In such circumstances, the pressure for teachers to conform to the expectations of custom, policy, and law may overpower their noble ideals about using assessment to guide and improve instruction first and foremost.

Additionally, the very different circumstances of educational professionals vis-à-vis other professionals must be kept in mind before we presume that the quality of a teacher can be determined by testing them or their students. Teacher evaluations are based on the performance of classes of learners who have not been selected by the practicing professional and whose performance is significantly determined by social factors (e.g., poverty, illness, prior educational experience, parental expectations and preparation, conditions of disability, etc.). This is quite different from professionals like private medical specialists, lawyers, and accountants who usually work with clients individually and whose customers have been screened for suitability and their ability to pay. Putting pressure on teachers through accountability testing creates invidious pressures to produce the result expected by superiors (Lerner & Tetlock, 1999), resulting in teacher cheating with punishments quite at odds with the impact of the crime relative to other offences (e.g., the sentencing of Atlanta teachers to jail for falsifying student test scores vs. actions of the bankers and traders who contributed to the 2008 global financial crisis which did not lead to jail time; Ravitch, 2015).

IN VIVO CULTURAL CONDITIONS

Cultural factors also come into play when determining the impact of assessment. Not only does the final section's discussion chapter (Ercikan & Solano-Flores, this volume) provide vivid examples of challenges in adapting assessments across societies and cultures and the bidirectional effect present between culture and assessment, but also gives a useful checklist of system capacity dimensions that need to be considered when approaching the phenomenon of assessment within any jurisdiction. Their chapter provides a guide to validity concerns when trying to improve the use of assessment within any jurisdiction and also a lens through which factors within a society can be isolated and considered.

Cultural differences in assessment emphases can be seen in the two cultural case studies included in this handbook. Confucian heritage societies (Kennedy, this volume) and Arabic, Islamic societies (Gebril, this volume) both rely heavily on public examinations, along with nations and societies not reported in this volume (e.g., India, much of Latin America, and Africa). This emphasis is, of course, different from that of the Anglo-American approach to school accountability testing (Lingard & Lewis, this volume; Nichols & Harris, this volume), since the public examinations are testing the individual students for selection and certification purposes. While in some countries, such exams may be legacies of colonisation (e.g., India, Hong Kong, Singapore), their implementation in post-colonial periods continues due to those societies' robust social commitments to mechanisms which are perceived to allow the most able, talented, and deserving candidates to be selected from wherever they may reside in the socioeconomic spectrum and physical geography of a jurisdiction.

While cultural values may be relatively constant in mono-ethnic societies, it is clear that multicultural diversity changes the makeup of test takers within most modern industrialised societies, with real implications for the meaning of test scores (van de Vijver, this volume). The greater challenge to assessment is that the patterns we detect within and across societal groups do not automatically apply to all individuals, who are self-regulating and autonomous in their own right. Indeed, emphasis on culturally responsive pedagogy and assessment (Bishop & Glynn, 1999; Hood, 1998), along with calls for differentiated assessment (Moon, this volume), suggest that assessments need not be standardised but rather functionally equivalent to better meet the social and individual diversity of learners. For educators, assessments that meet these challenges will generally not look like standardised formal assessments (i.e., in vivo does not equal in vitro), though culturally-responsive standardised testing for diagnostic in-school use have been developed (Keegan, Brown, & Hattie, 2013).

ASSESSMENT USING TECHNOLOGY

Technologies are being used to develop new and potentially powerful assessment practices (Katz & Gorin, this volume; Strijbos, this volume). However, current research into the student experience of novel assessments, including those within integrated technology, is not unequivocally favourable (Struyven & Devesa, this volume). While paper-based examinations and course work may still predominate, technology is making itself felt within all genres of assessment (Katz & Gorin, this volume).

The power of high-technology testing systems seems to be most frequently used within accountability policy implementations (Lingard & Lewis, this volume; Nichols & Harris, this volume; Teltemann & Klieme, this volume). However, these applications generally provide little value for the classroom practitioner, school administrator, parent, or student. Indeed, much of what we know about schools or countries through different low-stakes tests (e.g., NAEP, PIRLS, TIMSS, PISA, etc.) may have been 'contaminated' by the various elements discussed in this handbook (e.g., high cheating, low effort motivation, boredom, and anxiety emotions). This means that most of what we know about schools and countries through testing is substantially affected by error; indeed, a large body of research exists raising doubts about the validity of the PISA tests and reports (see Asil & Brown, 2016 for an overview). Hence, without substantially increased efforts around reducing these sources of error, collecting such data may not be worthwhile and may encourage inaccurate perceptions of schools and systems.

Discussion

As Cizek (2001) noted, scholars are much quicker to identify flaws in educational assessment practices than to provide potentially viable solutions. We have tried throughout this handbook to encourage authors to provide a fair and balanced perspective on the their topics, identifying benefits as well as limitations in relation to the human and social factors they have examined. We have also encouraged authors to be solutions focused, and here we provide our own ideas about ways forward in relation to the knotty problems identified within this volume.

STATISTICAL MODELS

It is clear that our current statistical models do not adequately encompass all the known factors impinging on a student's response or performance. Nonetheless, the conclusion for test score users seems simple: all of these factors are unstable and therefore impossible to incorporate into a statistical model for decision-making. It is important that classroom practitioners, parents, and other data users understand these factors and consider them when evaluating scores.

To be clear, we believe test developers and psychometricians have done significant work to model sources of score variation. Current item response theory (IRT) models take account of differences in item difficulty, item discrimination, and item pseudo-guessing in order to make a best estimate of student ability (Hambleton, Swaminathan, & Rogers, 1991). Extensions of IRT can handle or identify the effect of testlets and items that are polytomously scored (Samejima, 1969; Wright & Masters, 1982). Related statistical techniques are used to identify whether differences in response are biased or differential in their functioning according to student membership in a group (Zumbo, 1999). A myriad of techniques are being or have been developed to handle test dimensionality (Hattie, 1984), the structure of latent traits (Kline, 1994), the invariability of latent traits across groups (Vandenberg & Lance, 2000), the validity of diagnostic sub-scores (de la Torre, 2009), and so on.

Nonetheless, few of these technical and esoteric characteristics reflect the concerns of this volume. While statistical techniques for identifying lack of effort (Wise & Smith, this volume) and cheating (Murdock et al., this volume) have been identified, few operational systems are implementing these. Current research at the Leibniz Institute for Science and Mathematics Education at Kiel University is focusing on the variability of item parameters depending on their position and collocation in a test form (O. Köller, personal communication, 23 June, 2015). This process could mean that it would be possible to identify if items have different properties depending on where in a test they appear and on what items come before or after, with subsequent impact on score calculation.

However, these techniques presume computerised testing is how assessments will be administered, an assumption far from the practical realities of interactive and ephemeral assessment occurring via teacher-student and student-student interactions in classrooms. A further struggle in editing this volume was the dominance of tests in defining assessment; authors in this volume were asked to consider forms of assessment that were not tests or to draw implications for classroom processes that required observation, judgement, or interaction. Clearly, testing (online or on paper) is not the sum of assessment, and yet our psychometric industry defaults to 'assessment equals tests,' and this is clearly where the majority of research about important measures like reliability and validity has taken place. This may be a consequence of the origins, at least in the United States psychometric industry, of educational measurement being equated to standardised testing of achievement (Lindquist, 1951; Thorndike, 1971). Furthermore, current efforts in psychometrics tend to focus on achieving greater accuracy in score calculation. Hence, the implications for psychometrics when formal testing is not the norm are largely unrealised and relatively unexplored.

However, the development of quality standards for in vivo assessment methods has begun. For example, the use of multiple measures, multiple methods, and multiple opportunities for assessment are a standard convention of psychometrics (Joint Committee on Standards for Educational Evaluation, 2003). Research into the reliability of performance assessments, a major type of classroom assessment, has identified the need to have multiple samples, usually between five and nine, to make a reliable and generalisable estimate of ability (Brennan, 1996). Yet, while it is perfectly feasible in a classroom context to collect this many samples of a student's work, the circumstances of classrooms may invalidate such collection. In reality, multiple samples will probably be collected over quite a period of time (perhaps a semester or even a year). This means that only the last two or three samples actually represent the terminal state of the student's ability; with such a small sample, the validity of any conclusions about the student's achievement is jeopardised. Thus, the probability of being able to operationalise the ephemera of in vivo classroom assessments, let alone actually capture the data as it happens in the moment, and then be able to use that information to efficiently and rapidly modify the calculation of a 'true' score or form a valid judgment of ability, seems still quite low. Nonetheless, teachers need to make decisions about student achievement and learning needs long before sufficient in vivo evidence can be assembled to draw reliable conclusions.

Kane (2006) has made it clear that what makes an assessment valid in a classroom setting is quite different from a test. Classroom assessment practices are likely to be close in time and content to instruction, with strong potential to guide feedback to the teacher as to revisions needed in classroom planning. However, they are also threatened by the many construct-irrelevant sources of variance identified in this handbook's chapters. A suggestion made concerning self-assessment is that it should no longer be treated as assessment per se, but rather part of self-regulatory skills needed for life success (Brown & Harris, 2014). It may not be too much of a stretch to argue that all classroom interactions, despite their similarity to formal assessment practices, should be treated rather as teaching-learning or pedagogical interactions (Brown, 2013b; Stobart, 2006). This approach, while seemingly downgrading classroom interactions from the 'lofty' status of being assessment, would potentially free up such interactions from the burdens associated with evaluation and accountability and focus them more sharply on diagnosing needs and strengths and providing feedback and guidance for improved instruction and learning. Nevertheless, practitioners still need to be aware that in formatively setting targets, diagnosing needs, and providing feedback, there is still a strong possibility that the teacher or classmate will be wrong; the same factors that invalidate test scores exist in and impact on teacher judgements about children's achievement.

Unfortunately, standardised testing has become strongly associated with high-stakes consequences (Nichols & Harris, this volume; Teltemann & Klieme, this volume) and, even when this association is not implemented by policy makers, standardised tests often do not provide sufficient information (i.e., information beyond rank position or total score) to classroom practitioners to allow them to generate appropriate feedback and instructional planning (Brown & Hattie, 2012). However, this need not be the death knell of standardsed testing for formative classroom uses. Rather than attempt to generate new statistical formulae or modify conventional objectively scored items as recommended by Pellegrino and colleagues (2001), the approach taken in New Zealand's Assessment Tools for Teaching and Learning (asTTle) focused on better communication to teachers about the meaning of student performance (Hattie & Brown, 2008; Hattie, Brown, & Keegan, 2003; Hattie, Brown, Ward, Irving, & Keegan, 2006).

The asTTle approach centered on developing reporting systems that provided teachers and school leaders with rich diagnostic analysis of student performance relative to grade-appropriate norms, achievement objectives, and curricular levels. It also provided links to pedagogical and curriculum resources which could help teachers implement classroom activities, create groupings, and provide feedback designed to guide students to what they needed to do next to improve in reading comprehension, mathematics, or writing. The argument here is not that better testing or better statistics are required, but rather that better and more effective communication of information that teachers need and want is needed (Brown, 2013a; Hattie, 2010; Hattie & Brown, 2010). Evidence from New Zealand usage of the asTTle test system suggests that, with just single-parameter IRT score calculation, teachers and students can be shown 'who needs to be taught what next' and that student performance increases (Archer & Brown, 2013; McDowall, Cameron, Dingle, Gilmore, & MacGibbon, 2007; Parr, Timperley, Reddish, Jesson, & Adams, 2007).

Hence, perhaps the future for psychometrics is rather more an emphasis on communicating meaningful information more effectively to teachers (a concern identified some time ago by Hambleton & Slater [1997] and Wainer, Hambleton, & Meara [1999]) and other educational stakeholders so that formative responses can be made, notwithstanding the various errors contaminating scores. The asTTle example does not, of course, obviate the problem of error; hence, the asTTle team insisted that the standardised asTTle tests (a) were not the sole or best judgement of student performance, (b) should be used in conjunction with multiple methods of evaluating progress, and (c) ought not to be used more than three to four times per year (Brown, 2013a; Hattie et al., 2004). Thus, instead of attempting to eliminate error altogether, perhaps improved educational outcomes and teaching practices can be developed when better communication about student learning and needs occurs. This would require all participants to accept that there was error and agree that it was sufficiently controlled to permit discussion about decisions. Such a state of affairs is far from the naïve intuitive test theory presumption that test scores are correct; rather it requires a sophisticated and nuanced approach that takes test scores with a grain of salt in conjunction with the complementary and imperfect information derived from other approaches.

ASSESSMENT PURPOSES AND CONSEQUENCES

It is clear from many chapters in this volume that the decision as to what level of consequences should be attached to student and teacher mediated assessment is a vexed issue. In terms of ensuring motivation and effort, some sort of personal consequence may activate greater effort and often achievement (Wise & Smith, this volume); some level of anxiety can do the same (Vogl & Pekrun, this volume). However, when assessments matter, the relatively low risk of being caught means that cheating and dishonesty are also more likely (Murdock, Stephens, & Groteweil, this volume). Furthermore, it is clear that high-stakes consequences for schools and teachers appear to have largely invidious consequences (e.g., narrowing of curriculum, cheating) (Nichols & Harris, this volume). Accountability systems using a catch-and-punish mentality may encourage compliance (Lerner & Tetlock, 1999), but corruption of the assessment process is inevitable if the risk of being caught is low (Dixit & Nalebuff, 2008). Hence, some space between high-stakes consequences and no consequences is needed for an assessment to elicit positive attitudes and behaviours and minimise negative ones. While Assessment for Learning (Assessment Reform Group, 1999) policy advocacy seems to have grown from a rejection of high-stakes testing in England, the policy as a whole seems naïve to the intrapersonal and interpersonal problems identified in this handbook (specifically chapters by Andrade & Brown; Cowie & Harrison; Panadero; Strijbos, this volume), consequently threatening the validity of so-called formative assessments.

The argument made elsewhere (Hattie & Brown, 2008) is that assessment consequences need to be low, but simultaneously useful information to the system participants has to be high. Of course, students have to be sufficiently motivated to do their best and, at the same time, teachers need to care enough to implement approaches with fidelity and avoid practices which may undermine assessment validity; professional integrity and effort matter. Ideally, teachers and students should actively seek out feedback from assessment to deepen their teaching and learning, respectively, without need for any external reward or punishment consequence. Assessment consequences need to be sufficiently low as to allow teachers to discover any bad news; that is, 'my teaching has not been effective because the students still don't know or can't do what I've been teaching.' Research into teacher beliefs about assessment (Bonner, this volume) shows that teachers generally believe that improvement is the legitimating purpose of assessment, but that system pressure to generate high scores jeopardises that commitment. Likewise, if students will not apply themselves unless there are incentivising consequences, then the consequences must be balanced such that effort is high, but cheating is low. If consequences incentivise maximising the total score independent of substantive learning, then cheating is inevitable (Murdock, Stephens, & Groteweil, this volume; Nichols & Harris, this volume). Only when teachers discover what students do not know or cannot do, do they have the information they need to change their teaching. Likewise, only when students discover what they do and do not know when they did their best, do they have the information required to change their learning. But if the consequences make it difficult to discover unpleasant truths, then an assessment system will fail to lead to improved learning, although scores may rise.

The nature of the score information generated by a test also needs to change in order to minimise the temptation to attach consequences (Hattie & Brown, 2008, 2010). If an assessment provides nothing more than total score or rank order, its value is relatively low, since teachers usually already know, with reasonable accuracy, who is doing well or poorly in their class (Elley & Livingston, 1972). Providing rank or total scores reinforces the intuitive assumption that a small difference in rank or score is an accurate basis for judging between test takers, a fault demonstrated by the widespread response of nations to rank or change in rank in the PISA system (Teltemann & Klieme, this volume). Such 'simple' and 'straightforward' indicators actively facilitate stakeholder use of System I thinking rather than engagement in the more meaningful System II thinking necessary for diagnostic and formative uses of assessment. Hence, assessments that have high value to an educational system need to inform stakeholders, not only about student current attainment, but also most probable directions for progress, and should be presented in ways that support System II qualities of reflection before decision-making. Teachers wish to know more about student learning than if their pupils remember facts and details (i.e., surface learning; Biggs & Collis, 1982); they want to know if their teaching is helping students acquire the ability to (a) see things in a more meaningful way, (b) derive abstract principles, (c) understand relationships, and (d) understand new things for themselves (Brown, 2009). If tests, with low consequences, provide rich diagnostic information about these valued aspects of the curriculum, then asking schools why they have not used such tools to evaluate and guide improvements in schooling effectiveness (as per Lai & Schildkamp, this volume) becomes a legitimate and fair question. However, it would seem from both the U.S. (Nichols & Harris, this volume) and international (Lingard & Lewis, this volume; Teltemann & Klieme, this volume) systems, such rich information is relatively rare. While cognitive diagnostic models hold promise to help analyse student responses on tests (Huebner, 2010), practitioners can find sufficient guidance in judgment-based alignment of items and tasks to curriculum objectives and standards to deal with classroom realities (Brown & Hattie, 2012).

FUTURE ASSESSMENT

The future of educational assessment seems to involve major shifts in the mode and medium of assessment. For example, as Katz and Gorin (this volume) and Strijbos (this volume) discuss, improved technologies may make probing student cognition more efficient. Technology has already successfully shown that it can improve the accuracy and efficiency of objectively scored test items and, with continual improvements in automated essay scoring, even feedback about writing can be generated (Shermis & Hamner, 2012). Currently, there is evidence that initial encounters with novel machine-based assessments may be welcome when the stakes are low, but when important consequences arise, students prefer the tried and true (Struyven & Devesa, this volume). It may be easier for some students to receive critical feedback from a machine than from a teacher because it is difficult to take offence at the 'tone' of a machine's output; however, others may distrust and disregard such computer-generated feedback (Lipnevich, Berg, & Smith, this volume). Early research is suggesting that computer-based testing can monitor and prompt learners to maintain proper levels of effort throughout a test (Wise & Smith, this volume). The feasibility of difficulty customisation using computer-adaptive testing, now well established and commonly implemented (Katz & Gorin, this volume), has potential to improve student engagement and effort, and to lessen cheating (McMillan, this volume; Murdock, Stephens, & Groteweil, this volume; Wise & Smith, this volume).

However, reliance on technology raises concerns immediately about privacy (Tierney & Koch, this volume); should educational testing systems be allowed to examine so deeply the personal facets of human life? If the answer is yes, new questions arise: Does the nature of computer/learner interactions exclude some important aspects of the curriculum, meaning that only those parts of the curriculum or teaching that can be computerised count? Would it benefit society if only scores arising from a machine environment (i.e., in silico [Autoimmunity Research Foundation, 2012]) count as valid measures of student attainment? The doubts raised by Ellul (1964) about the dominance of technology over more humanistic methods are worth considering before we embark on completely technologising assessment.

A more expansive and pragmatic approach to fairness in classroom settings seems to be required, perhaps one in which consequences attached to teacher-student and student-student interactions are minimsed by not collecting the data as assessment at all. The challenges laid out in this volume on the educational, social, and affective psychologies involved in being evaluated suggest that assessment decisions needs to be pragmatic, and any decision to rely solely on automated assessment systems needs to take seriously overall effects. Perhaps we may need to utilise only in vitro types of assessments for decisions that require high levels of assurance, notwithstanding the threats to their validity, especially if one-off assessments are used or, otherwise, treat all assessment data as simply part of the complex matrix of information we use to build judgements and decisions.

RESEARCH DIRECTIONS

A number of knotty problems have been identified in this handbook. Some have already been discussed extensively, including the complexity and variability of classrooms and learners versus the simplicity and stability of formal testing, and tensions between improvement and accountability purposes. There are issues around equity due to uneven provision of educational resources within society and conditions of employment that interfere with the objectivity and dependability of assessment results. Additionally, what might be good for students (e.g., short tests with relatively easy items—Wise & Smith, this volume) might not be what is best for curriculum-based evaluation of student accomplishment and teacher effectiveness (i.e., understanding student abilities to handle the deeper or higher-order objectives). Vogl and Pekrun's (this volume) discussion of student emotions, along with Murdock, Stephens, and Groteweil's (this volume) analysis of cheating, have touched on tensions between what seem to be relatively stable conditions or traits and context-specific states in how students approach assessment. These findings speak to our increasing but inadequate ability to predict how a certain mode of assessment for a certain purpose will impact on learners and highlight the importance Parr and Timperley (this volume) place on understanding the impacts of context on stakeholder assessment beliefs and actions.

These chapters also identify that, when specifically considering assessment in K–12 schooling, developmental changes must be taken into account. Such assessments take place while children mature into adolescents and young adults with concomitant changes in physiological, social, emotional, and cognitive structures and relations. As cognitive and developmental changes are expected, even without the influence of instruction, clearly test scores and/or assessment results are unlikely to be consistent and stable throughout the student's schooling career. Schooling exists to create change and improvement, so logically we should not expect high levels of test-retest reliability to be present; one would hope that lower performance early in school would not necessarily predict low performance later in the school trajectory. Schooling is intended to cultivate intellectual abilities (Martinez, 2000), so persistence in rank may not arise despite the influence of social determinants of achievement. This disordering effect is on top of the changes students go through as they develop, potentially becoming more or less motivated and effortful in acquiring the skills and knowledge valued within educational assessments.

The authors in this handbook provide a number of useful frameworks that capture our current understanding and provide a basis for guiding further research into understanding and accounting for human and social conditions in assessment. For example, Brookhart's (this volume) model of co-regulation helps us understand both the individual contribution of teachers and students and their interaction in eliciting and creating an assessable response. McMillan's (this volume) structuring of the impact of assessment around the sequence of before, during, and after the assessable event assists us to become more aware of and able to integrate the various influences upon learners. Bonner's (this volume) framework helps us situate teacher practices in a space of contesting factors (e.g., learning theory, policy mandates, and system resources) impinging on teachers' capacity to enact assessment. Lai and Schildkamp (this volume) provide a framework situating teacher professional development in assessment around problem-based thinking about achievement phenomena in their own immediate work environments; this guides attention, especially of policy makers, to what has to be done to support them to create change and improvement (rather than just blame them for poor results).

At a more detailed level, the Wise and Smith (this volume) effort model provides a deeper understanding of how various motivational processes interact with environmental conditions in determining how much effort test takers expend and thus how valid a set of scores might be for intended purposes. Similarly, Lipnevich, Berg, and Smith (this volume) develop a framework of factors impinging on the design, delivery, and impact of feedback upon the learner. However, meta-frameworks that integrate across the assessment timeline, methods, and interactions have not yet been developed;

the field is still piecemeal and requires further coherence brought to it. For example, a matrix like that suggested by Parr and Timperley (this volume) which categorises assessment purposes, associated ways of obtaining information, and the potential consequences of these actions in ways that considers contexts, discourse, and diverse stakeholder perspectives and uses is yet to be realised. Nonetheless, ignoring these interactive processes is certainly a path to invalid scores, interpretations, and decisions. These frameworks provide a useful guide to future research to determine the stability of assessment processes across multiple social and human conditions.

CONCLUSION

The ultimate goals of an assessment system, in our view, should be to better education in ways that improve the quality of life or life chances of individuals within a society. Life chances are the sum and interaction of personal opportunities and social relations afforded by a society, such that quality of life is maximised when individuals get to do what they are personally interested in, without sacrificing the meaningful relations and roles they have in social communities in which they belong and have their identity (LeVine & White, 1986). If assessment practices also led to students having greater love for and joy in learning, then most national curriculum statements would also be fulfilled.

The key actors in education (i.e., students and teachers) need agency and autonomy to allow for flexible implementation and diversification of educational practice. This means respect for teachers' professional integrity and insights about who needs to be taught what next, supplemented at appropriate stages with formal evidence about teaching effectiveness and learning achievement. That will require a system wherein tests are an accepted part of the repertoire or toolbox of teachers, but where accountability systems rely more heavily on long-term gains across multiple measures of high-value outcomes. A second key stakeholder group often overlooked is the community of test takers; that is, the learners who are being assessed. Students are not necessarily opposed to being evaluated; indeed, endorsement of the legitimacy of being assessed has been associated with higher performance (Brown & Hirschfeld, 2008; Brown, Peterson, & Irving, 2009). Nonetheless, their views as to what are fair and valid approaches to evaluating their learning and assisting improvement provide important insights into advances that can be made to both in vitro and in vivo assessment. Raising the stakes of each and every assessment as suggested by Wise and Smith (this volume) seems highly likely to have a short-term impact on performance motivation, but perhaps at a cost of greater cheating and lower longer-term motivation for deep learning.

Perhaps greater benefit would arise if we understood more fully what students consider it is that tests, assessments, and teachers do that help them understand their accomplishments, needs, and next steps. Such feedback to teachers and assessment designers would help us prioritise their needs in the design of both in vitro and in vivo assessment systems. An important clue in student thinking about assessment is an intriguing result reported by Brown, Peterson, and Irving (2009), in which there was a positive regression from the belief that teachers use assessment to improve their teaching to test-like, teacher-controlled assessment practices and subsequently a positive regression to achievement. The researchers interpreted this to mean that students expect teachers to test them because teachers use such tools to improve teaching. Assessments that do not palpably contribute to the improved teaching of the individual student should probably be treated with disdain; systems need input from students (as well as teachers) as to what those assessments are and how they could be changed or improved.

The introduction of measurement-driven reforms in the late 1980s focused on designing tests that measured what the curriculum and society truly valued, expressed most eloquently in the acronym WYTIWYG (what you test is what you get) (Resnick & Resnick, 1989). Our formal testing systems generally do not yet achieve a robust focus on deep learning, which is what we should expect from our schools. The more classroom interactions that look like assessment (i.e., finding out what students know and can do by questioning, observing, or discussing with them) replicate inadequate forms of assessment, the worse our educational processes will be. Freeing classroom practice from the power of 'the accountability test' is likely to improve the quality of assessment and teaching practice and learning outcomes.

This take on assessment is not an anti-testing position. While it is relatively easy to see what is wrong with standardized tests used to evaluate schools and teachers (Cizek, 2001), it is much harder to design a framework that establishes and helps achieve what societies value in schooling. The New Zealand school system, despite having a long tail of underachievement among minority students (Hattie, 2008), has produced relatively high quality outcomes with a somewhat limited per capita budget partly because it encourages the use of tests diagnostically, while eschewing the dominance of tests as the arbiter of quality (Crooks, 2010). In that system, teacher intuitions based on in vivo classroom interactions lead to insights that parents and teachers have about student motivation, affect, and cognitive skills and abilities. This knowledge may not be organised and systematic (Hill, 2000), but it is valuable. These insights generate testable hypotheses about student needs or accomplishments, which schools can formally evaluate with a variety of diagnostic assessment techniques. Hence, the future of tests should be more about being an adjunct and handmaiden to good educational practice rather than their current role as the final arbiters of quality.

The reality is that each form of assessment has its threats to validity and can be negatively impacted upon by human and social factors; error will never be completely eliminated because humans are imperfect. However, if stakeholders at all levels can be made better aware of the limitations of particular practices and encouraged to draw on multiple sources of evidence, each of which has different validity threats, a more balanced and hopefully accurate picture of student learning could be gained to guide appropriate teaching and learning. Combining multiple sources of evidence to make a judgement, while simultaneously considering each source's limitations, forces stakeholders to use the more thoughtful System II thinking, which should always be employed when making important educational decisions. We hope this will be the future of assessment in light of this handbook.

REFERENCES

Archer, E., & Brown, G.T.L. (2013). Beyond rhetoric: Leveraging learning from New Zealand's assessment tools for teaching and learning for South Africa. *Education as Change: Journal of Curriculum Research, 17*(1), 131–147. doi:10.1080/16823206.2013.773932

Asil, M., & Brown, G.T.L. (2016). Comparing OECD PISA reading in English to other languages: Identifying potential sources of non-invariance. *International Journal of Testing, 16*(1), 71–93. doi: 10.1080/15305058. 2015.1064431

Assessment Reform Group. (1999). *Assessment for learning: Beyond the black box.* Cambridge, UK: University of Cambridge School of Education.

Autoimmunity Research Foundation. (2012). *Differences between in vitro, in vivo, and in silico studies.* Retrieved November 12, 2015 from http://mpkb.org/home/patients/assessing_literature/in_vitro_studies

Biggs, J. B., & Collis, K. F. (1982). *Evaluating the quality of learning: The SOLO taxonomy (Structure of the observed learning outcome).* New York: Academic Press.

Bishop, R., & Glynn, T. (1999). *Culture counts: Changing power relations in education.* Palmerston North, NZ: Dunmore Press.

Braun, H., & Mislevy, R. (2005). Intuitive test theory. *Phil Delta Kappan, 86,* 488–497.

Brennan, R. L. (1996). Generalizability of performance assessments. In G. W. Phillips (Ed.), *Technical issues in large-scale performance assessment (NCES 96–802)* (pp. 19–58). Washington, DC: National Center for Education Statistics.

Brookhart, S. M. (2013). The public understanding of assessment in educational reform in the United States. *Oxford Review of Education, 39*(1), 52–71. doi:10.1080/03054985.2013.764751

Brown, G.T.L. (2009). Teachers' self-reported assessment practices and conceptions: Using structural equation modelling to examine measurement and structural models. In T. Teo & M. S. Khine (Eds.), *Structural equation modeling in educational research: Concepts and applications* (pp. 243–266). Rotterdam, NL: Sense Publishers.

Brown, G.T.L. (2013a). asTTle—A national testing system for formative assessment: How the national testing policy ended up helping schools and teachers. In M. Lai & S. Kushner (Eds.), *A national developmental and negotiated approach to school and curriculum evaluation* (pp. 39–56). London: Emerald Group Publishing. doi:10.1108/S1474–7863(2013)0000014003

Brown, G.T.L. (2013b). Assessing Assessment for Learning: Reconsidering the policy and practice. In M. East & S. May (Eds.), *Making a difference in education and social policy* (pp. 121–137). Auckland, NZ: Pearson.

Brown, G.T.L., & Harris, L. R. (2014). The future of self-assessment in classroom practice: Reframing self-assessment as a core competency. *Frontline Learning Research, 3,* 22–30. doi:10.14786/flr.v2i1.24

Brown, G.T.L., & Hattie, J. A. (2012). The benefits of regular standardized assessment in childhood education: Guiding improved instruction and learning. In S. Suggate & E. Reese (Eds.) *Contemporary educational debates in childhood education and development* (pp. 287–292). London: Routledge.

Brown, G.T.L., & Hirschfeld, G.H.F. (2008). Students' conceptions of assessment: Links to outcomes. *Assessment in Education: Principles, Policy & Practice, 15*(1), 3–17. doi:10.1080/09695940701876003

Brown, G.T.L., Peterson, E. R., & Irving, S. E. (2009). Beliefs that make a difference: Adaptive and maladaptive self-regulation in students' conceptions of assessment. In D. M. McInerney, G.T.L. Brown, & G.A.D. Liem (Eds.), *Student perspectives on assessment: What students can tell us about assessment for learning* (pp. 159–186). Charlotte, NC: Information Age Publishing.

Cole, M. (2010). What's culture got to do with it? Educational research as a necessarily interdisciplinary enterprise. *Educational Researcher, 39*(6), 461–470. doi:10.3102/0013189X10380247

Cizek, G. J. (2001). More unintended consequences of high-stakes testing. *Educational Measurement: Issues and Practice, 20*(4), 19–27.

Crooks, T. J. (2010). Classroom assessment in policy context (New Zealand). In B. McGraw, P. Peterson, & E. L. Baker (Eds.), *The international encyclopedia of education* (3rd ed., pp. 443–448). Oxford, UK: Elsevier.

de la Torre, J. (2009). DINA model and parameter estimation: A didactic. *Journal of Educational and Behavioral Statistics, 34*(1), 115–130. doi:10.3102/1076998607309474

Dixit, A., & Nalebuff, B. (2008). Prisoners' dilemma. *The Concise Encyclopedia of Economics.* Library of Economics and Liberty. Retrieved September 1, 2015 from http://www.econlib.org/library/Enc/PrisonersDilemma.html

Elley, W. B., & Livingstone, I. D. (1972). *External examinations and internal assessments: Alternative plans for reform.* Wellington, NZ: New Zealand Council for Educational Research.

Ellul, J. (1964). *The technological society.* New York: Vintage.

Feldt, L. S., & Brennan, R. L. (1989). Reliability. In R. L. Linn (Ed.), *Educational measurement* (3rd ed., pp. 105–146). Old Tappan, NJ: MacMillan.

Haertel, E. H. (2006). Reliability. In R. L. Brennan (Ed.), *Educational measurement* (4th ed., pp. 65–110). Westport, CT: Praeger.

Hambleton, R. K., & Slater, S. C. (1997). *Are NAEP executive summary reports understandable to policy makers and educators?* (CSE Tech. Rep. 430). Los Angeles, CA: National Center for Research on Evaluation, Standards, and Student Testing. Graduate School of Education & Information Studies, University of California, Los Angeles.

Hambleton, R. K., Swaminathan, H., & Rogers, H. J. (1991). *Fundamentals of item response theory.* Newbury Park, CA: Sage.

Harris, L. R., & Brown, G.T.L. (2009). The complexity of teachers' conceptions of assessment: Tensions between the needs of schools and students. *Assessment in Education: Principles, Policy, & Practice, 16*(3), 365–381.

Hattie, J. A. (1984). An empirical study of various indices for determining unidimensionality. *Multivariate Behavioral Research, 19,* 49–78.

Hattie, J. A. (2008). Narrow the gap, fix the tail, or close the curves: The power of words. In C. Rubie-Davies & C. Rawlinson (Eds.), *Challenging thinking about teaching and learning* (pp. 19–23). New York: Nova Science Publishers.

Hattie, J.A.C. (2010). Visibly learning from reports: The validity of score reports. *Online Educational Research Journal*, 1–15. Retrieved July 11, 2011 from http://www.oerj.org/View?action=viewPaper&paper=6

Hattie, J.A.C., & Brown, G.T.L. (2008). Technology for school-based assessment and assessment for learning: Development principles from New Zealand. *Journal of Educational Technology Systems, 36*(2), 189–201. doi:10.2190/ET.36.2.g

Hattie, J. A., & Brown, G.T.L. (2010). Assessment and evaluation. In C. Rubie-Davies (Ed.), *Educational psychology: Concepts, research and challenges* (pp. 102–117). Abingdon, UK: Routledge.

Hattie, J.A.C., Brown, G.T.L., & Keegan, P. J. (2003). A national teacher-managed, curriculum-based assessment system: Assessment tools for teaching & learning asTTle). *International Journal of Learning, 10*, 771–778.

Hattie, J.A.C., Brown, G.T.L., Keegan, P. J., MacKay, A. J., Irving, S. E., Cutforth, S., . . . Yu, J. (2004, December). *Assessment Tools for Teaching and Learning (asTTle) Manual (Version 4, 2005)*. Wellington, NZ: University of Auckland/ Ministry of Education/ Learning Media.

Hattie, J. A., Brown, G.T.L., Ward, L., Irving, S. E., & Keegan, P. J. (2006). Formative evaluation of an educational assessment technology innovation: Developers' insights into assessment Tools for Teaching and Learning (asTTle). *Journal of MultiDisciplinary Evaluation, 5*(3), 1–54.

Hill, M. F. (2000). *Remapping the assessment landscape: primary teachers reconstructing assessment in self-managing schools*. Unpublished doctoral dissertation. Hamilton, NZ: University of Waikato.

Hood, S. (1998). Culturally responsive performance-based assessment: Conceptual and psychometric considerations. *The Journal of Negro Education, 67*(3), 187–196. doi:10.2307/2668188

Howe, M. (2014). *Fake engineer confesses after four decades*. Retrieved November 12, 2015 from https://sourceable.net/fake-engineer-confesses-four-decades/

Huebner, A. (2010). An overview of recent developments in cognitive diagnostic computer adaptive assessments. *Practical Assessment, Research & Evaluation, 15*(3). Retrieved from http://pareonline.net/getvn.asp?v=15&n=3.

Irving, S., Harris, L., & Peterson, E. (2011). 'One assessment doesn't serve all the purposes' or does it? New Zealand teachers describe assessment and feedback. *Asia Pacific Education Review, 12*(3), 413–426. doi:10.1007/s12564-011-9145-1

Joint Committee on Standards for Educational Evaluation. (2003). *The student evaluation standards: How to improve evaluations of students*. Thousand Oaks, CA: Corwin Press.

Kahneman, D. (2011). *Thinking, fast and slow*. London: Penguin Books.

Kane, M. T. (2006). Validation. In R. L. Brennan (Ed.), *Educational measurement* (4th ed., pp. 17–64). Westport, CT: Praeger.

Keegan, P. J., Brown, G.T.L., & Hattie, J.A.C. (2013). A psychometric view of sociocultural factors in test validity: The development of standardised test materials for Māori medium schools in New Zealand/Aotearoa. In S. Phillipson, K. Ku, & S. N. Phillipson (Eds.), *Constructing educational achievement: A sociocultural perspective* (pp. 42–54). London: Routledge.

Kline, P. (1994). *An easy guide to factor analysis*. London: Routledge.

Leahy, S., Lyon, C., Thompson, M., & Wiliam, D. (2005). Classroom assessment minute by minute, day by day. *Educational Leadership, 63*(3), 18–24.

Lerner, J. S., & Tetlock, P. E. (1999). Accounting for the effects of accountability. *Psychological Bulletin, 125*(2), 255–275.

LeVine, R. A., & White, M., I. (1986). *Human conditions: The cultural basis of educational developments*. New York: Routledge & Kegan Paul.

Lindquist, E. F. (Ed.). (1951). *Educational measurement*. Washington, DC: American Council on Education.

Linn, R. L. (2000). Assessments and accountability. *Educational Researcher, 29*(2), 4–16.

Martinez, M. E. (2000). *Education as the cultivation of intelligence*. Mahwah, NJ: LEA.

McDowall, S., Cameron, M., Dingle, R., Gilmore, A., & MacGibbon, L. (2007). *Evaluation of the literacy professional development project (RMR No. 869)*. Wellington, NZ: Ministry of Education.

Nichols, S. L., & Berliner, D. C. (2007). *Collateral damage: How high-stakes testing corrupts America's schools*. Cambridge, MA: Harvard Education Press.

Parr, J. M., Timperley, H., Reddish, P., Jesson, R., & Adams, R. (2007). *Literacy professional development project: Identifying effective teaching and professional development practices for enhanced student learning* (RMR. No. 851). Wellington, NZ: Ministry of Education.

Pellegrino, J. W., Chudowsky, N., Glaser, R., & National Research Council (U.S.). Division of Behavioral and Social Sciences and Education. Committee on the Foundations of Assessment. (2001). *Knowing what students know: The science and design of educational assessment*. Washington, DC: National Academy Press.

Ravitch, D. (2015, April 6). *Did Atlanta educators get justice before the law?* Retrieved November 12, 2015 from http://dianeravitch.net/2015/04/06/atlanta-cheating-scandal/

Resnick, L. B., & Resnick, D. P. (1989). *Assessing the thinking curriculum: New tools for educational reform*. Washington, DC: National Commission on Testing and Public Policy.

Samejima, F. (1969). Estimation of latent ability using a response pattern of graded scores. *Psychometrika Monograph Supplement, 34*(4, Pt. 2), 100.

Shermis, M. D., & Hamner, B. (2012). *Contrasting state-of-the-art automated scoring of essays: Analysis*. Paper presented at the annual meeting of the National Council for Measurement in Education, Vancouver, BC.

Stobart, G. (2006). The validity of formative assessment. In J. Gardner (Ed.), *Assessment and learning* (pp. 133–146). London: Sage.

Swaffield, S. (2011). Getting to the heart of authentic assessment for learning. *Assessment in Education: Principles, Policy & Practice, 18*(4), 433–449. doi:10.1080/0969594X.2011.582838

Thorndike, R. L. (Ed.). (1971). *Educational measurement* (2nd ed.). Washington, DC: American Council on Education.

Traub, R. E. (1994). *Reliability for the social sciences: Theory and applications*. Thousand Oaks, CA: Sage.

Vandenberg, R. J., & Lance, C. E. (2000). A review and synthesis of the measurement invariance literature: Suggestions, practices, and recommendations for organizational research. *Organizational Research Methods, 3*(4), 4–70.

Wainer, H., Hambleton, R. K., & Meara, K. (1999). Alternative displays for communicating NAEP results: A redesign and validity study. *Journal of Educational Measurement, 36*(4), 301–335.

Wright, B. D., & Masters, G. N. (1982). *Rating scale analysis: Rasch measurement*. Chicago, IL: MESA Press.

Wyatt-Smith, C., & Klenowski, V. (2012). Explicit, latent and meta-criteria: Types of criteria at play in professional judgement practice. *Assessment in Education: Principles, Policy & Practice, 20*(1), 35–52. doi:10.1080/0969594x.2012.725030

Wyatt-Smith, C., Klenowski, V., & Gunn, S. (2010). The centrality of teachers' judgement practice in assessment: a study of standards in moderation. *Assessment in Education: Principles, Policy & Practice, 17*(1), 59–75. doi:10.1080/09695940903565610

Zumbo, B. D. (1999). *A handbook on the theory and methods of differential item functioning (DIF): Logistic regression modeling as a unitary framework for binary and Likert-type (ordinal) item scores*. Ottawa, ON: Directorate of Human Resources Research and Evaluation, Department of National Defense.

Zumbo, B. D. (2015). *Consequences, side effects and the ecology of testing: Keys to considering assessment in Vivo*. Plenary address to the 2015 annual conference of the Association for Educational Assessment—Europe (AEA-E), Glasgow, Scotland.

CONTRIBUTING AUTHORS

Heidi L. Andrade, Ed.D., is Associate Professor of educational psychology and the Associate Dean for Academic Affairs at the School of Education, University at Albany–State University of New York. She received her doctorate from Harvard University. Her research and teaching focus on the relationships between learning and assessment, with emphases on student self-assessment and self-regulated learning. She has written numerous articles, including an award-winning article on rubrics for *Educational Leadership* (1997). She has edited or co-edited several books on classroom assessment, including the *SAGE Handbook of Research on Classroom Assessment* (2013) and the *Handbook of Formative Assessment* (2010), and has edited or co-edited special issues of *Theory Into Practice* (2009) and *Applied Measurement in Education* (2013).

David A. G. Berg, Ed.D., is a Lecturer at the University of Otago College of Education and former school deputy principal. His research interests include formative assessment, preservice teacher self-efficacy beliefs, and the work of teacher educators.

Sarah M. Bonner, Ph.D., is Associate Professor of educational psychology at Hunter College, New York. Her main area of research is the study of cognitive processes that underlie academic test performance and their relation to validity of test score interpretation. She also studies the relationship between theory and practice in classroom assessment. She teaches graduate courses in educational assessment, statistics, and measurement. Her research has been published in peer-reviewed journals such as *Applied Measurement in Education, Journal of Experimental Education*, and *Educational Assessment.*

Susan M. Brookhart, Ph.D., is an independent educational consultant and author. She also currently serves as an adjunct faculty member in the School of Education at Duquesne University. Her research interests include the role of both formative and summative classroom assessment in student motivation and achievement, the connection between classroom assessment and large-scale assessment, and grading. She was the 2007–2009 editor of *Educational Measurement: Issues and Practice*, a journal of the National Council on Measurement in Education. She has been named the 2014 Jason Millman Scholar by the Consortium for Research on Educational Assessment and Teaching Effectiveness (CREATE) and is the recipient of the 2015 Samuel J. Messick Memorial Lecture Award from ETS/TOEFL.

Gavin T. L. Brown, Ph.D., is Professor and Director of the Quantitative Data Analysis and Research unit in the Faculty of Education and Social Work at the University of Auckland, New Zealand. His research focuses on cross-cultural studies of conceptions and practices teachers and students have in response to assessment. He is lead author of New Zealand and Hong Kong textbooks on educational assessment; serves on the editorial boards of *Teaching and Teacher Education, Assessment in Education,* and *Educational Assessment* (among others); has published more than 100 journal articles, books, or chapters; and is a contributing author to two standardized test systems used in New Zealand schools.

Chad W. Buckendahl, Ph.D., is a psychometric consultant in Las Vegas, Nevada, U.S.A. His research interests are applied psychometrics including standard setting, legal issues, test evaluation, and validity. Dr. Buckendahl has designed and implemented validation studies for general education, end of course, alternate, and English language literacy assessments in education; language assessment for admissions, citizenship, and certification; and licensure and professional certification tests across a range of programs. He currently serves as a psychometric reviewer and Chair of the National Commission for Certifying Agencies (NCCA), an accrediting body for certification programs.

Bronwen Cowie, Ph.D., is a Professor and Director of the Wilf Malcolm Institute of Educational Research at the University of Waikato, Hamilton, New Zealand. Her research interests are in assessment for learning, classroom interaction, student voice, curriculum development and implementation, culturally responsive pedagogy, and assessment in science education. She has completed a number of large national research projects as well as in-depth classroom studies where she has worked collaboratively with teachers and students to understand and enhance teaching and learning for primary and secondary age students.

Joana Devesa holds a Master in Language and Literatures degree (New University of Lisbon) and recently graduated the Master in Educational Sciences program at VUB in Brussels. She currently teaches English as a foreign language to adult learners.

Daniel L. Dinsmore, Ph.D., is Associate Professor of educational psychology in the College of Education & Human Services at University of North Florida, Jacksonville. His areas of expertise include strategic processing, transfer of learning, expertise development, teacher mentoring and induction, and research design and analysis.

Kadriye Ercikan, Ph.D., is a Professor in the area of measurement, evaluation and research methodology (MERM) in the Department of Educational and Counselling Psychology and Special Education (ECPS) and Director of the Cross-Cultural Assessment & Research Methods in Education (CARME) Research Lab at the University of British Columbia, Vancouver, Canada. She has over 20 years of experience conducting research on assessment design, validity, and fairness issues in multicultural and multilingual assessments and psychometric issues in large-scale assessments. In the area of research methods, she focuses on research generalization and validity of research claims. She is currently Vice President for Division D of the American Educational Research Association and is Chair of the Scientific Committee for the 2016 biennial meeting of the International Test Commission.

Gayle E. Eyers, Ph.D., is an administrator in the Office of Initial Teacher Education and Undergraduate Studies in the Faculty of Education, The University of Waikato in Hamilton, New Zealand. Her recently completed doctorate, under the supervision of Mary F. Hill, focused on how preservice teachers reconceptualize assessment theory and practice in university and school practicum settings.

Atta Gebril, Ph.D., is an Associate Professor in the Department of Applied Linguistics, the American University in Cairo, Egypt. He obtained his Ph.D. from the University of Iowa in foreign language and ESL education with a minor in language testing. He teaches courses in language assessment and research methods in applied linguistics. His research interests include assessment literacy, test validation, teacher beliefs about assessment, and writing assessment. He serves on the editorial board of *Journal of Language Testing* and *Language Assessment Quarterly*. He has published in top-tier journals in his field including *Assessment in Education, Journal of Second Language Writing, Language Testing, Teacher Development, Language Assessment Quarterly*, and *Assessing Writing*. He has also worked on many test development projects worldwide, including in the U.S., Egypt, the UAE, Qatar, and Australia.

Joanna S. Gorin, Ph.D., is Vice President of Research at Educational Testing Service (ETS) in Princeton, New Jersey, U.S.A. As Vice President for Research, Dr. Gorin is responsible for a comprehensive research agenda to support current and future educational assessments for K–12, higher education, global, and workforce settings. Her research has focused on the integration of cognitive theory and psychometric theory as applied to principled assessment design and analysis. Prior to joining ETS, Dr. Gorin was an Associate Professor at Arizona State University where her research focused on the application of cognitive theories and methods to the design and validation of tests of spatial reasoning, quantitative reasoning, and verbal reasoning. She received her Ph.D. in quantitative psychology (minor: cognitive psychology) from the University of Kansas.

Morgan M. Grotewiel, M.A., is a doctoral candidate in counseling psychology at the University of Missouri-Kansas City, USA. Her research interests include motivation, flow, mindfulness, self-compassion, and the psychology of women. She is currently completing her predoctoral internship at the University of Iowa Student Counseling Service in Iowa City, Iowa, USA.

Lois R. Harris, Ph.D., is a Senior Post-doctoral Research Fellow in the School of Education and the Arts at Central Queensland University, Rockhampton, Australia. Her research has focused on the interplay between educational stakeholder beliefs and practices, with an emphasis on classroom assessment, feedback, student engagement, and literacy. Author of numerous journal articles and book chapters, she was recently the lead author of a paper that received the American Educational Research Association Classroom Assessment SIG Distinguished Paper Award.

Christine Harrison, Ph.D., is Senior Lecturer in science education at King's College London. She has worked on the King's-Medway-Oxfordshire-Formative Assessment project (KMOFAP), conducting action research work with science and mathematics teachers to help them focus on and improve their formative practice. More specifically, her work is acknowledged as contributing to theory and practice in classroom assessment, particularly how teachers conceptualize assessment practices and purposes and enact them in the classroom. Her teaching and research have centered on assessment, science education, cognitive acceleration, and the use of text and media in classrooms. Throughout all of these, she maintains an interest in professional learning, in working collaboratively with teachers, and in ensuring effective knowledge transfer.

Mary F. Hill, Ph.D., is Associate Professor, Deputy Head of School of Learning, Development and Professional Practice in the Faculty of Education and Social Work at the University of Auckland, New Zealand. Her work is grounded in the context of contemporary schooling and teacher education and the contribution that quality teaching makes to a socially just society. Her research interests include educational assessment, assessment education for pre and in-service teachers, practitioner inquiry, and the use of complexity theory and critical realism as explanatory theory for rethinking teacher education for equity.

Irvin R. Katz, Ph.D., is Senior Director of the Cognitive, Accessibility, and Technology Sciences Center at Educational Testing Service (ETS) in Princeton, NJ. He received his Ph.D. in cognitive psychology from Carnegie Mellon University. Throughout his 25 year career at ETS, he has conducted research at the intersection of cognitive psychology, psychometrics, and technology, such as developing methods for applying cognitive theory to the design of assessments, building cognitive models to guide interpretation of test takers' performance, and investigating the cognitive and psychometric implications of highly interactive digital performance assessments. Dr. Katz is also a human-computer interaction practitioner with more than 30 years of experience in designing, building, and evaluating software for research, industry, and government.

Kerry J. Kennedy, Ph.D., is Research Chair Professor of Curriculum Studies and Director of the Centre for Governance and Citizenship at the Hong Kong Institute of Education. He completed an M.A. and Ph.D. at Stanford University. His research interests are in curriculum policy and theory with a special interest in citizenship education. His co-authored book with Laurie Brady, *Curriculum Construction*, is now in its fifth edition (Pearson Education, 2014). He is the Series Editor of the *Routledge Series on Schools and Schooling in Asia* as well as the *Asia-Europe Education Dialogue Series*. In 2012 he was the co-winner of the Richard M. Wolf Memorial Award presented by the International Association for the Evaluation of Educational Achievement.

Eckhard Klieme, Ph.D., is Professor for Educational Sciences at the Johann Wolfgang Goethe-University and the German Institute for International Educational Research (DIPF) in Frankfurt/Main. He graduated from University of Bonn with master degrees both in mathematics and psychology, and a Ph.D. in psychology. He directed several video-based studies on teaching quality, longitudinal studies on school improvement, and large-scale assessment programs both at a national and an international level, including questionnaire development for PISA 2015. His publications focus on educational effectiveness, classroom teaching, and comparative studies.

Martha J. Koch, Ph.D., is Director of the School Experiences Office and Assistant Professor in Curriculum, Teaching and Learning at the University of Manitoba. Martha received a Ph.D. from the University of Ottawa in 2010 after working as a middle school teacher. She specializes in mathematics education and educational assessment. Through various forms of professional service, Martha works with preservice and in-service teachers as they continue to develop their practice in inquiry-based mathematics and classroom assessment. Her research focuses on gaining a better understanding of how classroom teachers gather information about teaching and learning and use that information to guide their practice.

Mei Kuin Lai, Ph.D., is Associate Director of the Woolf Fisher Research Centre and Senior Lecturer in the School of Curriculum and Pedagogy, Faculty of Education and Social Work, The University of Auckland. Mei has led or co-led national and large-scale projects on improving and sustaining students' literacy achievement across a variety of contexts, from high poverty multicultural schools to rural primary and high schools. Her recent projects are a national project to build evaluative capability in government funded schooling improvement initiatives and a regional intervention to improve reading comprehension and increase the numbers of students gaining national certificates. She is the co-author of *Practitioner Research for Educators,* which was nominated for the American Association of Colleges for Teacher Education (AACTE) Outstanding Book Award.

Steven Lewis is a full-time Ph.D. student in the School of Education at The University of Queensland, where he is completing his doctoral thesis, *Theorizing New Spaces and Relations of Global Governance: The OECD's 'PISA for Schools.'* He is also currently involved in a nationally funded research project that examines the role of data infrastructures, large-scale assessments, and new accountabilities across international schooling systems. Steven has published in the *Cambridge Journal of Education, Comparative Education Review,* and *Discourse: Studies in the Cultural Politics of Education,* and has co-edited a 2015 special issue of *Discourse: Studies in the Cultural Politics of Education,* addressing the effects of large-scale assessments on education policy and research.

Bob Lingard, Ph.D., is a Professorial Research Fellow in the School of Education at The University of Queensland. He is a sociologist of education who researches education policy. His most recent books include *Globalizing Educational Accountabilities* (Routledge, 2016) and *Politics, Policies and Pedagogies in Education* (Routledge, 2014). Bob is a Fellow of the Academy of Social Sciences in Australia and also a Fellow of the British Academy of Social Sciences. He is editor of the journal *Discourse: Studies in the Cultural Politics of Education.* With Trevor Gale, he has recently edited a special number of the *Cambridge Journal of Education* on Bourdieu.

Anastasiya A. Lipnevich, Ph.D., is Associate Professor of educational psychology at Queens College and the Graduate Center of the City University of New York. Anastasiya received her combined Master's degree in clinical psychology, education, and Italian language from the Belarusian State Pedagogical University, followed by a Master's in counseling psychology from Rutgers University. Her 2007 Ph.D. in educational psychology (learning, cognition, development concentration) won the Excellence in Dissertation Award from the Graduate School of Education, Rutgers University. She also received the New Investigator Award 2011 from Division 3 (Experimental Psychology) of the American Psychological Association. Her research interests include: instructional feedback, attitudes toward mathematics, affect, alternative ways of cognitive and non-cognitive assessment, and the role of non-cognitive characteristics in individuals' academic and life achievement.

James H. McMillan, Ph.D., is a Professor in the Department of Foundations of Education, Interim Associate Dean for Academic Affairs in the School of Education, and Executive Director of the Metropolitan Educational Research Consortium at Virginia Commonwealth University in Richmond, Virginia. His research interests include measurement and understanding of student perceptions of assessment, the effect of assessment on learning and motivation, and the nature of student mistakes and learning errors. Dr. McMillan is editor of the *Sage Handbook of Research on Classroom Assessment* (2013) and author of *Classroom Assessment: Principles and Practice for Effective Standards-Based Instruction* (6th ed.) (2014).

Tonya R. Moon, Ph.D., is a Professor in the Curry School of Education at the University of Virginia. She teaches courses in research design, is principal investigator for two research grants focused in the area of teachers' data use for instructional decision-making, and is a past president of the Virginia Educational Research Association. She is active in the American Educational Research Association, the National Council on Measurement in Education, and the National Association for Gifted Children. In 2003, she was awarded by the National Association for Gifted Children with the Early Scholar Award. Major research interests include issues associated with accountability, including the effects of high-stakes testing on classrooms, teachers, and students; assessment of gifted children; program evaluation; and research methodology.

Tamera B. Murdock, Ph.D., is a Professor in the Department of Psychology at the University of Missouri-Kansas Cityin Kansas City, Missouri, USA. Her research focuses on contextual factors that influence students' motivation for various achievement behaviors, including academic cheating. In addition to numerous empirical and conceptual articles on cheating that she has published in journals such as the *Educational Psychologist* and the *Journal of Educational Psychology*, she co-edited (with Eric Anderman) a volume *Psychology of Academic Cheating* that was published by Elsevier in 2011.

Sharon L. Nichols, Ph.D., is Associate Professor of educational psychology at the University of Texas at San Antonio in San Antonio, Texas. Dr. Nichols has authored over two dozen books, journal articles, and book chapters related to youth development and motivation and educational policy. She is coauthor of two books, including *Collateral Damage: How High-Stakes Testing Corrupts America's Schools* (with D.C. Berliner, Harvard Education Press, 2007) and *America's Teenagers—Myths and Realities: Media Images, Schooling, and the Social Costs of Careless Indifference* (with T. L. Good, Erlbaum, 2004). Her current work focuses on the impact of test-based accountability on teachers, their instructional practices, and adolescent motivation and development.

Ernesto Panadero, Ph.D., is a Researcher (Ramón y Cajal Programme) at the Faculty of Psychology, Universidad Autónoma de Madrid (Spain). His research interests are self-regulated learning and formative assessment, and one of his lines of work is how self- and peer assessment promote the regulation of learning. Dr. Panadero's publications have explored in great detail the effects of different assessment tools (such as rubrics) on the regulation of learning, reviewed the state of the art on formative uses of rubrics, and published an innovative study on peer assessment and the influence of friendship.

Judy M. Parr, Ph.D., is a Professor of education in the Faculty of Education and Social Work at the University of Auckland. Judy's research focuses on enhancing teacher practice and raising student achievement in literacy; mostly this has been collaborative research within major national projects for school improvement that emphasize the use of evidence. Her particular expertise is in writing, encompassing how writing develops and is assessed, and considerations of instructional issues like teacher knowledge and practice.

Reinhard Pekrun, Ph.D., holds the Chair for Personality and Educational Psychology at the University of Munich. His research areas include achievement emotion and motivation, personality development, and educational assessment. Pekrun pioneered research on emotions in education, originated the Control-Value Theory of Achievement Emotions, and developed the Achievement Emotions Questionnaire. He is a highly cited scientist who has authored 21 books and more than 200 articles and chapters, and is a Fellow of the American Educational Research Association and of the International Academy of Education.

Kim Schildkamp, Ph.D., is an Associate Professor in the Faculty of Behavioural, Management, and Social Sciences of the University of Twente. Kim's research, in the Netherlands but also in other countries, focuses on data-based decision-making and formative assessment. She is a board member of ICSEI (International Congress on School Effectiveness and Improvement), and she is chair of the ICSEI data use network. She has won awards for her work, and she has published widely on the use of (assessment) data. She developed the Datateam® procedure, and she is editor of the book *Data-Based Decision Making in Education: Challenges and Opportunities,* published by Springer.

Jeffrey K. Smith, Ph.D., is a Professor and Associate Dean, University Research Performance at the University of Otago in New Zealand. He conducts research into the relationship between assessment and achievement in schools, the psychology of aesthetics, and learning in cultural institutions. He is the author of *Natural Classroom Assessment, Educational Psychology: Reflection for Action,* and over 70 research articles on assessment and aesthetics. He is the former editor of *Educational Measurement: Issues and Practices,* and is a Fellow of the American Psychological Association. Prior to his current position, he was Co-Director of New Zealand's National Education Monitoring Project.

Lisa F. Smith, Ed.D., is Professor of education and Dean, University of Otago College of Education. Her research focuses on assessment issues related to standardized and classroom testing, preservice teacher efficacy, and the psychology of aesthetics. She serves on the editorial boards of several peer-review journals, on the Board of Governors of the International Association of Empirical Aesthetics, and as a Fellow of the American Psychological Association. She co-founded the APA journal, *Psychology of Aesthetics, Creativity, and the Arts.* She has received honors including the Rudolf Arnheim Award for Outstanding Achievement in Psychology and the Arts from Division 10 of APA, the Gustav Theodor Fechner Award for lifetime contribution to the field of empirical aesthetics from IAEA, and teaching awards in both hemispheres.

Guillermo Solano-Flores, Ph.D., is Professor of education at the Graduate School of Education, Stanford University. He specializes in the linguistic and cultural issues that are relevant to both international test comparisons and the testing of cultural and linguistic minorities. He is the author of the theory of test translation error. He has advised Latin American countries on the development of national assessment systems. Also, he has been the advisor to countries in Latin America, Asia, Europe, Middle East, and Northern Africa on the adaptation and translation of performance tasks into multiple languages. Current research projects examine academic language and testing, formative assessment practices for culturally diverse science classrooms, and the design and use of illustrations in international test comparisons.

Jason M. Stephens, Ph.D., is a Senior Lecturer in the School of Learning, Development and Professional Practice at The University of Auckland. His primary line of research focuses on academic motivation and moral development during adolescence. He is particularly interested in the problem of academic dishonesty and the incongruity between moral beliefs and behaviors related to cheating. He is a co-author of two books on schooling and moral development (*Educating Citizens* and *Creating a Culture of Academic Integrity*) as well as numerous journal articles and other publications related to academic motivation, moral judgment, self-regulation, and cheating behavior among secondary and post-secondary students.

Jan-Willem Strijbos, Ph.D., is Professor of research on learning and instruction in the Faculty of Psychology and Education at Ludwig-Maximilians-University, Munich, Germany. His research focuses on the design, implementation, and effectiveness of interactive learning practices (collaborative learning, peer assessment and feedback, learning communities) in physical and virtual settings.

Katrien Struyven, Ph.D., is an Assistant Professor at Brussels' VUB in the Educational Sciences Department. Her research focuses on the effects of instruction and assessment on student learning. She teaches introductory and advanced courses in didactics within the Bachelor-Master program of (Adult) Educational Sciences and within the Academic Teacher Education Program.

Janna Teltemann, Ph.D., is a senior researcher at the Research Center on Inequality and Social Policy (SOCIUM) at the University of Bremen, Germany. She holds a Ph.D. in sociology from the University of Bremen. Her research interests are quantitative methods, comparisons of education systems, educational inequality, and immigrant integration. She has published several papers on determinants of educational inequality, results and methodological implications of the PISA study, as well as on OECD activities in the field of migration.

Robin D. Tierney, Ph.D., is an independent research consultant at Research-for-Learning. She began her career in education as an elementary teacher with the Ottawa-Carleton District School Board in Ontario, Canada. Robin received a Ph.D. in teaching, learning and evaluation from the University of Ottawa (2010), and she serves as an Adjunct Professor with the University of British Columbia. She has designed, coordinated, and taught graduate-level courses on classroom assessment and research methodology. Her research interests and publications relate to the quality and ethics of classroom assessment, focusing particularly on the meaning of fairness, the use of assessment to support teaching and learning, and the role of teachers' professional judgment in assessment.

Helen S. Timperley, Ph.D., is a Professor in the Faculty of Education and Social Work at the University of Auckland, New Zealand. Her research focuses on policy, leadership, and professional learning and aims at promoting professional learning and schooling improvement through the development of adaptive expertise in ways that create better outcomes for student learners, particularly those underserved by education systems. She is a Companion to the New Zealand Order of Merit for services to education.

Fons J. R. van de Vijver, Ph.D., is Professor of cross-cultural psychology at Tilburg University (the Netherlands) and has extraordinary chairs at North-West University (Potchefstroom, South Africa) and the University of Queensland (Brisbane, Australia). He has (co-)authored over 450 publications, mainly in the domain of cross-cultural psychology. The main topics in his research involve bias and equivalence, psychological acculturation and multiculturalism, cognitive similarities and differences, response styles, translations, and adaptations. He is or has been supervising about 35 Ph.D. studies and five post-doc studies. He has teaching experience in cross-cultural psychology and methods/statistics. He has presented keynotes and invited lectures at various conferences and workshops in various countries. He is one of the most frequently cited cross-cultural psychologists in Europe.

Elisabeth Vogl, Ph.D., is a post-doctoral researcher for the Chair for Personality and Educational Psychology at the Ludwig-Maximilians University of Munich. Her research interests include the assessment of emotional, motivational, and cognitive states and traits in academic settings and the investigation of their interaction. Her Ph.D. thesis focused on "Antecedents and Effects of Epistemic Emotions" and the development of the Epistemic Emotion Scales (EES). In 2014 she won the Excellence in Dissertation Award granted by the Münchener Universitätsgesellschaft.

Hope E. Wilson, Ph.D., is an Assistant Professor in the College of Education & Human Services at University of North Florida. Her research interests include gifted identification, acceleration, academic self-concept, and arts integration for gifted students, using HLM and SEM, as well as qualitative methodologies. She is a co-author of *Letting Go of Perfect: Overcoming Perfectionism in Kids* (2009, Prufrock Press). Her cartoons are a regular feature in *Teaching for High Potential.*

Steven L. Wise, Ph.D., is a senior research fellow at Northwest Evaluation Association in Portland, Oregon (USA). Prior to coming to NWEA, he was a Professor in educational measurement and statistics for 25 years at the University of Nebraska and James Madison University. He is the author or co-author of over 100 publications, with research interests in applied measurement, especially computer-based testing and the psychology of test taking. For the past decade, he has focused primarily on test-taking motivation—its measurement and dynamics, and various methods for reducing its impact on the validity of scores from low-stakes assessments.

AUTHOR INDEX

SUBJECT INDEX